The Encyclopedia of Eastern Orthodox Christianity

Edited by
John Anthony McGuckin

Volume II
N–Z

WILEY-BLACKWELL

A John Wiley & Sons, Ltd., Publication

This edition first published 2011
© 2011 Blackwell Publishing Ltd

Blackwell Publishing was acquired by John Wiley & Sons in February 2007. Blackwell's publishing program has been merged with Wiley's global Scientific, Technical, and Medical business to form Wiley-Blackwell.

Registered Office John Wiley & Sons Ltd, The Atrium, Southern Gate, Chichester, West Sussex, PO19 8SQ, United Kingdom

Editorial Offices 350 Main Street, Malden, MA 02148-5020, USA
9600 Garsington Road, Oxford, OX4 2DQ, UK
The Atrium, Southern Gate, Chichester, West Sussex, PO19 8SQ, UK

For details of our global editorial offices, for customer services, and for information about how to apply for permission to reuse the copyright material in this book please see our website at www.wiley.com/wiley-blackwell.

Library of Congress Cataloging-in-Publication Data

The encyclopedia of Eastern Orthodox Christianity/edited by John Anthony McGuckin.
p.   cm.
Includes bibliographical references and index.
ISBN 978-1-4051-8539-4 (hardcover: alk. paper)
1. Orthodox Eastern Church–Encyclopedias.   I. McGuckin, John Anthony.
BX230.E53 2011
281′.503–dc22
                                                    2010029190

A catalogue record for this book is available from the British Library.

This book is published in the following electronic formats: ePDFs 978144439253; Wiley Online Library 9781444392555; ePub 9781444392548

Set in 9.5/11pt Minion by SPi Publisher Services, Pondicherry, India

BRIEF CONTENTS

N

Name (Name Day)

JOHN A. MCGUCKIN

Orthodox tradition from early times suggested to the faithful that their names ought to be taken from the lists of the great saints of the church, rather from the generally prevailing customs of the period that took names honoring the (pagan) gods or great heroes of the ancient world. Just as in most Orthodox countries (the Mediterranean Basin demonstrates it still) the names of the days of the week were wrested from the pagan cults (Sun day, Moon day, Wodin's day, Thor's day, and so on) so as to be "renamed" (Kyriake, or Lord's day instead of Sunday), so too on a personal level the clergy encouraged the faithful to reflect their religious commitments with different personal names. In the 3rd century the martyr Leontios of Alexandria and his son (soon to become) the great Christian theologian Origen, bear names that are indistinguishable from their pagan compatriots. Origen, named so presumably by his Christian father, bore a name derived from the Egyptian cult of Horus. In the later 4th century the Christian bishop and father of St. Gregory the Theologian (his own name reflected a Syrian title for the angels: "watchers") named his daughter Gorgonia (after the mythical monster!). Basil the Great was similarly designated from a common nickname ("royal one") also seen in the naming of Augustine ("little prince") by his parents in the 5th century.

At the end of the 4th century and into the 5th, however, a predominance of "Christian names" starts to show. Some were generic titles that had a common resonance with Christian and pagan culture alike, such as Athanasius ("immortal one"), but others were more explicitly Christian and biblically derived, such as Peter, or Timothy. By the end of the 6th century both those sets of earlier classical names that did not have biblical origins (Basil, Augustine, Macrina, Emmelia, Hilary, and the like) and those that did (Mary, Elizabeth, John, Peter, and so on) had accumulated "saints" to go with them, biblical or not. By the medieval period, in both the eastern and western churches the daily liturgical calendar of saints that were commemorated had grown apace; and Christian families were offered a very large choice of patronal names that had reference to the saints or the angels. By this stage it was common to suggest the dedication of a new Christian child to the saint on whose day it had been born (though this never completely superseded family choices according to ancestral traditions). Eight days after the birth, the child was named in a ceremony of prayers, so that it had a name already at its subsequent baptism. Nowadays at the reception of adult converts to Orthodoxy a new name is often suggested at the baptism or chrismation service (especially if the original one is not particularly "Christian") and the convert is known by that for the purposes of receiving communion and other

The Encyclopedia of Eastern Orthodox Christianity, edited by John Anthony McGuckin
© 2011 Blackwell Publishing Ltd.

mysteries, at least. Monastics also receive a new name, a new "dedication" at the time of their profession; a custom that is repeated sometimes if they are elevated to the episcopate. The fathers interpreted this process as being a displacement of "birth-days" so as to be able to celebrate the saint's day, which became known in Orthodox life as the celebration of the Name Day. The symbolism suggests that birth into the world, as such, is not a matter of rejoicing, for it is birth into mortality and suffering; whereas birth into the communion of the saints is a true occasion for joy. It is a widespread custom today among the Orthodox to send greetings and congratulations, and to meet for festive parties, on the occasion of a friend's Name Day. And most Orthodox will usually have about the house the icon of their "patronal" saint.

SEE ALSO: Baptism; Chrismation

Nativity of the Lord

DAN SANDU

The Nativity of the Lord is the liturgical feast commemorating the coming in flesh (incarnation) of the Second Person of the Holy Trinity: God made man, Jesus Christ, the Son of God among us. It is popularly known as Christmas. Jesus was born in Bethlehem of the Holy Virgin Mary, through the descent of the Holy Spirit, without the contribution of a human father. The Orthodox doctrine affirms the virginal conception and birth of the Lord and venerates Mary as the Ever-Virgin (*Aei-Parthenos*). Jesus was born during the reign of the Roman Emperor Caesar Augustus, in the year 754 *ab Urbe condita*, when a census was taking place in the Roman Empire.

The event has a universal dimension, as it is accomplished for and through the whole creation. The icon of nativity depicts hosts of angels singing joyous hymns, shepherds who come to worship the light in the cave and a star guiding the three wise men who traveled from the Far East to glorify the Holy Infant and offer precious gifts. The icon is inspired by the liturgy and reflects the biblical account, yet also includes elements handed down by tradition.

Nativity is celebrated on a fixed date (December 25) in the Orthodox Churches (those following the old calendar still celebrate it on that date, although they reckon it as falling 13 days later). It is one of the most important feasts in the calendar after the Great Feasts of Pascha and Pentecost. The dates of other fixed feasts (Annunciation, for example) are established in relation to it.

The Nativity of the Lord is to be understood as a spiritual symbol too, because Jesus must be born in the soul of each human being, a mystery which will determine an ontological change in those who accept Christ as Lord and Savior. His birth is the premise of all his redeeming work, through which human persons can attain godlikeness (Greek *theosis* or deification).

SEE ALSO: Deification; Incarnation (of the Logos); Nativity of the Theotokos; Theotokos, the Blessed Virgin

REFERENCES AND SUGGESTED READINGS

McKinion, S. A. (2000) *Words, Imagery, and the Mystery of Christ.* Leiden: Brill.
McGuckin, J. A. (2004) *St. Cyril of Alexandria: The Christological Controversy.* Crestwood, NY: St. Vladimir's Seminary Press.
Macleod, D. (ed.) (1998) *The Person of Christ.* Westmont, IL: InterVarsity Press.
O'Collins, G. (2002) *Incarnation.* London: Continuum.

Nativity of the Theotokos

JEFFREY B. PETTIS

The Orthodox ecclesiastical year is marked by the Twelve Great Feasts which commemorate the saving events of the life of Jesus Christ. Most of these are fixed calendar days. The Nativity of the Theotokos is the first of the Twelve Great Feasts. In this way the birthday of the Blessed Virgin Mary is celebrated as being that event in human history which makes possible all of the other Great Feasts of the year. The Nativity of the Theotokos is attested in two sermons by the theologian and hymn writer St. Andrew of Crete (ca. 660–740). In Byzantine and Latin liturgical tradition it is celebrated on September 8, the reason for the selection of this date being uncertain (the feast falls on May 1 for some Oriental Orthodox traditions). The liturgical title of the feast always associates the birth of Mary with her role as *Theotokos*, "Birthgiver of God," to show the theological significance of the event as the turning point of salvation history in the coming in the flesh of the Divine Word, the Son of God, through Mary the Virgin. The liturgical troparion of the Nativity of the Theotokos proclaims: "Your birth, O Virgin Mother of God, announces the joy of the whole world, for from you has come forth and shines out the Sun of Justice, Christ our God." The icon of the nativity of the Mother of God shows Anna the mother of Mary sitting upright in an inclined bed, as Joachim her husband looks down upon her from inside the window of his house. In the bottom right of the icon a midwife reposes with the infant Mary resting in her lap.

SEE ALSO: Nativity of the Lord; Theotokos, the Blessed Virgin

Nestorianism

TENNY THOMAS

The doctrine that emerged from the christological controversies of the 5th century, ascribed to Nestorius of Constantinople, that there were two separate persons in Christ, one human and one divine: the man Jesus and the divine Logos. Nestorianism grew out of the Christology developed at the school of Antioch by Diodore of Tarsus (d. before 394) and Theodore of Mopsuestia (ca. 350–428). Nestorius himself, arguably, did not actually teach a two separate person Christology as much as he was "heard" to teach one by the Alexandrian theologians. He himself was under the impression that he was representing the traditional Christology of Syria as exemplified in Diodore's and Theodore's Christologies, which stressed the need to preserve the distinct integrity of the two natures (divine and human) in Christ. One of the critical issues of the era was the lack of a distinct terminology for "Person," which was to be worked out in this dispute for the benefit of the wider church, introducing technical terms into the Christian theological vocabulary such as *persona, prosopon, hypostasis,* and *physis.*

Diodore and Theodore followed a tradition of historical exegesis very different from the allegorical tradition of the School of Alexandria. Diodore presented Christ as subsisting in two natures, human and divine. The images of temple and priest were central to this school's Christology. In the womb of Mary, the Logos had fashioned a temple for himself, in which he dwelt. This temple, the man Jesus, was the subject reference of Christ's human experiences of suffering. The full divinity of the Logos, he thought, was thus protected from any hint of diminishment. This idea was first developed by the Syrians against the heresies of Arius and Apollinaris. In refuting the christological monism that was Apollinarism, Diodore leaned heavily towards an opposing emphasis that at the time of the incarnation and after it, the divine and human natures of Jesus Christ were distinctly separate to such an extent that there was never an admixture or a union possible. This was meant to stress that the natures, created and uncreated, could not be confused, but it tended to underplay the sense in which the two natures dynamically interacted in the Lord's incarnation, and left unsaid in what medium they interacted.

Diodore prepared the way for the work of his student Theodore, who taught that there were two clearly defined natures of Christ: the assumed Man, perfect and complete in his humanity, and the Logos, the Son, true God of true God and consubstantial, complete, and perfect in his divinity. These two natures (*physeis*) were united by God in grace in one person (*prosopon*). The unity did not produce a "mixture" of the two natures but an equality in which each was left whole and intact. The older Syrian scheme of using the "Assumed Man" to refer to the human nature, here starts to be mixed with a newer attempt to conceive of the "person as a medium of interaction." This scheme has been known in shorthand as "Two Sons" Christology. Physis in the older sense meant not necessarily a nature (human or divine) as such, but also a concrete representation of something. The terminology was thus set on a course that was to cause much confusion as it negotiated the new theological waters of distinction of natures and singleness of personhood.

Theodore, horrified by the concept of "confusion" and "mixture that destroyed integrity," taught that the human and divine natures of Christ were so separate that there was only correspondence (*synapheia*) between them, but not union. In developing his ideas he wrote that the Man Jesus was born of the Virgin Mary completely

naturally and with all faults of men, and that God the Word (Logos), having foreknown the Man's triumph over sin, chose to redeem the human race through him by becoming united with him through grace (*kata charin*) from the time of his conception. Because of his triumph over sin, the Man Jesus was made worthy of being called Son of God at the time of the theophany. Then, after his complete triumph over sin during his Passion, he was united even more closely with the Divine Logos, becoming God's medium for the salvation of humankind. Theodore also stressed the theological significance of history as a progressive enactment of God's purpose and thereby justified theologically the Antiochene exegetical methods.

Based on these ideas, Theodore was one of the first to be opposed to the use of theological language that strictly applies to God, being affirmed as a description of things that apply to the human life of Jesus Christ. Thus, he was passionately opposed to the terms "God was crucified," "God suffered," or "God was born," because, he believed, only the Man Jesus was born and God dwelt in the Man Jesus. God could not die, only the human could die, and so on. For this reason, Theodore called Jesus the *Theophoros* (Bearer of God). Syrian thought after him referred commonly to the idea of "Two Sons," the divine Son of God and the human Son of Man. The idea of Jesus as High Priest was also used as a way of connoting how the human realities were "lifted up" so as to become redemptively significant.

the early 5th century it seemed to many Alexandrian thinkers, especially St. Cyril of Alexandria, that this was not so much a legitimate traditional way of Syrian theologians speaking about the diversity of the natures, as rather a novel form of teaching that a simple man, Jesus (Son of Man or Son of God understood merely honorifically) was associated in the work of salvation along with the Logos (Son of God). If there are two Sons, Cyril thought, there must be two subject centers in Christ: and who then is the human son? Cyril castigated the theological language of two persons in Christ as a betrayal of the fundamental belief in the union of Godhead and humanity in the single Christ: a union which was not a confusion of natures, but a dynamic coming together in the crucible of one single divine person (the Logos) who was the personal subject of both natures, and who, in that single personhood, united them both in a mystically dynamic synthesis. For Cyril, therefore, the Eternal Word was actually Jesus of Nazareth. Jesus' body was thus the body of God; and therefore statements like "the Sufferings of God" were not only admissible but expressed exactly what the incarnation achieved, the union (*henosis*) of God and humanity in the single person of the God-Man.

Nestorius first came to Cyril's attention because he was vehemently opposed to a term used in Alexandrian theology: *Theotokos* (Mary as the Birth-Giver of God). In contrast, Nestorius argued, Mary is not *Theotokos* because she gave birth only to the Man Jesus. Once again, and in less than careful language, he probably meant to say Mary gave birth only to Jesus' humanity, not his divinity (which has no earthly origination), but his language sounded to many ears as if Mary simply gave birth to an ordinary man, who was thereafter, somehow, "assumed" by a divine force (the old psilanthropist heresy of Paul of Samosata). Nestorius and Cyril engaged in a fierce controversy in the years leading up to the Council of Ephesus in 431 (the Third Ecumenical Council) and at that council Nestorius was condemned as a heretic who taught that two persons coexisted in Christ, and he was deposed amid a great scandal that involved all the great sees of Christendom, and which would run on in

the agendas of the next three international synods (Ephesus 449, Chalcedon 451, Constantinople 553). In 435 Emperor Theodosius II ordered his writings to be burned (only a few survived). In his postconciliar writings Nestorius condemned the heresy that had been attributed to him – the extreme view that the human Jesus and divine Christ were two different persons. For Nestorius himself, salvation required both the human and divine natures of Christ to be complete, to guarantee the integrity of the incarnation and to protect the divine Logos from what he most feared (and paradoxically what Cyril wanted to affirm by means of the theory of hypostatic union), namely the blasphemous assertion that God could suffer pain or weakness. Nestorius' Christology asserted that both natures were discrete and continued in the incarnation. "Two natures after the incarnation" was elevated in Syria as a refutation of "Union" language. He asserted sometimes that the natures were separate centers of operation (*prosopa*), a word that could hold this meaning, but also suggested "person" understood as a psychic subject (which caused the confusion). At other times, however, he went further (especially in his post-Ephesine book the *Tome of Heracleides* – first translated erroneously as the *Bazaar*), that a correlation or conjunction between the divine and human was effected in the "Prosopon of Union," which he designated by "common terms" and titles such as Christ, or Lord. In short, for Nestorius, purely human activities (eating, drinking) were to be designated by human titles (Jesus, Son of Man, and so on) and divine acts were to be attributed to the Logos, or Son of God, and "mixed activities" could be attributed to a "Prosopon of Union" (Christ, or Lord). The seeking after a more satisfactory concept of the christological term of association/union is marked in this late writing

of the *Tome of Heracleides*. It was only discovered in the early 20th century in Syriac,
and has caused much scholarly revision of
what Nestorius actually held and taught as
opposed to what he was heard as saying and
teaching at the time.

Diodore and Theodore were considered
"orthodox" during their lifetimes, indeed
as normative for much of Syrian theological
thought, but both of them came under post-
humous suspicion during the christological
controversies of the 5th century as the two
who had sown the seeds for Nestorian heresy.
The writings of both were also to be subsequently condemned, by virtue of their association with Nestorius. The condemnation of
Nestorius in 431 was the beginning of a
sustained attack on the early Syrian Christology across the next two centuries in the ecumenical synodical process. The great
controversies that then resulted led to major
disruptions in the life of the Eastern Churches
that have still not been resolved. The strongly
pro-Cyrilline Christology of Ephesus 431,
Ephesus 449, and Constantinople 553 is held
in some tension by the doctrine of the "two
unconfused natures" of Chalcedon 451,
where the di-physite language of Rome and
Syria was affirmed alongside the union language of Cyril (thus "Two natures after the
Union"). It is for this reason, perhaps, that
Chalcedon proved to be so divisive in the later
history of so many Eastern Churches.

SEE ALSO: Assyrian Apostolic Church
of the East; Council of Ephesus (431); St. Cyril
of Alexandria (ca. 378–444); Syrian Orthodox
Churches; Theotokos, the Blessed Virgin

REFERENCES AND SUGGESTED READINGS

Abramowski, L. and Goodman, A. E. (1972)
A Nestorian Collection of Christological Texts.
Cambridge: Cambridge University Press.

Bethune-Baker, J. F. (1908) *Nestorius and His
Teaching.* Cambridge: Cambridge University
Press.
Brock, S. P. (1992) *Studies in Syriac Christianity:
History, Literature and Theology.* Aldershot:
Variorum.
Clayton, P. B. (2007) *The Christology of Theodoret of
Cyrus: Antiochene Christology from the Council
of Ephesus (431) to the Council of Chalcedon
(451).* Oxford Early Christian Studies. Oxford:
Oxford University Press.
Driver, G. R. and Hodgson, L. (eds.) (1925)
Nestorius: The Bazaar of Heraclides. Eugene:
Wipf and Stock.
Greer, R. A. (1966) "The Antiochene Christology of
Diodore of Tarsus," *Journal of Theological Studies*
17, 2: 327–41.
McGuckin, J. A. (2004a) "Nestorianism," in *The
Westminster Handbook to Patristics Theology.*
London: Westminster/John Knox Press.
McGuckin, J. A. (2004b) *St. Cyril of Alexandria: The
Christological Controversy: Its History, Theology
and Texts.* Crestwood, NY: St. Vladimir's
Seminary Press.
McLeod, F. G. (1999) *The Image of God in the
Antiochene Tradition.* Washington, DC: Catholic
University of America Press.
McLeod, F. G. (2005) *The Roles of Christ's Humanity
in Salvation: Insights from Theodore of
Mopsuestia.* Washington, DC: Catholic Univer-
sity of America Press.
McLeod, F. G. (ed.) (2008) *Theodore of Mopsuestia.*
Early Church Fathers. New York: Routledge.
Norris, R. A. (1963) *Manhood and Christ: A Study in
the Christology of Theodore of Mopsuestia.*
Oxford: Clarendon Press.

Neumes *see* Music (Sacred)

New Martyrs
THOMAS KITSON

Orthodoxy calls those who died witnessing
to their faith in the eras following
Constantine's Edict of Milan (313) the
"New Martyrs." The title was first used for
the victims of heretical rulers during the
Byzantine Iconoclastic controversies that

preceded the Triumph of Orthodoxy in 843. While there was no systematic persecution during the Ottoman period, Christians were often punished for activities that directly threatened the Islamic faith. New Martyrs of the Turkish Yoke (commemorated on the third Sunday after Pentecost) suffered for openly preaching Christianity, for converting others (or reverting to the faith after adopting Islam), and for causing disturbances by promoting Christian revival (which, beginning with the 19th-century liberation movements, often carried ethnic and national overtones). There were numbers of New Martyrs in China and Japan also. The actively atheist Soviet government encouraged varying degrees of organized church persecution after the 1917 Russian Revolution, involving many thousands of martyrs. In 1981 the Russian Orthodox Church Outside of Russia recognized many Soviet victims, hierarchs, clergy, monks, and laity (including Tsar Nicholas II and his family) as New Martyrs and commemorates them on January 25, the date of Metropolitan Vladimir of Kiev's martyrdom in 1918. In recent years the Moscow patriarchate has also systematically extended the lists of the New Martyrs of Russia. Many other New Martyrs suffered under the Nazis (including Mother Maria Skobtsova) and their allies (the Serbian New Martyrs are commemorated on June 15), as well as subsequently under the violently repressive communist regimes in Romania, Bulgaria, Albania, and other parts of the Soviet Eastern bloc.

SEE ALSO: Albania, Orthodox Church of; Bulgaria, Patriarchal Orthodox Church of; Contemporary Orthodox Theology; Romania, Patriarchal Orthodox Church of; Russia, Patriarchal Orthodox Church of; St. Elizaveta Feodorovna (1864–1918); Serbia, Patriarchal Orthodox Church of

REFERENCES AND SUGGESTED READINGS

Cavarnos, C. (1992) *The Significance of the New Martyrs*. Etna, CA: Center for Traditionalist Orthodox Studies.
Papadopoulos, L. J. and Lizardos, G. (1985) *New Martyrs of the Turkish Yoke*. Seattle: St. Nektarios Press.
Polsky, M. (1979) *The New Martyrs of Russia*. Munich: St. Job of Pochaev Press.

Newly Revealed Saints

JOHN A. MCGUCKIN

The title of "Newly revealed" (*Neophaneis*) refers to those saints of the Orthodox Church whose relics have been discovered in relatively recent times, often after years of being lost or forgotten, and whose cult has accordingly revived. From the earliest times the concept of the "revelation of a saint" following a significant and wondrous event (*thauma*) or a dream in which the saint appears to an individual have been a commonly known part of the cult of saints in the Eastern Church. So it was that in the 5th century St. Cyril of Alexandria discovered the relics of Sts. Cyrus and John, Empress Eudoxia discovered the relics of St. Stephen the Protomartyr in Jerusalem, and the priest Nicholas Calligraphos discovered the relics of Sts. Andronikos and Junia at Constantinople. The cult of St. Phanourios of Rhodes developed in 1500 after an icon was discovered in a hidden chapel; and in 1798 a child's visions led to the discovery of the relics of the Megara martyrs, whose cult became especially popular after the Greek War of Independence. The relics of St. Patapios and companions were discovered in a cave church at Geraneia in 1904 and became a focus of much pilgrimage. The New Martyr Ephraim (martyred in the 15th century) was found after a series of visions by a Greek nun in 1950 at Nea Makri. Unknown saints' relics have also been discovered in the monasteries, such as St. Eudokimos found at Vatopedi in 1841, St. Basil of Akarnania found in 1923, and the relics found after a monk's grave started one day to emit a fountain of water at Neamt in Romania, after the fall of the communist regime there (St. Paisy Velichovsky's monastery).

SEE ALSO: Megalomartyr Saints; Military Saints; Myrobletes Saints; Unmercenary Saints

REFERENCES AND SUGGESTED READINGS

Anon. (1983) *Hagios Ephraim*. Nea Makri: n.p.
Gerasimos of Mikrayiannitis (1990) *Hosios Patapios*. Loutraki: n.p.
Mourtzoukou, D. (1984) *Ton en Megarois Athlesanton Neophanon Martyron*. Megara: n.p.

Nikephoros Blemmydes (1197–1272) *see* Lyons, Council of (1274)

Niptic Books (*Paterika*)

JOHN A. MCGUCKIN

This extensive corpus of monastic literature, in several different "sets" and collations, gains its collective title from the Greek word *nipsis* meaning "sobriety," a concept that was elevated to prominence in Orthodox thought after the 4th-century fathers applied the word and its cognate *sophrosyne* ("wise temperance") to be central terms of monastic spirituality, signifying the sober vigilance the ascetic ought to cultivate in the life of attentiveness to God. The Niptic fathers are thus the large assembly of Orthodox ascetical authors who wrote about the spiritual life. Over the course of the centuries many various editors collated the different ascetical writers into compendia and florilegia for ready access by monks to important formative literature. The collections are also known as *Paterika*, a word signifying "books of the (monastic) fathers." he single form, *Paterikon*, often simply means a monastery's special collation of primary monastic literature designed for exercises of spiritual reading and guidance. The Niptic books and *Paterika*, therefore, do not exhaust the monastic writings of the Eastern Church, which far exceed them in the amount of literature extant, but they do represent some of the most important collections of those texts which were felt to be standard and exemplary.

The first instances of Niptic books collected into *Paterika* were popularized in the 4th century as the monastic movement took shape. First at this early stage was the *Apophthegmata Patrum*, the sayings and deeds of the desert fathers, which were collated at Scete and other monastic centers, and from there passed on to have a wide readership in Byzantium. Latin translations were also made at a very early date. The 4th-century Byzantine writer Palladius, in his *Lausiac History* (stories of the monks sponsored by the Constantinopolitan aristocrat Lausos) produced an early exemplar that caused a literary sensation in its day (not only among ascetical readers) in the imperial capital, which was added to with the *History of the Monks in Egypt*, known often as the *Egyptian Paterikon*. The genre was very popular in classical Byzantine times. Cyril of Scythopolis produced a version outlining the deeds and miracles of the Palestinian monks in the 5th century and the *Evergetinon*, originating at the large Constantinopolitan monastery of Theotokos Evergetes, amounted to a large multi-volume *Paterikon* collection that had a massive distribution and subsequently formed generations of Orthodox in the "tales and deeds of the saints." To this day many Orthodox, not connected otherwise with the monastic movement, can recount stories and legends derived from this literature, which have become part of the folk memories of the different Orthodox countries. The *Philokalia* is another example of *Paterikon*, assembled in the 18th century from a wide body of patristic and later medieval monastic writings, and is perhaps the one most widely known today; but there were several others before it that had an influence on early Russian monasticism, and which continued to be produced in the later history of the Russian Church, such as the *Kiev Caves Paterikon* (13th century) associated with St. Mark of Pechersky Lavra, the *Skete Paterikon* (which is an old Slavonic version of the Egyptian desert literature), the *Valaam Paterikon*, the 16th-century *Volokolamsk Paterikon*, and others, including Romanian and Serbian *Paterika* collections.

SEE ALSO: Asceticism; Desert Fathers and Mothers; Elder (Starets); Monasticism; *Philokalia*; St. Paisy Velichovsky (1722–1794)

REFERENCES AND SUGGESTED READINGS

Harmless, W. (2004) *Desert Christians: An Introduction to the Literature of Early Monasticism*. Oxford: Oxford University Press.

Nissiotis, Nikos (1925–1986) *see* Contemporary Orthodox Theology; Ecumenism

Non-Possessors (Nil Sorskii)

KONSTANTIN GAVRILKIN

Monks from a number of Russian northern monasteries, associated with Nil Sorskii (1433–1508), who based his monastic rule on early Christian writers and advocated a moderate ascetic life in small communities, centered on contemplative prayer, discernment, and studying Scripture, with a focus on inner transformation of mind and heart. Nil criticized "external" asceticism and extensive decoration of churches, and argued that monastic landownership, despite its application for social welfare, corrupted the church. At the Moscow church council of 1503 he and his followers questioned the legitimacy of monastic estates, covering one third of Muscovy's territory at the time, and argued for their transfer to the poor. Eventually, they were defeated by their opponents the Possessors, led by Joseph of Volotsk.

SEE ALSO: Hesychasm; Monasticism; Possessors (Joseph of Volotsk); Russia, Patriarchal Orthodox Church of

REFERENCES AND SUGGESTED READINGS

Nil Sorskii (2008) *The Authentic Writings*, ed. and trans. D. Goldfrank. Kalamazoo: Cistercian Publications.
Pliguzov, A. I. (2002) *Polemika v russkoi tserkvi pervoi treti XVI stoletiia*. Moscow: Indrik.

Ode

DIMITRI CONOMOS

A liturgical composition, originally attached to the nine biblical canticles sung at Matins and related to these by means of corresponding poetic allusion or textual quotation. Each ode consists of an initial model troparion, the *heirmos*, followed by three, four, or more troparia that are exact metrical reproductions of the *heirmos*, thereby allowing the same music to fit all troparia texts equally well. The nine *heirmoi*, however, are metrically dissimilar but united musically by the same mode and textually by references to the general theme of the occasion as well as sometimes by an acrostic.

SEE ALSO: *Heirmologion*; Music (Sacred); Orthros (Matins); Troparion

Oktoechos

DIMITRI CONOMOS

The collection of eight modes forming the compositional framework of Christian chant. Each mode comprises a restricted set of flexible melody types peculiar to it. Byzantine theorists refer to them as Modes I–IV Authentic and I–IV Plagal. While the origins of the *Oktoechos* are obscure, by the 8th century the system had become established within the Greek liturgical orbit. St. John of Damascus (675–ca. 749) contributed significantly to the formation of the *Paraklitike* (*Oktoikh* in Russian), a liturgical book which allocates proper chants for the Office to the eight modes over a recurring cycle of eight weeks.

SEE ALSO: Liturgical Books; Music (Sacred); *Paraklitike*

REFERENCES AND SUGGESTED READINGS

Jeffery, P. (2001) "The Earliest Oktōēchoi: The Role of Jerusalem and Palestine in the Beginning of Modal Ordering," in P. Jeffery (ed.) *The Study of Medieval Chant, Paths and Bridges, East and West, In Honour of Kenneth Levy*. Woodbridge, UK: Boydell, pp. 147–210.

Old Believers

IRINA PAERT

Old Believers (*starovery*), also known as *staroobriadtsy* ("old ritualists"), is a generic term for the religious dissidents who split from the Russian Orthodox Church in and after the second half of the 17th century. Church reforms carried out in the 1660s under the leadership of Patriarch Nikon created a formal reason for the dissent. The changes introduced by the reformers in accordance with the contemporary Greek practice (concerning primarily language and ritual forms) alienated a large number of Russian Orthodox who adhered to the traditional Russian ritual practice, including baptism by immersion, the sign of the cross made by two fingers (rather than three), the spelling of the name of Jesus with one "I" (Isus) rather than two, double rather than triple Alleluias, the clockwise (rather than anticlockwise) order of liturgical processions in church, the use of seven rather than five prosphoras for the Eucharist, to name just a few. Moreover, the violent state-advocated methods that characterized the reformist behavior stimulated intense apocalyptic sentiment. Mass self-immolations took place among dissenters and continued until religious toleration was declared in the 1760s. The important centers of Old Believers in Tsarist Russia were in the northern Trans-Volga regions, the border between Russia and the Polish Common-wealth, the Baltic provinces, Bessarabia, Moscow, the Urals, and Siberia.

According to official data, 190,944 men and women registered as Old Believers under Tsar Peter I. However, the numerical strength of the Old Believers could not be determined precisely as many of them also formally belonged to the Orthodox Church. In 1912 there were 1,807,056 Old Believers, which made less than 2.5 percent of the population in the Russian Empire. Their geographical distribution was very uneven: while some regions had a high proportion, others had a more or less homogenous Orthodox population. However, the strength of the Old Believers lay not in their numbers but rather in their literacy, their economic power, and strong commu-nal identity. With the exception of the period of enlightened toleration between 1763 and 1814, the Imperial government did not recognize the legal rights of the Old Believers and tried to assimilate them into the Orthodox population. It was only in 1905 that they received equal legal rights with the members of the Orthodox Church. In the Soviet Union the number of Old

Believers dropped because of repression, with groups emigrating to China in the 1920s–1930s, and then to Australia and America. Apart from Russia, Old Believer communities can be found in Byelorussia, Ukraine, Latvia, Lithuania, Estonia, Poland, Romania, Bulgaria, Italy, Brazil, USA, and Canada. Following the breakdown of the Soviet Union, there has been a revival of Old Believer religious life, but its impact remains quite limited.

The main division is between the priestly (*popovtsy*) and priestless (*bespopovtsy*). The *popovtsy* Old Believers differed from the mainstream Orthodox Church only on the issues of ritual, while *bespopovtsy* justi-fied lay ministry and had fewer sacraments than the Orthodox Church (notably, the Eucharist is absent). The Old Believers who did not wish to part with holy orders and the Eucharistic communion continued to recruit priests from the Russian Ortho-dox Church, who thus received the popular name "fugitive priests" (*beglopopovtsy*). Following the conversion in 1846 of the retired Bosnian bishop Amvrosii (Pappa-Georgopoli) to Old Belief, the *beglopopovtsy* founded a hierarchy independent from the Russian Orthodox Church with the center in Belaia Krinitsa (then in the Austro-Hungarian Empire). In post-Soviet Russia, this section of Old Belief declared its independence from the Belokrinitskaia Old Believer church in Romania and has its center in the Rogozhskoe cemetery in Moscow. It consists of eleven dioceses and is headed by Metropolitan Kornilii. The *beglopopovtsy* reemerged in the 1920s when two Russian Orthodox bishops converted to Old Belief and founded the Russian Old Orthodox Church with its headquarters in Novozybkovo (Briansk Oblast). At the moderate end of the movement, there has been a union effected between Old Believers and the Orthodox Church, called *Edinoverie* (United Faith), which was officially approved in 1801. The priestless Old Believers have more internal divisions than the priestly section, splitting over the issue of the Antichrist (whether this can be understood as a spiritual force or a distinct person) and over the role of sacraments. Marriage, in particular, became a subject of fierce debates among the priestless: while some advocated celibacy as the only way of salvation on the basis of radical eschatological views, others practised marriage assisted by a non-ordained minister. Most radical offshoots (*spasovtsy, stranniki*) preached a total break with the world (refusing to hold passports, sabotaging state campaigns, and rejecting military service). As a rule, the priestless Old Believers require their new members to be re-baptized on the grounds that their previous baptism was invalid. They also maintain strict taboos regarding food and hygiene, often keeping separate dishes for use by outsiders. Ritual prohibitions typical for all sections of the Old Believers include shaving beards (for men) and smoking tobacco.

Old Believers preserved the medieval Orthodox rite and liturgy, including the monophonic (*znamennyi*) chant that has a Byzantine origin, traditional iconography, and a fascinating book culture. Old Believers were instrumental in the revival of interest for traditional Russian icon painting both in Russia and abroad during the first half of the 20th century. Generally, the Old Believer culture is regarded as a reflection of the way of life typical for Russia before the westernization introduced by Peter the Great. Like many religious dissenters in other cultures, Old Believers were active merchants and differed from the average Russian peasants by their well-organized and sustainable agricultural economy. Among them, both the priestly and priestless, the role of the laity was, and remained, very developed. Laymen

interpreted the scripture and participated in interconfessional debates. Women as a rule had a high status among the Old Believers both in everyday and in religious life. It was not unusual for women to carry out the roles of ministers among the priestless Old Believers.

SEE ALSO: Russia, Patriarchal Orthodox Church of

REFERENCES AND SUGGESTED READINGS

Crummey, R. (1970) *The Old Believers and the World of Antichrist: The Vyg Community and the Russian State 1694–1855*. Madison: University of Wisconsin Press.

Iukhimenko, E. I. (2002) *Vygovskaia staroobriadcheskaia pustyn'. Dukhovnaia zhizn' i literatura*, vols. 1–2. Moscow.

Michels, G. (1999) *At War with the Church: Religious Dissent in Seventeenth-Century Russia*. Stanford: Stanford University Press.

Paert, I. (2003) *Old Believers, Religious Dissent and Gender in Russia, 1760–1850*. Manchester: Manchester University Press.

Robson, R. (1996) *Old Believers in Modern Russia*. DeKalb: Northern Illinois University Press.

Rogers, D. (2009) *The Old Faith and the Russian Land: A Historical Ethnography of Ethics in the Urals*. Ithaca: Cornell University Press.

Old Testament

EUGEN J. PENTIUC

TWO TESTAMENTS, ONE BIBLE

The Jewish Bible, also known as Tanakh or Hebrew Scriptures, is for the Orthodox Church the first part of the Christian Bible or Holy Scripture. It is called by Christians the Old Testament in a precise theological balance to the affirmation of the New Testament. These terms were first signaled by Origen of Alexandria in the 3rd century and were developed into a theory of interpretation using Hellenistic hermeneutics where typology was used to read the Old Testament in the light of the New (Kannengiesser 2006). The early church's struggle with Marcion of Pontus over the Old Testament's place and role besides the emerging Christian scriptures occupied most of the 2nd century. Marcion (d. 160) rejected the Old Testament as having any authority for Christians. He argued that the God of the Jews was totally different from, and inferior to, the Christian God. His radical view, one that was often echoed by Gnostic teachers, accelerated the broader Christian embrace of the Hebrew Scriptures as a whole, and most scholars agree that the defeat of Marcion greatly helped to fix the church's canon of received scriptures. Another early danger, supersessionism, discernible in the indictment of the Parable of the Wicked Tenants (Mt. 21.33–46) and supported by Paul's teaching that the coming of Christ put an end to the custodian role of the Law (Gal. 3.24–5; Rom. 10.4; cf. Heb. 8.13), led to a premature devaluation of the Old Testament among some Christian commentators. The idea that the church and its new Scripture (New Testament) superseded the old Israel and its Hebrew Scripture is attested in many early Christian writings. Even so, the church as a whole has been able to keep the two Testaments in a dialectical unity, in the main avoiding factual reductionism and supersessionism as dangers. The centrality of the Christ event in Christian tradition, not least as a key hermeneutical principle, helped in reaching this objective.

THE RECEIVED TEXT

Although there is no clear conciliar statement on this topic, the Septuagint (*LXX*) remains the quasi-official form of the Old Testament for Eastern Orthodox Christianity. The popularity of this Greek text comes from its use by the New Testament writers and the Greek fathers. Accordingly, the Eastern Orthodox Church tends to rely on the Septuagint for its Old Testament teachings, and still uses it, at least in its Greek-language services. In recent times the wealth of Qumran findings and modern studies on the Dead Sea Scrolls has suggested the volatility of issues concerning the textual transmission of scripture in both Hebrew and Greek. Given this ethos of scholarly discovery, modern biblical scholars within the Eastern Orthodox tradition are now having to take a closer look at the long-neglected Hebrew text in conjunction with their traditional approach to the Greek *LXX*. Since the Eastern Orthodox tradition relies on the concept of the *phronema* or "mind" of the fathers in establishing a sense of interpretation of texts, rather than appealing to a fossilized patristic corpus of authorities (see Stylianopoulos 2006), it follows that Orthodox biblical scholars in this generation also have the noble duty of redeeming those Semitic nuances that may have been missed by those fathers who worked exclusively with the Greek text (see Pentiuc 2005).

CANON

According to the Roman Catholic Church following the Council of Trent (1545–6), the Old Testament contains forty-six canonical books (thirty-nine of the Jewish Bible and the seven "deuterocanonicals" of the Septuagint). Protestants, today, accept the same thirty-nine canonical books as the Jews. While accepting all thirty-nine books of the Jewish canon, the Orthodox have a peculiar view in relation to the Septuagintal additions. These are not considered "canonical" or "deuterocanonical" – to use the Roman Catholic terminology – but neither are they listed as "apocrypha" according to the Protestant terminology. On the contrary, since the time of St. Athanasius' 39th *Festal Letter* (367) they have been designated as the Anaginoskomena, the books that are "readable" (for the purposes of piety). This intricate and more relaxed view on canonicity aligns Eastern Orthodoxy closely with the position of pre-rabbinic Judaism, while it also recalls the situation of the historical era when the emerging church first used these Septuagintal additions as important proof-text material for their preaching of the Messiahship of Jesus.

INSPIRATION

The Eastern Orthodox view on the inspiration of the Old Testament text is perfectly exemplified in the writings of St. John Chrysostom, who applies the Greek word *synkatabasis* ("condescension") (see Chrysostom's *Homilies on Genesis*, PG 53.29A; 34B; 44A). This key term seeks to define God's ability and willingness to adjust himself to the *astheneia* or "weakness" (defectibility) of the human author, so that the scripture might be eventually acknowledged and praised for its *akribeia* (exactness, precision) being essentially God's word. A modern recast of such a balanced view might creatively employ two biblical paradigms. The first we can suggest as humanity's creation by God's breathing into the dust which thereby became a "living breath" (Gen. 2.7), and this understood as an analogy of how the human expressions of scripture are continuously infused by God's Spirit and thereby turned into a "living breath" of God for the church. The second paradigm, the incarnation of the preexistent Logos again accomplished through God's Spirit (Lk. 1.35), can point

to the comprehension of the scripture as a progressive enfleshing of God's eternal word. These two paradigms keep both communicative directions (from God' side to humanity and from humanity's to God) in a creative tension, as is revealed in this elaborate New Testament introductory formula: "What had been spoken by the Lord through the prophet" (Mt. 1.22; 2.15).

BYZANTINE MODES OF INTERPRETATION

There have been many various ways that the Eastern Orthodox have sought through history to assimilate, in a conscious manner, the Old Testament as scripture. Classic among them are the Byzantine modes of reception and interpretation which can be briefly summarized as follows. In the first place stand the patristic works (commentaries, biblical interpretations found in various writings, and *catenae* or florilegia of verse comments preserved in Greek, Syriac, and Coptic). What makes the patristic expositions of scripture valuable even in a postmodern world dominated by a hermeneutic of suspicion is the church fathers' persistent search for the *skopos*, the "goal" of the biblical text, its moral sense allied with a desire to apply an immediate pastoral application for it. Patristic exegesis with its overarching christological orientation and its typological searching moves from plain historical meanings (the literal sense) through allegorical reading, to search out higher moral and mystical senses. In the second place, Orthodoxy approaches the Old Testament through the major route of liturgy (hymnody, lectionaries, and liturgical symbolism as reflected in various Byzantine "rubrics"). The Old Testament texts and themes found so extensively in the Byzantine hymns show a very high degree of exegetical freedom within a dynamic liturgical setting. In the third place, Orthodoxy approaches and interprets the Old Testament through iconography (frescoes, icons, the arts of illumination), a process which sheds additional and sometimes invaluable light on the way the Byzantines read and understood the Old Testament in relation to the New. For example, the iconographic positioning of the ancient biblical episodes and figures in an Eastern Orthodox church can reflect the way in which specific Old Testament symbols were interpreted within the wider context of Byzantine tradition. The ascetical and spiritual tradition of Orthodoxy (Burton-Christie 1993) also determines how the Old Testament is seen within the church (monastic rules, canons, ascetical texts). Both cenobitic and individual forms of monastic spirituality are thoroughly regulated by specific scriptural readings, helping the ascetic and lay believer embark on what the fathers call the path of *theosis* or "deification." Lastly, it goes without saying that the dogmatic tradition of Orthodoxy is profoundly influenced by the Old Testament. Conciliar resolutions (creeds and decisions of local and ecumenical councils) crafted during the Byzantine period are based primarily on canonical scriptural texts, and the Byzantine modes of reception and interpretation of the Old Testament feature deeply within them (see Pentiuc 2011).

SEE ALSO: Bible; Canon (Liturgical); Christ; Church (Orthodox Ecclesiology); Judaism, Orthodoxy and

REFERENCES AND SUGGESTED READINGS

Breck, J. (2001) *Scripture in Tradition: The Bible and Its Interpretation in the Orthodox Church.* Crestwood, NY: St. Vladimir's Seminary Press.

Burton-Christie, D. (1993) *The Word in the Desert: Scripture and the Quest for Holiness in Early Christian Monasticism.* Oxford: Oxford University Press.

Hall, C. A. (1998) *Reading Scripture with the Church Fathers.* Downers Grove, IL: InterVarsity Press.

Heine, R. E. (2007) *Reading the Old Testament with the Ancient Church: Exploring the Formation of Early Christian Thought.* Grand Rapids, MI: Baker.

Kannengiesser, C. (2006) *Handbook of Patristic Exegesis.* Boston: Brill.

Magdalino, P. et al. (eds.) (2009) "The Old Testament in Byzantium," in *Dumbarton Oaks Byzantine Symposia and Colloquia.* Washington, DC: Dumbarton Oaks Research Library and Collection.

Oikonomos, E. (1992) "The Significance of the Deuterocanonical Writings in the Orthodox Church," in S. Meurer (ed.) *The Apocrypha in Ecumenical Perspective.* UBS Monograph Series 6. Reading, UK: United Bible Societies, pp. 16–32.

Pentiuc, E. J. (2005) *Jesus the Messiah in the Hebrew Bible.* New York: Paulist Press.

Pentiuc, E. J. (2011) *The Old Testament in Eastern Orthodox Tradition.* Oxford: Oxford University Press.

Stylianopoulos, T. G. (ed.) (2006) *Sacred Text and Interpretation: Perspectives in Orthodox Biblical Studies. Papers in Honor of Professor Savas Agourides.* Brookline, MA: Holy Cross Orthodox Press.

Sundberg, A. C. (1964) "The Old Testament in the Early Church," *Harvard Theological Review* 20: 205–26.

Optina

THOMAS KITSON

The Optina Hermitage (near Kaluga) promoted hesychast spirituality in 19th-century Russia, inspired by Sts. Paisy Velichkovsky and Seraphim of Sarov. Metropolitan Filaret Drozdov supported Abbot Moses' ambitious publishing program there of Russian translations from patristic works. The monastery's reputation, however, rested, until its closure in 1923, on its many renowned elders

Plate 44   Liturgical procession at Optina Hermitage. RIA Novosti/Topfoto.

Plate 45   Optina Hermitage recently restored. RIA Novosti/Topfoto.

(*startsy*) – especially Sts. Leonid, Macarius, and Ambrose – whose teachings on humility and obedience attracted several secular intellectuals, including Turgenev, Gogol, Dostoevsky, Leontyev, and others. The elders also filled a deeply felt spiritual need for the crowds of pilgrims who traveled to Optina to confess and receive their blessing. The Optina saints are commemorated on October 10.

SEE ALSO: Elder (Starets); Hesychasm; *Philokalia*; St. Filaret (Philaret) Drozdov (1782–1867); St. Paisy Velichovsky (1722–1794); St. Seraphim of Sarov (1759–1833)

REFERENCES AND SUGGESTED READINGS

Dunlop, J. (1972) *Staretz Amvrosy*. London: Mowbray.
Meletios of Nikopolis (1987) *Starets Varsanouphios*, 2 vols. Preveza: n.p.
Sederholm, C. (1990) *Elder Leonid of Optina*. Platina, CA: St. Herman of Alaska Press.
Sederholm, C. (1994) *Elder Antony of Optina*. Platina, CA: St. Herman of Alaska Press.

Ordination

JEFFREY B. PETTIS

The Orthodox Church looks upon ordination (derived from the Latin term for registering clerics in the official lists of the church), which it designates using the biblical term as the "laying on of hands" (*cheirotonia*), as the sacramental continuation of the setting apart of leaders for the Christian community. Ordination is the regular transmission through the ages of the church of the charism of priesthood, as derived from the apostolic succession the church protects within itself. The Book of Numbers 27.15–23 speaks of the setting apart of Joshua by the Lord to be a leader and shepherd of the congregation. Joshua is one who is "in the Spirit" (18), and Moses places him before the priest and the congregation, lays hands on him, and gives him a charge according to divine command (22–3; cf. Deut. 34.9). In the gospels Jesus himself sets apart for ministry the twelve apostles (Mt. 10.1–5; Mk. 3.13–19; Lk. 6.12–16). He also commissions the Seventy to do the work of evangelizing (Lk. 10.1). In Acts 14.23 the Apostle Paul lays hands (*cheirotonēsantes*) on designated church elders (*presbyterous*). The laying on of hands is the transmission of the sacred gift of the Spirit, confirming the gift given in Chrismation, for the special role of sanctifying, teaching, healing, and witnessing that constitutes the priestly service in the church. The Apostle Paul also refers to the bishop (*episkopos*) who tends the church of God like a shepherd (Acts 20.28; cf. Ignatius, *Eph.* 1.3; 2.1f.; 3.2; 4.1; 5.1f.). The *Didache* refers to the electing of bishops and deacons "who are worthy of the Lord, gentle men who are not fond of money, who are true (*alētheis*) and approved" (*Didache* 15). The earliest evidence for the church's formal service of ordination is found in the *Apostolic Tradition of Hippolytus* (ca. 215):

> He who is ordained as a bishop, being chosen by all the people, must be irreproachable. When his name is announced and approved, the people will gather on the Lord's day with the council of elders and the bishops who are present. With the assent of all, the bishops will place their hands upon him, with the council of elders standing by, quietly. Everyone will keep silent, praying in their hearts for the descent of the Spirit. After this, one of the bishops present, at the request of all, shall lay his hand upon him who is being ordained bishop, and shall pray. (*Apostolic Tradition* 2.1–5)

The Orthodox Church recognizes the transmission of the priesthood in three degrees, designated "major orders." These are bishop, presbyter, and deacon. The minor orders today include the subdeacon and readers (formerly there was a larger range of offices), who receive not the laying on of hands for admission into the priesthood but a lesser blessing (*cheirothesia*) to perform their special ministry. At an ordination a candidate is brought to the Iconostasis by fellow members of his rank (deacons by deacons, presbyters by deacons and presbyters) for "passing on" into the hands of ordained clergy of the rank to which he is being inducted. All priestly ordinations take place at the Eucharist, and only one ordination to any given rank can be celebrated at a single liturgy. The ordination of a bishop precedes the scripture reading and the Eucharistic Anaphora, in this way recognizing him as the expounder of the faith and celebrant of the mysteries. The candidate confesses his Orthodoxy and recites the creed, declares his fidelity to the canons and the ecumenical councils, vows to preserve the peace of the church and always to teach the people faithfully. Following the Trisagion chant the candidate is brought before the holy table and the book of the gospels is opened and placed upon his head. The presiding bishop offers a prayer and makes three crosses in the name of the Holy Trinity over the head of the initiate. The other bishops lay their hands upon his head while the consecratory prayers are said. Once ordained, he receives the *Sakkos* and other episcopal vestments. The presiding bishop places upon him the episcopal encolpion, the jeweled icon of Christ or the Mother of God which he will always wear upon his breast, the monastic mantle, the Komboskini rosary, and the pastoral staff.

The ordination of a presbyter directly follows the Eucharistic Great Entrance and thus again takes place before the Anaphora to show the presbyter's central office as celebrant of the mysteries. During the ordination the candidate is taken from the deacons by presbyters and led around the altar three times as he kisses the four corners, and reverences the ordaining bishop. He kneels at the altar bending both knees and places his head upon the holy table as the bishop lays hands on his head, to recite the consecratory prayer. He is then invested before the people with the priest's epitrachelion, zone (liturgical belt), and phelonion. He is also given the service book to guide his future ministry.

The ordination of deacons, whose chief service is to read the Holy Gospel and assist at the divine liturgy and the distribution of the Holy Gifts, comes after the consecration of the gifts and prior to Holy Communion, to symbolize that his is the office of assistance (not consecration). As the choir sings the deacon is led three times around the altar, the four corners of which he kisses, reverencing the bishop. Following his ordination, which takes place with a different prayer of consecration while he kneels at the altar on one knee, he receives the liturgical fan (rhipidion) as a symbol of his office.

Ordination to minor orders is performed by a bishop or monastic higumen who has received the blessing to do this, outside the sanctuary and at any communal worship service apart from the Eucharist. In the Orthodox Church all ordinations symbolically follow the consent given by the congregation and the clergy who say *Axios* when the candidate is presented by the bishop ("He is worthy to be ordained"). Because the nature of ordination is indelible, it can occur to the same rank only once and may never be repeated.

SEE ALSO: Anagnostes (Reader); Deacon; Deaconess; Episcopacy; Epitrachelion; Phelonion; Priesthood; Rhipidion (Fan)

REFERENCES AND SUGGESTED READINGS

Langford-James, R. (ed.) (1975) *A Dictionary of the Eastern Orthodox Church*. New York: Burt Franklin.
Litsas, F. (1984) *A Companion to the Greek Orthodox Church*. New York: Greek Orthodox Archdiocese.
Parry, K. et al. (eds.) (1999) *The Blackwell Dictionary of Eastern Christianity*. Oxford: Blackwell.

Oriental Orthodox

PETER C. BOUTENEFF

Oriental Orthodox is the name by which several "non-Chalcedonian Churches" have come to be collectively known. This category has tended to include the Syrian Orthodox Patriarchate of Antioch and All the East, the Coptic Orthodox Patriarchate of Alexandria, the Ethiopian Orthodox Tewahedo Church, the Eritrean Orthodox Tewahedo Church, the Armenian Apostolic Church, and the Malankara Orthodox Syrian Church.

Each of these churches has traditionally rejected the authority of what the Eastern Orthodox Church considers its Fourth Ecumenical Council, held in Chalcedon in the year 451. They recognize only three ecumenical councils: Nicea (325), Constantinople (381), and Ephesus (431). Although historical and political factors cannot be ignored, neither can the role of the *Tome* of Pope Leo I and its theologically controversial language. The chief theological rationale for their rejection of Chalcedon rests in the council's statement that Jesus Christ was known "in two natures." This statement was interpreted by the non-Chalcedonians as leading inexorably to a Nestorian understanding of Christ, i.e., seeing Christ as constituted by two personal subjects ("two Sons"), one divine and one human.

Plate 46 A Coptic monk in the Monastery of St. Antony, Egypt. Photo by John McGuckin.

Plate 47 Pope Shenouda, leader of the world's Coptic Orthodox faithful. Photo by John McGuckin.

The non-Chalcedonian Orthodox see Chalcedon's "in two natures" language as a betrayal of the formula identified with St. Cyril of Alexandria: "One incarnate nature of God the Word" (*mia physis tou theou logou sesarkomene*), alternately rendered "One nature of the divine Word incarnate" (*mia physis tou theou logou sesarkomenou*). Their preference for one-nature formulations has long earned them the collective title of "Monophysites." However, since (as twentieth-century dialogues have affirmed) the non-Chalcedonians insist upon Christ's consubstantiality (*homoousion*) with both God the Father according to his divinity, and with us according to his humanity, that title has increasingly been seen as misleading. Monophysitism, it is argued, best describes the radical (and bilaterally condemned) position of Eutyches the Presbyter, who rejected Christ's consubstantiality with humanity, and thus the non-Chalcedonians are sometimes called either "Henophysites" – the Greek *Hen* denoting a union rather than a radical monad – or "Miaphysites" – following the wording of the Cyrilline formula, again allowing for a union of divinity and humanity in one nature without separation, without confusion, and without change.

The title "Oriental Orthodox" arose in the context of the bilateral dialogues with the Eastern Orthodox Church, whose identity as a family or communion of autocephalous churches had been long established. The dialogues therefore played a vital role in establishing a rubric that would assemble the non-Chalcedonian churches and identify them as a coherent body. Calling these churches "Oriental" was not meant to elicit the stereotypic *Orientalism* of which Edward Said has written, but rather deliberately to evince a title that was essentially indistinguishable from "Eastern." The name "Orthodox," which did not figure previously into the self-appellations of all the churches (e.g., the Armenian Apostolic Church), was also meant to identify a parity of legitimacy and fidelity to world Orthodoxy through the ages.

These modern dialogues between the Oriental and Eastern Orthodox churches began unofficially, as a direct result of the multilateral ecumenical encounters through the World Council of Churches. Four unofficial meetings held from 1964 to 1971 were followed by a series of official dialogues constituted by church-appointed delegates from 1985 to 1993. These covered theological as well as pastoral issues, which in turn have been applied in local pastoral agreements, notably in the Middle East and in Egypt. While their theological conclusions were at points unequivocal – "both families have always loyally maintained the same authentic Orthodox Christological faith, and the unbroken continuity of the apostolic tradition" (Chambésy, 1990) – the dialogue statements have yet to be fully received or acted upon among the Eastern and Oriental churches in the wider sense.

SEE ALSO: Africa, Orthodoxy in; Armenian Christianity; Council of Chalcedon (451); Council of Constantinople I (381); Council of Ephesus (431); Council of Nicea I (325); Ecumenism, Orthodoxy and; Malankara Orthodox Syrian Church; Monophysitism (including Miaphysitism); Syrian Orthodox Churches

REFERENCES AND SUGGESTED READINGS

Gregorios, P. (ed.) (1981) *Does Chalcedon Divide or Unite? Towards Convergence in Orthodox Christology.* Geneva: World Council of Churches.
Ware, T. (1993) *The Orthodox Church.* London: Penguin.

Original Sin

M. C. STEENBERG

The term "original sin" is normally taken to indicate a specific view on the origin of sin and its effects in the world, as read through the perspective of the Genesis account of Adam and Eve in Eden (Gen. 2–3ff.). Specifically, it reads this text as suggesting a state of original perfection in which humanity was created and from which it "fell" through transgression. This fall affected the nature of humanity, such that it was to some degree imbued with sin, thereafter inherited by future generations. This condition of in-built sin (described in certain Latin authors as *concupiscence*, a process of being bound up in errant desire) is in moderate writers of the early Latin Church taken to indicate a general propensity or inclination toward error, while in more extreme exponents it has been developed into doctrines (particularly in post-Reformation western theology) of "total depravity" or an inheritance of the guilt of Adam's transgression.

The doctrine of original sin originates largely from St. Augustine and certain other writers of the patristic Latin West, such as Tertullian. From the outset it has been questioned by exponents of Orthodox theology. While the emphasis on the universal scope of sin is certainly consonant with Orthodox thought, notions of a perfect "pristine condition" and a fall from grace have often been seen as at variance with Orthodox anthropology – or at least as a reading of Genesis that puts excessive emphasis on a transformation of human nature that results from its first transgression. Orthodox writers have tended to emphasize the developmental nature of humanity's creation *into* perfection, rather than *as already perfected* before declining; and have resisted strongly the conceptions of inherited guilt that are often central to western expositions of original sin. As a result, there is a preference among some Orthodox writers in the modern era to use the phrases "ancestral sin" or "primal sin" as a means of distinguishing a non-"Augustinian" reading of the Genesis account of transgression from the understanding of original sin now dominant in the West. A precise definition of original sin is, however, difficult to pin down historically, and presentations of "Augustinian" doctrine in this regard are often generalized and imprecise, leading at times to a popular "East versus West" rhetoric on the point that has little concrete basis in the actual writings of the early church.

Nonetheless, what has become the popular definition of original sin (i.e., a perfect original state, a fall, a transformation of nature) does establish a point of contrast with traditional Orthodox anthropology and conception of sin, which is more dynamic, open-ended, developmental, and therapeutic. It thus forms an issue of ongoing disputation between Eastern and Western Christianity at large.

SEE ALSO: Humanity; Repentance; Soteriology

REFERENCES AND SUGGESTED READINGS

Williams, N. P. (1927) *The Ideas of the Fall and of Original Sin: Bampton Lectures for 1924*. New York: Longmans, Green.

Orthros (Matins)

JEFFREY B. PETTIS

The Greek word *orthros* translates as "dawn" or "early morning." In early Christian usage it referred to early morning prayer, or (as in monastic usage) dawn prayers after the night vigil (see Basil of

Caesarea, *regulae fusius tractatae* 37.3, 5 [PG.31.1013A,1016B]). After the 4th century the word came to designate the early morning service of psalms and canticles (a parallel to the western monastic services of Matins and Lauds) as one of the regular hours of Byzantine monastic prayer, in the sequence of Vespers, Compline, Midnight Office, Orthros, First, Third, Sixth, and Ninth Hours. In Greek practice Orthros is conducted by itself, or as the immediate prelude to the divine liturgy. In parishes it occurs chiefly on Sundays before the liturgy. In Russian practice it is often combined with preceding Sunday Vespers (on Saturday evening) as the Vigil Service. Orthros begins with the Trisagion prayers and the reading of the Six Psalms (Hexapsalmoi), and includes litanies alternating with hymns (especially in the form of canons) and recitations of appointed sections (kathismata) of the Psalter. In parish practice the psalm readings are much abbreviated. The service culminates with the reading of a resurrection gospel. If not followed by the liturgy, Orthros ends with the small doxology; if the liturgy follows the great doxology is used.

SEE ALSO: Canon (Liturgical); Eothina; Hexapsalmoi; Kathisma; Kontakion; Ode

REFERENCES AND SUGGESTED READINGS

Litsas, F. (1984) *A Companion to the Greek Orthodox Church.* New York: Greek Orthodox Archdiocese.

Patrinacos, N. E. (1984) *A Dictionary of Greek Ortho-doxy.* Pleasantville, NY: Hellenic Heritage Publications.

Taft, R. (2004) *The Liturgy of the Hours in East and West.* Collegeville, MN: Liturgical Press.

Ottoman Yoke

EVANGELOS KATAFYLIS

The Ottoman Yoke signifies the political and religious subordination of the Greek Christians to Islam after the fall of Constantinople in 1453 and the abolition of the Byzantine Empire. The Yoke is seen as having started to lift after the revolutionary declaration of Greek independence from the Turks in 1821. Though many parts of the Orthodox world (such as Egypt and Anatolia) never regained any form of political independence, other conquered Orthodox nations (especially in the Balkans) followed the Greek example soon after. After the fall of Constantinople the Orthodox Church was the only institution that continued the religious legacy of Byzantium, preserving and organizing Christianity throughout the sultan's extensive dominions. The conqueror, Sultan Mehmet II, recognized the Greek patriarch as the legal head of the Orthodox Christian community (*ethnarch*), and designated him supreme religious leader of all his Orthodox subjects (*dhimmi*) among whom he included non-Chalcedonian and non-Greek Orthodox too; allowing them freedom of worship under Ottoman protection provided the taxes of a subject nation were paid. Mehmet first appointed Gennadios Scholarios to take over the patriarchal office, giving to him and his successors full jurisdiction over the education of all the Orthodox Christians across the Ottoman Empire. The Orthodox Church was, at that time, the only organized institution which could represent Christians in their dealings with the Ottoman administration (*Porte Sublime*), and apart from the church, the Orthodox Christian population had no centrally surviving institutions.

Between the 15th and 16th centuries the Ottoman sultans succeeded in making Constantinople the center of their empire. It became a vibrant city, retaining Greek as the diplomatic language of the empire. When the empire became less tolerant of its Greek subjects, they were often forced to adopt a new way of life, for the sake of their survival. Accordingly, this period saw the progressive Islamicization of the

Christians, the phenomenon of crypto-Christianism, the recruitment of underage Christian children (*devşirme*) for the sultan's personal guard, the prohibition of the erection of churches (and often of their repair), the seizure and destruction of what church property remained after the conquest, the obstruction of Christian worship, the compulsory enlistment in the navy for Greeks, the growth of piracy and lawlessness against Christian merchants who were regarded as an easy target, and an oppressive poll tax (*haraç*) which was given to the patriarchate to enforce, thereby earning him unpopularity. This system of the patriarch acting as empire-wide ethnarch led to the rise of the so-called Phanariots, members of prominent Greek families in Constantinople who, from the second half of the 16th century until the 18th century, offered their services as *dragomans* (translators, or agents) to the Ottoman government, and thereby often commandeered leading political and ecclesiastic posts in all the Christian territories across Ottoman dominions.

The regime under which Christian subjects were living after the conquest was a harsh one, punctuated by many examples of captivities and persecutions, one that has been globally designated by the dramatic word *Yoke*, a term meaning "Slavery." Living under such conditions, many Greek Christians of the Turkish mainland emigrated to safer places in southern Italy, around the Danube, to Russia, Venice, or the Venetian colonies in Greece. Despite the migration, the spirit of Greek Orthodox culture continued to exist, with many eminent scholars of this time active on mainland Greece. The Greek Orthodox College, established in 1454 by Gennadios Scholarios, played an important role in continuing Orthodox Christian culture under the Yoke. In Crete and on Mount Athos,

Greek letters and iconic painting also flourished. The migrations were a demographic shift which significantly contributed to a wide dissemination of Greek culture and language in Orthodox lands, resulting in the establishment of schools and the publication of many books.

From the beginning of the 18th century the decline of Ottoman power in the face of European advances became increasingly evident. It led to a widespread sense among the Orthodox of the Ottoman domains that certain instances of independence could be achieved: something that became realized with the 1821 declaration of Greek independence. This led to rapid economic and cultural developments among the Greek and other newly independent Orthodox nations in the 19th century and beyond.

SEE ALSO: Constantinople, Patriarchate of; Mount Athos; Romania, Patriarchal Orthodox Church of; Scholarios, George (Gennadios) (ca. 1403–1472)

REFERENCES AND SUGGESTED READINGS

Chasiotes, I. (2001) Μεταξύ Οθωμανικής κυριαρχίας και Ευρωπαϊκής πρόσκλησης: Ο ελληνικός κόσμος στα χρόνια της Τουρκοκρατίας [Between Ottoman Domination and European Challenge: The Greek World in the Years of the Ottoman Yoke]. Thessaloniki: University Studio Press.

Metallenos, G. (1998) Τουρκοκρατία: Οι Έλληνες στην Οθωμανική Αυτοκρατορία [Ottoman Yoke: The Greeks in Ottoman Empire]. Athens: Akritas.

Vakalopoulos, A. (2001) Ιστορία του νέου Ελληνισμού [History of Modern Greece]. Thessaloniki: Hyrodotos.

Zakythinos, D. (1957) Τουρκοκρατία: εισαγωγή εις την νεωτέραν ιστορίαν του ελληνισμού [Ottoman Yoke: Introduction to Modern History of Hellenism]. Athens.

P

Panagia

JEFFREY B. PETTIS

The word *Panagia* is the Greek term (feminine form) for "She who is all holy." In common Orthodox usage today, Panagia is the most common title of honor for the Virgin Mary, the Mother of God. The word Panagia may also refer to the medallion icon of the Virgin that a bishop wears on his breast (*enkolpion*), or to the ritual blessing of a loaf bearing a stamped icon of the Virgin, usually held on feast days in monasteries.

REFERENCES AND SUGGESTED READINGS

Langford-James, R. (ed.) (1975) *A Dictionary of the Eastern Orthodox Church.* New York: Burt Franklin.
Litsas, F. (1984) *A Companion to the Greek Orthodox Church.* New York: Greek Orthodox Archdiocese.
Zernov, N. (1961) *Eastern Christianity: A Study of the Origin and Development of the Eastern Orthodox Church.* New York: Putnam's Sons.

Panikhida *see* Death (and Funeral); Kollyva

Pannychis *see* Kontakion

Pantocrator Icon

MARIA GWYN MCDOWELL

The broad range of Pantocrator ("Ruler" or "Preserver of all") icons of the Lord in majestic judgment and blessing serve as "a flexible spiritual aid for the devout viewer" (Onasch and Schnieper 1995: 129). Initially appearing on coins and in manuscripts, then domes and apses, Pantocrator icons proliferated during the high Middle Ages. A bearded Christ, hair neatly parted, sits on a throne (often absent), right hand raised in blessing, left hand holding the gospel, expression varying from severe to compassionate. The background may include a mandorla, angelic figures, and gospel symbols. Famous examples include the earliest known 6th-century Sinai encaustic and the 11th-century Daphni mosaic.

SEE ALSO: Deisis; Icons

REFERENCES AND SUGGESTED READINGS

Onasch, K. and Schnieper, A. (1995) *Icons: Fascination and Reality.* New York: Riverside Books.
Ouspensky, L. and Lossky, V. (1982) *The Meaning of Icons.* Crestwood, NY: St. Vladimir's Seminary Press.

The Encyclopedia of Eastern Orthodox Christianity, edited by John Anthony McGuckin
© 2011 Blackwell Publishing Ltd.

Plate 48 Coptic fresco of Christ in glory from the Monastery of St. Antony by the Red Sea. Photo by John McGuckin.

Papacy
AUGUSTINE CASIDAY

A statement of the Eastern Orthodox ideal of the papal office, and its role in relation to the churches, can be supplied from St. Ignatius of Antioch's salutation in his letter *To the Romans*, where he speaks of how the pope presides over the Church of Rome: "which presides in love." Similarly, the problems experienced by Orthodox Christians with respect to the papacy can also be summed up from Ignatius' further description of the Church of Rome as functioning to "maintain the law of Christ." Under the concept of "maintaining the law of Christ" can be accommodated many of the Eastern Christian world's experiences of the papacy that have been disagreeable,

ranging from doctrinal assertions to political interventions, with the result that Orthodox perspectives on the papacy and especially its ecclesiological theory of primacy, above all in the second millennium of Christianity, have frequently been negative. Attention to several key episodes and particular claims will substantiate and nuance this general view.

Ignatius' high regard was reinforced by Rome's ancient reputation for orthodoxy, unrivalled by any other major see in the early Christian world. Situated a convenient distance from an interfering emperor, the pope of Rome almost always spoke conservatively for the good of the churches, and with a degree of impartiality, even if that came occasionally at a steep price. During the 7th-century Monothelite controversy, Pope Martin I paid with his life for opposing imperial policy. During the same crisis, St. Maximos the Confessor exclaimed at his trial: "I love the Romans because we share the same faith, whereas I love the Greeks because we share the same language." But already by Maximos' day a far-reaching difference between Greek and Latin theology was emerging as a contested issue, namely, the broad-based western affirmation that the Holy Spirit proceeds from the Father "and from the Son" or, in Latin, *filioque* (Louth 2007: 84–6). Initially outside of Rome, and eventually in Rome itself, that clause was incorporated into the Nicene-Constantinopolitan Creed. Such a modification raised important questions about what kind of authority the pope claimed to alter the creed set out by an ecumenical council. It also created a symbolic issue of high theological significance over which Orthodox and Latin Christians would argue fiercely.

With the increasing social and political prominence of the Roman Church in post-Byzantine Italy, the parameters of papal leadership expanded and frequently clashed against the secular powers of the Franks, the Byzantines, the Lombards, and others (see Noble 1984). Religious clashes occurred, as we have noted, increasingly over the matter of the *filioque*. Was the pope's authority limited to final jurisdiction for appeals (as was the general eastern opinion in the first millennium) or did he enjoy the prerogative to intervene spontaneously whenever and wherever he considered such intervention justified (as became an increasingly affirmed Latin theory based on the idea of the pope as the extraordinary vicar of St. Peter)? What of the matter of jurisdictions extending as a result of sometimes competitive missionary activity (see Louth 2007: 167–92)? It was by no means unheard of for papal power to be exercised against the interests of the Christian East. Conflicting interests naturally led to confrontations, such as can be seen in Pope Nicholas I's interventions during the patriarchate of Photios (Chadwick 2003: 95–192). Nicholas eventually answered an appeal by Photios' deposed predecessor, but surely was also interested in the Christianization of Bulgaria, poised to come under either Roman or Constantinopolitan influence. For decades after this period, problems were rife between the Constantinopolitan patriarchate and the papacy, and matters only worsened as time went on. As Chadwick describes it: "In the century following the patriarchate of Photios, relations between Constantinople and Rome or the West generally fluctuated in close correspondence with political factors, and political concerns became a more potent factor than religious or theological matters" (2003: 193).

In 1054 another rupture opened in the tense existing communion between Rome and Constantinople, caused by diverging practices in liturgy and church discipline, and exacerbated by irreconcilable expectations about the exercise of authority in such cases (Chadwick 2003: 206–18; Louth 2007: 305–18). Although the mutual excommunications delivered in July 1054 were of doubtful importance, or even legality, in retrospect they more and more came to signify the formal separation of the Western Catholic Church from the Eastern Orthodox Churches. The events of 1054 certainly reveal "underlying issues of authority that were not to go away" (Louth 2007: 318).

That a confluence of competing political, doctrinal, and canonical interests contributed substantially to the estrangement of the Christian West from the Orthodox world is by no means solely a modern perception. The 12th-century historian Anna Comnena bundled ecclesiastical privileges together with political ascendancy in her claim for Constantinopolitan primacy: "The truth is that when power was transferred from Rome to our country and the Queen of Cities, not to mention the senate and the whole administration, the senior ranking archbishopric was also transferred here" (*Alexiad* 1.13). Her assessment suggests that 11th-century Rome was commonly seen by the Byzantines to lack ecclesiastical and political preeminence; and its claims for primacy as refuted in a reading of the Chalcedonian canons about jurisdictional precedence that interpreted Rome as having been subordinated to Constantinople. Such is Anna's brisk response to the Gregorian reforms of an ascendant papacy.

Relations between the sees of Rome and Constantinople continued to deteriorate during the course of the Crusades. Anna Comnena saw in them, from their inception, a sinister western plot to subvert Constantinople (*Alexiad* 10.5), an eventuality which indeed transpired in 1204. As the figurehead for the Christian West, the papacy's reputation in the East was enormously damaged by the fall of Constantinople to Latin Crusaders, and by the papacy's subsequent activities, installing parallel Latin patriarchates in the conquered territories.

The popes hosted several attempts at reconciliation between the churches, such as the Second Council of Lyons (1274) and the Council of Ferrara-Florence (1438–9). Sometimes the initiative in reconciliation came from the East, as with the Union of Brest (1596), or it may have been a personal initiative, such as the contributions by Leo Allatius (1648) or Vladimir Solovyov. But these attempts were all overshadowed by widespread Orthodox distaste for the "Unia," or Eastern-Rite Christian churches that accepted Papal obedience. The papacy's invitation to the leading Orthodox hierarchs to attend Vatican Council I in the mid-19th century drew from them only a formal rebuke of his jurisdictional pretensions. Much tension still exists in terms of the papacy's installation and continuing administration of a parallel Latin hierarchy in Orthodox lands (such as Russia).

In recent times, however, some Orthodox theologians have been revisiting the question of the papacy in a more pacific light (see Meyendorff 1992). The mutual excommunications of 1054 were rescinded on December 7, 1965 in a dramatic mutual gesture of reconciliation between Pope Paul VI and Patriarch Athenagoras of Constantinople (Abbot and Gallagher 1966: 725–7); and subsequent Constantinopolitan patriarchs have continued what has been called the "Dialogue of Love." It suggests that further developments of Orthodox reflection on the role and position of the papacy will be forthcoming.

SEE ALSO: Church (Orthodox Ecclesiology); Eastern Catholic Churches; Episcopacy; *Filioque*; Rome, Ancient Patriarchate of; St. Maximos the Confessor (580–662); St. Photios the Great (ca. 810–893); Sts. Constantine (Cyril) (ca. 826–869) and Methodios (815–885); Solovyov, Vladimir (1853–1900)

REFERENCES AND SUGGESTED READINGS

Abbot, W. and Gallagher, J. (ed. and trans.) (1966) *The Documents of Vatican II*. New York: Corpus Press.

Allatius, L. (1648) *De ecclesiae occidentalis atque orientalis perpetua consensione*. Cologne: Kalcovius.

Allen, P. and Neil, B. (ed. and trans.) (2004) *Maximus the Confessor and His Companions: Documents from Exile*. Oxford: Oxford University Press.

Chadwick, H. (2003) *East and West: The Making of a Rift in the Church*. Oxford: Oxford University Press.

Comnena, A. (1969) *The Alexiad*, trans. E. R. A. Sewter. London: Penguin.

Louth, A. (2007) *Greek East and Latin West: The Church AD 681–1071*. Crestwood, NY: St. Vladimir's Seminary Press.

Meyendorff, J. (ed.) (1992) *The Primacy of Peter*, 2nd edn. Crestwood, NY: St. Vladimir's Seminary Press.

Noble, T. (1984) *The Republic of St. Peter: The Birth of the Papal States, 680–825*. Philadelphia: University of Pennsylvania Press.

Paradise

PETER C. BOUTENEFF

The Greek *Paradeisos* (cf. the Persian *Pardez*, meaning "enclosure") in the Septuagint refers to any enclosed garden (cf. Num. 24.6; Neh. 2.8; Eccl. 2.5; Jer. 29.5), but remains particularly associated with the Garden in Eden (Gen. 2–3, 13.10; also Is. 51.3; Ezek. 28.13). In Second Temple Jewish literature (e.g., 1 Enoch 60.8, 23, 61.12; Apoc. Abraham 21.3, 6; 3 Baruch 4.10) as well as in the New Testament (Lk. 23.43; Rev. 2.7), Paradise comes to refer also to the destination of the righteous, whether it is an earthly or heavenly *topos*. St. Paul's mystical experience which associates Paradise with the Third Heaven (2 Cor. 12.2–3) has deeply influenced the Greek patristic literature, and is frequently cited.

PARADISE AS THE GARDEN OF HUMAN ORIGINS

Paradise as the earthly garden in Eden, into which the first-created humans were placed, and which Genesis 2 locates on Earth (in what is modern-day Iraq), is treated variously in the Greek fathers. Theophilus of Antioch, almost unique among the early writers for the absence of a typological (christological) exegesis of the Paradise narrative, is concomitantly almost unique in attempting to pinpoint the chronological dating of the events narrated in Genesis 1–3 (as did Eusebius of Caesarea, in his *Chronicle*, no longer extant). Conversely, and possibly following Philo (cf. *Laws of Allegory* 1.43), Origen practically mocks anyone who would interpret Paradise as an actual place with physical trees and chewable fruit (*On First Principles* 4.3.1). Precisely this notion, however, featured strongly in Ephrem's *Hymns on Paradise* (Brock 1990). Gregory of Nazianzus is open and provisional in his interpretation: God placed the human person in Paradise, "Whatever this Paradise actually was," and introduced him to trees which Gregory supposes might represent contemplation (*theoria*) (*Oration* 38.12).

Contemporary Orthodox theologians tend to follow the fathers in paying scant attention to the question of the physical historicity of the Paradise of Genesis 2–3, focusing rather on its existential significance or more often on its christological sense. Those who address the question of historicity answer it variously. Fr. Seraphim Rose insists on a literal reading of Genesis 1–3, rejecting any evolutionary theory and believing the universe to be less than ten thousand years old. Archbishop Lazar Puhalo associates the insistence upon the physical historicity of Genesis 1–3 with a weak faith in God, who quite evidently creates through an evolutionary means over the course of billions of years. A range of positions exists spanning these extremes, alternately accommodating or rejecting evolutionary theories and the scientific dating of the universe at 13.7 billion years. But again, most focus on the existential character of the narrative (Orthodox hymnography and patristic texts usually place "us" in the Garden, and lament "our" sin therein), or the christological (Adam being a type for Christ [Rom. 5.14], and the entire narrative describing what Christ comes to restore).

PARADISE AS DESTINATION

Some of the Greek fathers saw Paradise, albeit in various ways, as the resting place of the (righteous) dead. Some periodically distinguished Paradise from Heaven, the former being a kind of interim space before arrival in Heaven (cf. Origen, *First Principles* 2.11.6). Reckoning Paradise as the destination of the righteous relied on several factors that presented the age to come as a return to origins. One was the dynamic of typology, which related the events, personae, and even the "space" of Eden to the passion and resurrection of Christ. Christ is the New Adam, Mary the New Eve, the tree of the cross is the new tree of life, and the heavenly Paradise, and/or the church, is the new Eden. This manner of understanding the Scriptures came to a particularly full theological expression in St. Irenaeus's concept of recapitulation (*Adversus Haereses*).

Of related significance is the understanding of the age to come as a restoration (*apokatastasis*) (cf. Acts 3.21). "The end is always like the beginning," says Origen (*First Principles* 1.6.2). Although steeped in a classical Greek mindset which espoused a broadly cyclic understanding of time and destiny, he is here speaking of a restoration – through subjection to Christ in the Holy Spirit – to a single end which is like the single beginning. In so doing he articulates a consistent trajectory of thought in the Greek fathers. This is not properly understood as a return to a place or state that was ever historically realized, but rather as the realization of the divine will, the fulfillment of the original (or better, eternal) divine intention and principle (*logos*) for humanity, *unrealized* by Adam and Eve in the Garden of Eden. Frequently, then, the effective identity of end and beginning is expressed through this common *topos* of Paradise.

On this score, while the primeval Paradise was seen as an ideal place and condition, its human denizens (the biblical Adam and Eve) are not generally portrayed as icons of a fully realized state of human personhood. Maximus the Confessor asserts that humans fell "together with their coming into being" (*To Thalassius* 61). Irenaeus, Gregory of Nazianzus, and Ephrem the Syrian understood Adam and Eve to be "works in progress," innocent like children and, if anything, terribly weak. They partook of a fruit that was always intended for human consumption, but not for persons in their yet-underdeveloped state. The Eucharistic Anaphora of Basil the Great says that the human creature was placed in Paradise with "the *promise* of immortality." Adam and Eve represent an unrealized potential, while the icon of perfected, immortal humanity is the New Adam, Jesus Christ, through whom humans may now attain to the Paradise always intended for them, as a life in free and full communion with God – a place of ineffable, inexhaustible, and ever-surprising sweetness, beauty, and joy.

SEE ALSO: Ecology; Original Sin; Soteriology

REFERENCES AND SUGGESTED READINGS

Bouteneff, P. C. (2008) *Beginnings: Ancient Christian Readings of the Biblical Creation Narratives*. Grand Rapids, MI: Baker Academic.

Brock, S. (trans.) (1990) *St. Ephrem the Syrian: Hymns on Paradise*. Crestwood, NY: St. Vladimir's Seminary Press.

Rose, S. (2000) *Genesis, Creation, and Early Man: The Orthodox Christian Vision*. Platina, CA: St. Herman of Alaska Brotherhood.

Paraklesis

DIMITRI CONOMOS

A service of supplication and intercession. Loosely based on the structure of Matins, this unique service combines litanical prayer, a gospel reading, psalmody, and hymnody. It may be celebrated in church with a priest or at home as a service of the laity. Its function is to call upon Christ or one of his saints for succor, blessing, and mediation. The most popular (and presumably the model for subsequent imitations) are the Great and Small Parakleses to the Mother of God. Either one is chanted (often in alternation) each day during the fast of the Dormition (August 1–14).

Paraklitike

JEFFREY B. PETTIS

The *Paraklitike* is the Byzantine liturgical book containing the variable hymns of divine service. The texts are arranged according to the eight tones of Byzantine church music, each having its own hymns and antiphons. Accordingly, the *Paraklitike* is also known as the *Oktoechos* (Greek, "book of eight tones"). The texts are inclusive for All Saints Day (Sunday after

Pentecost) to the 4th Sunday before the Great Lent. St. Joseph the Hymnographer (9th century), a prolific composer of liturgical canons, gave the final form to the *Paraklitike*. St. John of Damascus (ca. 665–749) is also traditionally thought to have contributed to its composition.

SEE ALSO: *Anastasimatarion*; Hymnography; Liturgical Books; Music (Sacred); *Oktoechos*; St. John of Damascus (ca. 675–ca. 750)

Parousia

MATTHEW J. PEREIRA

The Greek term *parousia*, within the context of the New Testament, denotes the "presence" or "arrival" of Jesus Christ at the Eschaton (Matt. 24.3; 1 Cor. 15.23). Early Christian expectations of apocalyptic salvation were foreshadowed in Palestinian literature, as can be seen by reference to the Old Testament pseudepigrapha and the Qumran texts (Russell 1964). The early church's sense of the delay of the glorious return of Christ in judgment (Jn. 21.21–23) provided Christians the opportunity to rearticulate the Parousia in a manner that reflected their own theological concerns, which were shaped within specific social and ecclesial settings (Aune 1975). Beyond exclusively focusing on the "last days," patristic theologians extensively interpreted the Parousia as a present spiritual reality, part of the resurrection mystery, which pointed towards a future hope.

In the early church the Parousia denoted a wide range of spiritual realities, such as the nearness of the gospel, the day of resurrection, Christ's healing ministry, judgment, and accommodation to humanity. In his *Letter to the Philadelphians* Ignatius of Antioch (ca. 35–ca. 98/117) proclaimed that the gospel possesses the transcendent "appearance" of our Lord Jesus Christ, his passion

and resurrection (*Phil.* 9.2). Justin Martyr (ca. 100–165) interprets the Parousia as Christ's power, whereby the Lord resurrects the dead and heals the sick upon his arrival. In his *Dialogue with Trypho* Justin Martyr also interpreted the deluge as a Christ-event; Noah and his family totaled eight people and thus allegorically represented the eighth day, which is when Christ "appeared" (had his Parousia) and rose from the dead (*Dial.* 88.2). Further, in his *First Apology*, Justin parallels the prophecy of Isaiah with Christ's healing presence; it is at the Lord's "coming" that the "lame shall leap ... the lepers be cleansed, and the dead shall rise" (*I Apol.* 48.2). In the *Stromateis* Clement of Alexandria (ca. 150–215) argues that the "advent" of the Savior will divide the believers from the disobedient (*Strom.* 1.18). The Lord's arrival clearly reveals the spiritual state of each person, and thus ensures there will be only just judgment. Further, Clement teaches God has no natural relation with humanity, yet the Lord "accommodated" himself to our weakness (*Strom.* 2.16). In brief, Christian theologians in the first three centuries interpreted the Parousia as a fundamental christological event associated with Christ's resurrection power, healing, judgment, and nearness to redeemed humanity.

Origen of Alexandria (d. 253/254) enlarged the doctrine of the Parousia through emphasizing the possibility, for the spiritually advanced, to experience God in the present moment. While known for his speculative tendencies, Origen's pastoral concerns informed his theology of the Parousia (Etcheverría 1969; Daley 2003: 48). Origen predominantly understood the Apocalypse of John through the lens of Christ, rather than focusing on the "last days" (Daley 2003: 49). There is another "second coming," according to Origen, where the Lord becomes present to the souls who are being perfected. Overall, Origen interprets the "last times" in a manner that primarily is meant to illuminate Christian spiritual growth. The consummation of the world, according to Origen, involves the present process of spiritual growth realized within each soul (*De Principiis* 3.6.6). The Kingdom of God is already present in virtuous Christians, while not fully realized (*Comm. on Matt.* 12.14; *Or.* 25.2). The Parousia is presently experienced; however, the coming of Christ also remains a future hope only fully realized when "God becomes all in all" (*Comm. on Jn.* 20.7.47). God's presence, according to Origen, is experienced through contemplation. The heavenly banquet is analogous with contemplation of God, which is delimited by our human capacity (*De Princ.* 2.11.7). Further, Origen insists our knowledge of God will never be complete; rather, the sojourner is always spiritually advancing through entering deeper into the presence of God (*Hom. 17 on Numbers*).

With the ascendancy of Constantine as emperor (ca. 272–337) the church entered into an era of relative security. In this new situation a more church-centered eschatology became common; for example, Eusebius of Caesarea declared the first fruits of future rewards bring assurance to the faithful in their present state (*Vita Const.* 1.33; Thielman 1987). The first two ecumenical councils emphasized Christology and the doctrine of God; consequently, there was perhaps less of a lively theological interest in a future-looking eschatology throughout the 4th century. The Cappadocian fathers primarily understood the Parousia as a spiritual grace related to the process of divinization (Gross 1938). St. Basil of Caesarea (ca. 330–79) mediates between spiritual interpretations and a theology of apocalyptic judgment when reflecting upon the Lord's second coming. But of particular note

is the way in which St. Basil associates the coming of Christ with judgment when addressing monastic communities (e.g., *Ep.* 46.5). St. Gregory of Nazianzus (ca. 329/ 330–90) interpreted the Lord's presence as both a judgment and a grace (Mossay 1964). In his oration "On Holy Baptism" Gregory speaks of Christ's cleansing fire and then adds the caveat, "I know also a fire that is not cleansing, but avenging" (*Or.* 40.36). This fire, which represents Christ's judgment, is for the wicked that are in need of chastisement. Consequently, for Gregory, the fire, that is the presence of Christ, can be either blessing or bane. St. Gregory of Nyssa (ca. 335–94) developed Origen's doctrine of perpetual spiritual growth through his interpretation of the beatitude as *epektasis* (constant spiritual progress). In his *Life of Moses* Gregory asserts Christians are "never to reach satiety in one's desire," for they are inflamed with the desire to see more of God (*Life of Moses* 2.239).

The Parousia, therefore, had multiple and significant meanings throughout the Eastern Church, but ultimately each definition expressed some aspect of Christ's redemptive and lordly presence. The Parousia, for some theologians, was predominantly an eschatological event, whereas others emphasized the presence and coming of Christ in their present spiritual lives. Ultimately, Christians' ongoing experience of Christ is the basis for their future hope (e.g., St. John Chrysostom, *Homily on Philemon* 3.3; Daley 2003: 223). The Parousia, more than anything else, expresses the mystery of Jesus Christ, who is with humanity in the present situation and yet will come back again in his gloriously revealed resurrectional power (St. Cyril of Alexandria, *Commentary on 1 Cor.* 15).

SEE ALSO: Cappadocian Fathers; Eschatology; St. Constantine the Emperor (ca.

271–337); St. Cyril of Alexandria (ca. 378–444); St. John Chrysostom (349–407)

REFERENCES AND SUGGESTED READINGS

Aune, D. E. (1975) "The Significance of the Delay of the Parousia for Early Christianity," In G. F. Hawthorne (ed.) *Current Issues in Biblical and Patristic Interpretation.* Grand Rapids, MI: Eerdmans, pp. 87–109.

Daley, B. E. (2003) *The Hope of the Early Church: A Handbook of Patristic Eschatology.* Peabody, MA: Hendrickson.

Etcheverría, R. T. (1969) "Epidhimia y Parousia en Orígenes," *Scriptorium victoriense* 16: 313–37.

Florovsky, G. (1956) "Eschatology in the Patristic Age," *Greek Orthodox Theological Review* 2: 27–40.

Gross, J. (1938) *La divinisation du Chrétien d'après les pères grecs.* Paris: J. Gabalda.

Mossay, J. (1964) "Perspectives eschatologiques de Saint Grégoire de Nazianze," *QLP* 45: 320–39.

Russell, D. S. (1964) *The Method and Message of Jewish Apocalyptic, 200 BC–AD 100.* Philadelphia: Westminster Press.

Thielman, F. S. (1987) "Another Look at the Eschatology of Eusebius of Caesarea," *Vigiliae Christianae* 41: 226–37.

Pascha *see* Calendar; Feasts

Passion Bearers

JOHN A. MCGUCKIN

Passion Bearers are saints in the Orthodox Church who underwent cruelty and oppression in a spirit of meekness and non-resistance to evil, regarded as tantamount to the status of martyrdom, especially as that witnesses to the church the heroic gentleness of Christ. The most famous of the Passion Bearers are the 11th-century Rus princes Boris and Gleb, sons of Prince Vladimir, who offered no resistance to their brother Sviatopolk who murdered them to attain political eminence. Other Passion Bearers include the Serbian St. John Vladimir (d. 1015) and (as many consider) the more modern examples of the Romanov royal family, whose spiritual fortitude in their final days won wide admiration, and others such as Grand Duchess St. Elizaveta Feodorovna, killed by the Bolsheviks, and Mother Maria Skobotsova, who witnessed heroically in a Nazi death camp.

REFERENCES AND SUGGESTED READINGS

Demshuk, V. (1978) *Russian Sainthood and Canonization.* Minneapolis: Light and Life.

Lenhoff, G. (1989) *The Martyred Princes Boris and Gleb: A Socio-Cultural Study of the Cult and the Texts.* Columbus: Ohio University Press.

Paterikon see Niptic Books (*Paterika*)

Patristics

JOHN A. MCGUCKIN

A relatively modern term deriving from the Latin *Patres*, or "Fathers." It was also known as patrology up to the mid-20th century, though this latter designation has now been restricted mainly to signify reference manuals dealing with the works of the fathers of the church. The fathers were the bishops, outstanding theologians, and leading monastic elders of the early church, who left behind them authoritative bodies of spiritual, biblical, liturgical, and dogmatic writings. The age of the fathers is generally seen as extending from after the apostolic era (beginning of the 2nd century) to the 8th and 9th centuries, whose great luminaries then included St. John of Damascus and St. Photios the Great. John is, in many ways, a certain sign of the closing of the patristic age, with his works gathering together as a kind of encyclopedia of the earlier authoritative materials to form a synthesis of patristic theology for the later church's reference. In terms of Latin patristics, the traditional cut-off point has been significantly extended beyond this time, even up to the medieval western theologian Bernard of Clairvaux, who is sometimes called, in the Catholic Church, the "last of the fathers." Even so, there is not a hard and fast historical line, as Orthodoxy understands it, for some of the late Byzantine writers such as St. Symeon the New Theologian of the 11th century, or St. Gregory Palamas (1296–1359), for example, certainly enjoy a high "patristic status" in contemporary Orthodoxy. The word generally means, in Orthodox circles, those definitive and highly authoritative theologians of the church in its classical ages who represent purity of doctrine allied with great holiness of life; a life that manifests the indwelling of the Holy Spirit in their acts and their consciousness, such that they are not merely good speculative thinkers, or interesting religious writers, as such, but rather substantial guides to the will of God, and Spirit-bearers (*pneumatophoroi*) whose doctrine and advice can be trusted as conveying the authentic Orthodox tradition of faith and piety. This does not mean that every single thing any one of the fathers ever wrote is given "canonical" status. Orthodoxy admits that the general rule of human authorship applies even among the saints, for as the adage tells, "even Homer nods," but it does mean that collectively, and by the consensus of the fathers among themselves, and by the manner in which they stand in a stream of defense of the ecumenical faith of the church, they together comprise a library of immense prestige and authority. They are thus collectively strong and concrete evidence for the central tradition of the Orthodox Church. This is why the church affords them a very

high theological authority, not as great as the Scriptures or the ecumenical councils, but certainly alongside the latter; for it was from their writings that the doctrine of the great councils generally emerged.

The concept of "patristic witnesses" can be seen in the earliest writings of the church. Notable figures such as Ignatius, Polycarp, or Clement of Rome clearly enjoyed a significant status even in their own times as elders in the faith. But the formal growth of the idea that the "fathers" were a collective defense against heterodoxy was mainly a product of the anti-Arian writers of the 4th century, which came to be adopted passionately by the Greek and Latin churches of the 5th century and afterwards. One of the early and classical examples of this specifically happening is the hagiography of Antony the Great written by Athanasius of Alexandria (*Life of Antony*), which depicts him as one of the great fathers who personally represents a standard of truth, holiness, and orthodoxy. Another is the hagiography of Athanasius by St. Gregory the Theologian (of Nazianzus: *Oration* 21; see also *Oration* 33.5), which lauds Athanasius as a father and pillar of orthodoxy for his defense of Nicea (see also St. Basil the Great's *Epistle* 140.2). By the 5th century, the concept of "authoritative fathers" was being appealed to specifically and systematically to establish pedigree lines of doctrine; most notably by St. Cyril of Alexandria, who began to assemble florilegia of the "sayings of the orthodox fathers" in his conflict with Nestorius, thus beginning a style of theologizing that soon became a standard way of doing Orthodox theology ever after. The idea of bringing the evidence of the fathers together soon came into the synodical process of the ecumenical councils, which more and more, after the 5th century, saw themselves as the defenders and propagators of the "theology of the fathers" (see Canon 7 of the Council of Ephesus, 431; and the Acts of the Council of Chalcedon, 451; *Definition of the Faith* 2; 4). Patristics in this sense clearly corresponds to a certain vision of theology as the "defense and maintenance of Orthodoxy." This remains its essential meaning in the Orthodox Church today. Orthodoxy has generally accepted the great fathers of the Latin church as its own (Sts. Ambrose, Gregory the Great, Leo, and so on), though it has significantly distanced itself from many of the ideas of other influential early Latin thinkers (Arnobius, Tertullian), including St. Augustine, who so dominated the West's sense of patristic teaching, but hardly impressed himself upon the East.

In modern academic use "patristics" means something more general, less specific, than this idea of the "guides of Orthodoxy," and simply designates the study of Christian antiquity, leading to the often paradoxical position that much of modern academic patristic study is devoted to the heterodox writers of the ancient world: a thing which Orthodoxy would strictly exclude from the category of "patristics," though in so doing it has perhaps tended to narrow down the field in some unfortunate ways, leaving out some of the great contributors to Christian theology who were not bishops, or monastics, such as the numerous women saints from ancient times (who were literarily "invisible" in the main) or heterodox theologians of great merit (of significance, that is, beyond the specific "mistakes" of certain of their stances) such as Origen or Mar Theodore Mopsuestia (both of whom were major and lofty biblical interpreters of high spirituality but were the subjects of conciliar condemnations for specific doctrinal errors that caused their larger body of writings to be marginalized or lost). The massive 19th-century collections and editions of J. P. Migne (*Patrologia series graeca* and *series latina*) comprising hundreds of volumes of ancient and medieval Greek and Latin texts is a virtual canon of patristic literature (understood in the wider sense of a library of all the early theologians). Patristic theology today generally remains an important and valid branch of the theological disciplines, perhaps given a greater stress in Orthodox and Roman Catholic academies than Protestant, and one that enjoyed a veritable renaissance in the 20th century as many excellent critical editions of primary texts, and sophisticated historical analyses, enlivened the field.

SEE ALSO: Cappadocian Fathers; Christ; Ecumenical Councils; Fatherhood of God; Holy Spirit; Incarnation (of the Logos); Logos Theology; Philosophy; St. Athanasius of Alexandria (c. 293–373); St. Cyril of Alexandria (ca. 378–444); St. Gregory Palamas (1296–1359); St. John Chrysostom (349–407); St. John of Damascus (ca. 675–ca. 750); St. Maximos the Confessor (580–662)

REFERENCES AND SUGGESTED READINGS

Bardenhewer, O. (1908) *Patrology.* St. Louis: Herder.
McGuckin, J. A. (2004) *The Westminster Handbook to Patristic Theology.* Louisville: Westminster John Knox Press.
Prestige, G. L. (1940) *Fathers and Heretics.* London: SPCK.
Quasten, J. (1975) *Patrology,* vols. 1–3. Utrecht: Spectrum.

Pentarchy

GEORGE E. DEMACOPOULOS

Pentarchy refers to the ancient division of the Christian world into five autonomous and autocephalous jurisdictions, each under the leadership of a patriarch. Canon 28 of the Council of Chalcedon ranked the five sees in order of preeminence as Rome, Constantinople, Alexandria, Antioch, and Jerusalem. Both the principle and ranking were confirmed by Justinian's *Novella* 123, which asserted that each patriarch would serve as a court of last appeal for internal church legislative and disciplinary matters. Neither the borders that separate their jurisdictions nor the number of autocephalous churches remained static in the Byzantine period, but the original five have retained a measure of preeminence in the later expansion of the concept of Orthodox patriarchies.

SEE ALSO: Alexandria, Patriarchate of; Antioch, Patriarchate of; Constantinople, Patriarchate of; Council of Chalcedon (451); Jerusalem, Patriarchate of; Rome, Ancient Patriarchate of

Pentecost, Feast of

MARIA GWYN MCDOWELL

A great feast of the church observed fifty days after Pascha, celebrating the descent of the Holy Spirit, the full revelation of the trinitarian mystery, and the commencement of the church's mission in the world. On the Jewish pilgrimage feast of Pentecost commemorating the presentation of the law to Moses, the Holy Spirit descended upon the followers of Jesus gathered in Jerusalem, inspiring the preaching of the gospel in languages comprehensible to all present (Acts 2). A fulfillment prophecy (Joel 2.28–9) liturgically commemorated by the singing of Galatians 3.27, joyfully acknowledges the ongoing participation of the baptized, regardless of social status, in Christ through the Holy Spirit. At Vespers on this day solemn prayers of intercession are made.

SEE ALSO: Deification; Evangelism; Holy Spirit

Pentekostarion

SOTIRIOS A. VLAVIANOS

The *Pentekostarion* (meaning "the book of the fifty days"), alternatively known as the "Flowery Triodion" (still known as such in the Slavonic tradition), is the continuation of the *Lenten Triodion* book of liturgical texts. It contains the chanting and reading materials used in the services of the fifty-day season of Pentecost. The Pentecost season begins with Orthros (Matins) on Easter Sunday and lasts up until the Sunday of All Saints, following Pentecost Sunday. It has its roots in the *Triodion*, but by the 14th century it had evolved into a new book with its new name. Its initial version comprised short canons (*triodia*) that were gradually eliminated after the 14th century. The chanted material related to the saints (*Synaxaria*) of the Sundays and Feast-days, as composed by Nikiforos Kallistos Xanthopoulos, was also eventually incorporated into the *Pentekostarion* as it now stands. It is a book rich in theological content and spiritual teaching.

SEE ALSO: Canon (Liturgical); Feasts; Great Week; *Horologion*; Liturgical Books; *Menaion*; *Paraklitike*; Pentecost, Feast of; Resurrection; *Triodion*

REFERENCES AND SUGGESTED READINGS

Schmemann, A. (2003) *Introduction to Liturgical Theology.* Crestwood, NY: St. Vladimir's Seminary Press.

Taft, R. F. (1992) *The Byzantine Rite: A Short History.* Collegeville, MN: Liturgical Press.

Taft, R. F. (1997) *Beyond East and West: Problems in Liturgical Understanding,* 2nd edn. Rome: Pontifical Oriental Institute.

Penthos see Repentance

Perichoresis

THEODOR DAMIAN

The term *Perichoresis* indicates the mode of existence of the persons of the Holy Trinity characterized by interpenetration, co-inhabitation, mutual fellowship, surrounding, or indwelling. In Greek, *perichoreo* means to "make room," to "go or revolve around."

The basis of the doctrine of Perichoresis lies in Christ's declaration about the co-inhabitation between him and the Father ("I and the Father are one," Jn. 10.30; "I am in the Father and the Father is in Me," Jn. 14.11) which indicates a relation of consubstantiality (*homoousion*) of the trinitarian persons. Even so, the first application of the notion in patristic times was not in the context of trinitarian theology, but in Christology, and it was used in order to emphasize the unity of the one divine person and the distinctiveness of the two natures in Christ.

The idea appeared often in early patristic theological works (Justin the Martyr, Origen, Athanasius, Basil the Great) and though the term itself was also explicitly used in Sts. Gregory the Theologian and Maximos the Confessor, it was St. John of Damascus, in his work *Exposition of the Orthodox Faith,* who was really the church father to develop the term and concept most fully, especially where Perichoresis is used to describe the type of intra-trinitarian relationships. It was from the trinitarian context that St. John extrapolated the concept back to Christology; the perichoretical relations in the Trinity being used by him as a paradigm for the coexistence of the two natures in Christ.

The term Perichoresis essentially indicates that at the heart of God's life is supreme personal relationship; and that relation is one of total intimacy. According to St. John of Damascus, the persons of the Trinity live together in union in a relationship without coalescence or commingling; they cleave to each other and have their being in each other. When applied to the two natures of Christ, Perichoresis indicates their co-inhabitation and interpenetration, or mutual permeation, yet without any loss on the part of any of the two natures of its specific properties, and without any confusion or mixture. The *ekthesis* (credal definition) of the Council of Chalcedon expresses the idea succinctly. Trinitarian perichoresis also grew in the Orthodox tradition to become a paradigm for the spiritual union and interrelation of members of the Christian Church based on Christ's intentions as expressed in John 17.21: "That they all may be one; as You, Father are in Me, and I in You, that they also may be one in Us."

SEE ALSO: Church (Orthodox Ecclesiology); Council of Chalcedon (451); Holy Trinity; Patristics; St. John of Damascus (ca. 675–ca. 750)

REFERENCES AND SUGGESTED READINGS

Crisp, O. D. (2005) "Problems with Perichoresis," *Tyndale Bulletin* 56, 1: 119–40.

John of Damascus (1989) *Exposition of the Orthodox Faith,* in P. Schaff and H. Wace (eds.) *The Nicene and Post-Nicene Fathers,* Vol. 9. Grand Rapids, MI: Eerdmans.

Lossky, V. (1968) *The Mystical Theology of the Eastern Church.* Cambridge: James Clarke.

Prestige, L. (1928) "Perichoreo and Perichoresis in the Fathers," *Journal of Theological Studies* 24: 242–52.

Stăniloae, D. (1996) *Teologia Dogmatica Ortodoxa.* Bucharest: Editura Institutului Biblic si de Misiune al BOR.

Phelonion

PHILIP ZYMARIS

A Byzantine vestment equivalent to the western chausible. It has its origins in a poncho-like garment referred to by St. Paul (2 Tim. 4.13). It was once worn by bishops but was later replaced by the *sakkos*. Presently, priests wear them at all sacramental services.

Plate 49 Orthodox priest wearing the phelonion vestment and the pectoral cross (stavrophore). PhotoEdit/Alamy.

SEE ALSO: Epitrachelion; Sticharion; Vestments

REFERENCES AND SUGGESTED READINGS

Day, P. (1993) "Phelonion," in *The Liturgical Dictionary of Eastern Christianity.* Collegeville: Liturgical Press, p. 233.

Phountoulis, I. (2002) "Paradose kai exelixe leitourgikon hieron amphion," in *Ta hiera amphia kai he exoterike eribole tou orthodoxou klerou.* Athens: Church of Greece Publications, pp. 63–78.

Philokalia

ANDREW LOUTH

Philokalia is the Greek term for an anthology. Nowadays, *the Philokalia* virtually invariably refers to a collection of Byzantine ascetical and mystical texts published in Venice in 1782 by St. Macarius of Corinth and St. Nikodemos of the Holy Mountain, although there is another famous *Philokalia*, of extracts from Origen, mostly on the problem of free will and the interpretation of the Scriptures, composed 358–9 by St. Basil the Great and St. Gregory of Nazianzus. The 18th-century *Philokalia* is a collection of texts from the 4th to the 14th centuries, culminating in works drawn from St. Gregory Palamas and his circle, both predecessors and followers, representing "hesychasm," the monastic movement centered on the recitation of the Jesus Prayer which claimed that it was possible to behold the uncreated light of the Godhead in prayer. This claim was reconciled with the apophatic doctrine of God's unknowability by the distinction drawn by Gregory, based on earlier Greek patristic writings, between God's essence, which is indeed unknowable, and his uncreated (and therefore divine) "energies" or activities (*energeiai* in Greek) through which God makes himself known personally in the created world.

The texts in the *Philokalia* present a historical sequence of Byzantine ascetical texts, presented as the historical tradition leading up to Palamite hesychasm, but there is very little in them about the Jesus Prayer, and even less about the essence-energies distinction (the historical arrangement is probably due to St. Nikodemos, who had imbibed from the West a sense of history). Pride of place is given to St. Maximos the Confessor, Peter of Damascus, and St. Gregory Palamas himself, but many other important Byzantine ascetical writers are present, including Evagrios (both under his own name and that of Neilos), Mark the Monk, Diadochos of Photiki, John of Karpathos, Niketas Stethatos, and St. Gregory of Sinai. There are some, at first sight, surprising omissions: notably St. John of Sinai, author of the *Ladder of Divine Ascent*, and St. Symeon the New Theologian, who is represented by a few, unrepresentative, and even spurious, writings. St. John of Sinai is probably omitted because he was already well known in the Byzantine monastic tradition, his *Ladder* being read in the course of each Lent. The poor showing of St. Symeon is more mystifying, given that St. Nikodemos himself produced the first collected edition of his works.

Very little is known for sure about the origin of *Philokalia* and how the texts were selected. It belongs to a reform movement that sought to return to original monastic traditions of Athonite monks known as the "Kollyvades." However, in 1793, very shortly after the publication of the *Philokalia*, a Slavonic translation, called the *Dobrotolyubie* (a calque of *philokalia*), by the Ukrainian monk, St. Paisy Velichkovsky, was published in Iaşi in Moldavia (modern Romania). St. Paisy's

selection is smaller than the Greek version (and, in particular, omits the more intellectually demanding writers such as Maximos the Confessor and even Gregory Palamas), but draws on the same collection of material. His translation, which took some years, cannot be a selection from the printed Greek text, and must therefore be thought of as drawing from an already known – and presumably traditional – collection of ascetical texts, already current on the Holy Mountain. In 1822 a second edition of the *Dobrotolyubie* came out, supplemented by various other texts from the Greek *Philokalia*. Between 1877 and 1905 there appeared in Russia a further translation in five volumes, translated (into Russian) by St. Theophan the Recluse. This version restores Maximos and Palamas, omitted by St. Paisy, and considerably expands the list of philokalic fathers, including John of Sinai (in extracts), as well as the ascetics of Gaza, Barsanuphios, John, and Dorotheos, and St. Isaac the Syrian (in his lifetime a Nestorian bishop), as well as a more substantial group of texts by St. Symeon the New Theologian, and further texts from the original Greek *Philokalia*.

The immediate influence of the *Philokalia*, or rather *Dobrotlyubie*, was most immediately felt in Russia, where it was read by St. Seraphim of Sarov and the monks of Optina Pustyn', the monastery south of Moscow that became a center for the Slavophiles and other members of the Russian intelligentsia. It led to a revival of monasticism in Russia, in which stress was laid on the practice of private prayer, especially the Jesus Prayer, and the institution of spiritual fatherhood (*starchestvo*), echoes of which can be heard in Dostoevsky's *Brothers Karamazov*. It also inspired a revival of interest in the fathers, among whom the philokalic fathers formed a core. A work with a complex history, known in English as *The Way of the Pilgrim*, popularized the Jesus Prayer and (in its most common form) the institution of *starchestvo*, both in Russia and then through translations in the 20th century throughout the world. The Jesus Prayer, from being the preserve of primarily Athonite monks, came to gain a popularity that now reaches well beyond the bounds of Orthodoxy.

In the 20th century there were translations into many European languages, mostly selections from the Greek *Philokalia*. In the English-speaking world the first translations were from the Russian of St. Theophan's *Dobrotolyubie*, though there is a projected (not yet completed) translation of the whole Greek text of the original. Rather different is the Romanian translation, the work of the great Romanian theologian, Fr. Dumitru Stăniloae. This version is much longer than the Greek original, and often includes a more comprehensive selection of the works of the fathers included, as well as supplementing the selection found in the Greek version by other philokalic fathers, frequently following the example of St. Theophan. It also includes a commentary, recognizing that a reader of a printed book now cannot be sure of the guidance of a spiritual father, a thing taken for granted by the original compilers.

SEE ALSO: Elder (Starets); Hesychasm; Jesus Prayer; *Pilgrim, Way of the*; St. Gregory Palamas (1296–1359); St. Isaac the Syrian (7th c.); St. Maximos the Confessor (580–662); St. Nikodemos the Hagiorite (1749–1809); St. Paisy Velichovsky (1722–1794); St. Seraphim of Sarov (1759–1833); St. Symeon the New Theologian (949–1022); St. Theophan (Govorov) the Recluse (1815–1894); Sts. Barsanuphius and John (6th c.); Stăniloae, Dumitru (1903–1993)

REFERENCES AND SUGGESTED READINGS

Kadloubovsky, E. and Palmer, G. E. H. (1973) *Writings from the Philokalia on Prayer of the Heart*. London: Faber and Faber.
Palmer, G. E. H., Sherrard, P., and Ware, K. (1979) *The Philokalia*, Vols. 1– 4. London: Faber and Faber.
Smith, A. (2006) *The Philokalia: The Eastern Christian Spiritual Texts – Selections Annotated and Explained*. Woodstock, VT: Skylight Paths.

Philosophy
MARCUS PLESTED

Philosophy has long been integral to Eastern Orthodox theology, but the relationship has never been unproblematic. Distinct philosophical concerns can be traced in the earliest of the fathers, such as Justin Martyr, Theophilus of Antioch, or Clement and Origen of Alexandria, the latter being the first Christian philosopher of international stature. St. Basil the Great (and Augustine after him) regarded the church's use of philosophy as comparable to the manner in which the Jews escaping their servitude "despoiled the Egyptians"; and St. Gregory the Theologian used the memorable image of the Christian use of Greek philosophy as that of a gardener who carefully clips his roses of their thorns. Rooted in the patristic sense of the indispensability of a discerning use of human wisdom coupled with an understanding of Christianity as the true philosophy, Byzantine fathers such as St. Maximos the Confessor and St. John of Damascus make extensive use of philosophical categories and constructs. Maximos' theory of the divine *logoi*, the underlying principles of all things grounded in the *Logos*, clearly owes something to the Platonic understanding of Ideas but has been radically transformed in its christocentric focus and insistence upon the ontological gap between creature and Creator.

Between Maximos and John a general shift may be detected from a predominantly Platonic to a predominantly Aristotelian mode of discourse, without supposition of any incompatibility between the two. This Aristotelian preponderance was to obtain through the Byzantine and into the Ottoman era. Indeed, ongoing interest in Plato could often provoke controversy. The brilliant 11th-century writer Michael Psellos was appointed "Consul of Philosophers" by Constantine IX Monomachos at the newly established school of philosophy of the University of Constantinople. Psellos placed special emphasis on Plato and the Neoplatonic tradition, but was forced to clarify his position as to the ancillary status of philosophy in response to hostile criticism. His disciple and successor, John Italos, did not escape so lightly. John was indicted for heresy on a number of counts: for using reason to probe divine realities and for adhering to certain Platonic concepts, notably the reality of the realm of Ideas. Elements of his condemnation live on in the anathemas of the *Synodikon of Orthodoxy*.

St. Gregory Palamas is a useful example of the extreme care with which philosophy was employed in the later Byzantine era. Praised for his mastery of Aristotle in his youth, Palamas went on to draw on that expertise in his critique of Barlaam's theological agnosticism, asserting the propriety of apodictic argumentation in the articulation of divine revelation. Palamas excoriates philosophy when removed from its proper subservient status, but allows it when rightly ordered in the service of theology. The natural wisdom implanted in us can be cultivated through application and learning, including the standard curriculum of "outer learning." This outer learning has a role to play in the proclamation and defense of spiritual truths manifest in Scripture and witnessed in the lives of the saints. But it is always

relative and potentially dangerous when misused. Indeed, it is this misuse of our God-given endowments that St. Paul targets in his blistering critique in 1 Corinthians and not, Gregory is careful to point out, natural human wisdom *per se*.

Such strictly ordered use of philosophical argumentation remained normative down to the last days of the Byzantine Empire, as witnessed, for example, in the anti-Latin syllogisms of St. Mark of Ephesus or the thoroughgoing Aristotelianism of George (later Gennadios) Scholarios, who was Mark's successor as leader of the anti-unionist party. Scholarios' philosophical sensibilities fostered his warm embrace of Aquinas and his polemic against his enthusiastic Neoplatonist contemporary, the crypto-Pagan George Gemistos Plethon. Plethon's espousal of Plato greatly impacted the West but gained little purchase in the Greek world in which Aristotelianism retained its dominance, aided by figures such as Theophilos Korydaleus and Maximos Margounios. An indication of this ongoing preponderance is evident in the condemnation in 1723 of Methodios Anthrakites by the church authorities in Constantinople. Methodios was branded a modernist for rejecting alike the salutary philosophy of Aristotle and the divinely inspired teachings of the fathers, favoring instead the new philosophy of Descartes.

Enlightenment ideas developed significant currency in the Greek thought-world, attacked by philosopher-theologians such as Vincent Damodos but more sympathetically, if by no means uncritically, received by figures such as Eugenios Bulgaris. Bulgaris taught and translated Wolff, Leibniz, and Locke. In 1753 he was appointed head of the new patriarchal academy on Mount Athos. But while in many respects a deeply traditional and anti-Latin theologian, Bulgaris' cautious openness to modern philosophy earned him no little hostility on the part of the monks of the Holy Mountain and the academy was eventually forced to close. The ruins can still be seen today, close to the monastery of Vatopedi. Thereafter, Enlightenment ideas are associated with Greek nationalists and secularists such as Adamantios Koraes, but were generally eschewed by prominent churchmen such as St. Athanasius of Paros and St. Nikodemos the Hagiorite – forefather, with St. Macarius of Corinth, of a remarkable Hesychast renaissance.

In the Slavic world, a broadly scholastic mode of theologizing prevailed on the level of official church teaching and instruction. Resistance to this tendency took shape not only in the Hesychast revival spearheaded by St. Paisy Velichkovsky, but also with recourse to German Idealism. This latter dimension is particularly evident in the Russian "Slavophile" school. Kireevsky, for one, was delighted to find in the church fathers all the essential insights of Schelling. In 1860 Alexander Bukharev published a compelling case for explicit engagement with contemporary philosophy, arguing from the fact of the incarnation that such philosophy must contain, at the least, signs of redemption and glimpses of truth. German Idealism was to remain a vital force in Russian religious thought, notably within the powerful but perplexing phenomenon of Sophiology. Indeed, it served many key thinkers, such as Sergius (Sergei) Bulgakov and Nikolai Berdiaev, as a bridge from Marxism into Orthodoxy.

In the post-World War II period, Orthodox theology has often entered into a creative dialogue with contemporary philosophical concerns. The presentation of Orthodox theology by Vladimir Lossky and John Meyendorff certainly taps into and addresses French personalism and existentialism, as does Metropolitan John Zizioulas' deeply influential exploration of personhood. Christos Yannaras makes intriguing use of Heidegger in his exploration of the opposition between Orthodoxy and the West. So-called postmodernist philosophies have yet, however, to provoke any very substantial Orthodox response. In a nutshell, while philosophy has rarely, if ever, been determinative of Orthodox thought, let alone of Orthodox practice, it has always been very much close at hand, and used to a considerable extent.

SEE ALSO: Berdiaev, Nikolai A. (1874–1948); Bulgakov, Sergius (Sergei) (1871–1944); Contemporary Orthodox Theology; Gnosticism; Hesychasm; Logos Theology; Lossky, Vladimir (1903–1958); Patristics; St. Gregory Palamas (1296–1359); St. John of Damascus (ca. 675–ca. 750); St. Mark of Ephesus (1392–1445); St. Maximos the Confessor (580–662); St. Nikodemos the Hagiorite (1749–1809); St. Paisy Velichovsky (1722–1794); Scholarios, George (Gennadios) (ca. 1403–1472)

REFERENCES AND SUGGESTED READINGS

Hussey, J. M. (1937) *Church and Learning in the Byzantine Empire.* Oxford: Oxford University Press.

Tatakis, B. (1959) *La Philosophie byzantine.* Paris: PUF.

Photogogika *see* Exaposteilarion

Pilgrim, Way of the

KONSTANTIN GAVRILKIN

An anonymous Russian book first published in 1881, containing an account of the narrator's spiritual journey through life while studying the *Philokalia* and practicing the Jesus Prayer. The text in its

Plate 50   The medieval pilgrim's entrance gate to the Monastery of the Holy Trinity at Sergiev Posad, near Moscow. Photo by John McGuckin.

current version is the result of the editorial work of Bishop Theophan (Feofan) the Recluse, who also gave it the Russian title *Otkrovennye rasskazy strannika* (1884). For the authorship of the original text, see Basin (1996). The book was designed to popularize the radical development of the interior life in the spiritual tradition of St. Paisy Velichovsky and the Optina Elders, by showing that it could be adopted even by simple laity (the protagonist is a wandering peasant). The English translation received a wider notice in the West after its appearance in Salinger's novel *Franny and Zoey*.

SEE ALSO: Jesus Prayer; Optina; *Philokalia*; St. Paisy Velichovsky (1722–1794); St. Theophan (Govorov) the Recluse (1815–1894)

REFERENCES AND SUGGESTED READINGS

Basin, I. V. (1996) "Avtorstvo 'Otkrovennykh rasskazov strannika dukhovnomu ottsu svoemu,'" in *Arkhim. Mikhail Kozlov, Zapiski i pis'ma*, ed. I. V. Basin. Moscow: Bogoroditse-Rozhdestvenskii Bobrenev monastyr', pp. 123–56.

Pentkovsky A. (ed.) (1999). *The Pilgrim's Tale*, trans. A. Smith. New York: Paulist Press.

Platytera

JOHN A. MCGUCKIN

The word comes from the Greek, meaning "She Who is More Wide" (or more "spacious") and refers to a type of the iconography of the Blessed Virgin where she is depicted, frequently in the eastern apse of the churches, with arms held out wide in prayer (Orans) and often horizontally distorted to emphasize the verbal symbol. On the Virgin's breast is the figure of Christ Emmanuel (sometimes in a roundel – *clypeus*, an iconographic symbol of the Logos conceived in his mother, but not yet born; which is an iconic type often called, in the Russian church, the "Virgin of the Sign" after Isaiah 7.14, or in the Byzantine tradition *Blachernitissa*, after the palace chapel of that name in Constantinople). The Platytera icon is a Marian Christological symbol taken from the hymn "In You Rejoices All Creation" of the Liturgy of St. Basil, which speaks of the paradox of the incarnation, wherein the Logos who is greater than, and cannot be contained by, the heavens (as their Maker), is nevertheless perfectly fitted to the narrow constraints of the Virgin's womb. Accordingly, the Mother of God is shown to be "Wider than the Heavens," for she could contain the divine Lord whom the vast heavens could not.

REFERENCES AND SUGGESTED READINGS

Ryden, L. (1976) "The Vision of the Virgin at Blachernae and the Feast of the Pokrov," *Analecta Bollandiana* 94: 63–82.

Pneumatology *see* Holy Spirit

Pokrov see Protecting Veil

Poland, Orthodox Church of

JOHN A. MCGUCKIN

The Polish Orthodox Church takes its origins from two chief periods of establishment; the first in the 10th century, and the second revival after the political union of Lithuania and Poland in the 14th century. Its history and development have been closely bound up with the ebb and flow of the religious affiliations of the rulers of the area, the proximity and great influence of Russia, and the ascendancy of Catholicism. When the nation of Poland was politically dismembered in 1722, its Orthodox population was absorbed by the Russian church. When the country was reconstituted as a sovereign independent state after the cessation of World War I in 1918, her new borders contained about 4 million Orthodox faithful, mainly Ukrainians and Belo-Russians who inhabited the eastern part of the country. They had all belonged up to that time to the jurisdiction of the patriarch of Moscow. The Moscow patriarch of that time, St. Tikhon, was willing to grant autonomous status to the Polish church, but the new government, eager for all signs of national independence, was pressing the Polish hierarchy to declare their complete independence from Russian control by making a declaration of autocephaly. The senior Polish hierarch Archbishop George Yoroshevsky was attempting to resolve the tensions, and pressing towards a more limited autonomous status in 1923, when he was assassinated by a mentally deranged Russian monk who believed the hierarch was leading the Church into schism. The degree of scandal this murder caused occasioned the Polish government to appeal directly to the patriarch of Constantinople for the award of autocephalous status, and this was granted *sui jure* by Constantinople in a *Tomos* of 1924. The Moscow patriarchate did not recognize this situation until the country was subjugated under Russia's political control once more in 1945 and then, in 1948, the Moscow Patriarch Alexei wrote to the Phanar announcing that the Russian Orthodox Church had itself conferred autocephaly upon the Polish Orthodox. The

Catholic majority in Poland tended to regard the Orthodox now among them as former Greek rite Catholics (Uniates) who had been pressured to enter the Orthodox Church in the 19th century. Catholic missionary attempts in the prewar years over-zealously tried to persuade the Orthodox to come back into union; a process that involved many cases of law suits to claim back churches and buildings, allied with the forcible closures of Orthodox institutions. The heavy-handedness shown in this period extensively soured relations between the Orthodox and the Catholics for generations afterwards. Prior to 1918 the Orthodox had 10 bishops in their synod, 5 dioceses, 15 monasteries, and about 2,000 parishes with 4 million faithful. By 1960 the Orthodox totalled only 4,500 faithful. Today, there are eight dioceses (one providing military chaplains, another supervising Polish Orthodox parishes abroad) with 400 parishes with just over 1 million faithful. The senior hierarch of the Polish Orthodox is now known as the Metropolitan of Warsaw and All Poland. The church retains very close ecclesiastical links with the Moscow patriarchate.

SEE ALSO: Lithuania, Orthodoxy in; Russia, Patriarchal Orthodox Church of

REFERENCES AND SUGGESTED READINGS

Kloczowski, J. (2000) *A History of Polish Christianity*. New York: Cambridge University Press.
McGuckin, J. A. (2008) *The Orthodox Church: An Introduction to Its History, Theology and Spiritual Culture*. Oxford: Wiley-Blackwell.
Ramet, P. (1988) *Eastern Christianity and Politics in the 20th Century*. Durham, NC: Duke University Press.
Reddaway, W. F. et al. (ed.) (1950) *The Cambridge History of Poland*, 2 vols. Cambridge: Cambridge University Press.
Rowell, S. C. (1994) *Lithuania Ascending: A Pagan Empire within East Central Europe*. Cambridge: Cambridge University Press.

Pontike, Evagrios (ca. 345–399)

JULIA KONSTANTINOVSKY

The celebrated guide of semi-eremitic monks of the North Egyptian desert of Nitria; likewise a prolific biblical exegete and author of numerous ascetical and mystical treatises on the soul's ascent to God.

Born in Ibora on the Black Sea, Evagrios enjoyed a close connection with the Cappadocian fathers: a pupil of Gregory of Nazianzus, he was ordained reader by Basil. Later (380–1), he accompanied Gregory of Nazianzus to Constantinople as Gregory's theological assistant in the time he composed the Five Theological Orations. There he enjoyed acclaim for his success in disputes against Eunomians. Around 383, when Nektarios was patriarch, he fled Constantinople on account of its spiritual perils and in search of a life of stillness (*hesychia*). At the monastery on the Mount of Olives (near Jerusalem) he was tonsured a monk by Rufinus and Melania, then traveled via Alexandria to settle in the Nitrian desert as a solitary. Having spent several years under the spiritual direction of St. Macarius of Egypt and standing within the tradition of the desert fathers, Evagrios himself became a spiritual guide of great renown. His *Praktikos, Gnostikos, Chapters On Prayer, Antirrhetikos, On Evil Thoughts*, and *Commentary on the Psalms* were celebrated throughout late Antiquity and the Middle Ages. Styled as collections of mellifluous pithy maxims (*apophthegmata*), these expound the mind's journey of purification from obstreperous thoughts, the acquisition of virtues, and ascent to divine knowledge: the *praxis-contemplation-theology* trilogy. Via Cassian, Evagrios's ideas spread in the West at an early stage, while remaining ascetical classics in the Greek-speaking East. The late 5th century saw his writings translated into Syriac. He likewise authored other, more esoteric treatises (*Gnostic Chapters*, *Letter to Melania*) containing speculations about creation, Christ, and salvation, some of which were developed directly from Origen's works. There he argued that bodies and matter were fashioned subsequently to the creation of souls, as remedy for the souls' disobedience; Christ is not the divine *Logos* but is created; in the End of Things, all shall be saved (the Devil included, while bodies and material beings shall be destroyed). For these latter views, which first aroused the suspicions of Theophilus of Alexandria and Jerome (early 5th century), Evagrios was condemned as heterodox at the Fifth, Sixth, and Seventh Ecumenical Councils. Many of his Greek originals were destroyed, to remain only in Syriac translations. Other works survive under the names of persons of untainted reputation: notably, St. Nilus (*Chapters on Prayer*, in the *Philokalia*). Evagrios also appears in the *Philokalia* as Abba Evagrios the Monk (*On Eight Thoughts*). In later times Sts. John Climacus, Maximus the Confessor, and Symeon the New Theologian were deeply influenced by Evagrios's spiritual teachings; and in the later part of the 20th century he once again emerged as a spiritual master as his works found English translations.

REFERENCES AND SUGGESTED READINGS

Casiday, A. (2006) *Evagrios Ponticus*. Abingdon: Routledge.

Dysinger, L. (2002) *Psalmody and Prayer in the Writings of Evagrios Ponticus*. Oxford: Oxford University Press.

Evagrios (1972) *The Praktikos and Chapters on Prayer*, trans. J. E. Bamberger. Kalamazoo: Cistercian Publications.

Evagrios Ponticus (2003) *Ad Monachos*, trans. J. Driskoll. New York: Oxford University Press.

Konstantinovsky, J. (2009) *Evagrios Ponticus: The Making of a Gnostic*. Burlington, VT: Ashgate Press.

Palmer, G. E. H., Sherrard, P., and Ware, K. (eds. and trans.) (1979) *The Philokalia: The Complete Text*, 5 vols. London: Faber and Faber.

Sinkewicz, R. E. (trans.) (2003) *Evagrios of Pontus: The Greek Ascetic Corpus*. Oxford: Oxford University Press.

Possessors (Joseph of Volotsk)

KONSTANTIN GAVRILKIN

A loose translation of the Russian word *stiazhateli* (from the verb *stiazhat'*, "to acquire," "to gain"), a disparaging nickname given by the followers of Nil Sorskii to Joseph of Volotsk (1439–1515) and his associates, who defended strict ascetic life in big monastic communities, argued for the church's and monasteries' rights of landownership for administering social welfare, and justified the use of secular power in defense of Orthodoxy, including persecution of heretics. Joseph is the author of the first Russian dogmatic treatise "Enlightener" (*Prosvetitel'*), written in response to the so-called heresy of the Judaizers (late 15th century).

SEE ALSO: Non-Possessors (Nil Sorskii); Russia, Patriarchal Orthodox Church of

REFERENCES AND SUGGESTED READINGS

Goldfrank, D. (ed.) (2000) *Monastic Rule of Iosif Volotsky*, rev. edn. Kalamazoo: Cistercian Publications.

Volotskii, I. (1993) *Prosvetitel', ili, Oblichenie eresi zhidovstvuiushchikh.* Moscow: Valaamskii monastyr'.

Zimin, A. A. and Lur'e, I. S. (eds.) (1959) *Poslaniia Iosifa Volotskogo.* Leningrad: Izd-vo Akademii nau.

Prayer

THEODORE G. STYLIANOPOULOS

Prayer by means of words, thoughts, gestures, gifts, and rites is a universal religious phenomenon through which human beings have expressed their dependence on, or need of, assistance from a higher power. The Christian meaning of prayer is deeply rooted in the biblical understanding of God, his saving work and will. In Orthodox Christianity, prayer, both private and corporate, is absolutely central, as is manifest in Orthodox worship, piety, and spirituality. Energized by the Holy Spirit, prayer is the soul of the church and the breath of life for the striving believer.

The Old Testament is a treasure house of prayers of praise, glorification, and thanksgiving as well as of petition, confession, repentance, intercession, lament, and complaint to God. Such prayers are expressed through words, songs, and gestures such as standing, outstretched hands, kneeling, and prostration. Magnificent examples of prayers include the Song of Moses (Exod. 15.1–18), Solomon's prayer at the dedication of the Temple (1 Kings 8.22–53), the Prayer of Hannah in the dedication of Samuel (1 Sam. 2.1–10), the priestly benediction (Num. 6.24–26), and the prayers of Ezra (Neh. 9.6–37) and Daniel (Dan. 9.3–19) for the restoration of God's people. The Book of Psalms, the hymn book of Israel and later that of the church, is the primary Old Testament example of the rich variety of prayers already mentioned. Here also we find the astonishing dynamic of the human–divine relationship ranging from exultation and thanksgiving to bitter lament and despair, yet hanging on by faith in the God of steadfast love and mercy. St. Athanasius' *Letter to Marcellinus*, an extraordinary essay on the Psalms that classifies and explains their usage, likens the Book of Psalms to a garden offering many beautiful flowers and a mirror of the soul reflecting the whole range of human feelings and experiences with God.

The New Testament presupposes the stream of Jewish worship and prayer. The Gospel of Luke records exquisite prayers by the Virgin Mary (Lk. 1.46–55), the priest Zechariah (Lk. 1.68–79), and the elder Simeon (Lk. 2.29–32). Jesus himself, circumcised on the eighth day and presented at the Temple on the fortieth, grew up in the tradition of Jewish prayer and piety with frequent appearances at the Temple and the synagogue. He not only gave instructions on prayer but also practiced heartfelt prayer, seeking solitude in the hills where he could pray all night, not least before making important decisions (Mk. 1.35; Lk. 6.12). The personal depth of Jesus' prayers to God the Father breaks forth in dramatic moments of joyful confession (Mt. 11.25), the giving of the Lord's Prayer (Mt. 6.5–13), the high priestly prayer to the Father (Jn. 17), and the agony at Gethsemane (Mk. 14.33–5), all of which exemplify the intimate relationship with God as a personal and loving Father which Jesus lived and taught. While the early church inherited much of the Jewish tradition of prayer, it gradually moved away from the Temple worship and cultic practices such as animal sacrifices, circumcision, and kosher foods, regarded as no longer compatible with the gospel. Instead, the church focused on its own rites of baptism, the Mystical Supper or Eucharist, and other rites that gradually developed into a whole tradition of worship continuously elaborated in content and structure. St. Paul, large sections of whose letters read like prayers, is a primary figure of the Christian renewal of prayer and worship in trinitarian forms based on the view that each baptized Christian is a living sacrifice to God (Rom. 6.4, 13; 12.1) and the church is the body of Christ and the temple of the Holy Spirit (1 Cor. 3.16–17; 12.12–27). Stirring echoes of early Christian prayers and aspects of worship, replete with Old Testament language, frequently occur in the Book of Revelation, where the eschatological drama of salvation itself is recounted from the perspective of the worship of God (Rev. 4.4–11; 5.8–14; 7.9–12; 11.15–18; 12.10–12; 15.3–4; 19.1–8).

The biblical foundations of prayer – the accessibility of a personal and moral God worthy of all honor and praise, the reciprocity of the divine-human relationship in freedom and faith, and the active saving purpose of God to rescue from evil and sanctify all things in Christ and the Spirit – shine through the development of an immensely rich tradition of Orthodox worship, piety, and spirituality. In Orthodox worship, next to the main sacraments of baptism and Eucharist, numerous other sacraments and rites sustain the community's engagement with the mystery of God and invoke God's blessings on key events or moments of life, such as birth, marriage, the need for forgiveness and healing, ministry, and death itself. Orthodox piety seeks the sanctification of every conceivable human activity through prayers for the blessing of schools, programs, homes, buildings, fields, agricultural products, animals, and (in modern times) automobiles.

Orthodox spirituality, flourishing in monastic traditions but not to be separated from church worship and practice, celebrates prayer as a highly intentional and focused activity in pursuit of Christian perfection through inner cleansing and

sublime experiences of God. Origen, Gregory of Nyssa, Isaac the Syrian, Maximos the Confessor, Symeon the New Theologian, Gregory Palamas, the many authors included in the *Philokalia*, and modern saints and authors such as Theophan the Recluse and Silouan of Athos, are primary bearers of this Orthodox mystical tradition which has had significant impact on contemporary clergy and laity. The focus of this life of prayer is the recitation of the Jesus Prayer that, along with other ascetic disciplines, and above all reliance on God's grace, guide the Christian to deeper levels of prayer in the process of *theosis* (deification), including purification, illumination, and glorification. The striking metaphors – "heaven in the heart," "light of the mind," "food for the soul," "secret work of the heart," "spiritual breathing," "inner worship," "standing before God" – richly suggest the meaning and value of concentrated personal prayer. Prayer's ultimate purpose is the transformation of daily life into a sacrament of the presence, power, and holiness of God.

SEE ALSO: Baptism; Blessing Rituals; Deification; Eucharist; Jesus Prayer; Mystery (Sacrament)

REFERENCES AND SUGGESTED READINGS

Balentine, S. E. (1993) *Prayer in the Hebrew Bible.* Minneapolis: Fortress Press.

Bloom, A. (1970) *Beginning to Pray.* New York: Paulist Press.

Chariton, Higoumen. (1966) *The Art of Prayer: An Orthodox Anthology.* London: Faber and Faber.

Clément, O. (1996) *The Roots of Christian Mysticism.* Hyde Park, NY: New City Press.

Cullmann, O. (1995) *Prayer in the New Testament.* Minneapolis: Fortress Press.

McGuckin, J. A. (1999) "The Prayer of the Heart in Patristic and Early Byzantine Tradition," in

P. Allen, W. Mayer, and L. Cross (ed.) *Prayer and Spirituality in the Early Church*, vol. 2. Banyo: Australian Catholic University, Centre for Early Christian Studies, pp. 69–108.

Miller, P. D. (1994) *They Cried to the Lord: The Form and Theology of Biblical Prayer*. Minneapolis: Augsburg Fortress.

Palmer, G. E. H. et al. (eds.) (1979–95) *The Philokalia: The Complete Text*, vols. 1–4. London: Faber and Faber.

Payne, R. (1979) *The Classics of Western Spirituality: Origen on Martyrdom, Prayer, et al.* New York: Paulist Press.

Payne, R. (ed.) (1980) *The Classics of Western Spirituality: Athanasius, the Life of St. Anthony and the Letter to Marcellinus*. New York: Paulist Press.

Prayer of the Heart *see* Jesus Prayer; St. Isaac the Syrian (7th c.); St. Paisy Velichovsky (1722–1794)

Priesthood

GEORGE E. DEMACOPOULOS

The term "priesthood" (*hierosynes*) in Orthodox thought simultaneously refers to the clerical orders in general and the specific clerical rank of the priest or presbyter (*presbyteros*). The concept of Christian priesthood originated during the 1st and early 2nd centuries through a conceptual bridging of the Eucharistic meal and the ancient Hebraic practice (shared by many Greco-Roman cults) in which a specific group of leaders was responsible for making a sacrificial offering to God on behalf of the community. In Christian theology, of course, the Eucharistic meal is understood to be a bloodless sacrifice through which Christ himself, in the form of the High Priest (Heb. 2.17, 3.1, 4.14), offers the sacrifice of himself in order to reconcile to God those who consume the meal. In the celebration of the divine liturgy, the priest stands in the place of Christ, leading the community in the presentation of the bread and wine as the sacrifice. As a consequence, the celebrant is sometimes understood to represent Christ within the community of believers. With time, the function of the priesthood expanded greatly beyond its initial Eucharistic role to incorporate other sacramental, pastoral, and administrative responsibilities.

In the New Testament the terms for presbyter (literally, "elder") and bishop (*episkopos*, literally, "overseer") seem to be interchangeable (e.g., Titus 1.5–7). By the late 1st or early 2nd century, however, the bishop emerged as the clear leader of the local community. Presbyters played a subordinate role as teachers, administrators, and as a council of advisers, but were clearly seen to outrank the order of deacons. As Christianity expanded and local communities grew larger than a single (cathedral) city church could contain, both urban and rural bishops began to invest individual priests with the authority to celebrate the Eucharistic meal in outlying parishes and perform baptisms in their stead. In this early period the priest was only permitted to serve this function within those parishes directly under his bishop's jurisdiction and he was not permitted to serve private chapels (see Trullo, Canons 31, 59). Moreover, a priest was not permitted to move to another diocese without approval. Similarly, teaching authority remained technically within the bishop's domain, but parish priests increasingly assumed primary catechetical and doctrinal instruction for most Christian communities.

The New Testament does not offer specific instructions regarding the selection of presbyters. Both 1 Timothy and Titus list a number of regulations concerning the appointment of bishops and deacons and we might reasonably assume that the earliest selection of presbyters followed similar criteria. In the Byzantine period, canon law increasingly incorporated Old Testament proscriptions to block certain persons (e.g., the deaf, the blind, the deformed, proscriptions that were often subjected to allegorical interpretation) from the priesthood. Canon law also set a minimum age for ordination at 30 (by comparison, a deacon was required to be 25 and a bishop 35). And while ordination to the deaconate and the priesthood was certainly possible for married men (unlike bishops, who after the 4th century were drawn from the celibate clergy), most patristic descriptions of the ideal priest are laden with ascetic credentials.

Theological reflection on the priesthood began in earnest with Gregory the Theologian's (330–90) *Apology for Flight* (Oration 2), which was the first Christian treatise to explore in detail the criteria for ordination and the pastoral responsibilities for leadership. Written ostensibly at the time of his ordination to the deaconate, Gregory moves frequently between generic terms for Christian leadership and that of the bishop specifically. He argues that all Christian leaders should possess an advanced education and extensive ascetic experience. Gregory further suggests that the ideal leader must learn to strike a balance between private ascetic retreat, in order to experience the contemplative life, and active service in the form of ministering to others. His model of an "active contemplative" became the prevailing model for the priesthood in the Byzantine period and remains so for the Orthodox Church to this day. Not surprisingly, John Chrysostom's (349–407) rhetorical masterpiece, *On the Priesthood*, which borrows extensively from Gregory's *Apology*, cautioned that the balance between service and personal contemplation was often elusive. Like Gregory, Chrysostom typically employs the generic term *hierosynes*, rather than *presbyteros* or *episcopos*, in his description of the pastoral leader. While it did little to alter Gregory's theology of the priesthood, *On the Priesthood* enjoyed one of the largest readerships of any Greek text in the Middle Ages and did much to advance the idea of clerical importance. It suggests, for example, that the priest is more important than the angels because he, unlike they, baptizes and celebrates the divine liturgy.

The most sophisticated treatise of pastoral literature in the Orthodox tradition is the Treatise on Pastoral Care (*Liber regulae pastoralis*) by Pope Gregory the Great (540–604), which was the only Latin treatise of the Middle Ages to be translated into Greek and disseminated by imperial order during the author's lifetime. Like Chrysostom, Pope Gregory borrowed directly from Gregory the Theologian's concept of the active contemplative. He also greatly expanded the earlier Gregory's list of spiritual characteristics, which required individualized spiritual remedies. Indeed, the *Liber pastoralis* describes 72 spiritual personality traits set in pairs of opposites, for which he offers a corresponding regimen for spiritual therapy. The pastoral solutions, especially, demonstrate Gregory's extensive familiarity with the patterns of spiritual direction then operative in the ascetic community and represent a direct bridging of the monastic and lay patterns of spiritual direction.

In the modern Orthodox world the most thorough treatment of the priesthood came indirectly through the work of Fr. Nicholas Afanasiev (1893–1966), a prominent Russian theologian and member of the St. Sergius faculty in Paris. Afanasiev's Eucharistic ecclesiology radically challenged contemporary bifurcations between lay and cleric, priest and bishop, and local church versus institutional church. Afanasiev viewed the local Eucharistic community as a complete embodiment of the entire Christian community and held that the clergy and laity were ontologically equal. Relying on the biblical concept of a priesthood of all believers (cf. 1 Pet. 2.9) and the interchangeability of presbyter and bishop in the pastoral epistles, Afanasiev took aim at what he perceived to be an Orthodox form of clericalism that had initially developed in the Byzantine period, but also later seeped into the Orthodox tradition from Roman Catholic sources. The ritual for Orthodox priestly ordination states: "The divine grace which always heals that which is infirm and completes that which is wanting elevates through the laying on of hands, the Reverend Deacon -N- to be a priest." The secret prayers of the bishop accompanying the laying on of hands speak also about the "great grace of the Holy Spirit" which is to be conferred, the advancement to the degree of priesthood, the standing at the altar, the ministry of the word, the proclamation of the gospel, the offering of gifts, and the renewing of the people through baptismal regeneration.

SEE ALSO: Baptism; Contemporary Orthodox Theology; Deacon; Eucharist; St. John Chrysostom (349–407)

REFERENCES AND SUGGESTED READINGS

Afanasiev, N. (2007) *The Church of the Holy Spirit*, trans. V. Permiakov. Notre Dame: University of Notre Dame Press.
Brown, R. E. (1970) *Priest and Bishop: Biblical Reflections*. New York: Paulist Press.
Chryssavgis, J. (1992) "Ministry in the Orthodox Church," *Sourozh* 50: 27–30.
Gregory the Great, St. (2008) *Book of Pastoral Rule*, trans. G. Demacopoulos. Crestwood, NY: St. Vladimir's Seminary Press.
Gregory of Nazianzus, St. (1994) *Apology for his Flight (Oration 2)*. Nicene, Post-Nicene Fathers series, second series, vol. 7, trans. C. Browne. Peabody, MA: Hendrickson Publishers.
John Chrysostom, St. (1984) *On the Priesthood*, trans. G. Neville. Crestwood, NY: St. Vladimir's Seminary Press.
Norris, R. A. (1984) "The Beginnings of Christian Priesthood," *Anglican Theological Review*, Supplement Series 9: 18–32.

Proimion *see* Kontakion

Prokeimenon
JOHN A. MCGUCKIN

The Prokeimenon (the Greek word means "what precedes," that is, a prelude, or introduction) is a liturgical refrain taken from a verse of a psalm which is interspersed (usually by means of the cantor alternating in chant with the reader) with a selection of other verses, or half-verses, from that psalm. It serves to introduce the scriptural reading (the "Apostle") at the divine liturgy. Prokeimena also occur at the Vespers and Orthros services before the Old Testament readings (and even when these may not have scriptural readings appointed for the day). The current system of Prokeimena is a survival from earlier times in the liturgy when the entire psalm would have been read as part of the cycle of biblical readings in church. In current Greek practice the reading of the verses is relatively simple. In Slavic use it is a more extended antiphonal refrain.

Proskomedie (Prothesis)
JOHN A. MCGUCKIN

The ritual preparatory to the celebration of the divine liturgy, which is substantially the preparation of the *prosphora* or loaves of offering. Greek usage involves the cutting out, from a single large loaf, of a cube of bread marked on its surface with the cross-shaped ICXC NIKA cipher

("Jesus Christ Conquers") which has been baked into it. Slavic use generally employs five smaller prosphora, the first being used for the Eucharistic Lamb (*Amnos*) and the others for various commemorations. The priest who celebrates the Proskomedie (it is always celebrated by one priest alone) will leave some of the final elements unfinished if it is an episcopal service, since the presiding bishop will complete the prayers just before the Great Entrance. After the central cube of bread has been cut out, with attendant prayers, using a ceremonial knife (or *lance*), other particles of bread are also removed to symbolize the Blessed Theotokos, and the nine orders of saints (including angels, prophets, apostles, hierarchs ascetics, and martyrs), which conclude with the saint who composed the liturgy being celebrated (St. John Chrysostom, Basil, or James). These are laid on either side of the Lamb on the *diskos*. Particles are then removed to commemorate the ruling bishop, "the emperor" (civil authorities), the founders of the church, and those living and dead whom the priest wishes to remember. Wine is mixed with a little water in the chalice and the ritual concludes with the incensing of the veils that are laid over the sacred vessels in readiness for the Eucharist to begin. The faithful also provide other lists of names, and offerings of prosphora breads, to commemorate their own family lists (*diptychs*) for the living as well as the dead. The particles are placed into the chalice after communion with an intercessory prayer: "for all those commemorated here." In earlier times the Proskomedie was celebrated in a separate building (as at Hagia Sophia, Constantinople), but in most Orthodox churches today the northern side of the altar area is used, where a small altar of preparation (*prothesis*) can be found, usually adorned with iconic symbolism recalling the nativity.

SEE ALSO: Amnos; Eucharist; Lance

Prosomoia *see* Idiomelon

Prosphora *see* Lance; Proskomedie (Prothesis)

Protecting Veil

VERA SHEVZOV

The Protecting Veil (Greek *skepê, maphorion*; Russian, *Pokrov*), celebrated on October 1, is one of the most beloved Marian feasts on the Orthodox calendar in Slavonic Orthodox lands. The inspiration for the feast was a 10th-century vision in the Church of the Virgin of Blachernae, Constantinople, by the Blessed Andrew, the Fool for Christ, as recorded by the presbyter Nicephoros. According to the tradition, the Mother of God spread her protective veil, which "radiated the glory of God," over all those present in church. The celebration of the Protecting Veil thus recognizes the *Theotokos* as the universal heavenly protectress of all Christians. While there is scant evidence of any liturgical commemoration of this feast in Byzantium, it became immensely popular in Russia; whether developing from origins at Constantinople, Kiev, or Northern Russia remaining a point of controversy. By the end of the 19th century the feast was usually dated to the 12th century and was credited to the Grand Prince Andrei Bogoliubskii, who took St. Andrew as his patron saint. Liturgically, it parallels the feast of the Deposition of the Precious Robe of the Theotokos at Blachernae for July 2. The festal icon shows the central figure of the Mother of God spreading her protective veil, Blessed Andrew pointing

Plate 51   Icon of the Protecting Veil depicting the Holy Fool Andrew. Photo Temple Gallery, London.

her out to his disciple Epiphanius, St. John the Forerunner (who in Andrew's vision accompanied Mary into the Blachernae church), and St. Romanos the Melodist (whose commemoration also occurs on October 1).

SEE ALSO: Fools, Holy; Theotokos, the Blessed Virgin

REFERENCES AND SUGGESTED READINGS

Lyden, L. (1976) "The Vision of the Virgin at Blachernae and the Feast of the Pokrov," *Analecta Bollandiana* 94: 63–82.

Presbyter Nicephorus (1976) "Life of Andrew, the Fool for Christ," in J. P. Migne (ed.) *Patrologiae Graecae*, Vol. 111. Turnhout, Belgium: Brepols, cols. 620–887.

Prothesis *see* Proskomedie

Protodeacon
MARIA GWYN MCDOWELL

A rank of the diaconate, historically the protodeacon is a title of honor given to chief deacons who are not monastics. In contemporary practice the protodeacon is the senior deacon attached to a cathedral or principal church. The protodeacon is elevated, not ordained, to the new rank. The protodeacon can claim precedence when serving with other deacons. If more than one protodeacon serve together, precedence is given according to the dates of their elevation.

SEE ALSO: Archdeacon; Deacon; Deaconess; Ordination

Plate 52   Bishop in the Monastery of St. John on Patmos, Greece, talking to two monks. ILM Image Group/Alamy.

Protopsaltes *see* Music (Sacred)

Psaltes (Cantor)

DIMITRI CONOMOS

One of the minor clerical orders in those Orthodox Churches that employ monophonic chants. The chief cantor, the protopsaltes, initiates choral performances by intoning a conventional formula or, more frequently, by singing one or two starting notes to establish the pitch. The earliest testimonies to a solo cantor are from Constantinople (second half of the 4th century) where, in the responsorial execution of scriptural verse – especially psalmody – the cantor sang refrains which were repeated by the congregation. In Byzantium there were two choirs, each with its own leader: the protopsaltes for the right choir and the lampadarios for the left.

Psilanthropism

JOHN A. MCGUCKIN

From the Greek meaning "Merely a Man." It signifies the heretical doctrine that Jesus was a human being who was highly graced by God, as a Prophet, or Spirit-bearer (*pneumatophoros*), or even the greatest of all the saints; but was not, in the proper sense of the term, "divine." The heresy has appeared in numerous forms throughout church history, associated first with the Judeo-Christian Ebionite sect, and the 2nd-century "Modalists" who approached Christology in terms of a holy servant of God, Jesus, being caught up in the energy and work of the Spirit, and "manifested" as the Son of God in this sense, though not being divine in anything other than an exemplarist sense, a matter of honorific association of words. Paul of Samosata made this view notorious, and was one of the first public dissident bishops to be censured by a formal council of the church. In patristic times, however, the position was most closely associated with the person and teachings of Photinos, bishop of Sirmium (d. ca. 376), who was deposed for his christological views at the Council of Sirmium in 351 (Socrates, *Church History* 2.18, 29–30; Sozomen, *Church History* 4.6; Epiphanius, *Heresies* 71), and once more symbolically censured at the Council of Constantinople in 381, and yet again by the imperial decree of Theodosius II in 428. The heresy is thus also known in the Orthodox Church as "Photinianism."

Origen had partly clarified the Modalist problem, but also confused the matter for the 4th-century theologians, by his earlier and peculiar Christology that Jesus had to be distinguished from the Divine Logos, as being the bearer of the Logos, not synonymous with him. Origen, however, cannot rightly be classed as a Psilanthropist because his understanding of the "Preexistent Soul Jesus" belongs more to a category of Angelic Christology fused with a theology of the Incarnation of the Divine Logos. The Christology of Arius is more confused still, but it is clear enough that though he leaned away from seeing Jesus as the Divine Logos he nevertheless did not see him as "merely a man." Many of the ancient Orthodox polemicists were less careful in their analysis, and often fathered Psilanthropism onto their heterodox opponents in the course of the centuries when it seemed that they were advocating less than the full Nicene Christology (manifested in the Nicene Creed, St. Athanasius, St. Gregory the Theologian, and St. Cyril of Alexandria, for example): namely, that Jesus was synonymous with the Eternal and Divine Logos himself, as incarnated within history. For polemical reasons, therefore, several heterodox theologians of Antiquity such as Theodore Mopsuestia and Nestorius were erroneously accused of Psilanthropism. The heresy has been seen as a fundamental one, attacking the central and basic faith of the Orthodox Church that in the person of Christ Jesus we were "not saved by an angel, or a servant, but by God himself." Psilanthropism has been on the Christian horizons for a very long time, and its reappearance as widespread phenomenon in many parts of the modern world is nothing new, although the extent to which forms of Psilanthropism are now sustained among many western academic theologians (such as parts of the "Jesus of History" Movement, or aspects of the Liberation Christology movement) is unusual.

SEE ALSO: Christ; Council of Nicea I (325); Incarnation (of the Logos); Logos Theology; St. Athanasius of Alexandria (ca. 293–373); St. Cyril of Alexandria (ca. 378–444)

REFERENCES AND SUGGESTED READINGS

Bardy, G. (1935) "Photine," in *Dictionnaire de théologie catholique*, vol. 12, pt. 2. Paris: Letouzey et Ané.
Hanson, R. P. C. (1988) *The Search for the Christian Doctrine of God*. Edinburgh: T&T Clark.
McGuckin, J. A. (2000) "Quest for the Historical Jesus," in A. Hastings (ed.) *The Oxford Companion to Christian Thought*. Oxford: Oxford University Press. pp. 587–9.
Petavius, D. (1636) *De Photino Haeretico eiusque Damnatione*. Paris.
Simonetti, M. (1965) "Studi sull'Arianesimo," *Verba Seniorum* 5: 135–59.

Psychosabbaton

JEFFREY B. PETTIS

The Greek word *psychosabbaton* ("soul Sabbath") refers to the Saturdays in the Orthodox liturgical year set aside for a special remembering of the departed. On these "Sabbata" days special hymns are added to the divine service to commemorate the dead. The designation of the day of Saturday stems from its symbolic association with Christ's own entombment on that day. The designated days include the Saturday of Meatfare week, or the second Saturday before Great Lent; the Saturday before the Sunday of the Last Judgment; the second, third, and fourth Saturdays of Great Lent; the Saturday before Pentecost; and the Saturday prior to the Feast of St. Demetrius the Great Martyr. The divine service on these days has special hymns selected for the commemoration of the dead. Usually the memorial observance of the Panikhida follows the divine liturgy on Saturday morning, but it may also occur after Vespers on the preceding Friday evening (vigil of Saturday). Prayers are offered for the repose of those who have departed and for the comfort of the living. The service has a penitential emphasis, in that it calls believers to humility before the reality of the brevity of mortal human life. The service may include the use of the ancient tradition of Kollyva, a liturgical meal blessed and taken in memory of the dead. A service celebrated on behalf of an individual on these days will usually take place at the grave site, but memorial services for all the faithful who have departed occur in the church, as do services for those whose graves may be located at a far distance. In some cases the Saturday liturgy takes place in the cemetery chapel. The Orthodox Church additionally recognizes and prays for the dead on the holiday called "The Day of Rejoicing" which falls after St. Thomas Sunday in the post-Pascha Bright week.

SEE ALSO: Death (and Funeral); Kollyva

REFERENCES AND SUGGESTED READINGS

Krueger, D. (ed.) (2006) *Byzantine Christianity.* Minneapolis: Fortress Press.

Langford-James, R. (ed.) (1975) *A Dictionary of the Eastern Orthodox Church.* New York: Burt Franklin.

Quinisext Council (Council in Trullo) (692)

M. C. STEENBERG

The Quinisext Council (Latin, *quinisextum*, "fifth-sixth": so named as it was seen to complete the work of the fifth and sixth ecumenical councils) was convened in 692 by Emperor Justinian II and held in Constantinople's Trullo ("domed") palace, where the sixth council had convened in 681 (hence its alternate name, the Council in Trullo, or Troullo). Its purpose was to issue legislative canons, which neither the fifth nor sixth councils had done. These include injunctions against fasting on Saturdays, celebrating full liturgies on weekdays in Great Lent, and so on. Many of the canons address differences in Eastern and Western Church practice, and this, together with the lack of western representation at the council, ensured its disputed place in the ecumenical conciliar lists of the Western Churches, while in the Byzantine world it was widely assigned the same ecumenical status of its conciliar predecessors.

SEE ALSO: Canon Law; Ecumenical Councils

REFERENCES AND SUGGESTED READINGS

Davis, L. D. (1987) *The First Seven Ecumenical Councils: Their History and Theology.* Wilmington: Michael Glazier.

Meyendorff, J. (1989) *Imperial Unity and Christian Divisions: The Church 450–680 AD.* Crestwood, NY: St. Vladimir's Seminary Press.

R

Relics

MONICA M. WHITE

Relics – objects connected with a holy person or event – are venerated in all Eastern Churches. Primary relics are from the body of a holy person (usually bones, but also hair, blood, etc.), while secondary relics are objects from an event in sacred history or with which a holy person has come into contact, most famously the True Cross. Relics can play an important role in the cult of a saint. The discovery of incorrupt relics has often been taken as a sign of sanctity, particularly in Kievan Rus, although this has never been an official requirement for sainthood (Lenhoff 1993). Relics can also help spread a saint's cult by being broken up and distributed, or by exuding oil which can be collected by pilgrims.

The healing power of relics is attested in the Old Testament. In 2 Kings 13.21 a dead man was revived when his body touched that of Elisha. Although the New Testament makes no reference to human remains effecting cures, it does describe miracles accomplished through secondary relics, such as the woman with a haemorrhage who was healed by touching the hem of Christ's garment in Mark 5.25–9 (see also Acts 19.12).

These stories shaped Christian beliefs about relics, encouraging the idea that the body of a holy person had a power which could be transferred to objects with which it came in contact, both before and after death. The practice of keeping relics in homes and churches may have originated in Egypt, where it was not unusual for pagans and Christians alike to store the mummies of relatives in their homes. Christians may have begun distributing pieces of such mummies, particularly if they had belonged to martyrs or holy men, in the belief that they had healing properties (Wortley 2006: 12–14, 18–27).

Attempts by the authorities to discourage the distribution of relics (contrary to early Roman Law) were largely ineffectual, and their veneration quickly became widespread in the churches. As their popularity grew, so did the trade in them and the distribution of false relics. Athanasius of Alexandria and the Theodosian Code attacked these practices, apparently to no avail (Wortley 2006: 24–6).

In addition to curing individuals, relics took on broader political and ecclesiastical functions. Gregory the Illuminator, for example, brought relics with him to use in his work in Armenia. Despite his desire for his own body to remain concealed after his death, his relics were eventually discovered, and possession of them became a source of authority for heads of the Armenian Church from the 12th century onward (Kouymjian 2005: 221–5).

Constantinople soon after its foundation amassed a spectacular collection of relics from across the Christian world. They do not seem to have been banned during Iconoclasm, possibly because biblical

The Encyclopedia of Eastern Orthodox Christianity, edited by John Anthony McGuckin
© 2011 Blackwell Publishing Ltd.

Plate 53   Exhuming relics of the saints at Optina Hermitage. RIA Novosti/AKG.

Plate 54   A reliquary containing the remains of several saints. Relics are commonly found in Orthodox ritual and the saints are widely venerated by the faithful as vessels of the Holy Spirit, still active after their deaths. Photo by John McGuckin.

precedents existed for their veneration (Wortley 2003: 169–73). Particularly prized were the city's Marian relics, which included her milk, spindle, girdle, and robe. The robe, in particular, was believed to have saved the city from destruction on a number of occasions (Wortley 2005).

Relics were well represented in Byzantine iconography, and by the 10th century a complete graphic "life cycle" had been developed for them. This included the Invention or discovery of a relic, its Translation to a new city or church, the Adventus or formal greeting of the relic when it arrived, its Deposition in its new resting place, and its Veneration (Walter 1982).

Although relics were numerous, they came from a relatively restricted group of saints. In his survey of relics in the Greek Orthodox church, Otto Meinardus (1970/71) found evidence for 3,602 relics of 476 saints, out of the approximately 3,800 saints who were liturgically recognized by the late Ottoman period. Furthermore, five saints (Charalampos, Panteleimon, Tryphon, Paraskeva, and George) accounted for nearly a quarter of all relics.

Because relics were coveted, theft was common. The relics of many famous saints were taken to the West in the medieval period, and Constantinople lost most of its relics when the city was sacked in 1204 (Geary 1990). The Vatican has, however, returned a number of relics to various Eastern Churches since the mid-1960s as part of efforts to improve ecumenical relations (Meinardus 1970: 348–50).

Relics attracted international attention when the Russian government sponsored the exhumation of Tsar Nicholas II and his family, who were murdered by Bolsheviks and buried outside the city of Ekaterinburg in 1918. Although DNA tests made a strong case that the remains were those of the Romanovs, Patriarch Aleskii II refused to accept the findings and did not send a representative to the reburial ceremony on July 17, 1998. Nevertheless, the Russian Orthodox Church canonized the family, along with other new martyrs of the Soviet period, at a bishop's council in August 2000 (King and Wilson 2003: 381–503).

SEE ALSO: Ecumenism, Orthodoxy and; Healing; Iconography, Styles of; Myrobletes Saints; New Martyrs; Old Testament

REFERENCES AND SUGGESTED READINGS

Geary, P. (1990) *Furta Sacra: thefts of Relics in the Central Middle Ages.* Princeton: Princeton University Press.

King, G. and Wilson, P. (2003) *The Fate of the Romanovs.* Hoboken, NJ: John Wiley.

Kouymjian, D. (2005) "The Right Hand of St. Gregory and Other Armenian Arm Relics," in P. Borgeaud and Y. Volokhine (eds.) *Les Objets de la mémoire: pour une approche comparatiste des reliques et de leur culte.* Bern: Peter Lang, pp. 221–46.

Lenhoff, G. (1993) "The Notion of 'Uncorrupted Relics' in Early Russian Culture," in B. Gasparov and O. Raevsky-Hughes (eds.) *Christianity and the Eastern Slavs*, vol. 1. Berkeley: University of California Press, pp. 252–75.

Meinardus, O. (1970) "An Examination of the Traditions Pertaining to the Relics of St. Mark," *Orientalia Christiana Periodica* 36: 348–76.

Meinardus, O. (1970/71) "A Study of the Relics of Saints of the Greek Orthodox Church," *Oriens Christianus* 54/55: 130–278.

Walter, C. (1982) *Art and Ritual of the Byzantine Church.* London: Variorum.

Wortley, J. (2003) "Icons and Relics: A Comparison," *Greek, Roman and Byzantine Studies* 43: 161–74.

Wortley, J. (2005) "The Marian Relics at Constantinople," *Greek, Roman and Byzantine Studies* 45: 171–87.

Wortley, J. (2006) "The Origins of Christian Veneration of Body-Parts," *Revue de l'histoire des religions* 223: 5–28.

Repentance

ANDREI PSAREV

In Orthodox thought repentance is the blessed mourning of a person and longing for God (*penthos*) following after a sense of having moved away from him. It is a conversion to God and, as a result, is what scripture describes as radical change of mind or heart (*metanoia*, see Mk. 1.15). Christ came to save sinners having called them to repentance and belief in his gospel (Mt. 9.13). The parable of the prodigal son (Lk. 15.11) outlines the stages of how Orthodox understand the process of repentance: contrition, aversion from sin, repudiation of evil, confession, reconciliation with God and one's neighbor.

The words from the apostle about the impossibility of repentance for those who, by sinning, crucify Christ again (Heb. 6.4–6) reflect a dilemma of the early church; for in the 3rd and 4th centuries the Novatianists and Donatists permanently excluded from Eucharistic communion those who were guilty of serious sins. The greater church would not accept this rigorist approach, having prescribed in its canons various terms of abstinence from the Eucharist on account of grave sins; but no transgressor was ever to be deprived of the Eucharist at the time of their death (Nicea 1. Canon 13). There are no sins that may prevent a person from entering into the dedicated life of repentance which is monasticism (Quinisext Council. Canon 43). Repentance has been called in Orthodoxy the "second baptism."

Canon 12 of St. Gregory the Wonderworker (3rd century) defines how the church classifed penitents. In early times certain classes of sinners were debarred from full Eucharistic membership and had to stand apart from the community, in the narthex or outside the church building, sometimes for many years. St. Basil the Great (4th century) was not just occupied with the impact of sin on an individual, but also with the spiritual health of the entire congregation (St. Basil. Canon 88). In the same way as sin injures the body of the whole ecclesiastical community, through the healing of each member the entire church body acquires reconciliation with God (1 Cor. 12.26).

Although public ceremonies of repentance were already common in the time of St. Basil the Great, private repentance, appropriate for particular sins, was also in use (St. Basil. Canon 34). The successor of St. Gregory of Nazianzus, Nectarius of Constantinople, was the first major hierarch known to formally abolish the ecclesiastical office of public repentance in Constantinople in the late 4th century. By the 9th century, after the triumph of the monks over the iconoclasts, the practice of private monastic confession became standard. Nevertheless, the correspondence of Archbishop Demetrios Chomatenos demonstrates that the arranging of public penance was occasionally known even in 13th-century Byzantium. Current Orthodox practice is that a Christian repents secretly of personal sins, while a more public acknowledgment of repentance may be appropriate in case of widely known offenses. It is Christ himself who receives the believer's repentance. The priest, acting as confessor, is only a witness, a spiritual therapist who gives advice, or who may prescribe a penitential remedy (*epitimion*). The church annually assigns the time of Great Lent as an occasion for repentance. During this forty-day period Christians are called to turn from self-love towards deeper love of God and one's neighbor. Various ascetic and pious deeds – fasting, almsgiving, extended prayer with tears – may go along with the Orthodox practice of repentance.

According to the desert fathers, St. Gregory Palamas, and other church teachers, repentance signifies the beginning of the process of rebirth. Through this process a person becomes a participant in divine nature (2 Pet. 1.4). Repentance is not simply a matter of rejecting sin and leading a life of virtue, but rather a transformation that helps the person to discover in the soul's depths the very likeness of God.

SEE ALSO: Asceticism; Canon Law; Confession; Metanie (Metanoia)

REFERENCES AND SUGGESTED READINGS

Antonopoulos Nektarios, Archimandrite (2000) *Return.* Athens: Akritas Publications.
Chrysostomos, Archbishop of Etna (1997) *Repentance.* Etna, CA: Center for Traditionalist Orthodox Studies.
Chryssavgis, J. (1990) *Repentance and Confession.* Brookline, MA: Holy Cross Orthodox Press.
Erickson, J. H. (1991) "Penitential Discipline in the Orthodox Canonical Tradition," in *Challenge of Our Past.* Crestwood, NY: St. Vladimir's Seminary Press.
Melling, D. J. (2001) "Metanoia," in *The Blackwell Dictionary of Eastern Christianity.* Oxford: Blackwell.

Resurrection

THEODORE G. STYLIANOPOULOS

Belief in resurrection, and specifically resurrection from the dead, is a distinct biblical teaching that derives from Judaism and finds its full significance in the person and life of Jesus of Nazareth, historically proclaimed to have died, been buried, and risen from the dead. Much more so than in Judaism, resurrection is absolutely central to Christianity (1 Cor. 15.12–19), especially Eastern Christianity, because the death and resurrection of Jesus Christ constitute the foundational saving events, and the core of the gospel, which lie behind the birth and character of the church, the New Testament, and Christian theology and spirituality. While resurrection is chiefly tied to the resurrection of Jesus and to the hope of the resurrection of the dead at his glorious return, the term also carries diverse metaphorical meanings such as the historical restoration of a people, life after death, immortality of the soul, and even an experience of spiritual renewal in this present life. In ancient paganism the theme of resurrection was connected not to a historical person or historical event, but rather to mythological deities such as Isis and Osiris whose cult celebrated the annual rebirth of nature and the power of fertility, a phenomenon that scholarship has widely judged to be entirely different from the Christian understanding in origin, scope, and meaning.

In the Old Testament the focus was on this present order of life, the main arena of God's blessings and chastisements. Existence after death was viewed as virtual nonexistence, called Hades, a "land of forgetfulness," a place of shades (Ps. 88.10–12; 87.11–13 *LXX*), having no contact with the living and cut off from God himself (Ps. 6.5; 6.6 *LXX*). Exceptionally, some righteous persons such as Enoch (Gen. 5.24) and Elijah (2 Kings 2.11) escaped death not by resurrection but by direct transfer to heaven. In other rare cases, Elijah and Elishah revived dead children to ordinary life as apparent acts of healing (1 Kings 17.21–22; 2 Kings 4.34–5). Texts such as Hosea 6.1–3 and Ezekiel 37.1–14 look to the resurgence and restoration of Israel in space and time, although also easily seen by Christian interpreters as prophecies of the final resurrection of the dead. A singular text such as Isaiah 26.19 that foresees a resurrection of the dead is as

Plate 55   Icon of the myrrh-bearing women at the tomb. By Eileen McGuckin. The Icon Studio: www.sgtt.org.

rare as it is peripheral to classic Old Testament teaching. Regular belief in a future resurrection of the dead, especially of the righteous as reward for their persecution and martyrdom, developed among Jews after 200 BCE and is attested notably in Daniel 12.1–3 and 2 Maccabees 7.9, 22–9. By the time of Jesus, among other divergent views of the afterlife, this doctrine was firmly established among the Pharisees (in contrast to the Sadducees, Mk. 12.18) and subsequently became a key teaching of mainstream Christianity.

In the New Testament the accounts of Jesus' resurrection, based on apostolic memories and oral traditions, vary widely in detail. However, the fact and centrality of the resurrection constitute the bedrock of the Christian faith, attested by more than five hundred eyewitnesses (1 Cor. 15.5–8). The gospels indicate that Jesus anticipated his death as blood covenant renewal and viewed his resurrection as God's vindication of his ministry (e.g., Mk. 8.27–31; 14.22–5, 36, 61–2; cf. Acts 3.13–15). Matthew, Luke, and John link Jesus' resurrection with the gift of the Spirit and the inauguration of the early Christian mission (Mt. 28.16–20; Lk. 24.44–9; Jn. 20.19–23; cf. Acts 2.32–3). The Gospel of John magnificently integrates the life, death, resurrection, and enthronement of the Son of God as the mutual glorification between the Father and the Son, marking the decisive victory over the power of death and the gift of abundant life through the Spirit, available to believers in the present as well as the future (Jn. 1.14;

5.24–9; 7.37–9; 12.30–1; 14.15–24; 17.1–5). In this similar rich vein, the Apostle Paul provides the most detailed theological explication of the death and resurrection of the incarnate Son (Gal. 4.4–6; Rom. 1.1–4) and Lord of glory (1 Cor. 2.8; 15.1–4). For Paul, the death and resurrection of Jesus the Christ mark the cosmic shift from the old age of sin, corruption, and death to the new era of grace, life, incorruption, and transformed bodily immortality (Rom. 3.21–6; 5.12–21; 8.18–39; 1 Cor. 15.50–7). In Paul, as in John, God's powers of salvation are at work both now and in the future in those who are united with Christ through faith and baptism, and who enact the pattern of Jesus' death and resurrection by crucifying their sinful passions and offering themselves as living sacrifice to God (Rom. 6.1–23; 8.9–13; 10.9–13; 12.1–2; 2 Cor. 4.7–18; Gal. 3.16–24).

The New Testament includes mention of the resurrection of Lazarus and of several others who are returned to ordinary life and presumed that they will die again (Jn. 11.43–4; Mk. 5.41–2; Mt. 27.52–3). But Jesus' resurrection, and the expected future resurrection of the dead at the consummation, is of an entirely different order, involving God's decisive process of salvation and a radical transformation of soul and body in which "the corruptible must put on the incorruptible and the mortal must put on the immortal," and death will be swallowed up by life (1 Cor. 15.53–5). Thus the significance of Jesus' death and resurrection is summed up not only in resolving the problem of sin and guilt, but also in overcoming the tragic reality of decay and death through the new creation, the epoch of the Holy Spirit, moving toward the glorification of creation itself. Here lie the elements of the sharpest differences in theology between on the one hand medieval Western Christianity with its emphasis on the cross and penal theories of substitutionary satisfaction of the divine justice, and on the other hand the tradition of Orthodoxy with its emphasis on the resurrection and therapeutic views of salvation as rescue, healing, and liberation from humanity's true enemies – the powers of sin, corruption, death, and the devil.

SEE ALSO: Christ; Cross; Deification; Parousia; Soteriology

REFERENCES AND SUGGESTED READINGS

Athanasius, St. (1976) *On the Incarnation.* Crestwood, NY: St. Vladimir's Seminary Press.

Aulen, G. (1965) *Christus Victor: An Historical Study of the Three Main Types of the Idea of the Atonement.* London: SPCK.

Florovsky, G. (1976) *Creation and Redemption, Vol. 3: The Collected Works of Georges Florovsky.* Belmont, MA: Nordland Publishing.

Kirk, J. R. D. (2008) *Unlocking Romans: Resurrection and the Justification of God.* Grand Rapids, MI: Eerdmans.

Levenson, J. D. (2006) *Resurrection and the Restoration of Israel: The Ultimate Victory of God.* New Haven: Yale University Press.

Martin-Achard, R. and Nickelsburg, G. W. E. (1992) "Resurrection," in *The Anchor Bible Dictionary,* vol. 5, ed. D. N. Freedman. New York: Doubleday, pp. 680–91.

Pelikan, J. (1971) *The Christian Tradition, Vol. 1: The Emergence of the Catholic Tradition.* Chicago: University of Chicago Press.

Pelikan, J. (1974) *The Christian Tradition, Vol. 2: The Spirit of Eastern Christendom.* Chicago: University of Chicago Press.

Wright, N. T. (2003) *On the Incarnation of the Son of God.* Minneapolis: Fortress Press.

Rhipidion (Fan)

KENNETH CARVELEY

A round, sometimes "six-winged" disc placed on the end of a pole which was originally used as a liturgical fan to keep the Eucharistic elements free from flying insects. Symbolically, these represent the cherubim or angelic overshadowing and may reflect images from the mercy seat or Ark of the Covenant. Deacons are presented with these on their ordination for use during the anaphora, waving them over the elements until the elevation. Some rhipidia have bells attached. In the medieval West, these fans were known as *flabella*. Rhipidia are sometimes carried in procession at the Great Entrance of the Liturgy and are usually kept near the holy table.

REFERENCES AND SUGGESTED READINGS

Schuilz, H. J. (1986) *The Byzantine Liturgy.* New York: Pueblo.

Romania, Patriarchal Orthodox Church of

THEODOR DAMIAN

According to the census of 2002, 18,817,975 people out of the 21,680,974 inhabitants of Romania are Orthodox Christians; that is, 86.8 percent. In terms of population the Church of Romania is second in size only to Russia, and the most numerous Orthodox Church of any state of the European Union.

The Romanian Orthodox Church is an institution of apostolic origin. The Christian faith was known south of the Danube river, in the regions inhabited by Illyrians, Thraco-Dacians, and Greeks (today's Serbia, Bulgaria, and Greece), as far back as the second half of the 1st century, through the preaching of St. Paul and his disciples. More specifically, Christianity was spread through the preaching of the Apostle

Plate 56 The monastic cells (living quarters) of Rohia Monastery in Northern Romania. The monastery flourished even under communist oppression under the leadership of its higumen bishop, Justinian Chira. Photo by John McGuckin.

Andrew in what is today the Romanian province of Dobrogea, which, after the administrative reform of Diocletian, was called Scythia Minor. In local traditions St. Andrew is called the "Apostle of the wolves," which is historically significant in a context where the ethnic symbol of the Dacians was the wolf's head. In the northern part of the Danube river, in Dacia, which in 106 became a Roman province after being conquered by Trajan, the new faith arrived in the 1st, 2nd, and 3rd centuries, brought by merchants, colonists, and the soldiers of the Roman army who were settled in the newly occupied territory. After the retreat of the Roman legions to the south of the Danube (271) and later, after the promulgation of the Edict of Milan (313), through which Emperor Constantine the Great granted liberty for Christians, the new religion expanded. Significant Christian archeological evidence discovered in the northern territories, as well as all the words of Latin origin in the Romanian language which define fundamental notions of the Christian faith, stand as proof of this expansion. During the 4th century there also existed, on the eastern borders of the Danube, several diocesan seats such as Singidunum, Viminacium, Bononia, Ratiaria, Oescus, Novae, Appiaria, Abritus, and Durostorum, whose bishops took care of the spiritual needs of the faithful north of the Danube, too. There was a metropolitan seat at Tomis in Scythia Minor (today, Constanta) with as many as fourteen dioceses, active in the 4th century and led by diligent bishops (Bretanion, Gerontius, Teotim I, Timotei, Ioan, Alexandru, Teotim II, Paternus, and Valentinian). According to the historian Eusebius of Caesarea, a Scythian bishop was present at the First Ecumenical Council at Nicea (325) and other bishops who followed him took part in the works of the subsequent councils, as well as in the christological disputes of the time. There are also indications of the existence of diocesan seats in other towns. Well-known theologians from Scythia Minor are St. John Cassian and St. Dionysius Exiguus.

During the time of the persecution of Christians, many priests and faithful of the Danubian lands suffered martyrdom for Christ, such as Bishop Ephrem, killed in 304 in Tomis; the Daco-Roman priest Montanus and his wife Maxima, who were drowned, also in 304; and martyrs Zoticos, Attalos, Kamasis, and Filippos (whose relics were discovered in 1971 in a paleo-Christian basilica in Niculitel, Dobrogea). We also know of St. Sava called the Goth,

St. Niceta the Roman, and several others. Relics of martyrs who died in the Decian persecutions (249–51) have also been recently discovered by archeologists.

The second and fourth ecumenical councils put the territories north of the Danube under the jurisdiction of the patriarchate of Constantinople. Later, the faithful in the Dacian lands of present-day Romania, north of the Danube, were placed under the ecclesiastical jurisdiction of the archbishopric Justiniana Prima, founded by Emperor Justinian (535). The city of Sucidava, where probably a diocesan seat existed (the ruins of a basilica from the 4th to 5th centuries were discovered there), had an important role in the introduction of Christianity north of the Danube.

All these diocesan seats disappeared about the year 600, during the great Avaro-Slavic migration. During the 7th to 10th centuries the Slavs settled on the territories of present-day Serbia, Bulgaria, and their surroundings, and exerted a strong influence on Dacian Christianity to the point where even the Slavic language penetrated into Daco-Romanian worship, even if this language was not generally understood by the community. Thus, the Romanian people were the only people of Latin origin confessing the Orthodox faith to use the Slavic (Slavonic) language in worship until about the end of the 17th century. Starting in the early 16th century, Slavonic was slowly replaced by Romanian once more. The last liturgy in Slavonic was published in Wallachia in 1736 and in 1863 Romanian became the only official language of the church.

Information about the Christian life of the Daco-Romanians after 600 is scant. However, there are archeological vestiges of the 7th to 10th centuries that certify its continuity on the ancient territory of Romania: ruins of churches at Niculitel and Dinogetia, in the north of Dobrogea, the small rock churches at Basarabi near Constanta, the church ruins at Dabaca (Cluj district) and at Morisena-Cenad (Timis district). In the 13th century the Romanians had bishops of their own, as can be seen from a letter of Pope Gregory IX of 1234, as well as from other records.

After the founding of the two Romanian principalities of Wallachia or Muntenia (ca. 1330) and Moldavia (ca. 1359), metropolitan sees were established in the capitals of both countries. Since Dacia, south of the Danube river, was known as Greater Wallachia, in 1359 the ecumenical patriarchate acknowledged the metropolitanate of Ungro-Wallachia for Dacia north of the Danube, having its seat in Curtea de Arges, and Bishop Iachint of Vicina became its first metropolitan. At the beginning of the 16th century two other diocesan sees were founded, subject to the metropolitanate, at Ramnic and Buzau, which have continued to the present day.

In 1401 the ecumenical patriarchate acknowledged a second Romanian metropolitanate, that of Moldavia, with its seat at Suceava. At the beginning of the 15th century, two suffragan dioceses were founded at Roman and at Radauti, and later in 1598 another one at Husi. In Transylvania, under the rule of the Hungarian Catholic kings, three Romanian diocesan seats were created even though the Romanians were not officially recognized as a nation by the political authorities of the time. At the end of the 15th century St. Stephen the Great, prince of Moldavia, founded a diocesan see at Vad in the district of Cluj. The Romanian Orthodox metropolitanate of Transylvania did not have a permanent residence. Hence the metropolitan resided at Hunedoara, at Feleac in the vicinity of Cluj (at the end of the 15th century), at Geoagiu and at Lancram, near Alba Iulia (in the middle of the 16th century), and then at Alba Iulia.

This metropolitanate was suppressed by the Habsburgs in 1701.

With the help of the princes of Wallachia and Moldavia, the Romanian Orthodox Church started to flourish. Many of its hierarchs became eminent scholars, such as the metropolitans Macarie, Teofil, Stefan, Antim Ivireanul, Neofit Cretanul, and Grigorie Dascalul of Ungro-Wallachia and Anastasie Crimca, Varlaam, Dosoftei, Iacob Putneanul, and Veniamin Costachi of Moldavia. The first manuscript translations into the Romanian language were liturgical books (the Codex of Voronet, the Psalter of Scheia, and the Hurmuzaki Psalter). Book printing began in Wallachia in 1507 by the monk Macarie and was continued by Dimitrie Liubavici and the monk Lavrentie. They printed liturgical texts in the Slavonic language. In Transylvania in the 16th century the printing of books in the Romanian language was started by Filip the Moldavian at Sibiu and the deacon Coresi at Brasov.

Monasticism, always an important dimension of the Romanian Orthodox Church, began steady development from the 14th century when great monasteries began to be built, many of them existing to this day: Vodita, Tismana, Cozia, Cotmeana, Snagov, Dealu, Bistrita, and later Arges, Arnota, Caldarusani, Cernica, Hurezi in Wallachia; Neamt, Bistrita, Moldovita, Humor, and later still Putna, Voronet, Sucevita, Secu, Dragomirna in Moldavia; St. Michael at Peri in Maramures, Ramet, Prislop, and Sambata in Transylvania, Hodos-Bodrog and Partos in Banat, and also many others. The monasteries played not only an important religious role in the spiritual life of the faithful, but also a cultural one. In these monasteries diptychs and chronicles were written, liturgical manuscripts or teaching books in the Slavonic or Romanian languages were copied in beautiful calligraphy, and sacerdotal vestments and other liturgical objects were produced. It was in these monasteries that the first Romanian schools were founded: elementary and secondary first, later also encompassing higher education, such as the academies at St. Nicolae in Brasov-Schei, at Putna, at the Three Hierarchs in Jassy, St. Sava's Academy in Bucharest, and others.

The Romanian Orthodox Church contributed not only to the improvement and development of the moral, social, and cultural life of its people; it also supported other Orthodox Churches, by printing liturgical books in Greek, Slavonic, Arabian, and Georgian, and by other kinds of help offered to them. The princes of the Romanian principalities were generous founders and protectors of the monasteries at Mount Athos and Sinai, as well as benefactors of the patriarchates of Constantinople, Alexandria, Antioch, Jerusalem, and Georgia, and of other churches in many countries. The Romanian Church contributed to the strengthening and preservation of world Orthodoxy through the well-known work *The Orthodox Confession of Faith* written by the Metropolitan Peter Moghila of Kiev, a Moldavian by birth. This work was approved by a synod held in Jassy in 1642, at which representatives of the Greek, Russian, and Romanian Orthodox Churches were present.

Unlike the Church of Wallachia and Moldavia, the Church of Transylvania passed through numerous difficulties because of the proselytizing campaigns undertaken by the Roman Catholic Church (14th–15th centuries), the Calvinists (17th century), and again the Roman Catholics (18th century). The first two were not successful, but the third one, in 1698–1701, had a more lasting effect. Transylvania was then ruled by the Habsburgs. As a result of intrigues at the imperial court in Vienna and by the Jesuits of Transylvania, a small part of the Romanian Orthodox clergy and faithful embraced the "Union with Rome" (the *Unia*). This diocese resulting from the *Unia* was placed under the jurisdiction of the Roman Catholic archbishopric of Esztergom, which later moved to Fagaras and then to Blaj, where in 1853 it was raised to the level of a metropolitanate. The Orthodox Romanians remained without bishops until 1761, when the court in Vienna, compelled by the revolt led by monk Sofronie, appointed for them a Serbian Orthodox bishop. The Orthodox Romanians were granted the right to elect a Romanian bishop only in 1810. The most important Orthodox hierarch of this period was Andrei Saguna, bishop and (from 1864) metropolitan, who succeeded in reestablishing the ancient Orthodox metropolitanate of Transylvania and in restoring its former development. This situation lasted until 1948, when the clergy and faithful belonging to the *Unia*, under pressure from the communist regime, again merged with the old Romanian Orthodox Church.

In 1859, after the union of Wallachia and Moldavia into a single state called Romania, the issues of ecclesiastical unity and autocephaly were once more raised. In 1864 Prince Alexandru Ioan Cuza proclaimed the autocephaly of the Romanian Orthodox Church. In 1865 the metropolitan of Bucharest became "Metropolitan Primate." In 1872 the Holy Synod was created and in 1885 the Ecumenical Patriarch Joachim IV acknowledged its autocephaly. In 1925 the Romanian Orthodox Church became a patriarchate with the first patriarch as Miron Cristea (1925–39).

In parallel with these developments, in the 19th and early 20th centuries, as always during its history, the Romanian Orthodox Church was fully involved in the major events of the Romanian people. Thus in the 1848 revolutions in the three Romanian principalities of Moldavia, Wallachia, and Transylvania, hierarchs, priests, and monks militated energetically for the realization of the national ideals of liberty and unity. Some of the notables from this time were Bishop Andrei Saguna, the priests Ioan Popasu and Simion Balint of Rosia Montana (Transylvania), Metropolitan Meletie of Jassy (Moldavia), Bishop Filotei of Buzau, the priests Radu Sapca of Celei, Oprea and George (Wallachia), and many others.

In 1859, when the Union of Romanian Principalities (Moldavia and Wallachia) took place, the church expressed itself through numerous representatives from the ranks of the clergy. Actively involved were Metropolitan Sofronie Miclescu, Bishop Melchisedec Stefanescu of Roman, Hierarch Filaret Scriban and his brother archimandrite Neofit (Moldavia); Metropolitan Nifon, Bishop Filotei of Buzau, Bishop Calinic of Ramnic, and others, who delivered sermons, wrote letters, booklets, and articles in newspapers, addressed the authorities, and mobilized the faithful in favor of the political union. Some of them were co-presidents and members in the Ad-Hoc Council and the Electoral Assembly that elected Prince Alexandru Ioan Cuza as single ruler over both principalities, thus achieving the long fought-for dream of national unity.

In 1877 the church was actively involved in the war of independence from the Ottoman Empire. Many priests, monks, and even nuns enrolled in the army at different levels; others organized committees of support and collections of goods needed for the troops. Archimandrite Ignatie Serian and Ghenadie Merisescu, protosincel Sava Dumitrescu, and hieromonk Veniamin Alexandrescu are just a few. In World War I (1916–18) hundreds of priests went to serve; some were killed on the front lines, others taken prisoner, deported or exiled.

Another great event in the nation's history was the Great Union of 1918, when the Romanian principality of Transylvania was united with Romania (Moldavia and Wallachia). Among many clergy and hierarchs who took active part in this event were the priest Vasile Lucaciu of Sisesti, Bishops Ioan Papp of Arad and Dimitrie Radu of Oradea (who were co-presidents of the Great National Assembly of Alba Iulia where the Union was declared), and Metropolitan Miron Cristea (the future patriarch), who was the head of the delegation of the Romanians from Transylvania that presented to the authorities in Bucharest the document of the Union (December 1, 1918).

In 1925 the new patriarch Miron Cristea set among his priorities the construction of a new cathedral in Bucharest that he called the Cathedral for the Nation's Salvation. He also wrote and published several books on folklore and iconography, and collections of sermons; he supported the participation of Romanian theologians in international ecumenical congresses and meetings and initiated such events in Romania, too. He was followed by Patriarch Nicodim Munteanu (1939–48). Patriarch Nicodim excelled by translating and editing over one hundred theological works from Russian into Romanian. He wrote several original books and also was one of the translators of the Bible into Romanian. From 1948 to 1977 the Romanian Orthodox Church was led by Patriarch Justinian Marina. Under his leadership, although shadowed under the communist regime with all its restrictions and pressures, important events occurred in the life of the church, such as the organization and creation of new legislation in the church, the reintegration of the Eastern rite Catholic churches of Transylvania, the reorganization of theological education, the canonization of several Romanian saints, the reorganization of monastic life, the restoration of many ancient monuments of religious art, and the erection of new churches in villages and towns throughout the country. In his time the Romanian Orthodox Church reentered the World Council of Churches (New Delhi, 1961) and participated in all its Pan-Christian and Pan-Orthodox meetings, maintaining fraternal relations with the other Orthodox Churches, as well as with other Christian denominations.

The fourth patriarch of the Romanian Orthodox Church was Justin Moisescu, who carried out his responsibilities from June 19, 1977 until his death on July 31, 1986. It was through his special care that the church attained a notable level of development in the administrative, theological, and cultural fields, as well as in foreign ecclesiastic relations. On November 16, 1986 the leadership of the Romanian patriarchate was entrusted to His Beatitude Teoctist Arapasu. He was elected for this ministry, having served for four decades as a high prelate at the head of some of the most important dioceses of the Romanian Orthodox Church: in Bucharest as an assistant bishop to the patriarch; at Arad as diocesan bishop; at Craiova as a metropolitan; at the Jassy seat as metropolitan. He was also *locum tenens* for the metropolitan of Sibiu during the vacancy there.

On September 30, 2007 the sixth patriarch of the Romanian Orthodox Church was enthroned: His Beatitude Patriarch Daniel (metropolitan of Moldavia and Bucovina from 1990 to 2007). Under his leadership the new bylaws for the organization and functioning of the Romanian Orthodox Church were finalized. He created a new media system for the church, laid the cornerstone of the new patriarchal cathedral in Bucharest while consolidating the structures of the current one, established over a dozen social, cultural, charitable, and educational programs, created

new dioceses in the country, and canonized several new Romanian saints.

As of September 1, 2008 the Romanian patriarchate was made up of six metropolitan sees in the country and three metropolitan sees abroad (there are about 12 million Romanians living outside Romania), with forty-one eparchies: the Metropolitan See of Muntenia and Dobrogea at Bucharest, the Metropolitan See of Moldavia and Bucovina at Jassy, the Metropolitan See of Transylvania at Sibiu, the Metropolitan See of Cluj, Alba, Crisana and Maramures at Cluj, the Metropolitan See of Oltenia at Craiova, the Metropolitan See of Banat at Timisoara, the Metropolitan See of Bessarabia at Chisinau (Republic of Moldova), the Metropolitan See for Germany, Central and North Europe at Nurnberg, Germany, and the Metropolitan See for Western Europe at Paris. There is also the Romanian Orthodox archdiocese in the Americas based at Chicago. Other dioceses are in Hungary, at Gyula, in Serbia and Montenegro (Dacia Felix) at Varset, and the Romanian Orthodox diocese for Australia and New Zealand at Melbourne.

Of all Romanians living abroad today there are also many who belong to other ecclesiastical jurisdictions, such as the over eighty Romanian parishes in the United States and Canada that belong to the Orthodox Church of America (OCA) or the Romanians around the current borders of Romania who belong to the jurisdictions of their respective countries (Serbia, Bulgaria, Ukraine). There are other Romanian monasteries and churches in different places, such as Prodromou and Lacu sketes on Mount Athos, establishments in Jerusalem and Jericho, and parishes in Cyprus, Istanbul, South Africa, and other places.

The Republic of Moldova was in its entire history a Dacian and then Romanian territory. It was annexed by the Russian Empire in 1812, until 1918, when it was reunited with Romania. In 1944 it was reannexed by the Soviet Union and became a Soviet republic. In 1991 it became an independent state. At this time, the Romanian patriarchate created the metropolitanate of Bessarabia for the spiritual needs of all Romanians who (except during the time of the Russian Soviet occupation) had always belonged to the Romanian Orthodox Church and who now wanted to rejoin it. However, the government in Moldova did not allow the metropolitanate to function in Moldova officially. It was only in 2001 that the European Court ruled that the metropolitanate of Bessarabia was officially part of the Romanian patriarchate and allowed it to function there.

In the six metropolitanates in the country there is currently a total of 13,612 parishes and branches with 15,083 churches. There are also 637 monasteries and sketes with over 8,000 monks and nuns. At the central administrative level the Romanian Orthodox Church is structured as follows: Central deliberative bodies: the Holy Synod, the Standing Synod, and the National Church Assembly; central executive bodies: the Patriarch, the National Church Council, the Standing Committee of the National Church Council; Central administrative bodies: the Office of the Holy Synod and the patriarchal administration.

The highest authority of the Romanian Orthodox Church in all fields of activity is the Holy Synod, made up of the patriarch, as president, all the metropolitans, archbishops, eparchial bishops, vicar bishops, and all other serving bishops. Four synodal committees are appointed for preparing the sessions of the Holy Synod: the Pastoral, Monastic and Social Committee; the Theological, Liturgical and Didactic Committee; the Canonical, Juridical and Disciplinary Committee; the Committee for External Communities, for the Inter-Orthodox, Inter-Christian and Inter-Religious Relations. Between the sessions of the Holy Synod the Standing Synod is the central deliberative body which takes decisions for the life of the church. It is constituted by the patriarch, as president, the metropolitans and three other hierarchs appointed by the Holy Synod every year (an archbishop and two bishops). The central deliberative body of the Romanian Orthodox Church for all administrative, social, cultural, economic, and patrimonial issues is the National Church Assembly, made up of three representatives of each diocese (one clergy and two lay people), appointed by the respective diocesan assemblies for four years. The members of the Holy Synod take part in the meetings of the National Church Assembly with deliberative vote. The patriarch is the head of the hierarchs of the Romanian Orthodox Church and the president of its central deliberative and executive bodies. The full title of the current patriarch of the Romanian Orthodox Church is His Beatitude Daniel, Archbishop of Bucharest, Metropolitan of Wallachia and Dobrogea, *Locum tenens* of the Throne of Caesarea of Cappadocia and Patriarch of the Romanian Orthodox Church (or Patriarch of Romania).

The central executive body of the Holy Synod and of the National Church Assembly is the National Church Council, made up of twelve members of the National Church Assembly (one clergy and one lay person representing every metropolitan see of the country, appointed for four years). The members of the Holy Synod can participate with deliberative vote in the meetings of the National Church Council. The assistant bishops to the patriarch are lawful members of the National Church Council, with deliberative vote; the patriarchal administrative vicar, patriarchal counselors, and the general ecclesiastical inspector are standing members with consulting vote.

The Standing Committee of the National Church Council functions between the meetings of the National Church Council, as central executive body, made up of the patriarch, as president, vicar bishops to the patriarch, patriarchal administrative vicar, patriarchal counselors, and the ecclesiastical general inspector. The patriarch is assisted in the exercise of his duties as president of the central deliberative and executive bodies, as well as primate of the Romanian Orthodox Church, by the Office of the Holy Synod and by the patriarchal administration, with the following departments: theological-educational, social-charitable, economic-financial, cultural, patrimony, church and interreligious relations, external communities, communications and public relations, church monuments and constructions, patriarchal stavropegias and social centers, body for inspection and audit. At the local level, the component units of the Romanian Orthodox Church are the parish, monastery, protopresbyterate (deanery), vicariate, eparchy (archdiocese and diocese), and the metropolitanate.

During the communist regime, while it managed to survive and even have certain accomplishments, the church was severely restricted in its potential, mission, and activities. In the initial phases of communist rule in particular, the faithful were direct witnesses of the persecution, arrest, torture, and killing of thousands of Orthodox priests. One recent study documents that approximately 4,000 Orthodox priests were sent to communist prisons, sometimes two or three times, while others were killed. From the upper ranks of the hierarchy, seventeen bishops were demoted and fifteen were exiled. Many had to endure long years of detention (Caravia et al. 1999).

In a book published by the Romanian Academy, where the authors present a small, but representative selection of 180 informative notes, reports, referrals and accounts, addresses of various informers, militia and security agents, and administrative functionaries from the communist system at the local or national level, over 1,800 references are made to Orthodox bishops, priests, deacons, theology professors, theology students, monks, chanters, and believers who were opposing the regime and who were conducting so-called "anti-democratic" activities, speaking against the communist government or writing articles of anti-communist propaganda in the ecclesiastical press (Paiusan and Ciuceanu 2001). Though derided by communist propaganda it was because of Patriarch Justinian Marina's extraordinary skill and practical wisdom that while suffering this level of persecution the church could still not only hold on, but also develop and grow. In many other countries under communist rule such growth was not possible.

The church was forced to renounce its social philanthropic activities arising from its vocation of mercy; it had to strictly limit itself to the liturgical-sacramental dimension of its existence. The formation of priests and theologians was restricted to five theological seminaries at the high-school level (one at each of the five existing metropolitan sees) and two schools of theology at the university level. The patriarchate and each metropolitan see had its own theological journal published a few times a year, besides a pastoral guide published once a year. The communist government exerted strict control over their content. In the metropolitanate of Transylvania there was also a bi-weekly newspaper, *Telegraful Roman*, which was and still remains the only publication in the entire country to appear without interruption since its foundation in 1853.

After the fall of the communist regime in 1989 the Romanian Orthodox Church, which, according to repeated surveys, continues to enjoy the highest trust among Romanians, had a chance to develop at all levels. The church canonized thirty-six Romanian saints and extended the honoring at the national level of another forty-two local saints, so that the total number of Romanian saints, including those previously canonized, rose to ninety-seven. Some of these are Daniel the Hermit (Sihastrul), Evangelicus of Tomis, Gherman of Dobrogea, John Cassian, Gheorghe of Cernica, Nicodim of Tismana, Oprea Nicolae, Paisy Velichovsky of Neamt, Sofronie of Cioara, Visarion Sarai, and Voivode Stephen the Great.

One of the most important aspects of the church since 1989 has been its engagement in social work. At the central and regional levels, departments, programs, and branches were created that cover a vast and diverse area of social work. To enhance the efficiency of its philanthropic activity the church signed several protocols with the government and in 2007 it established the Philanthropic Federation of the Romanian Patriarchate. There are now in the Romanian patriarchate over forty offices of coordination of social work and assistance, with over 200 employees qualified in social work as well as theology. The number of social assistance establishments founded and administered by the patriarchate is over 350 and includes shelters for children (109) and for the elderly (51), soup kitchens and bakeries (106), clinics and pharmacies (37), counseling centers (33), centers for victims of human trafficking (2), and centers for assistance for families in difficulty (19).

These institutions are developing programs for the help of children who come from poor families, for the prevention of school drop-out, for orphan children, for those in correctional facilities, and for the help of the Roma population. There are also programs for religious assistance in hospitals, in nursing homes, and in homeless shelters, where well over 300 churches and chapels exist with over 300 priests; programs of religious assistance in prisons (over fifty churches and chapels with as many working priests), and programs of religious assistance in the military units (over eighty churches and chapels with about eighty military priests). The church trains its own workers in such fields. For this reason it introduced in theological schools at the university level sections, programs, and curricula of social assistance. Another expression of the social engagement of the church is evident in the constitution of local committees of bioethics in Cluj, Jassy, and Bucharest, and a National Committee on Bioethics with the special task to study and evaluate the specific issues raised by bioethics, such as abortion, contraception, genetic manipulation, *in vitro* procreation, and organ transplants. These committees are creating the documentation based on which the church will express its official position.

After 1989, religious education has been expanded at all levels. Religion has been reintroduced as a compulsory discipline in high schools, a subject taught by over 10,000 teachers. The number of Orthodox theological seminaries at high-school level has risen from five to thirty-nine (with over 700 teachers and over 6,000 students annually); there are now schools of religious chanters and post-high-school departments with double specialization in theology and social work; fifteen schools of theology at university level with eight specializations and approximately 450 professors teaching over 11,000 students (7,000 male and 4,000 female). There are master's programs at eleven of the fifteen schools of theology and doctoral programs at the theological schools in Bucharest, Sibiu, Cluj, and Oradea. The church offers scholarships for students from the Republic of Moldova and from other Romanian areas around the current borders of the country.

The Romanian Orthodox Church has a long and significant tradition of theological education. Among the best-known theologians, past and present, are Dumitru Stăniloae (dogmatic theology); Petru Rezus (fundamental theology); Ioan Zagrean (moral theology); Bartolomeu Anania, Vasile Tarnavschi (biblical studies); Mircea Pacuraru (historical studies); Ioan G. Coman (patristics); Liviu Stan (canon law); Ene Braniste (liturgics); Atanasie Negoita (Oriental studies); Ioan Bria (ecumenical studies). At the present time the most widely known Romanian theologian in Romania and abroad is Dumitru Stăniloae (1903–93). He taught at the theological schools of higher education in Sibiu and Bucharest, but also spent five years in communist prisons (1958–63). He published many books of dogmatic and moral theology, and translated works from the church fathers in a series called *Philokalia* that appeared in twelve volumes. His works have been translated and published in French, English, German, Greek, and Serbian. He is considered one of the most important theologians and Christian thinkers in the world today.

One of the most important achievements of the church after 1989 has been the unprecedented use of mass-media technology. In a world dominated by communication, the church remains faithful to the traditional means of conveying the right teaching of faith, but is open to modern technology in its missionary work. Thus the Basilica press center of the Romanian patriarchate was set up in Bucharest shortly after the inauguration of Patriarch Daniel Ciobotea in the fall of 2007. The new institution is seated in the patriarchal palace and made up of five branches: the Trinitas radio station, the Trinitas TV station, a group of three publications (*Lumina* – "The Light," a daily newspaper; *Lumina de Duminica* – "Sunday Light," a weekly publication; *Vestitorul Ortodoxiei* – "Herald of Orthodoxy,"

a monthly magazine), the Basilica news agency, and a press and public relations office. There is also a multitude of other magazines and publishing houses for religious books, from those belonging to major church dioceses, to those belonging to deaneries and even parishes. The radio stations and programs that were created at the diocesan centers are part of this revival, too, as well as numerous workshops where religious objects for liturgical use and daily spiritual needs are manufactured.

During its entire existence the Romanian Orthodox Church has brought its direct and effective contribution to the most important events that marked the history of the nation and to the development of Romanian culture, while maintaining the aspirations of the Romanian people for national liberty and social justice and helping strengthen the consciousness of national unity. The Romanian Orthodox Church is thus one of the most vigorous branches of world Orthodoxy. It is capable of a significant contribution for furthering the cause of Orthodoxy, to help improve ecumenical and brotherly relations among all Christian churches and denominations, and to promote peace and good understanding among peoples.

SEE ALSO: Canonization; Contemporary Orthodox Theology; Education; Newly Revealed Saints; *Philokalia*; St. John Cassian (ca. 360–ca. 435); St. Paisy Velichovsky (1722–1794); Stăniloae, Dumitru (1903–1993)

REFERENCES AND SUGGESTED READINGS

Caravia, P., Constantinescu, V., and Stanescu, F. (1999) *The Imprisoned Church: Romania 1944–1989*. Bucharest: Romanian Academy, National Institute for the Study of Totalitarianism.

Damian, T. (2005) "The Romanian Orthodox Church Between Deja-vu and Pas encore," *La voie de la Lumiere*, year 11, Nos. 129–30, Montreal.

Daniel, Patriarch of the Romanian Orthodox Church (2009) "Situatia Bisericii Ortodoxe Romane si Legaturile ei Ecumenice in Contextul Noii Europe (1989–2009)," *Meridianul Romanesc*, year 36, No. 13, Santa Clarita, CA.

Danila, N. (2001) *Daco-Romania Christiana: Florilegium Studiorum*. Bucharest: Danubius.

Diaconescu, M. (1999) *Istoria literaturii daco-romane*. Bucharest: Alcor Edimpex.

Metes, St. (1935) *Istoria Bisericii si a vietii religioase a romanilor din Transilvania*. Sibiu: Diecezana.

Pacurariu, M. (2002) *Dictionarul Teologilor Romani*. Bucharest: Editura Enciclopedica.

Pacurariu, M. (2006) *Istoria Bisericii Ortodoxe Romane*. Bucharest: IBMBOR.

Paiusan, C. and Ciuceanu, R. (2001) *The Romanian Orthodox Church under the Communist Regime, Vol. 1: 1945–1958*. Bucharest: Romanian Academy, National Institute for the Study of Totalitarianism.

Romanian Patriarchate (2009) *The Romanian Patriarchate: Mission, Organization, Activities*. Bucharest: Basilica.

Vicovean, I. (2002) *Istoria Bisericii Ortodoxe Romane*, Vols. 1 and 2. Jassy: Trinitas.

Rome, Ancient Patriarchate of

BRENDA LLEWELLYN IHSSEN

By the 5th century a system of pentarchy existed among the apostolic sees of Rome, Constantinople, Alexandria, Antioch, and Jerusalem. Though the patriarchates of Rome and Constantinople would eventually enter into periods of dispute and eventually schism, the ancient patriarchate of Rome was, in the first millennium of Christianity, held in high regard as a significantly important see due to multiple factors: the city of Rome was an early recipient of the Christian message; Rome was an apostolic foundation; it was a city where the foremost of the apostles, Peter and Paul, visited; it was where they were martyred; and it is where their bodies remain to this day. Rome was also a city noted for edifying resistance to Roman oppression on the part of many Christians, for the development of poor-relief programs, for strong resistance to internal schism and heresy, for lively theological discussion, and as an early model of noteworthy leadership for the international church. All of these factors would be significant in the initial development of the ancient patriarchate of Rome and contributed to the development of papal theory.

ROMAN CHRISTIANITY AND APOSTOLIC FOUNDATION IN THE FIRST CENTURIES

As the capital, Rome was a city of primary importance in a largely urban empire that was in the process of transforming itself in the 1st century. With a population of roughly half a million inhabitants, and with both people and philosophies arriving frequently, Rome was a natural goal. Evidence suggests that Christianity arrived in the city shortly after the death of Jesus, likely arriving in the 40s due in part to the migration of Jews as merchants, immigrants, or prisoners from Syria and Palestine to the Trastevere, the Jewish quarter of Rome. The constant flow of individuals, ideas, and influence between Rome and Jerusalem attests to the close relationship that the two cities shared prior to the rise of Christianity, a relationship that aided in the development of an immigrant Christianity when it arrived (Vinzent 2007).

Once in Rome, Christianity appears to have organized into various small cells and house churches of predominantly Jewish and then Greek-speaking gentiles in a fairly rapid and reasonably stable way, to the degree that it soon was a mission force. The author of Acts claims that the followers of Jesus present at Pentecost from Rome were both "Jews and proselytes" (Acts 2.10). Further, the Apostle Paul's Letter to the Romans, containing as it does fairly complex theology not suitable for a novice community, suggests that the recipients had by that time begun to move beyond basic organizational issues to address significant issues for the future of the Christian movement, specifically the potentially tense relationship between gentile converts and Jewish Christians, or even other competing Christian cells and philosophical schools of which, in a city of émigrés, there must have been several (Vinzent 2007; Hall 2007a). Evidence for the presence of Christianity in Rome as early as the 40s can also be found in additional passages in Acts (18.2–3), and exterior to the New Testament in the work of historian Suetonius, who wrote of Emperor Claudius' (41–54) expulsion of "Jews from Rome because of their constant disturbances impelled by Chrestus" (Suetonius, *The Lives of the Caesars II*, 25) – which suggests interference in worship-related activities on the part of Jewish Christians (Brown and Meier 1983).

Each of the ancient patriarchates of Rome, Constantinople, Alexandria, Antioch, and Jerusalem is traditionally held to have been founded by the most prominent among the apostles. Early sources, representing traditional stories more than hard historical data, maintain that Peter and Paul both traveled to Rome, where they established Christian communities. The New Testament evidence speaks only of Paul being in Rome (Acts 18). St. Clement of Rome (ca. 96) wrote in his *Epistle to the Corinthians* on behalf of the Roman Church only that Peter "went to the glorious place which was his due," and Paul, more specifically, "reached the limits of the West" (*I. Clement* 5). Ignatius of Antioch (35–107), when making his plea to the Christians in Rome to refrain from

interfering in his forthcoming martyrdom, wrote that he (Ignatius) does "not order you as did Peter and Paul" (*Ignatius to the Romans* 4), a statement which suggests relationship but not necessarily proximity. More specifically, Irenaeus of Lyons (135–200), writing on the importance of the succession of bishops in his treatise *Against Heresies*, says that this "tradition derived from the apostles, of the very great, very ancient, and universally known Church founded and organized at Rome by the two most glorious apostles, Peter and Paul" (*Against Heresies* 3.3.2). While Irenaeus' claim of apostolic foundation has been interpreted as evidence of Peter's personal activity in Rome, what is more evident, however, is the importance that will consistently be placed on the tradition of apostolic foundation itself, as well as the meaning that the tradition will hold in successive centuries for the subsequent Roman theory of primacy. It is worth noting that while these ancient writers do not leave the historian with incontestable evidence about any extensive activity of Peter's in Rome, they do leave the historian with evidence about Christian attitudes and structures in ancient Rome. Though there was likely at first no united single community, it was from earliest times to some degree organized, it already had a developing sense of its own history, and though archeology, epigraphy, and historical records indicate that Christianity flourished in the poorer districts, there were, even by the beginning of the 2nd century, Christians in Rome who enjoyed influence among the political powers and elite members of society.

THE CHALLENGE OF PAGAN ROME AND THE ROMAN RESPONSE

In addition to this early tradition that holds Peter and Paul as central to the foundation of Christianity in Rome, the ancient patriarchate of Rome was further enhanced by the various ways in which Christians responded to the surrounding community that threatened their religious identity. Christian intellectuals rose to the challenge of pagan apologists, whose opposition afforded them the opportunity to defend with eloquence a vigorous new faith against cults that promoted morally repulsive gods and goddesses. This apologetic process helped to shape both the public and internal self-identity of Roman (and other) Christians in relation to the Greco-Roman world. The anonymous 2nd-century (allegedly Roman) author of the *Epistle to Diognetus* argued the superiority of Christianity over paganism, idolatry, and Judaism's ritual rigidity, and defended the manner by which Christians live as citizens of one world but detached from it as citizens of another, presenting an eloquent explanation of God's plan for salvation in light of previous human understandings of God (Hall 2007b).

For those who lacked opportunity or intellectual ability, martyrdom also provided Christians the occasion to refute by use of the body what the scholarly did using their rhetorical skill (a few, such as Justin Martyr, had the opportunity for both forms of witness). Concerned and angered by what were regarded as the "sins" of an unauthorized religion, various pogroms took place to cleanse Rome and appease the authorities who were anxious to put down what they believed to be a dissident and seditious cult, or a repugnant sect of Judaism, too much like a conspiracy to be tolerated. Chief among the martyrs were Peter and Paul, but included among the many that perished in these first persecutions at Rome were notable figures such as Ignatius of Antioch (107), Justin Martyr (165), and Hippolytus (236). While hard historical evidence with respect to Christian

foundations at the direct hands of Peter and Paul is inconclusive, it is generally admitted that both apostles died in Rome during the purge of Emperor Nero, who was anxious to divert suspicion for a fire that destroyed ten of the fourteen districts of Rome in 64. Senator and historian Tacitus later wrote that Nero, the first of several emperors to inflict persecutions on this new sect, attempted to suppress rumors for his own responsibility for the fire by rounding up "the notoriously depraved group who were popularly called Christians" (*Annals* 15.44). Later described by Eusebius as the "first heralded as a conspicuous fighter against God" (*Hist. Eccl.* 2.25), Nero had Christians torn to pieces by dogs or burned alive, occasioning the pity of the Roman population who were witnesses to this cruel torture (Jeffers 1991). While Tacitus says nothing of the famous apostles perishing in this purge, Eusebius writes that during Nero's reign the apostles were murdered: "It is recorded that in his reign Paul was beheaded in Rome itself, and that Peter likewise was crucified, and the record is confirmed by the fact that the cemeteries there are still called by the names of Peter and Paul" (*Hist. Eccl.* 2.25). Eusebius includes in his *Ecclesiastical History* the valuable words of a churchman named Gaius who, in the late 2nd or early 3rd century wrote concerning their burial places that "I can point out the monuments of the victorious apostles. If you will go as far as the Vatican or the Ostian Way, you will find the monuments of those who founded this church" (*Hist. Eccl.* 2.25). In this passage we identify not only early public veneration of the space where the apostles were believed to be, but also clear indication that they are understood as the founders of Christianity in Rome. Further confirmation is offered by Eusebius in a letter written by Bishop Dionysius of Corinth to the Romans, who likens the two communities of Rome and Corinth as spiritually bound by apostolic foundation. However, what Rome has, that Corinth does not, is the site of the martyrdom of the apostles: "For both of them sowed in our Corinth and taught us jointly. In Italy too they taught jointly in the same city, and were martyred at the same time" (*Hist. Eccl.* 2.25).

Located today under an elaborate baldachin constructed by Bernini in 1633, the original cult center of a trophy (the "Red wall" shrine) identified as that of St. Peter's on Vatican Hill was originally quite inconspicuous among adjoining mausolea of adherents of multiple cults. Similar to Peter, Paul's body was buried in an ancient simple tomb over which a trophy was erected, and both apostles were venerated together in an equally unremarkable cult center located underneath *catacombo* San Sebastiano on the Via Appia, where the veneration of their relics (or at least a portion of them) was translated temporarily in 258 to protect them during the persecutions of Emperor Valerian (253–60) (Holloway 2004). The persecutions of Christians by the state were consistently interpreted apocalyptically and historically as manifestations of the secular world unleashing its venom and rage against the spiritual elect, who were honored and even envied for the opportunity to publicly portray their devotion to Christ through the offering of their bodies in imitation of the Passion. Those who survived the attempt on their lives (the *confessors*) emerged as respected leaders of various communities of Christians, wearing the evidence of their faith in sometimes quite visible ways in their flesh, and drawing support strong enough to enable them to challenge the decisions of local bishops (Hall 2007b). Christian Rome especially benefited by the prestige that the martyrs provided by their resolute resistance to the civil authorities and, for the future organization of the church, the martyrdoms of

Peter, Paul, and other leading Christians challenged the rising and developing episcopacy to love the church like a devoted spouse to the degree that they too needed to be willing to suffer martyrdom on her behalf. Finally, the point here must be emphasized: while the three most important cities in the empire – Rome, Jerusalem, and Antioch (though we might include also Corinth and others) – could claim association and relationship with Peter, only one city, Rome, could claim that they possessed the body.

THE ORGANIZATION OF CHRISTIANITY IN THE ANCIENT PATRIARCHATE OF ROME

Modern scholarly debate continues around the time frame of the development of the organization of city-wide Roman Christian leadership, and modern scholars generally believe that that the lineaments of a city-wide monarchical bishopric were retrojected with some hindsight (Hall 2007a). While Christianity came early to Rome, a single city-wide organization did not, and the very earliest Christian communities combined elements of philosophical school, extended household, oriental cult, and social club, and yet refrained from being truly any single one of those options. Recent studies suggest that only after the mid-3rd-century opposition to Pope Cornelius led by the intellectually gifted presbyter (later anti-pope) Novatian, does the issue of Roman Christian leadership emerge in terms of a series of recognizable central authority figures: *papae*. Before that time the various and sometimes quite disparate communities were held together in their commitment to being a household of God, a commitment that was reflected in the practice of sharing portions of the Eucharist bread among them (Vinzent 2007).

The earliest patristic literature maintains that the position of a monarchical bishop existed in Rome from the time of Peter himself, which reflects the strong desire of this patristic generation to set the monarchical episcopate on a firmer footing. Clement of Rome, a notable leader at the end of the 1st century, reproves the Corinthian church in his *Epistle* for community instability that culminated in the expulsion of their leadership. Clement advocates the recognition and support of the apostolic foundation and succession of the episcopate, which he asserts is a stabilizing factor for the normative Christian community:

> The Apostles received the Gospel for us from the Lord Jesus Christ, Jesus the Christ was sent from God. The Christ therefore is from God and the Apostles from the Christ. In both ways, then, they were in accordance with the appointed order of God's will.... They preached from district to district, and from city to city, and they appointed their first converts, testing them by the Spirit, to be bishops and deacons of the future believers.... Our Apostles also knew through our Lord Jesus Christ that there would be strife for the title of bishop. For this cause, therefore, since they had received perfect foreknowledge, they appointed those who have already been mentioned, and afterwards added the codicil that if they should fall asleep, other approved men should succeed to their ministry. (*I Clement* 42, 44)

Ignatius of Antioch, also writing at an embryonic time in the Roman church's developing episcopacy, also consistently raised in each of his letters to Christian communities the motif of the *single* bishop. Those who are subject to him, Ignatius says, are the ones subject to Jesus Christ himself: "See that you all follow the bishop, as Jesus Christ follows the Father.... Let no one do

any of the things appertaining to the Church without the bishop" (*Smyrn.* 8; *Trall.* 3.1).

As is the case in the development of any group dynamic, circumstances forged internal doctrinal debates that began to present difficulties first within the communities and then eventually among them. The 2nd-century *Shepherd of Hermas*, a text considered at one time for inclusion in the New Testament canon, speaks to the elasticity of many elements of the early Roman church, such as how to address the problem of sin committed after baptism. Eventually it was maintained that unity needed to be established and brought under the control of a central figure whose authority was neither ambiguous nor indistinguishable from presbyters. Such leadership would provide a necessary stability in the face of the more charismatic leadership provided by the prophet, martyr, confessor, and teacher. Writing during a time prior to publicly fixed creed or canon, and in opposition to those who maintained a secret oral knowledge apart from the gospels, Irenaeus of Lyons insisted that the true gospel was preserved through faithfulness to an apostolic succession and apostolic tradition that emerged and was witnessed in the churches of apostolic foundation. These were the pillars upon which the voice of authority should rest. Hinting at what will later be used to defend the specific issue of Roman primacy, Irenaeus claimed that the truth could be maintained solely in the churches tied to the apostles, and, more specifically, the church in Rome:

> Tradition derived from the apostles, of the very great, the very ancient, and universally known Church founded and organized at Rome by the two most glorious apostles, Peter and Paul; is also the faith preached to men, which comes down to our time by means of the

succession of bishops. For it is a matter of necessity that every Church should agree with this Church, on account of its preeminent authority, that is, the faithful everywhere, inasmuch as the apostolic tradition has been preserved continuously by those who exist everywhere. (*Adv. Haer.* 3.3.3)

Irenaeus' late 2nd-century thesis rests in the security of an apostolic foundation and succession that is difficult to correlate exactly with the historical condition of Christian social origins in Rome at that time, a reality in which communities largely managed their own local affairs. Nevertheless, Irenaeus himself was said to have journeyed to speak to the "Bishop" of Rome, Victor, on his mission to advocate for the Quartodecimans, and he clearly appeals to the concept of the monarchical bishop as an "apostolic" notion, to serve as a future norm for wider Christian organization. He also calls for Christians to reject innovations present in communities struggling with teachers of Gnostic Christology, and advises them to look to the faithful presentation of the gospel as it has been preserved in the church of Rome.

In addition to heresy (or internal debate) as an instigation for greater, overarching unity centered on a single apostolic bishop, threats of schism or external challenges to authority must also have prompted the move towards a more cohesive organization. Conflicts such as those waged by Cyprian of Carthage during the course of the mid-3rd-century persecution by Emperor Decius (and threats to do likewise by Emperor Gallus) needed the defense of a strong universal episcopate acting as a singular judge and authority over both individuals and communities (Hall 2007b). Facing division within the church over the restoration of the lapsed in the wake of persecution, the distribution of the sacraments at the hands of heretical clergy, and

direct challenges to the authority of the bishop by confessors and their supporters, Cyprian made it his life's work to establish, if not a sole authority, at least a monarchical authority within each location. Distinct from his claim in *De unitate ecclesiae* that Christ "set up one throne and by his authority appointed one source and principle of unity" (*Unit. Eccl.* 4) (a statement intended not to press for Roman primacy as would be later alleged, but directed against those who resist their bishop), a synod held in Carthage concluded that while Peter was a special symbol of authority, his preeminence did not extend to other bishops, but was a "charism" that was passed to every bishop who was "apostolic" (Cyprian, *Ep.* 69.17); namely the corporate body of bishops in the international Christian community (Hall 2007b).

Like martyrs resisting civil authorities, Roman leaders who resisted doctrinal innovations were regarded as particularly meritorious and therefore worthy of respect and honor. In time, Rome would be regarded as a model of moderation and conventionality, holding firm in the face of theological positions that would eventually be labeled heretical. Organization did not, however, simply emerge in defense of circumstances, but also through the need to respond to human despair in the city. Determined to meet slander head-on with public good works that could stand as evidence to their faithful citizenship for those who might have reason to judge them harshly, and following Jewish models of charity, Roman Christians established the practice of providing for the needy within the city. Following the biblical model set by Paul and his collection for the saints in Jerusalem (Rom. 15.25–26), contributions were gathered once a week by those in a position to give. Justin Martyr notes a variety of social services to which the Christians attended:

Those who prosper, and who so wish, contribute, each one as much as he chooses to. What is collected is deposited with the president, and he takes care of orphans and widows, and those who are in want on account of sickness or any other cause, and those who are in bonds, and the strangers who are sojourners among [us], and, briefly, he is the protector of all those in need. (*1 Apol.* 67.5–6)

And while texts such as the *Shepherd of Hermas'* careful castigation of the wealthy attest to the existence of predictable problems of avarice, nevertheless Clement of Rome writes of those in Rome who "have even given themselves into bondage that they might ransom others" (*1 Clem.* 55.2). Hippolytus notes the gifts for the sick, the widows, and the "bread for the poor" (*Apostolic Tradition* 24), and Bishop Cornelius' account of the synod of Rome attests to the "more than fifteen hundred widows and distressed persons" (*Hist. Eccl.* 6.43.11) who were supported by the church. By the end of the 3rd century giving and social programs were so central to the Christian mission at Rome that the need to coordinate charitable activities led, in part, to the need for a greater, city-wide organization. By the 5th century, in the absence of effective civil attention to such matters, the church in Rome was responsible for the care of widows, orphans and minors, prisoners, and public health and sanitation; further, it provided more than social services, for Rome was the logical launching point from which Christianity traveled to many parts of the Roman Empire, including parts of Africa, Spain, and Gaul, all of which looked in time to Rome as a leader and organizer of international Christianity (Dvornik 1966; Hall 2007a; Vinzent 2007; Winter 1994).

When Constantine arrived in Rome in 312, the Christian community there had certainly evolved beyond the early Jewish–Christian house churches gathered in the Trastevere. In less than 300 years it had been influenced in its organization and identity by the different types of people who embraced Christianity, by the traditions of Peter and Paul, by the resistance of Christians to the violent and public persecutions of the civil government, by the theological positions set up against pagan intellectuals, by Christian social practices, mission programs, resistance to internal heretical strains and schism, and by the rise of the Roman bishops, who were willing to care for, teach, preach to, die for, advise, and sometimes discipline Christian communities both in Rome itself and in various parts of the empire. These factors naturally contributed to the unwillingness of Rome to play any lesser role than that of a primary leader of international affairs in the church, as Christianity entered a new global era.

THE ANCIENT PATRIARCHATE OF ROME IN THE ERA OF CONSTANTINE

The first to favor Christianity so extensively, the Emperor Constantine (ca. 271–337) was apparently anxious (for diverse reasons) to incorporate the benefits of Christianity into the fabric of the Roman Empire. Social-scientific studies of Christianity estimate that at the time of Constantine's defeat of Emperor Maxentius in 312 there were approximately 9 million Christians, comprising roughly 15 percent of the population (Stark 2006). Neither large enough to pose too great a threat nor small enough to be safely ignored, Christians had become a part of the religious map of empire alongside Judaism, state cults, and eastern mystery cults. After promulgation of the emancipatory Edict of Milan with co-emperor Licinius, Constantine, the emperor in the western portion of the empire, demonstrated a steady interest in the doctrine and organization of Christianity, and his imperial generosity greatly enhanced Christianity in Rome. His wife's palace on the Lateran was donated in 313; he made grants of land to various churches and restitutions, as well as donations to the church of more than 400 pounds of gold per year. He promoted the building in 322 of a monumental church in honor of St. Peter on the Vatican Hill (its cut pillars are still visible in the crypt of St. Peter's). Clergy also rose in privilege and status both financially and jurisdictionally, becoming, in point of fact, a substructure of the civil administration (Cameron 2007; Holloway 2004). Within a short period of time ecclesiastical courts assumed responsibility for ruling in Christian municipal cases. So intimate was Constantine's involvement with church affairs that in 314, after an appeal by North African bishops, he appointed arbitrators headed by Miltiades, the bishop of Rome, to investigate the disturbance in the African church caused by Donatism and tensions among clergy in Carthage. It is noteworthy, however, that although the bishop of Rome headed this first inter-province council in the West, the Emperor did not take his pronouncement on the matter as final, for he called a second council the following year, which the current Pope Sylvester did not attend, though legates did. Pope Sylvester's legates also attended the first Ecumenical Council of Nicea, held in 325, where they were the first among all the bishops present to sign their names to the acts of the synod in agreement with the Nicene faith (Kelly 1996).

The transfer of the capital city of the empire from Rome to Constantinople in 324 altered the relationship between Rome and the other major eastern ecclesiastical centers in Antioch, and Alexandria. But while the site of the imperial residence and center of power had shifted, the "apostolic" status of Rome had not, and probably this challenge to its centrality contributed to the development by the Roman bishops of the *theologoumenon* of papal primacy, a doctrine that increasingly emerged in the latter half of the first millennium.

CLAIMS FOR PAPAL PRIMACY IN POST-CONSTANTINIAN ROME

The doctrine of papal primacy is dependent on acceptance of the three claims that Peter was the "prince" among the apostles, that he was the first "bishop" in Rome, and that he transferred to the leading authorities in the Roman Christian community only the authority which he received from Christ. The passage upon which this latter claim is dependent is Matthew 16.18–19. After Peter answers Jesus' question about his identity correctly with the confession that Jesus is "the Messiah, the son of the living God" (Mt. 16.16), Jesus' response to this admission of faith is "And I tell you, you are Peter, and on this rock I will build my church, and the gates of Hades will not prevail against it. I will give you the keys of the kingdom of heaven, and whatever you bind on earth will be bound in heaven, and whatever you loose on earth will be loosed in heaven" (Anastos 2001). Later inscribed in Greek around the base of the dome of St. Peter's in Rome, this passage was employed by Pope Callistus I in the early 3rd century as justification for a single papal (*papae*) decision on penance (*De Pudicitia* 1.6; 21.9), his understanding of which was vigorously contested by his opponent Hippolytus (Kelly 1996).

The church in the eastern provinces never contested Peter's signal symbolic importance for the city of Rome, but the problem that emerged in the relationship between the various sees was the question of the (honorific) primacy of the ancient patriarchate of Rome as distinct from ecclesiastical jurisdiction over the others. For the eastern churches, the organizing element of church jurisdiction was not so much an apostolic origin but rather how church government could be accommodated to the political regulation of the empire. This principle of conforming to civic administrative boundaries was sanctioned in Canon 4 of the First Ecumenical Council of Nicea (325), as well as in Canons 2 and 3 of the First Ecumenical Council of Constantinople (381), and it was upheld in the Synod of Antioch, and referenced by Pope Boniface (PL 20.773), who forbade metropolitans to exercise authority in other than their own provinces; as well as by Pope Innocent I (PL 20.548) (Anastos 2001).

The question of accommodation versus primacy deserves a longer treatment than can be offered here, but there are a few things worth noting. First, accommodation, which is also understood as an apostolic institution, was merely a natural outgrowth of the new social circumstances of a Christianized empire. Economic, social, judicial, and political life is naturally focused in any diocese on a central or capital city, and accordingly the bishop of that city would have to be a man of particular strength and character in order to meet the needs of the populace. It is understandable that over time the primary bishops of central cities in the empire would see themselves as more important than bishops in smaller, more backward towns, thus the origin of the concept of metropolitan archbishops. This applies all the more to the case of Rome because Rome was *the* central city of the empire, and not only was it "apostolic" in multiple ways, but it was the primary residence of the emperor. When the latter ceased to be the case, especially when Constantine shifted the capital to Constantinople, Rome remained apostolic but was no longer primary. Second,

even though the Eastern Churches made attempts to advance a literary tradition lauding the apostolic foundation of Constantinople (mainly originating after the construction of the Church of the Holy Apostles as a shrine for the relics of St. Andrew), nevertheless the roots of this principle were never deep (Anastos 2001). What mattered more to the Eastern Churches than a historically provable apostolic foundation of any see was the more compelling belief that all sees were apostolic by virtue of correct "apostolic" doctrine, maintained by the succession of legitimate teaching bishops.

Second-millennium focus on the conflicts between the sees of Constantinople and Rome has overshadowed the many years of concord that existed between these two preeminent patriarchates. Nevertheless, differences in language and culture added to the mix of things that brought about increasing liturgical and theological discord between the two sees. Because the political position of accommodation to civic borders in the eastern portions of the empire was of greater importance than the Roman *theologoumenon* of special apostolic status, the fathers of the Council of Constantinople (381) were happy enough to establish Canon 3 in their deliberations, which gave the bishop of Constantinople second rank in the ecclesiastical hierarchy because it was the "New Rome." While this preserved the honorific rights of Old Rome, it was seen as a natural result of the shift of the imperial residence to Constantinople, and an important safeguard against the aspirations of Alexandria (Anastos 2001; Dvornik 1966). The whole process of the rise of Constantinople to ecclesiastical eminence was bitterly resisted by Rome at first. Soon after the Council of Chalcedon (451), Pope Leo I declared its Canon 28 (which had just ratified Canon 3 of the Council of Constantinople) to be invalid

(Kelly 1996). Canons that were anti-Roman in character from the Constantinopolitan Council in Trullo (692) did not do much to ease relations between the sees, nor did Emperor Leo III and Pope Gregory II's late 8th-century dispute over images and taxes during the period of the first Iconoclastic Controversy (Noble 2009); nor Charlemagne's coronation on Christmas Day in 800 by Pope Leo III as *Imperator Romanorum*; nor the formal condemnation of Patriarch Photios in 863 by Pope Leo III (Anastos 2001). By the time of Photios' patriarchate, both Constantinople and the patriarchate of Rome functioned as largely independent sees, and the eventual fracture of the pentarchy was in process, accelerated by disputes over ecclesiastical jurisdiction in "new" Christian territories. Photios was one of the first patriarchs of Constantinople to entertain serious doubts over the continuing orthodoxy of Rome, not simply on matters of wider doctrine (the *filioque* issue), but also on the basis of the papal claims to special primacy as manifesting a form of ecclesiology not in harmony with the wider sentiment of the Eastern Churches. Growing fractures and theological differences were to come to a head as the tide of Islam pressured the Eastern Churches more and more, and Rome's papal monarchy rose to political precedence. The Crusades (especially the Fourth) left a lasting damage in relations; more so perhaps than the notional date of schism between the two patriarchates of 1054.

THE IMPORTANCE OF THE ANCIENT PATRIARCHATE OF ROME FOR ORTHODOXY TODAY

In October 2008 Pope Benedict XVI, the current leader of the world's more than 1 billion Roman Catholics, received as his guest in Vatican City the Ecumenical Patriarch Bartholomew I, and prayed with him in the Sistine Chapel. The two, who met together four times since the election of Pope Benedict, seemed eager for a continuing ecumenical dialogue in a world fractured by religious strife. The ecumenical patriarch described the service in the famous Sistine Chapel as a "joyous experience of unity, perhaps not perfect, but true and deep." While the place of the papal primacy among Christian hierarchs continues to be a strongly divisive and inflammatory aspect of the larger divisions between Eastern Orthodoxy and Roman Catholicism, nevertheless, both pope and patriarch are to be lauded for their willingness to work together for unity on wider church issues that can legitimately be undertaken in a spirit of Christian openness. If their joint works can contribute towards the healing of a planet that groans under the weight of significant social, ecological, and political challenges, it will be a blessing not only for Christianity, but even for the world at large.

SEE ALSO: Alexandria, Patriarchate of; Antioch, Patriarchate of; Constantinople, Patriarchate of; Iconoclasm; Jerusalem, Patriarchate of; Pentarchy; St. Constantine the Emperor (ca. 271–337); St. Photios the Great (ca. 810–ca. 893)

REFERENCES AND SUGGESTED READINGS

Anastos, M. V. (2001) "Constantinople and Rome: A Survey of the Relations between the Byzantine and the Roman Churches," in S. Vryonis, Jr. and N. Goodhue (eds.) *Aspects of the Mind of Byzantium: Political Theory, Theology and Ecclesiastical Relations with the See of Rome*, vol. 8. Aldershot: Ashgate/Variorum, pp. 1–119.

Brown, R. E. and Meier, J. P. (1983) *Antioch and Rome: New Testament Cradles of Catholic Christianity*. Mahwah, NJ: Paulist Press.

Cameron, A. (2007) "Constantine and the 'Peace of the Church,'" in M. M. Mitchell and F. M. Young (eds.) *The Cambridge History of Christianity: Origins to Constantine.* Cambridge: Cambridge University Press, pp. 538–51.

Dvornik, F. (1966) *Byzantium and the Roman Primacy.* New York: Fordham University Press.

Hall, S. G. (2007a) "Institutions in the pre-Constantinian *Ecclesia*," in M. M. Mitchell and F. M. Young (eds.) *The Cambridge History of Christianity: Origins to Constantine.* Cambridge: Cambridge University Press, pp. 414–33.

Hall, S. G. (2007b) "Ecclesiology in the Wake of Persecutions," in M. M. Mitchell and F. M. Young (eds.) *The Cambridge History of Christianity: Origins to Constantine.* Cambridge: Cambridge University Press, pp. 470–83.

Holloway, R. R. (2004) *Constantine and Rome.* New Haven: Yale University Press.

Jeffers, J. S. (1991) *Conflict at Rome: Social Order and Hierarchy in Early Christianity.* Minneapolis: Fortress Press.

Kelly, J. N. D. (1996) *The Oxford Dictionary of Popes.* Oxford: Oxford University Press.

Meeks, W. A. (1993) *The Origins of Christian Morality: The First Two Centuries.* New Haven: Yale University Press.

Meyendorff, J. (1996) *Rome Constantinople Moscow: Historical and Theological Studies.* Crestwood, NY: St. Vladimir's Seminary Press.

Noble, T. F. X. (2009) *Images, Iconoclasm, and the Carolingians.* Pittsburgh: University of Pennsylvania Press.

Stark, R. (2006) *Cities of God: The Real Story of How Christianity Became an Urban Movement and Conquered Rome.* San Francisco: Harper One.

Vinzent, M. (2007) "Rome," in M. M. Mitchell and F. M. Young (eds.) *The Cambridge History of Christianity: Origins to Constantine.* Cambridge: Cambridge University Press, pp. 397–412.

Winter, B. W. (1994) *Seek the Welfare of the City: Christians as Benefactors and Citizens.* Grand Rapids, MI: Eerdmans.

Royal Doors

DAN SANDU

The two, often elaborate, doors in the center of the iconostasis in Eastern Orthodox churches. They are called royal because Christ the Emperor mystically passes through them, and because the Byzantine emperor entered through these doors together with the patriarch or a bishop prior to the start of the Holy Eucharist. They are a sign of the unity of the two Testaments which are the pathway to the Kingdom of God, the Holy of Holies represented in the church by the Sanctuary.

On the royal doors there is a diptych icon of the annunciation, which symbolizes the fact that this event opened the gates of Heaven to humanity. The four corners of the double doors feature medallions of Sts. Matthew, Mark, Luke, and John, the authors of the gospel of Christ. Behind the doors there is often a velvet or cotton veil or curtain, which is opened and closed by being moved upward or to the side at specific moments during liturgical services. The royal doors are not used for regular access to the altar, and are only opened during the celebration of the mysteries, which offer redeeming grace and access to the heavenly kingdom. Only bishops and priests ever pass through them at designated moments in the liturgy. The doors are kept closed strictly outside religious ceremonies.

During the morning services the royal doors are kept closed until the Great Doxology as a reminder of man's banishment from heaven for failing to observe God's commandment. At the intoning of the Great Doxology – the hymn of praise based on the glorification by the angelic hosts of the nativity of Christ – the doors are opened to reflect the reopening of heaven following the coming of the Son of God into the world as a man and to proclaim the blessing for the start of the Holy Eucharist.

SEE ALSO: Diakonikon; Divine Liturgy, Orthodox; Iconostasis

Plate 57   The seminarians' chapel of Sergiev Posad Academy, near Moscow. Founded by St. Sergius of Radonezh, the monastery with its attached theological school is a center of Russian church life. Photo by John McGuckin.

REFERENCES AND SUGGESTED READINGS

Braniște, E. (2002) *Liturgica Generală* (General Liturgics). Galați: Editura Episcopiei Dunării de Jos.

Florensky, P. (1996) *Ikonostasis*. Crestwood, NY: St. Vladimir's Seminary Press.

Taft, R. F. (2004) *A History of the Liturgy of Saint John Chrysostom, Vol. 2: The Great Entrance*. Rome: Pontifical Oriental Institute.

Russia, Patriarchal Orthodox Church of

KONSTANTIN GAVRILKIN

The Russian Orthodox Church (hereafter, ROC), also known as the Moscow patriarchate, is ranked fifth in the listing of the autocephalous Orthodox Churches (after Constantinople, Alexandria, Antioch, and Jerusalem). The largest multinational church in the world, it has jurisdiction over most of the Orthodox parishes in Russia, Ukraine, Belarus, and other territories of the former Soviet Union (except for Georgia, which has its own autocephalous church), as well as a number of parishes in various regions of the world, organized in dioceses or under the direct authority of the patriarch of Moscow. There are also a number of ecclesiastical entities that emerged after the breakdown of the ROC caused by the Bolshevik Revolution of 1917 and incessant persecution of the church by the Soviet government (Tsypin 2006). Some were part of the massive Russian diaspora, others emerged from the Catacomb movement (Beglov 2008).

An outline of the history of the ROC helps to understand the difficulties

Plate 58   The Danilovsky Monastery, Moscow. Home of the Russian Orthodox Patriarchate. Photo by John McGuckin.

Plate 59   Patriarch Kiril, head of the Russian Orthodox Church. Photo by John McGuckin.

encountered when dealing with the complex phenomenon of Russian Orthodoxy.

KIEVAN RUS LATE 9TH–EARLY 13TH CENTURIES

In 988, Vladimir, the Grand Prince of Kiev (980–1015), ordered the inhabitants of the capital to be baptized in the Dnieper river, following his own baptism in Chersonesus earlier that year. There were, however, Christians in Kiev already by the mid-10th century, and their numbers grew after the conversion of Vladimir's grandmother Olga, who ruled in Kiev from 945 to 963 and was baptized in Constantinople in 954 (Golubinskii 1901). The missionary work of Sts. Cyril and Methodius, and especially their disciples in Bulgaria, who translated the basic corpus of Christian texts, including the liturgy, into Slavonic in the late 9th and early 10th centuries, were factors that eased the Christianization of the region. The mission was sponsored by the patriarchate of Constantinople, which exercised control over the ecclesiastical life of Ancient Rus and appointed all the Metropolitans "of Kiev and All Rus" until the mid-15th century (on the profound Byzantine legacy in Ancient Rus, see Thomson 1999).

Under Vladimir and his dynasty, Kiev and then such cities as Novgorod, Pskov, Vladimir, Rostov, and Suzdal' gradually emerged as important regional centers of Christian culture and spirituality. Kiev's Monastery of the Caves (later known as Kievo-Pecherskaia Lavra), founded in 1051 by St. Antonii Pecherskii, played a key role in shaping Russian monastic traditions and

Plate 60 The Monastery of the Holy Trinity, Sergiev Posad, one of the homes of the Moscow Patriarch. Photo by John McGuckin.

creating an original Christian literature, with its monks becoming the first Russian chroniclers, hagiographers, and spiritual writers.

The Mongol invasion of 1220–40 left most of the Kievan Rus in ruins. Afterwards came a short period of control by the principality of Vladimir-Suzdal', but in 1238 its capital, Vladimir, was itself destroyed, and in 1240 Kiev suffered a similar fate. After that point there followed dynastic and political reorganizations, and the northeastern lands became increasingly dominated by Moscow (Fennell 1983). Having recognized the long-lasting changes in the Russian political landscape, Maksim the Metropolitan of Kiev (1283–1305) abandoned the impoverished old capital and moved to Vladimir in 1299. His successor,

Metropolitan Peter (1308–26), moved his court to Moscow permanently.

RISE OF MOSCOW: 14TH–MID-15TH CENTURIES

The presence of the metropolitan's court in Moscow increased the authority and ambition of the local Muscovy princes to unify the land under their sole rule. The metropolitans, in turn, used the new situation to secure the stability of the ROC and inspire unity among the divided Russian principalities. Most of them, such as Theognostus (1328–53) and Photius (1408–31), were Greeks from Constantinople who were able to use diplomatic skill, wisdom, and personal courage in dealing with the rival Russian rulers on the one hand, and the Golden Horde on the other (Meyendorff 1981). Some were locals, like Metropolitan Aleksii (1354–78), who prior to his election was for many years an assistant to Metropolitan Theognostus and, at the latter's advice, was appointed his successor, ruling with authority and insight and striving to unite the Russian lands in their fight against Tatar oppression. His contemporary, St. Sergius of Radonezh (d. 1392), inspired a massive monastic movement that covered Russian territories with hundreds of monasteries, spreading the influence of hesychasm and ecclesiastical culture and further colonizing the land. The building of monasteries was accompanied by a broader cultural revival, one of the most remarkable examples of which was St. Andrei Rublev (d. 1430) and his school of iconography.

During the reign of Vasilii II (1425–62), the ROC underwent a dramatic change that redefined its identity. In the 1430s, Byzantine Emperor John VIII Palaeologus negotiated with Rome regarding the reunification of the Western and Eastern

Churches in order to save Constantinople from the looming takeover by the Ottoman Turks. His chief negotiator at the Council of Basle in 1434 was Bishop Isidor, who in 1437 was sent by the emperor to Moscow as Metropolitan of Kiev and All Russia in order to bring Muscovy into the union with Rome for the goal of the rescue of Constantinople. At the Council of Florence in 1439, Isidor was one of the chief Greek spokesmen for the reunion, and, upon signing the agreement, he was made by Pope Eugene IV the papal legate to All Russia and Lithuania and, later, Cardinal-Priest. When Isidor arrived in Moscow in the spring of 1441 as cardinal and papal legate he announced the union with Rome as official Orthodox Church policy. Vasilii II and the council of the Russian bishops rejected Isidor's authority: he was deposed and imprisoned, but allowed to escape in the autumn of 1441. At the end of 1448, a few weeks after the death of the Byzantine "unionist" Emperor John VIII, the council of the Russian bishops finally decided to act independently, and elected Jonah, Bishop of Riazan (who had been the local candidate to the metropolitan's office since 1431), who thus became the first head of the ROC not affirmed by Constantinople. The Church of Constantinople itself eventually rejected the union with Rome (1472), but its synod refused to recognize the ROC's claim to independence until the late 16th century.

In 1458 the uniate patriarch of Constantinople, Gregory III Mamma, who was living in Rome under papal protection, appointed the Bulgarian Gregory II as Metropolitan of Kiev, Galicia, and All Rus. Recognized by the Polish King Casimir IV, and with a unionizing policy in mind, Gregory's legitimacy was rejected by Moscow, and its choice of metropolitan Jonah was reasserted. The *de facto* existence of two Russian metropolias was finally resolved by all involved parties in 1460. And in 1461, after the death of Metropolitan Jonah, the Russian bishops elected Archbishop Theodosius of Rostov with the title "Metropolitan of Moscow and all Rus."

INDEPENDENCE: 1448–1589

The fall of Constantinople in 1453 made Muscovy the only free Orthodox country. Its leaders turned the tragedy of Constantinople into Moscow's triumph, claiming that their country providentially became the sole successor of the fallen Byzantine Empire. Ivan III (1462–1505) assumed firm control over most of the Russian lands through marriage, purchase, or war, tripling the size of the state. In 1478–88 he also crushed the Republic of Novgorod, which immediately became the source of a significant and lengthy ecclesiastical and political crisis, caused by the so-called "heresy of Judaizers" (Klier 1997), instigated (to believe Joseph of Volotsk, its chief prosecutor and author of *Prosvetitel'* [The Enlightener], a polemical treatise against the "Judaizers") by a certain learned Jew, Skhariia (Zacharia), who in 1470 came to Novgorod from Kiev. Under his influence, some Orthodox clergy secretly embraced a "Judaic faith" (circumcision and other customs and rituals) and secretly rejected Christian teaching on the Trinity and divinity of Jesus, icon veneration, monasticism, and church sacraments. Two of them, the priests Denis and Aleksei, were eventually brought by the Grand Prince Ivan III to Moscow to serve in the capital's cathedrals, where they managed to attract a significant group of followers in high places: the list of suspects included the Metropolitan of Moscow Zosima (1490–4), members of Ivan III's family, and his high officials. The Judaizers capitalized on the absence of the full Bible in Slavonic and a rudimentary knowledge of theology among the locals. To neutralize their influence, Archbishop Gennadii of Novgorod organized a circle of translators, both Orthodox and Catholic, to collect existing biblical texts and translate the missing ones, and by 1499 he assembled the first full Slavonic Bible. Historians argue that Gennadius' reliance on the expertise of a certain Dominican monk, Veniamin, could explain the favorable view of the Spanish Inquisition that he and Joseph of Volotsk seemed to display in their arguments and actions against the Judaizers, who were subjected to execution, imprisonment, and exile.

Simultaneously, Russian ecclesiastics were involved in the dispute regarding the nature of monastic life in relation to land ownership. Joseph of Volotsk and his party, heavily dependent on state protectionism, defended the vast monastic estates, covering one-third of the country at the time, as the basis of monasteries' wellbeing and intense involvement in social welfare. Their opponents, led by Nil Sorskii, defended contemplative monasticism and warned of the corruption of the church by power, both economic and political. The two parties also sharply disagreed in their attitude to heretics in general and to the Judaizers in particular. Joseph of Volotsk praised the Inquisition and justified violence against the heretics (including their public burning at the stake), while Nil Sorskii argued for tolerance and the arts of non-violent persuasion. The Josephites, as they were called, won the support of the Grand Prince and dominated the ecclesiastical life of Muscovy in the 16th century, for most of which Muscovy was ruled by two people: Vasilii III (1506–33) and his son, Ivan IV (1533–84). Crowned tsar in 1547, Ivan IV greatly expanded the state by war and conquest, and completed Muscovy's transition to autocracy by destroying regional elites and replacing them with his own appointees.

As long as it elevated and strengthened their authority, both subscribed to the ideology of Joseph of Volotsk, who, like his followers, was hopeful that a symphony of church and state in Muscovy was in sight. The whole 16th century, however, provides examples of how Russian rulers constantly kept their metropolitans in check: the latter always ran a risk of being deposed, imprisoned, and exiled (like Varlaam, 1511–21, or Ioasaf, 1539–42, or Dionisii, 1572–81), or even killed (like Philip, 1566–8), regardless of the significance of the issues involved.

Metropolitan Makarii (1542–63), himself a Josephite, became the most important figure in his century's Russian ecclesiastical, as well as cultural, life. While archbishop of Novgorod (1526–42), he initiated a complex program of collecting and organizing all available translations of ecclesiastical texts, as well as Russian original literature (compiled in the *Velikie Minei-Chet'i*). His further significance as the metropolitan was demonstrated graphically, one might argue, by the fact that Ivan IV's turn to uncontrollable violence (the so-called *Oprichnina*) took place after the metropolitan's death in December 1563. Makarii presided over a number of local councils – in 1547, 1549, 1551, and 1553–4 – some (the so-called *zemskie sobory*) with the ecclesiastical and secular authorities gathering together for the purpose of resolving both religious and secular issues. Among other actions, the councils canonized many Russian saints, certified legal codes (both secular and ecclesiastical), organized the life of monasteries and their estates, and codified liturgical rites and the calendar. Makarii also supervised an extensive building of new monasteries and churches throughout Muscovy.

AUTOCEPHALOUS PATRIARCHATE: 1589–1720

During the reign of Tsar Feodor 1 (1584–98), when the government was controlled by his brother-in-law, Boris Godunov (himself a tsar in 1598–1605), Russian authorities on a number of occasions attempted to engage the patriarchs of Constantinople, Alexandria, Antioch, and Jerusalem in negotiations regarding the establishment of the office of patriarch of Moscow and, *de jure*, recognition of the ROC's autocephaly. Only in 1589, however, when Patriarch of Constantinople Jeremiah II came to Moscow for help and alms after several years of harassment by the Turkish sultan, did the tide turn. Jeremiah had little choice but to agree to enthrone Job, metropolitan of Moscow since 1586, as the first Russian patriarch. The synods of Constantinople in 1590 and 1593 (in the latter case, with all Eastern patriarchs in attendance) confirmed Job's enthronement, accorded the ROC the fifth place in the diptych of the Orthodox Churches, and accepted the Muscovites' designation of their destiny, the only Orthodox country in the world, as now being the "Third Rome," the successor of Constantinople (i.e., the "Second," or New Rome, as the Greeks called their capital).

The 17th century became for the ROC a time of change and crisis. Several factors played a role in compromising what, after the establishment of the Russian patriarchate in 1589, looked like a bright and promising future. First were the developments in the neighboring Polish-Lithuanian Commonwealth, where the metropolia of Kiev broke down under pressure from the Polish government and Catholic propaganda, led by the Jesuit Order. By the 1590s many of the previously Orthodox nobles converted to Catholicism, practically all the Orthodox bishops favored the union with Rome, and only a few self-organized Orthodox brotherhoods, with the support of the monasteries and a few landowners, engaged in active self-defense through education and the printing of Orthodox literature, encouraged to that end by the patriarch of Constantinople. The declaration of the Union with Rome, signed by the Kievan hierarchy at the Synod at Brzezno (Brest), allowed the Polish authorities to deny the weakened Orthodox community in the Commonwealth their own legal hierarchy. Only in the early 1630s did the Polish King Ladislas IV (1632–48) agree to the consecration of Peter Moghila as Orthodox metropolitan of Kiev (1633–46) in the jurisdiction of Constantinople. Moghila believed that, in order to survive in Poland, the Orthodox needed education first and foremost, modeled after the European universities. He turned around the Kiev Orthodox Academy by introducing an eleven-year course of study and set it on the path to becoming an intellectual center of Eastern Orthodoxy for years to come. One of the immediate results of the Russo-Polish War of 1654–67 and Russia's annexation of the Left-Bank Ukraine was the migration of Ukrainian learned ecclesiastics, associated with the Kiev Academy, to Moscow at the invitation of Tsar Alexis Mikhailovich Romanov (1645–76) and his successors. Shortly after, they began to play prominent roles in ecclesiastical affairs, theology, and education (Saunders 1985). But their dominance and undermining of local (and "older," as their defenders claimed) traditions of religious and cultural practice began to generate strong resistance and opposition in Muscovy, erupting in the later 17th century in relation to the reforms of Patriarch Nikon (1652–66).

Another important factor was the increased authority of the Moscow patriarch, especially in the Time of Troubles (1603–13) and its aftermath. First, both Job (d. 1607) and Hermogen (1606–12) rejected two pretenders to the Moscow throne who relied on Polish troops and managed, albeit for a short time, to usurp the throne. Both ecclesiastics, together with Filaret, father of Tsar Michael Romanov (1613–45) and who would be a future patriarch himself (1619–33), became symbols of national resistance against the imposters and the Polish occupation. After the election of his son as the tsar in 1613, Filaret became the administrator of state affairs, accumulating in his hands that extensive personal authority which was later claimed for himself and his office by Patriarch Nikon, enthroned by Tsar Aleksei Mihailovich (1645–76).

By the mid-17th century the ROC was in need of reform. Liturgical abuses of various kinds, low moral standards, use of conflicting editions of liturgical texts, translated from varying sources both by Ruthenian and Muscovite printers, and the absence of the recognized experts in Greek and Latin to verify translations, created a conflictual situation requiring radical intervention. As soon as he was installed as patriarch, Nikon claimed absolute authority and power over the reform project, making changes in liturgical books according to the new Greek editions. The opponents of changes argued, however, that the traditional Russian practice originated from the earlier Greek sources and that the new editions all came from the Catholic countries and could not be relied on. Unwilling to take Nikon's side without negotiations, Tsar Aleksii eventually grew weary of the patriarch's overbearing personality, his constant demands of obedience, and refusals to collaborate. In 1666 Nikon was deposed and imprisoned in Ferapontov Monastery. Simultaneously, at the councils of 1666–7, the new rites were approved and the old ones condemned, together with the previous councils that endorsed them (the famous council of 1551, led by Metropolitan Makarii of Moscow). The opponents of the new practices were subjected to various forms of punishment after their refusal to accept the reforms. The leaders of what became known as the "Old Belief" (*staraia vera*, or *staryi obriad*) were executed, imprisoned, or exiled, while thousands escaped abroad or to Siberia; the persecution of the Old Believers continued until the 1905 Edict on Religious Tolerance.

SYNODAL PERIOD: 1721–1917

Peter I, who was in conflict with Patriarch Adrian (1690–1700) for most of the 1690s, did not allow for the election of his successor. Instead, in 1700 he established a commission for drafting new legislation limiting the privileges of the church and introducing taxation of dioceses. The reform, however, was delayed until 1721, when a manifesto on the establishment of the Spiritual Collegium (later, the Holy Governing Synod) was published, abolishing the office of the patriarch. In 1722 Peter I introduced the office of Chief Procurator of the Holy Synod (*oberprokuror*), who was directly appointed by the emperor from the ranks of career bureaucrats to supervise the daily operations of the holy synod. Until 1917 all resolutions of the synod of the ROC were published with the logo: "By decree of His Imperial Majesty." Soon after, he also secured the agreement of the Eastern patriarchs to treat the synod as the legitimate successor of the Russian patriarch in all ecclesiastical affairs of the ROC.

The state's encroachment on the ROC reached its peak after the ascension to power of Catherine II (1762–96), who in 1764 initiated a full secularization of ecclesiastical lands (they were confiscated with the attached serfs, almost a million of them) and sharply reduced the number and size of monasteries by dividing them into several categories: *shtatnye* (supported by the state) and *zashtatnye* (self-supporting), with each category subdivided into three classes according to the permitted number of monastics. The reform had a devastating effect on ecclesiastical life in general and monasticism in particular. Its opponents were subjected to a brutal persecution which made most of the bishops unwilling to voice their objections publicly, especially after what happened to the metropolitan of Rostov, Arsenii Matsisevich (d. 1772), who was deposed and imprisoned for the rest of his life.

Peter's reforms, and their later augmentations, created a centralized administrative system with effective control over all dioceses of the ROC (previously covering an enormous territory, they were gradually reduced in size, as were the number of parishes). On the parish level, the state's attempt to increase parishes' size by reducing their number in order to improve the clergy's material support, proved difficult. The liturgical burden of the priests increased considerably and left them with little time for educational and catechetical activities. Another government objective – the raising of the level of clerical education – was addressed only from the early 19th century onwards, when reforms in church education raised educational standards and significantly increased the number of seminary graduates among the clergy. This in turn, however, led to a new set of problems related to the hereditary structure of Orthodox clergy, a dynastic clerical tradition solidified by the legislation of the 18th century (Freeze 1977). Church schools, where only sons of the clergy could study, produced too many seminary graduates with a limited number of parishes to go to. Also, their appointment had little to do with professional or moral qualifications. Rather, it was based on the candidate's willingness to marry a priest's daughter and inherit the parish in due time (almost always, only after the death of the incumbent family-related priest). Even then, parish economy provided no adequate material support for priests, trained in superfluous subjects according to a Latin curriculum that laid emphasis on classical languages, as well as on agronomy, mathematics, medicine, and physics. In addition, priests depended on peasants' voluntary payments for services or on the small produce the priest's family could grow on the tiny land allotment belonging to the church, leaving little time for pastoral service.

Efforts by the government of Tsar Nicholas I (1825–54) to solve such problems proved insufficient (Freeze 1983: 3–187). A new attempt at reform of the ROC was made during the reign of Alexander II (1855–81), who had inherited the Russian Empire in a state of deep crisis, something that was abundantly revealed to him during the disastrous Crimean War (1853–6). The government was forced to reexamine the whole foundations of the Russian social and economic order, based on the labors of millions of enslaved serfs. Then the policy of *glasnost'* (openness) was deployed to engage the educated elite, alienated by Nicholas I, in debating the problems faced by the country. Major changes, initiated by the government, included the emancipation of the serfs (1861), establishment of representative local government (1861–4), and creation of an independent judicial system (1864), as well as the reforms of education (1863–4), municipal government (1870), the military (1874), and, finally, the ROC. While the reforms set the country on the path of rapid industrialization, they created new problems, caused by the inadequate legislation relating to the more than 20 million former serfs who were declared free without the legal right to the land they had formerly toiled. Millions moved to the sprawling cities and joined the quickly growing Russian proletariat, feeding the social unrest and the stormy revolutionary movement. This, in turn, gave rise to nationalism, xenophobia, and stubborn opposition to the reforms among the upper classes, thus further polarizing and destabilizing the country. On March 1, 1881, the very day when Alexander II approved a proposal for further and more substantial liberalization of the state policies on all levels – from the political structure of the empire to peasant land ownership – he was killed by a terrorist bomb, and the country was pulled back in the opposite direction by his son, Alexander III (1881–94), and his grandson, Nicholas II (1895–1917).

In the period of the Great Reforms, Russian ecclesiastics (bishops, priests, seminary professors, and synodal officials), as well as state bureaucrats and intellectuals, representing both liberal and conservative wings, got an opportunity openly to debate the situation of the church. The majority argued for the relaxation of state control over the church or even for the latter's full independence. The government, however, needed to make the church a more effective pastoral, educational, and ideological institution, providing Russian society with social and political unity and stability, which seemed to it to require more effective state control over the church.

These contradictory objectives defined the trajectory and dynamic of the reforms attempted in the 1860s and 1870s (Freeze 1983: 191–347). Parish councils were established in 1864 with the expectation that they would focus on improving the material conditions of clergy and schools.

The new seminary statute (1867) opened church schools to students of all social groups (estates), while allowing seminarians also to enter the universities. The ban on hereditary transfers of parishes (1867) was followed by a reorganization of the parishes in general (1869): cutting down their number, increasing the average size, and limiting clerical positions within them, aiming to improve the material conditions of the priest. A set of additional measures freed clerical children from previous limitations imposed by law: they were now free to pursue career and marriage outside of the clerical estate (1869–71). Parallel positive developments included the revival of preaching, mission, charity, and conciliar practices (such as the institution of diocesan councils).

A slow implementation of the reforms made their results visible only in the late 1870s to 1880s. Although the priesthood became a vocation and the identity of the Russian clergy was greatly strengthened in the public eye, the reforms disrupted the functions of many of the institutions they aimed to improve. Parish councils spent most of their allotted money on decorations, rather than on priests and schools. The best students were leaving seminaries to pursue secular careers through university education. Academic standards in seminaries declined and they experienced acute reductions in enrollment, and the resulting lack of candidates for ordination began to affect dioceses. If priests wanted their sons to study at seminaries, they now had to pay for them (prior to the reform, it was free). Closure of many parishes was accompanied by a widespread bitterness of affected parishioners who were neither consulted nor provided with means of traveling to now-remote parishes. It was not surprising that the parish clergy, who suffered the most by losing privileges of free seminary education, and who now faced a shortage of parish appointments, were among the largest group who saw the reforms as a disaster for the ROC. There were, however, positive developments in the life of the ROC as well. Many bishops and priests now came to service in the ROC from non-priestly backgrounds, and one could find among them charismatic figures of both peasant and aristocratic origin. Revival of monastic spirituality led to the repopulation of many previously deteriorated monasteries. Russian missionaries labored in various regions of the multiethnic and multireligious Russian Empire, as well as abroad (such as in Japan and the United States). Numerous charities were administered by the ROC on behalf of the poor and destitute families, mostly in the industrialized urban areas. The remarkable advancement in critical religious and theological studies in the late 19th and early 20th centuries, especially in the areas of church history, patristics, and comparative religion (albeit for missionary purposes), was another positive result of the educational reform of the 1860s. The Russian religious renaissance of the early 20th century would not have been possible without the groundwork provided by the graduates of the reform theological schools who served as professors in many Russian universities.

The appointment of K. P. Pobedonostsev, one of the major promoters of counterreforms under Alexander III, as chief procurator of the synod (1880–1905), reversed the changes of the reform period. The new statute of theological schools (1884) simplified the curriculum with a focus on "spiritual formation" rather than scholarly training, cancelled elections of rectors and deans, and gave overall control over the schools to diocesan bishops instead of faculty. Seminarians were no longer allowed to leave for universities. Seminaries were changing into caste training institutions once again, with rigid disciplinary regimes, places that were intolerant of critical thinking. In the late 1890s and 1900s riots and clashes between administrations and seminarians took place in a number of seminaries; in some schools, fewer and fewer students sought ordination, such as in the seminary of Blagoveshchensk, where no priest could be found among any of its graduates between 1903 and 1913 (Smolich 1996).

These and similar changes in other areas, suffocating creativity and initiative, as introduced by Pobedonostsev's policies, became another proof of the detrimental effects of state control over the church. A growing number of ecclesiastics, both liberal and conservative, began to raise voices in support of restoration of the office of Russian patriarch and called for a return to the principle of the administration of the ROC on the basis of canon law, rather than on the confusing, restrictive, and often arbitrary policies of the state. The whole synodal period became subject to critical reevaluation in the reign of Nicholas II, especially after the country's defeat in the war with Japan, and the political crisis of the revolution of 1905. The unrest was aggravated by the inconsistent policies of the imperial government, oscillating between reform and reaction. In the polarized empire, nationalist and monarchist groups sought the support of the church in their struggle against liberalism and socialism, while representatives of the liberal wing within society and the ROC were increasingly critical of the state policies and doubtful that the autocratic monarchy of the Romanovs was capable of leading the country out of its political and economic crises, especially as they had been exacerbated by World War I.

The empire's collapse in 1917 gave the ROC a chance finally to convene the All-Russian Church Council of August 1917–August 1918, which restored the office of the patriarch and proposed significant changes in the administration of the church on all levels. However, immediately after the Bolshevik Revolution in October 1917 the ROC came under increasing attack from the Soviet government, which immediately declared a separation of church and state only to unleash systematic propaganda against the church with openly repressive policies in the aftermath of the Civil War of 1918–22. Within twenty years, the country with more than 50,000 churches would see most of them destroyed or converted for different use (with only a few hundred deliberately kept open for propaganda purposes). Under the increasingly violent hostility of the Soviets most of the ROC's 200,000 clergy and monastics were killed or imprisoned, and around 1,000 monasteries closed (except for those in the territories that became independent).

SOVIET PERIOD: 1917–1988

The collapse of the Russian Empire and the Bolshevik Revolution disturbed the unity of the ROC. The Civil War, with quickly shifting frontlines and local governments and dislocation of hundreds of thousands, made it impossible for Patriarch Tikhon and the synod of the ROC to maintain normal communications with various dioceses in regions affected by unrest and bloodshed, or taken over by foreign armies, or even belonging to a separate state. In a few years a number of Orthodox entities in now independent and sovereign countries (Poland, the Baltics, Bessarabia, Ukraine, Georgia, the Far East) declared their independence from the administration of the ROC, which had no capacity to control the situation or assist them, or else they joined the patriarchate of Constantinople. Already in 1920, Patriarch Tikhon decided to give the former dioceses of the ROC freedom to

choose their own course of action: he issued a decree allowing diocesan bishops, who had no more contact with the administration of the ROC, to pursue the best solution to their immediate problems by uniting with the bishops of neighboring territories.

Some of the bishops, clergy, and the faithful began to reorganize already in the course of the Civil War but later, forced to escape, continued to maintain their temporary jurisdictional affiliations. The largest group of the Orthodox, represented by a group of exiled Russian bishops, took the next step when in 1920, in Constantinople, creating the Synod of the Russian Church in Diaspora (later, the Russian Orthodox Church outside Russia, or ROCOR), including also the Russian dioceses in Finland, China, Japan, and Manchuria. Led by Metropolitan of Kiev Antonii Khrapovitsky, in 1921 they moved to Yugoslavia. In 1936 a group led by Metropolitan Evlogy joined the patriarchate of Constantinople and has remained in its jurisdiction to this day. During and after World War II, a substantial number of Russian émigrés moved farther west into Europe, or to the Americas and Australia. Another part of the ROC, the American metropolia, maintained its operational independence from both the Moscow patriarchate and the ROCOR, until it was granted formal independence by the Moscow patriarchate in 1970, becoming the Orthodox Church in America (its autocephalous status has not been recognized by Constantinople and several other churches). After the collapse of the Soviet Union in 1991, it took more than fifteen years to see the ROCOR and the Moscow patriarchate sign the Act of Reunion in 2007, with ROCOR retaining its operational autonomy according to the agreement.

The main body of the ROC, led by Patriarch Tikhon, was subjected to brutal persecution. Within a few years of 1917, all theological schools were closed, printing of religious literature was prohibited, and most of the active and noteworthy clergy and monastics who had survived murder, torture, and execution were imprisoned in concentration camps. A short-lived attempt of the Renovationist movement, or the so-called "Living Church" (*obnovlentsy*), supported by the Soviet government so as to gain the trust of the Russian Orthodox and, simultaneously, pose as the "new," progressive church that embraced the Soviet ideology, ended in disgrace, soon exposed as a puppet organization controlled by the Soviet secret police.

With the beginning of World War II and the German occupation of a substantial part of the Soviet Union, thousands of churches were reopened in the occupied territories, reigniting anti-Soviet sentiments among the local population. To counteract the success of the Nazis in the region and encourage local support for the retreating Soviet troops, Soviet dictator Joseph Stalin met with a few Russian bishops in September 1943 and agreed to give the ROC some freedom in exchange for their visible public support of the regime. A few days later, the church council was convened and Sergey Stragorodskii (1867–1944), metropolitan of Moscow, who in 1927 had issued a "Declaration of loyalty to the Soviet government" (further antagonizing the Russian Orthodox outside the Soviet Union), was elected patriarch, only to die in 1944. In 1945 Alexey (Simanskii), metropolitan of Leningrad (formerly St. Petersburg), was elected patriarch (1945–70). Although thousands of churches were reopened, many bishops and priests released from prisons and camps, and a few theological schools and monasteries reestablished in the postwar years, the Soviet leader Nikita Khrushchev (1953–65) subjected the ROC to another wave of persecution that lasted, with different degrees of intensity, until the *perestroika* initiated under the leadership of Mikhail Gorbachev (1985–91).

CURRENT PERIOD

The beginning of the latest period of Russian Church renaissance could be linked either to the celebration of the millennium of the Baptism of Rus or to the collapse of the Soviet Union in 1991, when liberalization of Soviet policies towards the ROC gradually led to the latter's full independence. The year 1990 marked the election of Aleksii II as Patriarch of Moscow and All Russia (1990–2008), and he it was who oversaw the revival of the ROC after decades of violent and systemic repression, with the restoration of thousands of churches and monasteries, and the reopening of numerous dioceses and theological schools. Among other things, the ROC initiated the ongoing canonization of thousands of Russian Orthodox clergy and laity who had been persecuted and killed during the Soviet period, on the basis of the archival documents dispersed throughout the country.

Since the 1990s the ROC has had to deal with intra-Orthodox jurisdictional conflicts with the ecumenical patriarchate (over Estonia and Ukraine) and the Romanian Orthodox Church (over Moldavia); some of them are still unresolved. There are also, internally, a few minority groups (often vaguely) linked to the Catacomb movement of the Soviet period, claiming the status of the "true Orthodox Church" and accusing the ROC of being a "grace-less" political institution that has betrayed "true Orthodoxy." The ROC has also been deeply affected by the tides of widespread xenophobia, nationalism, fundamentalism, anti-Semitism, and even fascism that have washed over Russian society in the traumatic post-communist years. Since the collapse of the Soviet regime, the ROC has been also increasingly criticized in the Russian democratic press for being more interested in state protectionism, rather than in its own moral integrity and issues of spiritual freedom, criticized for restoring and guarding its privileged status, rather than addressing systemic social and economic problems, causing child abuse, alcoholism, prostitution, and drug use of catastrophic proportions. The church started to make its stance clearer in significant policy documents addressing moral and social problems, especially in the so-called "Social Contract Document" issued by the synod in recent times. In addition, as in other multiethnic and multireligious countries, the ROC has also been confronted with the increasingly difficult problem of finding a proper way for conducting missionary work without being accused of proselytizing among other religious minorities. It has objected loudly to proselytism from Catholic and Protestant "missionaries," which it sees as taking advantage of its long years of martyrdom, and often of being wholly ignorant of its enduring deep Christian roots in Russian culture and life.

The present leader (as of 2009) of the ROC is Patriarch Kiril. In terms of its institutional structure, the ROC is administered on the basis of the Church Statute of 2000 and includes the direct administration of all Orthodox parishes in Russia (or jurisdictional guidance for the autonomous churches, including the Autonomous Church of Japan; the self-ruling Churches of Latvia, Estonia, Moldova, and Ukraine; the Belorussian Exarchate). The ROC has 160 dioceses, including all regions of Russia; 24 synodal departments; 788 monasteries; 30,142 parishes; and numerous educational institutions of various types and levels such as universities, institutes, academies, and seminaries.

SEE ALSO: Berdiaev, Nikolai A. (1874–1948); Constantinople, Patriarchate of; Khomiakov, Aleksey S. (1804–1860); Men, Alexander (1935–1990); Moghila, Peter (1596–1646);

Non-Possessors (Nil Sorskii); Possessors (Joseph Volotsk); St. Andrei Rublev (ca. 1360–1430); St. Elizaveta Feodorovna (1864–1918); St. Filaret (Philaret) Drozdov (1782–1867); St. Ignatius Brianchaninov (1807–1867); St. Seraphim of Sarov (1759–1833); St. Sergius of Radonezh (1314–1392); St. Theophan (Govorov) the Recluse (1815–1894); St. Tikhon (Belavin) (1865–1925); Solovyov, Vladimir (1853–1900); Ukraine, Orthodoxy in the; United States of America, Orthodoxy in the

REFERENCES AND SUGGESTED READINGS

Aleksii, Patriarch of Moscow (ed.) (2000) *Pravoslavnaia entsiklopediia: Russkaia Pravoslavnaia Tserkov'.* Moscow: Pravoslavnaia Etsiklopediia.
Beglov, A. L. (2008) *V poiskakh "bezgreshnykh katakomb." Tserkovnoe podpol'e v SSSR.* Moscow: Izdatel'stvo Moskovskoi Patriarkhii.
Fennell, J. (1983) *The Crisis of Medieval Russia, 1200–1304.* London: Longman.
Franklin, S. (2002) *Writing, Society and Culture in Early Rus, c. 950–1300.* Cambridge: Cambridge University Press.
Franklin, S. and Shepard, J. (1996) *The Emergence of Rus, 750–1200.* London: Longman.
Freeze, G. L. (1977) *The Russian Levites: Parish Clergy in the Eighteenth Century.* Cambridge, MA: Harvard University Press.
Freeze, G. L. (1983) *The Parish Clergy in Nineteenth-Century Russia: Crisis, Reform and Counter Reform.* Princeton: Princeton University Press.
Golubinskii, E. E. (1901) *Istoriia Russkoi Tserkvi. Tom 1. Period pervyi, Kievskii ili domongol'skii,* 2nd edn. Moscow: *Universitetskaia tip.*
Klier, J. D. (1997) "Judaizing Without Jews? Moscow–Novgorod, 1470–1504," in G. D. Lenhoff and A. M. Kleimola (eds.) *Culture and Identity in Muscovy, 1359–1584.* Moscow: ITZ-Garant, pp. 336–49.
Kosik, V. I. (2008) *Russkoe tserkovnoe zarubezh'e: xx vek v biografiiakh dukhovenstva ot Ameriki do Iaponii.* Moscow: PSTGU.
Meyendorff, J. (1981) *Byzantium and the Rise of Russia: A Study of Byzantino-Russian Relations*

in the Fourteenth Century. Cambridge: Cambridge University Press.

Pliguzov, A. (1992) "Archbishop Gennadii and the Heresy of the 'Judaizers,'" *Harvard Ukrainian Studies* 16: 269–88.

Plokhy, S. (2006) *The Origins of the Slavic Nations: Premodern Identities in Russia, Ukraine, and Belarus.* Cambridge: Cambridge University Press.

Saunders, D. (1985) *The Ukrainian Impact on Russian Culture, 1750–1850.* Edmonton: CIUS Press.

Smolich, I. K. (1996) *Istoriia Russkoi Tserkvi*, Vol. 1. Moscow: Izd-vo Spaso-Preobrazhenskogo Valaamskogo monastyria.

Thomson, F. J. (1999) *The Reception of Byzantine Culture in Medieval Russia.* Brookfield, VT: Ashgate Press.

Tsypin, V. (2006) *Istoriia Russkoi Pravoslavnoi Tserkvi: Sinodal'nyi i noveishii periody*, 2nd edn. Moscow: Izd-vo Sretenskogo monastyria.

S

St. Alexis Toth *see* United States of America, Orthodoxy in the

St. Andrei Rublev (ca. 1360–1430)

KONSTANTIN GAVRILKIN

Little is known of the life of Russia's greatest icon painter. The indirect evidence suggests that he was born around the 1360s and settled in the Trinity Monastery (later, the Troitse-Sergieva Lavra) near Moscow shortly after the death of its founder, St. Sergius of Radonezh (1392), presumably already as a monk. Rublev is first mentioned in the *Chronicle of the Trinity Monastery* under the year 1405, when he is said to have worked on the frescoes and icons of the Annunciation Cathedral of the Moscow Kremlin together with Theophanes the Greek, a prominent Byzantine master who is believed to have been associated with the hesychast movement and who trained Andrei in icon painting. In this and other sources associated with the same monastery, Andrei is mentioned in later years as a man of holy life and master of remarkable talent who decorated churches in Moscow, Vladimir, and other places. The last place Rublev was known to be working was at the Moscow Andronikov Monastery, where he died around 1430. In the Soviet period this monastery was closed but has since reopened as the Andrei Rublev Museum of Early Russian Art, with a collection representing Russian works from the 15th to 17th centuries.

Although the authority of Andrei Rublev as model icon painter was recognized by the Stoglav Council of 1551, which declared that iconographers should follow the ancient standards of Greek icon painters, Andrei Rublev, and other famous masters (Lazarev 1966: 75–8), the decline of Russian iconography after the late 16th century led to a gradual loss of that knowledge and skill associated with Rublev and his school. By the 19th century virtually only the Old Believers who treasured the liturgical and spiritual traditions of the Muscovite Rus remembered his name without, however, being able to identify his works. With the beginning of the scholarly study of early Russian iconography at the beginning of the 20th century, the only starting point for the recovery of Rublev's legacy was the Icon of the Holy Trinity in the Trinity Cathedral of the Troitse-Sergieva Lavra, which, according to all the sources, was painted by Andrei Rublev alone. Cleaned in 1904, the icon provided iconologists with the stylistic and technical clues for further research. After a century-long study of his frescoes and icons, St. Andrei Rublev is recognized today as a great master of composition, light, and color, who was able to express through his works the peace and beauty of the world transformed by grace, the vision of the human being transformed by the Spirit into the true image and likeness

The Encyclopedia of Eastern Orthodox Christianity, edited by John Anthony McGuckin
© 2011 Blackwell Publishing Ltd.

of God. He was officially canonized as a saint by the Russian Church in 1988.

SEE ALSO: Iconography, Styles of; Iconostasis; Icons; Russia, Patriarchal Orthodox Church of

REFERENCES AND SUGGESTED READINGS

Alpatov, M. A. (1972) *Andrei Rublev.* Moscow: Iskusstvo.
Bunge, G. (2007) *The Rublev Trinity.* Crestwood, NY: St. Vladimir's Seminary Press.
Lazarev, V. N. (1966) *Andrei Rublev i ego shkola.* Moscow: Iskusstvo.
Lazarev, V. N. and Vzdornov, G. I. (eds.) (1997) *The Russian Icon: From Its Origins to the Sixteenth Century.* Collegeville, MN: Liturgical Press.
Shchennikova, L. A. (2007) *Tvoreniia prepodobnogo Andreiia Publeva i ikonopistsev velikokniazheskoi Moskvy.* Moscow: Indrik.
Vzdornov, G. I. (ed.) (1989) *"Troitsa" Andreia Rubleva.* Moscow: Iskusstvo.

St. Antony of Egypt (the Great) (ca. 251–356)

JOHN A. MCGUCKIN

St. Antony has a symbolic stature in the Orthodox world as the "first monk" of Christian tradition, There were, of course, ascetics and hermits before him, historically speaking, and even his *Vita* mentions that he placed his sister in the care of the city communities of virgin ascetics before he went off to the desert as an ascetic himself. But Antony was one of the most dramatic teachers of the early Egyptian desert, who adopted a life of profound seclusion (the "eremitical" life) when this was still very rare in Christianity (the city communities of ascetics being preferred as a *modus operandi* or settlements just on the outskirts of villages which allowed limited

communication). The *Life of Saint Antony* written by the great Egyptian hierarch and theologian St. Athanasius of Alexandria very shortly after Antony's death, became one of the most popular Christian texts of Antiquity and was responsible for making Antony paradigmatic for much of subsequent monastic theory. Athanasius' *Vita* sparked an interest in hagiography that would grow to immense proportions in later ages, and it set the terms of much that would follow in imitation. It is one of the earliest of all canonization narratives, and depicts the monastic life as a Christian parallel to the ancient Sophists.

The outline of Antony's career was that by the age of 20 he had inherited his father's wealth and became head of an Alexandrian merchant household. He experienced a dramatic conversion while hearing the gospel text read out in church: "Sell all that you have and come follow me." Taking it to heart, he dispossessed himself for the benefit

Plate 61 Icon of St. Antony of Egypt, father of monks. Photo by John McGuckin.

Plate 62   The tiny cave where St. Antony of Egypt spent forty years in solitary prayer. Now it is a shrine many hundreds of feet above the monastery dedicated to his name by the Red Sea in Egypt. Photo by John McGuckin.

of the poor, broke his familial ties, and left Alexandria for a life of ascetical seclusion in the semi-desert around the Nile, near Fayyum, which itself later became a great monastic center. He began his first exercises in the ascetical life near *fellahin* settlements and with some limited guidance from other desert dwellers (and from this period come the stories of his famous "wrestling with demons" in deserted tombs), but by 285 he moved deeper into the Egyptian desert seeking a more solitary lifestyle, at a place called Outer Mountain (*Pispir*). Here he organized a colony of disciples under a loose form of early communal "rule" (called "coenobitic" monasticism, from the Greek term for shared lifestyle). In 305 he moved even further into the wilderness to a place called Inner Mountain (*Deir Mar Antonios*) by the Red Sea. Here he presided over a much looser association of senior and experienced monks living as hermits. So it is that he traditionally came to be associated with the foundation of the three basic types of Christian monastic structure: communes (*koinobia*) under the direction of a senior monk (*abba* or *higumen*); *lavras*, where scattered groups of individual hermits would inhabit neighboring valleys and meet for Sunday vigil worship, under the spiritual authority of an elder (*geron*); and finally the eremitical life proper, where a monk would live in more or less complete seclusion.

Antony has several short letters attributed to him, which are generally regarded as genuine. His reputation as a leading "philosopher" is probably more a rhetorical *topos* of Athanasius'. The writings focus on the need to acquire freedom in the inner life, so that the vision of God could be sought with a focused heart. His reputation as a holy man, counselor, exorcist, and thaumaturg, even in his own lifetime, was such that the bishop of Alexandria, St. Athanasius, called on his assistance and used the power of his reputation to combat the Arian movement. Antony's final monastic settlement, Deir Mar Antonios, passed through numerous iterations, but today still functions as a living monastic settlement. It is located at the foot of the mountain in the face of which his tiny cave is still preserved as a shrine, in which he spent more than forty years of prayer.

SEE ALSO: Coptic Orthodoxy; Monasticism

REFERENCES AND SUGGESTED READINGS

Gregg, R. C. (1980) *Athanasius: The Life of Antony.* New York: Paulist Press.

Rubenson, S. (1990) *The Letters of Saint Antony: Origenist Theology, Monastic Tradition, and the Making of a Saint*. Bibliotheca Historico-Ecclesiastica Lundensis, 24. Lund: Lund University Press.

St. Athanasius of Alexandria (ca. 293–373)

TARMO TOOM

St. Athanasius, who is called "a pillar of orthodoxy" (festal troparion) by the Orthodox Church, is best remembered for his defense of Nicene theology and his role in promoting monastic ideals. In the writings of his friends, Athanasius is depicted as a "very dear brother" (Hilary, *Adversus Valentem et Ursacium* 1.3.1), but by his opponents, he was called a "villain" (ibid., 1.2.21).

Athanasius was born in Alexandria and served as a deacon and secretary of Bishop Alexander of Alexandria, whom he accompanied to the Council of Nicea in 325. In 328, after a disputed election, Athanasius was consecrated as the twentieth patriarch of Alexandria, and had to face immediately the assaults of Melitian and Arian opponents, and experience the wrath of unfriendly emperors, whose christological policy he opposed. At the Synod of Tyre in 335 Athanasius was accused of sacrilege, bribery, rape, and murder. Although none of these accusations stuck, Athanasius had to spend some fifteen years of his 46-year episcopacy in exile, where he established useful contacts with western theologians and Egyptian monks. After ordaining his successor Peter, "who followed him in all things" (*Historia Acephala* 13.19), Athanasius died in 373. Soon his corpus would gain a very highly authoritative status.

Athanasius' works are preserved in Greek, Coptic, and Syriac. A twofold apology *Against the Pagans* and *On the Incarnation* contends that the incarnation of the Son of God restored the damaged relationship between the Creator and the creation. "He was made human [both body and soul (Tom. 7)] so that we might be made God" (*On the Incarnation* 54). Among Athanasius' many anti-Arian works are *Orations against the Arians*, *Apology against the Arians*, *Defense of the Nicene Definition*, and the *History of the Arians*. For Athanasius, who was applauded as the first true trinitarian theologian by St. Gregory of Nazianzus (*Oration* 21.33), the Son is consubstantial and co-eternal with the Father. Even his enemies called him the "mighty champion of the consubstantialist doctrine" (Philostorgius, *Ecclesiastical History* 3.17). Athanasius also wrote many personal letters and, annually, the paschal *Festal Letters*. His *Letters to Serapion* defended the full divinity of the Holy Spirit, and his *Letter to Epictetus* presents an anti-Apollinarian Christology. All of these works were to gain a high authority in the next generation and to determine ecumenical conciliar Christology. His ascetical writings include the *Life of Anthony*, which presents the desert saint as an ideal Christian, the four *Letters to Virgins*, and the *Letter to Marcellinus* on biblical interpretation. Some fragments of his *Catenae* (isolated comments) on various biblical books are also extant. St. Athanasius' feast day is January 18, and he is also celebrated with St. Cyril of Alexandria.

SEE ALSO: Alexandria, Patriarchate of; Coptic Orthodoxy; Council of Nicea I (325); Deification; Desert Fathers and Mothers; Holy Spirit; Holy Trinity

REFERENCES AND SUGGESTED READINGS

Anatolios, K. (1998) *Athanasius: The Coherence of His Thought*. London: Routledge.

Barnes, T. D. (1993) *Athanasius and Constantius: Theology and Politics in the Constantinian Empire.* Cambridge, MA: Harvard University Press.

Dragas, G. D. (2005) "Saint Athanasius: Original Research and New Perspectives," in G. D. Dragas and D. R. Lamoureux (eds.) *Patristic Theological Library* vol. 1. Rollinsford: Orthodox Research Institute.

Martin, A. (1996) *Athanase d'Alexandrie et l'église d'Egypte au IVe siècle (328–373).* Rome: École Française de Rome.

Tetz, M. (1995) *Athanasiana: zu leben und lehre des Athanasius,* ed. W. Geerlings and D. Wyrwa. Berlin: De Gruyter.

Weinandy, T. G. (2007) *Athanasius: A Theological Introduction.* Aldershot: Ashgate Press.

St. Augustine of Hippo (354–430)

JOHN A. MCGUCKIN

St. Augustine, known commonly in the Orthodox Church as "the Blessed Augustine," is perhaps the single most important Christian writer of the ancient Christian West. He came from Thagaste, near Madauros, in Roman North Africa. His father Patricius was a pagan (until his deathbed), and his mother, Monnica, a Catholic Christian who enrolled her infant son as a catechumen. Augustine's talent was noticed early, and a wealthy patron, Romanianus, sponsored his education. He studied rhetoric at Carthage, where at the age of 19 he was powerfully attracted to the vocation of rhetor-philosopher by reading Cicero's (lost) treatise *Hortensius.* His mother pressured him to enrol for baptism but Augustine had already set up house with a concubine (whom he never names) to whom he was deeply attached, and he was not willing to threaten that relationship, or to submit himself to the doctrines of the Catholics, which he had come to regard as simplistic. He attached himself to the Manichean movement (as a "Hearer")

and belonged to them for the next ten years until 387.

Augustine's career took him from Carthage, to Rome, and eventually Milan, where he occupied the position of Rhetoric Professor, won for him by Manichean patrons. In Milan he became increasingly disillusioned with the Manicheans, and a series of crises shook his security; beginning with increasing asthmatic troubles (fatal for an ancient orator) and his agreement with his mother's plan to dismiss his partner of fifteen years' standing (the mother of his son Adeodatus) so that he could make a rich marriage to advance his career. His heartless agreement to her dismissal was soon followed by heartbreak at her loss, and his rapid employment of a sexual surrogate caused him to regard his philosophical aspirations with a depressed skepticism; but his increasing contact with one of the leading rhetorical and philosophical circles in the city (the group of theologians associated with the priest Simplicianus and Bishop Ambrose) opened up new vistas for him. He was greatly impressed by Ambrose, and began to consider the possibility of a similar career as ascetic philosopher. He describes his psychosexual and spiritual struggle in a famous autobiography (the *Confessions*) which he wrote many years later, and here he depicts the turning point of his life as occurring dramatically in a quiet Milanese garden when he abandoned his destiny to Christ and subsequently petitioned for admission to the church. For a while he stayed with Christian friends who formed a scholarly college around him. Soon, however, he returned to Rome, where Monnica died, and then he made his way back to Africa, in 388, where he intended to live with his companions (more cheaply) at Thagaste. One day in 391, while making a visit to the seaport of Hippo Regius, he was seized by local Christians and forcibly ordained priest by Bishop Valerius, so that he could help the old bishop in the church administration. He and his companions accepted the forced initiation into church administration, and by 395 Augustine was consecrated as Valerius' episcopal assistant and, soon afterwards, his successor. Local bishops in Africa regarded his promotion as canonically dubious, and even his baptism as somewhat irregular – for the news of his early life (both his sexual liaisons and his membership of the heretical Manichees) was common gossip in a church much troubled by the rigorist dissidents the Donatists. To defend himself Augustine composed treatises against the Manichees after his priestly ordination, and after his consecration as bishop wrote the *Confessions*, an exercise in how self-scrutiny can be a salvific reading of the story of God's providence in creation and in a human life. It was a brilliant answer to his episcopal colleagues who had criticized him for slipping through the rigorous baptismal "scrutinies" of the African church.

As bishop, Augustine made profound moves to resolve the schism of the Donatists, which led to his enunciation of important principles that would form the basic substructure of western Catholic ideas of sacramentality and ecclesial legitimacy. His works greatly developed the Latin Church's understanding of itself as both a heavenly and earthly body (like Christ himself – whose body it was – a complete and perfect synthesis of flesh and divine spirit). Opposed at first to applying secular pressure on dissidents, he reluctantly came to a position by 411 that allowed for the partial legitimacy of such a policy. His immediate context was the lively Donatist threat of violence against him, but his authority seemed to have been placed behind the idea of religious compulsion when necessary, and it was an authority much evoked to justify forms of ecclesiastical oppression in later centuries. The publication of his *Confessions* had caused some outrage in Rome, where a moralist preacher, Pelagius, was appalled by Augustine's apparently fatalist resignation of his salvation to God's grace. Pelagius called for a more robust personal commitment and moral effort, and so began a controversy that was to mark all of Augustine's later life, and cause him to elaborate a profound and careful doctrine of Grace that would become determinative for Western Catholicism. Augustine regarded humanity as having nothing on which it could base its salvation: all was a free gift of God. Humanity left to itself could only slip into the slavery of sin and corruption. His ideas were set out as a theology of praise for God's merciful providence, but in some, more negative, readings of his legacy, the pessimistic tone predominated in an unbalanced way, and Augustine in a real sense has to be seen as the author of a tendency in Latin theology to focus on the notions of Original Sin, and the corruption of the material world, along with an ever-present tendency of the whole race to depravity. Most Orthodox theological writers never laid such stress on this pessimism, and never adopted as elements of the faith (unlike subsequent Western Catholicism) what they regarded as peculiarities of Augustine's local church (*theologoumena*). After the sack of Rome in 410, Augustine began a work of large-scale apologetic to answer those who laid the blame for the decadence of the Western Empire at the door of the Christians. Between 412 and 427 he produced a monumental work called the *City of God*, where he elaborated the first extensively considered ethical and political view of what Christianity conceived of as a civilized order, in distinction to pre-Christian ideas. He stresses the earthly city's (human society's) radical dissociation from the true City of God (the eschatological realization of the kingdom), but makes a case for how the earthly city is informed and guided by heavenly ideals. Slavery is a prime symptom of the inherent corruption of the world's affairs. In the midst of endemic violence and disorder the church has the destiny to represent mercy and reconciliation, guiding society to a perfection it might never attain, but to which it is inexorably summoned.

To stand with the *Confessions* and *City of God*, in his triad of "world classics," we should add Augustine's monumental work of theology *On the Trinity*, composed between 399 and 419. In this he constructs a major anti-Arian apologetic around the Nicene faith in Christology and pneumatology. He demonstrates from a wide variety of triadic cosmic patterns the reasonableness of the trinitarian doctrine of three divine persons subsisting in one single divine nature. Much use is made of triadic patterns of human psychology (the soul as the image of God), and he emphasized once again his deeply sensed connection between self-scrutiny and theological method (something common to Augustine and the Platonic tradition). His vast corpus of writings became, of course, his own form of ascetical exercise. The great extent of his work made him function as an encyclopedic theological authority for the next millennium in the West. But he had only a very minor influence on the Eastern Church, though translations were made of him into Greek in the medieval period, and he had a small circle of interested Greek readers. His spiritual writings gave a great impetus to monasticism as the organizing structure of the Latin Church (something which Pope St. Gregory the Great later picked up and developed). He particularly stressed the element of true faith leading to a deep desire of the heart for God, an affective spiritual tradition that made him an attractive and highly approachable Christian writer – aspects that still appear from engagement with his work.

Only a few treatises can be singled out for special mention, such as *De Doctrina Christiana* which laid out his biblical hermeneutical philosophy, or *De Bono Conjugali* which argued (somewhat reluctantly) for the intrinsic holiness of sexuality in marriage (against St. Jerome's deeply hostile opinions). *De Peccatorum Meritis et Remissione* and *De Natura et Gratia* both demonstrate why he thought Pelagianism so destructive of Christian religious experience. The *Enchiridion* is a summatic handbook of theology, composed for reference. His greatest exegetical works are perhaps his Tractatus CXXIV in *Joannis Evangelium* and *De Genesi ad Litteram* (commentaries respectively on John's Gospel and the Book of Genesis). The commentary on the Psalms (*Enarrationes in Psalmos*) demonstrates his deep love for them as prayers. There is hardly a sermon, however, that is not an exposition of scripture, or a serious theological reflection, in the manner he approaches it. Augustine's friend and monastic companion Possidius wrote a biography soon after his death, and made an invaluable list of all his writings, most of which are still extant.

Augustine died as the Vandals were besieging his city on August 28, 430. One of his last instructions was to have his favorite psalms written in large letters around his walls so that he could read them as he died. Soon after his death, Prosper of Aquitaine began a process to lobby for Augustinianism as the standard theological system of the Latin West; a movement that slowly gathered momentum, culminating in Pope Gregory the Great's enthusiastic endorsement of Augustine as preeminent Latin theologian in the late 6th century.

SEE ALSO: Grace; Holy Trinity; Original Sin

REFERENCES AND SUGGESTED READINGS

Brown, P. (1967) *Augustine of Hippo: A Biography.* Berkeley: University of California Press.

Chadwick, H. (1986) *Augustine.* Oxford: Oxford University Press.

Fitzgerald, A. D. (ed.) (1999) *Augustine Through the Ages: An Encyclopedia.* Grand Rapids, MI: Eerdmans.

Schaff, P. (trans.) (1887–92) *Works of St. Augustine,* 8 vols. Grand Rapids, MI: Eerdmans.

Smith, W. T. (1980) *Augustine: His Life and Thought.* Atlanta: John Knox Press.

van der Meer, F. (1961) *Augustine the Bishop.* London: Faber and Faber.

St. Basil of Caesarea (Basil the Great) (330–379)

JOHN A. MCGUCKIN

Known even in his lifetime as the "Great Basil" (a title ascribed to him by his friend St. Gregory of Nazianzus), Basil was the most dynamic and politically active of the Cappadocian fathers, and if not the most intellectually original of them, certainly one of the leading intelligences of the early church. He was the son of a rhetorician, from a wealthy Christian family. He studied in Cappadocia (where he first met Gregory of Nazianzus), then in Constantinople, and finally for six years at Athens, where his friendship with Gregory was deepened into a lifelong alliance (one that witnessed some strain towards its end, on Gregory's part, though the final funeral oration Gregory delivered for Basil is one of the most famous of all Christian orations).

In 355 Basil returned to Cappadocia, expressing disillusionment with the academic life, and taught rhetoric for a restless year before he made his way (probably in the company of the radical ascetic Eustathius of Sebaste) to tour the ascetical communities of Syria, Mesopotamia, Palestine, and Egypt. He described this encounter with Christian asceticism as like waking up after a long sleep, and from that time onwards his religious life was given precedence over all other things. Basil was baptized on his return to Cappadocia and embraced the ascetical life under the influence of Eustathius and his own sister, Macrina, who had already adapted their country estate at Annesi in Pontus as a monastic retreat. Here he invited Gregory Nazianzen, though the latter found the style of monasticism not to his taste, preferring a more scholarly seclusion on his own estates. Gregory and Basil collaborated in producing the *Philocalia* (a first edition of selected passages on the subject of exegesis from Origen) as well as writings about the monastic life. This early work of writing manuals for the ascetics gathered around them (especially Basil's treatise *Asceticon,* though some see it as a work of Eustathius) had a historic impact in the form of the "Monastic Rules" which gave Basil the title of "Father of Eastern Monks"). The *Moralia* came first in 358, which was a largely traditional collection of ascetical maxims (each one attached to their suitable biblical proof text) and this work was followed by the *Asceticon* (ca. 363) (which is what most modern scholars refer to as the "Rule" of Basil, though it too is more in the form of generic maxim than detailed prescription).

Ordained a reader in 360 and then priest for the church at Cappadocian Caesarea in 362, Basil was actively involved in the resistance of the radical Arian party (the Heterousians or Anhomoians) led by Aetius and Eunomius. At first attached to the Homoiousian party which was dominant in Cappadocia, Basil increasingly aligned himself with the defense of the Nicene Creed (and the Homoousian party) as it had been orchestrated and aligned by the eminent figures of Athanasius in Egypt, and by Meletios of Antioch and Eusebius of Samosata in the provinces of the Orient. His attachment to Meletios was the reason Basil never quite gained Athanasius' complete trust. He fell out with his bishop, Eusebius, who seems to have been jealous of his younger assistant's capabilities, and to avoid rancor he retired to his estates until, in 364, the threat of an installation at Caesarea of an Arian bishop of the entourage of Emperor Valens brought him back to the service of the Caesarean church, and to the aid of his anxious bishop. Gregory Nazianzen mediated that return, and the threat from Valens was deflected. It won him friends and much popular acclaim, but also many enemies among the Caesarean clergy and the leading members of the local Curia.

In 368 he administered the church's relief effort for a great famine in the region and won the support of the people. Gregory of Nazianzen (Oration 14) preached the need for a large hospital facility attached to the Caesarean church, and the effort was successful: the creation of philanthropic institutions staffed by monastics becoming a great innovation introduced by Basil, that would have a long subsequent history in the church. In 370 he was elected bishop of his city, despite the opposition of the town officials and many neighboring bishops. Shortly afterwards, the great civil diocese of Cappadocia was divided in two, and to offset the influence of the new ecclesiastical metropolitan, Anthimos of Tyana, Basil desperately tried to fill small towns in his remaining district with episcopal appointments drawn from his circle of friends. It elevated Gregory of Nyssa and Gregory of Nazianzus to episcopal status, but also caused rifts among his immediate circle, who felt his machinations were chiefly squabbles about revenues dressed up as theological conflicts (Basil was anxious to

retain Caesarea as a significant metropolitan see staffed by Nicene believers).

As he moved more and more, as he grew older, to become the public face of the Nicene party, he stood in alliance with Meletius of Antioch, one of the few remaining first-generation Nicene stalwarts. This alliance (which brought him into conflict with Athanasius and Pope Damasus) he saw as fundamental for the Nicene cause in the East, and he was faithful to it, even though it alienated his old friend and mentor, Eustathius of Sebaste, who then went on to espouse the Pneumatomachian doctrine, denying the deity of the Holy Spirit. The public breach with Eustathius was marked by Basil's publication of a highly influential work, *On the Holy Spirit* (Books 1–3), where Basil affirms the deity of the Son and Spirit, and it paved the way for the full Neo-Nicene confession of the Trinity which Gregory of Nazianzus would elaborate at the Council of Constantinople in 381.

Basil died, worn out with his labors, in 379. His letters are major sources of information about the life of the church in the 4th century. His Hexaemeron, or interpretation of the creation through the Genesis account, is a masterpiece of early Christian scriptural theology, and shows him as a moderate Origenist, with a fine feel for the moral power of scripture. His treatise Against Eunomius was a major force revitalizing the Nicene resistance, and he did much in his time to persuade the Homoiousians that their position was in substance reconcilable with that of the Homoousians, something that historically speaking was a key element for the long-term success of the Nicene cause. His work in his church as teacher and public defender of his town, as well as his learned canonical writings (setting wise rules of governance that the Eastern Church formally endorsed as universal authorities at the Quinisext Council of 692), made Basil a model for future eastern bishops, and in

Byzantine times he was designated along with Gregory Nazianzen and John Chrysostom as one of the "Three Holy Hierarchs," the most important bishop theologians of the ancient period. His reputation as one of the most important early monastic theorists also gave him a reputation among the eastern ascetics akin to the greatest of the monastic theorists, Antony, and Theodore the Studite.

SEE ALSO: Cappadocian Fathers; Monasticism; St. Gregory of Nazianzus (Gregory the Theologian) (329–390)

REFERENCES AND SUGGESTED READINGS

Clarke, W. K. L. (1913) St. Basil the Great: A Study in Monasticism. Cambridge: Cambridge University Press.

Holman, S. R. (2001) The Hungry Are Dying: Beggars and Bishops in Roman Cappadocia. Oxford: Oxford University Press.

Jackson, B. (1989) St. Basil: Letters and Select Works. Grand Rapids, MI: Eerdmans.

Rousseau, P. (1994) Basil of Caesarea. Berkeley: University of California Press.

St. Constantine the Emperor (ca. 271–337)

JULIA KONSTANTINOVSKY

Constantine I was an enigmatic figure yet a unique saint in the Orthodox Church: the first Christian emperor (discounting the possible candidacy of Philip the Arab), Constantine abolished the persecution of Christians, making Christianity a favored state religion. His status as the benefactor of the church and Christ's emissary on earth is reflected in his titles in Orthodoxy as "the Great" and "Equal-to-the-Apostles."

Flavius Valerius Constantinus was born to the military officer Constantius and St. Helena, in Naissus (Nish in Serbia), on February 27 between 271 and 273. His youth corresponded to the time his father was a junior Caesar in the First Tetrarchy. Classically and militarily educated while held as Diocletian's hostage at the Nicomedian court, Constantine fought (in the 290s) under Diocletian and Galerius in Asia, witnessing the outbreak of the Great Persecution of Christians (303–13), though playing no role therein. Eusebius styles Constantine an early sympathizer of Christianity, while the pagan sources (notably Pan.Lat. 6.21.4–5) and coin evidence suggest his enduring links with the Apollinine Sol Invictus cult.

On his accession, which began the civil war, Constantine spent several years eliminating all of his political rivals. Assuming the purple in July 306 on the death of his father Constantius in York, Constantine defeated Maximian Daia Augustus (his father-in-law) in 310. In 312 he presided over a miraculous victory over Maxentius (Maximian's son) in the famous battle of the Milvian Bridge at Rome. Lactantius maintains (De Mortibus Persecutorum 44.5–6) that shortly before the battle Constantine had an epiphanic dream instructing him to inscribe "the heavenly sign of God" (the Chi-Rho shaped mark of Christ, labarum) upon his soldiers' shields. The ensuing victory convinced the emperor of Christ's divine power and his particular gift of favor to his dominion. By 323 he had become the empire's sole ruler.

After 312 Constantine manifested himself as a Christian and protector of the church by stopping the persecution of Christians (Edict of Milan, 313), initiating extensive construction of Christian buildings (notably Rome's Lateran Basilica, Bethlehem, and other buildings later in Rome and Palestine), ordering that the property of North African Christians confiscated in the persecutions should be restored, and addressing the North African Donatist problem. In 325 he was requested by Alexander Bishop of Alexandria to help resolve a bitter dispute (the Arian controversy) about the status of the Second Person of the Trinity. Constantine's response was to organize the first general church council at his palace in Nicea in 325. The resulting conciliar creed anathematized Arius, famously proclaiming the Son to be "consubstantial" (*homoousion*) with the Father, a mainstay of the Orthodox and many other Christian traditions. So overwhelming was the participant bishops' banquet at the emperor's palace that Eusebius (an eyewitness) strikingly likened it to the eschatological gathering of saints in Christ's kingdom, and compared Constantine to Christ. Constantine died on May 22, 337, having received baptism at the hands of bishop Eusebius of Nicomedia while on a military expedition.

Despite committing acts hardly compatible with Christian precepts (having his wife Fausta and son Crispus executed, 325), Constantine's impact on imperial Christianity was profound. By 337, Christianity had become the official state religion; public pagan sacrifices had become outlawed; Christian clergy had joined the state elite; Palestine had been reclaimed for Christianity; Constantinople, the new Christian capital named after Constantine, had replaced the old pagan Byzantium. The Orthodox Church commemorates him on May 21, together with his mother Helena.

SEE ALSO: Council of Nicea I (325); St. Athanasius of Alexandria (ca. 293–373)

REFERENCES AND SUGGESTED READINGS

Edwards, M. J. (ed.) (2003) *Constantine and Christendom: The Oration to the Saints.* Liverpool: Liverpool University Press.

Eusebius of Caesarea (1989) *Historia Ecclesiastica*, trans. G. A. Williamson. London: Penguin.

Eusebius of Caesarea (1999) *The Life of Constantine*, trans. A. Cameron and S. Hall. Oxford: Oxford University Press.

Lactantius (1886) *Of the Manner in Which the Persecutors Died (De Mortibus Persecutorum)*, trans. W. Fletcher, in A. Roberts, J. Donaldson, and A. Cleveland Coxe (eds.) *Ante-Nicene Fathers*, vol. 7. Buffalo: Christian Literature Publishing.

Lenski, N. (ed.) (2006) *The Age of Constantine.* Cambridge: Cambridge University Press.

St. Cyril of Alexandria (ca. 378–444)

JOHN A. MCGUCKIN

Although he himself saw his role as a continuator of St. Athanasius, and though the ecumenical conciliar tradition later wove in much of the Cappadocian fathers and Latin patristic thought into his conceptions, St. Cyril is undoubtedly the single most important theologian of the Orthodox tradition who wrote on the person of Christ (Christology). He was the major figure, both intellectually and politically, in the great crisis of doctrine in the international church of the 5th century, and presided over the Third Ecumenical Council of Ephesus (431), where the teaching of Nestorius was condemned, and his own teaching, that affirmed the single subjectivity of the Divine Logos personally present in Jesus, the incarnate Lord, was adopted. Cyril's teaching went on to determine the agenda of three following ecumenical councils up to the 7th century.

Cyril was a native of Egypt, and when his uncle Theophilus became the archbishop of Alexandria in 385, he brought the young man to Alexandria for advanced studies. In 403, when he was 25 years old, Cyril was ordained lector, and in the same year attended Theophilus at the notorious Synod of the Oak, which deposed John Chrysostom. At his uncle's death in 412,

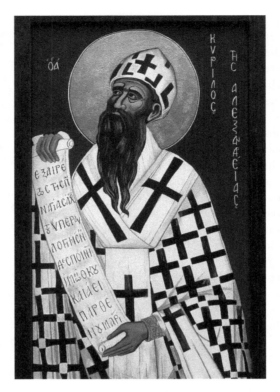

Plate 63   Contemporary icon of St. Cyril of Alexandria. By Eileen McGuckin. The Icon Studio: www.sgtt.org.

after a tumultuous election, Cyril was consecrated archbishop. His early years were marked by several major conflicts between the Christians and both the pagan and Jewish factions of the city. At the same time, he was using the monastic movement to advance the Christian evangelization of a country where the old religions still held considerable sway. After 428 Cyril was increasingly drawn into conflict with the new archbishop of Constantinople, Nestorius, who conceived of two centers of operation simultaneously present in the life of Christ: one human and one divine, with one sometimes predominating over the other. Cyril denounced this as heretical, insisting that Jesus was wholly and completely divine, thus only one single person, and that person God. For Cyril,

everything that Jesus did, whether it was a human act such as sleeping, or a powerful act such as raising the dead, was equally a work of the single divine Lord, now embodied within history. The divine power present in the humanity was also an archetype of how God had intended to "divinize" the human condition in the act of incarnation. Thus Christ is the pattern of the world's salvation. The process of deification is best exemplified in the reception of the Eucharist, the "life-giving blessing" of the divine flesh that immortalizes the believer. It was a dynamic Christology which eventually came to represent the classical statement of the Christian East, but not without major resistance on the way, especially from theologians in Rome and Syria. The Council of Ephesus, where Cyril was judge and jury simultaneously, caused great bitterness in its aftermath, and the emperor's negotiators had to work for several years to restore church communion, especially between Alexandria and Antioch. Eventually, in 433, a compromise was agreed on (the Formula of Reunion) where important points of the Antiochene position (Christ had two authentic natures – both human and divine) could be reconciled with Cyril's insistence that Christ was a single reality, one divine person, but the precise ramifications of that agreement still needed much clarifying debate, and in default of this it was inevitable that the whole argument would soon break out again. It did so with great force in the following generation. St. Cyril died on June 27, 444, a little short of his seventieth year. He is known in the church as the "Seal [*sphragis*] of the Fathers."

SEE ALSO: Christ; Deification; Eucharist; Nestorianism; Soteriology

REFERENCES AND SUGGESTED READINGS

McGuckin, J. A. (1994) *St. Cyril of Alexandria and the Christological Controversy: Its History, Theology and Texts.* Leiden: E. J. Brill.
Russell, N. (2000) *Cyril of Alexandria.* London: Routledge.

St. Dionysius the Areopagite

PETER C. BOUTENEFF

Acts 17.34 mentions one Dionysius the Areopagite among St. Paul's converts. Eusebius (*Church History* 3.4) identifies this figure as the first bishop of Athens. Later on the name came to be identified with St. Denys, first bishop of Paris. Yet the most enduring legacy associated with Dionysius the Areopagite is a corpus of four larger works and ten letters, these latter also constituting something like a self-contained treatise. These writings, appearing for the first time in the 6th century under this authorship, place themselves (pseudepigraphically) in the apostolic context: they are addressed to personalities such as John the Evangelist and speak of witnessing the darkening of the sun at Christ's crucifixion. Their provenance went virtually unquestioned until the late Middle Ages. Owing both to their content and their alleged sub-apostolic origins, they were deeply influential on subsequent Christian authors, notably Maximos the Confessor, John Scotus Eriugena, John of Damascus, Thomas Aquinas, Gregory Palamas, and the anonymous author of *The Cloud of Unknowing*, the very title of which is taken from Dionysius' *Mystical Theology*. Anachronisms in liturgical practice and in theologico-philosophical terminology have since conspired to make it impossible to date this corpus before the end of the 5th century or later. Certain liturgical details have suggested a Syrian monastic identity to an otherwise unidentified author. Orthodox theologians have tended to react ambivalently to the increasingly evident impossibility of identifying the 1st-century bishop with the written corpus, almost as if they ignore its significance. The Dionysian writings lose none of their credibility owing to the "problem" of authorship; they rise or fall in Orthodox esteem on the basis of their content alone. The feast day of St. Dionysius the Areopagite, October 3, officially commemorates one sole person, and the hymnography conflates the martyred bishop with the author-mystic.

Other controversies surround the content of the corpus itself: its message is expressed in the language of Middle-Platonism, and Jesus Christ is scarcely mentioned by name. A sympathetic appraisal, arguably regnant in contemporary

Orthodox scholarship (Golitzin 1994; Louth 2002), avers that the treatises were written as a missionary outreach to educated Platonists. The pseudonym itself, it is argued, was chosen to identify the works as the product of the "conversion" of Greek philosophy to the gospel of Christ. Others (Meyendorff 1975) have contested that the corpus effectively amounts to a Platonic treatise with merely a Christian veneer.

By the 20th century Dionysius' main influence on Orthodox theologians lay in his apophaticism. Vladimir Lossky, the title of whose flagship monograph *The Mystical Theology of the Eastern Church* testifies to his commitment to the Dionysian heritage, constructed his entire theological outlook on the basis of apophaticism as construed by Dionysius (and Eckhart), contrary to what he saw as a Thomist "essentialism." Christos Yannaras also steeped himself in Dionysius as a part of his broader engagement with Martin Heidegger, similarly taking God's radical and essential non-knowability as the starting point of any contemporary Orthodox theological reflection. Yannaras further explored implications of the apophatic semiotics of Dionysius' *The Divine Names*, which had also been taken up by Jean-Luc Marion and Jacques Derrida.

SEE ALSO: Angels; Apophaticism; St. Gregory Palamas (1296–1359); St. Maximos the Confessor (580–662)

REFERENCES AND SUGGESTED READINGS

Golitzin, A. (1994) "Et Introibo ad altare dei: The Mystagogy of Dionysius Areopagita," *Analecta Vlatadon* 59. Thessaloniki: George Dedousis.

Lossky, V. (1976). *The Mystical Theology of the Eastern Church*. Crestwood, NY: St. Vladimir's Seminary Press.

Louth, A. (2002) *Denys the Areopagite*. London: Continuum.

Meyendorff, J. (1975) "Pseudo-Dionysius," in *Christ in Eastern Christian Thought*. Crestwood, NY: St. Vladimir's Seminary Press, pp. 91–111.

Yannaras, C. (2007) *On the Absence and Unknowability of God: Heidegger and the Areopagite*. London: T&T Clark.

St. Dorotheos of Gaza (6th c.)

THOMAS KITSON

We know Dorotheos primarily from his own *Discourses* and from his correspondence with the "Old Men" of Gaza, Sts. Barsanuphius and John. He was born wealthy in early 6th-century Antioch and probably studied rhetoric at Gaza before entering the Monastery of Abbot Seridos at Tawatha, not far from the city. Seridos charged him with supervising the monastery's guest house and then, because he had medical knowledge, its infirmary, which was a donation of Dorotheos' brother. Dorotheos handled John's correspondence for nine years preceding the recluse's death in 543, when Barsanuphius decided to forego all human contact. Little is known of Dorotheos' subsequent life and whether or not he succeeded Seridos as abbot. He may have sought a more solitary contemplative life by moving from Tawatha's coenobium to the Lavra. John Moschos mentioned Dorotheos briefly in his *Spiritual Meadow*.

Dorotheos' *Discourses* may have been compiled before the 7th century, soon after his death. The earliest extant manuscripts of his work are in Arabic and Georgian (9th century), while the first Greek manuscript, including the Studite preface, dates to the 10th century. Dorotheos' main sources are scripture, especially the gospels and Psalms, and the *Apophthegmata* of the desert fathers, which he imbibed from Barsanuphius and John. He also cites liberally from the Cappadocian fathers, from Evagrios Pontike, and, it seems, from an early Greek translation of St. John Cassian's *Conferences*. Thus, he crucially combines the experience of the Egyptian desert with Syrian practices and the sophisticated theology of the Cappadocians to shape the ascetic life. Dorotheos exhorts listeners to cut off the will through humility and obedience, frequently citing Christ's injunction: "Learn of me, for I am meek and humble of heart, and you shall find rest for your souls" (Mt. 11.29). These themes ground the *Life of Dositheos*, Dorotheos' young disciple. They are also exemplified by Dorotheos' plain-spoken use of anecdotes from his own life, his willingness to risk losing the respect of his listeners by giving sometimes unseemly evidence against himself.

The christological and Origenist controversies that raged in Palestine during the 6th century colored the *Discourses*' initial reception. St. Theodore the Studite attested to their orthodoxy in the late 8th century, although it is possible that St. John Klimakos had already written the *Ladder of Divine Ascent* with them in mind. Dorotheos' influence spread with the Studite monastic reforms, especially to Mount Athos, and his works were read in refectories throughout the Greek East, along with those of St. Ephrem and the desert *Apophthegmata*. St. Nil Sorskii partially translated Dorotheos into Church Slavonic in the 15th century. Since Dorotheos' writings also indicate early traditions of the Jesus Prayer, they were incorporated into St. Paisy Velichovsky's hesychast renewal movement. St. Theophan the Recluse accordingly appended Dorotheos' works,

which had been translated and published separately by the Optina Hermitage in the 1850s, to the 19th-century Russian translation of the *Philokalia*.

SEE ALSO: Cappadocian Fathers; Desert Fathers and Mothers; Hesychasm; Jesus Prayer; Optina; *Philokalia*; Non-Possessors (Nil Sorskii); Pontike, Evagrios (ca. 345–399); St. John Klimakos (ca. 579–ca. 659); St. Paisy Velichovsky (1722–1794); St. Theophan (Govorov) the Recluse (1815–1894); Sts. Barsanuphius and John (6th c.)

REFERENCES AND SUGGESTED READINGS

Chryssavgis, J. (trans.) (2003) *Barsanuphius and John, Letters from the Desert: A Selection of Questions and Responses*. Crestwood, NY: St. Vladimir's Seminary Press.
Wheeler, E. (trans.) (1977) *Dorotheos of Gaza: Discourses and Sayings*. Kalamazoo: Cistercian Publications.

St. Elizaveta Feodorovna (1864–1918)

KONSTANTIN GAVRILKIN

Born as Princess Elizabeth Alexandra Luise Alice of Hesse, she was the older sister of Alexandra of Hesse, the future wife of Tsar Nicholas II (1872–1918). In 1884 Elizabeth became Orthodox and married Grand Duke Sergei (1857–1905), the fifth son of Emperor Alexander II (d. 1881). She assumed the name of Grand Duchess Elizaveta Feodorovna of Russia and quite soon became actively involved in various charities, especially for women and children from poor and destitute families, creating for them jobs, hospitals, schools, and affordable housing. In 1891 the couple moved to

GRAND DUCHESS ELIZABETH FEODOROVNA

Plate 64 Portrait of St. Elizaveta Feodorovna as Princess "Ella" before her widowhood and monastic profession. Topham Picturepoint/Topfoto.

Moscow, where her husband was to serve as governor general. In 1905 the terrorist Ivan Kaliaev assassinated Grand Duke Sergei by throwing a bomb at his carriage.

Widowed, Elizaveta decided to stay in Moscow and dedicate her life to poor and sick women and children through personally supervised charities in a convent she founded in 1907. The Marfo-Mariinskaia Obitel' Miloserdiia (Mercy Convent of Saints Martha and Mary) was established on the territory of the estate near the Kremlin, purchased with the funds raised from the sale of the Duchess's personal items and jewelry. It was rebuilt to include a hospital, pharmacy, and soup kitchen for the poor, a library, and school for girls and women, and was officially opened in 1909. In 1910 Grand Duchess Elizaveta became a nun herself. According to the statute of the convent, approved by the holy synod in 1911 (and revised in 1914), she was to remain the head of the convent for life. During World War I, Elizaveta helped with creating moveable hospitals, medical emergency teams, and commissions for accommodating the wounded who returned from the war zone and for helping the families of military personnel. Her convent was reorganized to accommodate a military hospital where 150 nuns worked under her direct supervision.

In addition, after the death of her husband who had chaired the Imperial Orthodox Palestine Society since its establishment in 1882, Elizaveta assumed his post and held it until her resignation after the February Revolution of 1917. The society supported Orthodox institutions in the Holy Land (churches, monasteries, hospitals, and schools), pilgrimages, and scientific studies of the region.

She refused to leave Russia after the Bolshevik coup in October 1917. Arrested in the spring of 1918 with the nun Barbara, her assistant, she was sent to Siberia, where other members of the Romanov family had also been imprisoned. In July 1918 she and others were thrown alive into a mine shaft a few miles from Alapaevsk. Their bodies were recovered in the fall of the same year by the White Army, which advanced to the region in October 1918. Eventually, the bodies of Elizaveta Feodorovna and the nun Barbara were taken to Jerusalem and buried in the Church of St. Mary Magdalene, according to the will of the Grand Duchess expressed in 1888 during her visit to Jerusalem. In 1992 the Moscow patriarchate canonized her and Barbara as new martyrs of Russia.

SEE ALSO: New Martyrs; Russia, Patriarchal Orthodox Church of; Women in Orthodoxy

REFERENCES AND SUGGESTED READINGS

Mager, H. (1998) *Elizabeth, Grand Duchess of Russia.* New York: Carroll and Graf.
Miller, L. (1991) *Grand Duchess Elizabeth of Russia.* Redding, CA: Nikodemos Orthodox Publication Society.

Tsitriniak, A. and Khemlin, M. (2009) *Velikaia kniaginia Elizaveta Fedorovna*. Moscow: Tsentr knigi VGBIL im. M. I. Rudomino.

Warwick, C. (2006) *Ella: Princess, Saint and Martyr.* Hoboken, NJ: John Wiley & Sons, Inc.

St. Ephrem the Syrian (ca. 306–373/379)

KENNETH CARVELEY

Ephrem was born to Christian parents in Nisibis. Legend describes his father as a heathen priest. During his youth he was influenced by Bishop Jacob (d. 338; present at Nicea 325, possibly with Ephrem) who appointed him as a church teacher. During the episcopate of Bishop Vologeses, the Persian Shapur II besieged the city and Ephrem migrated with the people to the Christian city of Edessa in 363, where he is said to have worked in the bath house. Teaching in the *schola* he defended the Orthodox Nicene teaching (the Edessene Orthodox group then called "Palutians," so named after Bishop Palut), and countered Arianism, Marcionism, the Bardesainians, and other Gnostic heresies. A prolific Syriac hymn writer, Ephrem wrote poetic homilies, biblical commentaries, and graceful hymns affirming Orthodox Christology, meant to counter the metrical hymns of Bardesanes' son Harmodios. He was possibly employed as liturgical chant writer for a community of Syriac women ascetics. His chief writings include *Carmina Nisibena, Hymns On Faith, Hymns on Paradise, On Virginity, Against Heresies*, and an (attributed) panegyric on St. Basil of Caesarea. His hymns, many of which mirror Hebraic parallel form, constitute part of the Syriac Church's liturgy, particularly for major feasts; a very popular prayer of repentance of St. Ephrem ("Lord and Master of my Life") is preserved in the regular Orthodox Lenten cycle of prayers. Sayings attributed to him appear in the *Apophthegmata Patrum*, and he had a distinctive influence over the traditions of Syro-Byzantine hymnody and liturgical chant. Scholars are still in the process, however, of disentangling the real Ephrem (the Syrian sage) from the so-called Greco-Byzantine Ephrem, with whom he was confounded at an early date. He supported the people of Edessa indefatigably during persecution by the Arian Emperor Valens (370–2) and in times of severe famine. Later Edessene hagiographic tradition developed his life and legend extensively.

SEE ALSO: Council of Nicea I (325); Gnosticism; Hymnography; Virgins

REFERENCES AND SUGGESTED READINGS

Brock, S. (1992) *The Luminous Eye: The Spiritual World Vision of St. Ephrem.* Kalamazoo: Cistercian Publications.

Brock, S. (1999) "St. Ephrem in the Eyes of Later Syriac Liturgical Tradition," *Hugoye Journal of Syriac Studies* 2, 1.

McVey, K. E. (trans.) (1989) *Ephrem the Syrian: Hymns.* New York: Paulist Press.

Mayer, R. T. (trans.) (1964) *Palladius: The Lausiac History.* New York: Newman Press.

Schaff, P. and Wace, H. (eds.) (1976) *Gregory the Great, Ephraim Syrus.* Aphrahat Select Library of Nicene and Post-Nicene Fathers, 2nd Series, vol. 13, part 2. Grand Rapids, MI: Eerdmans.

St. Feofan *see* Theophan the Greek (ca. 1340–1410)

St. Filaret (Philaret) Drozdov (1782–1867)

KONSTANTIN GAVRILKIN

Vasilii M. Drozdov was born into a clerical family in Kolomna and studied at the seminary in St. Sergius Lavra, where he also taught after graduation and was tonsured a monk with the name Filaret. Brilliant erudition, colorful preaching, and a gift for languages were decisive in his appointment in 1812 to the post of rector of St. Petersburg Theological Academy, where he had been teaching since 1810, and in 1817 he was elevated to the rank of bishop of Revel and vicar of St. Petersburg. During his rectorship (1812–19), Filaret completely revised the curriculum of all the Russian ecclesiastical schools, introduced the study of European scholarly literature, and practically created biblical studies as an academic discipline in Russia. Because of his organizational skills and effective leadership, he was also gradually introduced to a number of state and ecclesiastical committees, including the holy synod in 1819. Very shortly, however, because of intrigues and the growing influence of conservatives over Tsar Alexander I, he was removed from the capital though, after short terms at Tver' and then Iaroslavl', he was appointed archbishop of Moscow in 1821, becoming metropolitan in 1826.

From 1814 to 1826 Filaret was active in the Bible Society, believing that translation of the Scriptures into modern Russian (they were then available only in Church Slavonic) would revive the Russian Church. However, after printing a few books (the Psalms in 1822 and the New Testament in 1823) the society was closed down at the beginning of Nicholas I's reign (1825–55) amid accusations that its leadership, including Filaret, were "freemasons" seeking to destroy the Orthodox Church. Filaret remained at odds with Nicholaevan bureaucrats, and after the early 1840s would not attend meetings of the synod until the beginning of Alexander II's reign in 1855. Nevertheless, it was during the rule of Nicholas I that Filaret acquired the reputation of being a great hierarch. Despite his withdrawal

from the synod, he was consulted on every important question, and his opinions, decisions, and reviews of various ecclesiastical and secular subjects were regularly published. Even though he was academically brilliant, Filaret did not have the opportunity to develop truly scholarly work after he left St. Petersburg, although he continued to follow European scholarship throughout his life. Administrative and pastoral duties, together with frequent liturgical services and constant preaching, consumed his time. His ascetical lifestyle, pastoral wisdom, administrative efficiency, remarkable knowledge of the patristic tradition and of canon law, and, most of all, his unrivaled preaching, made him the most influential bishop of the Russian Orthodox Church in the 19th century, overshadowing every other Russian ecclesiastic from the 19th century onward. He was canonized in 1994.

SEE ALSO: Russia, Patriarchal Orthodox Church of

REFERENCES AND SUGGESTED READINGS

Filaret, Mitropolit of Moscow (1873–85). *Sochineniia: slova i rechi*, 5 vols. Moscow: A. I. Mamontov.

Filaret, Mitropolit of Moscow (1877–84) *Pis'ma k namestniku Sviato-Troitskoi Sergievy lavry arkhimandritu Antoniiu, 1831–1867*, 4 vols. Moscow: A. I. Mamontov.

Filaret, Mitropolit of Moscow (1885–8) *Sobranie mnenii i otzyvov po uchebnym i tserkovnym voprosam*, 6 vols., ed. Savva, Archbishop of Tver'. Moscow: Synod. Tip.

Filaret, Mitropolit of Moscow (1903–16) *Polnoe sobranie rezoliutsii*, 5 vols. Moscow: Dushepoleznoe chtenie.

Tsurikov, V. (ed.) (2003) *Philaret, Metropolitan of Moscow (1782–1867): Perspectives on the Man, His Works, and His Time*. Jordanville, NY: Variable Press.

St. Gregory the Great, Pope (ca. 540–604)

JOHN A. MCGUCKIN

Gregorius Magnus was one of the most important of the Late Antique bishops of Rome. He was a masterful political administrator and a significant theologian who, if not innovative in his writing, served to arrange and codify much that was important in the Latin theological tradition, and pass it on in a condensed form that would assume immense weight for the dawning medieval West. His work codifying and simplifying much of St. Augustine's complicated thought made it possible for Augustinianism to be passed on in a popular form, so as to become the most significant single strand of the later Latin tradition.

Gregory belonged to an aristocratic Christian family in Rome at a time when the fortunes of both Italy and the ancient city were in decline because of Justinian's wars of re-conquest, and later (from 586 onwards) because of raids from Lombardian brigands from the North. His father was a Christian senator, and in 573 Gregory himself became the prefect of Rome (the highest civic office possible). Soon afterwards he announced his retirement from public life and dedicated his extensive properties in Rome and Sicily to the cause of Christian asceticism, in the form of the retired life of the Sophist. His large villa on the Caelian hill, near the Colosseum, became his monastery of St. Andrew (still functioning), where he lived a life of scholarship and prayer with companions. As a dedicated ascetic, however, he fell under ecclesiastical obedience, and soon Pope Pelagius II ordered him to resume public service for the church. Accordingly, he was ordained deacon and sent as papal ambassador (*apocrisarius*) to Constantinople, where he lived from 579 to 586, engaging in dispute with the Patriarch Eutyches. In this period Gregory began one of his greatest works, the *Magna Moralia in Job*, designed as an ascetical commentary on the text of Job, for the use of his monastic companions. It assumed the status of a paradigmatic patristic book of exegesis for the later West, constantly seeking a moral end to scriptural reading.

After resuming his duties back in Italy as papal secretary at Rome, Gregory administered the church during the time of plague in the year 590, and on Pope Pelagius' death in that same year, he was himself elected pope (much against his inclination) as Gregory I. He rallied the city with extensive penitential processions to ask for God's mercy. Later tales spoke of a vision of an angel putting away his sword over Hadrian's mausoleum (now Castel San Angelo) where today the statue of the same is a familiar Roman landmark. Gregory began a highly efficient administration in Rome, a symbolic end to a long decline of the Roman church and city that began with Constantine's removal of the capital eastwards to Constantinople. He profoundly monasticized the Roman church administration, despite protests of the ordinary clergy, so beginning a long tradition along these lines that would mark western Catholicism ever afterwards. His successful leadership over Rome and its province led to his papacy becoming a symbol of how the papal office could develop in the future.

Gregory, realizing the futility of the local Byzantine imperial administration at Ravenna, independently negotiated peace with the Lombard invaders. Many later reforms (such as the liturgical changes that came to be called Gregorian chant) were retrospectively fathered on him. His writings on theological matters were chiefly pastoral, biblical, and hagiographical. His extensive biblical exegesis and theological comments were a moderated and simplified form of St. Augustine, and Gregory did more than any other (except perhaps the Latin theologian Prosper of Aquitaine) to elevate Augustine's influence over the whole western church, giving a theological preeminence to the doctrine of grace, and adding his own views on the need for a cleansing post-death purification of souls, a view that eventually grew into the distinctive Roman doctrine of Purgatory. His *Pastoral Rule* (written largely for his own guidance soon after he assumed the papacy) was designed as a manual of instruction for a bishop. It became a standard text in western church schools. In line with the central premise of the current educational system of his day, he elevates rhetoric as the chief tool of the leader. But he also adds that the bishop is above all else a pastor of souls, as well as the leader and expositor of the divine word of scripture. Gregory's exegetical works standardized the subsequent western view of biblical exegesis as the three stages of house-building, where the foundations were the exposition of the literal and historical sense of the text; followed by the roof and walls of the allegorical sense which interprets higher Christian mysteries present within the old narratives; and finally the beautiful decorations that perfect and finish off a building, in the form of moral counsels designed to elevate the lives of the hearers. His insistence that a preacher should pay attention to all three aspects of a text proved determinative for the later western Middle Ages. His *Dialogues* were also immensely popular. In these four books Gregory recounts the lives of Italian ascetic saints. The miraculous element abounds in them, marking an important stage in the development of the cult of the saint at a time when, both in Byzantium and the West, the fundamental idea on how to access the divine presence and favor was

undergoing radical reconstruction, and local democratization. In the second book of *Dialogues* Gregory popularized St. Benedict, the hermit of Nursia, thus providing an enormous impetus to the spread of Benedictinism as the central exemplar for Latin monasticism. His spiritual writings had a similarly determinative effect on the Latin Middle Ages insofar as he emphasized the monastic life as the "perfect" way of contemplation, far excelling the lay married state.

In the Orthodox tradition Gregory is mainly known for the liturgy attributed to him of the Presanctified Gifts, now celebrated in the course of Great Lent. This ritual is basically a communion service attached to a penitential form of Vespers, and served to allow the communion of the faithful on Wednesdays and Fridays in the course of the Great Fast, when the divine liturgy was not celebrated. The holy gifts are consecrated (presanctified) at the liturgy of the preceding Sunday. In the Orthodox tradition Gregory is known (from the title of his hagiographic work) as Pope St. Gregory the Dialogist.

SEE ALSO: Papacy; Vespers (Hesperinos)

REFERENCES AND SUGGESTED READINGS

Dudden, F. H. (1905) *Gregory the* Great, 2 vols. London: Longmans, Green.
Evans, G. (1986) *The Thought of Gregory the Great.* Cambridge: Cambridge University Press.
Markus, R. A. (1983) *From Augustine to Gregory the Great.* London: Variorum.
Richards, J. (1980) *Consul of God: The Life and Times of Gregory the Great.* London: Routledge and Kegan Paul.
Straw, C. (1988) *Gregory the Great: Perfection in Imperfection.* Berkeley: University of California Press.

St. Gregory of Nazianzus (Gregory the Theologian) (329–390)

JOHN A. MCGUCKIN

Gregory was the son of a wealthy land-owning bishop in Nazianzus, Cappadocia (also named Gregory). His father was the second bishop of the town, following after someone who was described as a "rustic," and after his consecration he built a splendid marble shrine to replace the old wooden church that had previously existed. In many ways Bishop Gregory the Elder and his more famous son demonstrate the "ascent" of the church in the Constantinian era. The younger Gregory received the finest local schooling, taught partly by his uncle, the rhetorician Amphilokios, and then (with his brother Caesarios) was sent to Alexandria, and finally to Athens, where he spent ten years perfecting his rhetorical style and literary education. Gregory the Theologian thus emerged as the finest Christian rhetorician of his day, and certainly the most learned bishop of the entire early church.

His sea journey to Athens in 348 was interrupted by a violent storm and, fearing for his life, Gregory seems to have promised himself to God's service, a vow he fulfilled by accepting baptism at Athens and beginning his lifelong commitment to the ascetical life. It was a dedication he saw as entirely consonant with the commitment to celibacy required of the serious philosopher. Gregory did much to advance the theory of early Christian asceticism, but always with the stress on seclusion in the service of scholarly reflection. He regularly described Christianity as "Our Philosophy." At Athens he shared lodgings with his close friend Basil of Caesarea, with whose later Christian career he was closely associated. Returning to Cappadocia, in 358, Gregory's plans to live in scholarly

retirement on his family estate were rudely interrupted by his father, who forcibly ordained him to the priesthood in 361. Gregory fled in protest to Basil's monastic estates at Annesi, where he edited the *Philocalia of Origen*, a collation of texts from the great Alexandrian theologian of the 3rd century, whose reputation was increasingly being attacked. The purpose of the edition was to focus on the exegetical brilliance of the Alexandrian scholar, and deflect attention from the metaphysical speculative elements that had tarnished his ecclesiastical reputation. Throughout all his later life Gregory represents a very profound, but also very skilfully moderated, form of Origenian thought.

As a priest, Gregory was no longer free to devote himself to the life of scholarly detachment that he had imagined for himself, and soon returned to assist in the administration of his local church alongside his father, whose increasing age and illness placed large demands on his son. His letters from this time give us the only window we possess on the life and conditions of St. Basil and St. Macrina's monastic foundation on the family estates. In 363 Gregory led the literary attack against Julian the Apostate's imperial policy of barring Christian professors from educational posts (*Invectives Against Julian*). In 364 he negotiated Basil's reconciliation with his estranged bishop, and eventually in 370 assisted him to attain the archiepiscopal throne at Caesarea. Thereafter began their long alienation. Basil (in his many fights) accused him of pusillanimity, and Gregory regarded Basil as having become too high and mighty. In 372 Basil and Gregory's father conspired, against his will, to appoint him as bishop of Sasima, and accordingly Gregory found himself placed as a suffragan bishop of Basil's in a rather miserable frontier town, at the center of a lively row with the neighboring metropolitan over church revenues. When he realized that he was supposed to galvanize street armies and thrash the followers of the rival metropolitan, he simply refused to occupy the see, leaving caustic (although funny) descriptions about it. He resumed duties of assisting his father as suffragan bishop of Nazianzus instead (quite oblivious to canons regulating episcopal successions), and began his series of episcopal homilies, all of which were taken down by scribes and edited at the end of his life for publication as a basic dossier of "sermons on every occasion" for a Christian bishop. In this guise they enjoyed an immense influence throughout the Byzantine centuries. His collected writings have been compared with the works of Demosthenes. In their purity and refinement of doctrine they have been rarely equalled. In the consummate power of their rhetoric, never.

From the outset Gregory stood for the Nicene cause of the *Homoousion* (the consubstantiality of the Son with the Father), and advanced it to the classic Neo-Nicene position of demanding that the *Homoousion* of the Holy Spirit (with the Father, and thus with the Son) should also be recognized. He thereby became one of the church's primary theological articulators of the classical doctrine of the Co-equal Trinity. He constantly pressured Basil to make his own position clear and led him, eventually, to break with his erstwhile mentor Eustathius of Sebaste and instead to declare openly for the deity of the Spirit of God, which he did in his famous classic *On the Holy Spirit*. On his father's death in 374 Gregory retired to monastic seclusion, but was summoned, after Valens' death gave new hope for a Nicene revival, by the hierarchs of the Council of Antioch (379) to assume the task of missionary apologist at Constantinople, where he had high-ranking family in residence. He began, in 379,

a series of lectures in Constantinople on the Nicene faith (the *Five Theological Orations*), and was recognized by the leading Nicene theologians, Meletius of Antioch, Eusebius of Samosata, and Peter of Alexandria (though not by Pope Damasus), as the true Nicene bishop of the city. When Theodosius took the capital in 380 his appointment was confirmed when the incumbent Arian bishop Demophilos was exiled. In 381 the Council of Constantinople was held in the city to establish the Nicene faith as standard in the eastern empire, and when its president, Meletius, died, Gregory was immediately elected in his place. His mild and reasoned leadership, and also probably his prosecution of the doctrine of the Homoousion of the Spirit, soon brought the council into crisis, for Theodosius was anxious that the party of 30 Pneumatomachian bishops (who admitted the inferior deity of, but denied the title "God" to, the Spirit) should be reconciled and Gregory was anxious that they should not. After they left the conciliar deliberations, refusing to admit any change to the pneumatological clauses of the creed, there were then calls for Gregory to initiate penal moves against dissidents. His response was that they ought to be forgiven as the gospel demanded, and that a mild treatment would be more likely to result in their return than any prosecution. This eirenic attitude lost him many friends at a time when scores were ready to be settled with Arians who had long been using state pressure against the Nicenes. Unable to convince the majority of the wisdom of his approach, Gregory bowed to increasing calls for his resignation, and decided to retire. He came back to his estates at Nazianzus and composed a large body of apologetic and theological poetry which gives crucial information on the controversies of the time. In his final years he focused chiefly on poetry (some of it very good) and prepared his orations for publication.

In the Byzantine era Gregory was the most studied of all the early Christian writers. His theological works against Apollinaris (especially *Letter 101 to Cledonius*) were cited as authorities at the Council of Chalcedon (451), where he was posthumously awarded the title "Gregory the Theologian." His writing on the Trinity was never rivaled in patristic times, and he is the chief architect of the church's understanding of how the divine unity coexists in three co-equal hypostases, as the essential dynamic of the salvation of the world.

SEE ALSO: Cappadocian Fathers; Council of Constantinople I (381); St. Basil of Caesarea (Basil the Great) (330–379)

REFERENCES AND SUGGESTED READINGS

McGuckin, J. A. (2001) *St. Gregory of Nazianzus: An Intellectual Biography.* Crestwood, NY: St. Vladimir's Seminary Press.

Norris, F. W. (1991) *Faith Gives Fullness to Reason: The Five Theological Orations of Gregory of Nazianzus – Text and Commentary.* Leiden: E. J. Brill.

Ruether, R. (1969) *Gregory of Nazianzus: Rhetor and Philosopher.* Oxford: Oxford University Press.

Winslow, D. F. (1979) *The Dynamics of Salvation: A Study in Gregory of Nazianzus.* Philadelphia: Philadelphia Patristic Foundation.

St. Gregory Palamas (1296–1359)

STEPHEN THOMAS

St. Gregory Palamas was born in 1296 in Constantinople into an aristocratic family, receiving a thorough education in Greek philosophy and rhetoric. His adoption of monasticism involved his whole family. Having tried this life on Mount Athos both as a solitary hermit and in a monastic community, he preferred to live with a small group of monks under the tutelage of a spiritual father. The writings of Barlaam the Calabrian led him to respond polemically, defending the hesychasts (those monks who practised inner stillness) against a philosophy so apophatic that it denied the possibility of experience of God. The whole of Palamas's theology addresses this question: if we cannot grasp God with the intellect, is he absolutely unknowable? Palamas argued that, just as the prophets of ancient Israel partially knew Christ as a foretaste of things to come, so do the hesychasts experience the glory of the Age to come in this life; it is a partially realized eschatology (Ware et al. 1995: 418). Palamas used a distinction between essence and energies to explain how God is knowable through divine revelation and can be experienced in the life of prayer: we know the uncreated energies of God, while his essence remains unknown. But while Palamas was competent in philosophy, especially that of Aristotle, and knew about the developments in the sciences of his time, he was not interested in an intellectual synthesis: having reviewed these, Palamas exclaims: "Where can we learn anything certain and free from deceit about God, about the world as a whole, about ourselves? Is it not from the teaching of the Spirit?" (Sinkiewicz 1988: 102–3; Ware et al. 1995: 354).

This is for from the medieval interest in human science burgeoning in the West during his time. Barlaam's teaching was universally rejected by the Orthodox Church, and he ended his days as a bishop, teaching Greek to Petrarch in Italy. A new challenge arose in Akyndinos, a former pupil of Palamas, who argued from a very static and formal view of tradition that the experiences of the hesychasts were not Orthodox. Against Akyndinos, Palamas eventually prevailed. He was appointed bishop of Thessalonica by the emperor, an appointment which saw him produce a series of pastoral sermons which encapsulate his teaching in a more popular way. He died in 1359 and was soon canonized (1368). His memory is celebrated in the liturgy on the second Sunday of Lent; no theologian is praised more highly as "a true follower and companion of thy namesake Gregory the Theologian" (Ware 1984: 318). Palamas was a theologian of "the glory of God," the light of Mount Tabor which shone upon three chosen apostles at the transfiguration of Jesus Christ (Mt. 17.1–8; Mk. 9.2–8; Lk. 9.28–36), these expressions being the biblical ones which correspond to the patristic formulations "divine or uncreated energy" and "uncreated light." This glory God chose to share with the human race. It is God's deifying grace transfiguring human life. That it is a matter of experience even in this earthly existence is the main feature of Palamas's understanding of Orthodoxy.

SEE ALSO: Deification; Grace; Hesychasm

REFERENCES AND SUGGESTED READINGS

Gendle, N. (trans.) (1983) *Gregory Palamas: The Triads*. London: SPCK.

Meyendorff, J. (1974) *St. Gregory Palamas and Orthodox Spirituality*. Crestwood, NY: St. Vladimir's Seminary Press.

Meyendorff, J. (1974) *A Study of Gregory Palamas*. Crestwood, NY: St. Vladimir's Seminary Press.

Sinkiewicz, R. W. (ed.) (1988) *Saint Gregory Palamas: The One Hundred and Fifty Chapters*. Toronto: Pontifical Institute of Medieval Studies.

Ware, K. and Mother Mary (eds. and trans.) (1984) *The Lenten Triodion*. London: Faber and Faber.

Ware, K, Palmer, G. E. H., and Sherrard, P. (eds. and trans.) (1995) *The Philokalia Volume IV*. London: Faber and Faber.

St. Herman of Alaska *see* Finland, Autonomous Orthodox Church of; United States of America, Orthodoxy in the

St. Ignatius Brianchaninov (1807–1867)

KONSTANTIN GAVRILKIN

Born to an aristocratic family, in 1822 Dmitrii A. Brianchaninov was sent by his father to St. Petersburg to enroll in the Imperial School of Military Engineers, despite his expressed desire to become a monk. While at school, Brianchaninov enjoyed the patronage of Tsar Nicholas I, as a student with exceptional intellectual and artistic gifts. During this time he also took part in the capital's literary circles, and this exposure to what became known as the Golden Age of Russian poetry played an important role in shaping the style of his religious writings, which have been praised for their literary quality and poetic eloquence. Although he graduated first in his class, Dmitrii immediately attempted to leave the military service for a monastic vocation, but Nicholas I refused his initial resignation in 1826. Only the next year, when Brianchaninov fell gravely ill and then repeated his request, did the emperor grant him release from military service.

In 1831 he was tonsured a monk with the name Ignatius, was ordained deacon, then priest, and for a short time he served as superior of a monastery in the Vologda diocese, only to resign a year later because of poor health. In 1833 Nicholas I made an imperial order to discover what had happened to his former protégé. Brianchaninov was then brought back to the capital and appointed higumen of the Troitse-Sergiev Monastery near Moscow. In the twenty-four years he spent there, the monastery was rebuilt, its liturgical life became exemplary, and Ignatius its superior became one of the prominent spiritual guides and writers of all Russia. In 1857 he was consecrated bishop of the Caucasus and Black Sea, although his tenure there lasted only four years: he had to resign in 1861 after falling seriously ill; and he spent the last years of his life at Nikolo-Babaevskii Monastery in the Kostroma diocese, where he died in 1867. He was canonized by the Russian Orthodox Church in 1988. His life and spiritual heritage can be properly understood in the context of the monastic revival associated with St. Paisy Velichkovsky, hesychasm, and the tradition of spiritual direction, of which the monastery Optina Pustyn' is the best-known example. He left a substantial body of writings, and it could be argued that many of his works are the finest prose ever written by a Russian ecclesiastic. The eight-volume Russian edition of his *Complete Works*, published in 2007 to celebrate the bicentennial of his birth, contains reflections on scripture and various theological subjects, writings on prayer and ascetic life, a Paterikon, poetic meditations, sermons, materials related to his episcopal administration, his reactions on contemporary political, ecclesiastical, and cultural life, and an extensive correspondence with state officials, clergy, monastics, and others. For a full bibliography of publications by and on Ignatii Brianchaninov (valid up to 2001), see Brianchaninov (2001–7, vol. 4: 644–776).

SEE ALSO: Hesychasm; *Philokalia*; Russia, Patriarchal Orthodox Church of; St. Paisy Velichovsky (1722–1794)

REFERENCES AND SUGGESTED READINGS

Brianchaninov, I. (1997) *The Arena: An Offering to Contemporary Monasticism*, trans. Fr. Lazarus. Joardanville: Holy Trinity Monastery.

Brianchaninov, I. (2001–7) *Polnoe sobranie tvorenii*, 8 vols., ed. A. N. Strizhev. Moscow: Palomnik.

Brianchaninov, I. (2006) *On the Prayer of Jesus*, trans. Fr. Lazarus. Boston: The New Seeds.

Sokolov, L. A. (1915) *Episkop Ignatii Brianchaninov: Ego zhizn', lichnost' I moral'no-asketicheskie vozzreniia*, 2 vols. Kiev: I-yi Kievskoi arteli pechatnago dela.

St. Innocent of Alaska *see* United States of America, Orthodoxy in the

St. Isaac the Syrian (7th c.)

JOHN A. MCGUCKIN

Also known as St. Isaac of Niniveh, one of the great ascetical and mystical writers of the Eastern Church. Isaac was a monk of the Chaldaean Church (or Assyrian Church of the East) from Beit Quatraye, possibly Qatar on the Persian Gulf. He was appointed bishop of Niniveh sometime before 680, but after a few months in the position resigned his charge and returned to the solitary life of an ascetic. In later life he became blind from his scholarly labors. His spiritual authority and the beauty of his writings on prayer and mystical experience made his works cherished by both the rival Monophysite and Nestorian factions of the Persian Church of his time. In the 9th century his texts on ascetical prayer were translated from the Syriac into Greek and Arabic versions, and came to Byzantium shortly after, where they had a large impact on the developing hesychastic spiritual theology. Isaac lays great stress on the sensibility of the grace of God in the heart, and is one of the most mature and gentle authors on the spiritual life from Christian antiquity. His writings were treasured on Mount Athos and highly regarded by St. Paisy Velichovsky in the time of the Philokalic revival (18th century) of Greek and Slavonic monastic spirituality. In recent years lost works have been rediscovered, and by virtue of new English translations he is once again becoming known as one of the great masters of early eastern Christian spirituality.

SEE ALSO: Assyrian Apostolic Church of the East; Hesychasm; Jesus Prayer; Monasticism; Monophysitism (including Miaphysitism); Nestorianism; *Philokalia*; St. Macarius (4th c.); St. Paisy Velichovsky (1722–1794)

REFERENCES AND SUGGESTED READINGS

Alfeyev, H. (2000) *The Spiritual World of Isaac the Syrian.* Cistercian Studies Series 175. Kalamazoo: Cistercian Publications.

Brock, S. (1995) Isaac of Niniveh (Isaac the Syrian): The Second Part. Chapters 4–41. Corpus Scriptorum Christianorum Orientalium 554–5; Scriptores Syri. 224–5. Louvain: Peters.

Miller, D. (trans.) (1984) *The Ascetical Homilies of St. Isaac The Syrian.* Boston: Holy Transfiguration Monastery.

Wensinck, A. J. (1923) *A Mystic Treatise by Isaac of Niniveh Translated from Bedjan's Syriac Text.* Amsterdam: Koninklijke Akademie van Wetenschappen.

St. John Cassian (ca. 360–ca. 435)

TARMO TOOM

St. John Cassian was a monastic writer, theologian, and renowned churchman. Little is known about his birth and upbringing.

Tradition suggests a Scythian origin and the Romanian Orthodox Church accordingly looks to him as a patron. Around 380, Cassian traveled to Bethlehem and then on to Egypt. In Scetis and Kellia Cassian learned the monastic wisdom from Abba Moses and Evagrios of Pontike (whose name Cassian never mentions for diplomatic reasons). The first Origenist crisis compelled him to move to Constantinople, where he was ordained to the diaconate by St. John Chrysostom. Here he became notable as an ecclesiastical diplomat. At Rome he sought help for John Chrysostom, and there Pope Leo asked him, as a bilingual westerner, to review and refute Nestorius's teachings (*On the Incarnation of the Lord* – written beween 429 and 430). Cassian was eventually ordained a priest and energetically promoted Egyptian monastic traditions in Gaul.

Although his conception of radical monastic asceticism was not generally or unqualifiedly accepted, Cassian nevertheless had a profound influence on western monasticism. St. Benedict recommended Cassian's *Conferences* and *Institutes* for the reading at Compline (Rule of Benedict 73) and Cassiodorus insisted that Cassian should be read "diligently" and "frequently" (Inst. 1.29) by all monks. Cassian is the only western father whose sayings have been included in the *Apophthegmata* and the collection of the *Philokalia* (1:72–108).

Gennadius (in *De Viris Illustribus* 62) gives a list of Cassian's works, noting that Cassian wrote "from personal experience." His two chief writings are the *Institutes* and the *Conferences*. The first is about the external aspects of monastic life and the eight evil thoughts, and the longer treatise of *Conferences* is about internal aspects, such as temptation, discernment, and chastity. *Conferences* 9–10, which include wonderful insights on unceasing and fiery prayer (see Ps. 70.1), were originally intended as the climax of the treatise. Purity of heart (Mt. 5.8) was Cassian's perceived goal (*scopos*) for all monastic striving, and the reign of God was its end (*finis*) (Conf. 1.4.1–3).

In the West, Cassian's admittance that "the slightest glimmer of good will" might be attributed to human effort was widely regarded as unacceptable in the light of the ascendant Augustinianism of the day (Conf. 13.7.1; cf. Prosper of Aquitaine, *Contra Collatorem*; Cassiodorus, *Institutiones* 1.29; *Decretum Gelasianum* V.7). Writing on this to the monks of Lerins, Cassian immediately added the qualification that even this good will arising from human effort was "stirred" by God (cf. Inst. 12.18; Conf. 13.9.5, 16.1). But it was enough to damage his later reputation. Cassian's emphasis on grace, as he speaks about free will, does not really allow one to accuse him of an alleged semi-Pelagianism (Inst. 12.14; Conf. 3.10, 15). He insisted that everyone was "in need of the Lord's help in whatever pertains to salvation" (Inst. 12.17). For him, sinlessness was an eschatological reality (Conf. 23). His liturgical feast day is February 29 (28).

SEE ALSO: Asceticism; Monasticism; *Philokalia*; Pontike, Evagrios (ca. 345–399); Prayer

REFERENCES AND SUGGESTED READINGS

Casiday, A. M. (2007) *Tradition and Theology in St. John Cassian*. Oxford: Oxford University Press.

Chadwick, O. (2008) *John Cassian*. Cambridge: Cambridge University Press.

Driver, S. D. (2003) *John Cassian and the Reading of Egyptian Monastic Culture*. London: Routledge.

Goodrich, R. J. (2007) *Contextualizing Cassian*. Oxford: Oxford University Press.

Merton, T. (2005) *Cassian and the Fathers*, ed. P. F. O'Connell. Kalamazoo: Cistercian Publications.

Stewart, C. (1998) *Cassian the Monk*. Oxford: Oxford University Press.

St. John Chrysostom (349–407)

TENNY THOMAS

St. John was born at Antioch in Syria of noble parents: his father was a successful civil servant in the bureau of the commander of military operations in the diocese of Oriens, the *magister militum per Orientem*. His father died soon after his birth and his mother Anthusa brought him up. He began his education under the renowned pagan rhetorician Libanius. He went on to study theology under the Syrian theologian Diodore of Tarsus and was baptized in 368, after which he spent the next three years as an aide to Bishop Meletius of Antioch. In 371 he was ordained reader and spent time in strict asceticism, though he was forced to abandon the monastic life because of the breakdown of his health. In 381 Flavian, the newly appointed archbishop of Antioch, ordained John deacon, and then priest in 386. Both as priest at Antioch and as archbishop of Constantinople he won the greatest renown as a preacher; hence his epithet *Chrysostomos* ("golden mouthed"), given to him posthumously.

His writings are most notable as expositions of pastoral teaching. His many biblical commentaries became a general model for ancient Christian preaching in the East; they wove together a straightforward narrative style with rhetorical flair and vivid moral instruction. The most valuable part of his works is perhaps his *Homilies* on various books of the Bible. He particularly emphasized almsgiving and was most concerned with the spiritual and temporal needs of the poor. He often spoke out against abuse of severe disparities of wealth and poverty in the cities of the empire, and the main themes of his discourses were eminently social, explaining the proper manner of a Christian's conduct in life.

In 387 after a riot in Antioch had destroyed statues of the emperor, threatening to bring down military punishment on the city, John delivered a series of passionate appeals for clemency (*Homilies on the Statues*), and his reputation was established. Against his wish, he was made archbishop of Constantinople in 398, and immediately set about the work of reforming the city, where the decadent standards of the court had been encouraged among the clergy by the worldly and princely style of his predecessor. His outspokenness and asceticism alienated many of the court and clergy, and especially the Empress Eudoxia. Theophilos of Alexandria saw his opportunity to assert dominance over the capital when Chrysostom gave shelter to the Tall Brothers, monks whom Theophilos had censured and exiled from Egypt because of their Origenism. At the Synod of The Oak, held with imperial approval at Chalcedon in 403, Theophilos tried and deposed John for canonical irregularities. The emperor deposed him, though shortly afterwards recalled him from exile. As soon as he was back in the city he renewed his reform program with even greater zeal, earning the undying enmity of the empress. He was exiled again, on the specious grounds that he had resumed his see after a synodical condemnation without canonical rehabilitation. At first John was sent to Antioch, but later his punishment was increased by an enforced winter march to Pityus, situated on the eastern shores of the Black Sea. John died in exile on September 14, 407, at Comana in Asia Minor. The Orthodox Church commemorates his feast day on November 13, and again in the company of Sts. Basil and Gregory the Theologian as one of the Three Holy Hierarchs.

REFERENCES AND SUGGESTED READINGS

Baur, C. (1959) *John Chrysostom and His Time.* Westminster, MD: Newman Press

Hartney, A. M. (2004) *John Chrysostom and the Transformation of the City.* London: Duckworth.

Kelly, J. N. D. (1995) *Golden Mouth: The Story of John Chrysostom – Ascetic, Preacher, Bishop.* London: Duckworth.

Maxwell, J. (2006) *Christianization and Communication in Late Antiquity: John Chrysostom and His Congregation in Antioch.* Cambridge: Cambridge University Press.

Mayer, W. and Allen, P. (2000) *John Chrysostom.* London: Routledge.

St. John of Damascus (ca. 675–ca. 750)

ANDREW LOUTH

Monk and theologian. Born probably in Damascus, John belonged to a family that had played a prominent role in the fiscal administration of Syria throughout the political changes of the 7th century, and he himself served under the caliph in Damascus. Probably early in the 8th century he left the service of the caliph and became a monk in or near Jerusalem (according to a late tradition at the Monastery of Mar Sava in the Judean Desert).

He was a prolific writer, most of his works being written while he was a monk. In his day, he had, as the chronicler Theophanes bears witness, a great reputation as a preacher, though only about a dozen of his homilies survive. He was also an important composer of liturgical poetry, much of which is still sung in the churches of the Byzantine tradition, and was one of the first to develop the genre of the canon, which forms the heart of the dawn office (Orthros). His prose works are mostly polemical or expository, defending and setting forth the theological tradition of the ecumenical councils against those groups who rejected it and had found relative religious freedom under the Muslim yoke. He is the first Christian theologian to write about Islam from direct knowledge. He also achieved renown in his own lifetime for his opposition to the Byzantine iconoclasm introduced by Emperor Leo V.

John saw himself as a defender of conciliar orthodoxy, as it had developed up to St Maximos the Confessor, and he epitomized the Greek patristic tradition in an important trio of works based on the genre of a century, primarily a vehicle for monastic meditation. These included a handbook of logic (*Dialectica*), which expounded a basically Aristotelian logic and the technical language of Greek theology; a century on heresies – the eighty chapters of an epitome of Epiphanios' *Panarion*, supplemented by twenty chapters of John's own composition, the last of which was on Islam; and a century summarizing the essential points of the Christian faith (*On the Orthodox Faith*, or *Expositio Fidei*) on the doctrines of God and the Trinity, creation (including a great deal of astronomical, geographical, physiological, and psychological learning), Christology, and various points concerned with Christian worship, the sacraments, icons, and the last things. *On the Orthodox Faith* was translated into many languages, including Latin, in which form it provided valuable access to Greek patristic theology for the Scholastics and later western theologians up to Schleiermacher. Perhaps his most creative theology is to be found in the three treatises John composed against iconoclasm, which contain a classical defense of icons in Christian worship, based principally on the doctrine of the incarnation, but which give imagery a central

epistemological role in Christian theology. The same use of imagery lies at the heart of his liturgical poetry. His treatises against the iconoclasts were translated into Slavonic in the early modern period and provided an Orthodox defense of religious painting against Calvinist Protestantism.

SEE ALSO: Canon (Liturgical); Hymnography; Iconoclasm; Orthros (Matins)

REFERENCES AND SUGGESTED READINGS

Anderson, D. (trans.) (1980) *St. John of Damascus: On the Divine Images.* Crestwood, NY: St. Vladimir's Seminary Press.
Chase, F. H. (trans.) (1958) *St. John of Damascus: The Fount of Knowledge.* Fathers of the Church 37. New York: Fathers of the Church.
Louth, A. (2002) *St. John Damascene: Tradition and Originality in Byzantine Theology.* Oxford: Oxford University Press.
Nasrallah, J. (1950) *St. Jean de Damas: son époque, sa vie, son oeuvre.* Paris.
O'Rourke-Boyle, M. (1970) "Christ the Eikon in the Apologies for Holy Images of John of Damascus," *Greek Orthodox Theological Review* 15: 175–86.
Sahas, D. J. (1972) *John of Damascus on Islam: The "Heresy of the Ishmaelites."* Leiden: Brill.
Salmond, S. (trans.) (1978) "St. John of Damascus: On the Orthodox Faith," in *The Nicene and Post-Nicene Fathers* vol. 9. Grand Rapids, MI: Eerdmans.

St. John Klimakos (ca. 579–ca. 659)

JOHN CHRYSSAVGIS

The ascetic author *par excellence*, John Klimakos (meaning John "Of the Ladder") lived on Mt. Sinai as a hermit and, later, abbot in the great monastery of St. Katherine there. The precise dates of his life are difficult to determine, but he is probably a contemporary of Maximos the

Confessor (580–662). It seems reasonable to place his dates between ca. 579 and ca. 659.

It is not known where John was born but he arrived at Sinai when he was only 16. When already quite advanced in age he accepted to write the *Ladder* at the request of another John, Abbot of Raithou. Originally entitled *Spiritual Tablets*, as many manuscripts indicate, it was the title *Ladder* which ultimately prevailed and which gives the book its unique flavor and feature. The *Ladder* consists of thirty steps (sections), including a range of virtues to acquire and vices to avoid. As a supplement to this John also authored a short treatise entitled *To the Shepherd*, describing the spiritual task of the abbot and likewise addressed to John of Raithou. Each step opens with a series of brief definitions, followed by a detailed exposition of the theme with illustrative anecdotes, and a terminal summary with inspiration.

John is deeply influenced by the early desert tradition of Egypt as well as the Gaza monastics, such as Barsanuphius and John. In some ways, he lays the foundations for the "school" of Sinaite spirituality commonly attributed to Hesychios and Philotheos. His extensive influence is witnessed in the writings of St. Symeon the New Theologian (especially in his teaching on tears) and the 14th-century hesychasts, such as St. Gregory Palamas (especially in his teaching on silence and prayer).

With the exception of the scriptures and the liturgical books, no other writing in Eastern Christendom has been studied, copied, and translated to the same extent as John's *Ladder of Divine Ascent*. It has shaped not only Eastern Orthodoxy, and especially its monastic tradition, but also the entire Christian world. Even today, the *Ladder* is appointed to be read aloud in churches or in the refectory, as well as privately in the cells of Orthodox monasteries, each year during Lent, a practice that may date back to the time of the author's life. There is no equivalent of the *Ladder* in the West, but its popularity may be compared with that of the *Imitation of Christ*, though the two books differ greatly in character.

Some of the key doctrines of the *Ladder* include the notion of spiritual direction (the separate treatise *To the Shepherd* is sometimes known as the "31st step"), the remarkable concept of joyful-sorrow (perhaps John's most original and most influential contribution), the emphasis on "divine eros" or "holy passion" (to describe the soul's mystical yearning for God), and certain key phrases that proved crucial passages in the development of the Jesus Prayer (John speaks of using a "single-phrase" or the "name of Jesus"). St. John Klimakos is liturgically commemorated on March 30 and on the fourth Sunday of Lent.

SEE ALSO: Jesus Prayer; St. Gregory Palamas (1296–1359); St. Maximos the Confessor (580–662); St. Symeon the New Theologian (949–1022); Sts. Barsanuphius and John (6th c.)

REFERENCES AND SUGGESTED READINGS

Chryssavgis, J. (2004) *John Climacus: From the Egyptian Desert to the Sinaite Mountain.* London: Ashgate Press.

Ware, K. (1982) "Introduction to John Climacus: The Ladder of Divine Ascent," in *Classics of Western Spirituality.* New York: Paulist Press.

St. Macarius (4th c.)

MARCUS PLESTED

This anonymous author (also known as Macarius-Symeon or pseudo-Macarius) stands as a principal source of Orthodox mystical and ascetic theology. He flourished in Syro-Mesopotamia between ca. 370 and ca. 390. His writings were variously ascribed to a Macarius (of both Egypt and Alexandria) or, later, Symeon – hence the many names of this elusive theologian.

The direct experience of God forms the cornerstone of the Macarian vision. He speaks with astonishing precision and poetry of the operation of the Spirit. Bestriding Greek and Syriac thought-worlds, Macarius was able to combine the philosophical reflection of the Greek fathers with the vivid symbolism of the Syriac tradition. His writings call every Christian to directly experience the triune God, an experience described as the vision of uncreated light, a formulation of great import for later Orthodox teaching.

The tone of Macarius' call to perfection is compelling and encouraging. The writings use an exuberant abundance of imagery and metaphor to convey the progressive deification of the Christian, setting out a dizzying vision of the mutual indwelling of man and God. Macarius is a key witness to the patristic doctrine of deification, insisting on the perfect union of man and God without ever compromising their ontological discontinuity and hypostatic distinctness.

His is a heart-centered anthropology. The heart is the point at which soul and body meet and the dwelling-place of the intellect. It is the deep self, the battleground between good and evil. In and through the struggle of the heart Christ restores man to the primal state of Adam and grants him in addition the grace of the Holy Spirit. Through cooperation (synergeia) with divine grace the perfect grace of baptism is manifested and revealed.

His legacy began to take shape with Gregory of Nyssa's reworking of the Macarian Great Letter (Epistola Magna) as his own De Instituto Christiano. Works of Macarius rapidly appeared under an array of illustrious names and in numerous translations. Many of the authors of the Philokalia stand in the Macarian tradition, most obviously Sts. Mark the Monk, Diadochus of Photice, Maximos the Confessor, and Gregory Palamas. Macarius himself is also included in that seminal publication and went on to play a major role in the Hesychast revival of late-imperial Russia.

Much was made in the early 20th century of the apparent connection with the condemned propositions of the Messalian heresy, an ascetic tendency that allegedly held prayer, and not the sacraments, to be the only sure vehicle of grace. Recent researches have established Macarius as a reformer of the nascent Messalian tendency, not an adherent. The way is now clear for further explorations of the impact and importance of this most blessed of spiritual masters.

SEE ALSO: Jesus Prayer; St. Isaac the Syrian (7th c.)

REFERENCES AND SUGGESTED READINGS

Dörries, H. (1978) Die Theologie des Makarios-Symeon. Göttingen: Vandenhoeck and Ruprecht.
Plested, M. (2004) The Macarian Legacy: The Place of Macarius-Symeon in the Eastern Christian Tradition. Oxford: Oxford University Press.
Stewart, C. (1991) "Working the Earth of the Heart": The Messalian Controversy in History, Texts and Language to AD 431. Oxford: Clarendon Press.

St. Mark of Ephesus (1392–1445)

A. EDWARD SIECIENSKI

Mark Eugenicus was metropolitan of Ephesus and leader of the anti-unionist party during and after the Council of Florence (1438–9). He claimed that the Western teachings on purgatory and the filioque were heretical, and were supported by the Latins only on the basis of corrupted and spurious texts. He alone among the Greek delegates refused to sign the *Tomos* of union, returning east to lead the campaign against it until his death in 1445.

SEE ALSO: Ecumenism, Orthodoxy and; *Filioque*; Florence, Council of (1438–1439)

REFERENCES AND SUGGESTED READINGS

Constas, N. (2002) "Mark Eugenicus," in C. Conticello and V. Conticello (eds.) *La Théologie byzantine et sa tradition*, vol. 2. Turnhout: Brepols, pp. 411–75.

St. Maximos the Confessor (580–662)

ANDREW LOUTH

Monk and theologian. Born in Constantinople (though an alternative nearly contemporary Syriac life makes him a native of Palestine), in 610 Maximos became the head of the imperial chancery under Emperor Herakleios. Soon, he withdrew from public life and became a monk, first at Chrysopolis, opposite Constantinople, and later at Kyzikos, on the Erdek peninsula. When the Persians laid siege to Constantinople in 626, he fled with other monks to North Africa. As a monk he retained his contacts with the court, as his correspondence demonstrates, and quickly became a renowned theologian. His early works – up to the early 630s – are addressed primarily to monks, and are concerned with the ascetic life and the interpretation of Scripture and the fathers. One besetting problem in the monastic circles known to Maximos was Origenism, which had provided a metaphysical context for understanding monastic asceticism. In these early works, Maximos corrects Origenist errors and provides an alternative metaphysical understanding of the goal and purpose of asceticism. Drawing on the Cappadocian fathers and the Alexandrine tradition of Athanasius and Cyril, combining this with the ascetic wisdom of Evagrios Pontikos and the Egyptian desert, and also with Dionysius the Areopagite's cosmic, liturgical vision, Maximos set out a theology cosmic in scope, with intensely practical ascetic implications, that focused on the church's liturgy, where the drama of salvation drew in the participation of humankind.

The Persian occupation of the eastern provinces of the empire in the 610s and 620s exposed the weakness of the empire caused by christological divisions, and led to attempts to reconcile those who accepted the Christology of Chalcedon (451) and those, called by their opponents "Monophysites," who rejected it. In 633, during Maximos' African sojourn, a dramatic reconciliation was achieved in Egypt, on the basis on the doctrine that Christ had a single "divine-human" (theandric) activity, the doctrine known as "Monoenergism." This was opposed by Sophronios, Maximos' abbot in North Africa, soon to be patriarch of Jerusalem. Next, a refinement of Monoenergism known as "Monothelitism," the doctrine that Christ had a single (divine) will, became the favored imperial christological compromise, and from the end of the 630s Maximos took on Sophronios' mantle and became the principal theological opponent of Monothelitism, arguing that it compromised Christ's perfect human nature. He sought to solve the problems raised by Christ's having two wills by distinguishing between the natural will (Christ having both a divine and human natural will) and the gnomic will (*gnômē*: Greek for "opinion") involved in deliberating over moral decisions, that was absent in Christ. His attack on Monothelitism eventually took him to Rome, where the christological heresies were condemned at the Lateran

Synod of 649. By this time it was Islam that threatened the empire; Maximos and Martin's actions were regarded as seditious. The architects of the synod – Pope Martin and Maximos – were arrested, condemned, and exiled: Martin to the Crimea, where he died in 655, and Maximos to Lazica, in Georgia, where he died in 662.

SEE ALSO: Council of Constantinople III (680–681); Monophysitism (including Miaphysitism); Monothelitism

REFERENCES AND SUGGESTED READINGS

erthold, G. (trans.) (1985) *St. Maximus the Confessor*. Classics of Western Spirituality. New York: St. Paul Press.

Louth, A. (1996) *Maximus the Confessor*. London: Routledge.

Thunberg, L. (1965) *Microcosm and Mediator: The Theological Anthropology of Maximus the Confessor*. Lund: C. W. K. Gleerup.

St. Nicholas Cabasilas (ca. 1322–ca. 1391)

A. EDWARD SIECIENSKI

Byzantine theologian and spiritual writer known chiefly for his books *The Commentary on the Divine Liturgy* and *The Life in Christ*. Born Nicholas Chamaetos in 1322, he was the nephew of Nilus Cabasilas (1298–1363), whose surname he used throughout his life. Nilus had succeeded Gregory Palamas as archbishop of Thessalonica and was the author of several important anti-Latin tracts later used at the Council of Florence (1438–9). Although born in Thessalonica, Nicholas was educated at Constantinople and entered the imperial service, later becoming an official and friend of John VI Cantacuzenos (1347–54). During the civil war between John VI

and John V Palaeologus (1341–91), Cabasilas sided with Cantacuzenos, who entrusted him with several important diplomatic missions and (briefly) considered him as candidate for patriarch following the deposition of Callistus I. When in 1354 John VI Cantacuzenos was deposed, Nicholas retired from public life and concentrated his energies on theological matters. He was once thought to have succeeded his uncle Nilus as archbishop of Thessalonica; however, it is more likely that he entered monastic life, serving as a priest at the Manganon monastery near Constantinople.

Cabasilas's hospitable open-mindedness has led some to believe that he was influenced by the so-called "Latin-minded" theologians surrounding his contemporary, Demetrius Cydones (1324–98). However, among Cabasilas's works are a firm defense of hesychasm against Nicephorus Gregoras (ca. 1295–1360) and a new edition of his uncle's book against the Latins on the procession of the Holy Spirit. He also wrote several homilies and hagiographical works, many of which manifest a particular concern for social justice and the need to redress economic and institutional inequities.

Cabasilas's two most famous works are his *Life in Christ* and *Commentary on the Divine Liturgy*. The *Life in Christ* emphasized the synergy of divine and human activity in the process of salvation, the role of individual and public prayer, and the union with Christ made possible by the mysteries of baptism, chrismation, and Eucharist. Although thoroughly Eastern in its outlook, the influence of Latin theology can be seen in Cabasilas's explanation of the atonement, which closely follows Anselm of Canterbury's satisfaction theory. His *Commentary on the Divine Liturgy* (a work that found admirers in the West and was even quoted favorably by the Council of Trent) spoke of the transformative and mystical aspects of the liturgy, especially as it related to the eternal, heavenly liturgy. It became, alongside the earlier work of Patriarch Germanus of Constantinople (715–30), the most significant commentary on the Byzantine liturgy in the Eastern tradition.

SEE ALSO: Divine Liturgy, Orthodox; Mystery (Sacrament)

REFERENCES AND SUGGESTED READINGS

Cabasilas, N. (1960) *A Commentary on the Divine Liturgy*, trans. J. M. Hussey and P. A. McNulty. London: SPCK.
Cabasilas, N. (1974) *The Life in Christ*, trans. C. de Catanzaro. Crestwood, NY: St. Press.

St. Nicholas the Wonderworker

MARIA GWYN MCDOWELL

A "super-saint" (Onasch 1963: 205) in whom the "Church sees ... a personification of a shepherd, of its defender and intercessor" (Ouspensky and Lossky 1982: 120), the received story of St. Nicholas the Wonderworker is a conflation of the 4th- century Nicholas of Myra and the historical 6th-century Nicholas of Sion (d. 564).

Nicholas of Sion's cult was well established by the end of the 6th century, aided by his Life written soon after his death by a disciple (Ševčenko and Ševčenko 1985: 11). To this abbot of the Monastery of Holy Sion and later bishop of Pinara belong the popular birth miracles, felling of the cypress tree, miracles at sea, and many healings (ibid.: 13). Exemplifying a "down-to-earth piety" (ibid.: 15), the Life is modeled after the New Testament and Psalms. Its historical credence is partly due to its detail, which likely reflects first-hand knowledge of itemized monastery records; for example, the amount of oxen Nicholas ordered slaughtered to feed the populace after the bubonic plague of 541–2. The Life also refers to the earlier St. Nicholas who had a coastal shrine in or near Myra. This earlier saint's small 6th-century cult engulfed that of Nicholas of Sion by the 10th century – the distinction between the two saints blurred by the extensive borrowing of Byzantine hagiographers from the later Life on behalf of St. Nicholas of Myra.

The earliest known account of Nicholas of Myra is likely the *Vita per Michaelem* from the 10th century, though isolated stories appear earlier. Eustratios of Constantinople (late 6th century) cites the story of the falsely accused generals, while the terminology of the *On the Tax* indicates a 9th- or 10th-century composition. Icons of the saint often feature two medallions of Christ and the Virgin, alluding to St. Nicholas' presence at the Council of Nicea in 325. Angered, Nicholas is said to have slapped Arius, resulting in the suspension of his episcopal office and the removal of its attributes – the Gospel Book and Omophorion. In the icons, Christ and the Virgin Mary return these items to Nicholas, reflecting their appearance in dreams to the emperor's advisers advocating his reinstatement. This event, as well as his appearances to Constantine I (d. 337) in a vision on behalf of the three generals and a dream in which Nicholas receives a chrysobull exempting the city of Myra from taxation, place his activity in the early 4th century. However, there is no historical evidence of such a bishop nor any official written record of his presence at the council.

Issues of historicity aside, by the time of iconographic portraiture the two saints had merged into Nicholas the Wonderworker whose miracles during and after his life produced an extraordinary cycle of icons. Maguire attributes his immense popularity, second only to the Theotokos by the

Plate 65   Icon of St. Nicholas, 10th century (tempera and gold leaf on panel), from the Monastery of St. Catherine, Mount Sinai, Egypt. Ancient Art and Architecture Collection/The Bridgeman Art Library.

12th century, to his being "somewhat of a generalist" (Maguire 1996: 169). The many, often mundane miracles depicted in spare iconographic detail allow for a wide range of intercessory prayers by the patron saint of mariners, scholars and students, merchants, marriageable women, bankers, thieves, and pugilists.

SEE ALSO: Communion of Saints; Iconography, Styles of

REFERENCES AND SUGGESTED READINGS

Maguire, H. (1996) *The Icons of Their Bodies: Saints and Their Images in Byzantium*. Princeton: Princeton University Press.

Onasch, K. (1963) *Icons*. London: Faber and Faber.
Ouspensky, L. and Lossky, V. (1982) *The Meaning of Icons*. Crestwood, NY: St. Vladimir's Seminary Press.
Ševčenko, I. and Ševčenko, N. P. (1985) *The Life of St Nicholas of Sion*. Brookline, MA: Hellenic College Press.
Ševčenko, N. P. (1983) *The Life of Saint Nicholas in Byzantine Art*. Turin: Bottega d'Erasmo.

St. Nikodemos the Hagiorite (1749–1809)

CYRIL HOVORUN

Leading spiritual writer and Kollyvadic Father. He was born Nikolaos Kallivourtsis on the island of Naxos in 1749, and died a leading monastic theologian, canonist, and hymnographer on Mount Athos in

1809. He spent much of his life as a hermit, and in his writings advocated frequent participation in the Holy Eucharist. Nikodemos composed numerous books on ascetical and pastoral theology, canon law, hagiography, and exegesis of the Holy Scripture and liturgical texts. He adapted the writings of St. Symeon the New Theologian and St. Gregory Palamas for modern Greek readers, and was the author of more than fifty liturgical hymns. He had profound knowledge of Latin spiritual traditions and made Greek adaptations of Ignatian and Theatine spiritual texts such as the *Exercises* and the *Spiritual Combat*. He is chiefly known today as the co-editor of one of the major collections of Eastern Christian spirituality, the *Philokalia*, as well as codificator and commentator on the Eastern Canon Law (the *Pedalion*, or Rudder).

SEE ALSO: Kollyvadic Fathers; *Philokalia*; St. Gregory Palamas (1296–1359); St. Symeon the New Theologian (949–1022)

REFERENCES AND SUGGESTED READINGS

Chamberas, R. (trans.) (1989) *Nikodemos of the Holy Mountain: A Handbook of Spiritual Counsel*. New York: Paulist Press.

St. Paisy Velichovsky (1722–1794)

JOHN A. MCGUCKIN

Also known as St. Paisy of Neamt, from the Romanian monastery where he did most of his publishing work. He was a very important disseminator of the spiritual tradition of the *Philokalia* to the Slavic Orthodox lands. Along with the original Greek editors of the *Philokalia* – St. Nikodemos the Hagiorite and St. Macarius of Corinth – he

is one of the major early modern Philokalic fathers. His intense labors for the rediscovery of the classical hesychastic tradition bore fruit in many revivals across the Orthodox world, lasting to the present. He was a native of the Ukraine, son of the dean of Poltava Cathedral. Orphaned at an early age and brought up by his elder brother, the priest John, the child learned to read from the holy books (scripture and the *Menaion*) and developed a great love for the works of the Fathers. He entered the Kiev Mohyla Academy (1735–9) but was attracted to the ascetic life, and in 1740 entered the monastery of Lubetch, moving soon after to St. Nicholas' monastery where he was tonsured in 1741. It was a time when many Orthodox monasteries were being forcibly closed. He himself took refuge with Hieromonk Michael in 1743, who brought him to the Romanian Skete of St. Nicholas at Traisteni. After two years there, following Athonite observance, he left to study under the hermit Onuphrios in Wallachia, and in 1746 finally made his way to Mount Athos, where he entered the Great Lavra before moving to settle at St. Panteleimon's. In 1750 he was admitted to the Lesser Schema and began accepting disciples. His first followers were Romanians, and shortly after he accepted Russian monks, making his foundation a dual-language community. In 1758 he was ordained priest and became a highly regarded spiritual father on Athos. His community grew rapidly and he first realized the need to provide serious spiritual seekers with a library of patristic advice. He commissioned several monks to translate patristic mystical texts into Slavonic. This labor was carried with his community when it relocated to Romania in 1764, at Dragomirna, and would be constitutive of the mission of the Paisian houses. In 1775 the Austrian forces captured Bukovina, and Paisy was forced to relocate once more. In

Plate 66   Domes of the Kiev Pechersky Lavra. Photo © Sergey Kamshylin/Shutterstock.

1779 he was given charge of the monastery of Neamt. His community here soon numbered more than 700. After the publication of the Greek *Philokalia* in 1782, Paisy made a version in Slavonic (*Dobrotoloubié*) which from its appearance in 1793 electrified the Russian monastic world. In 1790 he was given the Great Schema and made archimandrite, and died at Neamt on November 15, 1794, aged 72. Mount Athos and the Romanian Church were the first to venerate him as a saint, and this was followed by the Russian Synod in 1988. Paisy's main labors were the dissemination of Philokalic texts, but he also presided over a radical reorganization of the monastic Typikon or structure of the daily life in Athonite-style monasteries. His purpose (causing controversy at the time) was to bring back into cenobitic houses a greater flexibility which would allow monastics greater possibilities for solitude and prayer. The later Russian hesychastic tradition owes much to him, including such figures such as St. Seraphim of Sarov, the Optina Elders, Bishop Ignatius Brianchaninov, and St. Theophan the Recluse.

SEE ALSO: Hesychasm; *Philokalia*

REFERENCES AND SUGGESTED READINGS

Chetverikov, S. (1933) *Paisius: Starets of Neamt Monastery in Moldavia. His Life, Teaching, and His Influence on the Orthodox Church* (Romanian text). Neamt, Romania: Neamt Monastery.

Joanta, S. (1992) *Romania: Its Hesychastic Tradition and Culture.* Wildwood. CA: St. Xenia Skete, pp. 128–57.

Tachiaos, A. E. N. (1986) *The Revival of Byzantine Mysticism among Slavs and Romanians in the 18th Century: Texts Relating to the Life and Activity of Paisy Velichovsky* (Greek and Slavonic texts). Thessalonica.

Zaharia, C. (1985) "Paissij Velichovskij et le role oecumenique de l'Église Orthodoxe Roumaine," *Irenikon* 58: 3–27.

St. Photios the Great (ca. 810–ca. 893)

BRENDA LLEWELLYN IHSSEN

St. Photios was an intellectual, a member of Byzantine aristocracy, and a teacher, theologian, and bibliophile. He remains one of the most highly venerated patriarchs of Constantinople, a position he held from 858 to 867 and again from 877 to 886.

Photios was born to aristocratic Christian parents and was related to both the imperial family and the ecumenical patriarch. Devoted at a young age to scholarship, at the completion of his education he became a teacher of philosophy and dialects, and was eventually appointed to the position of Protoasecretis in the Byzantine bureaucracy. Though a layman, Photios was elevated to the ecumenical patriarchate when Patriarch Ignatios was forced to resign by Caesar Bardas, uncle of Emperor Michael III. Though widely admired as an intellectual and administrator, Photios himself was surprised at the high clerical appointment he had not sought, not least because of his lay status.

Pope Nicholas I, who along with the other three patriarchs received the customary letter declaring Photios' dedication to Orthodoxy, had previously been contacted by supporters of Ignatios, and sent delegates to a synod in 861 to investigate the resignation of Ignatios and the elevation of Photios. Further complicating the situation was the dispute over the territories of Sicily, Calabria, and Illyricum, which had been removed from Roman jurisdiction and transferred to Constantinople during the first phase of iconoclasm. The question of the jurisdiction of the newly formed Bulgarian Church was aso a lively issue at this time. While the papal legates found Photios' election legal, Nicholas subsequently declared that he had deposed Photios and reinstated Ignatios; pronouncements which the East at first ignored.

Photios' denunciation in 867 of Nicholas' claims for papal primacy, and his critique of the Latin innovation of the *filioque*, manifested to Christianity the first clear sign of significant theological differentiation and large-scale division between the churches of the East and of the West.

At the death of Emperor Michael III in 867, Emperor Basil I sought reconciliation with Rome. Ignatios was elevated to the patriarchate for a second term, while Photios was deposed and subsequently condemned and anathematized at the Fourth Council of Constantinople (869–70). This synod is not recognized as having ecumenical status by the Orthodox Church. After Ignatios died, Photios was again reinstated as patriarch until his forced resignation in 886, after which he devoted the remainder of his life to his academic pursuits.

Details of the schism with Rome tend to overshadow Photios' additional accomplishments, including his support of vigorous missionary activity to the Bulgars, Georgians, Moravians, and Khazars; achievements which were not divorced from his advancement of Hellenic culture, his noble leadership in the city during the siege of the Rhos (Rus) and their subsequent baptism, and his development of a refined prospectus on the relationship between church and state. Furthermore, Photios' scholarly contributions are remarkable in both quantity and diversity of subject matter. He wrote extensively not just on theology and philosophy, but also on scientific matters, on history, mathematics, astronomy, music, poetry, and law. One of his most important theological contributions is *The Mystagogy of the Holy Spirit*, a sweeping indictment of the major theological distinction between Orthodox and Latin Christianity, the *filioque*. He is one of the first, and the most significant, to set out the critical issues involved.

SEE ALSO: *Filioque*

REFERENCES AND SUGGESTED READINGS

Dvornik, F. (1948) *The Photian Schism, History and Legend*. Cambridge: Cambridge University Press.

Farrell, J. P. (trans.) (1987) *Patriarch St. Photius, The Mystagogy of the Holy Spirit*. Brookline, MA: Holy Cross Orthodox Press.

Hergenröther, J. (1867–9) *Photios, Patriarch von Constantinopel*, 3 vols. Regensburg.

Kallos, J. (1992) *Saint Photios: Patriarch of Constantinople*. Brookline, MA: Holy Cross Orthodox Press.

Photios (1959) *Homiliai*, ed. V. Laourdas. Thessaloniki: Hetaireias Makedonikon Spoudon.

Treadgold, W. (2002) "Photius Before His Patriarchate," *Journal of Ecclesiastical History* 53, 1: 1–17.

White, D. S. (1980) "Patriarch Photios – A Christian Humanist," *Greek Orthodox Theological Review* 25, 2: 195–205.

White, D. S. (1982) *Patriarch Photios of Constantinople*. Brookline, MA: Holy Cross Orthodox Press.

White, D. S. (2000) "The Dual Doctrine of the Relations of Church and State in Ninth Century Byzantium," *Greek Orthodox Theological Review* 45, 1–4: 443–52.

St. Romanos the Melodist (6th c.)

DIMITRI CONOMOS

The greatest of all Byzantine poets. Little is known about his life, but it is likely that he was born in the city of Emesa, Syria, and that he was of Jewish origin. As a young man he served as deacon at the Church of the Resurrection in Beirut, before coming to Constantinople during the reign of Anastasius I (491–518), where he was attached to the Church of the Virgin in the Kyros quarter of the city. At an unknown time after his death (late 6th century) he was canonized as a saint of the Orthodox Church (his feast day is October 1).

Eighty-five kontakia attributed to Romanos have survived, thirty-four of which are on the person of Christ; the rest deal with other figures of the New and Old Testaments. Around sixty out of the eighty-five (those with his name as part of the acrostic) are considered to be genuine. A great number appear to be spurious (probably all those on martyrs and saints), for it has been proved that the acrostics were frequently falsified to include the poet's name. The grand christological kontakia bear vivid dramatization; monologues are used to reveal the inner mind of his agents and dialogues to explain the motives of their actions. Opinions would no doubt differ as to which are the best, but *On the Nativity*, *On the Presentation in the Temple*, *On Mary at the Cross*, and *On the Resurrection VI* would be a reasonable shortlist. Romanos did not avoid contemporary topics, however, and the hymn *On the Earthquake and Fire* depicts the Nika Riots (532) and praises "the new Solomon," Justinian I, for the restoration of Hagia Sophia.

Romanos' language is the Atticizing "literary *koine*" or Hellenistic Greek, which does not escape the influence of the simple spoken language or that of the Scriptures, with their many Jewish-Greek elements. His style is marked by simplicity, dignity, and emotional directness, the sentences moving in short and uninvolved phrases well adapted to the intricate meters of which he is a master. In one kontakion only, *On Judas*, does he make use of rhyme, following the example of the *Akathistos*. His dialogues are embellished by rhetorical devices such as parallelism, oxymoron, and word play. Clarity of style, striking imagery, arresting similes, bold comparisons, sharp metaphors, irony, and a dexterous use of discourse characterize his writing and add dramatic tension.

The full texts of Romanos' hymns first appear, without musical notation, in manuscripts of the 11th century. The music of the hymns of Romanos is unfortunately lost, but the dramatic character of their content suggests that they were chanted in a kind of recitative, resembling oratorio. Originally, the poems would have been recited in full during the services, and since the texts are very long, the musical texts were probably syllabic. This theory is partly based on the assumption that Romanos' metrical system is stable and conforms to the principles of *homotonia* (identical stress patterns in corresponding verses) and *isosyllabia* (identical number of syllables in corresponding verses).

SEE ALSO: Kontakion; Music (Sacred)

REFERENCES AND SUGGESTED READINGS

Brock, S. (1989) "From Ephrem to Romanos," *Studia Patristica* 20: 139–51.

Carpenter, M. (ed.) (1970–3) *Kontakia of Romanos*, 2 vols. Columbia: Missouri University Press.

Grosdidier de Matons, J. (ed.) (1964–81) *Romanos le Mélode: Hymnes*, 5 vols. Paris: Cerf.

Grosdidier de Matons, J. (ed.) (1977) *Romanos le Mélode et les origines de la poésie religieuse à Byzance*. Paris: Beauchesne.

Lash, E. (trans.) (1995) *St Romanos "On the Life of Christ": Kontakia*. San Francisco: Harper Collins.

St. Seraphim of Sarov (1759–1833)

KONSTANTIN GAVRILKIN

St. Seraphim belongs to that tradition of monastic spirituality which was brought to Ancient Rus from Mount Athos in the early 11th century and revived in the late 18th to 19th centuries by Paisy Velichovsky and his followers, among whom one should note St. Ignatius Brianchaninov, St. Feofan (Theophan) the Recluse, and the Optina elders.

Prokhor Moshnin (Seraphim's name prior to his monastic tonsure) was born into a pious merchant family in Kursk. In 1776 he visited the Kiev Caves Monastery, where the elder Dosifei advised him to practice the Jesus Prayer continuously and to enter the Sarov monastery (in Nizhnii Novgorod province). He arrived there in 1778, took monastic vows in 1786, and received the name Seraphim. From his disciples and early biographers, who relied both on his personal testimony and eyewitness accounts, we know that he had multiple mystical experiences, including revelations of Christ and many visitations by the Virgin Mary who guided him throughout his 55-year monastic life and healed him on a number of occasions from severe illnesses and injuries. Between 1794 and 1810 Seraphim lived a reclusive life in the forest outside the monastery, spending his time in the practice of the Jesus Prayer, reading Scripture and patristic literature, and engaging in manual labor. One day he was savagely beaten by robbers who left him crippled for the rest of his life; when the attackers were later arrested, he persuaded the authorities to let them go. He returned to the monastery in 1810, but remained in seclusion until 1825, when, at the command of the Virgin Mary, he began to receive people seeking his guidance and healing, and became one of the most renowned *startsi* of Russia.

Seraphim's extraordinary asceticism and mystical life were witnessed by several of the inhabitants of the Sarov monastery and by visitors whose lives were dramatically changed by their encounter with the saint. In his later years some of the nuns of the Diveyevo Convent of the Holy Trinity, which was under his personal supervision, also witnessed his spiritual gifts and power of prayer. The most famous description of the latter is found in the recollections of N. A. Motovilov (1809–79), a lay disciple who was particularly close to Seraphim and left

Plate 67   St. Seraphim of Sarov. RIA Novosti/Topfoto.

autobiographical notes, a fragment from which was published in 1903 (Nilus 1903), the year St. Seraphim was canonized at the initiative of Nicholas II. It contained Seraphim's conversation with Motovilov on the meaning of Christian life, defined by the saint as the "Acquisition of the Holy Spirit" (hence the known title of the fragment). During Seraphim's explanation of what it meant "To be in the Spirit," both he and Motovilov went through a number of mystical experiences of illumination similar to those described by St. Symeon the New Theologian and mystical writers of other periods, giving the most striking demonstration of what the concept of theosis means within the Eastern Orthodox tradition.

SEE ALSO: Jesus Prayer; Monasticism; Russia, Patriarchal Orthodox Church of; St.

Paisy Velichovsky (1722–1794); St. Theophan (Govorov) the Recluse (1815–1894)

REFERENCES AND SUGGESTED READINGS

Arkhimandrit Sergii (1851) *Skazanie o zhizni i podvigakh blazhennyia pamiati ottsa Serafima, Sarovskoi pustyni ieromonakha i zatvornika, s prisovokupleniem dukhovnykh ego nastavlenii*, 3rd edn. Moscow: A. Semena.

Nilus, S. (1903) *Dukh Bozhii, iavno pochivshii na ottse Serafime Sarovskom v besede ego "O tseli khtistianskoi zhizni."* Moscow: Universitetskaia tipografiia.

Veniamin (Fedchenkov) (1996) *Vsemirnyi svetil'nik prepodobnyi Serafim Sarovskii.* Moscow: Palomnik.

Zander, V. (1997) *St. Seraphim of Sarov.* Crestwood, NY: St. Vladimir's Seminary Press.

St. Sergius of Radonezh (1314–1392)

KONSTANTIN GAVRILKIN

Founder of the Trinity Monastery, now known as Troitse-Sergieva Lavra (Sergiev Posad, north of Moscow), St. Sergius of Radonezh is considered the most influential saint of the Russian Orthodox Church. Together with his great contemporary Alexii, Metropolitan of Moscow in 1354–78, he is credited with the spiritual revival of Ancient Rus at the time of the Mongol invasion and, ultimately, with liberation from that oppression. Sergii, known before monasticism as Bartholomew, was born to a noble family near Rostov, but in the late 1320s the impoverished family moved to the Moscow region and settled in the town of Radonezh (10 miles from Sergiev Posad). His parents eventually became monastics in a local monastery, and after their death the youth Bartholomew himself began an ascetic life, joined by his widowed brother Stefan. In 1335, on a site occupied by today's Cathedral of the Holy Trinity, he built a wooden church with the same name. When his brother left for a Moscow monastery, he invited another monk, Igumen Mitrofan, to join him as a replacement companion. Mitrofan tonsured Bartholomew with the name Sergius. Within a few years, other ascetics, attracted by Sergius' strict ascetic life, discipline of prayer, humility, and wisdom, came to join him, and in 1345 they officially established the Holy Trinity Monastery. Although Sergius demanded that all monks sustain the monastery by their manual labor, with time the community grew and among those who joined it were people of different ranks and means – from peasants to princes – who often donated their wealth to the monastery. Patriarch of Constantinople

Plate 68   Icon of St. Sergius of Radonezh, founder of the Sergiev Posad monastery, and one of the most important saints of Russian Church history. Photo by John McGuckin.

Philotheus (1300–79) advised Sergius to introduce the coenobitic rule. With the blessing of Metropolitan Alexii of Moscow, he followed the advice; within a few decades his disciples founded many monasteries of the same style in various Russian principalities. In his late years, Alexii of Moscow urged Sergius to became his successor, but the latter would not abandon his monastery for the metropolitan throne. Sergius is credited with playing a peacemaking role in the disputes among Russian princes whose dynastic quarrels divided and weakened Rus at the time of the Mongol oppression, and encouraging their union with the Moscow principality and its ruler Dmitrii Ioannovich (1350–89), who in 1380 led the united Russian forces to victory against the Golden Horde in the Battle of Kulikovo.

Epifanius the Wise (d. ca. 1420), the disciple of the saint, wrote the first biography (*Zhitie*) of Sergius, which was later revised by the famous hagiographer Pachomius the Serb. Prior to the mid-16th century the Russian Church did not have a formal process of canonization, but according to the available sources Sergius of Radonezh was venerated as saint already in the 15th century for his spiritual wisdom, his asceticism, and the power of his healing prayer.

SEE ALSO: Monasticism; Russia, Patriarchal Orthodox Church of

REFERENCES AND SUGGESTED READINGS

Golubinskii, E. E. (1892) *Prepodobnyi Sergii Radonezhskii i sozdannaia im Troitskaia Lavra.* Sergievskii Posad: A. I. Snegireva.

Kloss, B. M. (1998) *Izbrannye trudy. T. 1: Zhitie Sergiia Radonezhskogo.* Moscow: Iazyki russkoi kul'tury.

Kovalevsky, P. (1976) *Saint Sergius and Russian Spirituality*, trans. W. Elias Jones. Crestwood, NY: St. Vladimir's Seminary Press.

Tsurikov, V. (ed.) (2004) *The Trinity: Sergius Lavra in Russian History and Culture.* Jordanville, NY: Holy Trinity Seminary Press.

St. Silouan of Athos (1866–1938)

JULIA KONSTANTINOVSKY

St. Silouan of Athos, also known as Silvanus, was born Simeon Ivanovich Antonov of Russian peasant origin, and became a schema-monk of the St. Panteleimon monastery on Mount Athos. He was a revered mystic and spiritual director (*starets*) of monastics and laypeople alike. St. Silouan was the spiritual father of Archimandrite Sophrony (Sakharov), who, on Starets Silouan's request, edited and published his handwritten notes on the spiritual life and salvation. Archimandrite Sophrony likewise prepared an introduction to St. Silouan's writings, expounding the teachings from the perspective of the Orthodox ascetic tradition (*Saint Silouan the Athonite*, first published in Paris, 1948). Largely because of the testimony of this spiritual biography, which elucidates the inner progress of Silouan's life, St. Silouan was canonized as a holy Orthodox ascetic (*hosios, prepodobny*) in 1987 by the ecumenical patriarchate of Constantinople. The Orthodox Church commemorates him on September 24, the day of his repose. Through his prayer, life, and writings, St. Silouan delivered a potent message about the boundlessness of God's love, forgiveness, and healing, which has been widely received as strikingly modern, pertinent to the contemporary social predicament. Silouan, therefore, became acknowledged as "the saint for the present day." Although possessed of little secular learning and never ordained as a priest, through years of monastic training St. Silouan became a spiritual giant, achieving a full measure of "passionlessness" (*apatheia*).

While standing firmly within the continuity of the patristic tradition, he also possesses striking originality. His contribution to Orthodox theology and soteriology encompasses the chief following ideas: unbounded love; prayer for the whole world; the prioritization of the love of "enemies"; stress on the power of repentance; and Christ-like humility.

St. Silouan's teaching on the love of all humanity and the love of "enemies" is the guiding tenet of his thought, proceeding from his understanding of the fundamental requirement of Christian charity towards all people in general, good or bad. To him, this was the essence of the human being's likeness to God and perfect discipleship of Christ. St. Silouan, strikingly, asserts that if one fails to love one's enemies, one's salvation is not assured. Having received in his youth a mystical vision of the merciful Christ, Silouan viewed the attainment of "the humility of Christ" as the highest degree of Christian perfection, that which in patristic tradition was frequently termed "deification." However, having had this vision of the glory of the humble Lord, Silouan likewise experientially knew that the greatest misfortune a human being can suffer is to lose touch with Christ through wrongful actions and even mere evil thoughts (*pomysly*), pride being the deepest root of sin. He thus saw pride as the origin of all evil and suffering in the world, what he called "the seed of death and despair." For this reason Silouan concentrated all his powers upon striving relentlessly, through the gospel commandments, to overcome pride in himself and to obtain "Christ-like humility." St. Silouan stands as the icon of Christ's saint: the one who presents to the world the Lord's own depths of humility and love to all humankind.

SEE ALSO: Asceticism; Elder (Starets); Monasticism; Sophrony, Archimandrite (1896–1993)

REFERENCES AND SUGGESTED READINGS

Larchet, J. C. (2001) *Saint Silouane de l'Athos*. Paris: Editions du Cerf.
Sophrony, Archimandrite (Sakharov) (1985) *We Shall See Him as He Is*. Maldon, UK: Monastery of St. John.
Sophrony, Archimandrite (Sakharov) (1999) *Saint Silouan the Athonite*. Crestwood, NY: St. Vladimir's Seminary Press.

St. Symeon the New Theologian (949–1022)

JOHN A. MCGUCKIN

St. Symeon is a major mystic, a precursor of the hesychasts, emphasizing the themes of illumination by the Spirit, the role of the spiritual father, the importance of the gift of tears, and the necessity of personal experience of God. He was a controversial figure in his time. His *Discourses* re-present much of the classical Studite monastic teaching but with a deeply personal charismatic spirit. Symeon's aristocratic father brought him to Constantinople in 960, and his uncle (killed in the Phocas riots of 963) advanced his career until the young man assumed senatorial rank. In 969 he first encountered the monk Symeon Eulabes who became a father-confessor. In the time of the Tzimisces revolt, he was sheltered by Symeon Eulabes, who ever after appeared to him as a mediator of Christ's salvation. He tells how, once when he was overwhelmed by a consciousness of his sinfulness, he saw during his evening prayer a brilliantly shining light, and behind that an even greater radiance. He interpreted the vision as his spiritual father interceding for him with Christ.

In 976 another palace coup brought Basil II to power and marked the end of Symeon's political life. He took refuge with his confessor and once again experienced a vision of the light of Christ, which became for him a definitive moment of conversion. He entered the monastic state. In a short time (979) he became the higumen of the St. Mamas monastery in Constantinople and refurbished it. The traditional morning *Catecheses* to the monks have survived as a central body of his work. Some time between 995 and 998 the growing opposition to his discipline broke out as a revolt by a section of his community. Patriarch Sisinnios II (995–8) heard charges against him and found in his favor; but Patriarch Sergios II (999–1019) opened new legal proceedings against him (instigated by the court). In 1003 an attempt was made to entangle him in a public theological dispute (it produced as his response the *Theological Chapters*). His answer took the form of an excoriation of the synod's chief theologian and confidant to the Emperor, Stephen of Alexina, for attempting to theologize without first having experienced the divine light. In 1005 he was subjected to house arrest and exile followed in 1009.

Symeon regarded the *casus belli* as his claim that the present generation had the same charismatic right to live in the freedom of the ancient saints. In exile he bought the oratory of St. Marina at Chrysopolis and wrote some of his most famous works, including the *Hymns of Divine Love*, a classic of mysticism. He died aged 73 in 1022. His relics were not admitted back into the capital until 1054, when Niketas Stethatos composed a *Vita* for the occasion. Symeon was revered as a great master of the inner life by the Hagiorites. In recent decades he has attracted much scholarly attention. His teaching is important both for the light it throws on a dark period of Byzantine affairs, but more so for the spiritual themes it treats with such vigor. He is a major advocate of the power of repentance: a force that is not simply for "beginners" in the ascetical life, but which makes the human soul into the "friend of Christ." His descriptions of visions of the divine light inspired generations after him, as did his devotion to the Eucharist. The practice of the Jesus Prayer, however, does not make much of an appearance. Symeon is also important for the doctrine of Spiritual Fatherhood which had a marked impact on Orthodox spiritual praxis in the time of the 18th- century Philokalic revival.

SEE ALSO: Hesychasm; Jesus Prayer; *Philokalia*; Stethatos, Niketas (ca. 1005–1085)

REFERENCES AND SUGGESTED READINGS

de Catanzaro, C. J. (trans.) (1980) *Symeon the New Theologian: The Discourses* [Catecheses]. New York: Paulist Press.

Golitzin, A. (1995–7) *St. Symeon the New Theologian* [trans. of "The Ethical Discourses"], 3 vols. New York: St. Vladimir's Seminary Press.

Hausherr, I. (1928) "Un grand mystique byzantin: Vie de S. Syméon le Nouveau Théologien [par Nicétas Stéthatos]," *Orientalia Christiana* 12, 45.

Holl, K. (1898) *Enthusiasmus und Bussgewalt beim griechischen Mönchtum, eine Studie zu Symeon dem Neuen Theologen.* Leipzig.

Krivocheine, B. (1987) *In the Light of Christ.* New York: St. Vladimir's Seminary Press.

McGuckin, J. A. (1996a) "St. Symeon the New Theologian and Byzantine Monasticism," in A. Bryer (ed.) *Mount Athos and Byzantine Monasticism.* London: Variorum Press, pp. 17–35.

McGuckin, J. A. (1996b) "St. Symeon the New Theologian (d. 1022): Byzantine Theological Renewal in Search of a Precedent." In R. N. Swanson (ed.) *The Church Retrospective: Studies in Church History*, vol. 33. Oxford: Boydell Press.

McGuckin, J. A. (1996c) "The Notion of Luminous Vision in 11th C Byzantium: Interpreting the Biblical and Theological Paradigms of St. Symeon the New Theologian." In *Acts of the Belfast Byzantine Colloquium – Portaferry 1995* (The Evergetis Project). Belfast: Queen's University Press.

McGuckin, P. (1994) *Symeon the New Theologian: Chapters and Discourses.* Kalamazoo: Cistercian Publications.

Maloney, G. (1975) *The Hymns of Divine Love.* New Jersey: Dimension Press.

Maloney, G. (1975) *The Mystic of Fire and Light.* Denville, NJ: Denville Books.

Palmer, G., Sherrard, P., and Ware, K. (1995) *Philokalia*, vol. 4. London: Faber and Faber, pp. 11–75.

Turner, H. J. M. (1990) *St. Symeon the New Theologian and Spiritual Fatherhood.* Leiden: E. J. Brill.

St. Theodore the Studite (759–826)

JOHN A. MCGUCKIN

Theodore was the aristocratic abbot (higumen) first of the Sakkudion Monastery (founded with his uncle Platon on family estates in Bithynia) and then, in 798, of the large and important Stoudium Monastery at Constantinople (by the patronage of Empress Irene). His monastic reforms (refining and systematizing the ascetic corpus of St. Basil the Great) led to his Studite Typikon becoming a "standard" model for the majority of Eastern Orthodox monasteries in the Byzantine era. He encouraged the many hundreds of monks of his cenobitic establishment to engage in literary, as well as liturgical, activities; and scholars have surmized that it was in the scriptoria of the Stoudium that the minuscule script was invented. He was a vigorous defender of the rights of the monastics against both the imperial and patriarchal throne when he felt canonical limits had been transgressed; and was particularly noted as a strong advocate of the Iconodule cause in the second phase of the Iconoclastic crisis, beginning in 814. After the Triumph of Orthodoxy, in 843, his memory was elevated along with that of St. John of Damascus as among the chief of the Iconodule saints, and his treatise *On the Holy Images* has been an influential text.

SEE ALSO: Iconoclasm; Icons; Monasticism

REFERENCES AND SUGGESTED READINGS

Roth, C. P. (trans.) (1981) *St. Theodore the Studite: On the Holy Icons.* Crestwood, NY: St. Vladimir's Seminary Press.

St. Theophan (Govorov) the Recluse (1815–1894)

KONSTANTIN GAVRILKIN

Born into the family of a rural priest, after the seminary Georgii V. Govorov continued his studies at Kiev Theological Academy, where, under the influence of the Kievan Cave Monastery, he decided to become a monk. Prior to his graduation in 1841, he was tonsured (with the name Theophan) and ordained deacon and priest shortly afterwards. For a few years he served as instructor and administrator at a number of ecclesiastical schools, but in 1847 he resigned from St. Peterbsurg Theological Academy in order to join the Russian Mission in Jerusalem, where he studied Greek, Hebrew, Arabic, and French. He also traveled throughout the Middle East and visited many holy places in Syria, Egypt, and Palestine. In 1854, because of the Crimean War, the Mission was closed, and upon his return to Russia he was appointed again to St. Petersburg Academy, and then, five months later, to the Olonetskaia Seminary (Petrozavodsk).

Less than a year later he was sent to the Russian Embassy Church in Constantinople. In the summer of 1857 he was made dean of St. Petersburg Theological Academy, only to be consecrated bishop of Tambov in 1859 and moved again in 1863 to the see of Vladimir. In 1866, tired of his endless transfers and busy administrative life, he petitioned the synod to allow him to resign and live as a "simple monk" in a monastery of his choice in order to dedicate his life to the study of Scripture, prayer, and writing. The synod (after launching an inquiry into his "unusual" request) accepted his resignation, and Theophan moved to Vyshenskaia Pustyn' (Tambov province).

For six years he followed the monastery's regular life, but in 1872 withdrew from direct contact with all people, both inside and outside the monastery, except for the abbot, his father-confessor, and the *keleinik*, a monk assigned to assist him. His life in seclusion followed a classic monastic model: prayer, study, manual labor. For the first ten years he served liturgy on Saturdays and Sundays, and for the last twelve he did so every day. He sent out between twenty and forty letters a day in response to people seeking his spiritual advice. His ever-expanding library contained several encyclopedias in various languages, Migne's *Patrologia*, Russian editions of the fathers of the church, books of the liturgical cycle, many theological journals, commentaries on Scripture, and such like. He wrote continuously, authoring more than fifty books by the end of his life: commentaries on Scripture, manuals on Christian life and prayer in particular, meditations on various subjects, theological treatises, and collections of letters of spiritual direction. In addition, he translated two volumes of Symeon the New Theologian, the *Unseen Warfare* in the version of Nicodemus the Hagiorite, as well as texts of the major ascetic writers, included in his five-volume *Philokalia*,

which was supplemented by a volume including the monastic rules of Pachomius, Basil of Caesarea, John Cassian, and Benedict of Nursia. In the last years of his life, Theophan suffered from a number of ailments, including blindness in one eye. He died on the Feast of Theophany, January 6, 1894. Having become one of the most popular and influential spiritual writers of the Russian Orthodox Church in the 19th and 20th centuries, he was canonized in 1988.

SEE ALSO: Monasticism; Russia, Patriarchal Orthodox Church of

REFERENCES AND SUGGESTED READINGS

Amis, R. (ed.) (1991) *The Heart of Salvation: The Life and Teachings of Russia's Saint Theophan the Recluse*, trans. E. Williams. Newbury, MA: Robertsbridge.

Theophan the Recluse (1997) *The Path to Salvation: A Manual of Spiritual Transformation*, trans. S. Rose. Platina, CA: St. Herman of Alaska Brotherhood.

St. Tikhon (Belavin) (1865–1925)

KONSTANTIN GAVRILKIN

Vasilii I. Belavin was born into a priestly family in the Pskov diocese. He studied at the Pskov Seminary and St Petersburg Theological Academy, became a monk with the name Tikhon in 1891, and was ordained to the diaconate and priesthood shortly after. After a few years at the Kholm Seminary, where he became the dean, he was consecrated bishop of Lublin, vicar of the Kholm-Warsaw diocese, in 1897, but a year later was sent to the United States as bishop of the Aleutians and Alaska, and he

Plate 69   Portrait of St. Tikhon (Belavin). Topfoto.

remained there until 1907. In his nine years in America, Tikhon reorganized and expanded the diocese, initiated a number of missions, and encouraged the use of the English language (instructing that Anglican prayer books should be used until translations of Orthodox texts could be published). He provided pastoral care for diverse ethnic groups of Orthodox immigrants from the Old World, since the Russian Church was the only autocephalous church with a proper administrative presence and resources in the United States at the time (the situation dramatically changed after the collapse of the Russian Empire in 1917, when its material support of the church also evaporated). By 1907 the now archdiocese of the Aleutians and North America had two vicar bishops (in Alaska and Brooklyn) and

St. Tikhon's Monastery in Pennsylvania was under construction, together with new churches in various regions.

In 1907 Tikhon was summoned back to Russia and appointed first to Yaroslavl', then to Vilnius (1913), and finally to Moscow (June 1917). When the Council of the Russian Orthodox Church was convened in Moscow in August 1917 for the first time since the 17th century, Tikhon was elected its chairman and elevated to the rank of metropolitan. The council continued its work despite the Bolshevik *coup d'état* in October and the beginning of the new regime's persecution of the church, which intensified after the outbreak of the Civil War in 1918. Among the council's primary goals was reestablishment of canonical order in the administration of the church and, first of all, the restoration of the office of patriarch, which had been abolished by Peter the Great in the early 18th century. After a few rounds of voting, Tikhon was elected out of the three leading candidates by the drawing of lots.

Tikhon led the Russian Church in the period of persecution by the hostile regime, when virtually all of its infrastructure was destroyed and internal divisions weakened its unity. In addition, the Bolshevik government used various provocations to undermine Tikhon's authority and legitimacy, and his condemnation of the violent repression of the church was widely publicized as anti-Soviet ideology. Eventually, in order to protect thousands of people from certain death, the patriarch appealed to the clergy to abstain from direct involvement in the political struggle, but this measure did not change the Bolsheviks' attitude to the church or alleviate mass repressions of the Orthodox clergy and laity. Between 1922 and 1925 Tikhon was practically under house arrest in the Donskoi Monastery in Moscow, where he died in 1925. He was canonized in October 1989. His shrine is today in the Donskoi monastery church.

SEE ALSO: New Martyrs; Russia, Patriarchal Orthodox Church of; United States of America, Orthodoxy in the

REFERENCES AND SUGGESTED READINGS

Gubonin. M. (ed.) (2007) *Sovremenniki o Patriarkhe Tikhone*, 2 vols. Moscow: PSTGU.
Lobanov, V. V. (2008) *Patriarkh Tikhon i sovetskaia vlast' (1917–1925 gg.)*. Moscow: Panorama.
Swan, J. (1964) *The Biography of Patriarch Tikhon*. Jordanville, NY: Holy Trinity Russian Orthodox Monastery.

St. Tikhon of Zadonsk (1724–1783)

JOHN A. MCGUCKIN

Russian bishop and spiritual theologian of the baroque era. He was born Timothy Sokolov, son of a village church lector, who died when he was a child, leaving the family impoverished. He entered the Novgorod seminary (with a very pro-western curriculum) where his extreme poverty evoked ridicule from other students, but eventually became a professor, and rector of the Tver seminary. His lectures on dogmatics were later published and focus on the doctrine of the redemption in western terms of atonement. In 1758 he was tonsured as a monk and priested, and in 1760 he became head of the Otroch monastery. In 1761 he was consecrated as assistant bishop in Novgorod, and two years after that was appointed bishop of Voronezh. He was active in restoring the diocesan seminary and trying to institute schemes to raise the standard of the diocesan clergy. But in 1767 he suddenly, and without explanation, sought permission to retire into an obscure monastery, settling at Zadonsk, where he stayed until he died in 1783, aged 59.

All his life he found it difficult to engage with people. He suffered from irritability, and what his first biographer, Bishop Eugene Bolkhovitinov, described as a "melancholy nervous illness" and which we today would probably call serious bi-polar disorder. One of his monastic assistants, after his death, spoke about his nervous hypochondria. His forced involvement in the state-mandated deposition of Metropolitan Arseniy Matsievich in Moscow in 1763 deeply disturbed him. Tikhon always preferred to avoid social engagement, making an exception (which he had to force against his inclination) to visit the imprisoned, and minister to the peasants, whom he helped from his state pension while living in great personal simplicity.

Tikhon was canonized in 1861. His spiritual work, mostly composed in solitude in Zadonsk, is typical of much that was happening in 18th-century Russia, and shows familiarity with western pietistic and evangelical trends. His *Spiritual Treasure* is an Orthodox adaptation of *Occasional Meditations* by the 17th-century Anglican theologian Joseph Hall, bishop of Norwich. Johann Arndt's treatise *True Christianity* also was a strong influence on him, though in his own book, of the same title, Tikhon moderated Protestant pietism with deep currents from Russian Kenoticism that were familiar to him. Fedotov, in his study of Russian spiritual masters, says that his "personality is much more interesting than his writings. He is the first 'modern' among the Russian saints, with his interior conflicts, his painful groping for his spiritual way – the constant shift of light and shadow, of ecstasy and depression" (Fedotov 1950: 183–4). At Zadonsk, Tikhon devoted every night to prayer, sleeping only at sunrise. When he was overcome with depression he would ceaselessly chant: "Lord have mercy on me. Lord forgive. Giver of life have mercy on me." And when he was happy he would replace the invocation with "Praise the Lord in heaven." Late in life he received ecstatic visions of Christ, the Theotokos, and the joy of heaven. In his writing profound devotion and love for Christ crucified are manifested. His path to sanctity was one that was navigated through many psychological fragilities; a fact that makes him unusual in the annals of Orthodox spiritual writing of the modern period. Dostoevsky saw in Tikhon a model of spirituality that he reflects in several of his writings.

SEE ALSO: Russia, Patriarchal Orthodox Church of

REFERENCES AND SUGGESTED READINGS

Bolshakoff, S. (1980) *Russian Mystics*. Kalamazoo: Cistercian Publications, pp. 61–78.

Fedotov, G. P. (ed.) (1981) *A Treasury of Russian Spirituality*, 3rd edn. London: Sheed and Ward, pp. 182–241.

Spidlik, T. (1991) "Tikhon de Zadonske," in *Dictionnaire de spiritualité*, Vol. 15. Paris: Beauchesne, cols. 960–4.

Sts. Barsanuphius and John (6th c.)

JOHN CHRYSSAVGIS

In the early 6th century Barsanuphius, an Egyptian monk, entered the hilly region of Thavatha in Southern Palestine (near Gaza) as a recluse, acquiring a remarkable reputation for discernment and compassion. Abba Seridos, who attended to Barsanuphius as his scribe, was later appointed abbot of a monastery created to organize the increasing number of monks that gradually gathered around the elder. The community included workshops, two guest-houses, a hospital, and a large church where women, too, could receive instruction. Seridos acted as mediator for those wishing to submit questions in writing. Since Seridos did not know Coptic, he would write in Greek. Some time between 525 and 527, another hermit, John, came to live beside Barsanuphius, who became known as the "Great Old Man"; John was called the "Other Old Man." The two shared the same way of life and supported one another's ministry. John's attendant and scribe was Dorotheus of Gaza (later an important spiritual writer in his own right).

John's letters were more "institutional," responding to practical matters; those of Barsanuphius were more "inspirational," responding to spiritual problems. Their authority is uniquely refreshing. At a time when monastic life in the West was becoming increasingly more regulated, Palestinian monasticism preserved flexibility and fluidity. The letters are not a monastic "rule"; they are very personal in style and content.

While scholarship sometimes emphasizes the more "extraordinary" characteristics of the desert elders, Barsanuphius and John are less spectacular. Sensational miracles and exceptional charisms are hardly the most striking feature of their spirituality; they defy the romanticized hagiographical picture of the Late Antique holy man. They do not provide wisdom on request; nor do they attempt to solve all problems presented before them. Their purpose is to inspire and to exhort.

In all, there are approximately 850 letters. Almost 400 of these letters (the longer ones) belong to Barsanuphius, while almost 450 letters belong to John. Whereas early monastic literature has concentrated on monastic development, the correspondence of Barsanuphius and John redresses a balance in this regard, focusing much attention on the concerns of lay persons. The letters involve more or less all of the main actors of the period, with the exception of women. They include monks from the monastery of Abba Seridos and simple laypersons from the surrounding community, through to high-ranking political officials and ecclesiastical leaders; bishops ask about ordinations; lay people inquire about illness and healing, legal and economic matters, marriage and death, property rights and popular superstitions. The ascetic teaching of the letters includes such concepts as gratitude in all circumstances and constant joy, as well as two terms that they coin, namely "not reckoning oneself as anything" and avoiding "the pretense to rights."

Beyond scriptural references, relatively few proper names are recorded in the letters, which continue the tradition of the Apophthegmata Patrum. Through Dorotheus of Gaza, Theodore the Studite also accepts the authority of their teachings, whose extensive influence is evident in John Klimakos and, through John, in Symeon the New Theologian and the 14th-century Hesychasts. Barsanuphius and John are liturgically commemorated on February 6.

REFERENCES AND SUGGESTED READINGS

Chryssavgis, J. (2003) *Letters from the Desert: A Selection of the Spiritual Correspondence of Barsanuphius and John.* Crestwood, NY: St. Vladimir's Seminary Press.
Hevelone-Harper, J. L. (2005) *Disciples of the Desert: Monks, Laity, and Spiritual Authority in Sixth-Century Gaza.* Baltimore: Johns Hopkins University Press.

Sts. Constantine (Cyril) (ca. 826–869) and Methodios (815–885)

BRENDA LLEWELLYN IHSSEN

Brothers Constantine-Cyril and Methodios were born, raised, and educated in Thessaloniki, an area populated by Slavs for several centuries before them. Their heritage is uncertain, but their home was probably bilingual, Greek and Slavic. Constantine studied at Constantinople under the guidance of future patriarch Photios, and was elevated to chartophylax, a position he resigned in favor of a monastic vocation. Constantine was appointed professor of philosophy at the imperial university, his brother Methodios was appointed archon of an unnamed Slavic territory, a position he also renounced in favor of monasticism. The brothers were united again for a diplomatic and religious mission in the Crimea, where their talents with languages and apologetics were tested in conversation with Jewish and Islamic-influenced Khazars, as well as the Rus.

Facing territorial pressure from Germans and Bulgars, Moravian Prince Rastislav requested that Byzantine Emperor Michael III (842–67) send a bishop and teacher to provide ecclesiastical instruction in Slavonic for building national unity and consciousness, and intellectual and religious culture among various tribes in the territory known to historians as "Greater Moravia." A secondary goal was a diplomatic alliance with Byzantium, which would be able to provide political protection for Moravia from menacing neighbors. The brothers, with language and diplomatic skills recently tested on their mission in the Crimea, were suited for the appointment. Prior to the departure and under Cyril's supervision, a team translated sacred texts from Greek into Slavonic using a rough Slavic alphabet that possibly existed in a rudimentary form prior to Rastislav's request. As developed and finally attributed to Constantine, Glagolitic is a creative and original alphabet that is a testament to his talents as a philologist.

Though the embassy was received favorably in Moravia, German Catholic clergy bitterly opposed their work on the grounds that the gospel ought to be preached only in three languages: Hebrew, Greek, or Latin (trilingualism). This argument would be dismissed by Pope Hadrian II, who greeted the brothers when they arrived to appeal in Rome in 867 with native Slavic clergy to be ordained, and offering the relics of St. Clement (currently at rest in the Basilica di San Clemente). While in Rome the brothers learned of Emperor Michael III's death and the deposition of Patriarch Photios; Constantine, who was ill, recognized that he would likely die in Rome, and subsequently took solemn monastic vows, electing the name "Cyril." Since transfer to Constantinople was impractical, Cyril's body was also buried in the Basilica di San Clemente at Methodios' request.

Methodios was consecrated as archbishop and returned to Moravia, where he faced mounting opposition from Frankish clergy. After successfully defending his Orthodoxy in Constantinople he returned to Moravia and labored to complete a full translation of the Bible into the vernacular before he died in 884.

The brothers are central figures in the history of Slavic Orthodoxy. In addition to the alphabet and the transmission of sacred texts, they were responsible for transmitting the wider context of meaning for what was translated. Subsequently, the Slavic world inherited the harvest of their labors in the form of a literary, spiritual, theological, and artistic tradition which is marked to this day in the unique character of the Slavic Orthodox people.

SEE ALSO: St. Photios the Great (ca. 810–ca. 893)

REFERENCES AND SUGGESTED READINGS

Dvornik, F. (1970) *Byzantine Missions Among the Slavs: SS. Constantine-Cyril and Methodius.* Piscataway, NJ: Rutgers University Press.
Soulis, G. C. (1965) "The Legacy of Cyril and Methodius to the Southern Slavs," *Dumbarton Oaks Papers* 19.
Tachiaos, A. N. (2001) *Cyril and Methodius of Thessalonica: The Acculturation of the Slavs.* Crestwood, NY: St. Vladimir's Seminary Press.
Vlasto, A. P. (1970) *The Entry of the Slavs into Christendom: An Introduction to the Medieval History of the Slavs.* Cambridge: Cambridge University Press.

Schmemann, Alexander (1921–1983) *see* Contemporary Orthodox Theology

Scholarios, George (Gennadios) (ca. 1403–1472)

A. EDWARD SIECIENSKI

George Scholarios was a great admirer of Thomas Aquinas and an advocate of union with Rome at the Council of Florence (1438–9). However, following the death of his friend and teacher Mark of Ephesus in 1445, Scholarios became a staunch anti-unionist and then first patriarch of Constantinople (as Gennadios II) following the fall of the city in 1453.

SEE ALSO: Ecumenism, Orthodoxy and; Florence, Council of (1438–1439); *Filioque*; St. Mark of Ephesus (1392–1445)

REFERENCES AND SUGGESTED READINGS

Petit, L. and Jugie, M. (eds.) (1928–36) *Oeuvres complètes de Georges (Gennadios) Scholarios*, 8 vols. Paris: Maison de la bonne presse.
Tinnefeld, F. (2002) "George Gennadios Scholarius," in C. Conticello and V. Conticello (eds.) *La Théologie byzantine et sa tradition*, vol. 2. Turnhout: Brepols, pp. 477–549.

Semandron

DIMITRI CONOMOS

A struck instrument used on Mount Athos and in many other Orthodox monasteries. Its rhythmic percussions call worshippers to a service or to a meal. On important occasions its resonating claps lead an outside litanical procession. Semandra are made of wood or metal. If wooden, it is either a long plank, grasped by the player's left hand and struck by the right with a wooden mallet, or a larger and heavier timber block suspended by chains and struck by one or two mallets. The metallic semandron is not portable, but often horseshoe shaped and struck by a metal mallet.

Serbia, Patriarchal Orthodox Church of

GORDON N. BARDOS

In the ecclesiastical hierarchy of the Orthodox Church, the autocephalous Patriarchal Church of Serbia ranks sixth in terms of primacy (behind the patriarchates of Constantinople, Alexandria, Antioch, Jerusalem, and Russia). Since the Middle Ages, the Serbian Church has been spread territorially across many parts of the Balkan peninsula, from southern Dalmatia on the Adriatic coast, to parts of present-day Albania, Bosnia and Herzegovina, Kosovo and Metohija, Macedonia, and Serbia.

Today, as a result of centuries of migrations and emigrations, the Orthodox Church of Serbia consists of approximately thirty dioceses worldwide, governed by a standing holy synod of bishops representing the highest executive and judicial body within the church. The holy synod of bishops is composed of the patriarch (*ex officio*) and four bishops who are elected bi-annually by the holy assembly of bishops of the Serbian Orthodox Church. The holy assembly of bishops, in turn, is a body which represents all of the metropolitans and bishops in the church.

Throughout its history, the Serbian Orthodox Church has portrayed itself, and has been widely perceived by the Serbian public, as being the most consistent, strongest, and sometimes the sole, defender of the Serbian people. This has on occasion led to charges that the Serbian Orthodox Church is overly nationalistic, yet it is a phenomenon common to most of the religious organizations in Southeastern

Europe. Because of a variety of historical and cultural circumstances, religion and ethnicity have become strongly intertwined in the Balkans; in this sense, the relationship between the Serbian Orthodox Church and the Serbian people follows the general Balkan rule, rather than being an exception.

CONVERSION OF THE SERBS TO CHRISTIANITY

Along with other Slavic tribes, the Serbs migrated to the Balkan Peninsula in the 7th century. In the 10th century, followers of Sts. Cyril and Methodios converted the pagan Serb tribes to Christianity. In the late 12th century a powerful Serb state emerged during the rule of Stefan Nemanja (1109–99), centered on the mountainous regions straddling the borders of modern-day Kosovo and Metohija. Serbs commonly refer to Kosovo as "Kosovo and Metohij." The word *Metohija* is derived from the Greek meaning "land of the monasteries." It specifically refers to the many monasteries spread throughout northern and western Kosovo, Serbia, and Montenegro. Under Nemanja and his heirs, the Serbian state grew and expanded territorially until the mid-14th century, largely at the Byzantine Empire's expense. The history of medieval Serbia and, by extension, the medieval Serbian Church, is intimately connected with the Nemanjić dynasty, so much so that most of the rulers from the Nemanjić dynasty were canonized as saints by the Serbian Church. The most important and venerated figure in Serbian history is Stefan Nemanja's son, Ratsko (1175–1235), who left his father's court for Mount Athos, became a monk, and adopted the monastic name of Sava. After his death he was canonized by the Serbian Church, thereafter becoming known as St. Sava the Enlightener.

St. Sava played a crucial role in forming the Serbs' religious and national identities. Given the Balkan Peninsula's geographical location between East and West, for several centuries it remained unclear whether the Serbs as a people would ultimately fall under the fold of the Western Church, with all of the political and cultural implications that entailed, or accept Orthodox Christianity, and thereby draw their spiritual and cultural inspiration from Constantinople and the Byzantine world. St. Sava was a determined proponent of the latter. A few years after moving to Mount Athos, Sava was joined there by his father, Stefan Nemanja, who also became a monk and adopted the monastic name of Simeon. Together, Simeon and Sava founded one of the most important religious and cultural centers of the Serbian people, the Monastery of Hilandar on Mount Athos. Hilandar's (and, by extension, Mount Athos') influence on Serbia's subsequent development would be of tremendous importance, as many of Sava's Serb contemporaries and successors would spend their spiritually and intellectually formative years there.

Simeon and Sava returned to Serbia in approximately 1196–7 to develop spiritual and religious life in the Serbian lands. Coinciding with the Latin conquest of Constantinople in 1204, the subsequent weakness of the Byzantine Empire at this time allowed Sava to build a strong, indigenous church organization. In 1219, during the Byzantine court's exile in Nicea, Sava convinced the patriarch of Constantinople, Manuel I, to grant the Serbian Church autocephaly. In granting his assent, Patriarch Manuel also consecrated Sava the first archbishop of the autocephalous Serbian Church.

Upon his return to Serbia, Sava reorganized Orthodoxy in the Serbian lands, consecrating new bishops, creating new dioceses, and founding new monasteries to serve as episcopal seats. Many of the monasteries built during the Nemanjić period, such as Studenica, Gračanica, Visoki Dečani, the Peć Patriarchate, Sopoćani, and Žića, are considered to be the most important cultural, spiritual, and historical landmarks of the Serbian people. Sava was also careful at this time to give the newly autocephalous church a distinctively Serbian national character; thus, for instance, he ordered that the abbots of the leading monasteries be Serb rather than Greek, and also that inscriptions on church buildings or frescoes be in Slavonic rather than Greek. St. Sava the Enlightener's legacy would prove to be profound. Largely thanks to his efforts and personality, both the Serbian state and the Serbs as a people became firmly anchored in the Orthodox world, and would in subsequent centuries come to represent the westernmost frontier of Orthodoxy.

A century after Sava's death, during the reign of Serbia's most powerful medieval ruler, Stefan Dušan Nemanjić (the "Mighty"), the Serbian state expanded to the point of becoming an empire that included most of the southern Balkans, and Dušan's ambitions had grown to include capturing Constantinople itself. Towards this end, he had the Serbian archbishopric elevated to the status of a patriarchate (without, however, the blessings of the ecumenical patriarch in Constantinople), which was given the name of the patriarchate of Peć. In 1346 in Skopje, the newly installed Serbian patriarch, Joanikije II, crowned Dušan "Emperor and Autocrat of the Serbs and Greeks." Dušan also had the new patriarchate assume jurisdictional authority over several traditionally Greek metropolitan sees throughout the southern Balkans, further alienating and deepening the hostilities between him and his Byzantine rivals. In 1353 Ecumenical Patriarch Kallistos excommunicated Dušan, Joanikije, and the Serbian Church as a whole.

Dušan's empire, however, was short-lived. Upon his death in 1355, his successors began to compete for different parts of his realm, while the simultaneous Ottoman advance into southeastern Serbia proved unstoppable. Some degree of reconciliation between the Serbian Church and the ecumenical patriarchate was achieved under Dušan's eventual successor, Prince (popularly called Tsar) Lazar Hrebljanović, although the precise details of this reconciliation remain unclear. The Serbian state gradually collapsed between the Battle of the Maritsa in 1371, the famous Kosovo battle of 1389, and the final fall of the last Serbian capital, Smederevo, in 1459. The patriarchate of Peć itself became vacant with the death of Patriarch Arsenije II in 1463.

CULTURAL HERITAGE OF SERBIAN ORTHODOXY

Although the medieval Serbian state drew most of its spiritual and cultural inspiration from the Byzantine Empire and the Orthodox East, Serbia's geographical location ensured that it would also be significantly affected by intellectual and artistic influences from the West. In the late 9th and early 10th centuries the Serbs had already adopted a modified version of the Glagolithic script devised by Sts. Cyril and Methodios. The new version, known as Cyrillic, was created by St. Clement of Ohrid. Many of the earliest written works produced in Serbia in the medieval period were based on translations of various Greek (or in some cases, Bulgar) biblical, patristic, and liturgical texts.

In later centuries, influences from the Latin West and Old Muscovy became more apparent. Monasteries built during the 12th and 13th centuries, such as Studenica (founded in 1190), represent a particularly Serbian blend of both Byzantine and

Romanesque architectural styles which became known as the Raška School, described as a style linking "Latin rationalism with Greek mysticism" (Peić 1994: 29). Thus, Serbian monasteries during this period were frequently built by Adriatic stonemasons, while the frescoes inside the churches were drawn by Greek painters. The frescoes of this period, most especially in monasteries such as Studenica and Sopoćani, are frequently described as "monumental," in the sense that themes such as the crucifixion are often 8–10 feet tall.

In the 14th century, partly under the influence of the Palaeologue Revival in Constantinople, Serbian art and architecture evolved into a more purely Byzantine/Orthodox form. Monasteries such as Gračanica (built 1313) were constructed using the standard Greek cross floor plan, with anywhere from one to five domes. The years before and after the famous Battle of Kosovo in 1389 saw a final flourishing of Serbian art exhibiting many indigenous qualities in which Roman and Byzantine influences were less obvious. This new style came to be known as the Morava School. Examples of the Morava School include Ravanica (built 1375), Kalenić (ca. 1407), and Manasija (also known as Resava, ca. 1407).

As throughout medieval Europe, monasteries in the Serbian lands served both as spiritual centers and as centers of great learning and artistic creativity. Thus, Serbian monasteries were frequently multipurpose enterprises, incorporating icon studios, woodworking shops, scriptoria for producing and reproducing Bibles, liturgical texts, and biographies of the saints, and medical centers.

SERBIAN CHURCH UNDER OTTOMAN AND HABSBURG RULE

The demise of the medieval Serbian state in the 14th and 15th centuries, and the imposition of Ottoman rule in the Balkans, significantly changed the position and role of the Orthodox Church in Serbian society. The Ottoman *millet* system was a form of indirect rule and corporate self-government by ethno-confessional groups first established in 1454 by Sultan Mehmet II after the fall of Constantinople. The *millet* system has been described by Sugar (1977: 44) as "basically a minority home-rule policy based on religious affiliation," whose roots can be found in Ottoman rule in Sassanid Iran, and even in some of Justinian's edicts concerning Jews in the Byzantine Empire. Sugar notes that under the *millet* system:

> Besides full ecclesiastical powers and jurisdiction, the patriarch acquired legal powers in those cases, such as marriage, divorce, and inheritance, that were regulated by canon law.... certain police powers that even included a patriarchal jail in Istanbul. Naturally, the church was also permitted to collect the usual ecclesiastical dues, but it was also made responsible and was often consulted in the assessing and collecting of taxes due the state. Finally, ecclesiastical courts had the right to hear and decide cases in which all litigants were Christians, provided they voluntarily submitted their cases to church courts rather than to the kadi. (Sugar 1977: 46)

In the Serbian case, somewhat paradoxically, the practical result of the *millet* system was that the church became a more powerful institution among the Serbian people under the Ottomans than it had been while the Serbs had their own native rulers, with the Serbian people's ecclesiastical leaders henceforth becoming their secular leaders as well.

Historical records of this period in Serbian Church history are scarce. Soon after the fall of Smederevo, in 1463 the Ottoman state abolished the patriarchate of Peć and ecclesiastical authority over the Serbs was turned over to the archbishop of Ohrid. Some one hundred years later, however, the rise to power of a Bosnian Serb boy, Mehmet Paşa Sokollu (in Serbian, Mehmet Paša Sokolović, 1506–79) to the position of grand vizier of the empire would lead to the reestablishment of the patriarchate of Peć in 1557, when Sokollu installed his relative Makarije Sokolović as Orthodox Serbian patriarch. Territorially, the reestablished patriarchate of Peć stretched from southern Hungary in the north to Macedonia in the south, and from the Dalmatian coast (as far north as Šibenik) to parts of western Bulgaria in the east.

The existence of the Peć patriarchate provided the Serbs with a symbolic reminder of their lost medieval state, and was consequently a natural focal point for Serb insurrections against the Ottoman Empire. During this period, monasteries frequently served as natural places for insurrections to be planned and proclaimed. In April 1594, to discourage further Serb revolts, Turkish troops removed the relics of St. Sava from Mileševo Monastery and burned the remains on the site of Vračar, one of Belgrade's most prominent hills. The Serbian Orthodox Church since the 19th century had plans to build a monumental memorial temple to St. Sava on the site. Construction began after World War I, but completion was delayed by World War II and then by the communist government. In the late 1980s work resumed in earnest, and today construction on the Temple of Saint Sava (*Hram Svetog Save*) has been completed. It is one of the largest Orthodox Churches in the world.

The Ottoman conquest of Southeastern Europe had another important effect on the Serbian Orthodox Church, inasmuch as large numbers of Serbs fleeing Ottoman rule spread the Serbian Church territorially and jurisdictionally to many parts of the Habsburg Empire as well. From the 15th century onwards, large-scale migrations pushed the Serbs from their historic religious and cultural homelands in Kosovo, Montenegro, and the Sandzak, northwards to the Krajina in central and western Croatia, and the Vojvodina region north of Belgrade, bounded by the Danube and Tisa rivers.

One of the most important of the Serb revolts under Turkish rule occurred in 1690, when Patriarch Arsenije (Crnojević), seeing a strategic opportunity arise after the Habsburgs went to war with the Ottoman Empire, decided to support the Austrians in a bid to liberate the Serbs from Ottoman rule. The Ottomans, however, ultimately proved successful in the conflict, as a result of which Arsenije led a legendary "Great Migration" of several tens of thousands of Serbs from present-day Kosovo and Metohija northwards into Habsburg territory.

As a result of centuries of Ottoman persecution and out-migrations, by the 18th century the Serbian Church under Turkish rule had become a very weak institution. In 1766 the patriarchate of Peć was again abolished, whereupon the Serbian Church in the Ottoman Empire again fell under the jurisdiction of the ecumenical patriarch, beginning a period of attempted Hellenization of the Serbian Church led by Greek Phanariot bishops. Ultimately, however, these efforts made little headway because of the social and cultural distance between the Greek hierarchy and lower-ranking Serb clerics and laity.

In the Habsburg Empire during this same period, the Serbs populated what became known as the "Military Frontier" (*vojna krajina*) of the Habsburg territories, where they enjoyed special forms of self-government in return for serving as full-time soldiers protecting the imperial borders. Importantly, the Habsburgs adopted many features of the *millet* system, insofar as the Serbs' spiritual and ecclesiastical authorities again became intermediaries between the Habsburg monarch and their own people in secular matters. The Serbian Church organization in the Habsburg monarchy was centered on the metropolitan of (Sremski) Karlovac, which in 1710 the patriarch of Peć, Kalinik I, recognized as autonomous. In 1848, during the general uprisings against absolutism in the Habsburg monarchy, a Serb revolt against Magyar rule proclaimed the metropolitan of Karlovci, Josif Rajačić, as "patriarch." His successors continued to use that title until 1913, although the metropolitans of Karlovci are not generally considered to be successors to the patriarchs of Peć.

The Serbian Church in Montenegro developed along somewhat different lines. Given Montenegro's forbidding geography, after the Battle of Kosovo in 1389 Serbian religious and even political life was able to continue in somewhat freer circumstances, and with considerable autonomy. Although in the 18th century Montenegro was essentially composed of a collection of extended mountain clans formed into "tribes," a rudimentary form of state, led by the metropolitan of Montenegro, continued the Serbian state traditions from the Nemanjić period and drew its legitimacy and inspiration from them. By the 18th century, Montenegro had evolved into a form of theocracy in which secular power was passed down from the metropolitan (who, by tradition, came from the Petrović-Njeguši clan) to his nephew. By tradition, the Montenegrin prince-bishops went to Moscow for their consecration. The greatest of these religious-secular rulers, Bishop Petar II Petrović Njegoš, became one of the greatest poets of the South Slavs. By the mid-19th century, however, Montenegro's hereditary theocracy died out, and a more formal secular government was formed.

LIBERATION AND REUNIFICATION

As the Ottoman Empire began a slow but steady decline in the latter part of the 17th century, the Balkan Christian peoples again began to contemplate their liberation from Turkish rule. In 1804 the Serbs began the first Balkan Christian revolt under the leadership of Djordje "Karadjordje" Petrović. Although Karadjordje's insurrection was defeated after a few years, in 1815, the Serbs launched a second, ultimately more successful insurrection under the leadership of Miloš Obrenović. By 1830 the sultan was forced to recognize Serbian autonomy, and with it religious autonomy; henceforth, the Serbs would be allowed to elect their own metropolitans and bishops, who were only required to go to Constantinople for their consecration by the ecumenical patriarch.

At the Congress of Berlin in 1875 the Serbian principality was recognized as an independent state, and consequently, in 1879, the ecumenical patriarch granted the church in Serbia proper full autocephaly. Nevertheless, the various branches of the Serbian Church still found themselves disunited during this period. The Serbs in Bosnia and Herzegovina were still under the spiritual authority of the ecumenical patriarch in Constantinople, while the Serbian Church organizations in Austria-Hungary and Montenegro had *de facto* (although not canonical) autocephaly.

The full reunification of the Serbian Orthodox Church only became possible after World War I, with the collapse of the Austro-Hungarian and Ottoman Empires, and the creation of the Kingdom of Serbs, Croats and Slovenes (renamed the Kingdom of Yugoslavia in 1929). In 1919 the ecumenical patriarch recognized the will of the Serbian Orthodox jurisdictions within the new kingdom to unite in one church organization, and in 1920 the modern patriarchate of Serbia was proclaimed. The first modern Serbian patriarch, Dimitrije, assumed the title "Archbishop of Peć, Metropolitan of Belgrade-Karlovci, and Serbian Patriarch."

WORLD WAR II

The Axis invasion and dismemberment of Yugoslavia in April 1941 led to one of the most difficult periods in the history of the Serbian Orthodox Church. Under Nazi sponsorship, a political puppet *Nezavisna Država Hrvatska* ("Independent State of Croatia," hereafter, NDH) was created which incorporated most of present-day Croatia, Bosnia and Herzegovina, and parts of Vojvodina. An extreme fascist group, the Ustaša, were brought to power in the NDH, and initiated what proved to be one of World War II's most horrific reigns of terror. Tens of thousands of Serbs, Jews, Roma, and anti-fascist Croats were liquidated in the NDH during World War II, with the Serbian Church becoming a special target of the Ustaša. The Ustaša-led NDH was a criminal regime of almost incomprehensible brutality, mainly targeted against the Orthodox population of Croatia and Bosnia and Herzegovina. The Roman Catholic bishop of Mostar, Monsignor Alojzije Mišić, communicated some of these crimes against the Serb population of Herzegovina to the archbishop of Zagreb, Alojzije Stepinac, in a letter in August 1941:

> Men are captured like animals. They are slaughtered, murdered; living men are thrown off cliffs.... From Mostar and Čapljina a train took six carloads of mothers, young girls, and children ten years of age to the station of Šurmanci. There they were made to get off the train, were led up to the mountains, and the mothers together with the children were thrown alive off steep precipices. In the

parish of Klepci 700 schismatics from the surrounding villages were murdered. Must I continue this enumeration? In the town of Mostar itself, they have been bound by the hundreds, taken in wagons outside the town, and there shot down like animals. (Tomasevich 2001: 57)

Together with the general Serb Orthodox population of the NDH, Serb hierarchs and clerics were also especially targeted by the Ustaša regime. The ferocity of the Ustaša attack on the Serbian Orthodox Church can be seen in the following figures: in April 1941 the Serbian Orthodox Church had eight bishops and 577 priests in the territories which comprised the NDH. By the end of 1941, three bishops and 154 priests had been killed outright, while three bishops and some 340 priests were expelled from the NDH or fled of their own accord. It is estimated that only approximately eighty-five Serbian Orthodox priests remained on NDH territory by the end of 1941. Nor did the Ustaša spare the physical and material infrastructure of the church. For instance, in the Orthodox diocese of Plaški-Karlovac alone, of the 189 Orthodox churches in that bishopric, the Ustaša destroyed eighty-eight and badly damaged a further sixty-seven.

Serbia itself was divided and occupied by Nazi Germany and its fascist allies, Hungary and Bulgaria. To further weaken popular resistance to Nazi rule, the Nazis deported the Serbian Patriarch Gavrilo (Dožić) and interned him in the Dachau concentration camp during the war, along with Bishop Nikolai (Velimirović), generally considered the most important Serbian theologian of the 20th century.

The Serbian Orthodox Church in Bulgarian-occupied southeast Serbia, Kosovo, and Macedonia was also persecuted. The Bulgarian occupying forces in these regions expelled Orthodox clerics considered to be Serbs, including the metropolitan of

Skopje, Josif. In the parts of Kosovo and Macedonia annexed to the Nazi-sponsored "Greater Albania," the church administration was incorporated into the expanded Albanian Orthodox Church. Many of these changes were reversed after the war, however, as with the victory of Tito's communist movement, Yugoslavia was reestablished in its prewar borders, and some attempt was made to go back to the official *status quo ante* in these areas.

Nevertheless, the war and the communist takeover of Yugoslavia did have long-lasting repercussions for the Serbian Orthodox Church. In Bosnia and Herzegovina and Croatia, the Ustaša persecution of the Serbs and the Serbian Orthodox Church poisoned interethnic relations in ways that would become all too apparent two generations later. But World War II also had repercussions in places such as Macedonia. In October 1943, in the middle of World War II, a communist-sponsored organizing committee for church affairs in Macedonia was held which marked the first move by Macedonian clerics to break with the Serbian Orthodox Church. This meeting was followed by a National Church Assembly held in Skopje in March 1945, which, among other things, called for reestablishing the ancient archbishopric of Ohrid, making the Macedonian Church autocephalous, and insisted that only Macedonian nationals be allowed to serve as bishops and clerics in Macedonia.

COMMUNIST RULE

Due to its immense human and material losses during World War II, and the opposition many church hierarchs exhibited to the Nazi occupation, the Serbian Orthodox Church emerged from World War II with considerable prestige. Yugoslavia's postwar communist regime, led by Josip Broz Tito,

however, came to power with the intent of severely limiting the role of religious organizations in the state. Toward this end, various proscriptions were placed on the activities of the Serbian Orthodox Church, as well as on other religious communities in the country. These included placing limits on the construction of new church buildings (or limiting the reconstruction of churches destroyed during the war). The most famous example of such legal and bureaucratic persecution and harassment was the placing of various obstacles in the way of completing the construction of the Temple of St. Sava in Belgrade.

The church's life in communist Yugoslavia was also affected by such things as a ban on religious education in schools and limitations on the ability of refugees to return to their prewar homes. This was particularly the case with respect to Kosovo and Metohija, where the communist government prevented tens of thousands of Serbs who had lived in Kosovo before 1941 from returning, effectively shifting the demographic balance in the province decisively in favor of the Albanian (Muslim) population.

Tito's communist government also attempted to weaken the Serbian Orthodox Church by promoting various schisms within it. In this it was somewhat successful. The most important example of such efforts was government pressure and support for the creation of the Macedonian Orthodox Church. In the general exhaustion and confusion of the immediate postwar years, relations between the Serbian Orthodox Church and the church in Macedonia were tenuous, but in 1957 Macedonian clerics recognized the Serbian patriarch as their head. The reconciliation was only nominal, however, and in July 1967 church leaders in Macedonia formally broke with the Serbian patriarchate, declared their church autocephalous, and elected the archbishop of Ohrid and metropolitan of Macedonia as the leader of the "Macedonian Orthodox Church." Neither the Serbian patriarchate nor other Orthodox Churches around the world, however, recognized this as a move that was canonically valid.

In the 1960s the Serbian Orthodox Church was also afflicted by a schism in its overseas dioceses, primarily those in Western Europe and the United States, the basis of which could largely be found in postwar anti-communist émigré politics. Although only a minority of the Serbian churches abroad supported the clergy who accepted the break with the Serbian patriarchate, the schism nevertheless proved to be a long, costly, and painful problem for the church.

AFTER COMMUNISM AND THE YUGOSLAV WARS

The fall of communism throughout Eastern Europe marked the beginning of the Serbian Orthodox Church's reemergence as a major social, cultural, and even political force in Serbia. Unfortunately, this was also the precise historical moment at which the former Yugoslavia began to collapse amid widespread interethnic violence. The Serbian Church found itself in an especially challenging situation, most especially because it had adherents and churches in all of Yugoslavia's republics and provinces.

The most difficult situation confronting the church was in Croatia and Bosnia and Herzegovina. As noted above, these two Yugoslav republics had together comprised most of the World War II "Independent State of Croatia," and the survivors of the NDH genocide against the Serbs were particularly alarmed that the political and security guarantees they enjoyed in Yugoslavia would be eliminated or reduced in the newly independent states, where Serbs would constitute a distinct minority

vis-à-vis the Croats in Croatia and the Muslims in Bosnia and Herzegovina.

During the wars in Bosnia and Herzegovina, Croatia, and Kosovo, the Serbian Orthodox Church and its hierarchs had to walk a fine line between defending the legitimate interests of their flock while at the same time avoiding dangers of becoming an overtly nationalist organization that engaged in dealings with actual or perceived war criminals. Some members of the clergy managed to navigate successfully and honorably through those times; the behavior of others was more questionable. Undoubtedly, however, the most famous denunciation of the wars in Bosnia and Croatia, and of the nationalistic excesses that accompanied them, was made by Patriarch Pavle, who said during this period:

> If a "Greater Serbia" has to be maintained through crime, I would never accept that. Let Greater Serbia disappear, but to maintain it through crime, never. If it would be necessary and needed for Little Serbia to be maintained through crime, I would not accept that either. Let Little Serbia disappear as well, rather than having it exist through crime. And if we would have to maintain the last Serb, and I was that Serb, but to do it through crime, I do not accept that, let us cease to exist, but let us cease to exist as human beings, because then we will not cease to exist, we will as living beings go into the arms of the living God.

One of the most delicate balancing acts of all concerned the Serbian Orthodox Church's position vis-à-vis the regime of Slobodan Milošević, president of Serbia. As early as 1992, many Serbian Church officials, most prominently the bishop of Zahumlje-Hercegovina, Atanasije (Jevtić), had publicly called on Milošević to resign. Other members of the church hierarchy, however, were more sympathetic to Milošević and his regime (Bardos 1992). Nevertheless, most of the church opposed Milošević, and during the 1990s many opposition leaders in Serbia sought the church's support for their efforts.

PERSECUTION IN KOSOVO AND METOHIJA

Throughout the 20th century the Serbian Orthodox Church's position in Kosovo had been especially threatened. Albanian–Serb relations have been exceptionally hostile, with the two groups taking turns at being the oppressor and the oppressed as historical circumstances have varied. The rise in Albanian nationalism after Tito's death in 1980 marked the start of a new period of persecution for the Serbian Orthodox Church and Serbian Orthodox Christians in Kosovo. Throughout the 1980s, extremists engaged in various forms of harassment and intimidation against the Serbs in Kosovo, such as stealing livestock or engaging in various forms of verbal and physical harassment. In 1981 arsonists set part of the patriarchate of Peć on fire, and a few years later the bishop of Raška-Prizren, Pavle (later to become patriarch of the Serbian Church), was beaten on the streets so severely by youths that he had to spend several weeks in hospital.

Albanian–Serb tensions finally exploded into full-scale violence in 1998, and in March 1999 the North Atlantic Treaty Organization (NATO) initiated a three-month bombing campaign of the Federal Republic of Yugoslavia to wrest control of the province of Kosovo from Serbia. During the conflict, Serb government and paramilitary forces expelled tens of thousands of Albanians from the province and destroyed or damaged dozens of mosques. Under the terms of United Nations Security Council Resolution 1244, in June 1999 the conflict came to an end, and the UN, together with NATO, assumed responsibility for governing Kosovo.

During the UN–NATO occupation of Kosovo, some 200,000 Serb Orthodox Christians have been driven from Kosovo by ethnic extremists. Most of the remaining Serb Orthodox population in Kosovo lives in what are essentially ethnic ghettoes. During this time, over 130 Serbian Orthodox monasteries and churches have been destroyed, along with numerous cemeteries and other church properties. In just one outburst of anti-Serb pogroms in March 2004, extremists destroyed approximately thirty Orthodox churches, including priceless monuments of Byzantine culture in the Balkans, such as the Church of the Virgin Mother in Prizren. In February 2008, Albanian authorities in Kosovo unilaterally declared independence according to the terms of a plan drawn up by former Finnish president Marti Ahtisaari. The so-called "Ahtisaari Plan" provides for significant self-government of the Serb population in Kosovo and includes various protections for the Orthodox religious and cultural sites in Kosovo, but it remains to be seen whether and how these protections will be implemented in practice.

FUTURE CHALLENGES AND PROSPECTS

In November 2009 the highly respected and much beloved patriarch of Serbia, His Holiness Pavle, died after a long illness. In January 2010 the holy assembly of bishops of the Serbian Orthodox Church elected the bishop of Niš, Irinej, as Pavle's successor to the throne of the Orthodox Archbishopric of Peć, Metropolitan of Belgrade-Karlovci, and Serbian Patriarch.

Patriarch Irinej's early pronouncements suggest that the Serbian Church is ready to take some decisive steps on two issues of some debate within the church over the past several years. The first concerns promoting a rapprochement with the Roman Catholic Church. The late Pope John Paul II had been keenly interested in making a pilgrimage to Serbia, but many Serbian Church hierarchs opposed such a visit until the Vatican issued some form of acknowledgment or apology to the Serbian Orthodox Church for the role played by Catholic clerical officials in the genocide committed against the Serbs in the NDH during World War II. Upon assuming office, Patriarch Irinej suggested the possibility that John Paul II's successor, Pope Benedict XVI, might be invited to Serbia in 2013 to attend the commemoration of the 1,700th anniversary of Constantine the Great's proclamation of the Edict of Milan in Constantine's birthplace, the Serbian city of Niš. While it remains to be seen whether an official invitation to Pope Benedict will ultimately be issued, the fact that senior church officials are now suggesting such an invitation would be possible indicates that resistance to such a papal visit to Serbia is eroding.

Patriarch Irinej is also believed to be eager to resolve the long-running dispute with the Macedonian Orthodox Church. As bishop of Niš, Irinej had been personally involved in the near-successful negotiations in that city with Macedonian Church officials in 2002 to resolve the uncanonical status of the Macedonian Church and bring it back into communion with the Serbian Church and the rest of the Orthodox world. Patriarch Irinej's initial public statements suggest that the Serbian Church is ready to devote more effort to the problem of relations with the Macedonian Church than had been possible during Patriarch Pavle's illness. The persistent persecution by Macedonian authorities of Archbishop Jovan of Ohrid, who has remained in canonical unity with the Serbian Church, nevertheless suggests that finding a compromise solution will remain difficult. Because of the Macedonian government's persistent attacks on him, Archbishop Jovan has been named a prisoner of conscience by Amnesty International.

Patriarch Irinej is also firmly committed to defending the Serbian Orthodox Church's existence and position on Kosovo and Metohija. In recent years, church hierarchs in Kosovo have been fiercely divided among themselves over how best to deal with both international officials in Kosovo and with the Albanian authorities there. More focused leadership on the part of the patriarch and the holy synod in Belgrade may help the church develop a more coherent policy on these issues.

The Serbian Orthodox Church also has to deal with a minor schism in Montenegro, where a so-called "Montenegrin Orthodox Church" has been proclaimed by a few defrocked clergy. The schismatic Montenegrin organization has no canonical standing and little popular acceptance. Even after Montenegro declared its independence in June 2006, for instance, the Serbian Orthodox Church in Montenegro, represented by the metropolitanate of Montenegro and the Littoral, continues to be one of the most widely respected institutions in Montenegro. Nevertheless, extremists within the schismatic organization regularly try to occupy churches and other properties belonging to the Serbian Church.

In many ways, the 20th century has proved to be one of the most turbulent and traumatic episodes in the history of the Serbian Orthodox Church. During the first decade of the 21st century the church entered somewhat calmer waters, but it still faces numerous challenges. It does so, however, with its reputation as the most trusted institution among the Serbian people largely intact.

SEE ALSO: Constantinople, Patriarchate of; Mount Athos; Russia, Patriarchal Orthodox

Church of; Sts. Constantine (Cyril) (ca. 826–869) and Methodios (815–885)

REFERENCES AND SUGGESTED READINGS

Alexander, S. (1979) *Church and State in Yugoslavia since 1945*. Cambridge: Cambridge University Press.

Bardos, G. N. (1992) "The Serbian Church Against Milosevic," *RFE/RL Research Report* 1, 31 (July 31).

Mileusnić, S. (1996) *Duhovni genocide, 1991–95*. Belgrade: Muzej Srpske Pravoslavne Crkve.

Pavlovich, P. (1989) *The History of the Serbian Orthodox Church*. Toronto: Serbian Heritage Books.

Peić, S. (1994) *Medieval Serbian Culture*. London: Alpine Fine Arts Collection.

Perica, V. (2002) *Balkan Idols: Religion and Nationalism in Yugoslav States*. New York: Oxford University Press.

Slijepčević, D. (1962) *Istorija Srpske Pravoslavne Crkve*, vols. 1–3. Belgrade: Bigz.

Slijepčević, D. (1969) *Srpska Pravoslavna Crkva, 1219–1969*. Belgrade: Sveti Arhijerejski Sabor Srpske Pravoslavne Crkve.

Sugar, P. (1977) *Southeastern Europe under Ottoman Rule, 1354–1804*. Seattle: University of Washington Press.

Tomasevich, J. (2001) *War and Revolution in Yugoslavia: Occupation and Collaboration, 1941–45*. Stanford: Stanford University Press.

Velimirović, N. (1989) *The Life of St. Sava*. Crestwood, NY: St. Vladimir's Seminary Press.

Sexual Ethics

MARIA GWYN MCDOWELL

Human beings are sexual; human bodies are places where love, affection, and respect are often accompanied by physical desire; places, therefore, of both great joy and struggle. Orthodoxy recognizes the tension which often exists between love, desire, and respect. Questions of sexual ethics are dependent on an understanding of the

human person as participating in an ongoing transformation into the likeness of God, one that includes joy and blessing as well as sin and repentance As unique, irreducible, and dynamic spiritual realities, personhood and relationship cannot be reduced to matters of "natural" or civil law. The pertinent questions for ethical decision-making are who am I/we becoming and how does a particular relationship, sexual behavior, or action enable me/us to be more like God; that is, to better love God and neighbor.

Modern Orthodox sexual ethics must honestly confront an ambiguous past history. While the written tradition has known outspoken defenders of the body and the value of sexual relations in the context of marriage, it has produced many detractors as well. Nor can we ignore the fact that while both men and women are ostensibly called to the same standards of virtue and sexual integrity, double standards existed and still exist which uncritically accepted preexisting cultural assumptions about women's weakness and supposedly greater struggle for virtue, which over-sexualized women and meted out harsher penalties for wrongdoing. This imbalance has not gone unnoticed by the tradition, but the misogyny pervasive in Late Antique and Byzantine cultures nonetheless affected the development and application of much Orthodox canon law, theology, and pastoral care. This is especially important to bear in mind as Orthodoxy now makes its home in western cultures and encounters feminist insights regarding the shared dignity of men and women, and new opportunities for articulating gender roles and responsibilities. Reenvisioning such roles must grapple with the difficulty engendered by phrases such as the "Manly-woman of God," something that was meant as a compliment in Late Antique discourse but which is completely lost on women today.

Discerning pastoral care is increasingly important in the Orthodox Church to modify rhetorically extreme views of sex and the body. It is increasingly important to move beyond a dominant monastic frame of discourse and acknowledge loving marital relationships as God-given and potentially deifying. Comparing the early with the late works of both Gregory of Nyssa and John Chrysostom evinces this shift from an initial idealization of virginity to a recognition of the life-giving potential of faithful, married intercourse. The early work of these fathers begins in the ascetic abstract ideal, but new-found pastoral involvements faced them with the grief and life-giving joy that marriage brought to their congregants. Consequently their attitudes shifted. It is paradigmatic of attitude changes Orthodoxy needs to articulate again.

Orthodox canon law regarding sexual behavior was developed mainly to address problematic behavior. It is not a manual of good practice, therefore, but an indication of appropriate boundaries. Further, given the contextual nature of the canons, their application in varying social contexts and relationships requires the careful exercise of discernment and compassionate application by all parties involved (the tradition of *oikonomia*).

Sexual expression is a way of one child of God relating to another, and the same criteria for Christian relationships (that is, the treating one another as "neighbor," granting love, dignity, respect, and joy to the other) govern sexual behavior. Pornography, prostitution, domestic abuse, and sexual exploitation of any kind deny and deface the image of God in another person. Sexual relations are best entered into, articulated, and sustained through relationships committed to all these elements. Orthodoxy always presumes a faithful marriage as the place of settlement

where all this happens under a covenantal blessing.

Marriage is intended as a means to deification. Families are characterized as a "domestic church." Children are a blessing and parenthood is a respected and vital task. This ethos of respect underlies Orthodox critiques of social movements and systems which denigrate, or make difficult, motherhood or fatherhood. Traditionally, contraception has been forbidden by Orthodox teachers; not only because of the value of children and the issue of love's openness to life, but because in Antiquity contraceptives were largely synonymous with abortofacients. Non-abortofacient contraception, possible today, allows for discerning family planning. Couples who choose to plan or limit their families are unfortunately often still characterized as selfish by some Orthodox theologians; but even so *oikonomia* respects that many factors contribute to the decision and ability to bear or adopt children.

The church holds that life begins at conception. Modern science recently has greatly contributed to the understanding of the process of human life's development, but does not indicate when personhood is granted by God and the community to the child. Abortion has been consistently rejected by Orthodox tradition, and is frequently referred to as murder for which canon law prescribes a period of excommunication as penance. However, the church also recognizes that threats to the life of the mother, abject poverty, and the helplessness of women often complicate the ethical dimensions of what many portray as a simple issue. Orthodox pastoral practice is widely experienced on the individual level as being compassionate to parents who have been involved with abortions and repent of it. Further, modern Orthodoxy recognizes that social circumstances often aggravate beginning-of-life decisions, and advocates for the creation of conditions that protect parenthood, encourage adoption, and generally address dire circumstances of life, of which abortion is a symptom, not a cause.

The cultural androcentrism of Orthodoxy is particularly evident in some liturgical practices, especially those for miscarriage and the churching of infants. Traditionally, miscarriage has been attributed to a mother's sinfulness and forgiveness is requested on her behalf. Likewise the rite of the forty-day presentation of a newborn prays for the restoration of purity to the mother, strongly implying that the birth process renders her unclean and defiled. The longstanding dispute regarding women not receiving the Eucharist during *menses* reflects an ancient social context in which blood and purity held significantly different meanings to those they have today. Many priests now modify prayers to remove elements which impute sin or project shame or wrongdoing on women and parents involved in these moments, and some priests church male and female babies identically: either bringing both of them, or neither of them, into the altar area. The 20th century has seen increased conversation among the Orthodox regarding the whole issue of women's place in the church's ministries, and the related issues of how sexuality and gender stand in need of extensive reconsideration in the church today, in the light of how different philosophical and social conditions illuminate in new ways the ancient yet ever fresh and responsive Orthodox tradition of the appropriation of the gospel.

SEE ALSO: Bioethics, Orthodoxy and; Chastity; Deaconess; Deification; Ethics; Fasting; Humanity; Original Sin; Repentance; Women in Orthodoxy

REFERENCES AND SUGGESTED READINGS

Council of Russian Bishops (2000) *The Orthodox Church and Society: The Basis of the Social Concept of the Russian Orthodox Church.*
Guroian, V. (2002) *Incarnate love: Essays in Orthodox Ethics.* Notre Dame: University of Notre Dame Press.

Sin *see* Original Sin; Soteriology

Sinai, Autocephalous Church of

JOHN A. MCGUCKIN

One of the most venerable monasteries in the Orthodox world, St. Catherine's, is located in a powerfully dramatic setting at the foot of Mount Sinai in Egypt. The great mountain (Jebel Musa) that broodingly hangs over it is a sacred site to three world religions. The rocky area began to be occupied by hermit monks (it was and remains a true wilderness) who occupied caves in the region, and probably had a communal settlement there before the 4th century, since parts of the present Justinianic site (dating from the 6th century and beyond) already incorporated Constantinian-era fortifications in the innermost buildings.

From ancient times, Sinai, and the monastic community which settled around it, was a major pilgrimage destination for Christians. It is first mentioned in Christian literary sources in the *Voyages of Egeria*, a travelogue written by a western lady (possibly a nun) from the late 4th century. Pilgrims were attracted there to see the site of the Burning Bush, the mountain top where the revelation of the covenant to Moses took place, and also because of the

Plate 70   The fortified monastery of St. Catherine at Sinai, built by Emperor Justinian in the 6th century to protect the monastic community who had been living there from the 3rd century. Photo by John McGuckin.

increasing reputation of the monastery's ascetics. Later in the monastery's history its dedication changed from the Transfiguration, and also the Virgin of the Burning Bush (an incarnational typology of the *Theotokos* in which she was compared to the bush that blazed containing the presence of God but could not be consumed by the flames) to that of St. Catherine the Great Martyr of Alexandria (patron of the "Catherine Wheel"), whose relics were laid in the monastery church and attracted large numbers of medieval pilgrims. The basilical church's apsidal end still contains the small Chapel of the Burning Bush, whose roots were originally here, but whose branches are now cultivated outside the eastern wall of the church so that pilgrims can take souvenir leaves. All entering this chapel still must remove their shoes, as Moses was once commanded by God.

By the late 7th century Sinai had produced (or influenced) some of the leading ascetical theorists of the Christian world, and was "in the mind" of world Orthodox leaders, who patronized it throughout its long history: from the Byzantine emperors, to the Romanian Voivodes, to the last tsar of Russia. The Sinai community first heard rumors of the Bolshevik Revolution of 1917 months afterward, when they were puzzled as to why the usual Romanov tributary caravan of supplies had not reached them from Cairo. One of its higumens was St. John Klimakos, who wrote his 7th-century text *The Ladder of Divine Ascent* for the instruction of the Sinai novices. It remains as one of the charter documents of Orthodox monastic spirituality. Anastasius of Sinai, Stephen, and Neilos are just a few of the other great saints the monastery produced.

Plate 71   Once the only way into the Sinai monastery was to be wound up in a wicker basket on a rope, into the entrance high up in the wall. Photo by John McGuckin.

By the late 5th century the desert monasteries of Egypt, including Sinai, were suffering increasing depredations from tribal raiders, as the Byzantine hold on the territories was increasingly relaxed. Mount Sinai itself was threatened on several occasions with complete extinction as a Christian settlement, but the Emperor Justinian, with an eye to the venerability of the site, as well as its strategic advantage as a military post, deliberately fortified the buildings in a massive set of works in the 6th century, and stationed a garrison there, resettling several villages of Christians nearby for the service of the monks and the military garrison. Those who remain today as the tiny lay membership of this church often claim to be the descendants of those settlers, though the majority of the Bedouin (especially the Jelabiya tribe) are now Islamic. The architecture at St. Catherine's today is still largely from this period, with some

medieval (the old refectory and the bell tower particularly) and modern additions (the rather awful library and monastic cell block in modern concrete). The refectory graffiti has the names of Crusader pilgrims, some of whom went on to scratch their names in other ancient pilgrim sites: the same culprit's handiwork being found scrawled on the walls of St. Antony's Church by the Red Sea, too. Today, St. Catherine's is unique among all Orthodox monasteries for having a small Fatimid mosque built within its grounds (now unused). The local Bedouin who serve the monastery themselves worship in their own mosque not far away from Jebel Musa.

The basilical church with world-renowned 6th-century apsidal mosaics of the transfiguration is one of the most venerable buildings in all the Orthodox world, largely untouched from the time of its first building. The monastery collection of manuscripts and icons is undoubtedly the most ancient and important in the Orthodox world, too. The library not only had some of the most important manuscripts of the New Testament; the *Codex Sinaiticus* for example (which was controversially removed from the site by Tischendorf, and which was probably one of the Pandects that Constantine the Great commissioned for the new churches of Palestine that he was building), but it is probably the most important single library in the world for the history of the binding of books. New manuscripts and icons are still coming to light, even in recent times, and in each instance it causes the textbooks to be rewritten. Sinai contains most of the known surviving pre-Iconoclastic icons that there are, and several of its old collection (including the Sinai Christ, the Sinai St. Peter, the Virgin attended by soldier saints, and the Ladder of Divine Ascent) are among the greatest iconic art pieces in existence. Today, St. Catherine's is one of the last surviving monasteries of a once flourishing circle of Greek-speaking ascetic sites spread like a pearl necklace across the Middle East.

Sinai, therefore, is justifiably a world heritage center, a veritable jewel box of ancient and wonderful things in terms of art, manuscripts, and relics; but the monks who still live there point also, with a deep sense of satisfaction, to something they hold as even more precious than their treasures, namely their fidelity to the ascetical evangelical life after so many unbroken centuries of witness in the wilderness, which is one of the chief *raisons d'être* of Sinai as an Orthodox holy place apart from its geographical location. From the very beginning, the monks of Sinai kept up livelier relations with the Jerusalem patriarchate (of easier access) than with Alexandria, and eventually this was reflected in the structures of ecclesiastical organization, for Sinai became

a monastery under the care of the Jerusalem church. At the height of its flourishing it had *Metochia*, or dependent monasteries and estates, in Egypt, Palestine, Syria, Crete, Cyprus, Romania, and Constantinople, which supported it financially and ensured its effective independence during the long years when (like the Athonite communities) it had to buy the patronage of its Islamic overlords at great expense.

All these important supports eventually eroded, but not before Sinai had more or less successfully asserted its importance and its claims for autonomous governance over and against the patriarchate of Jerusalem, which itself had fallen onto hard times. It's ecclesiastical independence (against the initial grumblings of Jerusalem) was affirmed by the patriarchate of Constantinople in 1575, and confirmed again in 1782. Today, the monks of the community (only a few dozen still resident there) elect one of their own number as the abbot and also as the prospective archbishop of Sinai. The patriarch of Jerusalem always has the right to perform the consecration (which fact, along with the peculiar smallness of the "Church of Sinai," limits its complete claim to autocephaly). After that point, however, the archbishop, with his synaxis, or monastic assembly and council, entirely governs the affairs of the monastery-church. The archbishopric also includes the churches of Pharan and Raithu (by the Red Sea shore) which are now only tiny outlying parish centers, but which were once monasteries of great repute in their own right. Sinai is thus the smallest independent church of the entire Orthodox world: a unique and special instance, poised between autocephalous and autonomous condition. The charnel house at Sinai contains the bones of its many saints and ascetics, piled up rank on rank. As a monastic of the community recently said while introducing visitors to it: "Although we have one of the world's most ancient libraries on site, this is the real library where a Christian must learn about life."

SEE ALSO: Iconography, Styles of; Monasticism

REFERENCES AND SUGGESTED READINGS

Galey, J. (2003) *Katherinenkloster auf dem Sinai.* Stuttgart: Belser.
Nelson, R. S. and Collins, K. M. (eds.) (2006) *Holy Image, Hallowed Ground: Icons from Sinai.* Los Angeles: J. P. Getty Museum.
Rossi, C. (2006) *The Treasures of the Monastery of Saint Catherine.* Vercelli, Italy: White Star Press.
Soskice, J. M. (2009) *The Sisters of Sinai: How Two Lady Adventurers Discovered the Hidden Gospels.* London: Chatto and Windus.
Walsh, C. (2007) *The Cult of St. Katherine of Alexandria in Early Medieval Europe.* Aldershot: Ashgate Press.
Weitzmann, K. (1973) *Illustrated Manuscripts at Saint Catherine's Monastery on Mount Sinai.* Collegeville, MN: St. John's University Press.
Weitzmann, K. (1976) *The Monastery of Saint Catherine at Mount Sinai: The Icons.* Princeton: Princeton University Press.

Skoupho *see* Kalymauchion

Solovyov, Vladimir (1853–1900)

KONSTANTIN GAVRILKIN

Russia's most significant religious thinker, Vladimir Solovyov experienced a crisis of faith in his youth but returned to Christianity through the study of philosophy. His teaching career was short: after graduation from Moscow University in 1874, he taught until late March 1881, until the occasion when, during a public lecture, he challenged the government of Alexander III to spare the lives of the terrorists who had assassinated his father, Alexander II, earlier that month. Shortly afterwards, he left university life and dedicated himself to writing.

His early texts focus on western rationalism, and only in the *Lectures on Godmanhood* (1878–81) did he turn to the problems of religion. There he presents the history of humanity as leading inexorably to the incarnation of Divine Logos in the person of Jesus of Nazareth (cf. Alexander Men's *History of Religion*, which was inspired by Solovyov). The next important work, the *Spiritual Foundations of Life* (1882–4), deals with Christology and the sacramental and spiritual life of the church, as well as the realization of salvation in human history. The union of divine and human natures in Christ, or his Godmanhood, given through the church to the world, is viewed by Solovyov not as an abstract principle, but as a living source of political, social, and cultural transformation of the world through a free choice of autonomous human beings. This vision would inform Solovyov's approach to all problems related to Christianity. The assassination of Alexander II, the wave of anti-Jewish pogroms of 1881–2, and the counter-reforms of Alexander III prompted Solovyov's turn to the question of religion and politics. Ancient Israel, Byzantium, Roman Catholicism, Poland, and Russia were interpreted by him as a series of failed theocracies (*The Great Debate and Christian Politics*, 1883; *Jewry and the Christian Question*, 1884; *History and the Future of Theocracy*, 1885–7). At the same time, while raising many of the problems of the later ecumenical dialogue, Solovyov saw relations between Russia and Roman Catholicism in the light of their mutual responsibility for the realization of Christian mission in history (Solovyov 1966–70, Vol. 11).

During the 1880s and 1890s Solovyov wrote extensively on Russian identity, Slavophilism, nationalism (Solovyov 1966–70, Vol. 5), the religious traditions in Judaism, Islam, and China (Solovyov 1966–70, Vol. 6.), Russian literature, and philosophy, especially in relation to the multi-volume *Brockhaus-Ephron Encyclopedic Dictionary*, then appearing, for which he wrote numerous entries as chief author responsible for the philosophy section. In the 1890s he also published his key works: *The Meaning of Love* (1892–4) and the massive *Justification of the Good* (1897), which was his *magnum opus* on ethics. His collection of poetry, including meditations on the encounters with what he called Sophia, the divine feminine (Solovyov 1966–70, Vol. 12), were published in the 1890s as well. Finally, in his last year of his life Solovyov wrote *Three Conversations on War, Progress, and the End of History*, an apocalyptic drama inspired by the philosopher's premonitions of the disasters facing the 20th century.

Although his writings played a key role in the Russian religious renaissance of the 20th century, Solovyov's legacy was viewed rather negatively within conservative ecclesiastical circles because of his sympathy for Roman Catholicism, his mysticism, and his sometimes sharp criticism of the Russian Church and of Slavophilism. While Sophiology has been sometimes attributed to him retrospectively, its significance in Solovyov's own corpus of texts is often overrated.

SEE ALSO: Russia, Patriarchal Orthodox Church of; Sophiology

REFERENCES AND SUGGESTED READINGS

Solovyov, S. M. (2001) *Vladimir Solovyov: His Life and Creative Evolution*, trans. A. Gibson. Fairfax, VA: Eastern Christian Publications.

Solovyov, V. S. (1966–70) *Sobranie sochinenii*, 13 vols. Brussels: Zhizn's Bogom.

Sutton, J. (1988) *The Religious Philosophy of Vladimir Solovyov: Towards a Reassessment*. Basingstoke: Macmillan.

Sophiology

JUSTIN M. LASSER

In Orthodox theology Sophia represents an evocation of the mystical apprehension of the divine mysteries in the life of the Godhead and the symphonic apparatus of the cosmos. The term derives from the Greek word for "wisdom" (*Sophia*). It is the Greek translation of the biblical Hebrew concept *Hokhma* (wisdom) in the Old Testament scriptures, which contain a rich and diverse tradition about "divine wisdom" (Deut. 34.9; 2 Sam. 14.20; 1 Kings 4.29; Job 12.13; Ps. 104.24; Prov. 3.19; Prov. 8.22–31; Sirach (Ecclesiasticus) 1.4, 7; 8.34). This tradition was taken up extensively, out of the biblical Wisdom literature, and also with reference to Greek philosophico-religious cosmology, and used by the Logos theologians of the early church to sketch out cosmological Christology. The concept of God's creative wisdom is deeply rooted in many ancient religious cosmologies (not least pre-biblical Egyptian). In their use of Wisdom Christology the fathers followed Greek and Hebrew sages before them in personifying the divine wisdom, hypostatically, under the feminine figure of Sophia. This tradition continued despite the overall preference of the patristic era for the (masculine) equivalent "Logos" (Word or Reason of God) which was used heavily in the conciliar christological tradition. The poetic play between creator and created, as evidenced in the Sophianic Wisdom literature (see Prov. 8.22), precipitated a fierce debate in the 4th-century Arian crisis. It is the ambiguity of Sophia's nature that lends her so easily to theological speculation. Sophiology, although subordinated after the 4th century to the terms of Logos theology, remained a significant part of the Orthodox mystical tradition, and was used to connote the eternal, creative, and preexistent Son of God, who entered into human history at the incarnation, and as "Wisdom of the divine" permeates the substructure of the entire cosmos which that Divine Wisdom personally shaped, and made, into a vehicle of revelation and grace. It is clear from this how pneumatology was closely related to Sophia. In the hands of later Orthodox thinkers (including Sts. Maximos the Confessor and Gregory Palamas) the study of Sophia became an issue of mystical initiation into the communion of the divine life of the Godhead, a way of considering Deification Christology with more of a cosmological stress, an approach that emphasized that true knowledge was not summed up solely in the domain of facts, or Kataphatic discourse, but rather pointed to the way that material realities open out beyond the world to signal the domain of mystical apprehension. In this sense Sophiology is inherently an esoteric venture. Sophiology, as it became increasingly known in later times, became one of the controversial centerpieces of early 20th-century Russian theology in the writings of Solovyov, Berdiaev, Florensky, and Bulgakov. It was Bulgakov who perhaps most made it a central pillar of his theological work, and most explicitly tried to demonstrate its central position in Orthodox dogmatics. It was certainly this aspect of his thought that occasioned most resistance from other Orthodox theologians of his time, not least Georges Florovsky and the Synod of the Russian Church in exile, fearing what they felt was its overly close association with similar esoteric trends in Rosicrucianism and other heterodox gnoseological approaches. Nevertheless, Orthodox understandings of Sophiology

differ from gnoseology in this respect, that it stands for a summation of ways of "living in," more than ways of "knowing about," the Godhead. As Fr. Pavel Florensky wrote, Sophia is "not a fact, but an act" (Florensky 1997: 237).

Like her symbol, the great imperial church of Hagia Sophia in Constantinople, Holy Wisdom takes her place at the very center of Orthodox life. It is the Logos, yet it is also the outreach of the Logos to the world, in the intimacy of the human comprehension, as the scripture reveals. Sirach (Ecclesiasticus) 8.34 teaches that Sophia "is an initiate in the mysteries of God's knowledge. She makes choice of the works God is to do." Thus to learn wisdom (*Sophia*) is to be united to God. She exists as *the* choice of God, and yet she makes God's choices. Baruch 3.31–2 declares that "no one knows the way to her, no one can discover the path she treads. But the one who knows all knows her, for God has grasped her with God's own intellect." The Sophiological tradition in Orthodoxy, with various degrees of success, is the continuing contemplation of this ambiguity – the mystical path of the study of wisdom. Sophia is manifested as teacher, bride, lover, and Christ; both as within and without the human mind and soul. To acquire Sophia is not to acquire scientific knowledge but to begin to see the totality of knowledge from the right perspective.

SEE ALSO: Berdiaev, Nikolai A. (1874–1948); Bulgakov, Sergius (Sergei) (1871–1944); Florensky, Pavel Alexandrovich (1882–1937); Florovsky, Georges V. (1893–1979)

REFERENCES AND SUGGESTED READINGS

Bulgakov, S. (1993) Sophia, the Wisdom of God: AnOutline of Sophiology. Library of Russian

Philosophy. Great Barrington, MA: Lindisfarne Books.

Donskikh, O. A. (1995) "Cultural Roots of Russian Sophiology," *Sophia* 34, 2: 38–57.

Florensky, P. (1997) *The Pillar and Ground of Truth*, trans. B. Jakim. Princeton: Princeton University Press.

Sergeev, M. (2007) *Sophiology in Russian Orthodoxy: Solov'ev, Bulgakov, Losskii, Berdiaev*. Lewiston, NY: Edwin Mellen Press.

Sophrony, Archimandrite (1896–1993)

JULIA KONSTANTINOVSKY

Archimandrite Sophrony (Sergey Symeonovich Sakharov) was an outstanding Christian Orthodox ascetic, spiritual director, and theologian of the 20th century. Spiritual son of St. Silouan of Athos, Archimandrite Sophrony was the founder in 1959 of the Stavropegic Monastery of St. John the Baptist (Essex, UK) under the jurisdiction of the ecumenical patriarchate of Constantinople. He is the author of several major works on the spiritual and ascetical life in Christ and on Christian personhood, among them *Saint Silouan the Athonite*, *His Life is Mine, We Shall See Him As He Is*, and *On Prayer*. An accomplished artist, he also founded a unique school of iconography. Born in Moscow, he then lived most of his life in the West, a revered theologian and elder for the entire Christian world, Orthodox and non-Orthodox alike.

Fr. Sophrony was born into a bourgeois Russian Orthodox family and trained as an artist in the Academy of Arts and Moscow School of Painting, Sculpture, and Architecture. Arriving in Paris in 1922 to further his career, he underwent a profound conversion back to the Christian faith of his childhood, which compelled him to renounce his art and embrace a life of prayer. In 1924 he joined the Russian Saint-Panteleimon Monastery on Mount Athos, spending the next twenty years first as a coenobitic monastic and subsequently a hermit. Ordained to the priesthood in 1941, he acted as father confessor to numerous Athonite monks. After World War II he returned to France to write his highly acclaimed work on Starets Silouan. Enduring health problems prevented him from returning to Athos. Soon, an ascetic community, men and women, gathered around him in Paris. In 1956 it moved to Essex, England, where the present-day Monastery of St. John the Baptist was established.

Influenced by Lossky and Bulgakov, Fr. Sophrony's thought is nevertheless deeply original. Its fundamental principle is Christian personalism, whereby the Person/Hypostasis (*Lichnost'/Ipostas'*) is the *arche* of all being, Uncreated, as well as created. In his essence, the divine Absolute is personal: it is the Trinity of three divine hypostaseis indissolubly united by one common divine essence. This trinitarian principle is kenotic: the three hypostaseis inhere within one another through mutual self-emptying love. God's disclosure of himself as a Person to Moses (Ex. 3.10) is the beginning of all theology, its fulfillment consisting in Christ's self-revelation in his voluntary kenosis "for us men and for our salvation."

There is commensurability between the personal divine being, on the one hand, and the human person, on the other. Christ is the measure of man: just as he reveals and personifies the perfection of divinity and humanity, so equally man is able to comprise the fullness of the human and divine being (the latter by grace, not by nature). Archimandrite Sophrony saw this possibility as the foundation of the human freedom and of man's being in God's image (cf. Gen. 1.26). The following three principles sum up Archimandrite Sophrony's ecclesiology: there is no faith without doctrine; there is no Christianity outside the church; there is no Christianity without asceticism.

SEE ALSO: Elder (Starets); Monasticism; Mount Athos; St. Silouan of Athos (1866–1938)

REFERENCES AND SUGGESTED READINGS

Archim. Sophrony (1988) *We Shall See Him As He Is.* Maldon, UK: St. John's Monastery.
Archim. Sophrony (1997) *His Life is Mine.* Crestwood, NY: St. Vladimir's Seminary Press.
Archim. Sophrony (1998) *On Prayer.* Crestwood, NY: St. Vladimir's Seminary Press.
Archim. Sophrony (1999) *Saint Silouan the Athonite.* Crestwood, NY: St. Vladimir's Seminary Press.
Archim. Zacharias (Zacharou) (2003) *Christ, Our Way and Our Life: A Presentation of the Theology of Archimandrite Sophrony.* South Canaan, PA: St. Tikhon's Seminary Press.
Sakharov, N. V. (2002) *I Love Therefore I Am: The Theological Legacy of Archimandrite Sophrony.* Crestwood, NY: St. Vladimir's Seminary Press.

Soteriology

STEPHEN THOMAS

The ecumenical councils of the Orthodox Church do not give a soteriology or doctrine of salvation, but offer rather a rich and exhaustive Christology. Nevertheless, there is a profound soteriology underlying the Christology which the fathers used to support it. The main idea of salvation found in the eastern fathers, as well as western fathers such as Pope St. Leo the Great of Rome, concerns the victory over death which Christ won, and the victory over all the morbid limitations which humanity has acquired though sin, the alienation from God. Orthodox soteriology is extremely hopeful because it thinks of salvation as a victory over the malicious powers exercised by the demons

(Heb. 11.35). It has two elements, which complement one another: salvation is, firstly, therapy, and, secondly, deification or divinization.

The victory motif dominates Orthodox liturgical texts, especially in the paschal liturgy. Continually repeated during the paschal season is the following poem: "Christ is risen from the dead, trampling down death by death, and on those in the graves, bestowing life" (*Pentekostarion* 1990: 27).

In Orthodox soteriology sin and death are personified as forces which belong to the sphere of the Devil and the demons, who, through divine respect to their free-will, are still active until the judgment. Christ's voluntary sacrifice on the cross brought the depths of suffering into intimate contact with the divine light, so that suffering could be transfigured and conquered. The victorious Christ descended to Hades, conquered the power of the Devil, and brought out the souls imprisoned there. While this idea is found in medieval Catholicism, in the form of the harrowing of hell, it is not as prominent as it is in the Orthodox services which accord to Holy Saturday an essential role in the process by which Christ saves humankind: "He quenched Death by being subdued by Death. He who came down into Hades despoiled Hades; And Hades was embittered when he tasted of Christ's flesh" (*Pentekostarion* 1990: 37).

Therapy, the dominant Orthodox expression of salvation theology (Larchet 2000), consists of the transformation of the human situation which has been damaged by sin, liberating it from its subordination to corruption, an ephemeral life of passion turned away from God which leads to death. Orthodoxy teaches that humanity was seduced by the Devil at an early stage in its development, and the whole human race contracted illness, which is both spiritual (sin, passion) and physical (illness and death), a malaise not caused or willed by God (Larchet 2002: 17). Particular sins issue from this sickness and are a form of madness or blindness rather than a deliberate revolt, provoking the divine compassion. The union of the divine and human natures in Christ heals the damaged human nature in its root. In these terms St. Athanasius explains why the divine Word and Son of God had to become human: only a divine nature could raise up the human nature (Athanasius 1971: 185). Equally, Christ had to have a human nature: St. Gregory of Nazianzus argues that Christ had to have a human intellect, in addition to the divine mind, because the mind especially was in need of salvation (Hardy 1995: 221). While the cross is the victory, the whole incarnation is saving, since every aspect of the human nature is healed by contact with the divinity, during the course of the Savior's earthly life. The sacraments, or mysteries, heal the various dimensions of human life, the Eucharist having a special place in divinizing the human person through reception of the holy gifts, Christ's deifying body and blood. However, salvation also means more than healing. Salvation is the process of the believer's deification, establishing the likeness to God intended for the original creation. The rays of God's goodness, being uncreated, draw humankind up into the uncreated dimension.

The various theories of the atonement in Catholic and Reformed Christianity, which present a rationale for Christ's death upon the cross, are foreign to Orthodoxy. In *Cur Deus Homo*, Anselm of Canterbury explained the relationship of incarnation to salvation very differently from St. Athanasius. Anselm uses the idea of the infinite offense to the honor of the deity, which Christ put right by his death upon the cross, a sacrifice earning an infinite treasury of merit upon which sinful Man could draw (Anselm 1998: 283). Calvin thought in terms of the infinite majesty of God and the wrath provoked by human sin, which Christ suffered instead of us. But in Calvinism

grace attained by the sacrifice is only received by those who are predestined to receive it; in this sense, the sacrifice is not for all. Orthodoxy, however, teaches that Christ offered "the life-giving and unslain sacrifice" (*Pentekostarion* 1990: 30) for all people. There was no debt required by God to appease his wrath or satisfy justice, and there is no transaction between Father and Son to effect human salvation. In Orthodox soteriology God goes far beyond justice; his mercy is paramount, (Alfeyev 2000: 292–7), still less is there predestination to hell (Isaac of Nineveh 1995: 165). Christ's sacrifice was that he "did not count equality with God a thing to be grasped but emptied himself taking the form of a servant, being born in the likeness of men" (Phil. 2.7). Christ obeyed the Father, becoming "obedient unto death, even death on a cross" (Phil. 2.8), in the sense that he united his will to that of the Father and assumed a human nature in order to heal and deify it: to save it from corruptibility and the sinking into nothingness, by offering Life.

SEE ALSO: Cross; Deification; Ecumenical Councils; Eucharist; Healing; Judgment; Mystery (Sacrament)

REFERENCES AND SUGGESTED READINGS

Alfeyev, H. (2000) *The Spiritual World of Isaac the Syrian*. Kalamazoo: Cistercian Publications.

Anselm (1998) *The Major Works*, ed. B. Davies and G. R. Evans. Oxford: Oxford University Press.

Athanasius (1971) *Contra Gentes and De Incarnatione*, ed. and trans. R. W. Thomson. Oxford: Clarendon Press.

Aulen, G. (2003) *Christus Victor*. Eugene, Ontario: Wipf and Stock.

Hardy, E. R. (1995) *The Christology of the Later Fathers*. Philadelphia: Westminster/John Knox Press.

Isaac of Nineveh (1995) *The Second Part*, trans. S. Brock. Louvain: Peeters.

Larchet, J.-C. (2000) *Thérapeutique des maladies spirituelles*. Paris: Cerf.

Larchet, J.-C. (2002) *Theology of Illness*, trans. J. and M. Breck. Crestwood, NY: St. Vladimir's Seminary Press.

Pentekostarion (1990) Boston: Holy Transfiguration Monastery.

Stăniloae, Dumitru (1903–1993)

ARISTOTLE PAPANIKOLAOU

Dumitru Stăniloae was born in Vladeni in the Romanian province of Transylvania. After studying in Romania, Athens, and Germany, Stăniloae began teaching in 1929 at the Theological Institute in Sibiu. Between 1946 and 1973 he taught at the Theological Institute in Bucharest, though between 1958 and 1962 he was incarcerated as a political prisoner at Aiud Prison. Early in his theological career, Stăniloae rejected the Orthodox dogmatic manuals, which he felt, together with his Russian émigré counterparts in Paris, Vladimir Lossky and Georges Florovsky, were under a "western captivity." In his initial theological studies he noticed that the spirituality of hesychasm and the thought of St. Gregory Palamas were offering a different theological vision than that presented in the manuals. His life work is a labor of attempting to articulate an Orthodox dogmatic theology that is existentially relevant and not simply a set of propositional truths. The fruit of this work began with the publication of his study on Palamas, *The Life and Teaching of Gregory Palamas* (1938), and culminated with his three-volume *Orthodox Dogmatic Theology* (1978). Stăniloae was also responsible for translating the *Philokalia* into Romanian (a larger edition by far than that of St. Nikodemos; nine volumes between 1946 and 1980). Up until his death, Stăniloae published numerous books and articles, achieved a national reputation as a public intellectual commenting on the political and cultural issues of Romania, and acquired an internationally recognized ecumenical stature, with his work continuing to exercise influence in both Orthodox and non-Orthodox circles alike. He is one of the best-known, respected, and influential Orthodox theologians of the 20th century.

Among the many theological insights contained within Stăniloae's corpus, two stand out as distinctive. First, Stăniloae insisted that trinitarian theology must articulate more explicitly the proper relation of the Son to the Spirit. Against what he saw as Lossky's separation of the work of the Son and the Spirit, Stăniloae argued that the Spirit proceeds from the Father and rests on the Son as the Father's love for the Son, and is reflected back from the Son to the Father as the Son's active love for the Father. Stăniloae rejects the *filioque* because it inevitably makes the Son a Father of the Spirit, rather than seeing the relation between the Son and the Spirit as a reciprocity that has its source in the Father, and one that allows for humans to share in the Son's filial relationship with the Father. The second distinctive aspect of Stăniloae's theology is his notion of creation as God's gift that initiates the possibility of an exchange of gifts between God and human beings, who function as priests of creation. This exchange of gifts is simultaneously a dialogue of love enabling a personal communion between God and creation. The fact that the world was created for the purpose of communion between the personal God and human persons is not simply a truth of revelation, but is indicated, for Stăniloae, in the iconic human experience of freedom and relationality.

SEE ALSO: *Filioque*; Holy Trinity; *Philokalia*; Romania, Patriarchal Orthodox Church of; St. Gregory Palamas (1296–1359)

REFERENCES AND SUGGESTED READINGS

Louth, A. (2002) "The Orthodox Dogmatic Theology of Dumitru Staniloae," *Modern Theology* 13, 2: 253–67.
Neamtu, M. (2006) "Between the Gospel and the Nation: Dumitru Stăniloae's Ethno-Theology," *Archaeus: Studies in History of Religions* 10, 3: 4.
Turcescu, L. (ed.) (2002) *Dumitru Stăniloae: Tradition and Modernity in Theology*. Palm Beach: Center for Romanian Studies.
Turcescu, L. (2005) "Dumitru Stăniloae," in J. Witte and F. Alexander (eds.) *The Teachings of Modern Christianity on Law, Politics, and Human Nature*, 2 vols. New York: Columbia University Press, vol. 1, pp. 685–711; vol. 2, pp. 537–58.

Starets *see* Elder (Starets)

Stavrophore

JOHN A. MCGUCKIN

Greek term signifying "cross-bearer." Its most frequent use is in reference to Orthodox monastics. In the entrance into monastic life there are several degrees. The first level, that of the Novice, can be left freely. The novice will wear the black cassock (*anterion, raso*) and headgear (*skouphos*) of the monk, but is not as yet tonsured and takes no vows. After tonsuring the novice is formally given the black habit (*raso*) consisting of the inner cassock with leather belt, the outer clerical robe with wide sleeves, and hat with black veil. He is now known as a Rassophore. If the monk perseveres and reaches a degree of maturity and asceticism deemed appropriate by his higumen (abbot) he may be initiated into a higher degree of monastic life known as the Little Schema. At this time the monastic makes formal vows of stability, poverty, chastity, and obedience, and may receive the more ample form of the outer cassock, along with the monastic mantle, and especially a symbolic garment known as the *paramandyas*. This is a square of black cloth worn on the back, embroidered in red with the instruments of the Passion, and connected by ties to a wooden cross worn over the heart. It symbolizes how the monk must bear the "yoke" of Christ. It is the act of putting on this cross which entitles the monk to be known as Stavrophore or Cross-bearer. The last and highest degree of monastic life is the Great Schema. The term *Stavrophore* can also refer to a priest who is awarded the right to wear a cross as a sign of special honor. In Russian tradition all priests wear the silver cross. A gold cross can be awarded as an honor. The gift of the "jeweled cross" is a significant award of honor to a priest from a bishop. In the non-Russian traditions, only those priests wear the cross who have received it as a special honor from the bishop or patriarch (equivalent to the jeweled cross). In the Greek custom their rank is designated as Oikonomos, in other churches they are known as Stavrophore.

SEE ALSO: Cross

Stethatos, Niketas (ca. 1005–1085)

JOHN A. MCGUCKIN

Niketas is an important but neglected Byzantine writer who composed treatises on mystical prayer, as well as being involved with the troubled relations between Patriarch Michael Caerularios and the papal legates leading up to the rupture of communion between Rome and Constantinople in 1054. Niketas entered the Studios monastery as a young man and eventually became its higumen (after 1076). In his youth he met St. Symeon the New Theologian (d. 1022). After the latter's death in exile, he became a dedicated follower, attributing the change to a vision he had of the saint (ca. 1035). He zealously defended Symeon's memory and teaching, publishing and editing his *Discourses* and *Hymns*, as well as composing a Life of the Saint, and arranging for the return of the saint's relics to the capital. In his own spiritual teachings (*Three Centuries of Practical and Gnostic Chapters*) Niketas largely follows Symeon in laying stress on the importance of the gift of tears, and on the role of the spiritual father. He also composed apologetic works against the Latins, the Armenians, and the Jews. In his minor works he often discusses the nature of the soul and the afterlife, and is thought to be part of the wider reaction to controversies initiated by Michael Psellos. Niketas' theology is very aware of the concept of hierarchy as mediated by Pseudo-Dionysius the Areopagite, and in this sense (emphasizing the parallels between heavenly and earthly hierarchy) he moderated Symeon's public hostility to the patriarchate and court. He is influenced by the spiritual tradition of Evagrios Pontike and St. Maximos the Confessor, mixing metaphors of divine union as brilliant illumination, with references to the Dionysian darkness of unknowing. He also has resonances from some of the teaching of Isaac the Syrian. Some think that he gained his nickname *Stethatos* ("big-heart" or "courageous one") because of his criticism in ca. 1040 of the relations between Emperor Constantine IX Monomachos and his mistress Skliraina.

SEE ALSO: Caerularios, Michael (d. 1059); Pontike, Evagrios (ca. 345–399); St. Maximos the Confessor (580–662); St. Symeon the New Theologian (949–1022)

REFERENCES AND SUGGESTED READINGS

Niketas (1928) "Vie de s. Syméon le Nouveau Théologien," ed. I Hausherr. *Orientalia Christiana* 12, 45.

Niketas (1961) *Opuscules et lettres*, ed. J. Darrouzes. *Sources Chrétiennes*, vol. 81. Paris.

Niketas (1995) *Centuries of Practical and Gnostic Chapters*, ed. G. Palmer, P. Sherrard, and K. Ware. London: Faber and Faber.

Solignac, A. (1982) "Niketas Stethatos," in *Dictionnaire de spiritualité*, vol. 11. Paris: Beauchesne, pp. 224–30.

Van Rossum, J. (1981) "Reflections on Byzantine Ecclesiology: Niketas Stethatos' *On the Hierarchy*," *St. Vladimir's Theological Quarterly* 25: 75–83.

Volker, W. (1974) "Nicetas Stethatos als mystischer Schriftsteller und sein Verhaltnis zu Symeon dem Neuen Theologen," in *Praxis und Theoria bei Symeon dem Neuen Theologen*. Wiesbaden, pp. 456–89.

Sticharion

VALENTINA IZMIRLIEVA

The sacramental vestment (Russian *Podrizhnik*) worn as an outer garment by deacons and sub-deacons and as the undergarment by bishops and priests. It is a long narrow robe that buttons down both sides and features an embroidered cross on the back. Its symbolic prototypes are Aaron's robe (ποδήρης, Ex. 25.7, 28.4) and Christ's "seamless tunic" (Jn. 19.23). It is usually white, symbolizing purity and the light of divine glory (Rev. 7.14). The priest's garment is covered by the *phelonion* and made of simple white fabric with narrow sleeves tied at the cuff. The wider-sleeved deacon's garb, usually made of brocade, bears decorative stripes that symbolize the power and grace bestowed through Christ's bonds.

SEE ALSO: Phelonion

Sticheron

DIMITRI CONOMOS

An appointed troparion inserted between, and providing poetic commentary on, psalm verses in the course of Byzantine Vespers and Matins. Stichera idiomela are sung to a unique melody; stichera automela function as melodic and metrical patterns for generating stichera with borrowed melodies (*contrafacta*) that are called *prosomoia*. In Byzantine manuscripts, sticheron melodies are generally syllabic; that is, they have one or two notes per syllable, although short melismas may occur on accented syllables or on words or phrases requiring special emphasis. Stichera for major feasts also may have more extensive ornamentation. Cadences are marked by recurring melodic formulae.

SEE ALSO: Idiomelon; Troparion

Stylite Saints

AUGUSTINE CASIDAY

Asceticism in the form of ascending a column (in Greek, *stylos*) and remaining there for extended periods as a "column-dweller" or *stylite* is a distinctive feature of Eastern Christianity. This way of life was pioneered in 5th-century Syria by Simeon the Stylite (ca. 389–459). From the 430s Simeon built his column and gradually extended it to a height of some 16 meters in order to escape the crowds who gathered around him, and to pray. But he did not sever his connections with the faithful. On the contrary, pilgrims came from afar to marvel at Simeon, seeking support and even adjudication of legal and political matters, no less than spiritual guidance from him (Theodoret, *Historia Religiosa* 26.26; Syriac, *Life of Simeon* 56, 60, 77; Brown 1971:

90–1). At least one pilgrim to Simeon's column actually followed his example: Daniel the Stylite (*Life of Daniel* 6, 21). In 460 Daniel (403–93) ascended his pillar near Constantinople, which allowed him to continue exercising influence albeit now within the imperial capital (Brown 1971: 92–3): "The Emperor Zeno is said to have taken his advice" (*Life of Daniel* 55).

Images and pilgrim tokens of the great stylites circulated within their own lifetimes as far away as Rome and Gaul. This probably explains how Walfroy of Carignan (d. 596 or 600) found out about Simeon Stylites. Unique among western ascetics, Walfroy set up a column near Trier, but he was sharply rebuked by bishops who compared him unfavorably to Simeon and then demolished the column to make sure he would not ascend it again (Gregory of Tours, *History of the Franks* 8.15). Walfroy's Byzantine contemporary, Simeon the Younger (521–96), was also precocious and more accepted. He took to a pillar when he was only seven. Some years later, he relocated to the Wondrous Mountain where a monastery formed nearby. Simeon left behind several writings, which may perhaps be compared to the case of the *Chronicle* of the wars between Byzantium and Persia which was purportedly written in 504 by Joshua the Stylite. These few men are the most eminent examples from a "golden age" of stylite asceticism.

From the Iconoclast controversies through the 9th century, the prominence of stylites began to wane. This is not to say that no stylites are found thereafter. We know of Luke the Stylite in the 10th century. Similarly, Lazarus of Mt. Galesios (ca. 972–1053) lived on a pillar near Ephesus where he was surrounded by three monasteries he had founded. And in the 12th century, Nikita the Stylite was a revered figure whose reputation spread from Pereyaslavl throughout the Slavic world. Reverence for stylites, however, was increasingly directed to historical figures of the past. So, for instance, in *The Travels of Macarius* 4.7.1, Paul of Aleppo reports on the Muscovites' special devotion to Simeon the Stylite on the first day of the year and describes its rites in some detail for the mid-17th century. A stylite monk lived on the top of one of the large columns in Hadrian's temple in Athens in the 19th century. Stylites became rare, then, but their memory has endured. Elevated between earth and sky, the stylites have for centuries directed the eyes – and sometimes the lives – of Orthodox Christians heavenward.

SEE ALSO: Asceticism; Iconoclasm; Monasticism

REFERENCES AND SUGGESTED READINGS

Brown, P. (1971) "The Rise and Function of the Holy Man in Late Antiquity," *Journal of Roman Studies* 61: 80–101.

Dawes, E. and Baynes, N. H. (1977) *Three Byzantine Saints*. Oxford: Mowbray.

Delehaye, H. (1923) *Les Saints stylites*. Brussels: Société des bollandistes.

Doran, R. (1992) *The Lives of Symeon Stylites*, CS 112. Kalamazoo: Cistercian Publications.

Schachner, L. A. (2009) "The Archaeology of the Stylite," in D. Gwynn and S. Bangert (eds.) *Religious Diversity in Late Antiquity*. Late Antique Archaeology 5.1. Leiden: E. J. Brill.

Subdeacon *see* Ordination

Syrian Orthodox Churches

JUSTIN M. LASSER

Christianity in the lands of the Tigris and Euphrates and the Syrian Orient has both a rich and diverse history. The Syrian Christians represent some of the last remnants of the Aramaean civilizations that populated the region for millennia. The glories of these civilizations and cultures are not merely preserved by modern Syrian Christians, but lived out. Though their numbers in the original homelands have been steadily decreasing over the past centuries, their vitality has not. Most *Sūryāyē* (Aramaean and Assyrian) peoples trace their origins to a region occupying the northern limits of the Tigris and Euphrates rivers, now composed of southeastern Turkey, northern Iraq and Iran, Jordan, and Syria.

The Aramaean language that the *Sūryāyē* preserve in their hymns and holy books is a West-Semitic language, which is related to the Aramaic language of Jesus' world. The *Sūryāyē* also trace their Christian roots to the cultural world of Jesus and the earliest apostles. According to traditional accounts, St. Thomas "the Twin" served as the apostle to Syria and the accounts of his adventures are recounted in the Syriac *Acts of the Apostle Thomas*. The Osrhoene region (now southeastern Turkey) was a crucible for new ideas and cultural exchanges between the Hellenistic West and the Orient. Many literary works existed in both Syriac and Greek, which often stimulated intriguing syntheses, but also precipitated unfortunate linguistic and cultural misunderstandings (e.g., the Messalian, Nestorian, Gnostic, and Monophysite crises). From earliest times the two pearls of the Osrhoene region, the cities of Edessa and Nisibis, made great strides in translating the indigenous Syriac Christian experience and vocabulary into the Hellenistic and Byzantine West. Even the name of the Apostle to Syria, St. Thomas, illustrates this attempted cultural transmission. The name "Thomas" derives from the Aramaic word for "twin" (*tōma*). In the gospel attributed to St. Thomas, his name is presented as

"Judas, Didymus Thomas," which uses both the Greek and Aramaic locutions for "twin." This construction is intriguing in that it doubles "Judas'" name so that it reads, "Judas twin twin," emphasizing that the Apostle Judas Thomas was "*twice* twin" and an apostle to both the Greeks and the Aramaeans.

One of the earliest documents from Syria, the *Doctrine of Addai*, recounts the alleged correspondence between Jesus and King Abgar of Edessa. While the tradition is not historically demonstrable from any other sources, it does reveal important aspects of early Syrian Christianity. According to the tradition, King Abgar sent a letter to Jesus in Jerusalem asking him to come to the city of Edessa. Though Jesus turned down the request, he blessed King Abgar and promised to send one of his disciples to heal all of the infirmities of the king and his subjects. But before the king's entourage departed, Hannan, the king's "painter," tried to paint the likeness of Jesus and bring it to King Abgar. This tradition, as well as the variant version that recounts Jesus impressing his face upon a cloth (the *icon-painted-without-hands*), represents the central role that icons have played in Syrian Christianity from the beginning. After Christ's ascension, the tradition recounts how the Apostle Thomas sent Addai, one of the seventy, to Abgar to heal the sick in Edessa and to preach the gospel. The *Doctrine of Addai* represents one of the earliest attempts to weave together the diverse traditions associated with the advent of Christianity in Syria. It specifically merges the Thomas tradition with the Addai tradition, which may have developed in different locales and time periods. It is important to note that the Manichean "apostle" to Osrhoene was also an "Addai," which may suggest that the tradition in the *Doctrine of Addai* may be a later Orthodox response to the success of

the Manichean missions in Syria in the 3rd century.

The traditions preserved in the *Doctrine of Addai* and in Eusebius' *Church History* describes how a certain Palūt was consecrated as the first bishop of Edessa (ca. 200) by Serapion, the bishop of Antioch. This story was also intended to establish the patriarchal jurisdiction of Antioch. However, these foundational stories must be tempered by the remembrance that the Orthodox in early Syria probably held a minority status. According to St. Ephrem, the greatest hymnographer in Syrian Christianity, the Orthodox were not first referred to as "the Christians" but rather as the "Palūtians" (*Contra Haereses* 22, 6, in Vööbus 1958: 4), that is, "the Nicene party." Though a bishopric was established for the Orthodox in Osrhoene in the 2nd century, the church had to operate outside the Roman fold in a world where a wide diversity of Christian expressions was the norm. Within the 2nd-century crucible of the Syrian Orient there existed a variety of groups, including the Ebionites, "Jamesian" Christians, Jewish-Christians, Mandaeans, and the groups associated with the Pseudo-Clementine literature, in addition to many others.

The earliest chronological source for Syrian Orthodox Christianity exists in the *Chronicle of Arbēl*, which recounts the beginnings of Christianity in the environs of the great Syriac city of Hadiab in the villages of Arbēl. The tradition connects the work of Mar Addai with a certain Mar Peqida, whom Addai consecrated the first bishop of Hadiab (Vööbus 1958: 5). If the chronology can be trusted, it seems that Orthodoxy was established in the Arbēl region in the first quarter of the 2nd century, which suggests that Christianity had already made prior inroads into the Syrian Orient.

Beyond the traditional Orthodox foundational stories exists the tradition associated with the Apostle Thomas, which is, in all probability, the earliest Christian tradition in Syria. This tradition is recorded in the *Gospel of Thomas*, the *Book of Thomas the Athlete* (also the earliest Syrian ascetic text), and the *Acts of the Apostle Thomas*. The tradition represents a surprisingly coherent "school-of-thought" that spanned more than three centuries. One of the earliest specifically Syrian titles for Christ is represented in the Coptic *Acts of Peter and the Twelve Apostles*. This Syrian text describes how a certain *Lithargoēl*, playing the part of a pearl merchant, traveled the world offering pearls for free. In the story, the wealthy ignore this *Lithargoēl*, while the poor seek merely to catch a glimpse of the pearls. The pearl in question, of course, was a metaphor for the experience of the Kingdom of God, echoing Jesus' Parable of the Pearl Merchant (Mt. 13.45–6). The name *Lithargoēl* is Syriac for the "the light, gazelle-like stone," who in this story is the risen Christ offering the pearls of the kingdom. The pearl motif plays a central role within Syrian Christian spirituality, which is preserved in the *Acts of Thomas* as the *Hymn of the Pearl*. The later Syrian ascetical writers often depicted themselves as "pearl divers" seeking after the glories of the kingdom.

The temperament of the early Syrian Christians was often ascetically very severe. They are particularly known for their profound adherence to poverty and their strict exhortations toward virginity, self-flagellation, and constant prayer. One of the earliest groups was known as the *benai* and *benat qeiama*, Syriac for "the sons and daughters of the oath (or covenant)." These early Orthodox Christians swore an oath together, binding themselves in collective prayer, in a condemnation of wealth, in the struggle against the "world," and to a state where spiritual marriages would replace sexual marriages. It is important to note that this group was composed of both males and females without any identifiable leadership roles. Some scholars of Christian origins now believe that at one time (an "Encratite" position destined to give way before wider church practice) celibacy was required of early Syrian baptismal candidates, thus leaving a majority in the church in the condition of a long-term catechumenate. The origins of this movement are paralleled in the hermeneutical shifts reflected in the *Gospel of Thomas* and the *Book of Thomas the Athlete*. Later parallels are also manifested in the Syriac *Ketaba de Maskata* or *Book of Steps*. This uniquely Syrian late 4th-century text exhibits evidence of a gradually progressing moderation of the early Syrian severity. The *Book of Steps* details the responsibilities of two groups within Syrian Orthodoxy – "the Perfect" (*gmîrê*) and the "Upright" (*kênê*). The Upright were exhorted to live lives worthy of Christ while supporting the Perfect, who continued the practices of absolute poverty, virginity, and constant prayer. The great Aphrahat of Syria, author of the influential *Demonstrations*, was also a member of these *benai qeiama*.

Unlike the ascetics in the West, these "single ones" (Syriac: *ihidaya*) were both wanderers and active participants within village life. They often lived on the outskirts of villages and actively prayed for the communities that supported them. Their particularly severe form of asceticism is recounted in Theodoret of Cyr's *History of the Monks of Syria*. These ascetics would deprive themselves of sleep, mortify their bodies, chain themselves, bury themselves in caves, and walk naked during the winter, among a whole host of other practices. With their long fingernails, perched atop mountains, and with their long wild hair, these monks appeared to resemble eagles more than humans. In the eyes of many, these spiritual athletes had already taken flight into the world of the purely spiritual. This "perching" above the world in prayer and fasting was imitated by the early Syrian "stylites" (from the Greek *stylos*, "pillar"). These stylites would sit atop pillars acting as intercessors between the world below and the heavens above. According to tradition, the first to ascend a pillar was St. Simeon Stylites in the first quarter of the 5th century. This practice continued in Syria and the wider Orthodox world for centuries.

Any account of early Syrian Christianity would be incomplete without mentioning the towering character of Tatian (ca. 150). Traditionally a student of St. Justin Martyr, Tatian had renounced Hellenistic philosophy and embraced the Christian asceticism of his Syrian homeland. His greatest contribution was the *Diatesseron*, a Syriac harmony of the four gospels and other extra-canonical gospels. This harmony of the gospels remained one of the most important texts in Syriac history. St. Ephrem wrote a commentary on the *Diatesseron* and its influence beyond Syria is attested throughout the Mediterranean world and Northern Europe. Other important documents for early Syrian spirituality include the *Odes of Solomon*, the *Gospel of the Nazoreans*, the *Gospel of the Ebionites*, the *Psalms of Thomas*, and the works of Bardaisan of Edessa.

The remarkable richness of the Syrian Christian spiritual vocabulary was a cause for both controversy and inspiration. The cultural and linguistic divide widened as Byzantine control over the Osrhoene region decreased. The spiritual practices of the Syrians did not always translate easily into the Byzantine Orthodox world. These confusions were certainly manifested in the 4th century during what became known as

the "Messalian controversy" (from the Syriac *meššalīm*, "prayers"). Though the controversy was primarily the result of linguistic and cultural confusion, there were particular Syrian elements that caused a stir in Byzantine quarters. It seems the Syrian distinction between the "Perfect" and the "Upright" did not translate well into the established hierarchal church structures at Antioch or other Byzantine centers on the border with Syriac speaking lands. That the controversy was primarily linguistic is evinced by the extraordinary influence of the writings of St. Macarius. Most scholars agree that the writings of St. Macarius (*Fifty Spiritual Homilies* and the *Great Letter*) were actually written by a Syrian Orthodox Christian, which has led many to prefix Macarius' name with "pseudo," thereby dubbing him "Pseudo-Macarius." If so-called "Messalian" spirituality was unorthodox it would be difficult to make sense of Pseudo-Macarius' popularity among so many later mainline Orthodox mystics and saints, from the time of St. Gregory of Nyssa to St. Symeon the New Theologian. The primary linguistic misunderstanding derived from the Syrian proclivity to describe the spiritual struggle of the Christian in terms of the coexistent dwelling of both a demon (tendency to evil) and the Spirit of God (tendency to holiness) within the heart. Another important difference between Syrian and Greek spiritual traditions relates to the state of *apatheia*, or the advanced ascetic's release from the tyranny of the passions. This state, which many Greeks assumed was impossible – or at least delusional – was for the Syrians, the natural progression of the "Perfect." This association between perceived pride and Syrian spirituality eventually produced a unique spiritual experiment in the form of the "holy fool" as expressed, for example, in the *Life of St. Symeon the Holy Fool*.

The holy fool combined the severity of Syrian spirituality with a guard against the "demon" of pride. The holy fool "mocked the world" and acted in such a way that would constantly cause him to be humiliated.

These linguistic, cultural, and theological differences eventually came to a head in the Council of Ephesus I (431). After Nestorius, bishop of Constantinople, was deposed, seen as a progressive silencing of the ancient Syrian church language in Christology, the Syrians were progressively cut off from the rest of the Byzantine world. Later, attempts at reunification were tried, but with little success. In time the Syrian Christians splintered into two main groups, now often pejoratively referred to as "Nestorian" and "Monophysite." The increased alienation of Syria made them particularly vulnerable to foreign attack. The isolated Syrians were finally completely cut off with the advent of Islam. Since the 7th century, Syrian Christians have existed as a persecuted church. Despite their tenuous status, there continued a rich literary and spiritual tradition within the Christian Orient. St. Isaac of Nineveh represents one of the few Syrian voices that influenced the entire Christian world. The last flowering of Syrian spirituality is represented in the comedic and penetrating works of Barhebreus, bishop of Baghdad. He also epitomizes one of the most fruitful exchanges between the Islamic faith and Orthodox Christianity.

Today, the Syrian Christians are divided into a number of different churches. The Oriental Orthodox accept the first three ecumenical councils but reject the Council of Chalcedon. They are sometimes referred to as Monophysite or Jacobite Syrians. The Assyrian Church of the East represents the Oriental Christians of Syrian origin who affirm the paradigmatic standing of Nicea (325) and accept the dogmatic construct of the first two ecumenical councils, but reject the Council of Ephesus I, and advocate Christian positions dependent on the traditional saints of their church: Theodore Mopsuestia, Diodore of Tarsus, and Nestorius of Constantinople. The Assyrian Church of the East has also been referred to in earlier literature as the "Syrian Church," the "Persian Church," and the "Assyrian Orthodox Church." These are not to be confused with the "Oriental Orthodox" or the Chalcedonian/Byzantine Syrian Orthodox Christians. The Syrian Orthodox Christians, in the Byzantine sense (i.e., those that accept all seven ecumenical councils), are part of the Eastern Orthodox family of churches and belong either to the Greek Orthodox Patriarchate of Antioch and All the East or the Antiochian Orthodox Church. The Syrian Christians in communion with the Roman Catholic Church who are thus part of the family of Eastern Catholics comprise the Syriac Catholic Church, the Maronite Church, the Melkite Greek Catholic Church, the Chaldean Catholic Church, and the Syro-Malankara Catholic Church.

SEE ALSO: Antioch, Patriarchate of; Apostolic Succession; Assyrian Apostolic Church of the East; Council of Chalcedon (451); Council of Ephesus (431); Gnosticism; St. Ephrem the Syrian (ca. 306–373/379); St. Isaac the Syrian (7th c.); St. Macarius (4th c.)

REFERENCES AND SUGGESTED READINGS

Baker, A. (1965–6) "The 'Gospel of Thomas' and the Syriac 'Liber Graduum'," *New Testament Studies* 12: 49–55.

Brock, S. (1988) *Syriac Fathers on Prayer and the Spiritual Life*. Collegeville, MN: Cistercian Publications.

Brock, S. (1992) *The Luminous Eye: The Spiritual World Vision of Saint Ephrem*. Collegeville, MN: Cistercian Publications.

Brock, S. and Harvey, S. A. (1987) *Holy Women of the Syrian Orient*. Berkeley: University of California Press.

Klijn, A. F. J. (trans.) (1962) *The Acts of Thomas*. Supplement to *Novum Testamentum* 5. Leiden: E. J. Brill.

Quispel, G. (1964) "The Syrian Thomas and the Syrian Macarius," *Vigilae Christianae* 18: 226–35.

Stewart, C. (1991) '*Working the Earth of the Heart': The Messalian Controversy in History, Texts, and Language to* AD *431*. Oxford: Clarendon Press.

Vööbus, A. (1958) *History of Asceticism in the Syrian Orient*. Louvain: Secretariat of the Corpus Scriptorum Christianorum Orientalium.

T

Teretismata *see* Music (Sacred)

Theophan the Greek (ca. 1340–1410)

THOMAS KITSON

Only two of the master icon painter Theophan's works in the Russian lands remain: the frescoes in Novgorod's Transfiguration Church (1379) and the deisis row of the iconostasis in the Annunciation Cathedral of Moscow's Kremlin (before 1405), where he worked with his student, St. Andrei Rublev. Nothing of his earlier life is certain, though he possibly came from Constantinople to Novgorod around 1370. He may have been influenced by the 14th-century hesychast controversies in Constantinople. His striking Novgorod frescoes emphasize ascetic labor with an ethereal, nearly monochromatic, reddish-brown palette, over which white, green, and blue brushstrokes create lightning-like effects. Rublev adopted but softened his highly individual treatment of faces and hands.

SEE ALSO: Hesychasm; Iconography, Styles of; Icons; Russia, Patriarchal Orthodox Church of; St. Andrei Rublev (ca. 1360–1430)

REFERENCES AND SUGGESTED READINGS

Hamilton, G. H. (1983) *The Art and Architecture of Russia*. London: Penguin.

Parry, K. (2001) "Theophan the Greek," in K. Parry et al. (eds.) *The Blackwell Dictionary of Eastern Christianity*. Oxford: Blackwell.

Theophany, Feast of

DAN SANDU

Theophany (Greek for "Manifestation of God") is the feast (January 6) celebrating the revelation of the Trinity at the river Jordan (Mt. 3.13–17). The troparia of the feast emphasize the divinity of Christ who was sent forth into the world by the Father through the Holy Spirit. The commemoration on January 6 derives from the 4th century, when eastern and western liturgical traditions were becoming united. Theophany marked three "revelatory" moments in the life of Jesus: the baptism in the Jordan, the adoration of the Magi, and the miracle at Cana. Solemn blessings of water occur in (and outside) churches on this day.

REFERENCES AND SUGGESTED READINGS

Gillquist, P. E. (2001) *Becoming Orthodox: A Journey to the Ancient Christian Faith*. Ben Lomond. CA: Conciliar Press.

Theokritoff, E. (2009) "Theophany," in M. B. Cunningham and E. Theokritoff (eds.) *The Cambridge Companion to Orthodox Christian Theology*. New York: Cambridge University Press.

Tradigo, A. (2006) *Icons and Saints of the Eastern Orthodox Church*. New York: Oxford University Press.

Plate 72   Ukrainian folk group celebrating the feast of the Theophany in the open-air Museum of Folk Architecture and Rural Life, Pyrogovo. Photo © Viktor Mikheyev/Shutterstock.

Theophylact of Ohrid (ca. 1050–1108)

A. EDWARD SIECIENSKI

Byzantine theologian and ecclesiastic, Theophylact of Ohrid was born in Euboea, Greece, and became a student of Michael Psellos. He was appointed archbishop of Ohrid (in Bulgaria) in 1090, writing learned commentaries on both the Old and New Testaments. In his dealing with the West, Theophylact defended the traditional Eastern position on the *filioque* and the papacy, while simultaneously urging the Byzantines to charity with regard to other Latin divergent ecclesiastical practices.

SEE ALSO: Ecumenism, Orthodoxy and *Filioque*; Papacy

REFERENCES AND SUGGESTED READINGS

Mullett, M. (1997) *Theophylact of Ochrid: Reading the Letters of a Byzantine Archbishop.* Birmingham Byzantine and Ottoman Monographs 2. London: Variorum.

Obolensky, D. (1988) "Theophylact of Ohrid," in *Six Byzantine Portraits.* Oxford: Clarendon Press, pp. 34–82.

Theotokion

JOHN A. MCGUCKIN

From the Greek meaning "Pertaining to the Mother of God." It denotes a short hymn (troparion or sticheron) in the Orthodox offices of prayers, which celebrates the role of the Virgin in the history of salvation and calls upon her help for the Church. A Theotokion occurs in each service and usually occupies a place at the end of a series of hymns. The Theotokion that occurs in Vespers after the "Lord I have Cried" hymn, and just before the Entrance, is called the Dogmatik since it contains a dense synopsis of the doctrines of Incarnation and Salvation. On Wednesdays and Fridays, and in prayer services focused on the Passion, the hymn is designated as Stavro-Theotokion (Cross-Hymn to the Virgin) and evokes the sorrow of the Virgin as she laments the sufferings and death of her Son.

SEE ALSO: Hymnography; Music (Sacred); Sticheron; Troparion

Theotokos, the Blessed Virgin

ANTONIA ATANASSOVA

The Blessed Virgin Mary has an indisputable place of honor in Orthodox Christianity. She is revered as "our all-holy immaculate, most blessed, and glorious Lady Theotokos and Ever-Virgin Mary," for through her the Word of God becomes incarnate. In Scripture her special status is foretold in the words of the angel Gabriel for whom she is "blessed among women" and "full of grace" (Lk. 1.26–38). Mary's motherhood serves in restoring the relationship between God and the human race, in fulfillment of Isaiah's prophecy of a virgin bearing a son who is "God with us" (Isa. 7.14). Her quiet acceptance of God's will: "Here am I, the servant of the Lord; let it be with me according to your word," her magnificent song of praise extolling God's care for the lowly (Lk. 1.46–55), and the blessing she receives from Elizabeth, the mother of John the Baptist, mark the

incarnation as a pivotal moment of history, and Mary as the ideal follower of God. Throughout the course of her son's ministry, the Virgin plays a central role, from its inception at the wedding in Cana, where her intervention leads to the first sign of Jesus' exalted destiny, to its bitter fulfillment at the foot of the cross where Jesus commits her into the beloved disciple's care (Jn. 2.1–11; 19.25–7). In sum, the evangelists' account of Christ's life and mission recognizes the presence of his mother as no less than indispensable to the unfolding of the divine economy.

Scriptural references to Mary are further supplemented by a variety of beliefs widely held in Orthodoxy, many of which stem from devotional practices. In the popular apocryphon *The Protoevangelium of James*, Mary is described as a "creature of exceptional purity" set aside for a divine purpose from the moment of her conception. We meet her parents, Joachim and Anna, who surrender their only child in service to the Temple in Jerusalem and leave her there throughout her childhood, to converse with angels and weave a scarlet and purple veil for the Holy of Holies. Eventually, the Virgin leaves the Temple to be betrothed to Joseph and even in the context of her marriage remains perpetually virginal, since Jesus' brothers and sisters mentioned in Scripture are traditionally considered to be a part of a larger kinship group, not the offspring of Mary and Joseph. Orthodox traditions speak of Mary as receiving special revelation of Christ's resurrection at the first Pascha, and after Jesus' ascension tell of her being accompanied by John the Evangelist to Ephesus. Many devotional writings from the 6th century describe how she "falls asleep" in Jerusalem, surrounded by the apostles, and as her grave is opened to show her body to the latecomer, Thomas, it turns out to be empty. The liturgical hymns commemorating the greatest

Plate 73   Mother of Tenderness. By Eileen McGuckin. The Icon Studio: www.sgtt.org.

Marian feast, the day of her Dormition (August 15), sing of how Mary has joined the Lord in heaven, in body and soul. This glorious exaltation of the Virgin stands in Orthodoxy as a sign of eschatological hope and a foretaste of the reward reserved for the blessed at the end of time.

Historically speaking, the collage between scriptural record and traditions of piety provoked from early times the need for an explanation as to how and why the presence of the Virgin is essential to the Christian faith. Orthodox Marian theology developed in close correspondence with larger christological questions about the authenticity of Jesus' humanity, the manner of the incarnation, and the nature of the union of natures in Christ. It is a recurring motif and principle that the glorification of the Virgin Mary stems from her contribution to the incarnation, as explicitly stated in the Symbol of Faith accepted at the Council of Nicea (325). Far from being a mere footnote to the christological question, the recognition granted to Mary is a necessary corollary of the fact that, in her womb, the Word of God is made flesh "for our salvation."

The veneration of Mary as the one who gives birth to God (*Theotokos*) originated in Alexandria as early as the 3rd century, marking a rising tide of Marian piety that would soon encompass the Eastern Christian Empire. The title did not gain universal acceptance immediately, and in 427 the Syrian archbishop of Constantinople, Nestorius, challenged it as reminiscent of paganism and logically untenable. He proposed that Mary be called *christotokos* (Christ-bearer), that is, mother only of the human nature of the incarnate Son. His opponent Cyril, archbishop of Alexandria, saw the rejection of the Theotokos title as a direct assault on the unity of the person of the Lord, on the creed of Nicea, and the legacy of the fathers. For Cyril, the title encapsulated the very meaning of salvation by underscoring the double generation of the Divine Logos: the "incomprehensible manner" of the Son's generation from the Father and the fact that "for our sake he economically underwent a self-emptying" (McGuckin 1994: 321, 324). In the Virgin's womb, Cyril argued, the union between God and humanity becomes a reality whose ultimate goal is the restoration and sanctification of all creation in God. Accordingly, to recognize and confess Mary as Theotokos is a safeguard against heretical perceptions of the christological union. At the Council of Ephesus in 431, Cyril's Marian theology was vindicated and the title Theotokos was confirmed as a fitting designation of Mary's special status in salvation history. It would also form an integral part of the theological definition of Christ's personhood promulgated at the Council of Chalcedon in 451.

To this principal Marian title of Theotokos, the Council of Constantinople added a second one of *Aei-Parthenos* or "Ever-Virgin" (553). Mary's perpetual virginity, before, during, and after Jesus' birth, is a fundamental tenet of Orthodox incarnational theology; it illustrates the divine identity of her son as well as her own cooperation in the history of salvation. Iconographically, its symbolism is conveyed by three stars embroidered on the Virgin's veil (*mapharion*). Its theological significance is well attested in early Christian literature and a parallel is often drawn between the two archetypal virgins, Mary and Eve. Unlike her biblical counterpart, Mary the Second Virgin proves herself to be obedient and faithful. Her virtue reverses the divine condemnation of Eve which has led the female race to lust after a husband and bear children in pain (cf. Gen. 2.16). In the words of Proclus, 5th-century archbishop of Constantinople, Mary's virginal womb is the bridal chamber uniting God and creation where she gives birth without pain (Constas 2003: 263).

The Virgin Mary is the perfect prototype of a pure and holy life and the primary model for a life of asceticism and self-denial. Unsurprisingly, the first recorded Marian appearance in the church is in a vision ascribed to the ascetic Gregory Thaumaturgus (PG 46:1133D–1136B). Gregory of Nyssa, who relates the story of the apparition, praises Mary's chastity, her purity of body and soul, as a "frontier between life and death" reestablished by faithful Christians in the act of imitating Mary's piety. Textual evidence is complemented by formal cultic recognition of Mary as the champion of virginity as early as the 4th century, with the Jerusalem feast of the *Hypapante* celebrating Mary's purification and Jesus' presentation in the Temple. Another feast dedicated to the commemoration of Mary and the merits of virginity is recorded in Constantinople in the first half of the 5th century; most likely, it formed part of the Nativity liturgical cycle. During the 5th-century Theotokos controversy in Constantinople, this feast provided the occasion for Proclus' delivery of the first of several influential Marian homilies in the presence of Nestorius himself. Proclus praised Mary with the support of the monks and the ascetics who proved to be most vocal defenders of the Theotokos. In line with this tradition, the Virgin Mary is considered to be the primary benefactor and protectress of the autonomous monastic republic on Mount Athos, often described as "the garden of the Virgin." In the broader sense, the Theotokos is revered in Orthodoxy as the paragon of holiness to which the church, the bride of God, aspires as a whole. In this context Mary is a shining example of the rewards of a life of humility and obedience to God, the greatest of all the saints, and an eschatological intercessor at the throne of Christ.

The formal recognition of Mary in the doctrines of the church is complemented and (as in in the case of Ephesus 431) even pre-dated by a steady rise of her prominence in liturgical life and devotional practice. Early Marian veneration was especially notable in Constantinople, the capital city which, according to Byzantine legend, was dedicated to the Virgin by Constantine himself. The cult of Mary developed there under generous imperial patronage with the building of three major churches commemorating the Virgin: the Blachernae, the Hodegoi, and the Chalkoprateia. Priceless Marian relics and objects of pilgrimage were kept in those establishments, including the Virgin's belt and veil. Devotional objects related to Mary and Marian icons were exhibited on the city walls and carried not only in liturgical processions, but also in battle, by both Byzantine and Slav rulers, fortifying popular acclaim of the Virgin and highlighting her intercessory and protective powers (the Akathist designates her as *Promacheia* – "defending warrior"). The Virgin's glorification as the defender of the Christian empire and a military and civil leader *par excellence* is amply reflected in iconic depictions of Mary enthroned with the holy child in her lap and surrounded by angels and saints. In the Eastern Christian world victories on the battlefield and miraculous rescue were often ascribed to the Virgin. In Byzantium the Virgin protected her city from Slav, Persian, and Arab enemies; in Russia, miracle-working Marian icons were thought to have repeatedly saved Moscow, Kiev, and Novgorod from invasion. The Russian liturgical calendar records three occasions when the Virgin of Vladimir is said to have delivered Russia from the Tatars (Tradigo 2006: 28).

The fervor of Marian devotion reflects the fact that, by virtue of its intimate connection with the Savior, Mary is uniquely suited for the role of the most effective intercessor the church has on its behalf. The earliest extant prayer to the Theotokos (*sub tuum praesidium*) evokes the eagerness with which her protection was sought: "Under your mercy we take refuge, *Theotokos*, do not reject our supplications but deliver us from danger" (Limberis 1994: 104). In Eastern Christian art this entrusting of the prayers of the faithful to the Virgin would come to be depicted in the iconic composition of the Deisis, a grouping of Christ enthroned in glory with his mother to his right and John the Baptist to his left. As the iconostasis screen developed in Orthodox churches, the Deisis would come to be situated in its upper center, emphasizing the value and importance attributed to the Virgin's intercession. As a result of a Marian vision to St. Andrew the Fool in the church of the Blachernae, the Virgin's protective powers also acquired a separate liturgical feast, called the Feast of Protection or the Feast of the Protecting Veil (*Pokrov*, October 1/14), which remains highly popular in Russia.

Icon-centered liturgical iconography in the East uses Marian depictions in a variety of settings and always in a place of prominence. Traditionally, Mary's image is found above the sanctuary (Virgin *platytera*; "More Spacious than the Heavens"), where she presides over the consecration of the Eucharist as the Mother of the incarnate Word and a symbol of the church. The annunciation scene with Mary and the angel Gabriel bringing her the good news, flanks the royal doors leading to the altar area in Orthodox churches; the Deisis scene is situated above them. Mary is the central figure in icons related to her liturgical feasts:

her nativity (September 8) and presentation in the Temple (November 21), the annunciation (March 2) and her Dormition (August 15), the post-Easter Feast of the Theotokos Life Giving Font, and the Protection of the Theotokos. An additional number of iconic types illustrate her instrumentality in the divine economy and the many roles she would come to play in response to the spiritual needs of the faithful. Marian typology is embedded in her depictions as a burning bush, an enclosed garden, and an unfading rose; other iconographic formulas have her nursing the holy child, contemplating the inevitability of his passion, or lamenting his death. The best known of those formulas is the canonical representation of the Virgin as *Hodegetria* ("The One Who Shows Us the Way"), in which Mary offers her child to the world as the way to salvation. A variation of the Hodegetria evolved into the image of the Virgin *Eleousa* ("Virgin of Mercy or Lovingkindness"), particularly widespread in the Balkans and in Russia. The Virgin of Vladimir is a famous example of the mixing of the *Eleousa* type and the Virgin of the Passion; the mutual embrace of mother and child in this icon reflects Mary's role as an intercessor as well as offering the assurance that Christ listens to his mother's prayers. The Virgin is also portrayed in the traditional posture of prayer (*Orans*), sending the supplications of the church to heaven, or enthroned with Jesus in her lap and accompanied by saints, apostles, emperors, or benefactors of the particular temple in which the icon resides. Of Russian origin is the popular representation of the Virgin as the Joy of All That Sorrow.

The wealth of Marian iconic types corresponds to the substantial liturgical hymnography dedicated to the Virgin. Each Orthodox service proclaims that "it is meet and right" to praise the Virgin as "more honorable than the cherubim and more glorious beyond compare than the seraphim" because of her contribution to the history of salvation. Early examples of liturgical poetry are found in the hymns of Ephrem the Syrian (4th century) and the *kontakia* of Romanos the Melodist (6th century). These works rely on a deeply evocative language which is redolent with scriptural allusions and highlights Mary's distinctive status in relation to "all created women": she is the most joyous of all, for she has conceived God in flesh, and most "magnified," for she has given birth to him (McVey 1989: 77). In an array of breathtaking images, Ephrem delights in outlining the paradox of how Mary suckled the Word while he, the incarnate God, nourished the world with the restoring power of his life. Similarly, in his *kontakia* on the nativity and death of Christ, Romanos turns to Mary as a narrator and imagines her son's Passion through her eyes. The most impressive assembly of Marian praises is found in the Akathist, a (processional) hymn written after the Council of Ephesus and sung today on Fridays during Great Lent. The Akathist praises Mary redeemer of the ancient curse of Eve, as well as the "womb of the divine Incarnation." Particularly noteworthy is the insistence on presenting the Virgin as a "container of the uncontainable God." Mary is emphatically depicted as the God's indwelling and the new locus of salvation: she is an "ark gilded by the Spirit," an "immovable tower" of the Church, an "impregnable wall," a pillar, a tabernacle, a bridal chamber, a bridge, and a ladder. As the woman who unites God and humanity, the Akathist proclaims, the Virgin is the one who will always protect Christians, assure victory, and heal souls and bodies.

On the whole, the significance of the Virgin Mary in Eastern Christian culture and theology is clearly central. In consenting to do the will of God, Mary becomes the mother of the incarnate Word and makes salvation come true. She brings the human race back to the garden of life from which Adam and Eve were exiled and shines as the embodiment of eschatological hope. The veneration accorded to her is also an acknowledgment of the salvific power of Christ of which she is the first recipient. The church accordingly teaches that while the saints rightly receive honor (*douleia*), she alone of all creatures is appointed by God to receive "high honor" (*hyperdouleia*). As a popular hymn attributed to John Damascus aptly puts it, this is why "in you all creation rejoices, o full of grace."

SEE ALSO: Council of Chalcedon (451); Council of Ephesus (431); Eleousa (*Umilenie*); Iconography, Styles of; Iconostasis; Icons; Panagia; Platytera; Protecting Veil; St. Cyril of Alexandria (ca. 378–444); St. Ephrem the Syrian (ca. 306–373/379); St. Romanos the Melodist (6th c.)

REFERENCES AND SUGGESTED READINGS

Constas, N. (2003) *Proclus of Constantinople and the Cult of the Virgin in Late Antiquity*. Leiden: E. J. Brill.

Limberis, V. (1994) *Divine Heiress: The Virgin Mary and the Creation of Christian Constantinople*. New York: Routledge.

McGuckin, J. A. (1994) *St. Cyril of Alexandria: The Christological Controversy, Its History, Theology, and Texts*. Leiden: E. J. Brill.

McGuckin, J. A. (2008) *The Orthodox Church: An Introduction to Its History, Doctrine, and Spiritual Culture*. Oxford: Blackwell.

McVey, K. (ed. and trans.) (1989) *Ephrem the Syrian: Hymns*. New York: Paulist Press.

Tradigo, A. (2006) *Icons and Saints of the Eastern Orthodox Church*. Milan: Mondadori Electa.

Tradition

JOHN A. MCGUCKIN

"Tradition" is a central term for Orthodox theological life. The church understands the "Holy Tradition" (by no means signifying every ecclesiastical custom) to be the essence of the evangelical experience as it lives it out fully, and mediates it through each generation to the world. Orthodoxy is itself the embodiment of the essential Christian tradition in time and space. The Latin term *traditio* ("handing on") and its Greek counterpart *paradosis* both acquired technical meanings from the New Testament onwards (cf. 1 Cor. 11.23), signifying tradition as the central core of evangelical experience that was communicated from Jesus to the apostles and through them to the Christian world.

The concept of tradition was clarified and elevated by St. Irenaeus in the 2nd century as the ultimate safeguard against Gnostic "innovations," in an age when Christian self-identity was being publicly challenged by numerous speculative streams of redefinition. It was he who, in the *Adversus Haereses*, popularized the model of tradition as a conservatory force (not necessarily a conservative one) that guarded the transmission of the message of salvation, through a regularly constituted order (*taxis*) from Jesus, to the apostles, to the early episcopate, who maintained the apostolic succession of the *Kerygma*. Tradition, as St. Irenaeus understood it, was the vital force of evangelism, as much as (if not more than) it was the mechanism whereby the church was able to filter out what it felt was inauthentic in relation to its central self-identity, from generation to generation. Jesus himself was less than patient with those who could not differentiate between the "customs of men" and the perennial demands of the Word of God. His anger was directed at those who resisted the dynamic process of the saving Spirit, by opposing against it deliberately "deadening" appeals to past "traditions" (Mk. 7.13). In his argument with the Pharisees over the significance of traditions, the Lord was not opposing a developmental sense of theology to a "static" or "traditionalist" one; rather, he was opposing a concept of living tradition to a traditionalist attitude that opportunistically served to screen the elect community from the ever-present demands of God.

In the apostolic age, St. Paul operated with a double sense of tradition. At some times he is conscious of how carefully he must deliver to others "what I myself received" (1 Cor. 11.2, 23; 15.1–4), especially when it concerns traditions about the Lord, or liturgical process. At other times, in advancing the cause of the church's effective preaching of the message of salvation, he is more than conscious of how the Risen Lord has empowered him to "seize the moment" (*Kairos*), and how he himself authoritatively transmits his own contribution to the tradition, with the authority of no less than Christ, whom he serves apostolically. The first concept of tradition Paul sees as an unchanging verity. The second he sees as economically related to the saving *Kerygma*, and changing across the times as the servant of the efficient proclamation of the gospel in various conditions (1 Cor. 7.10–12, 25, 40). In his times of conflict with other apostolic missionaries of the Jerusalem Church, who resisted his boldly "innovative" apostolate to the Gentiles, Paul is ready to use this missionary sense of tradition not merely as a flexible kerygmatic tool – "To be all things to all" (1 Cor. 9.22) – but even in a fixed and canonical sense. He warns his disciples in several places to keep fast to the traditions he gave them, and to keep away from those who did not live accordingly (1 Thes. 2.15; 3.6). The generation after Paul, less confident than their teacher, represents a correspondingly more cautious attitude and speaks of that "deposit" of tradition that has to be preserved by the church with nothing added or taken away (1 Tim. 6.20). The sense of kerygmatic adaptability was being conditioned at this period, on the cusp of the 1st and 2nd centuries, by an imminent sense of the End Times approaching.

In the writings of Clement of Rome, later in that same generation, one witnesses the first attempt to make the tradition synonymous with that which the presbyters and bishops of the church both represent and protect. This first attempt to make the tradition align very closely with "authoritative preaching" on the part of church leaders was really the first formally elaborated patristic concept of tradition (more exactly, in this case, a doctrine of the episcopal inheritance of the charism of authority). It proved insufficiently flexible to meet the large range of challenges to church unity that the 2nd century threw out. In the following generation, witnessed both in Tertullian and Irenaeus, who were both much exercised with the problem of how to distinguish authentic tradition from heretical imposture, the broader principle of an appeal to the community's sense of basic truths was more noticeably elevated. For Irenaeus, the question of what was true tradition could be proven by appeal to the record of the main apostolic centers, the ancient and leading churches. He further developed his thought by suggesting that the apostolic churches possessed the "charism of truth" in a special way (*Adversus Haereses* 4.26.2). This was manifested above all in the manner in which they interpreted the Scriptures, soberly and with catholic consensus. In this context he developed his famous image of the interpretative "key" (*hypothesis*) which the church owned but which others do not possess. It was to grow into the fuller patristic concept of the *Mens Ecclesiae*, the "Mind of the Church," what St. Athanasius was later to call the church's *dianoia* and its instinctive sense of the true intentionality (*skopos*) of both scripture and tradition; that is, the comprehensive overview given to the Spirit-illumined faithful, which was radically partialized and distorted by heretical dissidents. Irenaeus added further to the fundamental vocabulary of the theology of tradition when he developed the argument that the key to biblical interpretation was the "Canon of Truth" (*Adversus Haereses* 3.2.1), which in the Latin version of his works gave to the West (decisively so in the hands of Tertullian) the principle of the Rule of Faith: *Regula Fidei* or *Regula Veritatis*. This *Regula*, Irenaeus says, is the strongest refutation of heretical variability, for it is maintained in all the churches and goes back to the apostles. Apostolic succession, then, is not primarily a matter of succession of individual bishops one after another, but the succession of apostolic teaching from the time of the apostles to the present.

When the Arian controversy caused a crisis in the 4th-century church over the precise nature of fundamental truths (the divinity of Christ, the Trinity), the Orthodox fathers reacted instinctively by appealing to an older process of solving problems from the end of the 2nd century: that is, by holding regional synods where the church leaders would decisively address problems and offer solutions in a synodal consensus. At first, the "international" (ecumenical) synodical principle had a hopeful beginning, but soon the restless policy changes of the Imperial house and the party strife of bishops left the aspirations for public harmony in tatters. The 4th century saw the hope of an ecumenically led

principle of synodical government heavily compromised as one synod countermanded and anathematized another.

The question of how to recognize the identifying marks of tradition rose again acutely at the end of the Arian period, over the issue of the deity of the Holy Spirit. Here, significant theologians such as Sts. Athanasius, Basil, and Gregory of Nazianzus all consciously theologized about the way in which tradition could make new statements about fundamental matters of faith that had not been explicitly witnessed hitherto. Gregory's *Oration 31* describes his own role in proclaiming the *homoousion* of the Holy Spirit (despite any lack of precedent) as a herald of God speaking in the time of a new "seismic shaking" of the world order. Similarly, Basil (typically, more cautiously) appeals to the range of "unwritten traditions" in the church's liturgical life (*On the Holy Spirit* 27) to justify the principle that the real inner life of the church (its core tradition) is something more extensive than its canonical or written traditions. This more or less stabilized the nexus of the ancient church's overall doctrine of tradition, apart from two last movements: one eastern and the other western. The christological crisis of the 5th century was so fast, furious, and subtle, that many of the same problems over discerning "true tradition" that had occupied Irenaeus rose again in this period. The 5th-century answer (as manifested in the Acts of the Councils from Ephesus in 431 to Nicea II in 787) was to assemble dossiers of patristic evidences. The very notion of "patristic theology" was born in this era. Fathers of the church were regarded as possessing significantly elevated authority, and when accumulated in a *florilegium*, collectively they made a powerful testimony for authentic tradition. After this period, most Latin and Greek theology was constructed on the basis of assembling *florilegia*.

In the West, Augustine's long fight with the Donatists had led him to elevate the principle of catholicity (a universal solidarity as opposed to a provincial regionalism) as a handy guide to authentic tradition. Catholicity was thus a necessary factor alongside antiquity (apostolic or scriptural status). This view of truth manifested by its geographical extension was always closely allied in the Western Churches with the principle of communion with the Roman see. It led inexorably to the famous formula of Vincent of Lerins, commenting on Augustine, who argued that "oral tradition" must always be subordinated to Scripture (*Commonitorium* 2.1–2) as being purely its exegesis. It was he who also defined the authentic Christian tradition as that which is held to be such "by everyone, always, and in all places." This gave rise in later Latin thought to the doctrine of the clear distinction of Scripture and tradition (as two sources of Christian *kerygma*). The Orthodox Churches never followed this latter path, seeing always Scripture itself as one of the primal (but not exclusive) manifestations of the core tradition of the gospel *kerygma*, of which the inner life of the church was certainly another; as were also the other principles of tradition-discernment it had elevated across the centuries as a closely meshed interwoven web: namely the scriptural (canonic) principle, the apostolic principle, the episcopal, the synodical, the conciliar, the pneumatic, and the canonical principle (legislative decrees). All these things together, harmoniously commenting upon one another, their balance discerned by spiritual *Diakrisis*, manifested authentic tradition in each age of the church. The Orthodox Christian doctrine of tradition is thus an ancient and richly complex idea, which is no less than an investigation of the inner roots of Christian consciousness in history; and indeed more than this – for it is the tracing of the presence of the Divine Spirit in Christ's church across the ages.

SEE ALSO: Apostolic Succession; Bible; Ecumenical Councils; Episcopacy; Gnosticism; Heresy; Holy Spirit; Patristics

REFERENCES AND SUGGESTED READINGS

Bouyer, L. (1947) "The Fathers of the Church on Tradition and Scripture," *Eastern Churches Quarterly* 7 (special volume dedicated to scripture and tradition).

Florovsky, G. (1971) *Bible, Church and Tradition: An Eastern Orthodox View*, in *Collected Works* Vol. 1. Belmont, MA: Nordland.

McGuckin, J. A. (1998) "Eschaton and Kerygma: The Future of the Past in the Present Kairos: The Concept of Living Tradition in Orthodox Theology," *St. Vladimir's Theological Quarterly* 42, 3–4: 225–71.

Reynders, B. (1933) "Paradosis: Le progrès de l'idée de tradition jusqu'à S. Irenée," *Recherches de théologie ancienne et médiévale* 5: 155–91.

van den Eynde, D. (1933) *Les Normes de l'enseignement chrétien dans la littérature patristique des trois premiers siècles*. Paris: Gembloux-Paris.

van Leer, E. F. (1954) *Tradition and Scripture in the Early Church*. Assen, Netherlands.

Triodion

SOTIRIOS A. VLAVIANOS

The *Triodion* (Greek: Τριῴδιον, "book of the three odes") is a liturgical book that contains service material from the Sunday of the Publican and the Pharisee (tenth Sunday before Easter) up until the night of Great Saturday. The name of this lengthy liturgical season (encompassing Great Lent) is both taken from and identified with this book. The title *Triodion* refers to short canons with only three odes which are sung at Orthros (Matins) on the weekdays of Great Lent. The book evolved around the 9th century and was largely the work of Studite monks from Constantinople. Currently, the texts found in the *Triodion* reflect the liturgical tradition of Jerusalem from various time periods: some early, some later. The *Triodion* used to be divided into two parts, the *Lenten Triodion* and the *Festal Triodion*. The *Festal Triodion* covered the liturgical cycle beginning on Easter up to the Sunday of All Saints. Eventually, the latter was incorporated into the *Pentekostarion* around the 14th century, when it then had its short canons (*triodia*) eliminated.

SEE ALSO: Canon (Liturgical); Great Week; Ode; *Oktoechos*; *Paraklitike*; *Pentekostarion*

REFERENCES AND SUGGESTED READINGS

Savas, S. J. (1983) *The Treasury of Orthodox Hymnology – Triodion: An Historical and Hymnographic Examination*. Minneapolis: Light and Life Publications.

Schmemann, A. (1974) *Great Lent: Journey to Pascha*. Crestwood, NY: St. Vladimir's Seminary Press.

Taft, R. F. (1985) *The Liturgy of the Hours in East and West: The Origins of the Divine Office and its Meaning for Today*. Collegeville, MN: Liturgical Press.

Troparion

DIMITRI CONOMOS

A short, monostrophic chant in rhythmic prose. The oldest stratum of hymnody for Vespers and Matins, the troparia constitute by far the largest body of sung texts in the Byzantine rite. The *kata stichon* hymns, of Syrian and Palestinian monastic origin, are important early examples. They exhibit the same number of syllables (usually eleven) and the same number of accents in every line. Although no music for primitive troparia survives, it is generally held that they were sung to unpretentious tunes, generally composed on the rule of one tone to each syllable, to render them suitable for congregational singing.

REFERENCES AND SUGGESTED READINGS

Conomos, D. (2008) "What is a Troparion?" *Sobornost* 30, 2: 59–80.

Trypanis, C. A. (1981) *Greek Poetry from Homer to Seferis*. London: Faber and Faber.

Tropes *see* Music (Sacred)

U

Ukraine, Orthodoxy in the

TODD E. FRENCH

The Ukraine is host to the rich history of the conversion of the Rus to Orthodoxy, which led to the further spreading of Christianity in Asia. Its capital city, Kiev, has served as the focal point of political maneuvering in the Slavic territories from the conversion of the Rus down through to modern times. It is worth noting that the history of this conversion, commonly associated with Vladimir in 988, overrides numerous alternative conversion stories. Ancient Christian legend tells that St. Andrew the "First-Called" embarked on a mission to convert the Scythians in the year 55. Evidence only becomes clearer in the later medieval period, when one starts to find several clues to Christianity's influence on the Rus. Although the term "Rus" is used to describe the people of a diocese in Tmutorokan as early as the 860s, the Rus are historically associated with the Kievan centered kingdom. The distance between these two cities being roughly a thousand miles has raised questions about whether the two Rus settlements are both Slavic kingdoms or if the Black Sea Rus were the same as the Goths mentioned by St. John Chrysostom in the 4th century, as being an important community for missionary enterprise.

Few were more influential in the growth of Christianity in the Ukraine than St. Constantine (tonsured Cyril before his death) and his brother St. Methodios. They were chosen to lead a mission to the Slavic kingdom of Moravia in 864. Prior to their departure they devised an alphabet (Glagolitic) into which many texts were translated. Their successors, Clement and Naum of Ohrid, were instrumental in the development of the Cyrillic alphabet, named for their teacher.

Kiev, however, was a good distance from Tmutorokan and the story of the Kievan Rus conversion proper begins with two princes, Askold and Dir. A popular version of the story tells how after attempting to seize Constantinople, the princes saw their fleet destroyed through a miracle which they believed to have been called down by the Patriarch St. Photios and the emperor. This led to the baptism of the defeated (and impressed) leaders. A more textured account survives in Greek chronicles relating the defeat of Askold and Dir by Prince Oleg, who made Kiev his capital. Vladimir, one of four successor princes, was a pagan like his forebears but perhaps saw the need for a unifying religion that resonated with the population both within his kingdom and in neighboring lands, especially Byzantium. After dismissing the claims of Judaism and Islam, Vladimir settled on Christianity, but relied on ambassadors to the Latins and Greeks in order to decide on his preferred style. His emissaries returned explaining that they were not sure whether they were in heaven or on earth during a service at St. Sophia's. The decision was

The Encyclopedia of Eastern Orthodox Christianity, edited by John Anthony McGuckin
© 2011 Blackwell Publishing Ltd.

Plate 74 The Kiev Mohyla Academy, founded by the great Ukrainian hierarch Peter Moghila for raising the standards of the education of clergy. It was the center of a great revival in Orthodoxy after the 18th century. Photo by John McGuckin.

made for Byzantine alliance and the Orthodox Church began to fuel Ukraine's religious history. In 988 Vladimir was baptized at Chersonesus. Following that, there were mass baptisms of the people in the river Dnieper.

The conversion of Vladimir has been attributed to his Christian grandmother St. Olga and his political connections with the Byzantine ruler, Basil II (the "Bulgar Slayer"). Regardless of its origin, its spread was initiated from the ruling classes down through Slavic society by incentive and coercion. The Byzantine church maintained important links with Vladimir's kingdom through missionaries and an appointment of a metropolitan archbishop in Kiev. Vladimir's son, Yaroslav, consolidated his rule in 1036 and was able to build many churches. Among them was the renowned cathedral of St. Sophia (1044), built to rival its sister in Constantinople. Yaroslav

organized the translation of important religious texts into the liturgical language of Church Slavonic. In 1051 he appointed the first non-Greek archbishop, Ilarion.

Ukrainian monasticism was first founded in the Kievan caves (Pechersky Lavra) in the 11th century. Built into the banks of the river Dnieper, the lavra's catacombs are a treasury of relics uniquely preserved through mummification and attesting to the rich history of saints this land has produced. The golden age of Kievan Rus began to deteriorate in the 12th century when princes began to challenge Kiev for autonomy in their territories. The result was a fractured kingdom with numerous claims to power. Disunity allowed for a national defeat when in 1237 Genghis Khan's grandson, Batu, invaded the northeastern Rus territories. By 1240, Kiev had fallen and its churches were burned by the Mongol invaders. Perhaps even more significant

Plate 75   St. Jonah's skete in midtown Kiev. The monastery was destroyed by the Soviets and the church turned into a warehouse. Today it has been refounded and the monastic life thrives there with a young community. Photo by John McGuckin.

than the loss of the capital was the shift of the metropolitan archbishop's seat from Kiev to the city of Vladimir in 1299 and then on to Moscow.

After Kiev fell, Danylo, the ruler of Galicia-Volhynia (1237–64), attempted to recapture the prominence of Kievan Rus by waging war against the Mongols. Although his efforts at first failed, he and his successors were finally able to wrest the kingdom back. After the archbishopric was moved and Kiev was destroyed through multiple wars, the Lithuanians, a pagan community living along the Baltic Sea, saw an opportunity in these lands. They invaded what is now Belarus and made their way to the Ukraine. Under Grand Prince Algirdas, the Lithuanians declared all of Rus to belong to the Lithuanians and in 1340 they made their move into the Ukraine. By 1362 they had taken Kiev and they definitively defeated the

Mongols shortly after. Lithuanian power was rooted in their amenability to Rus law (as constituted by Yaroslav), culture, and language. Their rule was preferred over Mongol rule and thus the pagan Lithuanians gradually became the Orthodox-leaning Slavic state. This was once again to be challenged by the invasion of Polish Catholic interests in 1340, which promoted a westward leaning affiliation. Acquiring all of Galicia-Volhynia by 1366, the Poles ended the notion of Ukrainian self-rule in 1471 when they officially incorporated the Ukraine.

Meanwhile, Moscow imposed a decisive defeat on the Mongols in 1480 and was quickly emerging as the prominent power of the region. When the Ottoman Turks invaded Constantinople in 1453, Moscow emerged as a "Third Rome" and the dominant sustainer of Orthodox belief. The Orthodox in Ukraine found themselves in a strange relationship with this new power. It had lost its senior metropolitan status to Moscow, but also desperately needed Moscow's support in maintaining any hope of an Orthodox Ukraine.

In 1448 the hierarchy of the Orthodox Church was in division over the issue of the Imperial Byzantine policy for Union with Rome; and because of this Moscow was able to declare some independence from Constantinople. This move promoted the development of the Russian Orthodox Church. The Union of Lublin in 1569 brought together the Lithuanian and Polish states, which housed nearly all of Ukrainian territory. This combined power rivaled Moscow for a time, but eventually found itself divided internally between powerful, landed nobility and peasant, Ruthenian Orthodox who worked the agricultural lands.

In 1589 the metropolitanate of Moscow became fully autocephalous and the Ukrainian Orthodox were subsequently organized as a dependent ecclesial domain. Along with the rapid rise of Muscovite political control, there was a counterbalancing call in Ukraine for independence from Moscow. This move toward independence partially came to fruition in an attempt to organize a Greek Catholic church. In the Polish-Lithuanian Union, Catholics stood to gain political privilege and preference over their Orthodox counterparts. In the interest of unity, the nobles proposed the conversion of the Ruthenian Orthodox quarter of their population by establishing a Greek church that maintained its Orthodox rules and rites but was subject to the pope. Orthodox communities did not give in easily, however, and in 1578 their cause was championed by Konstantyn Ostrozky, who built a printing press at Ostrih in Volhynia. Famously publishing the first Slavic Bible in 1581, Ostrozky was instrumental in building an Orthodox rival to the Catholic schools of the West. The school, however, was turned

over to the Jesuits in 1608 by his Catholic granddaughter, Anna.

Conflicts began to rage over properties and rights between the Greek Catholics and Orthodox, costing many clerics their lives. In 1632 the Polish government proposed a compromise in which the Orthodox hierarchy was recognized and properties were divided. Peter Mohyla (Moghila), the new archimandrite of Pechersky Lavra and eventual chief hierarch of Kiev, utilized the peace after 1632 to print the first Slavic Orthodox catechism.

Khmelnytsky's uprising of 1648 showed what a united Ukraine was capable of accomplishing. Revoking the Polish magnates' power, the Cossacks overthrew the political regime with a bloody revolution. Needing to call upon foreign assistance, Khmelnytsky first considered the Ottoman Porte, but ultimately secured the might of the Muscovites and their tsar, Aleksei Mikhailovich. The appeal was answered with a nod to the shared vision of Orthodoxy. At the time of Khmelnytsky's death, 17 percent of the land formerly in Polish hands was designated as the property of the Orthodox Church. The metropolitanate of Kiev was subsumed by the patriarch of Moscow in 1686.

Eventually, Russia, Prussia, and Austria divided Poland-Lithuania among themselves and by the late 18th century Russia was in control of 62 percent of the Ukrainian territories. There was a steady ongoing struggle between the tsars and Ukrainian notions of self-government. The period of imperial rule was marked with important moments for the Orthodox Church. During General Dmitri Bibikov's rule (1837–52) the aim was to convert the 2 million remaining Catholics to Orthodoxy through willful tactics such as deportation and executions.

When the tsarist regime collapsed in 1917 the Ukraine quickly responded with the formation of the Central Rada. A rival to

Bolshevik power, it was ultimately put down by the Germans. The resulting Ukrainian Soviet government held some sovereignty until 1923. Orthodoxy in the Ukraine suffered significant setbacks during the communist era, but was never extinguished. When communism began to wane in its appeal, the Ukrainian Catholic Church began to move toward the restoration of its properties to its 5 million members. The Russian Orthodox Church responded to this development by changing its name to the Ukrainian Orthodox Church in 1990, but remained under the supervision of the Moscow patriarchate.

The Ukrainian Autocephalous Orthodox Church (UAOC) had been created in 1921 with Vasyl Lypkivsky as its metropolitan. The UAOC grew quickly and was initially favored by the Soviets because of the challenges it posed to the Russian Orthodox Church. Once the movement took hold, however, it too became another threat for the Soviets to extinguish. Dismantled after the 1930s in the homeland, but enjoying a time of development in the diaspora countries of the West, the UAOC came back as a significant factor in Ukrainian church life after the fall of communism, and reaffirmed their distance from the Moscow patriarchate in 1990. They now are represented by 1,650 parishes. Under the persecution of Soviet rule, several diaspora parishes submitted to the leadership of the patriarch of Constantinople. In the US and Canada the UAOC communities have recently declared their independence from the phanar.

When President Kravchuk came to power in 1990, after the fall of the Soviet satellite system, there was the hope that the diverging religious communities of the Ukraine might be united under one unified church. For this reason the new Kiev patriarchate of the Independent Ukrainian Orthodox Church was formulated. It was largely composed of those communities who wished to place distance between themselves and the Moscow patriarchate, which they characterized as a tool of oppression. The new political leadership of independent Ukraine fostered these ambitions for separate status. Wider world Orthodoxy, however, did not regard the Independent Ukrainian Orthodox Church as having legitimate canonical status. Its first claimant as patriarch, Filaret of Kiev, was unable to sustain unity and suffered the severe censure of the Russian Orthodox Church. The Moscow patriarchate, in response to these calls for Ukrainian autonomy, declared the canonical autonomous status of the Ukrainian Orthodox Church, which was no longer to be called simply the "Russian Church," although it remained in the wider system of the synod of the Moscow patriarchate: autonomous not autocephalous.

Currently, the largest of the communities in the Ukraine is the Ukrainian Orthodox Church under the Moscow patriarchate. They represent 6,000 parishes mainly in the East and South. Their liturgical language remains Church Slavonic rather than the vernacular Ukrainian used by other communities such as the UAOC. Representing over 27 million Orthodox parishioners, the Ukraine is a major center of Orthodox energy and culture. This new vitality after communism, however, has found itself divided on account of its liminal position between Europe and Asia. Depending on Russia for 90 percent of its oil and 77 percent of its natural gas, the Ukraine has often found itself in a difficult relationship with Moscow power bases, both secular and ecclesiastical. Politically, the Ukraine often leans toward cooperation with Europe and the United States, as can be seen in numerous treaties and disarmament proposals, but they continue to find themselves in a difficult geographical and political position with regard to Russia's interests. These colliding trajectories also affect church life and will for the foreseeable future.

SEE ALSO: Lithuania, Orthodoxy in; Sts. Constantine (Cyril) (ca. 826–869) and Methodios (815–885)

REFERENCES AND SUGGESTED READINGS

Kubicek, P. (2008) *The History of Ukraine*. Westport: Greenwood Press.

McGuckin, J. A. (2008) *The Orthodox Church*. Oxford: Blackwell.

Pospielovksy, D. V. (1998) *The Orthodox Church in the History of Russia*. Crestwood, NY: St. Vladimir's Seminary Press.

Prokurat, M., Golitzin, A., and Peterson, M. D. (1996) *Historical Dictionary of the Orthodox Church*. Lanham: Scarecrow Press.

Subtelny, O. (2000) *Ukraine: A History*. Toronto: University of Toronto Press.

Uniate *see* Eastern Catholic Churches

United States of America, Orthodoxy in the

THOMAS FITZGERALD

THE ALASKAN MISSION

The Alaskan territory became part of the United States in 1867 when it was sold by Imperial Russia. The Orthodox Church had a significant presence in the territory dating from 1794. In that year, eight monks and two novices from the Church of Russia established the first mission in Alaska. Led by Archimandrite Joseph Bolotov, the missionaries departed St. Petersburg on December 25, 1793 and arrived on Kodiak Island on September 24, 1794. They had traveled about a third of the circumference of the earth. Discovered and explored by Russian explorers from 1741 onwards, the Alaskan coastland and the numerous islands between North America and Siberia were claimed by Imperial Russia. A colony had been established in 1784 on Kodiak and became the center of trade.

While these early missionaries confronted numerous difficult challenges, their work in Alaska in the late 18th and early 19th centuries was remarkable. Spreading from its center on Kodiak to other populated regions, the Alaskan Mission was one of the largest and most significant missionary endeavors guided by the Church of Russia and supported by the imperial government. As a sign of its significance, the Church of Russia selected Fr. Joseph the head of the mission to serve as the first bishop in Alaska in 1796. After traveling to Siberia for his consecration, however, the new bishop died in a shipwreck before returning to Kodiak.

Two missionaries during this period have attracted particular attention. With little formal education, the monk Herman (1760–1837) came to exemplify the best qualities of the early missionaries in Russian Alaska. As one of the first missionaries, Herman, who was not ordained, instructed the natives both about Christianity and about agricultural techniques. He staunchly defended the rights of the natives in the face of exploitation by many Russian merchants and traders. By 1812, Herman moved to Spruce Island, three miles from Kodiak, and established a chapel, an orphanage, and a hermitage. Not long after his death in 1837, the natives began to honor him as a saint. They collected stories about his service and recorded the miracles attributed to his intercession. His formal canonization took place in 1970.

Fr. John (Innocent) Veniaminov (1797–1879) and his family arrived on the island of Unalaska in 1824. As part of his missionary work, the young priest created an Aleut alphabet based upon Cyrillic characters. This was followed by a dictionary and grammar. These provided the basis for his translation of the Gospel of St. Matthew and portions of the liturgy. John also wrote a basic catechism entitled *Indication of the Pathway into the Kingdom.*

Like Herman, Fr. John was concerned with the needs and activities of the natives. He taught them agricultural techniques, carpentry, and metalworking. During ten years on Unalaska, Fr. John constructed a school, an orphanage, and a number of chapels. Moving to New Archangel (Sitka) in 1834, he continued his remarkable missionary work among the Tlingits, a tribe generally hostile to the Russian merchants. Fr. John also traveled to other missionary outposts. He visited Fort Rus in Spanish Northern California in 1836. He also visited a number of Roman Catholic missions and met with the missionaries.

Following the death of his wife, Fr. John became a monk and took the name Innocent. He subsequently was elected bishop of Kamchatka, the Kurill and Aleutian Islands. With his return to New Archangel (Sitka), a new period of missionary activity developed. Regarded as a great educator, he created schools offering a wide variety of subjects. In 1841 he opened a seminary at Sitka which included courses not only in religious but also in native languages, Latin, trigonometry, navigation, and medicine. He insisted that his priests learn native languages and customs. Innocent was elected metropolitan of Moscow in 1868 and established the Russian Orthodox Missionary Society before his death in 1879. He was canonized a saint in 1977 and given the title "Apostle to America."

Following the sale of Alaska to the United States, many Russian merchants and fur traders in Alaska subsequently returned to their homeland or traveled to San Francisco where there was a sizeable Russian colony. The formal interest of the Church of Russia in Alaska also diminished. Few competent clergy remained in Alaska to care for the faithful, which numbered about 12,000 gathered into about 43 communities. A new diocese encompassing Alaska and the Aleutian Islands was established in 1870, but the episcopal see was moved to San Francisco in 1872 and its affairs developed with less regular connection with the Russian synod.

The sale of Alaska also opened the territory to Protestant missionaries from the lower United States. Having little appreciation of the Orthodox Church, the Protestant missionaries proselytized among the native Orthodox, and showed little regard for their indigenous history and culture. Native languages and customs were discouraged. Assimilation was demanded. Despite this, the Orthodox Church continued to maintain a weakened presence in the Alaskan territory, and the mission continued to influence the subsequent development of Orthodoxy in the United States. The various Russian Orthodox jurisdictions which developed in the United States in the early 20th century claimed a direct continuity with the Alaskan Mission.

EARLY ORTHODOX IMMIGRATION AND CHURCH DEVELOPMENT

The focus of Orthodox Christianity in the United States dramatically shifted to the east coast in the late 19th and early 20th centuries as a consequence of mass immigration. Thousands of Orthodox immigrants from Greece, Asia Minor, Carpatho-Russia, the Ukraine, and the Middle East came to the United States. Lesser numbers came from Serbia, Bulgaria,

Romania, and Russia. Almost immediately, the immigrants set about establishing parishes, to construct church buildings, and to find a priest to serve their community. This was done often with little or no formal direction from church authorities either here or in the Old Country.

A number of the earliest parishes began as pan-Orthodox communities containing immigrants from various ethnic backgrounds. Among these parishes were those in New Orleans (1864), San Francisco (1868), and New York City (1870). There, a notable attempt to introduce Orthodox Christianity to the wider society in New York was made by Fr. Nicholas Bjerring (1831–84). Between 1879 and 1881 his journal, the *Oriental Church Magazine*, published essays on Orthodox teachings and liturgical texts in English.

As the number of Orthodox immigrants increased, these early parishes and most subsequent Orthodox parishes began to serve particular ethnic and linguistic groups. Since many immigrants intended to return to their homeland, the parishes became centers in which not only the faith was preserved but also the language and customs of the old country were carefully maintained. The church buildings were a place for worship. They also offered a secure place for fellowship and mutual support. There was a natural link between the family and the parish. There was also an intimate link between faith and the culture and language of the old world. Therefore, there was little contact among these parishes with other Orthodox groups and little sense of mission beyond the needs of a particular ethnic family. The large urban centers of the United States during the late 19th and early 20th centuries contained neighborhoods where the various immigrant groups could maintain their faith, culture, and language, somewhat insulated from the wider society. This was true not only for the various Orthodox immigrant groups. It was also true for certain Roman Catholic and Protestant immigrants.

The accomplishments of these early Orthodox immigrants were truly remarkable. By 1920 there were about 300 organized parishes composed primarily of Orthodox immigrants. As centers of religious and cultural life in a new country, set up and financed by the laity in the main, these parishes were usually built and maintained with very little formal direction from the hierarchical authorities.

EARLY GREEK ORTHODOX DEVELOPMENTS

The largest single group of Orthodox immigrants in this period were the Greeks. Although a community of Greek Orthodox workers came to New Smyrna, Florida in 1768, there is little evidence of organized Orthodox religious life. The great wave of Greek immigration occurred in the late 19th and early 20th centuries. By 1920 there were about 300,000 Greek immigrants in the United States organized into about 135 parishes. With few exceptions, these parishes in the early years sought to maintain some connection with dioceses of the Church of Greece or the ecumenical patriarchate of Constantinople. Many of the early Greek immigrants saw themselves as temporary residents in the United States and kept in close contact with families back home.

From the early decades of the 20th century the patriarchate of Constantinople affirmed its responsibility for all Orthodox living in America. This was done in accord with Canon 28 of the Council of Chalcedon in 451 and subsequent practical precedents. According to the commonly held Greek interpretation of the Chalcedonian canon, the ecumenical patriarchate had responsibility for all the Orthodox in territories beyond the canonical borders of other autocephalous churches. However, because of the acute political and financial difficulties which the patriarchate experienced throughout the late 19th and early 20th centuries, it was not in a position to assert its prerogatives or to exercise its ministry adequately in America. Orthodox church life in the United States continued to develop during this period with very little hierarchical supervision and not always in harmony with accepted church polity and canonical order.

Ecumenical Patriarch Meletios (Metaxakis) of Constantinople (1871–1935) envisioned a united Orthodox Church in the United States in his enthronement address in 1921. The patriarchate subsequently established the Greek Orthodox Archdiocese of North and South America as a canonical province. Prior to his election as ecumenical patriarch, Meletios, as archbishop of Athens, visited the United States in 1918 and 1921 and had begun to organize the Greek Orthodox parishes he found there. Nevertheless, the Greek Orthodox parishes in the Americas were deeply divided in the 1920s and 1930s because of political differences between royalist and republican sympathizers as these parties had arisen in Greece. Between 1931 and 1948, Archbishop Athenagoras Spirou (1886–1972), later patriarch of Constantinople, labored greatly to heal the divisions and to unify the Greek archdiocese. Faced with the specific pastoral needs of the Greek immigrants and with the acute divisions among them, however, little at that time could be done to broaden the patriarchate's embrace to include all Orthodox faithful in the Americas.

EARLY RUSSIAN ORTHODOX DEVELOPMENTS

The late 19th century also witnessed the emigration of more than 150,000 Carpatho-Russians from the Austro-Hungarian Empire. In their homeland they had been Eastern Catholics, sometimes called "Greek Catholics." Their union with Rome dated from the 16th century. While permitted to maintain Eastern liturgical practices and a married priesthood, the Carpatho-Russians had accepted the ultimate authority of the pope. The basis for the "return" of many Carpatho-Russians to the Orthodox Church after they arrived in America was primarily the refusal of local Roman Catholic bishops and priests in the United States to honor the Eastern Catholic traditions, particularly the married priesthood. Beginning in 1891, Fr. Alexis Toth (1853–1909; now canonized as St. Alexis of Wilkes-Barre), a former Eastern Catholic priest, led about 65 parishes with about 20,000 Eastern Catholics into the Russian Orthodox archdiocese. By 1917 about 160 former Eastern Catholic parishes with about 100,000 faithful had become Orthodox. The Carpatho-Russian immigrants formed the foundation of a newly energized Russian Orthodox archdiocese.

Because of the increase of parishes in eastern America, the Russian Orthodox diocesan see was moved to New York in 1905 under Bishop Tikhon Belavin (1865–1925), later patriarch of Moscow, and canonized as St. Tikhon). The rapid increase of Russian Orthodox parishes comprising Carpatho-Russian immigrants radically changed the character of the Russian Orthodox Church in the United States. The Church of Russia in 1900 approved the request of Bishop Tikhon to change the diocese's title to the Diocese of the Aleutians and North America. Granted the title of Archbishop, he subsequently consecrated in 1904 a bishop for Alaska and Fr. Raphael Hawaweeny (1860–1915; now canonized as St. Raphael of Brooklyn) as bishop of Brooklyn to serve to oversee about six Syrian Orthodox parishes. Archbishop

Tikhon subsequently presented a plan to the Church of Russia in 1905 which envisioned a unified church in America under the jurisdiction of the Moscow synod. About 200 parishes were part of the Russian Orthodox archdiocese. In addition to parishes of the Carpatho-Russian and Syrian immigrants, the Russian Orthodox archdiocese also included in the early 20th century parishes of Serbian Orthodox, Syrians, Romanians, Bulgarians, and Albanians.

Additional diocesan developments rapidly took place among the Russian Orthodox. Following the Bolshevik Revolution of 1917 in Russia, the administration of the Russian Orthodox archdiocese and its parishes was profoundly disrupted because of the effects of the political and religious developments in Soviet Russia, and because of the loss of imperial financial support for church affairs. There were at least four major Russian Orthodox jurisdictions in the United States by the year 1933. The largest was the Russian Orthodox Greek Catholic Church, frequently referred to as the "Metropolia," which declared itself temporarily independent from the Church of Russia in 1924. Its authority was challenged by a small number of clergy and laity associated with the Russian "Living Church" movement, especially between 1922 and 1943. A diocese of the Russian Orthodox Church Abroad was established in 1927 serving Russian immigrants with monarchist sympathies who refused to acknowledge the official leadership of the Church of Russia in the period after Patriarch Tikhon, who died in 1925. Repudiating both these jurisdictions, the beleaguered Church of Russia headed by Metropolitan Sergius as acting patriarchal *locum tenens* established an exarchate in the United States in 1933. Each of these rival jurisdictions claimed to be the historic continuation of the Alaskan Mission in the United States. Each also expressed very different attitudes toward the Church in Russia and the communist regime in the Soviet Union.

OTHER DIOCESAN DEVELOPMENTS

In the wake of further immigration and unsupervised parish development, other autocephalous Orthodox Churches also acted to establish dioceses in the United States so as to serve their immigrant faithful. After preliminary local foundations in each case, new dioceses were subsequently established by the Church of Serbia in 1921, of Antioch in 1924, of Romania in 1930, of Albania in 1932, and of Bulgaria in 1938. The ecumenical patriarchate also established dioceses for Ukrainian parishes in 1937 and Carpatho-Russian parishes in 1938, and received Albanian parishes under its jurisdictional care in 1949.

The varied political allegiances of the immigrant communities often led to the creation of some separatist parishes and dioceses which were not part of the jurisdiction of any autocephalous Orthodox Church. With each wave of immigration, fresh political divisions in the homeland of the immigrants frequently manifested themselves in the church life of the Orthodox in the United States. Claiming to be united in faith, the Orthodox were actually fractured into numerous diocesan jurisdictions. Most had an "Old World" orientation and served a particular ethnic population. Some followed the "Revised Julian (New) Calendar" inaugurated in 1923 and others the "Old Calendar" (called the "Julian" because it was established by Julius Caesar in 45 BCE). Many parishes were marked at this time by a strong emphasis upon congregationalism which frequently challenged the leadership of the clergy. Attitudes of nationalism and parochialism pervaded much of church life. By 1933 there were no fewer than fifteen separate Orthodox jurisdictions comprising parishes serving particular ethnic communities and often reflecting political perspectives related to the old homeland. At that time, there were over 400 Orthodox parishes overall, serving about half a million believers.

A TIME OF TRANSITION

Facing divisions both within and beyond their flocks, Archbishop Athenagoras and Metropolitan Antony Bashir (1898–1966) of the Syrian (Antiochian) Orthodox archdiocese recognized the need for greater cooperation. Metropolitan Antony advocated the greater use of English in liturgical services and envisioned a more united church in the United States. Together with Metropolitan Antony, Archbishop Athenagoras proposed a pan-Orthodox seminary in 1934 and a pan-Orthodox journal in 1941. Strife among the Russian jurisdictions prevented common action on these proposals. However, the Federated Orthodox Greek Catholic Primary Jurisdictions in America was established in 1943. This voluntary association brought together the primates of six Orthodox jurisdictions which were in communion with one of the patriarchates. During its early years the federation did much to achieve greater recognition of the Orthodox Church, especially by governmental agencies. Because it was not then in communion with the Moscow patriarchate, the Russian Orthodox metropolia, the largest of the Russian jurisdictions, was not a member of the federation. Its absence was a major weakness in the federation, which ceased to function by 1949.

The decades following World War II marked an important period of transition for the Orthodox in the United States. Demographics were changing. There was

a notable decrease in immigration of Orthodox by the 1920s. Many parishes began to lose their predominantly immigrant character. At the same time, new parishes were being established in the suburbs beyond the center of immigrant life in the inner city. Born and educated in America, most parishioners became less and less in contact with the land of their grandparents and their political concerns. There was an increase in Orthodox marrying beyond their ethnic communities. There was also a gradual increase of marriages between Orthodox and Catholics or Protestants. Moreover, persons coming from other religious traditions were beginning to embrace the Orthodox Church and its teachings. This movement would increase as time went on.

The education of clergy and lay leaders acquired new significance. Following earlier attempts to establish pastoral schools, new theological schools came into existence. The Greek Orthodox archdiocese established the Holy Cross Greek Orthodox School of Theology near Boston in 1937. Likewise, the Russian Orthodox metropolia founded St. Tikhon's Seminary near Scranton, Pennsylvania, and St. Vladimir's Orthodox Theological School in Crestwood, New York in 1938. Since that time, these institutions have been responsible for educating most clergy and theologians in the United States. Their presses have also published a significant number of Orthodox theological books in English.

There was also an increase of pan-Orthodox endeavors. Orthodox from various jurisdictions began to recognize that they shared not only the same faith but also the same challenges and obligations within American society. A number of avenues of cooperation were established, especially in the areas of retreats, religious education, and campus ministry. New catechetical materials in the English language were published. There was growing use of English in the liturgy and other services as a result of translation efforts. Joint liturgical services began to become more common in larger cities, especially on the first Sunday of Great Lent, celebrated as the Sunday of Orthodoxy. Pan-Orthodox clergy associations and councils of churches also began to appear.

These developments were not without difficulties. New tensions developed in some jurisdictions related to these developments. Some felt that the role of the church as the preserver of a particular ethnic identity was being destroyed by the tendency toward greater cooperation. Indeed, additional divisions developed as new Orthodox immigrants arrived in the 1950s and 1960s, fleeing political changes in Eastern Europe. Opposing the communist governments there, rival dioceses developed among the Bulgarians in 1947, the Romanians in 1951, the Ukrainians in 1950 and 1954, and the Serbians in 1963. The larger jurisdictions, however, continued on a trajectory which recognized the growing American identity of its faithful.

THE STANDING CONFERENCE
OF BISHOPS

The establishment of the Standing Conference of Canonical Orthodox Bishops in America (SCOBA) in 1960 marked a significant move towards greater cooperation and unity among the Orthodox jurisdictions. Under the leadership of Archbishop Iakovos (1911–2005) of the Greek Orthodox archdiocese, SCOBA initially brought together the presiding bishops of eleven jurisdictions and developed a number of committees to deal with common challenges. Although SCOBA was not a formal synod, in canonical terms, many viewed it as the first step towards greater administrative and canonical unity.

Each jurisdiction continued to maintain its own identity, yet SCOBA provided a significant means of cooperation. Unlike the earlier federation, SCOBA included the Russian Orthodox metropolia as well as the Moscow patriarchal exarchate. The Russian Orthodox Church Outside of Russia (the Synod Abroad) refused to cooperate at this time, citing its opposition to those who recognized the leadership of the Church of Russia.

SCOBA set about coordinating various national pan-Orthodox activities which had begun in earlier decades. These included programs related to religious education and campus ministry. An Education Commission and a Committee on Scouting were established in 1960. These were followed by a Campus Commission in 1965. The Orthodox Theological Society was established in 1965. With the development of the ecumenical movement, SCOBA became responsible for establishing formal bilateral theological dialogues with the Episcopal Church (1962), the Roman Catholic Church (1966), the Lutheran Church (1968), and the Reformed Churches (1968). A commission for dialogue with the Oriental Orthodox Churches was established in 2000.

In more recent years, SCOBA has formally sanctioned the establishment of a number of additional agencies. Among the most notable are the International Orthodox Christian Charities (1991), the Orthodox Christian Mission Center (1994), and the media outreach of the Orthodox Christian Network (2003). A Military Chaplaincy Commission supports chaplains for Orthodox Christians serving in the armed forces. In addition, seven other pan-Orthodox organizations have received SCOBA's endorsement. All the activities of SCOBA have provided rich opportunity for clergy and laity to join together in pan-Orthodox witness. These activities also served to deepen a desire for greater Orthodox unity.

The initial achievements of SCOBA occurred at a time when the Orthodox Churches on a global level were also engaged in a process of renewed conciliarity. Between 1964 and 1968, four pan-Orthodox conferences took place and began to address issues affecting all the autocephalous Orthodox Churches. These meetings led to the establishment of a conciliar process designed to prepare for the convocation of a Great and Holy Council. Among the topics which deserved attention by the churches was the so-called "Diaspora," the developing Church in America, Western Europe, and elsewhere.

In the light of these developments, the bishops of SCOBA in 1965 proposed to the autocephalous churches that it should be recognized as an episcopal synod having full authority to govern the life of the Church in America within the jurisdiction of the ecumenical patriarchate. A similar proposal was made in 1968 with the request that the American situation be placed on the agenda of the global pan-Orthodox conferences. While no action was taken by the ecumenical patriarchate or the other autocephalous churches, the appeals of SCOBA indicated that the situation in the United States could not be long ignored.

The conciliar process both in America and at the global level was, to an extent, disrupted in 1970 when the patriarchate of Moscow moved to grant autocephaly (self-governing status) to the Russian Orthodox metropolia. From then, the metropolia has been known as the Orthodox Church in America (OCA). This action regularized the formal relationship between the metropolia and the Church of Russia which had been lost in 1924, but the grant of autocephalous status to the OCA was not recognized by the ecumenical patriarchate or by most of the other autocephalous churches. This

disputed status of the OCA immediately increased tensions among the jurisdictions in the United States. Eventually, it led to new discussions related to the presence of Orthodoxy in the United States and the meaning of autocephaly. Currently, while continuing not to recognize the autocephaly of the OCA, the ecumenical patriarchate determined to cooperate with it in the hope of encouraging a more comprehensive resolution of the overall canonical position of Orthodoxy in America.

Throughout the early 1970s the ecumenical patriarchate initiated a number of discussions on themes preparing for a Great and Holy Council. A list of ten topics for study was agreed upon by the representatives of the autocephalous churches in 1976. This list included the topics of the so-called "Diaspora" and the question of autocephaly. After dealing with a number of other topics, the theme of Diaspora was examined in meetings of the pre-conciliar committees in 1990, 1993, and 1995. In light of these discussions, a historic meeting of all Orthodox bishops in the United States was held in 1994. On the eve of a new millennium, the bishops issued a historic pastoral letter entitled *And the Word Became Flesh and Dwelt Among Us*, which spoke about the responsibilities of the church and Orthodox Christians in contemporary society. Subsequent meetings of all the bishops were held in 2001 and 2006.

A number of significant developments occurred in several of the jurisdictions. Divisions among the two rival Syrian Orthodox (Antiochian) jurisdictions were healed in 1975, creating a unified Antiochian Orthodox Christian archdiocese. This provided a basis in 1987 for the reception of a number of convert clergy and 20 parishes of various evangelical Protestant traditions. The Serbian Orthodox dioceses healed their internal divisions in 1988. The two Romanian Orthodox jurisdictions began a dialogue aimed at reconciliation in 1992. The ecumenical patriarchate in 1996 restructured the Greek Orthodox archdiocese into an archdiocesan district and eight metropolises. In 1995 it also regularized the canonical status of a number of Ukrainian Orthodox bishops, clergy, and parishes. Likewise, the Antiochian Orthodox archdiocese in 2003 received a "self-rule" status from the Church of Antioch which also established nine dioceses. These new developments, as well as leadership changes and some financial difficulties in the OCA, led to some internal strife. The difficulties often served to highlight the need for greater unity among the Orthodox in America.

The SCOBA member jurisdictions as of 2010 are: the Albanian Orthodox diocese (Bishop Ilia), the American Carpatho Russian Orthodox diocese (Metropolitan Nicholas), the Antiochian Orthodox Christian archdiocese (Metropolitan Philip), the Bulgarian Eastern Orthodox Church (Metropolitan Joseph), the Greek Orthodox archdiocese (Archbishop Demetrios), the Orthodox Church in America (Metropolitan Jonah), the Romanian Orthodox archdiocese (Archbishop Nicolae), the Serbian Orthodox Church, the Ukrainian Orthodox Church (Metropolitan Constantine), and the Representation of the Moscow Patriarchate in America.

THE NEW EPISCOPAL ASSEMBLY

In October 2008, at a special synaxis of the heads of Orthodox Churches which he called at Constantinople, Patriarch Bartholomew (b. 1940) proposed that renewed attention be given to the so-called "Orthodox Diaspora." His proposal was unanimously accepted by hierarchs representing the other thirteen autocephalous churches. This historic gathering led directly to the Fourth

Preconciliar Pan-Orthodox Conference, which met in Geneva on June 6–12, 2009. This meeting approved the creation of an Episcopal Assembly in North and Central America, as well as in eleven other regions. The new Assembly would bring together all the canonical Orthodox bishops from all jurisdictions in North and Central America to strengthen the unity of the church and to address together critical issues. At that time, there were over fifty canonical Orthodox bishops in this region.

During his visit to the United States in October 2009, Patriarch Bartholomew met with the presiding bishops of the SCOBA jurisdictions under the leadership of Archbishop Demetrios (b. 1928) of the Greek Orthodox archdiocese and exarch of the ecumenical patriarchate. Patriarch Bartholomew formally announced the decision of the synaxis in 2008 and the more recent decision of the fourth Preconciliar Pan Orthodox Conference. He urged the SCOBA bishops to begin the process of establishing the new Assembly. This body would build upon the significant work begun by SCOBA in 1960, and would be envisaged as succeeding and replacing SCOBA. Unlike SCOBA, however, the Assembly would now have the full recognition and support of the ecumenical patriarchate and the other autocephalous churches.

The new Assembly provides an important opportunity for the Orthodox Church to address the serious challenges and opportunities it has placed before it. The ongoing division of Orthodoxy in the United States into separate jurisdictions continues to weaken its mission and witness. Within most of the jurisdictions, the process of acculturation has not always been easy. As some of the jurisdictions move beyond their reliance upon ethnic loyalties, however, they are obliged to speak more clearly about the distinctive features of the Orthodox Christian faith within a religiously pluralistic society. They must express the Orthodox faith in terms which are understandable and develop ministries which respond to the spiritual need of persons living in this complex modern American society. The Orthodox in this context now need to distinguish between old world cultural practices, perspectives that are not essential to the faith, and those essential affirmations which are at the heart of the faith. Without diminishing the importance of worship, the Orthodox are challenged to enable greater participation in liturgical life, and relate this to all aspects of life. This will mean that a new spirit of mission must be cultivated and that a proper relationship between clergy and laity must be expressed at all levels of church life. In addition, the role of women and their contribution to the church will need to be appropriately recognized. With its profound affirmations about the loving triune God, the theocentric nature of the human person, and the deep divine blessing within the creation, Orthodox Christianity has much to offer American society and to contemporary Christianity in America. Even so, this offering can take place only if the Orthodox themselves take seriously their responsibility to this society and to all its people.

There are today about 3 million Orthodox Christians in the United States gathered in more than 1,500 parishes. The church has about twenty monasteries, three graduate schools of theology, a college and a number of other schools and charitable institutions. The Orthodox in the United States sponsor missions in Africa, Albania, and Asia. Likewise, the International Orthodox Christian Charities presently provide humanitarian assistance in over a dozen countries. Through their books and lectures, Orthodox theologians from the United States are influencing the church

in many other parts the world. The Church in the United States is composed primarily of American members of a wide variety of racial, ethnic, and religious backgrounds who treasure the faith of Orthodox Christianity.

SEE ALSO: Constantinople, Patriarchate of; Greece, Orthodox Church of; Russia, Patriarchal Orthodox Church of; St. Tikhon (Belavin) (1865–1925)

REFERENCES AND SUGGESTED READINGS

Bogolepov, A. (2001) *Toward an American Orthodox Church: The Establishment of an Autocephalous Church.* Crestwood, NY: St. Vladimir's Seminary Press.
Bolshakov, S. (1943) *The Foreign Missions of the Russian Orthodox Church.* London.
Constantelos, D. J. (1967) *The Greek Orthodox Church: Faith, History, Practice.* New York: Seabury Press.
Litsas, F. K. (ed.) (1984) *A Companion to the Greek Orthodox Church.* New York: Greek Orthodox Archdiocese of North America.
McGuckin, J. A. (2008) *The Orthodox Church: An Introduction to Its History, Theology and Spiritual Culture.* Oxford: Wiley-Blackwell.
Ware, K. (1997) *The Orthodox Church.* London: Penguin.

Unmercenary Saints

SUSAN R. HOLMAN

"Unmercenary saints" were physicians, often martyrs of the late 3rd century, who healed without taking payment (known in Greek as *anargyroi*, "without money"). Ancient supplicants at their healing sanctuaries practiced incubation (sleeping at the shrine) and were sometimes healed through dream therapy; the saints treated or prescribed cures as the patient slept. This practice, similar to that of the pre-Christian healing sanctuaries of Asclepius, continued well into late Christian Antiquity.

The appendix to Dionysios of Fourna's 18th-century *Painter's Manual* lists forty-one *anargyroi*. The most popular, usually paired as siblings or co-workers, include Cosmas and Damian, Cyrus and John, Panteleimon and Hermolaos, Sampson and Diomedes, Photius and Antiketos, Thalleios and Tryphon, and sometimes the evangelist Luke. Of these, the two pairs best documented in contemporary scholarship are Cosmas and Damian and Cyrus and John.

The veneration of Cosmas and Damian was first mentioned by Theodoret of Cyrrus in the late 4th century (PG 83.1373; PG 84.747). Their images are present in the life-size mosaic of calendrical saints in the rotunda Church of St. George in Thessalonica. Accounts of their miracles exist in six series totaling forty-eight stories; Ludwig Deubner's (1907: 52ff.) claim originating their cult in the pagan mythos of Castor and Pollux is now dismissed by most scholars. Festugière (1971: 87) notes that the early editor of Series 6 speaks of "the most ancient church situated at the famous monastery of the Cosmidion" at Constantinople, built ca. 439. The Emperor Justinian (527–65), finding the building in ramshackle condition, renovated and embellished it after being healed there. A monastery existed by 518. Both monastery and church were destroyed by the Avars, but in 1261 Michael VIII the Palaeologue spent the night at the site. Different dates for the saints' feast (September 27, July 1, and November 25) and several pairs with the same name attest to Cosmas and Damian's popularity in both East and West.

Sts. Cyrus (a physician) and John (a soldier martyred with him) were first venerated in the 4th century (McGuckin 1992); their shrine at Menouthis near Alexandria in Egypt and their miracles are attested by only one surviving text, by Sophronius of Jerusalem (d. 638). Sophronius notes that Cyril of Alexandria discovered them and translated their bones to Menouthis ca. 427/428 (celebrated on June 28). Scholars debate whether Cyril merely revived the shrine and cult or if it was founded after the destruction of the Isis sanctuary at Menouthis ca. 489. Sophronius' *Miracles of Saints Cyrus and John*, written after a healing at the sanctuary, emphasize Sophronius' opposition to the aphthartodocetic heresy and his defense of Chalcedonian orthodoxy. Neil (2006: 188) suggests that the text may have traveled to Rome when the saints' relics were transferred there in 634. Their festival is January 31.

Frescoes of several *anargyroi*, including Cosmas, Damian, Cyrus, and John, from both Greek and Syriac tradition were recently discovered at Deir al-Surien in Egypt (Innemée and Van Rompay 2002).

The Unmercenary Saints are evoked frequently throughout the healing services of the Orthodox Church, especially the healing ritual of the sacrament of anointing.

SEE ALSO: Healing; Relics; St. Cyril of Alexandria (ca. 378–444)

REFERENCES AND SUGGESTED READINGS

Deubner, L. (1907) *Kosmas und Damian: Texte und Einleitung.* Leipzig: Teubner.

Duffy, J. (1984) "Observations on Sophronius' Miracles of Cyrus and John," *Journal of Theological Studies* 35: 71–90.

Festugière, A.-J. (ed. and trans.) (1971) *Sainte Thècle, Saints Côme et Damien, Saints Cyr et Jean (extraits), Saint Georges.* Paris: Éditions A. et J. Picard.

Gascou, J. (2006) *Sophrone de Jérusalem: miracles des saints Cyr et Jean (BHG I, 477–479).* Paris: De Boccard.

Holman, S. R. (2008) "Rich and Poor in Sophronius of Jerusalem's Miracles of Saints Cyrus and John," in S. R. Holman (ed.) *Wealth and Poverty in Early Church and Society.* Grand Rapids, MI: Baker Academic, pp. 103–24.

Hronas, G. (1999) *The Holy Unmercenary Doctors: The Saints Anargyroi, Physicians and Healers of the Orthodox Church: Translated from the Greek Great Synaxaristes of the Orthodox Church.* Minneapolis: Light and Life Publishing.

Innemée, K. C. and Van Rompay, L. (2002) "Deir al Surian (Egypt), New Discoveries of January 2000," *Hugoye, Journal of Syriac Studies* 3 (2); available online at www.syrcom.cua.edu/Hugoye/Vol3No2/HV3N2PRInnemee.html.

McGuckin, J. A. (1992) "The influence of the Isis cult on St. Cyril of Alexandria's Christology," *Studia Patristica* 24: 191– 9.

Neil, B. (2006) "The Miracles of Saints Cyrus and John: The Greek Text and Its Translation," *Journal of the Australian Early Medieval Association* 2: 183–93.

Skrobucha, H. (1965) *The Patrons of the Doctors.* Pictorial Library of Eastern Church Art 7. Recklinghausen, Germany: Aurel Bongers.

V

Vespers (Hesperinos)

M. C. STEENBERG

Vespers (Greek, *Hesperinos*) is the divine service associated with the setting sun, and thus the beginning of the liturgical day in the Orthodox Church. It is made up of three broad parts: the great psalm of creation (Ps. 103 *LXX*) followed by the hymn "Lord, I have cried . . ." and its associated verses (*stichera*); the christological "Hymn of Light"; and the Aposticha and Song of Symeon ("Lord, Now Lettest Thou Thy Servant"). With these are interspersed various litanies and other prayers.

Theologically, Vespers signifies the calling out of creation for its Redeemer, who is encountered in the incarnate Jesus Christ: hence its focus on the created world (e.g., "There is the great and wide sea, wherein

Plate 76 An Orthodox bishop wearing the mantya robe and carrying the episcopal staff (rabydos) presides over the Vespers service. Pascal Deloche/Godong/Corbis.

The Encyclopedia of Eastern Orthodox Christianity, edited by John Anthony McGuckin
© 2011 Blackwell Publishing Ltd.

are creeping things innumerable," Ps. 103.25), expectation, and the encounter with Christ ("O Gladsome Light of God the Father's glory"; "Now Lettest Thou Thy Servant Depart in Peace," etc.). Liturgically, Vespers constitutes the shift from one day to the next (technically, this takes place at the prayer "Vouchsafe, O Lord"), building upon the biblical ordering of a "day" as starting with the night ("And there was evening and there was morning: one day," Gen. 1.5). Vespers can be served on its own, or (a common practice in the Russian parishes) as part of the monastic All-Night Vigil, where it is combined (abbreviatedly) with Matins (Orthros) and the First Hour.

SEE ALSO: Apodosis; Apolytikion; Aposticha; *Hieratikon, Horologion*; Kathisma; Orthros (Matins); Prokeimenon; Sticheron

REFERENCES AND SUGGESTED READINGS

Taft, R. (1985) *The Liturgy of the Hours in East and West*. Collegeville, MN: Liturgical Press.

Vestments

TENNY THOMAS

Sacred garments (*vestimenta* – Latin for "clothing") of the clergy worn for liturgical celebrations, and some also worn outside the church. The dress of Orthodox clergy is now held to symbolize the vestments of the Aaronic priesthood (see Exod. 28.2–43; 39.1–31), but it originated in the styles of ordinary costume of the Greco-Roman upper classes in the ancient Christian world. While a better form of dress was probably used at sacred functions during the earliest centuries, the development of specific clerical costume occurred between the 4th and 9th centuries, the church

retaining antique dress in liturgy long after everyone else. Outside the celebration of liturgical service, Orthodox clergy usually wear a black under-cassock (*rason*) under a larger outer-cassock (*exorason*, like an enveloping overcoat with ample bell sleeves). The specifically liturgical vestments are different for each order of clergy. The deacon wears a *sticharion* (white robe) with separate brocade cuffs (*epimanikia*) and a diagonally worn *orarion* (stole) on top. The latter can also be worn (girded in a cross shape over the body) by subdeacons, and even by tonsured altar servers in the Greek tradition. The priest wears the *epimanikia*, the *sticharion*, and a stole falling vertically from the neck in the form of the *epitrachelion*. He belts the *sticharion* and *epitrachelion* with the *zone*, and on top of all else wears the sleeveless enveloping outer-garment known as the *phelonion*. Bishops and senior priests may also wear a *hypogonation* (a diamond-shaped stiff embroidery suspended on the right side, a remnant of what was once a purse). In the liturgy the bishop wears over all the priestly vestments (except the *phelonion*) the distinctive garment of the *sakkos*, a T-shaped brocade garment that once signified high rank in the imperial court. On the seams are sewn bells to remind the worshippers of the robes of the High Priest in the Temple (Exod. 28.33). On top of the *sakkos* he wears a distinctive episcopal stole called the *omophorion* (a wide cloth band draped about the shoulders). All priests of the Russian tradition also wear a silver (sometimes gold) cross over the *phelonion* or cassock. Greek and other Orthodox clergy only wear the pectoral cross (usually a jeweled or enameled cross) if they have been awarded this as a mark of special honor. The jeweled cross is also reserved for very senior priests in the Slavic Orthodox tradition. The bishop wears, in and out of church, a jeweled medallion or

Plate 77   A convent workshop in Romania. The monastics support themselves from their own labors. Photo by John McGuckin.

panagia over the chest of his cassock, normally featuring an icon of the Virgin Mary. Archbishops and metropolitans are denoted by a second *engolpion* (meaning "that which is worn on the breast") featuring Christ, or a jeweled pectoral cross alongside the *panagia*. In the liturgy the bishop also wears the mitre which is modeled on the ancient Byzantine imperial crown. In some Slavic traditions the mitre can be awarded as a sign of honor to an archpriest or higumen. The bishop's mitre is surmounted by a cross, while a mitred-archpriest's is not. A bishop will also carry a pastoral staff, usually T-shaped, symbolizing authority to govern. From early medieval times a code of vestment colors was developed to reflect the liturgical seasons: gold or white for normal Sundays, green for feasts of the Spirit, red for the Lord's festivals, purple for Holy Week, and white for Pascha.

SEE ALSO: Divine Liturgy, Orthodox; Episcopacy; Epitrachelion; Phelonion; Sticharion

REFERENCES AND SUGGESTED READINGS

Chrysostomos, A. (1981) *Byzantine Liturgical Dress*. Brookline, MA: Holy Cross Orthodox Press.

Cope, J. (1986) "Vestments," in J. G. Davies (ed.) *A New Dictionary of Liturgy and Worship*. London: SCM Canterbury Press.

McGuckin, J. A. (2004) "Vestments," in *The Westminster Handbook to Patristics Theology*. London: Westminster/John Knox Press.

Mayo, J. (1984) *A History of Ecclesiastical Dress*. New York: Holmes and Meier.

Pavan, V. (1992) "Liturgical Vestments," in A. Di Berardino (ed.) *Encyclopedia of the Early Church*, vol. 2. Cambridge: James Clarke.

Pocknee, C. E. (1960) *Liturgical Vesture: Its Origins and Development*. London: A. R. Mowbray.

Virgins

MARIA GWYN MCDOWELL

An order of the church primarily composed of women dedicated to God through renouncing marriage and committing to a life of holiness.

Basil the Great in the 4th century says that "She is named a virgin who has willingly consecrated herself to the Lord, and has renounced marriage and preferred the life of holiness" (*Ep.* 99; Elm 1996: 139). St. Basil is here defining and regulating a popular and varied group of early ascetics which existed from at least the early 3rd century and was in need of reform. The earliest textual witnesses to such women (and men) are of Syriac provenance ("Sons and Daughters of the Covenant"). Ignatius in his *Letter to the Smyrneans* refers to "widows who are called virgins." The well-established order of widows supplied a model for the newly developing order of virgins discussed in the *Apostolic Constitutions*, a 4th-century text based in part on the early 3rd-century *Didascalia*. Possibly, the orders were closely related; it is unclear whether the ambiguous term for widow assumed a deceased spouse or if a virgin was necessarily unmarried. Basil's sister Macrina, whose ascetic lifestyle and charitable service provide the basis for his regulations, insists on becoming a "virgin widow." Her "widowhood," however, is the result of the death of her fiancé, *not* her husband. The conflation between widows, virgins, and the deaconess makes it difficult to discern distinct functions, relationships, and the manner in which the rise of one may have precipitated or encouraged the demise of another.

As celibacy was increasingly esteemed in the patristic-era church, so too were the virgins. Seating arrangements in the liturgical assembly indicated rank, and virgins

Plate 78   Romanian nun of the community of Voronets engaged in making candles. Photo by John McGuckin.

eventually preceded widows. Vowed virginity allowed women to escape marriage and devote themselves to the service of God while remaining within social proprieties. A virgin might live with her family, in a community of women, in ascetic communities with men, even in popular but controversial "spiritual marriages." If wealthy, she might live in her own home. Virgins were present in urban centers and small towns. They had no apparent role in the ecclesial framework, though they engaged in charitable work (Macrina) and could wield considerable power (Empress Pulcheria). All followed very similar principles of self-control, fasting, and continence. By the 4th century the order was increasingly institutionalized, requiring a free confession at the age of reason, a period of trial to discern intention and suitability, and financial remuneration. Female monasteries resulted from the popularity of the order, but only became a viable option by the late 4th century, becoming the major social matrix of organized Christian virginal life thereafter.

As an eschatological sign, virginity indicates complete dedication to God as brides, as well as a rising above sexual passions. The ideal virgin in the Orthodox religious tradition is the holy Theotokos, whose faithfulness to God alone is the model for all Christians. The restoration of the order of virgins today (apart from female monasteries) seems difficult given radically different understandings of anthropology and social *mores*. What remains enduringly valuable about the virginal witness is the praxis of prayerful lives dedicated to God in charitable service to others in the midst of urban living rather than social separation.

SEE ALSO: Asceticism; Cappadocian Fathers; Chastity; Deaconess; Widows

REFERENCES AND SUGGESTED READINGS

Elm, S. (1996) *Virgins of God: The Making of Asceticism in Late Antiquity*. Oxford: Clarendon Press.

War

PERRY T. HAMALIS

"War" carries multiple meanings and describes phenomena from varied contexts within Eastern Orthodoxy. In addition to the common understanding of war as "organized violence carried out by political units against each other" (Bull 1977: 184), Orthodox sources discuss war as encompassing both the personal and communal, the physical and spiritual, the bloody and bloodless. St. John Chrysostom writes: "There are three very grievous kinds of war: The one is public, when our soldiers are attacked by foreign armies; the second is when, even in time of peace, we are at war with one another; and the third is when the individual is at war with himself, which is the worst of all" (*Hom. 7 on 1 Tim.*). In each of these contexts (interstate, interpersonal, and intrapersonal) the Orthodox Church has a threefold response: it proclaims the ideal of authentic peace, acknowledges the spiritual roots and implications of warfare, and affirms the sinfulness of physical violence even if such violence may be tragically necessary given humanity's fallen condition.

The ideal of authentic peace, while not unique to the Christian East, has been upheld as normative and is reflected clearly within the Orthodox tradition (cf. Harakas 1999; McGuckin 2006; Webster 1998). The Eastern Church's divine services, oriented toward the eschatological peace of God's kingdom, are replete with petitions for "peace from above" and "peace in the world," as well as with exhortations to pray "in peace." This focus reminds worshippers that the Lord being praised is the "Prince of Peace" (Isa. 9.6) who proclaimed a "gospel of peace" (Eph. 6.15), and that their identity as the church cannot be separated from their calling to be "peacemakers" and imitators of the non-violent Christ (cf. Mt. 5; Rom. 12; Heb. 12).

Notwithstanding their eirenic ideal, voices within Orthodoxy also express an acute sense of the depths of human corruption and resist naïve optimism about the possibility for peace on earth. For the Orthodox, the problem of violence and war within human social history goes all the way back to Cain's act of fratricide (Gen. 4), and stems from the passions that corrupt human beings' souls. Furthermore, the activity of war tends to exacerbate and institutionalize those same sinful proclivities that sparked conflict in the first place (cf. Harakas 1999). Thus, from an Orthodox perspective, the only truly effective response to the fundamentally spiritual roots of war begins with baptism and continues through a lifetime commitment to wage spiritual warfare against both human passions and the forces of evil in the world. Waging spiritual warfare in the intrapersonal context, then, is the necessary basis of a proper response to war in the interpersonal and interstate contexts. For the Orthodox, such spiritual warfare is the only legitimate "holy war" (cf. Dennis 2001).

Like many ethical issues, the topic of war developed differently within Orthodoxy than it did within Western Christianity – both Roman Catholic and Protestant. Despite the reality of war in Byzantium, there was no single eastern father who wrote extensively and systematically on the subject of war in the way that, for example, St. Augustine, Gratian, Thomas Aquinas, or Erasmus of Rotterdam did in the West. Neither was there a controversy in the Orthodox Church like the one between the Reformers (e.g., Martin Luther and John Calvin) and the Radical Reformers (e.g., Thomas Münzter and Menno Simons) that engaged the questions of Christians' military service and use of the sword. Furthermore, the Orthodox Church never endorsed or practiced "crusades" (cf. Dennis 2001; McGuckin 2006). In fact, Orthodox Christians were the victims when, during the Fourth Crusade, Latin Christians turned their weapons against the citizens of Constantinople. In short, the different histories and theological styles of Western and Eastern Christianity led to different approaches to war ethics. The predominant categories used by Western Christian ethicists – "pacifism," "just war theory," "Christian realism," "just peacemaking," and "crusade" – do not exactly fit, therefore, within Orthodoxy. Strictly speaking, the Orthodox Church is not "pacifist" because, during the reign of the Emperor Constantine and, subsequently, in other predominantly Orthodox nations, military service by Christians became necessary (although canonically forbidden among clergy and monks). Important recent research, however, highlights the ways in which Orthodox Christian sensibilities shaped Byzantine military practices, reflecting a pro-peace bias (Miller and Nesbitt 1995). Similarly, "just war theory" is incompatible with both the spirit and substance of most Orthodox sources (Harakas 1999; McGuckin 2006). The Eastern Church, particularly in its canon law, acknowledges the tragic necessity of defensive wars in some circumstances, but resists efforts to justify wars according to formal criteria, which can easily be preempted by those in power, and affirms the need for repentance among all who are complicit in physical violence. Some debate within Orthodoxy has ensued recently over whether war is best described as a "necessary evil" or as a "lesser good" (Harakas 1999; Webster 2003), with the majority of Orthodox thinkers supporting the "necessary evil" position.

SEE ALSO: Ethics; Military Saints; Original Sin; St. Constantine the Emperor (ca. 271–337)

REFERENCES AND SUGGESTED READINGS

Bull, H. (1977) *The Anarchical Society*. New York: Columbia University Press.

Dennis, G. T. (2001) "Defenders of the Christian People: Holy War in Byzantium," in A. Laiou and R. P. Mottahedeh (eds.) *The Crusades from the Perspective of Byzantium and the Muslim World*. Washington, DC: Dumbarton Oaks, pp. 31–9.

Harakas, S. (1999) "The Teaching on Peace in the Fathers," in *Wholeness of Faith and Life: Orthodox Christian Ethics: Part One – Patristic Ethics*. Brookline, MA: Holy Cross Press, pp. 137–61.

McGuckin, J. A. (2006) "Non-violence and Peace Traditions in Early and Eastern Christianity," in K. Kuriakose (ed.) *Religion, Terrorism, and Globalization: Nonviolence: A New Agenda*. New York: Nova Science Publishers, pp. 189–202.

Miller, T. and Nesbitt, J. (eds.) (1995) *Peace and War in Byzantium: Essays in Honor of George T. Dennis, SJ*. Washington, DC: Catholic University Press.

Webster, A. F. C. (1998) *The Pacifist Option: The Moral Argument Against War in Eastern Orthodox Theology*. Lanham, MD: Rowman and Littlefield.

Webster, A. F. C. (2003) "Justifiable War as a 'Lesser Good' in Eastern Orthodox Moral Tradition," *St. Vladimir's Theological Quarterly* 47: 3–57.

Wealth

JUSTIN M. LASSER

From time immemorial Orthodox Christianity has struggled to harmonize the stringent ethical demands of the Lord (not least as they relate to personal economies) with the material realities of life in the world. Jesus' demands upon the wealthy are manifested paradigmatically in his encounter with a rich man (Lk. 18.18–25). The rich man wanted to know what he should do in order to inherit eternal life. He felt he had fulfilled all of the commandments but, Jesus told him, "There is still one thing lacking. Sell all that you own and distribute to the poor, and you will have treasure in heaven: then come follow me." But when the rich man heard this startling demand of Jesus he went away despondent. Jesus responded by saying, "How hard it is for those who have wealth to enter into the Kingdom of God! Indeed, it is easier for a camel to go through the eye of a needle than for a rich man to enter the Kingdom of God." Such is a stinging account of Christ's view of wealth.

The gospels at many instances denounce wealth, such as the occasion of Zaccheus' renouncing half his fortune, and paying back fourfold anyone he had cheated (Lk. 19.1–10). The severity of the gospel message concerning the necessary readiness to renounce wealth was sustained in the early apostolic era, as depicted in the Acts of the Apostles. In that time the followers of Christ held all things in common and "no one claimed private ownership" (Acts 4.32). Only Ananias and his wife Sapphira kept back some money privately from the sale of their property (Acts 5.1–11). St. Peter interprets such an action as the inspiration of Satan, and the death of Ananias and Sapphira soon after is lifted up as a mark of divine judgment against them.

In the post-apostolic period of the church this early attitude to wealth as a severe "problem" (a hard saying) is progressively relaxed. One can note four stages in a developing attitude to wealth in the wider church: first, the softening of these hard passages in patristic reflection (their "spiritual" exegesis); second, the abstraction of poverty and wealth from immediate economic realities and transmutation more into symbolic or "intentional" status; third, the institution of almsgiving as a redemptive force in wealth possession; and fourth, the use of public and private wealth, administered by both clergy and laity, in the service of the poor and in upbuilding the church's philanthropic institutions. It is important to note, however, that there have always existed specific Christian groups that did try to adhere to the radical ethical-economic demands of Christ without softening them, without realigning their apocalyptic bluntness in terms of the vicissitudes of "normal fiscal responsibility" in daily life. We can cite the instance of the early monks of Syria, the Ebionites, the Donatist Circumcellions, and the followers of Eustathius of Sebaste, as a few examples. The later Russian Non-Possessors are examples of similar tendencies in the church.

The softening of Jesus' demands is readily apparent in Matthew's transformation of the Beatitudes text "Blessed are the poor" into the version "Blessed are the poor, *in spirit*." This minor variant opened the door to a variety of interpretations, to the effect that what was being called for was not literal poverty (or fiscal simplicity – living for the day) but a right attitude (of course, how attitude would manifest in right action was sometimes glossed over). Clement of Alexandria (2nd century) was one of the first theologians to respond reflectively to the issues of wealth and poverty for Christians in Greco-Roman society. In his treatise

Who is the Rich Man that can be Saved?
Clement asks: "What would there be left to
share among people, if nobody had anything?" (*Quis. Div.* 13). Clement argued
that the literal meaning of Christ's call for
poverty could not have been what he meant.
It would be senseless if God intended all to
be poor. Clement was responding to a larger
community that was antagonistic toward
the wealthy. Being in the minority of the
literate middle-class intelligentsia, Clement
was evidently concerned with legitimizing
the possession of wealth, and does so on
the philosophical basis of advocating
a "detachment" from the allure of riches,
on the moral basis of adopting a simple
(non-excessive) lifestyle, and on the biblical
basis of symbolic (typological) rather than
literal interpretation of the Scriptures.
Origen of Alexandria would follow him in
all three things, and establish this as the
church's standard intellectual approach in
later ages. Following the author of the *Shepherd of Hermas* Clement advocated the
divine economy of "redemptive almsgiving." The terms of this economy are that
the wealthy were to use their resources in
the service of the poor, and would receive in
return the intercessions of the poor who
prayed for them. This approach, unfortunately, tended to justify the chasm that
existed in antique society between rich and
poor, by obscuring it. Clement sees it as
a solution, an alternative economy: "What
beautiful trade, what divine business! One
buys incorruptibility with money, and by
giving the perishable things of the world
one receives an eternal abode in exchange"
(*Quis. Div.* 32).

Clement stood at a transition point when
for the first time, perhaps, a notable
element of the church had excess wealth.
For most of its existence, even now perhaps,
the Orthodox Church has been chiefly composed of the poor (or relatively poor). The
institution of redemptive almsgiving may

partially succeed in reconciling the wealthy
and intellectual elite with the overwhelming
majority of the church's community of the
poor, but the tendency of theologians to
abstract and spiritualize the term of poverty
has tended to lead not to the liberation of
the poor but rather to specious justifica-
tions of their being (and remaining) poor.
The best aspects of Orthodox thought on
wealth and poverty have tended to stress the
supreme generosity of God as common
Father of men and women in the world,
and to speak of the duty of philanthropy
(especially to the suffering) as a necessary
characteristic of a true disciple. The church
has not always been so successful in elevat-
ing systematic ideas about wealth and its
just distribution in society, preferring
often an individual perspective.

The problem with constructing a work-
able modern Orthodox theory of wealth
and poverty, built out of biblical or patristic
sources and principles, is that the ancient
authorities of the church always speak from
a particular period in which they were
located. In Antiquity there were vast disparities between a tiny minority of the wealthy
and a mass of poor. In modern economies
the terms of transaction have changed so
vastly that new iterations are called for
to clarify the perennial Christian principle
of philanthropy (love for the neighbor as
the mode of one's love for God) and how it
can apply in modern society. In Orthodox
theology, from ancient times, the bishop
has always been the particular spokesman
for, and defender of, the poor. A genuinely
Orthodox response to the challenges posed
on Christians by poverty, and by the possession of wealth or the desire to acquire
it, can be offered in the lives of the saints,
especially in those many who were the
noted advocates of the poor. St. John Chrysostom has always been one to whom
Orthodox turn for such an example.
He expressed the problem, and the great

Christian challenge it contains, in the following words : "If you cannot remember everything, instead of everything, I beg you, remember only this without fail, that not to share our own wealth with the poor is the same as theft from the poor and deprivation of their means of life. It is not our own wealth that we are clinging on to, but theirs" (*Second Sermon on Lazarus* 55).

SEE ALSO: Charity; St. John Chrysostom (349–407)

REFERENCES AND SUGGESTED READINGS

Holman, S. R. (2001) *The Hungry are Dying: Beggars and Bishops in Roman Cappadocia.* Oxford: Oxford University Press.

Holman, S. R. (ed.) (2008) *Wealth and Poverty in Early Church and Society.* Grand Rapids, MI: Baker Academic.

John Chrysostom, St. (1984) *On Wealth and Poverty,* trans. C. P. Roth. Crestwood, NY: St. Vladimir's Seminary Press.

Western Europe, Orthodoxy in

JOHN A. MCGUCKIN

Orthodoxy in Western Europe remains a small, but significant, church minority and presence. Though there were earlier Orthodox visitors, the establishment of a permanent and noticeable Orthodox presence in Western Europe (chiefly France, Britain, and Germany) really came about as a result of two specific waves of Orthodox immigration in the early and the late 20th century. In both cases the Orthodox presence was in the form of "diaspora" communities. The diaspora consists of the Orthodox faithful of the patriarchal, autocephalous, or autonomous Orthodox Churches (often

referred to as "the jurisdictions") who have moved elsewhere in the world and are, in their new countries, looked after by bishops appointed by the home synods of their originating churches. Only in America has there been any move to establish an indigenous Orthodox Church out of a diaspora community (the Orthodox Church of America). Throughout Western Europe the Orthodox institutional presence entirely relates back to missionary communities of the older churches. All Greeks (including Cypriots) living in the diaspora (a large number indeed) now fall under the jurisdictional care of the patriarchate of Constantinople, which has exarchates and missions in most western countries, given that the modern Greeks (like their ancient forebears) traveled far and wide. The Russian Orthodox also had a large diaspora population, especially after the great political upheavals caused by the Russian Revolution. Its diaspora institutions have also been profoundly complicated by those political troubles. The other larger churches that had a considerable number of faithful living abroad either set up pastoral missions for them, or knew that they could be pastorally cared for by the existing Greek and Russian ecclesiastical provisions.

In more recent times, following on the collapse of totalitarian communist regimes in Eastern Europe, and also on the lifting of border restrictions within the parameters of the European Union, there has been considerable mobility in Western Europe among younger Romanians and naturally an extension of the pastoral provision for Romanian Orthodox in Europe and America has followed. It has been organized by the Patriarchal Synod of Romania, with specific reference to the pastoral needs of the Romanians in the diaspora, with an archbishop in Western and Central Europe, respectively, and also one in America. All of them are members of the Patriarchal Synod.

"Diaspora church" in this sense means an outlying "mission" of the original church. Problems arise, of course, as to how long a church mission can be established in a land without becoming indigenized. It is invidious, to the Orthodox, to establish churches where the church has historically already been established under the protection of an ancient patriarchate (the West falling under the aegis of the Roman patriarchate). The overlaying of a separate ecclesial structure (indigenous dioceses and synods, for example) is regarded by the Orthodox as proselytism, not true missionary activity, and is taken as a sign of a profoundly defective ecclesiology when it is forced upon the Orthodox in their own countries by so-called Western Christian "missionaries" who are really proselytizers. This situation holds in reverse, even after the long-established secession of the Roman patriarchate from the Orthodox pentarchy of leading sees. Diaspora churches, therefore, which are in the traditional territories of the Roman patriarchate (which covers all Western Europe) are in a very different situation from those in the "New World" (Asia, Australasia, the Americas), a situation which was envisaged canonically by the fathers of Chalcedon in 451, who laid responsibility for authentically "new" missions (to the "barbarians") with the patriarchate of Constantinople. The patriarchate of Constantinople regularly refers to the Chalcedonian canon in the sense that it ought to have supervision of all Orthodox communities all over the world who are outside the geographical territories of historically established Orthodox Churches. However, its radical interpretation of this conciliar decision is challenged by several other churches (especially Russia), and also by the facts of history, for it has never been as simple as this in "real life." The establishment of Orthodox mission churches has always followed

the natural process of the establishment of trade with new countries, that immediately required the setting up of missions to care for the pastoral need of the traders from their different national churches. This particularly had reference to the Russians, who had an expanding empire of great proportions while the rest of the Orthodox world was politically in bondage under the Turkish yoke; but in more recent times it has also applied equally to a wide variety of ethnic Orthodox groups who moved to the West either for trade purposes or to escape persecution. Indigenous Orthodox hierarchies will not, then, be declared in the traditional regions of the Western (Catholic) Church but can, and perhaps ought to, be declared in the "new lands" that are neither part of Western Christianity nor Eastern Christianity. This whole, troubled, question of diasporas and jurisdictions is scheduled to be high on the agenda for the forthcoming Great Pan Orthodox Council which (it is hoped) may be convened before the new century grows old.

The Greek churches of the diaspora in Western Europe are the simplest to account for. All of them are under the immediate jurisdiction of the patriarchate of Constantinople. The largest grouping is the Greek Orthodox Archdiocese of Thyateira and Great Britain. There are a few communities in Ireland and Scotland which are part of the Thyateiran jurisdiction. Thyateira, named from an extinct see in Asia Minor and led by an archbishop with several assistant bishops, enjoys a large measure of autonomous government but is, canonically speaking, simply an extension of the Church of Constantinople in foreign parts. Its archbishop is a member of the Constantinopolitan Synod. It was founded earlier but grew in stature after a large wave of Cypriot immigration to England in the middle part of the 20th century, and the large majority of its clergy and people are of Cypriot ancestry, though today there are increasing problems as many of the children of the third generation are losing their grip on Greek language and customs. The church has attracted a small number of English converts, chiefly from Anglicanism (more have gone to the Russian parishes in England, which had a more developed sense of liturgical accommodation to English), and there are several parishes now that offer the divine liturgy with regular amounts of English in the service. A small minority (such as the mainly English community in Chester with an English priest) or the joint Russian-Greek parish in Oxford where Metropolitan Kallistos serves, offer the divine services more or less entirely in English.

The other largest Orthodox group comprising the Western European diaspora is the Russian Orthodox outside of Russia. This diverse and extended community of Orthodox faithful has been heavily disrupted both socially and ecclesiastically by the aftermath of the Bolshevik Revolution. Resulting from this time of persecution, and the considerable refugee problem resulting from it, the Russian Orthodox community abroad fragmented into several divisions. One of these groups is composed of those dioceses outside Russia that remained loyal to the allegiance of the Moscow patriarch. There are a number of such parishes, in Britain, France, and Germany. Well known is the British Russian Archdiocese of Sourozh, formerly led by the renowned Metropolitan Antony Bloom. Throughout his life he retained full relations with the Moscow patriarchate. After his death small parts of the Sourozh diocese preferred to place themselves under the jurisdiction of the Russian Archdiocese of Western Europe under the Omophorion of the patriarch of Constantinople.

The second division was composed of the group of churches organized after the Karlovtzy Synod (1921). St. Tikhon, the last patriarch of Russia before the communist yoke was imposed with a vengeance, disseminated an encyclical in 1920 that laid down emergency plans if communication between the Russians abroad and the patriarchate at home should become problematized. In 1921 the bishops of the Russian Orthodox Church outside the borders of Russia who were free to act, met at the invitation of the patriarch of Serbia to discuss how to organize themselves in those difficult times. It was decided that the final authority over this "Russian Church Outside Russia" (ROCOR) would be vested in the holy synod of the free bishops, who should meet every year at Karlovtz (Sremsky Karlovtzy) in Yugoslavia. After World War II and the fall of Yugoslavia to communist control, it moved its headquarters to Munich, and after 1949 to buildings on the Upper East Side of New York City. Archbishop Antony Khrapovitsky, the former metropolitan of Kiev who had been exiled by the Bolsheviks, was elected as the synodical president. They had the allegiance and good will of many of the Russian exiles abroad, but by no means all of them, and not all were willing to recognize their authority when they constituted themselves, more and more, as an "alternative" to the Russian hierarchy in Russia. In 1921 a statement they issued declaring themselves for the restoration of the monarchy made their identification as "reactionaries" easy for Bolshevik propaganda at home, and caused much unease among the wider Russian Church, which did not universally have rosy memories of life under the tsars.

After the Bolshevik arrest (and suspected torture) of Tikhon (1922–3), he issued a statement expressing dissatisfaction with the way the Karlovtzy synod had arranged matters and appointed one of the leading Russian hierarchs, Metropolitan Evlogy (Georgievski) of Paris, to work out a new plan for the governance of the ROCOR. This, too, was adopted by the synod outside Russia, but received no official endorsement from Tikhon. Tikhon established Evlogy as his personal representative for Western Europe, and Bishop Platon (Rojdestvensky) for North America. At first the ROCOR synod was very anxious to keep Evlogy and Platon closely bound to its decisions, but the tension was soon to prove too much. After Tikhon's death in 1925 (thought by many to be another of Stalin's clandestine assassinations) the succession to the newly reestablished patriarchate was somewhat irregular, and Sergius of Moscow was widely seen in Western Europe as a communist puppet. In 1927 the ROCOR synod issued a condemnation of Evlogy and Platon. In the following year it flatly refused any ecclesiastical obedience to Patriarch Sergius following on his demand that all exiled Russian bishops should cease from political activities of any kind, and it was, in turn, condemned by the patriarch and the Russian synod. Evlogy was reconfirmed in his role as representative of the Russian Church in Western Europe by Sergius, but in 1930 he was relieved of his duties in a blatantly political move. From the death of Tikhon onwards the ROCOR synod was immensely suspicious of the Russian hierarchs, regarding them as tools of the state. In their turn they have been denounced and pilloried. In the decades following the fall of communism in Russia, however, there were strong moves for reconciliation. In autumn of 2006 the hierarchs declared their decision for the restoration of full canonical union with the patriarchate, though retaining the autonomous administration of their parishes and clergy. The reunion finally took place in 2007, and as a result the ROCOR parishes in America, France, Britain, and Germany were restored to full communion with the Moscow patriarchate. Some few

ROCOR parishes, in Britain and America, refused to accept the union.

Metropolitan Evlogy of Paris continued to lead the major group of the Russian Orthodox diaspora in France. After 1926 he ceased to attend any meetings of the ROCOR synod. Separating from them, he had intended to keep lines of communication open with Patriarch Sergius in Moscow, but in 1927 he was denounced by the ROCOR synod for vacillation, and in 1930 he was personally disowned by Sergius for having had the audacity to pray in public for "persecuted Christians in Russia" when there was "no such thing." By 1931, therefore, Evlogy realized that his hope of keeping formal lines of connection open under such bizarre circumstances was not realistic, and he placed himself and his parishes under the jurisdictional care of the patriarch of Constantinople, despite the loud protests of both Moscow and the ROCOR synod. Evlogy was never happy with this arrangement, however, and at the end of his life was personally reconciled with the Moscow patriarchate, but the parishes of his jurisdiction had no desire to follow his example, seeing the communist powers in Russia gaining more and more of a stranglehold over their church and homeland. The ecclesiastical arrangement of Constantinopolitan supervision of the Russian parishes abroad was suspended in 1965 (one presumes after protests by Moscow), but even at that stage many Russian parishes in Western Europe harbored deep suspicions of the intentions of the Moscow patriarchate, and refused to return to its allegiance, continuing their independent existence. In 1971 the patriarchate of Constantinople once more assumed a supervisory position. It was the French group of Russian Orthodox who had a massively important role in raising the consciousness of the Western Churches in regard to Orthodoxy after World War II.

The White Russians in Paris were among the first to bring to the attention of most Europeans (especially French Catholics and British Anglicans) the beauties of the Orthodox liturgy, and the strengths of Orthodox theology. Many theologians were among the group of exiles: Bulgakov, Florovsky, Frank, Lossky, Zernov, and Evdokimov chief among them; and their works gained a large and sympathetic attention in Europe.

One of their number, Sergius Bulgakov, was instrumental in founding the Society of Sts. Alban and Sergius which did so much to open up friendly relations between the Anglican Church and the Russian Orthodox in exile. Bulgakov was a brilliant teacher and writer, a protégé of Evlogy of Paris, who appointed him as a professor in the Theological Institute of St. Sergius which he had founded in 1925, and which remains as the most prestigious Orthodox theological academy in Western Europe. Bulgakov's trial and condemnation for heretical teaching by the Karlovtzy Synod hierarchs was a *cause célèbre* at this period, and further complicated relations among the Russians in exile.

Today, the older disposition of Orthodoxy in Western Europe as a balance between Russians and Greeks is now triangulated as a result of the large, young, and relatively vigorous Romanian presence around the Mediterranean and in Germany. There are also smaller Orthodox communities of Bulgarians, Ukrainians, and Serbs in Germany, France, and Britain. Western European Orthodoxy has not seen any real rapprochement between the various ethnic jurisdictions, although a recent initiative in England has seen the establishment of a second theological institute (after St. Serge) based at Cambridge, and designed as a pan-Orthodox establishment to serve both clergy and laity (and function as an indigenous seminary course for Thyateiran ordinands). In France there is the well-known monastery of Bussy-en-Othe in Burgundy, and the largest in England is the Stavropegial foundation of St. John in Essex. In recent years a small Lavra of the Romanians has been established in England and a larger coenobitic hesychasterion in Nuremberg. The Orthodox presence in England owes a great deal to the generosity and warm hospitality of the Anglican Church, who welcomed and helped it considerably in its early stages of growth.

SEE ALSO: Bulgaria, Patriarchal Orthodox Church of; Constantinople, Patriarchate of; Cyprus, Autocephalous Orthodox Church of; Romania, Patriarchal Orthodox Church of; Russia, Patriarchal Orthodox Church of; Serbia, Patriarchal Orthodox Church of; Ukraine, Orthodoxy in the

REFERENCES AND SUGGESTED READINGS

McGuckin, J. A. (2008) *The Orthodox Church: An Introduction to Its History, Theology and Spiritual Culture.* Oxford: Wiley-Blackwell.

Widows

VALENTINA IZMIRLIEVA

Widows were the most prominent group of women in the first three centuries of the Christian church. The Greek term for widow, χήρα (etymologically related to the preposition "without"), meant not merely a deceased man's wife, but any woman *without* a husband. Used as a cover term for celibate women living outside traditional matrimonial structures (whether widowed, separated, divorced, or unmarried) it became associated in the Christian context with *charisma*, following the Pauline treatment of celibacy as a spiritual gift (1 Cor. 7.7–17). Given the patristic understanding of virginity as a spiritual state that can be regained through continence, widows were often linked to virgins: Ignatius of Antioch hails "the virgins who are called widows" (*Smyrn.* 13.1), while Tertullian of Carthage commends the widows for "becoming virgins" (*Exhortation to Chastity* 1; *To His Wife*, 2.8). Thus, for the early Christian communities, widowhood came to represent an ideal lifestyle, a privileged opportunity for spiritual progress through chastity and service, offering a new social role for independent women that granted them respectability outside the patriarchal constraints of their society.

In the biblical tradition, widows and their children (the orphans) symbolize all powerless people in society and fall directly under divine protection. Christian law, drawing on both its Jewish roots (Exod. 22.22; Ps. 68.5) and the personal example of Jesus (Mk. 12.38–44; Lk. 7.11–17), made widows the financial responsibility of the church (Acts 6.1–7). Not all widows in Late Antiquity, however, were in need of support. Upperclass widows could inherit substantial property under Roman law. Such financially independent women, who were often also highly educated, were among the most generous benefactors of the Christian communities and the ecclesiastical elite.

The early church generally encouraged widows of childbearing age to remarry (1 Tim. 5.11–14), even though St. Paul considered those who remain widows "more blessed" (μακαριωτέρα; 1 Cor. 7.39–40). Only menopausal widows (the age limit fluctuates between 60 in 1 Tim. 5.9 and 50 in the *Didascalia Apostolorum*) were entrusted with responsibilities toward their communities in exchange for subvention. To qualify for service, these "real" (ὄντως)

widows had to have married only once, distinguished themselves by good deeds, and pledged a life of celibacy. They were appointed mostly for prayer, since the Lord never ignores the pleas of widows (Sirach 35.17–22) and a widow personifies the New Testament ideal of incessant prayer (Lk. 18.1–8). Yet both Tertullian and the *Didascalia Apostolorum* refer to more extensive communal duties (teaching, anointing the newly baptized, caring for the sick).

At the peak of their prominence in the 3rd century, widows personified active lay service in the church, rivaling the liturgical role of female deacons in later times, and offering a strong model of female Orthodox ministry. Vehement arguments against ordaining widows, especially in *Traditio Apostolica*, indicate that their exclusion from the clergy was hardly a matter of course. The "office" of widows stood for radical charismatic leadership and, as such, was not sufficiently under the control of the ecclesiastical hierarchy. It was eventually superseded by the clerical office of deaconesses.

SEE ALSO: Deaconess; Virgins

REFERENCES AND SUGGESTED READINGS

Eisen, U. (2000) *Women Officeholders in Early Christianity.* Collegeville, MN: Liturgical Press.

McNamara, J. (1979) "Wives and Widows in Early Christian Thought," *International Journal of Women's Studies* 2: 575–92.

Osiek, C. (1983) "The Widow as Altar: The Rise and Fall of a Symbol," *Second Century* 3: 159–69.

Stählin, G. (1985) "Hera," in G. Kittel (ed.) *Theological Dictionary of the New Testament.* Grand Rapids, MI: Eerdmans, pp. 440–65.

Thurston, B.B. (1989) *The Widows: A Women's Ministry in the Early Church.* Minneapolis: Fortress Press.

Women in Orthodoxy

NIKI J. TSIRONIS

The relatively marginal place of women in the contemporary Orthodox Church (as compared with the Western Christian denominations) might lead the casual observer to the assumption that this has always been the case in the tradition of Eastern Christianity. However, this would be far from the truth, as women have played an essential role in the spread of Christianity during the first centuries of our own era, as well as in the foundational development of the Orthodox world during the Byzantine era. Their role is testified in the written sources as well as in the material remains of the ancient and medieval periods. Women in Byzantium remained to a large extent anonymous and despite the flourishing of gender studies in recent years history cannot go back to retrieve all the anonymous women who so fundamentally and basically served society and the church. Speaking about women in Orthodoxy, we refer not only to the extraordinary amount of martyrs and saints, but also empresses and lay anonymous women who played an important part in the Orthodox tradition. This article will concentrate on the Byzantine period, as it was during that time that the presence of women marked the formation of the church.

In the context of the ancient Greco-Roman world, the role of women as taking precedence in religious rites and rituals (especially those of the home) was self-evident. This spirit seems to have been maintained in the early Christian centuries. In the gospels the place of women appears to have been crucial, as they were the first to hear the message of Christ and to witness his teaching, his mission, his sacrifice on the cross, and his resurrection. Mary Magdalene and the other Marys are only a few of the women who

surrounded Christ during his earthly life. The Mother of God holds a unique place among women in the church ("our tainted nature's solitary boast") as she was the one through whom the Word of God was made incarnate. According to Orthodox tradition, Mary was not only present at the crucifixion but was also the first of all the disciples to witness his glorious resurrection. In the course of centuries the figure of Mary attained increasing importance and from the 9th century onwards she became the symbol *par excellence* of the mystery of the incarnation. In this sense a female icon carries the great weight of the representation of Christ among the world.

The early Christian period is marked by the multitude of female martyrs who – even with their blood – helped the message of

Plate 79   A nun of the Romanian community of Voronets outside the famous "painted church." Photo by John McGuckin.

Christianity reach contemporary society. In the New Testament (Lk. 8.2–3) we encounter references to women as sponsoring patrons of the early missionary efforts of Christianity. Priscilla and Aquila, a notable couple within the Pauline circle, probably sustained in a most decisive way the activity of St. Paul. The earliest reference to a deaconess is encountered in the Pauline Epistle to the Romans (16.1) and refers to Phoebe, a young sister from Kenchreae (near Corinth) whom Paul commends to the Romans. In the same chapter of his epistle, Paul refers to another nine women out of a whole of twenty-four notable people mentioned; among them, the above-mentioned Priscilla, the scholarly missionary and patron of the churches in Corinth and Ephesus. The notable female disciple Junia (mentioned together with Andronicus) is explicitly referred to as an Apostle; and she along with many other women (such as the explicitly named Mary, Tryphosa, Tryphaena, Persis, and so on) recall for us the early, apostolic, Christian environment where women played a vital role in the life of the church and its proclamatory mission. It seems that the role of the deaconess designated an ordained member of the church with specific duties and obligations. Sixty-four inscriptions from the Eastern Roman Empire testify to the existence of ordained deaconesses, while a few others refer to female presbyters (the meaning of which is not entirely clear).

Part of the body of Christian texts which did not find their way into the New Testament, such as the apocryphal *Acts of Paul and Thecla*, recount the fascination of the young betrothed virgin who for three days and three nights, without eating or drinking, remained fastened to the window like a spider listening to the words of Paul (Kraemer 1988; Lipsius and Bonnet 1891). According to the *Acts*, Thecla followed Paul and when thrown to the lions she was miraculously saved. It is interesting that when Paul declined to baptize her, Thecla baptized herself in a ditch of water. Although the events related are probably legendary, it remains significant that the icon of Thecla as a leading female apostle was still convincing, and was set out in this literature to encourage Christian disciples in the post-apostolic generation. The place where Thecla is said to have spent the last years of her life, in Seleucia of Asia Minor, became the focal point of her cult which – as surviving ampullae found in the area show – was very popular and attracted large numbers of pilgrims from all over the Mediterranean. The Emperor Zeno built a large basilica there in 476. The remains of the basilica are surrounded by a large number of monastic dwellings, which further testify to the popularity of her cult and her continuing role as a patron of female ascetics. In the mid-4th century it was a place to which Gregory the Theologian retired for a time to prepare his ministry in Constantinople when he preached the Five Theological Orations.

The cessation of persecutions and the foundation of Constantinople, the capital of the Eastern Roman Empire that was to survive from the 4th to the 15th centuries, were times and events also marked by a distinguished female figure, namely the Empress Helena, mother of the first Christian emperor, Constantine the Great. The two were celebrated together as saints of the church on their Feastday of May 21. Empress Helena through her patronage of church life in Jerusalem became the one who discovered the True Cross of the Lord, in 326. Following this event the empress ordered a church to be built at the site of the discovery: it was the Church of the Holy Anastasis (Holy Sepulchre, as it is known in the West), which was consecrated in 335. The event is still commemorated every September 14, the Feast of the Elevation of the True Cross, and it represents one of the most important festivals of the Orthodox Church.

The 4th century is also marked by the Cappadocian fathers, who faithfully combined Christian doctrine with Greek thought. More important for our present purposes is the fact that they molded the profile of the women of their entourage in a way that greatly influenced Christian *mentalités* regarding the role and activity of women at home and society. Macrina, the eldest child of Basil of Caesarea and Gregory of Nyssa's family became the subject of a *Vita* written by St. Gregory of Nyssa in the form of a letter addressed to the monk Olympius. Macrina became the higumen of a monastery at the banks of the river Iris (a place of outstanding beauty) even before her brother St. Basil the Great had started his monastic settlement nearby after visiting Pachomius' coenobitic monastery at Tabennisi, in Egypt. In this same convent lived the mother of Macrina, Aemilia, with whom the saint, as it is said in the *Life*, had decided never to separate after the death of the young man to whom her parents had betrothed her. Macrina had a reputation as an ascetic that led many contemporaries to compare her to Thecla herself. The *Vita* tells that at the hour of Macrina's birth, Aemilia had a dream in which a radiant figure addressed the child she was carrying by the name of Thecla. The life and works of Macrina are narrated by her brother Gregory most vividly and the figure of the saint is fashioned on a hagiographical model, so as to be held up for emulation by future generations. Rarely had female figures been ever held up in this way in previous Greek literature. In doing this the Cappadocian fathers set out a new basis and status of Christian women in society. St. Gregory the Theologian does much the same in relation to his sister Gorgonia, using her funeral oration to elevate her as an ascetic example. The virtues that led Macrina to sanctity include chastity, the mortification of her body, obedience to her mother, humility in all respects, poverty, and almsgiving to everybody in need. Macrina's *Life* shows the way in which in the 4th century, martyrdom is being replaced by the new martyrly witness of virginity. Later in life and while higumen at her convent, Macrina acquired the power of healing, the casting out of demons, and also prophecy. There are also stories of how her giving of food to the poor miraculously did not cause her monastery's store of supplies to be diminished. Macrina's virtues echo the expectations of Orthodox Byzantine society of women. In the first Christian centuries, the renunciation of the body became a central issue in the practice of Christianity and undoubtedly it is linked to the rise of monasticism (both in its eremitic form initiated by Antony the Great (ca. 290–346) and in the coenobitic form propounded first by Pachomius and then by Basil the Great).

Women of authority had a massive influence over the development of Orthodoxy in its history. Christian empresses exercised their power carefully and wisely on many occasions for the benefit of the church (Holum 1982; Connor 2004). One of the most characteristic examples was the Augusta Pulcheria, who acted as a regent to her younger brother Theodosius II, who later married Athinais Eudocia. Pulcheria took vows of chastity and according to the sources transformed the imperial palace almost into a convent. She opposed fervently the doctrines of Nestorius and Eutyches, and was a passionate advocate for the title Theotokos, seeing in the Virgin Mary a powerful advocate for all humankind. She modeled herself on the intercessory role of the Blessed Virgin, a fact which

Nestorius objected to, as well as to her defense of the Theotokos title (McGuckin 1994).

Almost a century later, the reign of Justinian, the most noteworthy emperor of the early Byzantine era, was enhanced by the role of his wife, the Empress Theodora, who (although of lowly origins, according to the historian Procopius) is probably the only woman of the Byzantine Empire that a non-specialist might have heard of. Theodora's Miaphysite christological sympathies influenced the theological developments of the 6th century, and were behind Justinian's regular efforts to reconcile the Egyptian and Syrian anti-Chalcedonian parties after her death, not least his desire to reconcile the schism definitively at the Council of Constantinople II in 553. Similarly, the presence of empresses during the Iconoclastic era immeasurably assisted the cause of the Iconophiles during the century-long debate over the veneration of images. The issue of the relationship between women and the veneration of icons is still an open field of discourse in modern scholarship. Two figures need to be mentioned at this point: first, the Empress Irene who put an end to the first phase of the Iconoclastic controversy; and secondly, the Empress Theodora. Irene, the wife of Emperor Leo IV, acted as regent to her son Constantine VI when the emperor died in 780. Irene, with the support of Patriarch Tarasius, summoned the Seventh Ecumenical Council, which ratified the cult of icons and the relics of the saints. Similarly, Theodora, the wife and later widow of Emperor Theophilus, in 843, who acted as regent to her son Michael, reinstated the cult of images which was celebrated as the Triumph of Orthodoxy (still celebrated in the Orthodox Church every first Sunday of Lent). St. Theodora is portrayed along with her young son at the upper register of the prototype icon of the Triumph of Orthodoxy (two examples of this iconographic type survive today, one at the British Museum in London and another at the Benaki Museum in Athens). In subsequent centuries, one should add to this list women of the imperial court like Anna Comnene, the daughter of Alexius I Comnenos, but also Zoe and innumerable other Byzantine aristocratic women who used their ability to be involved in societal life (because of their gifts of wealth, talent, and education) in ways that greatly advanced the life and mission of the church.

Another example of female talent used to powerful theological ends is the 9th-century poet Cassia, a legendary figure most commonly associated with her troparion on the repentant harlot which is still sung in the Orthodox Church on Tuesday in the Holy Week. Cassia's biographical details have not been established with any certainty but, judging from her surviving works, she must have been of aristocratic descent. In her poetry, Cassia propounds the veneration of icons and exalts the role of women in the fight against Iconoclasm. She is one of the very few women whose poetry came down to us signed in her own name (Tsironis 2002).

In Orthodox hagiography, over a wide span of time, women appear in a number of capacities: as mothers, daughters, nuns and higumens, providers of charity, compassion, and philanthropy. In the narratives, they often give the impression they are transparent to the grace of God and to visions revealing divine grace. The earliest tales of martyrs from the first Christian centuries are followed in the history of hagiography by tales of "transvested" nuns and female saints in the 5th and 6th centuries, who dressed as men in order to assume the most severe forms of ascetical life (sometimes merging as unknown "beardless eunuchs" in the life of male communities). From the 6th century onwards we also encounter narratives focusing on coenobitic nuns and married laywomen, who dominate the scene through the 8th and 9th centuries. Starting from Mary of Egypt, the exemplary harlot whose repentance and total renunciation of the body led her to sanctity, to women of a domestic environment who attained sanctity through charity and endurance of many sorrows (one case records the abuse of husbands as a cause of martyrdom), Byzantine hagiography covers the whole range of paradigms of the multiple ways which may lead a woman disciple to sanctity. Despite its ancient character and limited range of socially open roles, this suggests that the road to holiness is broad and wide for women disciples, just as it is for men; that they have equal challenges and capacities in their Christian lives. At the same time these texts reveal to the reader the multiple functions of women in the context of medieval society and the Orthodox Church of the time. The case of the transvested ascetic female saints is of great significance for understanding the challenges faced by women in Orthodoxy. The *Life* of St. Mary/Marinos is not the first instance where a woman puts on men's clothing in order to escape societal expectations and pursue an ascetic life. St. Thecla is also reported in her *Life* to have put on men's clothes in order to continue her pursuit of St. Paul at Myra. Nicholas Constas, in his study of the cult of the Virgin in late Antiquity, analyzes the symbolism and the complex issues underlying this form of cross-dressing: "Through the medium of clothing, individuals could achieve relative autonomy or advantage in interaction with others" (2003: 353). Clothes were thought of as absorbing the qualities of the people wearing them and in this respect the otherwise deviant act of wearing male clothes was accepted as an action through which women negated the seductive nature of their sex in pursuit of the Kingdom of God. St. Mary/Marinos – venerated both in East and West – dressed like a man and entered a monastery together with her father, aiming to lead an ascetic life (see Constas, in Talbot 1996: 1–12). A similar pattern of seeking anonymity and freedom to follow God despite all accusations and challenges is encountered in the *Life* of St. Matrona of Perge, a fervent defender of Chalcedonian Orthodoxy against the Monophysite policy of the Emperor Anastasius I (491–518), who spent her early years in disguise in the monastery of Bassianos in Constantinople (*Acta Sanctorum Novembris* 3). More than ten lives of transvested nuns survive from the period from the 5th to the 9th centuries and they testify to the need of women to supersede gender boundaries, even by deception if necessary. As Judith Herrin puts it, in an essay entitled "In Search of Byzantine Women": "The monastic disguises adopted by women enabled them to simulate a holiness reserved by male ecclesiastical authorities to men only. To the church fathers, the very idea of a holy woman was a contradiction in terms, which women could only get round by pretending to be men" (Cameron and Kuhrt 1983: 179).

Byzantine hagiography gives us an insight into various other kinds of female sanctity. Ascetics and hermits like Mary of Egypt and Theoktiste of Lesbos attained to holiness through the renunciation of the body; coenobitic nuns like Elizabeth the Wonderworker and Athanasia of Aegina, through their miracles during their lifetime or after their death; housewives paid for their benevolence by suffering death from their husbands' violent hands, like Mary the Younger or Thomais of Lesbos (Talbot 1996). The women who became saints during this time were thus married or unmarried, pursued an ascetic way of life or not, defended the true dogma of the church or lived quiet lives, as the case may be. Sanctity thus follows no fixed recipe and women arrive to the state of holiness from many various paths and ways. Their lives provide an example which sustained women during the Byzantine and post-Byzantine era.

The period from 1453 to the present has not witnessed major new developments as far as the role of women in a male-dominated environment has been concerned. The dawn of the new millennium found the Orthodox Church relatively well behind Western Christian denominations, which had made considerable efforts to include women in the official, liturgical, and pastoral life of the church. However, Orthodox women continued as usual setting an example of Christian love and sacrifice within the church. The figure of Mother Maria Skobtsova (married, divorced, and with children before becoming an ascetic), who dedicated her life to the service of the poor and the persecuted, and who died in a Nazi concentration camp on the last day of German occupation at Ravensbruck, is not unique, even though it is exemplary (Hackel 2003). Her recent canonization by the Russian Orthodox Church has elevated a remarkable woman, the twists and turns in whose life were all raised up in the end by her complete dedication to God. In modern times Orthodox women still work for the glory of God and the spread of his kingdom, motivated by a deep belief in the royal priesthood of believers and in the responsibility of the creature towards its Creator. The place of women in the counsels of the church for the future; their place in its offices of authority, and its common social and missionary strategies for the centuries ahead, is something that remains to be worked out and something that calls to be worked out, for the newly ascendant education and professional eminence of so many modern women demands an extensive reconsideration of the role of women in the Orthodox Church worldwide. Such a

discussion has been partially initiated in the modern era, but a long road lies ahead, demanding much Christian honesty and willingness in all the Orthodox communities – not only those that already have large numbers of professionally educated women, but also those (for historical reasons) with less.

SEE ALSO: Contemporary Orthodox Theology; Deaconess; Marriage; Monasticism; St. Elizaveta Feodorovna (1864–1918); Virgins; Widows

REFERENCES AND SUGGESTED READINGS

Cameron, A. and Kuhrt, A. (eds.) (1983) *Images of Women in Antiquity*. Detroit: Wayne State University Press.
Connor, C. (2004) *Women of Byzantium*. New Haven: Yale University Press.
Constas, N. (2003) *Proclus of Constantinople and the Cult of the Virgin in Late Antiquity*. Leiden: Brill.
Hackel, S. (2003) *Pearl of Great Price: The Life of Mother Maria Skobtsova 1891–1945*, Crestwood, NY: St. Vladimir's Seminary Press.
Holum, K. (1982) *Theodosian Empresses: Women and Imperial Dominion in Late Antiquity*. Berkeley: University of California Press.
Kraemer, R. (1988) *Maenads, Martyrs, Matrons, Monastics*. Philadelphia: Fortress Press.
Lipsius, R. A. and Bonnet, M. (1891) *Acta Apostolorum Apocrypha*. Leipzig: Mendelssohn.
McGuckin, J. A. (1994) *St. Cyril of Alexandria: The Christological Controversy*. Leiden: E. J. Brill.
Talbot, A. M. (1996) *Holy Women of Byzantium*. Washington, DC: Dumbarton Oaks.
Tsironis, N. (2002) Κασσιανή η Υμνωδός. Athens.

World Religions, Orthodoxy and

TIMOTHY J. BECKER

The Orthodox Church understands itself as the full completion of the covenant with

Israel. From the outset, Orthodoxy has claimed continuity with a Jewish past, and so has assumed its monotheism, Scriptures, and critique of idolatry. Yet it has also stood in significant discontinuity with that past heritage, orienting the Jewish dispensation according to Jesus Christ, whom it proclaims as the true goal of the Law and the Prophets, and who exceeds them all (cf. Mt. 12.6; 12.41–2).

However, most who became Orthodox Christians came from the nations surrounding Israel and, while accepting the Jewish critique of their cults, progressively resisted Jewish culture. This differentiation between cult and ethnic culture saw the emergence of the new and distinctive category of "religion," in which cult took precedence but no longer necessarily corresponded to a particular culture. Thus, Orthodoxy has encountered the world with a restricted cult but an unrestricted attachment to culture; in this sense every culture can house Orthodoxy, while Orthodoxy can house only one cult, which it offers to all nations as the fulfilment of their own cultures.

Nearly all the fathers of the church saw Judaism in a closely relational mode to Christianity. Even those hostile to it were hostile likely because of local tensions rather than systematic theological reasons. The religions of other nations around them, however, were not seen positively. St. Athanasius (296–373) taught that the pagan cults were failures (at a basic logical and moral level) at assessing the innate Image of God properly, which was a live possibility. In a very influential early 4th-century treatise on the pagan cults, he said that rather than worshipping their uncreated Master, humans were swayed by evil to establish created things as God. Evil, which lacks existence, is thus the cause of false gods, which also lack existence (*Contra Gentes* 1.8). For Athanasius, the religions are not just errors

in religious style, they are metaphysically the undoing of the world, the deification of ontologically diminishing forms of existence. Athanasius is also clear that this practice is widespread, implicating, among others, the Phoenicians, Egyptians, Persians, Syrians, Indians, Arabs, Ethiopians, and Armenians (*Contra Gentes* 1.23).

Two centuries later, Pseudo-Dionysius (early 6th century) wrote that the religions of the nations derived from their rejection of angels. God had assigned an angel to each nation for oversight and divine illumination (*The Celestial Hierarchy* 9.2–4; cf. Dan. 10.13–21), which for Pseudo-Dionysius, explains the priesthood of Melchizedek (see Gen. 14.18–20; Ps. 110.4; Heb. 5.6), in the sense that he was faithful to angelic revelation. However, the vast majority of the nations had wandered from their angelic overseers and turned to false gods. Only Israel remained faithful to their angel, Michael, and so received illumination. Thus, for both Athanasius and Pseudo-Dionysius, the religious state of the world was a result of free will. All the nations could have been endowed with the true worship which Israel accepted, but have chosen otherwise because of moral and intellectual failures.

What this false worship would entail for the pagans at the Judgment was a matter of some reflection among the early fathers. A general sentiment, witnessed in the Egyptian desert literature, is that all followers of the cults were eternally lost. John of Damascus (655–750) summed up this view, teaching that repentance was not possible after death (*On the Orthodox Faith* 2.4). Gregory of Nyssa (331–95), following Origen (186–255), held that all things would make eternal progress towards God; though this has always been a minority position within Orthodoxy and was formally condemned as a dogmatic proposition in the 6th century. Nevertheless, Isaac of Nineveh (7th century) wrote in his recently discovered treatises (*The Second Part*) that God's mercy was greater than could be imagined; and one is also reminded of the celebrated saying of Silouan the Athonite (1866–1938): "Lord stand me at the gates of Hell and I shall see no one ever enters."

While uniformly rejecting "false gods," "demons," and "idols," the Orthodox theologians, always within an active missionary and evangelistic awareness given to them by a vastly pluralistic ancient world, have generally sought to claim for themselves elements within other religions that they have regarded as culturally valuable, as partially "compatible" with Christian truth. Chief among these characteristics have always been a prevalence towards monotheistic worship, an attachment to a rational mode of life, and the elevation of moral standards that were akin to those of the church. So, Justin Martyr (d. 165) argued that all who lived reasonably throughout history were in a real sense partakers of the Word, Jesus Christ (*First Apology* 46) and, as such, partial knowers of Christ (*Second Apology* 10). Justin retrospectively claimed for Christ the achievements of figures as prominent as Socrates and Heraclitus. In some Greek churches it is not unknown to see, occasionally, the great philosophical figures, Socrates and Plato, depicted in the frescoes of the Narthex, as some form of Hellenic preparation (*propaideusis*) for the gospel.

Orthodoxy after the 3rd century was active in deliberately reconfiguring the theological and metaphysical systems of the Greek philosophers, in order to harmonize elements of them with the scriptural teachings about God and the world. For instance, Platonism regarded God as an impersonal ultimate principle, with which the soul had a necessary kinship. While Orthodoxy drew on Platonic conceptual patterns, it thoroughly reworked them. For the patristic

tradition, God was a Person, to whom the soul related as a creature with no natural bonding, only a connection by God's graceful mercy that bridged an otherwise impassable chasm between Creator and creature. Thus, the fundamental cultural distinction between the immaterial soul and material body had become one between the Uncreated Maker and everything else, which had been created out of nothing and which (without God's vivifying grace) would lapse back into nothing. Athanasius epitomized this insight when he argued in the *Contra Gentes* that idolatry involved the worship of anything other than the Uncreated Creator.

In the early centuries of the church, reflection on the "other religions" was heavily conditioned by the pluralistic cultic scene of the late Roman Empire. There were regular persecutions of the church by the imperial authorities in this period, attacks which the Christians attributed to the hostility of demons roused by the church's refusal to pay homage to them, and which local pagan communities also articulated in similar ways, from a slightly different angle, accusing the Christians of being worthy of death because of their "atheistic" rejection of the ancient cults. Such a context was not likely to lead towards much positive regard for alternative religious systems, and the positive reflections of the "philosophical fathers" probably did not carry much beyond the intellectual class.

Within a few centuries, the church had spread across the Mediterranean world and into Ethiopia, Arabia, Armenia, Persia, and India. By the 7th century the East Syrian Church had even reached China, where it survived active until the close of the 10th century. By the 9th century, Orthodoxy began its movement among the Eastern European tribes of the Slavs, Moravians, Bulgars, Serbs, and Rus. Thus, at the end of its first millennium, Orthodoxy, and Eastern Christianity more generally, had encountered tribal religions from Africa to Arabia to Europe as well as Judaism, Zoroastrianism, Platonism, Hinduism, Buddhism, and Islam. Each new religion it discovered was assessed with reference to its own classical past and long experience of evangelization in pluralistic environments.

Among all the religions, Orthodoxy's relationship to Islam is distinctive. Islam is the only religion to have politically superseded Orthodoxy in homelands where once it was a majority. Between the 7th and 15th centuries, Orthodoxy moved from a position of power to that of an oppressed minority in Egypt, Palestine, Syria, Persia, Armenia, and finally the Levant. In the times of the Byzantine ascendancy, Islam was generally regarded in a hostile way (Muhammad as a false prophet). In times when the church was subject to Islamic control, there were more attempts to have a sympathetic understanding, and some degree of accommodation could be witnessed (along the lines that Muhammad had brought monotheism to his people, together with a sense of reverence for Scripture, and a moral code – all of which spoke of elements of divine inspiration).

When Muslim Turks finally overcame the Byzantine Empire in the 15th century, the remaining Orthodox stronghold became Russia. Through the extending of the Russian Empire, the Orthodox eventually came into contact with the religiously plural Mongol Empire (before it became Muslim), as well as with Buddhism, Shintoism, and Shamanism in Alaska. And throughout the 20th century the Orthodox in Russia and much of Eastern Europe had to struggle with communism, an atheistic system with religious roots and characteristics.

The 20th century also saw the large-scale movement of Orthodox into an increasingly religiously plural West. This, together with its involvement in the Christian ecumenical world, is leading Orthodoxy to become aware of its minority status within the global religious climate. The Orthodox today are faced, even in traditionally Orthodox countries, with making the transition, once again, from a context of power to one of weakness. In the West they are also faced with large-scale problems of the loss of religious identities, and a vastly greater pluralism than they had hitherto imagined. There are many challenges for the Orthodox Church in terms of what its future response will be. One thing is clear: the old attitudes that relied on clichés about other religions will have to be replaced by a deeper and closer study of what these religions actually do and teach. Many resources exist for such an extension of *caritas*. Patristic theology set up terms of rapprochement based upon the common heritage of humanity (all men and women of all religions) as made in the Image and Likeness of the Divine Logos who is the center of the worship of the Orthodox Church: the selfsame Lord, with a desire to save all humanity. The church, however, is governed by its divine commission to evangelize (Mt. 28.18–20), and pluralism in the form of accepting other religions as "equal or valid" alongside Orthodoxy is not seen as a viable path forward, or as compatible with its fundamental mission in the world to bring all to Christ and to witness to all the authentic traditions of the gospel in its own lifestyle and Christian culture. The exact resolution of many of these issues of Orthodoxy's relations to other religions remains to be clarified in the future. What is unarguable, however, is that Orthodoxy has a vast experience of living in a religiously plural world from its earliest origins, and that its relations with Judaism will remain on a different basis from all others. However, Islam also constitutes a special, though lesser, case because of its own origins with so many Jewish and Christian influences in its foundational Scriptures.

SEE ALSO: Ecumenism, Orthodoxy and; Evangelism; Islam, Orthodoxy and; Judaism, Orthodoxy and

REFERENCES AND SUGGESTED READINGS

Boyarin, D. (2003) "Semantic Differences; or 'Judaism'/'Christianity,'" in A. H. Becker and A. Y. Reed (eds.) *The Ways That Never Parted: Jews and Christians in Late Antiquity and the Early Middle Ages*. Tübingen: J. C. B. Mohr (Paul Siebeck).

Griffith, S. H. (2008) *The Church in the Shadow of the Mosque: Christians and Muslims in the World of Islam*. Princeton: Princeton University Press.

Louth, A. (2007) Th*e Origins of the Christian Mystical Tradition: From Plato to Denys*, 2nd edn. Oxford: Oxford University Press.

McGuckin, J. A. (2008) *The Orthodox Church: An Introduction to Its History, Doctrine, and Spiritual Culture*. Oxford: Wiley-Blackwell.

Moffett, S. H. (2003) *A History of Christianity in Asia, Vol. 1: Beginnings to 1500*. Maryknoll, NY: Orbis.

Pospielovsky, D. (1998) *The Orthodox Church in the History of Russia*. Crestwood, NY: St. Vladimir's Seminary Press.

Sunquist, S. W. (ed.) (2001) *A Dictionary of Asian Christianity*. Grand Rapids, MI: Eerdmans.

Y

**Yannaras, Christos
(b. 1935)** *see*
Contemporary Orthodox
Theology

The Encyclopedia of Eastern Orthodox Christianity, edited by John Anthony McGuckin
© 2011 Blackwell Publishing Ltd.

Appendix

Foundational Documents of Orthodox Theology

Contents

These documents are adapted from the source collections presented in the *Nicene and Post-Nicene Fathers of the Church* (series 2), Eerdmans, Grand Rapids; and T&T Clark, Edinburgh. Especially NPNF: vol. 7, 1893 (St. Gregory of Nazianzus), vol. 9, 1899 (St. John of Damascus), and vol. 14, 1900 (Seven Ecumenical Councils). Texts modernized and clarified by the editor. Original text and all secondary references related to it can be accessed from www.ccel.org/fathers.html.

Introduction

The range of the *Encyclopedia of Eastern Orthodoxy* is immense in both geographical and temporal terms. Its topical coverage, from the front of the alphabet to the end, allows for easy access for a researcher on any major theme that they may wish to follow up. This appendix tries to offer more. It is attached to the main body of the articles, in a sense as if it were the words of the ancients themselves (indeed, that is chiefly in what it consists) telling of the Orthodox faith directly, *viva voce*, rather than having it presented by contemporary commentators and exegeted in historical context. Both things, of course, are useful and necessary, and should complement one another invaluably. But if

The Encyclopedia of Eastern Orthodox Christianity, edited by John Anthony McGuckin
© 2011 Blackwell Publishing Ltd.

someone were to ask, "What are the essential primary texts of the Orthodox faith?" it might be easy enough to answer that here in this appendix one will meet with a good collection of them. Not all of them, by any means, but a representative sample of what the major theologians and dogmatic bishops (fathers) of the early church thought were essential architectural elements of the building.

The proper answer to what are the essential primary documents of Orthodoxy would be: the gospels, the Old Testament, the liturgical and sacramental texts used in worship, the statements and definitions of the ecumenical councils, the canons and disciplinary decisions of the great councils of the church, and the writings that have been afforded "patristic" status by the church over the generations (whether those were writings of sub-apostolic times, patristic-era theologies, or even writings of considerably later saints and doctors, whose opinions and decisions have been widely held among the Orthodox to affirm and express authentic Orthodox attitudes and values). In that list the biblical material has pride of place of course (see "Tradition" in the encyclopedia articles) and the conciliar and patristic materials are regarded as fundamental commentary upon it. The liturgical prayers and hymns, gathered together over the centuries as the church corporately worshipped, have a unique ethos and character for revealing the essential spirit of Orthodoxy. Here the old Latin adage holds true still: *Lex orandi, lex credendi* (the rule of prayer is the rule of faith). The text of the liturgy is widely accessible (numerous versions of it are freely available on the Worldwide Web, for example). It was composed at the dawn of the life of the church and reached its polished form in the golden age of patristic theology. The liturgies of St. John Chrysostom, or St. Basil, or St. James, to take the main instances, are replete with prayers of extreme beauty, simplicity, and profundity. There are also several available examples of "Orthodox prayer books" extant; three common and useful instances giving a broad coverage of typical Orthodox prayers being those from St. Vladimir's Seminary Press, New York, St. Tikhon's Seminary Press, Pennsylvania, and the Fellowship handbook of the Society of Sts. Alban and Sergius, Oxford. Another, of my own editing, also appears later this year with Paraclete Press. Perusing such a book of devotional materials shows, as it were, the inside of the cathedral: just as important for giving a true ethos, but often not as monumental or awe-inspiring as the outside façade.

For such reasons I have not included any of what might be called "devotional" material here (if that is not too weak a word for such essential theology). Instead, the appendix offers the main historical line of "dogmatic" literature that Orthodoxy advanced before itself as it made its way through the first eight centuries of its existence. This material was often set out in the face of major controversies and crises (clashes of theological schools, or Christian cities) and is (obviously) not in the mood for any further argument. It more or less claps its hands and calls for a stop. Then it teaches. It sets out what is to be held and affirmed in the churches. This is why (from the Greek word *dogma*, meaning teaching) it is "dogmatic theology" in essence: *the* theology of the Orthodox Church: then, as now.

The first exemplar of this basic Orthodox dogmatics has to be the Nicene Creed. This began life as a prayer for catechumens as they approached baptism. The fathers elevated it, after an early and great internal crisis known as Arianism, as a common prayer that summed up the faith. It has remained as an "ecumenical" (the word signifies meriting worldwide attention) standard of Christian faith ever since. The Nicene Creed is the tent pole of this appendix. The second creed that follows it, that of Constantinople I (381), is a commentary upon it, extending and clarifying the doctrine of the Trinity. It is this later statement which is popularly called the "Nicene Creed" (since the fathers of the council of 381 used the statement of 325 as their starting point). After this follows the *Ektheseis* (Formal Statements) of all the great and ecumenical councils up to the seventh and last of them at Nicea in 787. The historical contexts of the councils can be read up, separately, in the articles. But it is invaluable to have these core documents here at first hand also. In addition to the seven councils, the appendix contains the work of the three fathers whose dogmatic theologies most succinctly digested classical Orthodox theology. St. Cyril of Alexandria summed up and systematized his predecessor, the great Athanasius. The work of St. Gregory the Theologian (of Nazianzus), whose *Five Theological Orations* (Orats. 27–31) were once regarded as sufficient in themselves to present to a student the whole ethos of the theology of the church, is a classic of trinitarian, pneumatological, and anthropological doctrine. Lastly, we add the work (in selections) of St. John of Damascus. This 8th-century scholar and monk, hymnographer and politician, was a major source of inspiration even for Aquinas; and served the function in the East of synopsizing almost every aspect of theological inquiry into an ordered form in his great *Treatise On the Orthodox Faith*. Sections from this have been included to cover Christology and Trinity, but also a wider range of questions such as God's providence over the world, the nature of angels, what the sacraments are, why icons and relics of the saints matter, and what honor is due to the Blessed Virgin Mary. John wrote in the midst of the ascent of Islam in the Eastern Christian provinces of the Middle East and felt pressed by the decline of the church that he had already seen forced upon the conquered Christian cities of Syria and Egypt. His work has the character of a synopsis of authentic Orthodox faith as if, before a coming storm, one urgently needed to "batten down the hatches." It was a masterly summing up by one of the great fathers, and one of the leading scholastics among them. It has always been a core text of Orthodox theological schools ever since its appearance in the 8th century. While John is seen as the most authentic synopsizer of all the patristic writers on the widest range of other subjects, Cyril is regarded by the church as the paragon of christological teaching, the "Seal of the Fathers"; and Gregory is seen as the deepest of the trinitarian masters (the "Theologian" *par excellence*).

There I leave it. There are many other things that could have gone in, but where would have been the end? The so-called "symbolical books" (largely 18th-century responses to problems and challenges raised by Orthodoxy's encounter with an expanding Post-Tridentine Catholicism, as well as with Lutheranism and Calvinism first appearing on Orthodox horizons) might have deserved an appearance, but then again there are many today who raise an eyebrow at these documents (once so proudly advanced in the Baroque and Early Modern eras as definitive statements of Orthodox faith, as distinct from Catholic and Protestant positions) because, simply put, the apologetic context colored these statements of Orthodoxy perhaps too much. Sometimes the very terms of the arguments were unconsciously too heavily conditioned by the affairs, interests, and controversies of the West. Some have even called this era of the symbolical books a kind of Babylonian Captivity of Orthodox thought. It is not that their doctrine is being controverted of late; rather, their modes of expression, their range, and their tonality.

The present appendix therefore represents purely the classical formulations of the first eight centuries of the church. It contains the main seam of the gold mine, as it were. It is dense material, not given to much dialogue, entirely didactic and non-compromising in its form. It arises from the context of an ancient school, not a modern one, where we are accustomed now to learn through dialogue, questioning, and perhaps querulous dissent. This ancient teaching (*didache*) refuses to leave the doctrinal tradition of the Christians open to any doubt. It is *didache* with a rhetorical thump on the table, as was the manner of most ancient teaching situations. The word "dogma" in those days carried no negative connotations, as it might do today to listeners who grew up in the teaching traditions of the Humanities. We ought to imagine the material being presented here more in the manner of an early medical school lecture, where the class is still expected to write down the basic information, preferably without diverging from it, at all. Though it is far from easy material, it collectively comprises a veritable foundation course in the core teachings of the Orthodox Christian faith. It will also be recognized as the foundational elements of all the Western Churches too. Anyone interested in understanding the foundations of the Christian Church ought to be familiar with this material; and it is in this spirit that the appendix is offered, as the capstone and completion, as it were, of these volumes of contemporary research. I have used the material as it was collated and edited by scholars collaborating from Oxford University and Union Theological Seminary in the 19th century: that great collection of patristic texts known as the Post-Nicene Fathers series, and still in common use today, widely accessible on the Worldwide Web, and downloadable in full (even with notes and references, which I have here omitted). The translations found there, however, have "drooped" with the weight of time. Some of those venerable texts (notably the *Theological Orations* of St. Gregory) were in hardly comprehensible English versions to begin with. So I have thoroughly modernized all of them as I have selected them, with a view to making them clear, comprehensible, endowed with the grace of their (very) elegant Greek originals. The little polish added deoxidizes them sufficiently to allow us to see that there are even several jokes in the writings of these major saints. They breathe, graciously, even while teaching about "That Life which is the light of all humanity" (Jn. 1.4).

John A. McGuckin

1   The Creed of the Council of Nicea, 325 (First Ecumenical Council)

The Ekthesis (Formal Statement) of the Synod at Nicea

> We believe in One God
> The Father, All-Powerful Master [*Pantokrator*],
> The Maker of all things that are visible and invisible;
> And in One Lord Jesus Christ,
> The Son of God,

The Only Begotten [*Monogenes*] of His Father,
Of the being [*Ousia*] of the Father,
God from God,
Light from Light,
True God from True God,
Begotten [*gennethenta*] not made,
The same in being [*homoousios*] as the Father;
And by him all things were made,
All things in Heaven, and all on earth.
For us humans and for the sake of our salvation
He came down [from the heavens],
And was incarnate [*sarkothenta*],
and was made a man [*enanthropesenta*].
He suffered, and on the third day he rose again,
And he ascended into heaven.
And he shall come again to judge both the living and the dead.
And [we believe] in the Holy Spirit.

The Credal Anathemas

Whosoever shall say that "there was a time when he was not"
   Or that before he was begotten he was;
Or that he was made of things that once were not;
Or that he is of a different substance or essence [*heteras ousias*];
Or that he is a creature;
Or is subject to change or alteration [*treptos*];
All that say such things – the Catholic and Apostolic Church anathematizes.

2 The Nicene Creed in the Edition of the Second Ecumenical Council of Constantinople, 381

I believe in one God, the Father All Powerful Master,
The Maker of heaven and earth, and of all things visible and invisible.
And in one Lord Jesus Christ, the Only-Begotten Son of God,
Begotten of the Father before all Ages;
Light of Light, True God of True God, Begotten, not Created,
Of one Being with the Father
Through Whom all things were made.
Who for us and for our salvation came down from heaven
And was incarnate of the Holy Spirit and the Virgin Mary,
And became man.
He was crucified for us under Pontius Pilate, and suffered and was buried;
And He rose on the third day, in accordance with the Scriptures.
He ascended into heaven and is seated at the right hand of the Father;
And He will come again in glory to judge the living and dead.
His Kingdom shall have no end.
And in the Holy Spirit, the Lord, the Creator of life,

Who proceeds from the Father,
Who together with the Father and the Son is worshipped and glorified,
Who spoke through the prophets.
In One, Holy, Catholic, and Apostolic Church.
I confess one baptism for the forgiveness of sins.
I look for the resurrection of the dead and the life of the age to come.
Amen.

3   The Documents Defining the Faith Issuing from the Third Ecumenical Council, Ephesus, 431

St. Cyril of Alexandria's First Letter to Nestorius, Endorsed by the Ephesine Council (Excerpt)

The holy and mighty Synod therefore said that the Only-begotten Son himself, Begotten by Nature of God the Father, Very God of Very God, Light of Light, him through whom the Father made all things, himself came down and was made Flesh and became Man, suffered, rose the third day, and ascended into the Heavens. And so, these words and doctrines we also must follow, considering what the "Word of God made Flesh and Man" might signify. For we do not say that the Nature of the Word was changed and made into flesh, nor that it was changed into a whole man, of soul and body: but we affirm this rather, that the Word having personally united to himself flesh ensouled with reasonable soul, in an ineffable and incomprehensible way, was made Man and was called Son of Man, not in respect of God's favor only or his will [*kata thelesin monen e eudokian*], nor yet by adding person to person. But, although the natures which are gathered together into true Union are diverse, even so there is One Christ and Son out of both, not implying the diversity of natures was rendered void because of the Union, but rather that the Godhead and Manhood make up One Lord and Son through their indescribable and ineffable consilience to Unity.

This is why it is said, that although he had his being from before the ages and was begotten of the Father, he was also born in accordance with the flesh, born of a woman; meaning not that His Divine Nature received the beginning of its Being in the holy Virgin, nor that a second birth was needed on its own account, along with his birth from the Father. For it would be both idle and foolish to say that he who is before every age and is Co-eternal with the Father, needed a second beginning of his Being. But since for us and for our salvation, the Word having united Human Nature to himself personally, came forth of a woman, he is accordingly said to have been born in the flesh. For it was not a mere man that was first born of the holy Virgin, and then consequently the Word of God came down upon this man; On the contrary, united from the very womb, he himself is said to have undergone birth in the Flesh, and is said to have made that birth of his own Flesh his very own. This is why we say that he both suffered and rose again, not as meaning that God the Word suffered in his own nature either lashes, or piercings of nails, or the other wounds (for the Godhead is impassible because it is also incorporeal), but since that which had been made his own body suffered these things, so it is that he is said to suffer for us; since the Impassible One was in the suffering body. In the same way we also conceive of his Death. For the Word of God is by Nature Immortal and Incorruptible and is both Life and Life-giving: but since his own Body by the grace of God (as Paul says) tasted death for every man, he himself is said to have suffered death for us; not meaning as though he had experienced death as far as pertains to his own Nature (for it would be off the point to say or think this) but because (as I said earlier) his flesh had tasted death. So too, when his Flesh was raised, the Resurrection is said to be his own, not as though he had fallen into decay (God forbid!) but because it was his body that was raised. This is how we confess One Christ and Lord; not as if co-worshipping a man alongside the Word, in order that we do not introduce even a hint of separation by adding the prefix "co" [*syn*]. No, we say that we worship One and the Same, because the body is not alien to the Word, that body with which he sits down with the Father; not as though two sons sat with the Father but only One, in union with his own Flesh. And if we reject the concept of personal [*hypostatic*] union as either being impossible or as unseemly, we shall lapse into confessing two sons; and then we will of necessity split him apart and say that the one is man by himself, honored with the title of Son; and another, separate, is the Word of God, who naturally possesses both the name and reality of Sonship.

We must, therefore, never divide the One Lord Jesus Christ into two sons, for it will not help the correct expression of the Faith so to do; even if one should still allege the unity of persons. For the Scripture did not say that the Word united to himself the person of a man, but says rather that the Word was made flesh. And the Word's being made flesh means nothing else than that he partook of flesh and blood, like ourselves, and made our body his own and came forth as a man of a woman, even so never casting away his existence as God and his birth from God the Father; but even while assuming flesh he remained what he was.

This is what the utterance of the Orthodox faith everywhere declares to us. This is what we shall find the holy Fathers thought. For this reason they made bold to call the holy Virgin Mother of God [*Theotokos*]: not meaning that the nature of the Word or his Godhead took its beginning of existence from the holy Virgin, but rather that in the holy body endowed with a rational soul that was born of her, which the Word personally united to himself, the very Word is said to have been born after the flesh.

I write these things to you out of love in Christ and I encourage you as a brother and adjure you before Christ and the elect Angels, to agree to these ideas, and teach them along with us, so that the peace of the Churches may be preserved intact and that the bond of harmony and of love should abide indissoluble among the priests of God.

St. Cyril's Third Letter to Nestorius (Excerpt)

The Council of 431 endorsed the theology of the Third Letter but held back from synodically endorsing the contents of the Twelve Anathemas appended to its end. The substance of the Twelve Anathemas was subsequently endorsed at the Second Council of Constantinople in 553, which elevated Cyril as the "Seal" of the Fathers, and the Orthodox Church's leading christological articulator.

We have subjoined to this our letter the things that you must hold and teach and those things from which thou must abstain: for what follows is the Faith of the Catholic and Apostolic Church, to which all the Orthodox Bishops throughout the West and East adhere:

> We believe in One God the Father, All Powerful Master, Maker of all things visible and invisible, and in One Lord Jesus Christ, the Son of God, the Only-Begotten, Begotten of the Father, that is of the Essence [*ousia*] of the Father, God of God, Light of Light, True God of True God, Begotten not made, Consubstantial with the Father, through whom all things were made, both those that are in Heaven and those that are on earth, who for us and for our salvation came down and was made flesh and was made man; suffered and rose on the third day, ascended into the Heavens, and comes again to judge the living and the dead; And in the Holy Spirit.

And as for those that say: There was a time when He was not, and: Before He was begotten He was not, and: He was made of things that are not, or that say that the Son of God is of some other Hypostasis or Essence, or is subject to change or variation … these the Catholic and Apostolic Church anathematizes.

Following in all respects the confessions of the holy Fathers which they have made through the Holy Spirit who was speaking within them, and tracing out the aim of their ideas and, as it were, setting off along the royal road, we say that the Only Begotten Son of God himself, who was begotten of the very being of the Father, who is True God of True God, Light of Light, he through whom all things were made, both those in Heaven and those on earth, having for our salvation come down and abased himself and emptied himself out, was the one who was made flesh and made man. In other words, having taken flesh of the holy Virgin and made it his own from the womb, he underwent birth as we do, and came forth as man of a woman; not losing what he was, but even though he assumed flesh and blood, even so remaining what he was, that is God by nature and in truth. We do not say that the flesh was turned into the nature of Godhead nor that the ineffable nature of God the Word was borne aside into the nature of the flesh; for it is unchangeable and invariable, ever abiding wholly the same, in accordance with the Scriptures. And so, he was seen, even as a baby and in swaddling clothes, and though he was in the lap of the Virgin that bore him, he was even so filling the Creation as God, and sitting alongside the Father. For the Godhead is without quantity and size and will not endure limitation.

And so, confessing that the Word was personally [*hypostatically*] united to flesh, we worship One Son and Lord Jesus Christ. We do not set apart or parse up Man and God, as though they were connected with each other only by the unity of dignity and authority (for this would be empty speech and nothing more). But neither do we call the Word of God a separate Christ, and likewise the one that was born of the woman another separate, as if he were a different Christ. No, we know only One Christ, the Word of God the Father together with his own flesh (for he was anointed as Man along with us, even though he himself gives out the Spirit to those who are worthy of it, and does so without reserve, as the blessed Evangelist John tells us [Jn. 3.34]). Nor do we say that the Word of God dwelt in the one who was born of the holy Virgin as if indwelling a mere man, in case Christ might be imagined as only a God-clothed human being. For even though "The Word dwelt among us," [Jn. 1.14] and dwelt in Christ too, nonetheless it is said that "All the fullness of the Godhead dwelt bodily in him" [Col. 2.9]. Similarly we do not imagine that when he was made Flesh, this indwelling was comparable to the way he is said to dwell in the saints, but rather that he was united in a natural way but not turned into flesh, he made the indwelling of such a kind as the soul of a man might be said to have in relation to its own body.

There is, therefore, only One Christ, and Son, and Lord; not as though this meant a man had a simple connection with God on the level of a unity of dignity or of authority (for equality of honor does not unite natures, and indeed Peter and John were of equal honor one with another, insofar as they were both Apostles and holy disciples, but even so the two were not one), nor do we reckon the mode of connecting in terms of juxtaposition (for this is not sufficient to describe a natural unity). Nor do we imagine it in terms of an external participation, in the sense that it is written that "We who are joined to the Lord, become one spirit with Him" [1 Cor. 6.17]. On the contrary, we refuse the term "connection" as being insufficient to express the Union. But this does not mean we call the Word of God the Father, the God or the Lord of Christ, again so that we do not blatantly cut in two the single Christ and Son and Lord; for then we would incur the charge of blasphemy, as making him God and Lord of himself. For the Word of God united (as we already before said) in a personal way to the flesh, is God of all, and rules over all, but is himself neither servant nor lord of himself. It would be both silly and blasphemous to say or think this. For he called the Father his God [Jn. 20.17], even though he is God by nature and of God's very being. We know, of course, that along with being God, he also became Man (who is under God, according to the Law that befits the nature of the humanity) but how can he be God or Lord of himself? It follows, then, that it is as Man and insofar as relates to the degree of the kenotic "emptying out," that he says that he stands alongside us under God. In just the same way was he placed under the Law too, even though he himself spoke the Law and, as God, is the Lawgiver.

Moreover, we refuse to say of Christ, "For the sake of him that bore, I reverence that which is borne; for the sake of the Invisible I worship that which can be seen." Apart from this, it is a terrible thing to say: "He that is assumed shares the name of God with him that assumed him." For whoever speaks like this once again cuts Christ into two, and sets the man apart by himself and a God likewise: and such a person manifestly denies the union, on the basis of which we rule out that one is worshipped alongside another, or one is nominally given divine titles alongside the other thought of as encompassing him. We, however, understand quite simply that there is one Christ Jesus, the Only Begotten Son, worshipped with a single worship, together with his own flesh. And we confess that it is the Son begotten of God the Father, that is the Only-Begotten God himself, even though he is impassible in his own nature, who has suffered for us in the flesh [1 Pet. 4.1] in accordance with the Scriptures. And we say that he was in his crucified body making the sufferings of his own flesh into his very own in an impassible manner. And by the grace of God he tasted death [Heb. 2.9] for the sake of every one, even though he was by nature, himself both Life and Resurrection [Jn. 11.25]. For (as we said earlier) in order that he might become the Firstborn of the Dead [Col. 1.18] and the First Fruits of those who slept [1 Cor. 15.20], and might make a way for human nature to return to incorruptibility by the grace of God, he trampled down death with his ineffable power in his own flesh first of all. He tasted death on behalf of every man, and lived again after three days, having despoiled Hades; so that even though the Resurrection of the Dead [1 Cor. 15.21] can be said to have been accomplished through man, even so we conceive that the Word of God was made Man and that it is through him that the power of Death has been unraveled. And he shall come finally as One Son and Lord in the glory of the Father, to judge the world in righteousness [Acts 17.31], as it is written.

We also feel it necessary to add this as well: for we declare the Death in the flesh of the Only-Begotten Son of God, who is Jesus Christ, and we confess His coming to life from the dead and his assumption into Heaven, and thus we celebrate the unbloody liturgy in the churches, and thereby approach to the mystic blessings, and are sanctified, changed into participants of the holy flesh and precious blood of Christ the Savior of us all. This does not happen as though we were receiving common flesh (God forbid!) nor yet the flesh of a man who has been sanctified and was connected with the Word in terms of a unity of dignity, or someone who enjoyed a type of divine Indwelling; no, but rather as receiving the truly life-giving and very-own flesh of the Word himself. For since the Word is God and Life by nature, since he became One with his own Flesh, He rendered that flesh Life-giving. So that even though he might say to us: "Truly truly, I say to you, unless you eat the flesh of the Son of Man, and drink his blood" [Jn. 6.53], we do not thereby understand this flesh to be the same as one of us (for how can a man's flesh be life-giving in its own nature?) but on the contrary, as something that has truly become the very own flesh of him who for our sakes both became, and was named, the Son of Man.

In addition we do not ascribe the words of our Savior in the Gospels to two different hypostases or persons (for the one and only Christ is not two-fold, even though he can be conceived to have been composed out of two diverse things that were gathered into an inseparable unity, in just the same way as a human being can be conceived as composed of soul and body, but is not thereby two-fold, but is rather One from out of both). On the contrary we think correctly, and we maintain that both the human and the divine expressions [of the Gospels] have been spoken by one and the same. For when he says in a divine manner about himself: "whoever has seen me has seen the Father," [Jn. 14.9] or again: "I and the Father are one" [Jn. 10.30], we are led to think of his divine and ineffable nature, wherein he is truly one with his own Father by reason of identity of essence, and the "Image and impress and brightness of his Glory" [Heb. 1.3]. But on the other hand, when he accepts the limits of human nature and thus addresses the Jews, saying: "Now are you seeking to kill me, a man who has told you the truth" [Jn. 8.40], here, we recognize no less he who is truly God the Word in equality and likeness of the Father, even though he is in the limits of his humanity. For if, as we ought, we believe that he is God by nature, and that he was thereby made flesh, or rather made man endowed with a reasonable soul, then why on earth would one feel ashamed of his words, if they are spoken in a manner appropriate to a man? For if he despised words that betoken humanness, who was it that compelled him in the first place to become a man like us? Why would he scorn words that fit the experience of the human emptiness when he elected to abase himself in a voluntary emptying-out for our sake? This is why we must attribute all the sayings in the Gospels, to one person, one incarnate hypostasis of the Word: for there is only one Lord Jesus Christ, according to Scriptures.

And even though he can be called the "Apostle and High Priest of our confession" [Heb. 3.1], insofar as he ministers to God the Father the confession of our faith which we offer to him, and through him to God the Father, and to the Holy Spirit also; even so we affirm once more that he is by nature the Only Begotten Son of God. Accordingly we do not assign to a man, different to him, the name of priesthood and its reality. For he himself became the Mediator of God and Man [1 Tim. 2.5], and the Reconciler to Peace, who offered himself to God the Father like an odor of a sweet savor. This is why he also said: "Sacrifice and offering you did not desire, holocaust sin-sacrifices were not pleasing to you, but you preferred to prepare a body for me. This is why I said: Behold I am coming ! In the scroll of the book it stands written that I should do your will O God" [Heb. 10.5–7, as derived from Ps. 40.6–8]. For he offered his own Body on our behalf as an odor of a sweet savor. He did not offer it on his own behalf. For what offering or sacrifice would he need for his own self, since he is far above all sin, as God? For even if all had sinned and fell short of the glory of God [Rom. 3.23], simply because humans are inclined to stray aside, and man's nature is sick from the disease of sin; even so, this is not the case with him. We may well have fallen short of his glory: but how can we doubt that it was for our sake, on our account, that the True One was sacrificed? And to reply to this that he must have offered himself for both his own sake as well as for ours, will certainly incur the charge of blasphemy. For he has not transgressed in any way at all; nor has he committed any sin; and so what offering did he need to bring for himself when there was no sin to which an offering rightly pertains?

And when he says of the Spirit: "He shall glorify me" [Jn. 16.14], we also understand this in the correct way, as not denoting him as Christ and Son, taking glory from the Holy Spirit, as if from outside. For his Spirit is not superior to him or above him. It was to demonstrate his own Godhead that he used his own Spirit for the work of mighty deeds, and this is what he means when he says that he is glorified by him. It is just as if one of us, for example, were to refer to his own faculties of strength or understanding, and say that they will be our glory. For even though the Spirit exists in his own person, and is conceived of discretely, insofar as he is the Spirit, and is not the Son, even so the Spirit is not alien from Christ, for he is called the Spirit of Truth [Jn. 15.26], and Christ himself is the Truth [Jn. 14.6], and the Spirit proceeds from him, just as it does from God the Father. The Spirit worked miracles even through the hands of the holy Apostles after our Lord Jesus Christ had gone up into heaven, and in doing so glorified him. What is more, he himself worked through his own Spirit, and so it was believed that he was God by nature. This is why he said: "He shall take of what is mine, and declare it to you" [Jn. 16.14]. This is why we do not say that the Spirit is wise and mighty on account of participation [*methexis*] because the truth is that he is all-perfect and stands in need of nothing good, but we say this on account of him being the Spirit of the Father's own Wisdom and Might, who is none other than the Son. For it is the Son who is Wisdom and Might personified.

And since the holy Virgin bore in the flesh he who was God hypostatically united to the flesh, this is the reason that we say that she is also Mother of God [*Theotokos*]. This does not mean that the nature of the Word took a beginning of its existence from flesh, for "It was in the beginning and the Word was God, and the Word was with God" [Jn. 1.1], and is himself the Maker of the Ages, co-eternal with the Father and the Creator of all things. No, what it means, as we have explained earlier, is that he personally united human nature to himself and underwent fleshly birth from the very womb. This was not done out of necessity or for the sake of something his own nature required, as if needing a temporal birth in the last times of the world; no, it was done in order to bless the very beginning of our being. It was done so that once a woman bore him united to the flesh, the curse against our whole race could finally be stopped, that curse which sends our earthly bodies down into death. Through him those words uttered against us: "In sorrow shall you bear children" [Gen. 3.16], were abolished, and he revealed as true that saying of the prophet: "Death in its might has been swallowed up, and God wiped away every tear from every face." [Is. 25.8 *LXX*]. This is the reason too that we speak according to the economy, and say that he also blessed marriage, and when invited to Cana of Galilee went there along with the holy Apostles.

All these things we have been taught to hold by the holy Apostles and Evangelists and all the God-inspired Scripture, and by the true confession of the blessed Fathers. To all of them Your Reverence [Nestorius] should also give his assent and agreement, without any subterfuge.

I have added as an appendix to this Letter the things which it is necessary for Your Holiness to condemn:

The Twelve Anathemas

1   If any one will not confess that Emmanuel is truly God, and that the holy Virgin is therefore the Mother of God (since she bore in the flesh, the Word of God made Flesh); Let him be Anathema.
2   If any one will not confess that the Word of God the Father has been hypostatically united to flesh and that he is One Christ together with his own flesh, the selfsame God and Man; Let him be Anathema.
3   If any one should divide the persons of the One Christ after the union, connecting them with only a connection of dignity, or authority, or influence; and not rather with a natural consilience into unity; Let him be Anathema.
4   If any one should ascribe as to two persons or Hypostases, the sayings in the Gospels and Apostolic writings, spoken either of Christ by the saints or by him of himself; and should refer some to a man conceived of by himself apart from the Word of God, and ascribe others as more divinely appropriate to the Word of God the Father alone; Let him be Anathema.
5   If any one should dare to say that Christ is a God-bearing man, and not rather that he is truly God insofar as he is the Only Son by nature, since the Word has been made flesh, and has shared in blood and flesh like us [Heb. 2.14]; Let him be Anathema.
6   If any one should say that the Word of God the Father is the God or Lord of Christ, and does not rather confess that the same one is both God and Man, insofar as the Word has been made flesh, according to the Scriptures; Let him be Anathema.

7   If anyone should say that Jesus was humanly energized by God the Word and that the Glory of the Only-Begotten was wrapped about him, as from a different being than he; Let him be Anathema.

8   If any one should dare to say that the man that was assumed ought to be co-worshipped with God the Word and co-glorified and co-named God as one standing in another (for the prefix "co-", so repeatedly added, forces our imagination) but rather does not honor Emmanuel with a single worship and attribute to him a single doxology, insofar as the Word has been made flesh; Let him be Anathema.

9   If any one should say that the One Lord Jesus Christ has been glorified by the Spirit, and used his Power as though it were that of someone different, and has received from the Spirit the power of working against unclean spirits and of accomplishing divine signs upon men; but does not rather say that the Spirit is his very own, through whom he has accomplished the divine signs; Let him be Anathema.

10 The Divine Scripture says that Christ has been made the High Priest and Apostle of our confession [Heb. 3.1] and he has offered himself for us as an odor of sweet savor to God the Father. If any one, therefore, should say that it was not the true Word of God who was made our High Priest and Apostle when he was made flesh and became man as we are, but rather that it was a man of a woman, different from himself and other than he, who was made the priest: or if any one should say he offered the sacrifice on his own behalf too and not simply for our sake alone (for he who does not know sin needed no offering); Let him be Anathema.

11 If any one will not confess that the flesh of the Lord is life-giving and that it is the true flesh of the true Word of God the Father, but says instead that it belongs to another than he, someone connected with the Word in terms of dignity or as possessed of a divine indwelling only; but will not say rather that it is life-giving (as we said) because it has been made the very flesh of the Word who is powerfully able to give life to all things; Let him be Anathema.

12 If any one will not confess that the Word of God suffered in the flesh and was crucified in the flesh and tasted death in the flesh and was made First-born of the Dead; insofar as he is, as God, both Life and Life-giving; Let him be Anathema.

4   The Tomos (Conciliar Definition of Faith) of the Fourth Ecumenical Council of Chalcedon, 451

Following the holy Fathers we teach with one voice that the Son [of God] and our Lord Jesus Christ is to be confessed as one and the same [person], that he is perfect in Godhead and perfect in manhood, very God and very man, consisting of a reasonable soul and [human] body, consubstantial with the Father with regard to his Godhead, and consubstantial with us in regard to his humanity; "Made in all things like us," sin only excepted; begotten of his Father before the ages according to His Godhead; but "in these last days" "for us and for our salvation" born [into the world] of the Virgin Mary, the Mother of God according to His humanity. This one and the same Jesus Christ, the only-begotten Son [of God] must be confessed to be in two natures that are united unconfusedly, immutably, indivisibly, and inseparably; and that without the distinction of natures being taken away by such union, but rather the peculiar property of each nature being preserved and being united in one person and subsistence, not as separated or divided into two persons, but rather that there is one and the same Son and Only-Begotten, God the Word, our Lord Jesus Christ, as the prophets of old have spoken concerning him, and as the Lord Jesus Christ himself has taught us, and as the Creed of the Fathers has delivered to us.

And so, insofar as we have expressed these things with the greatest accuracy and attention, the holy Ecumenical Synod defines that no one shall be permitted to bring forward a different faith, nor to write one, or to put one together, or to speculate on one, or to teach one to others. Whoever shall dare either to put together another faith, or to bring forward or teach or deliver a different creed to those who wish to be converted to the knowledge of the truth, either from among the pagans, or the Jews or any one of the heresies, if they be bishops or clerics let them be deposed; the bishops from the episcopate, and the clerics from the clergy; but if they be monks or laity let them be anathematized.

After the reading of the definition, all the most religious bishops thereupon cried out: "This is the Faith of the Fathers!" ... "This is the faith of the Apostles!" "This is where we all stand." "This is what we all profess."

5 The Conciliar Decree and Anathemata of the Fifth Ecumenical Council of Constantinople II, 553: Against the Three Chapters

We learn from the parable in the Gospel, that our Great God and Savior Jesus Christ distributes talents to each person according to their ability, and at the appropriate time demands an account of the work that has been done by each. If he to whom only one talent was entrusted was condemned because he did not develop it, but only kept it safe; then how much greater and more horrible a judgment will that person be subject to, who not only is he negligent in his own affairs, but even lays down a stumbling-block and scandal in the way of others? Since it is obvious to all the faithful that whenever any question concerning the faith arises, not only that an irreverent man should be condemned, but so too anyone who has the power to make things right but will not exercise himself in that task. It is for this reason, then, that we who have had entrusted to us the office of ruling the Lord's church, fearing the curse which hangs over those who negligently perform the Lord's work, make haste to keep the good seed of faith pure from the weeds of wickedness which are being sown by the enemy.

When, therefore, we saw that the followers of Nestorius were attempting to introduce their wickedness into the church of God through the vile Theodore, who was bishop of Mopsuestia, and through his wicked writings; and even through those same things which Theodoret wrote, and through the vile epistle which is said to have been written by Ibas to Maris the Persian; then moved by all these sights we rose up for the correction of what was going on, and assembled in this royal city called here by the will of God and the command of the most religious Emperor.

It came to pass that the most reverent [Pope] Vigilius then resident in this royal city, was present at all the discussions with regard to the Three Chapters, and even though he had often condemned them verbally as well as in writing, nevertheless afterwards he also gave his agreement in writing to be present at the Synod, there to examine with us the Three Chapters, so that a suitable definition of the right faith might be set forth by us collectively. Moreover the most pious Emperor, according to what had seemed good between us, exhorted both him and ourselves to meet together, because it is only fitting that the priesthood should only impose a common faith after common discussion. On this account we petitioned his reverence to fulfil his written promises; for it was not right that the scandal with regard to these Three Chapters should go any further, or that the Church of God should be disturbed by it. Accordingly we brought to his remembrance the great examples left us by the Apostles, and the traditions of the Fathers. For although the grace of the Holy Spirit abounded in each one of the Apostles, to the extent that none of them needed the counsel of another in the execution of his work, even so they proved unwilling to make definitive statements on the question that had then been raised in relation to the circumcision of the Gentiles, until after having gathered together they had confirmed their own individual opinions by the testimony of the divine Scriptures. By this means they arrived unanimously at this conclusion, which they wrote to the Gentiles: "It has seemed good to the Holy Spirit and to us, to lay upon you no other burden than these necessary things, that you should abstain from things offered to idols, and from blood, and from things strangled, and from fornication."

But it is also common knowledge that the Holy Fathers too, who in previous times met in the four holy councils, following the example of the ancients, have by a common discussion, disposed of the heresies and new problems by a fixed decree, because when the matter in dispute was presented by each side, as a result of common discussion the light of truth expelled the darkness of falsehood. Nor is there any other way in which the truth can be made manifest when there are disputations concerning the faith, since each one needs the help of their neighbor, as we read in the Proverbs of Solomon: "A brother helping his brother shall be exalted like a walled city; and he shall be as strong as a well-founded kingdom." And again in Ecclesiastes it says: "Two are better than one; because they have a good reward for their labor." So also the Lord himself says: "Truly I say to you that if two of you shall agree upon earth about anything they need, they shall have it from my Father who is in heaven. For wherever two or three are gathered together in my name, there am I in the midst of them."

Nevertheless, even when he had been often invited by us all, and when the most glorious judges had been sent to him by the most religious Emperor, Vigilius promised to give sentence himself on the Three Chapters. And when we heard this answer, we had the Apostle's admonition in mind, that "Each one must give an account of himself to God" and we feared that judgment which hangs over those who scandalize even one of the least important, being aware also how much worse it must be to give offense to an Emperor who is so deeply Christian, and even to the people, and to all the churches. Moreover we called to mind what was said by God to Paul: "Do not be afraid, but speak out, and do not be silent, for I am with you, and no one can harm you." Therefore, we gathered together in synod, and before doing anything else we briefly confessed that we hold that faith which our Lord Jesus Christ, the true God, delivered to his holy Apostles, and through them to the holy churches, the same which they, who after them were holy fathers and doctors, handed down to the people entrusted to them.

We confessed, therefore, that we hold, preserve, and declare to the holy churches that confession of faith which the 318 holy Fathers set forth more fully, those who were gathered together at Nicea, who handed down the holy creed. And we agree also with the 150 gathered together at Constantinople who set forth our faith, who followed that same confession of Nicea and explained it. And we follow the 200 holy Fathers gathered for the profession of the same faith in the first Council of Ephesus; as well as the same things that were defined by the 630 gathered at Chalcedon for the profession of the very same faith, which they themselves both followed and taught. As for those who from time to time have been condemned or anathematized by the catholic church, and by the aforesaid four councils, we confessed that we ourselves hold them condemned and anathematized. And after we had thus made our profession of faith we began the examination of the Three Chapters.

First we brought under review the matter of Theodore of Mopsuestia; and when all the blasphemies contained in his writings were made manifest, we wondered at the long-suffering of God, that the tongue and mind which had framed such blasphemies were not immediately consumed by the divine fire. And we never would have permitted the reader of the aforementioned blasphemies to go any further (since we were afraid of the anger of God hearing them read out on record, since each blasphemy surpassed its predecessor in the magnitude of its impiety and shook the minds of the hearer from their foundations) except for the fact that we understood that certain people who gloried in such wickedness required to be put to the confusion which would result from having these things brought to light.

So it was that all of us, moved with indignation by these blasphemies against God, both during and after their reading, broke forth into denunciations and anathematisms against Theodore, as if he had been living and present. "O Lord be merciful," we cried, "For not even devils have dared to utter such things against you. O intolerable tongue! O the depravity of the man! O that high hand he lifted up against His Creator!" For the wretched man who had promised to know the Scriptures, had no recollection of the words of the Prophet Hosea: "Woe to them! For they have fled from me: they have become notorious because they were impious in regard to me, and spoke iniquities against me, and when they had thought them out, they spoke violent things against me. Therefore shall they fall in the snare by reason of the wickedness of their own tongues. Their contempt shall turn against themselves: because they have transgressed my covenant and have acted impiously against my laws." To these curses the impious Theodore is justly subject. For he rejected the prophecies concerning Christ and hastened to destroy, insofar as he had the power to do it, the great mystery of the economy of our salvation. He attempted in many ways to show the divine words to be nothing but fables, for the amusement of the gentiles, and he spurned the other prophetic announcements made against the impious, especially that which the divine Habakkuk spoke about those who teach falsely, "Woe to that man who gives his neighbor strong drink, that gives the bottle to him to make him drunk so that he can look upon His nakedness," a reference that signifies their doctrines full of darkness which are altogether foreign to the light.

And why do we need to add anything further? For anyone can take up the heretical writings of the impious Theodore or those chapters which we took from him to place in our synodical Acts, and find there the incredible foolishness and detestable things which he said. As for ourselves, we are afraid to proceed further with them, or to call to mind these infamies.

On that occasion we had read to us the things that had been written by the holy Fathers against him and his foolishness which exceeded that of all prior heretics, and in addition the Histories and the imperial laws that declared his impiety from early times. Even after all this there were some who defended his impiety, protecting the damaging things he uttered against his Creator, who said that it was not right to anathematize him after death. Even though we knew the ecclesiastical tradition concerning the impious, that even after death heretics should be anathematized, we nevertheless thought it only right that we should look into that question, and so it was that we found in the records how many different heretics had been anathematized after death. It was thus manifest to us in many ways that those who were advancing this position simply did not care for the judgment of God, or the Apostolic announcements, or the patristic tradition. So we would like to ask of them what they have to say in relation to the Lord's saying about himself: "Whoever has believed in him, is not judged: but whoever does not believe is already judged, because he has refused to believe in the name of the Only Begotten Son of God," or about that exclamation of the Apostle: "Even if we or an angel from heaven were to preach to you another gospel than the one we have preached to you, let it be anathema: As we have said, so now I say again – if anyone preach to you another gospel than the one you have received, let him be anathema." For when the Lord says: "Such a person is judged already," and when the Apostle is ready to anathematize even an angel if they should teach anything different from what we have preached, then how can even the most audacious persons presume to say that these words refer only to the living? Is it that they are ignorant? Or is it not rather the case that they are pretending ignorance of the fact that the judgment of anathema is nothing else than that a declaration of alienation from God? For the heretic, although he may not have been verbally anathematized by anyone, nevertheless he is truly anathematized, because he has separated himself from the true life by his wickedness.

And what answer do they have to give when scripture says, "A man that is a heretic you should reject after the first and second corrections. And know that such a man is perverse, and sins, and is self-condemned." In accordance with these words Cyril of blessed memory, in the books which he wrote against Theodore, said as follows: "They are to be avoided who are in the grasp of such awful crimes whether they be among the living or not. For it is necessary always to flee from whatever is harmful, and not to have respect of persons, but to consider instead what is pleasing to God." And again the same Cyril of holy memory, writing to John, bishop of Antioch, and to the synod assembled in that city concerning Theodore who had been anathematized together with Nestorius, says this: "It was therefore necessary to keep a brilliant festival, since every voice which agreed with the blasphemies of Nestorius had been cast out no matter whose. For it proceeded against all those who held these same opinions or had at one time held them, which is exactly what we and your holiness have said: We anathematize those who say that there are two Sons and two Christs. For as we have repeatedly stated, Christ, the Son and Lord, whom we preach, as the wise St. Paul says, is One single reality even as he was begotten as man." And also in his Letter to Alexander and Martinian and John and Paregorius and Maximus (presbyters and monastic fathers, and the solitaries attached to them), he says this: "The holy synod of Ephesus, gathered together according to the will of God against the Nestorian perfidy, condemned him with a just and keen sentence along with the empty words of those who might afterwards embrace (or whoever had in times past embraced) the same opinions as he had. The synod laid a condemnation of same severity against those who presumed to say or write any comparable thing. For it is logical that if a single person is condemned for such profane vacuity of speech, the sentence is not merely individual but generically applies to all similar heresies or calumnies, which that kind of person utters against the pious doctrines of the Christ: whoever worships two Sons, for example, or whoever divides the indivisible, or introduces the crime of man-worship into both heaven and earth. For along with us on earth the holy hosts of the heavenly spirits adore one single Lord Jesus Christ." In addition to this, several letters of Augustine, of most religious memory, who shone forth resplendent among the African bishops, were read at the synod, showing that it was quite proper that heretics should be anathematized after death. And this ecclesiastical tradition, the other most reverend bishops of Africa have preserved: and the holy Roman Church itself has anathematized certain bishops after their death, even though they had not been accused of any falling from the faith during the course of their lives. In relation to each instance we hold the evidence in our hands.

But since the disciples of Theodore and his impiety, who are so manifestly enemies of the truth, have attempted to exegete certain passages of Cyril of holy memory and of Proclus, as though they had originally been written in favor of Theodore, it is the appropriate moment to apply to them the words of the prophet when he says: "The ways of the Lord are right and the righteous walk in accordance with them; but the wicked falter in them." For these people have received what was once fittingly and rightly composed by the holy Fathers in a wicked manner, and have quoted them as if to make an excuse for their sins. The Fathers do not deliver Theodore from anathema, even if they seem to do so, but what they have done is economically to use certain expressions on account of those who once defended Nestorius and his impiety, so that they might draw them away from their error, and to lead them into perfection and teach them to reject not only Nestorius, the disciple of that impiety, but also Theodore who was His teacher. This is why in their economical teachings the Fathers show their intention on this same point, namely that Theodore should also be anathematized; a point that has been abundantly demonstrated by us in the synodical acts out of the writings of Cyril and Proclus of holy memory, in relation to the condemnation of Theodore and his wickedness. The same kind of economy is found in divine Scripture too: for it is evident that Paul the Apostle made use of it in the beginning of his ministry, in relation to those who had been brought up as Jews, for then he circumcised Timothy, so that by this economy and condescension he might lead such people on to perfection. But afterwards he strictly forbade circumcision, writing to the Galatians as follows: "Behold, I Paul say to you, that if you become circumcised Christ will be of no use to you at all."

We found out that the supporters of Theodore had done that which heretics often do, namely cut up the writings of the holy Fathers so as to intrude and jumble up with them certain falsities of their own. This was how they tried, by citing a letter of Cyril of holy memory as though using a patristic testimony, to liberate the aforementioned impious Theodore from anathema. But the matter was revealed when the mutilated text was read in its original order, for the truth of the affair was then perfectly evident, and the lie was unmasked by the collation of the truth. In all these things, those who perpetrated such vanities trusted in falsehood, as the scripture says: "They trust in falsehood, and speak vanity; they conceive grief and bring forth iniquity, weaving a spider's web."

And so, after we had so passed judgment on Theodore and his impiety, we took care to have proclaimed and inserted in the synodical acts a few of those propositions which had been scandalously written by Theodoret against the Orthodox faith and against the Twelve Chapters of St. Cyril and against the first council of Ephesus. We included also certain things written by him in defence of the heretics Theodore and Nestorius, for the peace of mind of the reader; so that all might know that these men had been justly cast out and anathematized. In the third place the Letter which is said to have been written by Ibas to Maris the Persian, was brought up for examination, and we found that this too deserved a public hearing. When it was read out, its impiety was immediately manifest to all. And so it was right to formalize a condemnation and anathematization of these "Three Chapters" that we have been speaking about, since even to the present time there has been some question on the subject. Because the defenders of the impious Theodore and Nestorius continued scheming in various ways to rehabilitate these persons and their heresy, and were arguing that this impious letter of Ibas, which praised and defended Theodore and Nestorius and their false teaching, had been received by the holy Council of Chalcedon, we thought it necessary to show that the holy synod was altogether free of the impiety which was contained in that letter. We wanted it to be clear that those who claimed the contrary did not do so with any approval from this holy council, but on the contrary only confirmed their own wickedness under the title of this script. And it was also shown in the synodical acts that in former times Ibas had been accused because of the very impiety which was contained in this same letter; namely first of all by Proclus, of holy memory, the bishop of Constantinople, and then afterwards by Theodosius, of pious memory, and by Flavian, who was ordained bishop in succession to Proclus, who delegated the examination of the matter to Photius, the bishop of Tyre, and to Eustathius, bishop of the city of Beirut. After this the same Ibas, who had been found guilty, was deposed from his see. These are the facts of the case, so how can anyone dare to say that this impious letter was received by the holy council of Chalcedon and that the holy council of Chalcedon entirely agreed with it? Nevertheless, so that these calumniators of the holy council of Chalcedon may have no further opportunity afforded them, we ordered the decisions of the holy synods to be publicly proclaimed, namely Ephesus (431), and Chalcedon, especially the Epistles of Cyril of blessed memory and those of Leo, of pious memory, former Pope of Old Rome. And since we learned from these sources that nothing written by anyone else ought to be received unless it had been proven to agree with the Orthodox faith of the holy Fathers, we then interrupted our proceedings so as to recite also that definition of the faith which was proclaimed by the holy council of Chalcedon, in order that we might compare the things in Ibas' Epistle with this decree. As soon as we had done this, it was perfectly clear that the contents of the epistle were entirely contradictory to those of the definition. For the definition was in harmony with the single unchanging faith set out also by the 318 holy Fathers (of Nicea) and also by the 150 (of Constantinople I) and by those who assembled at the first synod at Ephesus (431). But that impious letter, on the other hand, was full of the blasphemies of the heretics Theodore and Nestorius, and defended them, calling them doctors, while at the same time calling the holy Fathers heretics.

We made all of these things manifest to all, and stated that we had no intention of superseding the Fathers of the first and second synods, which the followers of Theodore and Nestorius had cited as supporting their position. But once we had read them along with the other synods, and had examined their contents, we adjudicated that the aforesaid Ibas should not be permitted to be received unless he anathematized Nestorius and his impious teachings, which were actually defended in that epistle. All the reverent bishops agreed to this, as they did in relation to those other two writings (of Theodore and Theodoret) which some had been trying to apply. In the case of Theodoret, the bishops responded by requiring the anathematization of all those things of which he stood accused. Since they were willing to accept Ibas as long as the impiety contained in his letter was renounced, and as long as he concurred with the definition of faith adopted by the council, how can his supporters now try to make out that this impious letter was received by the same holy council (of Chalcedon)? For as we have been taught: "What fellowship is there between righteousness and unrighteousness? And what communion does light have with darkness? And what concord does Christ have with Belial? Or what relation does a believer have with a non-believer? And what agreement does the temple of God have with idols?"

And so, having so set out in detail all our proceedings, let us state again that we confess that we receive the four holy Synods, that is, the Nicene, the Constantinopolitan, the first of Ephesus, and that of Chalcedon, and we have taught, and continue to teach all the things that they defined in relation to the one faith. As for those who do not receive these things, we account them to be alienated from the catholic Church. In addition, we condemn and anathematize, together with all the other heretics who have been condemned and anathematized by the same four holy Synods, and by the holy catholic and apostolic church, Theodore the former bishop of Mopsuestia, along with all his impious writings. We do the same in regard to those things which Theodoret impiously wrote against the Orthodox faith, and against the Twelve Chapters of the holy Cyril, and against the first Synod of Ephesus, and also those things which he wrote in defense of Theodore and Nestorius. In addition to these texts we also anathematize the impious Epistle which Ibas is said to have written to Maris, the Persian, which denies that God the Word was incarnate of the holy Mother of God, and Ever-Virgin Mary, and which accuses Cyril of holy memory (who taught the truth) of being heretic; charging him as holding the same sentiments as Apollinaris, and blaming the first synod of Ephesus for deposing Nestorius without examination or enquiry, and calling the Twelve Chapters of the holy Cyril heretical, and contrary to the Orthodox faith, all the while defending Theodore and Nestorius, along with their impious dogmas and writings. For this reason, therefore, we anathematize the Three Chapters we have been speaking of; namely, the impious Theodore of Mopsuestia, with his execrable writings; the things which Theodoret impiously wrote; and the impious Letter which is said to be from the hand of Ibas. And with this we also include all their defenders, and those who have written or continue still to write in defense of them, and those who dare to say that these men are correct, and those who have defended or still attempt to defend their impiety by appending to it the names of the holy Fathers, or that of the holy Council of Chalcedon.

We have thus settled all these matters with the fullest exactitude. We bear in mind the promises made respecting the holy church, and who it was that said that "The gates of hell shall never prevail against her" (meaning the deadly tongues of heretics) and we also remember what was said in prophecy about the church by Hosea: "I will betroth you to myself in faithfulness, and you shall know the Lord." And so we number along with the devil, that father of lies, the unbridled tongues and texts of heretics who persevered in their wickedness even to death, and we apply that scripture to them: "Behold, you have all kindled a fire, and have caused the flame of the fire to grow strong. So you shall walk in the light of your fire, and in the flame which you have kindled." As for our part, we have received the commandment to encourage the faithful with Orthodox doctrine, and to speak to the heart of Jerusalem, that is, the church of God, that it should "Act rightly, make haste to sow in righteousness, and reap the fruit of life."

Kindling for ourselves the light of knowledge from the holy Scriptures, and the doctrine of the Fathers, finally we have considered it necessary to sum up in selected chapters of our own this matter of the declaration of truth as well as the condemnation of the heretics and their wickedness.

The Chapters of the Fifth Ecumenical Council, Constantinople II, 553

1. If anyone will not confess that the nature or essence of the Father, the Son, and the Holy Spirit is one, as also is their force and power; [and if anyone will not confess] the consubstantial Trinity, one Godhead to be worshipped in three subsistences or Persons: Let him be anathema. For there is only one God: even the Father from whom are all things, and one Lord Jesus Christ through whom are all things, and one Holy Spirit in whom are all things.
2. If anyone will not confess that the Word of God has two nativities, the one timeless and bodiless, from all eternity from the Father; the other in these last days, when he came down from heaven and was made flesh of the holy and glorious Mary, Mother of God and Ever-Virgin, and was born of her: Let him be anathema.
3. If anyone should say that the wonder-working Word of God is one [person] and the Christ that suffered is another; or should say that God the Word was with the woman-born Christ, or was in him as one person [dwelling] in another, instead of affirming that he was one and the same, our Lord Jesus Christ, the Word of God incarnate and made man; or if anyone should say that his miracles and the sufferings which he voluntarily endured in the flesh were not of the same [person]: Let him be anathema.
4. If anyone should say that the union of the Word of God with man was only a matter of grace, or energy, or dignity, or equality of honor, or authority, or relation, or effect, or power, or

according to God's favor (in the sense that God the Word was pleased with a man, or that he loved him for his own sake, as the senseless Theodore said); or [if anyone should say that the union is] merely a similarity of title as the Nestorians understand it, who call even the Word of God Jesus and Christ, and honorifically ascribe to "the man" the names of Christ and Son, but all the time are evidently referring to two persons, and being disingenuous about the fact that they are only really ascribing the glory, dignity, and worship, to one of those persons, and one of those Christs; Or if anyone will not acknowledge in accordance with the teaching of the holy Fathers, that the union of God the Word is made with flesh animated by a reasonable and living soul, and that such union is made synthetically and hypostatically, and that therefore there is only one person, and that person our Lord Jesus Christ, who is one of the Holy Trinity: then let him be anathema.

Now, as a matter of fact the word union [*Henosis*] has many possible meanings, and the partisans of Apollinaris and Eutyches have affirmed that these natures are confounded with one another, and have asserted a union produced by the mixture of both. On the other hand the followers of Theodore and Nestorius have delighted in the separation of the natures, and have taught only a union of relationship. Meanwhile the holy church of God, condemns equally the wickedness of both sorts of heresies, recognizing the union of God the Word with the flesh synthetically, that is to say, hypostatically. For in the mystery of Christ the synthetical union not only preserves those natures which are united in an unconfused manner, but also allows for no separation between them.

5.   If anyone understands the expression "One single Person of our Lord Jesus Christ" in the following sense: that it signifies the union of several hypostases, or if such a person attempts in this way to introduce into the mystery of Christ two hypostases, or two persons, and, after having effectively introduced two persons, speaks of one person only as a matter of dignity, honor or worship (a thing which both Theodore and Nestorius have foolishly written); Or if anyone should calumniate the holy Council of Chalcedon, and pretend that it employed the term [one hypostasis] in this heretical sense; Or if anyone will not recognize that the Word of God is united with the flesh hypostatically, and this is the reason why there is only one hypostasis and only one person, and this is exactly how the holy Council of Chalcedon professed the single person of our Lord Jesus Christ: then let him be anathema.

For since one of the Holy Trinity, God the Word himself, has been made man, the Holy Trinity has by no means been increased by the addition of another person or hypostasis.

6.   If anyone will not affirm the holy, glorious, and Ever-Virgin Mary, to be truly the Mother of God in the exact sense of those words, but only in a false or a relative sense, believing that she bore only a simple man and that God the Word was not made incarnate of her, but rather that the Incarnation of God the Word resulted solely from the fact that he united himself to a human being who was born from her; Or if anyone shall calumniate the holy synod of Chalcedon as though it had affirmed the Virgin to be Mother of God [*Theotokos*] in the heretical sense Theodore meant it; Or if anyone should call her the "Mother of a man" [*Anthropotokos*] or the "Mother of Christ" [*Christotokos*], as if Christ were not himself God; Or if anyone will not confess that she is exactly and truly the Mother of God, since God the Word (who before all the ages was begotten of the Father) was in these last days made flesh and born of her; Or if anyone will not confess that it was exactly in this sense that the holy Synod of Chalcedon professed her to be the Mother of God: then let him be anathema.

7. If anyone using the expression "In two natures" does not confess that our one Lord Jesus Christ has been revealed in the divinity and in the humanity, so as to designate by that expression a difference of natures out of which an ineffable union is unconfusedly made; a union in which the nature of the Word was not changed into that of the flesh, nor the nature of the flesh changed into that of the Word, for each remained what it was by nature, and the union was a hypostatic one; Or if anyone shall take the expression [union] in relation to the Christ mystery in a sense that separates the parties, or while recognizing the two natures in the One Lord Jesus, God the Word made man, such a person does not rest content with taking in a theoretical manner the differentiation of the natures which compose him (a difference which is not destroyed by the union between them, for one is composed of the two and the two are in one), but rather makes use of the number [two] to effect a division between the natures or to make of them discretely separate persons: then let him be anathema.

8. If anyone should use the expression "Out of two natures" to confess that a union was made of the Godhead and of the Humanity, or should use the expression "The One Enfleshed Nature of God the Word," and will not understand those expressions in the way the holy Fathers have taught, to the effect that a hypostatic union was made between the divine and human natures, from which is the single Christ; but rather attempts to introduce from these expressions the concept of one nature or substance derived from the Godhead and manhood of Christ; then let him be anathema.

    For in teaching that the only-begotten Word was hypostatically united [to humanity] we do not mean to profess that a mutual confusion of natures occurred, but we understand, rather, that while each nature remained what it was, the Word was united to the flesh. And this is why there is one Christ, who is both God and man, consubstantial with the Father as regards his Godhead, and consubstantial with us as regards his manhood. And so whoever it is that divides or separates the mystery of the divine Economy of Christ, or whoever introduces confusion into that mystery, they are equally condemned and anathematized by the church of God.

9. If anyone shall take the expression "Christ ought to be worshipped in his two natures" in the sense that they wished to introduce two adorations; one in particular reference to God the Word and the other in relation to the man; Or if anyone wanting to get rid of the flesh, or to mix up together the divinity and the humanity, should speak outrageously about one single nature or essence [*physis* and *ousia*] of the united natures, and worships Christ in this way, instead of venerating God the Word made man, together with his flesh, with a single adoration, just as the holy church has taught from the beginning: then let him be anathema.

10. If anyone will not confess that our Lord Jesus Christ who was crucified in the flesh is true God, and the Lord of Glory, and one of the Holy Trinity: then let him be anathema.

11. If anyone does not anathematize Arius, Eunomius, Macedonius, Apollinaris, Nestorius, Eutyches and Origen, as well as their impious writings, as also all the other heretics who have already been condemned and anathematized by the holy catholic and apostolic Church, and by the aforementioned four holy synods; Or if anyone does not anathematize all those who have held, and still hold, and even now persist in their impiety so as to adhere to the same opinion as those heretics just mentioned: let him be anathema.

12. If anyone defends the impious Theodore of Mopsuestia, who has said that the Word of God is one person, but that Christ is another person, troubled by the sufferings of the soul and the desires of the flesh, and separated only a small degree above our inferior condition, who improves by his advancement in good works and becomes irreproachable in his manner of life,

and as a mere man was baptized in the name of the Father, and of the Son, and of the Holy Ghost, and so obtained by this baptism the grace of the Holy Spirit, and became worthy of Sonship, and worthy to be worshipped by reference to the person of God the Word (just as one worships the image of an emperor) and that he became, after the resurrection, unchangeable in his thoughts and altogether sinless; moreover, that same impious Theodore who also said that the union of God the Word with Christ is like to that which the Apostle said to exist between a man and his wife, "The two shall be in one flesh"; for the same [Theodore] has dared, among numerous other blasphemies, to say that when after the resurrection the Lord breathed upon his disciples, saying, "Receive the Holy Spirit," he did not really give them the Holy Spirit, but breathed on them only as a sign; he likewise has said that the profession of faith made by Thomas when after the resurrection he touched the hands and the side of the Lord, namely "My Lord and my God," was not said in reference to Christ, but that Thomas, filled with wonder at the miracle of the resurrection, was thereby addressing thanks to the God who had raised up Christ; and moreover (which is still more scandalous) this same Theodore in his Commentary on the Acts of the Apostles compares Christ to Plato, Mani, Epicurus and Marcion, and says that like each of these men, once having discovered his doctrine, had given the name Christians to his disciples; If, therefore, anyone shall defend this most impious Theodore and his impious writings, in which he vomits the blasphemies mentioned above, and countless others besides against our Great God and Savior Jesus Christ, and if anyone does not anathematize him or his impious writings, as well as all those who protect or defend him, or who assert that his exegesis is orthodox, or who write in favor of him and of his impious works, or those who share the same opinions, or those who have shared them and still continue unto the end in this heresy: let him be anathema.

13.   If anyone shall defend the impious writings of Theodoret, directed against the true faith and against the first holy synod of Ephesus and against St. Cyril and his Twelve Anathemas, and [defends] that which he has written in defense of the impious Theodore and Nestorius, and of others having the same opinions as the aforesaid Theodore and Nestorius; if anyone admits them or their impiety, or shall give the name of heretic to the doctors of the Church who profess the hypostatic union of God the Word; and if anyone does not anathematize these impious writings and those who have held or who hold these sentiments, and all those who have written contrary to the true faith or against St. Cyril and his Twelve Chapters, and who die in their impiety: let him be anathema.

14.   If anyone shall defend that letter which Ibas is said to have written to Maris the Persian, in which he denies that the Word of God incarnate of Mary, the Holy Mother of God and Ever-Virgin, was made man, but says that a mere man was born of her, whom he styles a Temple, as though the Word of God was one person and the man another person; in which letter also he accuses St. Cyril of being a heretic, when in fact he teaches the right faith of the Christians, and there charges him with writing things like the wicked Apollinaris; in addition to this he vituperates the first holy council of Ephesus, asserting that it deposed Nestorius indiscriminately and without examination. The aforesaid impious epistle styles the Twelve Chapters of Cyril of blessed memory, impious and contrary to the right faith and defends Theodore and Nestorius and their impious teachings and writings; And so, if anyone shall defend that epistle [of Ibas] and shall not anathematize it and those who defend it and say that it is right or that a part of it is right, or if anyone shall defend those who have written or shall write in its favor, or in defense of the impieties which are contained in it, as well as those who shall presume to defend it or the impieties which it contains, in the name of the Holy Fathers or of the Holy Synod of Chalcedon, and shall insist on supporting these offenses: let him be anathema.

6   The Statement of the Sixth Ecumenical Council, Constantinople III, 681

The Definition of Faith

The holy, great, and ecumenical synod which has been assembled by the grace of God, through the Sacra of the most religious, faithful, and mighty Sovereign Constantine, in this God-protected and royal city of Constantinople, the New Rome, in the Hall of the imperial Palace, named the Troullos (Great Domed Hall), has decreed as follows:

The only-begotten Son, and Word of God the Father, who was made man, who was in all things like us though without sin, Christ our true God, has expressly declared in the words of the Gospel, "I am the light of the world; whoever follows me shall not walk in darkness, but shall have the light of life." And again: "My peace I leave with you, my peace I give to you." Our most gentle Emperor, the champion of Orthodoxy, and opponent of evil doctrines, being reverentially led by this doctrine of peace spoken by our God, and thus having convened this present holy and ecumenical assembly, has assembled together the judgment of the entire Church. For this reason, our holy and ecumenical synod has driven away the impious error which had prevailed for a certain time until the present, and has kept strictly to the path of the holy and approved Fathers, and has thus reverently given its full assent to the five holy and ecumenical Synods (that is to say, the 318 holy Fathers who assembled in Nicea against the raging Arius; and the next in Constantinople of the 150 God-inspired ones who withstood Macedonius the Spirit-Fighter, and the impious Apollinaris; and also the first Synod in Ephesus of the 200 venerable ones convened against Nestorius the Judaizer; and that of Chalcedon of the 630 God-inspired fathers convened against Eutyches and Dioscorus the enemies of God. And in addition to these, to the most recent one, that is the Fifth holy synod assembled in this city, against Theodore of Mopsuestia, Origen, Didymus, and Evagrius, and the writings of Theodoret aimed against the Twelve Chapters of the celebrated Cyril, and the Epistle which was said to be written by Ibas to Maris the Persian, a synod that set out to universally renew the ancient decrees of religion, and chase away the impious doctrines of irreligion. And this our own holy and ecumenical God-inspired synod has set its seal to the Creed which was put forth by the 318 Fathers, and later reverently confirmed by the 150, which the other holy synods also cordially received and ratified for the abolition of every soul-destroying heresy.

[There follow the Nicene and the Niceno-Constantinopolitan Creeds]

Furthermore, the holy and ecumenical synod confesses that this reverent and orthodox creed of the divine grace ought to have been sufficient for the full knowledge and confirmation of the Orthodox faith. But the author of evil (the same who, in the beginning, used the serpent to bring the poison of death upon the human race), has never ceased his labors, and even in this age has found suitable instruments for working out his will: by this we mean Theodore, who was bishop of Pharan, Sergius, Pyrrhus, Paul and Peter, who were Archbishops of this royal city, and in addition Honorius who was Pope of Old Rome, Cyrus bishop of Alexandria, Macarius who was lately bishop of Antioch, and Stephen his disciple. The evil one has actively employed all of them in raising up for the whole Church the stumbling-blocks of "one will" and "one operation" in the two natures of Christ our true God, who is one of the Holy Trinity. In this way he has disseminated among the orthodox the novelties of a heresy similar to the mad and wicked doctrine of the impious Apollinaris, Severus, and Themistius. He has endeavored craftily to destroy the perfection of the incarnation of the same Lord Jesus Christ, our God, by blasphemously arguing that his flesh which was endowed with a rational soul was devoid of will or operation. For this reason Christ our God raised up our faithful Emperor, as a New David, having found him a man after his own heart, who as it is written, "Has not suffered his eyes to sleep nor his eyelids to slumber," until he has found a perfect declaration of Orthodoxy from this our God-assembled and holy synod. As it is said in the words of our God: "Where two or three are gathered together in my name, there am I in the midst of them."

So it is that the present holy and ecumenical synod also faithfully receives and salutes with uplifted hands the suggestion sent to our most pious and faithful Emperor Constantine by the most holy and blessed Agatho, Pope of Old Rome, which named and rejected those who taught or preached one will and one operation in the economy of the incarnation of our Lord Jesus Christ, our true God. And it has similarly adopted the other synodical suggestion which was sent by the Council held under the presidency of the same most holy Pope, composed of 125 God-beloved Bishops, addressed to his God-instructed Serene Majesty, as being fully in harmony with the holy Council of Chalcedon and with the Tome of the most holy and blessed Leo, Pope of Old Rome, which was originally addressed to St. Flavian, which this Council, in its turn, designated as a "Pillar of Orthodox Faith"; for it also agrees with the Synodical Letters written by blessed Cyril against the impious Nestorius and addressed to the Oriental Bishops.

So it is that, following the five holy Ecumenical Councils and the holy and approved Fathers, with one voice we define that our Lord Jesus Christ must be confessed as true God and true man, one of the holy and consubstantial and life-giving Trinity, perfect in deity and perfect in humanity, true God and true man, subsisting of a reasonable soul and human body; consubstantial with the Father as regards his divinity and consubstantial with us as regards his humanity; in all things like to us, sin only excepted; begotten of his Father before all ages according to his divinity, but who in these last days for us men and for our salvation was made man of the Holy Spirit and of the Virgin Mary, who is strictly and properly the Mother of God according to the flesh. We confess one and the same Christ, our Lord, the only-begotten Son, recognized unconfusedly, unchangeably, inseparably and indivisibly in two natures, the peculiarities of each nature not being lost by the union but rather the proprieties of each one being preserved, concurring in one person and in one subsistence, not separated or divided into two persons, but one and the same Only-Begotten Son of God, the Word, our Lord Jesus Christ; just as the prophets of old have taught us and as our Lord Jesus Christ himself has instructed us, and the Creed of the holy Fathers has handed down to us. In defining all this, we likewise declare that in him there are, indivisibly, inconvertibly, inseparably, and unconfusedly, two natural wills and two natural operations according to the teaching of the holy Fathers. And these two natural wills are not contrary to one another (God forbid!) as the wicked heretics assert; because his human will follows after his divine and omnipotent will, never as a resisting and reluctant entity, but rather in true submission. For it was fitting that the flesh should only be moved in subjection to the divine will, as the most wise Athanasius taught. For as his flesh is called, and indeed is, the flesh of God the Word, so also the natural will of his flesh is called, and is, the proper will of God the Word. It is, as he himself says: "I came down from heaven, not that I might do my own will, but the will of the Father who sent me!" And here he calls his own will, the will of his flesh, insofar as his flesh was also his own. For as his most holy and immaculate animated flesh was not destroyed because it was deified, but rather continued in its own state and nature, so also his human will, even though it was deified, was not suppressed, but was rather preserved according to the saying of Gregory the Theologian: "His will is not contrary to God but is altogether deified."

And so, we glorify two natural operations existing indivisibly, immutably, unconfusedly, and inseparably in the same Lord Jesus Christ our true God; that is to say a divine operation and a human operation, according to the divine preacher Leo, who most distinctly asserts as follows: "For each form does in communion with the other what pertains properly to it; the Word, that is, doing that which pertains to the Word, and the flesh that which pertains to the flesh." And so we refuse to admit one natural operation in God and in the creature, because we will not exalt into the divine essence that which is created; nor will we bring down the glory of the divine nature to that place suited to a creature. We recognize the miracles and the sufferings as belonging to one and the same [person], but as appropriate to one or the other nature out of which he is, and in which he subsists, as Cyril admirably puts it.

And so, preserving the unconfusedness and indivisibility, we briefly make this whole confession, believing our Lord Jesus Christ to be one of the Trinity and our true God. After the incarnation we say that his two natures shone forth in his single subsistence in which he both performed the miracles and endured the sufferings through the whole of his economic engagement, and he did not do this in appearance only but in true actuality, because of the difference of nature which must be recognized in the same person, for although they are joined together even so each nature wills and does the things that are proper to it, acting together indivisibly and unconfusedly. This is why we confess that there are two wills and two operations which very appropriately concur in him for the salvation of the human race.

Since we have formulated these things with all diligence and care, we define that it shall never be permissible for anyone henceforth to bring forward, or to write, or compose, or think, or teach, a different faith. Whoever shall presume to compose or propose a different faith, or to teach a different creed or hand one over to those wishing to be converted to the knowledge of the truth, whether from the Gentiles or the Jews, or from any heresy; or whoever tries to introduce a new discourse or speech designed to subvert these matters which now have been determined by us: whoever they are, if they are bishops or clerics let them be deposed; the bishops from the episcopate, the clerics from the ranks of clergy; but if they are monks or laity: let them be anathematized.

7 Statement of Faith of the Seventh Ecumenical Council, Nicea II, 787

The holy, great, and ecumenical Synod which by the grace of God and the will of the pious and Christ-loving Emperors, Constantine and Irene, his mother, was gathered together for the second time at Nicea, the illustrious metropolis of Bithynia, in the holy church of God which is named Sophia, having followed the traditions of the catholic church, has defined the following:

Christ our Lord, who has granted to us the light of his knowledge, and has redeemed us from the darkness of mad idolatry, has espoused to himself the holy catholic church without spot or defect, and promised that he would always preserve her. And he gave his word to this effect to his holy disciples when he said: "Behold! I am with you always, even to the end of the world." This promise he made, not only to them, but to us also who afterwards should believe in his name through their word. But there are some who did not consider this gift, who became fickle through the temptations of the crafty enemy, and who thus fell away from the Orthodox faith. Withdrawing from the traditions of the catholic church, they wandered from the truth. As the Book of Proverbs put it: "The husbandmen have gone astray in their own husbandry and have gathered emptiness in their hands." Indeed, certain priests, who were priests in name only (but not so in truth) dared to speak out against the God-approved ornament of the sacred monuments. It was about these that God cried aloud through the prophet, saying: "Many shepherds have corrupted my vineyard, and have polluted my portion." And, in truth, following the lead of profane men, and led astray by their carnal sensibilities, they calumniated the church of Christ our God, which he has espoused to himself. They failed, accordingly, to distinguish between what is holy and what is profane, describing the icons of our Lord and of his saints with the same designation as the statues of diabolical idols. Seeing these things, our Lord and God, who is never willing to stand by while his people are corrupted by such manner of plague, was pleased to call his chief priests together from every quarter. We are thus moved with a divine zeal and brought here by the will of our princes, Constantine and Irene, so that the traditions of the catholic church may receive stability from our common decree.

And so, with all diligence, after having made a thorough examination and analysis, and following the path of the truth, we have diminished nothing; we have added nothing. On the contrary we have preserved unchanged everything pertaining to the catholic church. Following the six ecumenical synods, especially that which met in this illustrious metropolis of Nicea, and also that which was afterwards gathered together in the God-protected Royal City we declare our belief:

[There follows the Niceno-Constantinopolitan Creed]

We detest and anathematize Arius and all the sharers of his absurd opinion; also Macedonius and those who following him are well styled "Fighters against the Spirit" [*Pneumatomachi*]. We confess that our Lady, the holy Mary, is properly and truly the Mother of God, because she was the Mother after the flesh of one of the persons of the

Holy Trinity, namely, Christ our God, just as the council of Ephesus had already defined when it cast out of the church the heretic Nestorius with his colleagues, because he taught that there were two persons [in Christ].

Along with the Fathers of that synod we confess that he who was incarnate of the immaculate Mother of God and Ever-Virgin Mary has two natures, recognizing him as perfect God and perfect man, as also the Council of Chalcedon declared when it expelled Eutyches and Dioscorus from the divine atrium for their blasphemy and placed Severus, Peter and a number of others who had blasphemed in different forms, in that same category of sacrilege. Moreover, along with these we anathematize the fables of Origen, Evagrius, and Didymus, in harmony with the decisions of the Fifth Council held at Constantinople. We affirm that in Christ there are two wills and two operations according to the reality of each nature, as also the Sixth Synod, held at Constantinople, taught, casting out Sergius, Honorius, Cyrus, Pyrrhus, Macarius, and those who agreed with them, and all those who were unwilling to be reverent.

To make our confession short, we keep unchanged all the ecclesiastical traditions handed down to us, whether in writing or verbally, all of which are interconnected and related; and one of which is the making of pictorial representations, agreeable to the history of the preaching of the Gospel. For this is a tradition useful in many respects, but especially in this regard that the incarnation of the Word of God may thus be depicted as real and not merely imaginary.

And so, we follow the royal highway and the divinely inspired authority of our holy Fathers and the traditions of the catholic church (because, as we all know, the Holy Spirit dwells within her). And we define with all certitude and all accuracy that just as the symbol of the precious and life-giving Cross should be set up in the holy churches of God, and placed on the sacred vessels and on the vestments and on hangings, and in pictures both in private houses and by the wayside, so also should the venerable and holy icons be set up, both in painted form and in mosaic, and any other appropriate materials. This includes the figures of our Lord and God and Savior Jesus Christ, our Immaculate Lady, the Mother of God, the honorable Angels, and all the Saints and holy ones. For the more often they can be seen in artistic representation, so much more readily will believers be lifted up to the memory of their prototypes, and to a longing after them. Due salutation and honorable reverence [aspasmon kai timetiken proskynesin] should be given to the icons, which is assuredly not that true adoration [latreian] which pertains only to the divine nature. Even so, incense and lights can be offered before the icons, in accordance with ancient and reverent custom, just as we do before the symbol of the precious and life-giving Cross, and also to the Book of the Gospels and to other holy things. This is because the honor which is paid to the icon passes on to that which the icon represents. So it is that whoever venerates the icon venerates within it, the subject that is represented. For this is the teaching of our holy Fathers, and this is the tradition of the catholic church, which from one end of the earth to the other has received the Gospel, and is established.

So it is that we follow Paul, who spoke in Christ, and the whole divine apostolic company and the holy Fathers, holding fast to the traditions which we have received.

So we sing prophetically the triumphal hymns of the Church, "Rejoice greatly, O daughter of Sion; Shout, O daughter of Jerusalem. Rejoice and be glad with all your heart. For the Lord has taken away from you the oppression of your enemies. You are redeemed from the hand of your enemies. The Lord is a King in your midst. No longer shall you look upon evil things, and peace will be yours forever."

Accordingly, those who dare to think or teach otherwise; Or those who like wicked heretics spurn the traditions of the church in order to invent novelties, or else to reject some of the customs which the church has received, such as the veneration of the book of the Gospels, or the image of the cross, or the pictorial icons, or the holy relics of a martyr; Or those who wickedly and caustically devise anything subversive of the lawful traditions of the catholic church; Or those who turn to common use the sacred vessels or the venerable monastic houses; if they are bishops or clergy, we command that they be deposed; if monastics or laity, let them be anathema.

8   The Five Theological Orations of St. Gregory of Nazianzus (the Theologian)

On the Holy Trinity, Orations 27–31

St. Gregory of Nazianzus, Oration 27: The First Theological Oration

A Preliminary Discourse Against the Eunomians

Orat. 27.1. I am about to speak against those who pride themselves on their eloquence; so, to begin with a text of Scripture, "Behold, I resist you who are so proud," and this applies not only with regard to their system of teaching, but also to their way of listening and to their mentality. For there are certain persons whose ears and tongues are itching for our words and, as I can now see for myself, for some here present even their fists are itching too. They take delight in profane babblings, and the puzzles of what is wrongly called knowledge or else in word clashes, all of which tend to be profitless; for was it not Paul, the preacher and establisher of the "Abbreviated Word," that disciple and teacher of the Fishermen, who said this about all that is excessive or superfluous in discourse? But as to those to whom we refer, I wish that they, whose tongue is so voluble and so clever in applying itself to noble and approved language, would equally pay some attention to deeds. For then perhaps in a little while they would become less sophistical, and less absurd as bizarre word-jugglers, if I may be allowed to use a ridiculous expression about a ridiculous subject.

27.2. However, since they neglect all the paths of righteousness, and look only to this one point, namely, which of the propositions submitted to them shall they bind or loose, like professional wrestlers in the theatres – you know, not that kind of wrestling match in which the victory is won according to the rules of the sport, but rather the sort that is set up to deceive the eyes of an ignorant audience and to catch applause. Every market place, therefore must buzz with their talking; and every dinner party has to be worried to death with silly chat and boredom; and every festival must be made unfestive and full of dejection, and every occasion of mourning needs to be consoled by an even greater calamity, namely their syllogisms. Every women's quarters, formerly accustomed to simplicity, is now thrown into confusion and robbed of its flower of modesty by the torrent of their words. Well, I might tell you, this is an intolerable evil and an insufferable state of affairs. Our Great Mystery is in danger of being made a thing of small account. Well then, let these spies bear with us, moved as we are with fatherly compassion, and as holy Jeremiah says, "torn in our hearts." Let them bear with us so far as not to give too savage a reception to our oration upon this subject; and let them (if indeed they are able to), restrain their tongues for a short while and lend us their ears. But whatever the case may be, you shall suffer no loss tonight. For either we shall have spoken in the ears of those ready to hear, and our words will bear some fruit, namely offer an advantage to you (since the sower sows a good word into every kind of mind; and those which are good and fertile will bear fruit), or else you will leave us, scorning this discourse of ours as you have scorned that of others, and may draw from it further material for contradiction and mockery of our party, upon which you can feast yourselves even more. And do not be astonished if I speak a language which is strange to you and contrary to your custom, you who profess to know everything and to teach everything in too impetuous and prolix a manner (for I will spare your feelings and not say that it is an ignorant and rash style).

27.3. My friends, it does not pertain to everyone to philosophize about God; no, certainly not to everyone. The subject is not so cheap and low; and I might add, nor is it a suitable topic to lay before every audience, nor at any time, nor in relation to all aspects of the theme; for it should be done only on certain occasions, and before certain persons, and within certain limits.

I say not to everyone, because such discourse is permitted only to those who have been proven, and are validated masters in meditation, and who have been previously purified in soul and body, or at the very least are in the state of being purified. For the impure to touch the pure is, we may safely say, not safe at all, just as it is unsafe to fix weak eyes upon the sun's rays. And what is the permitted occasion? It is when we are free from all external defilement or disturbance, and when that power which rules within us is not confused with vexatious or erring images; like persons mixing up good writing with bad, or filth with the sweet odors of perfumes. For in order to know God it is necessary to be truly at rest; and then when we can find the appropriate time, to see where lies the royal highway of divine matters. And who are the permitted persons? Those to whom the subject is of real concern, and not those who make it a matter of pleasant gossip, like any other topic, a chitchat for after the races, or the theatre, or a concert, or a dinner party, not to mention still lower occupations. To such men as these, idle jests and pretty contradictions about high subjects are a part of their amusement.

27.4. Next, on what subjects and to what extent may we philosophize? On matters within our reach, and to such an extent as the mental power and grasp of our audience may extend. Go no further, because just as excessively loud sounds can injure the hearing, or excess of food can damage the body, or (if you like) as excessive burdens beyond our strength can injure those who bear them, or excessive rains can damage the earth; so too, they run the risk of being pressed down and overburdened by the stiffness (if I may use this expression) of the arguments and can even lose what strength they once started out with.

27.5. Now, I am not saying that it is not important to remember God at all times. I must not be misunderstood on that score, or I shall be having these nimble and quick people down upon me again. For we ought to think of God even more often than we draw our breath; and if the expression is permissible, we ought to do nothing else. Yes, I am one of those who entirely approve that text which bids us meditate day and night, to pray "evening, morning and noontide," and so praise the Lord at all times; or, to use Moses' words, "when we lie down, or rise up, or walk by the wayside," or whatever else we are doing; and by this recollection we shall be molded in purity. So it is not the continual remembrance of God that I would hinder, but only a continuous talking about God. Not that even this in itself is wrong, but only when it is unseasonable talk; not that all teaching is wrong, but only that which lacks moderation. Even in regard to sweet honey, too much and too often can make us sick. As Solomon says (and I agree), "there is a season for every thing," and that which is good ceases to be good if it is not done in a good way; just as a flower is quite out of season in winter, and just as man's clothing does not look right on a woman, or vice versa. Just as uproarious laughter would be seriously out of place at a funeral, or bitter tears shed at a party. Shall we in this case of theology alone disregard the issue of the proper time, a matter in which most of all, the issue of due season should be respected? Surely not, my friends and brethren (for I will still call you my brethren, even though you do not behave like brothers). Let us not think that, and let us not try, like hot tempered and hard mouthed horses, to throw off our rider who is Reason, or buck Reverence, which keeps us within due limits, or run far away from the Hippodrome's turning post; but rather let us philosophize within our proper bounds, and not be carried away into Egypt, or be swept down into Assyria, and let us not "sing the Lord's song in a strange land," by which I mean in front of any kind of audience, strangers or kindred, hostile or friendly, kindly or the opposite, who watch what we do with too obsessive a care, and would like the spark of whatever is wrong in us to burst into flame, and who secretly desire to kindle and fan it so as to raise the blaze to heaven with their breath and make it higher than that Babylonian flame which burned up everything around it. For since their strength hardly lies in their own [pagan] dogmas, they have to hunt for contradictions in our weak points. And therefore they apply themselves to our (shall I say "misfortunes" or "failings") like flies to wounds. But at least let us determine to be no longer ignorant of what we do, or pay too little attention to the concept of due order in these matters. And if it is not possible to put an end to the existing hostility, let us at least agree upon this point: that we will utter Mysteries under our breath, and speak of holy things in a holy manner, and that we will not cast before profane ears that which ought not be uttered, or give evidence that we possess less gravity than those who worship the demons, and attach themselves to shameful fables and deeds. For the pagans would sooner give their blood to the uninitiated than their secret words. But let us recognize that, just as is the case in relation to dress and diet and laughter and demeanor, where there is a certain decorum that applies, so there is also in relation to speech and silence. Indeed, among so many titles and powers of God, we pay the highest honor to "The Word." For this reason let even our disputations be kept within bounds.

27.6. But why should someone who is a hostile listener to such words as these be allowed to hear about the generation of God, or his creation, or how God was made out of things which had no existence, or of terms like section, analysis and division in the Godhead? Why should we make our accusers into our judges? Why should we put swords into the hands of our enemies? How do you think the arguments about such subjects would be received by the likes of those who think there is nothing wrong with adulterers or paedophiles, the likes of those who worship their passions and can conceive of nothing more lofty than their bodily desires? Types who until very recently were still setting up idols in their houses, and worshipping gods who were also famous for their filthy deeds. Would such people not hear and understand us solely from a material standpoint, in a shameful and ignorant way, and only in the sense to which they are familiar with such terms? Would such a person not make our theology a defense for the conduct of his own gods and his own passions? For if we Christians misuse these terms in a reckless way it will be a long time before we shall be able to persuade them to accept our philosophy. And if our hearers are the type who like to invent evil things, surely they would jump at the chance to grasp at the opportunity? This is what is likely to happen when we engage in a contest. This is what is likely to happen to those who fight for the Word, but use means other than the Word approves. For they are like the deranged, who set their own house on fire, or maul their own children, or claim that they do not recognize their own parents, but look on them as strangers.

27.7. So first let us put out of the conversation those [pagans] who are strangers to it. Let us send the great legion on its way to the abyss in the herd of swine. Now, the next thing to do is to look to ourselves, and polish our theological self to beauty like a statue. The first point to be considered is this: What is this great rivalry of speech and endless talking among us? What is this new disease of insatiability? Why have we tied our hands and armed our tongues? We have stopped praising our common values of hospitality, and brotherly love, and conjugal affection, and virginity. We have stopped admiring liberality to the poor, or the chanting of Psalms, or nightlong vigils, or spiritual tears. We have neglected the mastery of the body by fasting, and the ascent to God by prayer. We have failed to subjugate the worse to the better (I mean the dust to the spirit) as the wise would do, who hold a correct view about the synthetic nature of humanity. We have stopped making our life a preparation for death; and have neglected the task of the mastery of our passions out of our mindfulness of heavenly nobility. We have not tamed our anger when it swells and rages, or our pride that leads us to a fall. We have not moderated our unreasonable grief, or set a bound on our pleasures and salacious laughter. We have not disciplined our eyes, or our insatiable ears, or excessive talk, and our absurd thoughts. We have not guarded against all the occasions which the Evil One uses against us from sources within ourselves, in order to bring upon us that death that comes "through the windows," as holy Scripture says; that is, through the senses. Far from it in fact; for we do the very opposite, and we have given liberty to the external passions, just as kings, in honor of a victory, give free pardons on the condition that the parties attach themselves to their side. But then the passions make their assault upon

God even more boldly, and more impiously. And we give them an evil reward for their bad behavior, license of tongue in return for their impiety.

27.8. Even so, you wordy dialectician, I will ask you one small question, and as God said to Job, giving divine admonitions through whirlwind and cloud: "I expect you to answer me." It is this: Are there many mansions in God's house, as you have heard, or only one? Of course, you will admit that there are many, and not one only. Now, I ask you, Are they all to be filled, or only some of them? leaving some empty, and prepared to no purpose? Of course, you will say, all will be filled, for nothing which has been done by God, can be in vain. In that case can you tell me what you consider this Mansion to be? Is it the rest and glory which is in store there for the Blessed, or is it something else? No, you say, nothing else? Since we are in agreement upon this point, let us further examine another issue. Is there anything that wins these Mansions (as I think there is) or is there nothing that can merit them? Certainly there is, you say. Then what is it? Is it not that there are various modes of conduct, and various purposes, one leading one way, another a different way, according to the proportion of faith, and these we call ways? And should each one of us travel along all (if that were possible) or just along some of these ways; or at least travel along as many of them as we can? It seems to me that even if we cannot manage all of them at least it would be an excellent thing to travel along one way in as excellent a manner as possible. What is that you say: I am right in my supposition? In that case I ask you when you hear that there is only one way, and that it is a very narrow one, what do you make of this term? Does it suggest to you that there is only one way that is truly excellent? I think that it is indeed a single way, even thought it might be divided into several parts. It is narrow because it is difficult, and because it is walked by comparatively few compared with the crowds that walk along the road of wickedness. You think the same too, you say? Well, then, good friend, if this is the case, why do you condemn our party's doctrine for a certain intellectual poverty, and then insist on rushing headlong down the road of arguments and speculations, though I would call it a road of frivolities and nonsenses? Let Paul himself correct you with those bitter reproaches he raises after he had listed the graces in his Letter when he says: "So are all to be Apostles? Are all to be Prophets?"

27.9. Well enough of that. Let us suppose you are a superior person, superior even to the superior, even above the very clouds, even (if you insist) one who can look upon things invisible and listen to things ineffable; someone who has ascended in the train of Elijah, and who in Moses' footsteps has been found worthy of the vision of God, or like Paul has been lifted up into heaven. Then why would you want to form the rest of your companions into saints in the space of one single day, and ordain them as theologians as if you were breathing learning into them, or making them seminar participants in regard to oracles they cannot comprehend? Why do you entangle the weak in your spider's web, as if this were something great and wise? Why stir up a hornet's nest against the Faith? Why suddenly flood us with dialectics, as the old fables tell us about the inundation of the giants? Why have you collected together a torrent of all the frivolous and effeminate class of men, like a rabble, and having made them more effeminate by flattery, formed a new workshop, cleverly making a harvest for your school on the basis of their lack of understanding? Will you deny that this is the truth of the matter? And are my other points not relevant to you either? Is your tongue master come what may – so that you cannot restrain the birthpangs of your speech? Well, if so, you can find many other honorable subjects for discussion. Turn your disease of loquacity to these topics with some advantage. Attack the topic of Pythagorean silence, or that of Orphic beans, or the latest style of: "The Teacher Said." Hold forth about the ideas of Plato, and the trans-migrations and paths of our souls, and their reminiscences, or even the unlovely loves of the soul for lovely bodies. Attack the atheism of Epicurus if you like, and his atomic theory and his far-from-philosophic pleasure principle; or Aristotle's petty ideas on Providence, and his artificial system, or his discourses about the mortality of the soul, and his general humanitarianism. If you need to, attack the superciliousness of the Stoics, or the greed and vulgarity of the Cynics. Attack the doctrine of the "Bathos and the Pleroma" (what a load of nonsense there!), and all the details about the gods and their sacrifices, and the idols and the demons, whether beneficent or malignant, or all the tricks that people play with regard to divination, either the evoking of the gods or spirits, and the power of the stars. But if these topics strike you as unworthy of discussion, being rather petty and already often refuted, and you have to hold your ground and seek to satisfy your ambition, then even so allow me to provide you with some good paths to follow up. Why not philosophize about the world or numerous worlds; about matter; about soul; about natures endowed with reason, good or bad; about resurrection, about judgment, about reward, or about the sufferings of Christ. For in these subjects if you are able to hit the mark it would prove very useful, but if you miss it then it would not involve you in danger.

But with respect to God himself, know this – we can have converse as long as we are in this world only in a very small degree; afterwards, it may turn out to be a matter more perfectly apprehended, in the same Lord Jesus Christ, to whom be glory for ever. Amen.

St. Gregory of Nazianzus, Oration 28: The Second Theological Oration

28.1. In the former oration I set out clearly what sort of character the theologian ought to have, and on what kind of subjects he should philosophize, and also when, and to what extent, he should do this. We concluded that a theologian ought to be as pure as possible so that that "Light can be apprehended by light"; and that he ought to consort with serious men, so that his word will not be fruitless, falling on unfruitful soil. The proper "when" for all this is when we have interior calm, detached from the whirl of outward things; so that we will not lose our breath like madmen in whirl; and the "extent" to which we may go is that limit to which we have ourselves advanced, or to which we are advancing. Since this is the case, and we have made a start in ploughing the field of theology (so as not to sow upon thorns), and since we have leveled the ground (being shaped by Holy Scripture and shaping others in it), then now let us enter upon theological questions proper. We place at the head of our concerns: the issue of Father, Son and Holy Spirit; so that the Father may be well pleased, and the Son may help us, and the Holy Spirit may inspire us; or rather so that one illumination may come upon us from the One God, who is one in diversity, and diverse in his unity, which is a wonder to start with.

28.2. I am eager to climb the mountain. Or to speak more truly, I long so much to enter inside the Cloud, and hold converse with God (for so God commands it), but I am at the same time afraid; the one because of my hope and the other because of my weakness. If anyone is an Aaron, let him go up with me, and let him stand near, being ready, if it must be so, to remain outside the Cloud. But if anyone is a Nadad or an Abihu, or belongs to the Order of the Elders, let him ascend by all means, but let him stand afar off, according to the quality of his purification. If anyone belongs to the multitude who are unworthy of this height of contemplation, and if they are entirely defiled, then he should not approach at all, for it would be dangerous for such a man. But if a person is at least temporarily purified, let him remain below and listen only to the voice, and the trumpet crash, and the simple words of piety, and let him see the Mountain smoking and flashing, at once a source of terror and of wonderment to those who cannot ascend. But if any person is an evil and savage beast, and altogether incapable of taking in the subject matter of contemplation and theology, let them not lurk malignantly and violently in their wild dens, trying to leap out and seize some poor dogma or saying, and tear sound doctrine to pieces by their misrepresentations. But let them stand far off, and withdraw from the holy mountain altogether, or else they shall be stoned and crushed, and shall perish miserably in their wickedness. For sound orations are just like stones for those who are like wild beasts. If such a person is like a leopard let him die with his spots. If he is a ravening and roaring lion, seeking for something to devour from our souls or from our words; or a wild boar, trampling the precious and translucent pearls of the truth under foot; or a foreign Arabian wolf, or one that is even keener than any of these in tricks of argument; or a fox, that is a treacherous and faithless soul, changing its shape according to circumstances or need, feeding on dead or putrid bodies, or on little vineyards when the larger ones have eluded them; or any other carnivorous beast, rejected by the Law as unclean for food or enjoyment: in these cases our discourse must withdraw from such as those and be engraved on solid tables of stone. This is necessary on both sides: because the Law is in part visible, and in part hidden; the one part belonging to the mass who remain below, the other to the few who press upward into the mountain's heights.

28.3. Well, now what has happened to me, dear friends, and initiates, and fellow-lovers of the truth? I was running to lay hold on God, and so I went up into the mountain, and drew aside the curtain of the Cloud, and entered away from matter and material things, and as far as I could I withdrew within myself. But then when I looked up, I could only with great difficulty see the hind parts of God; although I was sheltered by the Rock, that is the Word that was made flesh for us. And when I looked a little closer, I saw, not the First and Unmingled Nature, known only to Itself (to the Trinity, I mean); not that nature which dwells within the first veil, and is hidden by the Cherubim; but only that Nature, which at last reaches out even to us. And that is, as far as I can make out, the Divine Majesty, or as holy David calls it, the Glory, which is manifested among the creatures which it has itself produced and governs. For these are the "hind parts" of God, which he leaves behind him, as tokens of Himself like the shadows and reflection of the sun in the water, which show the sun to our weak eyes, because we cannot look at the sun itself, since its unmediated light is too strong for our power of perception. This is the way, therefore, that you ought to speak about God; even if you were a Moses who was "a god to Pharaoh"; even if you were caught up like Paul into the Third Heaven, and had heard ineffable words; even if you were raised above them both, and exalted to an Angelic or Archangelic stature and dignity. For even if something was entirely heavenly, or even above heaven, and stood far higher in nature and nearer to God than we are, even so it would be much further removed from God and from the complete comprehension of his Nature, than it would be lifted above our complex, humble, and earth-declining composition.

28.4. And so, we must begin again in this manner. It is difficult to conceive of God; but to define him in words is an impossibility, as one of the Greek theological teachers taught, not without some degree of craftiness, as it appears to me; with the intention that he might be thought to have apprehended God. For note how he says that it is a hard thing to do; and yet he tries to escape being convicted of ignorance because he speaks of the impossibility of giving expression to the apprehension. But my opinion of the matter is that it is impossible to express God, and still more impossible to conceive of him. For whatever can be conceived can partly be clarified by language, if not completely then at any rate imperfectly, to any one who is not quite deprived of his hearing, or utterly slothful in understanding. But to comprehend the whole of so great a subject as the deity is quite impossible and impracticable, not merely to the utterly careless and ignorant, but even to those who are highly exalted, and who love God. Indeed it is impossible to any created nature; seeing that the darkness of this world and the thick covering of the flesh is an obstacle to the full understanding of the truth. I do not know whether it is the same with the higher natures and purer Intelligences [of the angels] which because of their nearness to God, and because they are illumined with all of his light, may possibly see, if not the whole reality, then at any rate, may see more perfectly and distinctly than we do; some of them perhaps more, and some less than others, in proportion to their rank.

28.5. But enough has been said on this point. Now what really matters is not only the "Peace of God which passes all understanding and knowledge," and not just the things that God has promised for the righteous, which "Eye has not seen, nor ear heard, nor mind conceived" except in a very small degree, and not even the accurate knowledge of the Creation. For even in regard to the latter I would have you know that you possess only a shadow when you hear those words, "I will consider the heavens, the work of your hands, the moon and the stars," and all their fixed order. Something was not indicated at that time, but was promised for the future. But far in advance of all these things is that nature which is above them, and out of which they spring, the Incomprehensible and Boundless nature; and this not in respect of the fact that God is, but rather in relation to how God is. But our preaching is not empty, and our faith is not vain, and this is not the doctrine we are proclaiming; so I would not have you take our candid statement [about the limits of knowledge] as a starting point for a quibbling denial of God's existence, or an arrogant assertion of agnosticism. For it is one thing to be persuaded of the existence of a reality, and quite another to know what it consists of.

28.6. Now our very eyes and the Law of Nature itself teach us that God exists and that he is the efficient and maintaining cause of all things: our eyes, because they fall on visible objects, and see them in beautiful stability and progress, immovably moving and revolving if I may so describe it; and Natural Law, because through these visible things and their order, one is able to reason back to their Author. For how could this Universe have come into being or could it have been composed, unless God had called it into existence, and sustained it? For every one who sees a beautifully made lyre, and considers the skill with which it has been fitted together and arranged, or who hears its melody, will think directly of the lyre-maker, or the lyre-player, and will mentally reflect on him even though he might not know him by sight. In the same way we have a manifestation of the one who made and moves and preserves all created things, even though he might not be comprehended by the human mind. It would be a foolish person indeed who would not follow us in pursuing these natural proofs; but not even this argument about what we have imagined or postulated, or which reason has sketched out for us, actually proves the existence of God. And if you can grasp the significance of this, then consider: how is it possible to demonstrate the being of God? Who could ever reach this extremity of wisdom? Who was ever deemed worthy of so great a gift? Who has opened the mouth of his mind so as to draw in the Spirit, in order to take in God by means of the one who searches all things, even the deep things of God? Who is there that no longer needs to progress, since he already possesses the extreme object of all desire, and that reality to which all societal life and all the keen perception of the best of all men strains after?

28.7. For if you rely on the approximations of human reason what will you conceive the Deity to be? Or where will human reason carry you, most philosophic of men and finest of theologians, you who boast of your familiarity with the Unlimited? Tell me: is he a body? If so how can he be the Infinite and Limitless; the Formless, Intangible, and Invisible? Are such things the attributes of a body? It would be arrogant to say so: for this is not how we describe a body. Or would you say that God has a body, but not these attributes? Well that would be foolishness to imagine the Deity should possess nothing more than we have. For how can he be an object of worship if he is circumscribed? Or how could he escape being made of constitutive elements, and therefore subject to being reduced into them again, or even altogether dissolved? For every compound is a starting point of strife, and strife of separation, and separation of dissolution. But dissolution is something altogether foreign to God and to that Primary Nature. Accordingly, there can be no separation in God, so that there may be no dissolution; and no strife so that there may be no separation; and no composition so that there may be no strife. In short it follows that there must be no body [in God], that there may be no composition. In this way the argument is established by going back from the last principle to the first.

28.8. However, if God only partly contains and is partly contained, then how shall we maintain the truth that the divinity pervades and fills all things, as it is written of him: "Do not I fill heaven and earth? says the Lord," and again: "The Spirit of the Lord fills the whole world?" For either God will occupy an empty Universe, and so all things will have vanished for us, with this result, that we shall have insulted God by making him into a body, and by robbing him of all the things he has made; or else he will in fact be a body contained within other bodies, which is impossible; or he will be enfolded in them, or contrasted with them, for example as liquids are mixed, and one divides and is divided by another, which is a view which is even more absurd and feeble than the atoms of Epicurus. In short, this argument concerning the divine embodiedness will fall through, and itself will lack any body and have no solid basis at all. But if we are to assert that God is immaterial (as for example that he is that "Fifth Element" which some have imagined), and that he is carried round in a heavenly circular movement, then let us assume that he is immaterial, and that he may even be that Fifth Element; and, let him even be bodiless as well, in accordance with the independent drift and arrangement of their argument; for I will not presently differ with them on this point. In that case I ask them in what respect will God be one of those things which are in movement and agitation? For I will say nothing about the insult involved in making the Creator subject to the same movement as that governing creatures, or making the One that carries all (I presume they would allow this point) one with those whom he carries. Moreover, what is the force that moves your Fifth Element, and what is it that moves all things? And if you have an answer tell me what is the force that moves that; and then the force that moves that too? And so on *ad infinitum*. And how can God help being altogether contained in space if he is subject to motion? But if they assert that he is something other than this Fifth Element; suppose it is an angelic nature that they attribute to him, how will they show that the Angels are corporeal, or what sort of bodies they have? And in that case how far could God, to whom the Angels are said to minister, be considered as superior to the Angels? And if he is above them, there would again be introduced an irrational swarm of bodies, and a depth of nonsense, that has no possible foundation on which to stand.

28.9. For these reasons we see that God is not a body. For no inspired teacher has yet asserted or admitted such a notion, nor has the sentence of our own Council [of the Church] allowed it. Nothing then remains but to conceive of God as incorporeal. But this term incorporeal, though granted, does not yet set before us, or contain within itself God's essence, any more than the term Unbegotten, or Unoriginate, or Unchanging, or Incorruptible, or any other predicate which is used concerning God or in relation to him. For what effect is produced upon his being or his substance by the fact of his having no beginning, and his being incapable of change or limitation? Indeed, the whole question of God's being is still left open for the further consideration and exposition of whoever it is who truly has the mind of God and is advanced in contemplation. Because to say "It is a body," or "It was begotten," is not enough to give a clear presentation to the mind of the various objects of which these predicates are used, and you will find that you must also express the subject about which you use these predicates, if you want to present the object of your thought clearly and adequately. For each of these predicates, corporeal, begotten, mortal, can be used in reference to a man, or a cow, or a horse. Well, in the same way, whoever is eagerly pursuing the question of the nature of the Self-Existent will not stop at saying what God is not, but must go on beyond what he is not, and say what he is. For it is easier to take in some single point than to go on disowning point after point in endless detail, in order, by the elimination of negatives and the assertion of positives, to arrive at a comprehension of this subject. But someone who states what God is not, without going on to say what he is, acts much in the same way as that person who, when asked how many twice five make, should answer: "Not two, nor three, nor four, nor five, nor twenty, nor thirty, nor in short any number below ten, nor any multiple of ten";

but would consistently never give the answer: "ten," or condescend to settle the mind of his questioner upon the firm ground of such an answer. In short, it is much easier, and much quicker, to show what a thing is not from what it is, than to demonstrate what it is by stripping it of what it is not. And this point is surely evident to all.

28.10. Now since we have ascertained that God is incorporeal, let us proceed a little further with our examination. Is God nowhere or somewhere? For if he is nowhere, then some person of a very inquiring turn of mind might ask: How is it then that God can even exist? For if the non-existent is nowhere, then that which is nowhere is also perhaps non-existent. But if God is somewhere, then he must either be in the Universe, or above the Universe. And if he is in the Universe, then he must either be in some part of it, or in the whole. If in some part, then he will be circumscribed by that part which is less than himself; but if everywhere, then he will be circumscribed by something which is greater and more extensive, I mean the Universal, which contains the particular; that is if the Universe is to be contained by the Universe, and no place is to be free from circumscription. This follows if God is contained in the Universe. And besides, where was God before the Universe was created, for this is a point of no little difficulty? But if he is above the Universe, is there nothing to distinguish this from the Universe, and where is this above situated? And how could this transcendence and that which is transcended be distinguished in thought, if there is no limit now to divide and define them? Is it not necessary that there must be some measure to mark off the Universe from that which is above the Universe? And what could this be but a place, which we have already rejected? For I have not yet brought forward the point that God would be altogether circumscript, if he were even comprehensible in thought: for comprehension is one form of circumscription.

28.11. Now, why have I gone into all this? And perhaps done it too exactly for most people to listen to, and why did I do so in the modern style of theological orations which despise noble simplicity, and have introduced a crooked and intricate style? I did it so that the tree may be known by its fruits; I mean, that the darkness which is at work in such teachings may be known by the obscurity of the arguments. For my purpose in doing this was not to get credit for myself for amazing utterances, or because of my excessive wisdom demonstrated through tying knots and resolving difficulties (wasn't this the miraculous gift of Daniel?), but instead to make clear that point at which my argument has aimed from the very outset. And what is it? Namely that the divine nature cannot be apprehended by human reason, and that we cannot even represent to ourselves all its greatness. And this does not derive from envy, since envy is far removed from the divine nature which is passionless, and purely good, and Lord of all; and especially not envy of that which is the most honorable of all his creatures. For what does the Word prefer to rational and vocal creatures? Why, even their very existence is a proof of God's supreme goodness. Nor is the divine incomprehensibility for the sake of his own glory and honor, since he is the Complete One, and his possession of his own glory and majesty do not depend upon the impossibility of anyone approaching him. For it is utterly sophistical and foreign to the character, I will not say of God, but of any moderately good man, who has any right ideas about himself, to seek his own supremacy by throwing a hindrance in the way of another.

28.12. But whether there are other causes for the divine incomprehensibility, let those judge who are nearer God than we are, and who are eye witnesses and spectators of his unsearchable judgments; if there are any who are so eminent in virtue, and who walk in the paths of the Infinite, as the saying goes. However, as far as our own limits apply, who measure with our little measure things so hard to be understood, perhaps one reason for it is to prevent us from too readily throwing away the possession because it was so easily come by. For people cling tightly to that which they have acquired with much labor; but whatever they acquire easily they quickly throw away, because it seems it can be easily recovered. And so the divine incomprehensibility is turned into a blessing, at least to all sensible people, so that this blessing should not be too easy. Or perhaps it is in order that we may not share the fate of Lucifer, who fell; so that we might not receive the full light and then stiffen our pride against the Lord Almighty, and suffer a most pitiable fall from the eminence we had attained. Or perhaps it may be to give a greater reward hereafter to those who have been purified here below, and have exercised long patience in respect of their desired goal, because of their labors and their glorious life. And so, this darkness of the body has been placed between us and God, like the ancient cloud placed between the Egyptians and the Hebrews; and this is perhaps what is meant by "He made darkness his secret place," namely our dullness, and because of this only the few can see even a little. But as to this point, let those discuss it whose business it is; and let them ascend as far as possible in the examination. To us who are (as Jeremiah says), "prisoners of the earth," and covered with the denseness of carnal nature, we can at least know this as true, that just as it is impossible for a person to step over their own shadow, however fast they may move (for the shadow will always move on as fast as it is being overtaken) or, just as it is impossible for the eye to draw near to visible objects apart from the intervening air and light, or just as a fish cannot glide around outside the water; so too it is quite impossible for those who are still in the body to be conversant with the objects of pure ideation which is altogether separate from bodily objects. For something in our own environment will always be creeping in, even when the mind has most fully detached itself from visible reality, and recollected itself, and is attempting to apply itself to those invisible matters which are most akin to itself.

28.13. Let me demonstrate this to you as follows: Spirit, Fire, and Light, Love, Wisdom, and Righteousness, Mind and Reason – and the like, are they not all suitable titles for the Primary Nature? And so, can you conceive of Spirit apart from motion and diffusion; or conceive of Fire without the concept of fuel, or its upward motion, its proper color and form? Or conceive of Light unmingled with air, or detached from that which is, we may say, its father and source [the sun]? And how do you conceive of a mind? Is it not something inherent in a person and not freestanding; and are not thoughts its movements, whether silent or spoken? And as for Reason, how else can you imagine it other than its silent state within us, or its expressed state? And if you reflect on Wisdom, what is this other than the habit of mind which you recognize, which is concerned with either divine or human contemplations? And as for Justice and Love, are they not praiseworthy dispositions, the one opposed to injustice, the other to hate, and at one time intensifying themselves, at another relaxed, now taking possession of us, now leaving us alone; and in a word, making us what we are, yet also changing us as colors change bodies? Or should we perhaps leave all these matters aside and consider the Deity absolutely, as best we can, collecting a fragmentary perception of what it is from its images? What is this subtle thing, therefore, which is of these things, and yet is not these things? or how can that Unity which is in its Nature incomposite and incomparable, still be all of these, and each one of them, perfectly? In this way our mind falters and faints, unable to transcend corporeal things so as to consort with the incorporeal, stripped of the clothing of corporeal ideas, as long as it has to look through its innate weakness at things that are far above its strength. For every rational nature longs for God and for the First Cause, but is unable to grasp him, for the reasons I have mentioned. And so, faint with the desire, and being restless and impatient with its disability, the mind tries a second way: either to study visible things, and out of some of them to fashion a god (a poor contrivance, for in what respect and to what extent can that which is seen ever be higher and more godlike than that which does the seeing, that the one should worship the other?) or else through the beauty and order of visible things to attain to that which is above sight; but not to suffer the loss of God through the magnificence of visible things.

28.14. Because of this, some have made the Sun into a god, and others have done so with the Moon; others have deified the host of stars, or the heaven itself with all its hosts, and have attributed to them the guiding of the Universe, according to the quality or quantity of their movement. Others have deified the elements: earth, air, water, and fire, because of their useful nature, since without them human life cannot possibly exist. Yet others have worshipped random visible objects, setting up the most beautiful things they saw as their gods. And there are others who worship pictures and images, beginning with their own ancestors (for this is what the more affectionate and earthly types did) so as to honor the departed with memorials; but afterwards men of later generations honored and worshipped even the images of strangers who were separated from them by a long interval. They did this through ignorance of the Primal Nature, subsequently observing these traditional honors as lawful and necessary; for custom when confirmed by time has been held to be Law. And I think that some who were courtiers of arbitrary power and who extolled bodily strength and admired beauty, made a god in time out of various people whom they honored, perhaps using some fable or other to help on their masquerade.

28.15. And those who were most subject to passion actually deified their passions, or honored them among the gods; Anger and Blood-thirstiness, Lust and Drunkenness, and every similar wickedness; for they made out of this an ignoble and unjust excuse for their own sins. And some of these gods they left on earth, and some they hid beneath the earth (this being the only sign of wisdom they still retained!) and others they raised up to heaven. What a ridiculous carving up of an inheritance! Then they gave to each of these concepts the name of some god or demon, by the authority and private judgment of their error, and set up statues whose costliness was a snare, and they thought they would honor them with blood and the steam of sacrifices, and sometimes even by most shameful actions, with frenzies and manslaughter. Even so, such honors were the fitting due of such gods. And even up to this time men have degraded themselves by worshipping monsters, and four-footed animals, and other most vile and absurd creeping things, and have made an offering to them of the glory of God. The result is: it is not an easy matter to decide whether we ought to despise most the worshippers, or the objects of their worship. Probably the worshippers are far the most contemptible, for though they were of a rational nature, and had received grace from God, even so they set up what was far worse as if it were the better part. All this was the trick of the Evil One, who abused good to an evil purpose, as in most of his evil deeds. For he laid hold of their desire as it wandered round in search of God, so that he could distort the power to himself, and steal the longing, leading it by the hand, like a blind man asking his way; and he hurled some down and scattered them in one direction and some in another, yet into the same pit of death and destruction.

28.16. This was what they did, then. But as for us, it was reason that received us in our desire for God, and reason that gave us the sense of how impossible it was to be without a leader and guide. It was reason that made us apply ourselves to visible matters and engage with the things which have been established since the beginning; and it was reason that would not stay within these limits either. For Wisdom refused to grant sovereignty to things which are, as our observation could tell us, of equal rank with us. By such observations it leads us to that which is above these things, the very source from which being is given to such things as these. For what is it that first ordered things in heaven and things on earth, and those things which pass through the air, and those which live in the water; or rather the things which subsisted before all of these, namely heaven and earth, air and water? Who was it that mingled these, and distributed them? What is it that each has in common with the other, and what constitutes their mutual dependence and agreement? For I would highly commend any man, even though he were a pagan, who could tell me what it was that gave movement to these things, and which drives their ceaseless and unhindered motions? Is it not the maker of all things who implanted reasoned order in them all, in accordance with which the Universe is moved and controlled? Is it not the one who made them and brought them into being? For we cannot attribute such a power to the Accidental. For if we suppose that its very existence is accidental, how can we at all account for its order? And even if, for argument's sake, we grant you the idea of accidental: how will you account for its preservation and protection in accordance with the terms of its first creation? Do such things belong to the Accidental, or to something else? Surely not to the Accidental. But what can this "Something Else" be, other than God? So it is, that reason which proceeds from God, which is implanted in all of us from the beginning and which is the first law in us, and is bound up in all of us, leads us all up to God through visible things. Let us begin afresh, then, and reason this matter out.

28.17. No human being has ever yet discovered or can ever discover what God is in nature and essence, Whether this is something that will ever be discovered is a question which whoever wishes to can examine and decide at leisure. In my opinion the answer will be discovered when that within us which is godlike and divine, I mean our mind and reason, shall have mingled with its Like, and the Image shall have ascended to the Archetype, of which it now has but the desire. And this I think is the solution of that vexed problem over the text: "We shall know even as we are known." But in our present life all that comes to us is merely a small effluence, that is a small effulgence, from a great

Light. In other words if anyone ever has known God, or has had the testimony of Scripture to his knowledge of God, we should understand such a person to have possessed a degree of knowledge which gave him the appearance of being more fully enlightened than another who did not enjoy that same degree of illumination; and this relative superiority is spoken of in terms suggestive that it were absolute knowledge: not because it is really such, but merely by comparison with the power of the other person.

28.18. So it was that Enoch is said to have "Hoped to call upon the name of the Lord." Here he is commended for his hope, not for the fact that he truly did know God, rather that he should call upon him. And Enoch was translated, but it is not yet clear whether this was because he already comprehended the Divine Nature, or in order that he might begin to comprehend it. And Noah's glory was that he was pleasing to God; he who was entrusted with the rescue of the whole world from the waters, or rather the rescue of the seeds of the world which escaped the Deluge in a small Ark. And Abraham, great Patriarch though he was, was justified by faith, and offered a strange victim, the type of the Great Sacrifice. Yet he did not see God as God, but rather gave food to him in the form of a man. He was approved because he worshipped to the extent that he was able to comprehend. And Jacob dreamed of a lofty ladder and a stairway of angels, and in a mystery anointed a pillar; perhaps to signify the Rock which was anointed for our sake. And thus he gave the name of the House of God [Bethel] to a place in honor of the one whom he saw; and he wrestled with God in human form (whatever this wrestling of God with a man may mean). Possibly it refers to the comparison of man's virtue with God's; for Jacob bore on his body the marks of the wrestling, denoting the defeat of the created nature. As the reward of his reverence he received a change of name; being called Israel instead of Jacob, a great and honorable title. Even so, neither he nor any one associated with him even to this day, of all the Twelve Tribes who were his children, could boast that he was able to comprehend the whole nature or the pure sight of God.

28.19. As far as Elijah was concerned neither the strong wind, nor the fire, nor the earthquake, as you can learn from the story, adumbrated the presence of God but only light breeze; and even this did not reveal his divine Nature. And who was this Elijah? No less than a man whom a chariot of fire took up to heaven, signifying the superhuman excellency of that righteous man. And are you not also amazed at Manoah the ancient Judge, or Peter the disciple of the latter days; for the one was unable to endure the sight even of an image representing God, for he said: "O wife, we are undone, for we have seen God"; speaking as though even a vision of God could not be grasped by human beings, let alone the Nature of God; and the other was unable to endure the presence of Christ in his boat and therefore begged him to depart, even though Peter was more zealous than the others for the knowledge of Christ, and received a blessing on this account, and was entrusted with the greatest gifts. What would you say about Isaiah or Ezekiel, who were eyewitnesses of very great mysteries, or about the other prophets; for the first saw the Lord of Sabaoth sitting on the Throne of Glory, and encircled and praised and hidden by the six-winged Seraphim, and was himself purged by the live coal, and thereby equipped for his prophetic office. And the other described the Cherubic Chariot of God, and the Throne set upon them, and the Firmament over it, as well as the One that showed himself in the Firmament, not to mention other voices, and powers, and mighty deeds.

And whether this was a daytime apparition, as such only visible to saints, or a reliable epiphany of the night, or an impression on the mind engaging the future as if it were the present, or whether it was some other ineffable form of prophecy, I cannot say; the God of the prophets is the One who knows, and those who have been so inspired. Even so, not one of these I have been talking about, or any of their like, ever stood before the Council and Essence of God, as it is written, or ever saw, or proclaimed the Nature of God.

28.20. If it had been allowed to Paul to speak of what the Third Heaven contained, and his own advance, or ascension, or assumption, there, perhaps we might know something more about God's Nature, if this was the mystery of the rapture. But since it was ineffable, we too must honor it by silence. But this much we should allow Paul to say about it: that "we know only in part and we prophesy in part." This, and many comparable statements, are the confessions of someone very advanced in knowledge, a great doctor and champion of the truth, who constantly proves that it was Christ speaking in him. This is why it is his opinion that all knowledge on earth is "through a glass darkly," since it is based upon little images of the truth. Now (and I hope I don't appear to anyone as being too careful or over-anxious about the examination of this matter), perhaps it was about this same exact thing that the Word himself spoke when he intimated that there were things which could not now be borne, but which should be borne and cleared up hereafter, and which John the Forerunner of the Word and great herald of the Truth declared that even the entire world could not contain.

28.21. The fact is the Truth, and the Word, is altogether full of difficulty and obscurity; and when we pursue the knowledge of the Self-Existent by means of that terribly small instrument of human reason, then we are undertaking a great work indeed. This is because we have to do it in company with our senses, certainly not apart from them, and these carry us here and there and often lead us into error, since we apply ourselves to searching after things which can only be grasped by the mind, and we are unable to approximate any more closely to the truth by means of encountering naked reality with naked intelligence, and thus molding the mind by reference to its ideas. Now the subject of God is harder to come at, to the degree that it is more perfect than any other; and it is open to more objections, and their solution is more demanding. For every objection, however small it may be, blocks and hinders the course of our argument, cutting off its further advance, just like men who suddenly rein in horses which are in full flight, and turn them right round by the unexpected shock. So it was that Solomon, that wisest of all men, whether of those who lived before him or in his own time, to whom God gave breadth of heart and a profundity of contemplation, more abundant than the sand, even he found that the more he entered into the depth, the more dizzy he became, and so it was that he declared that the summit of wisdom was the discovery of how very far off she was from him. Paul also tried to arrive at (I will not say the Nature of God, for this he knew was utterly impossible, but only) the judgments of God. But he could find no way forward, and no resting place on the ascent, and since his mind's earnest searching after knowledge could not end in any definite conclusion, since new and unattained aspects were being continually disclosed to him (a wonderful thing too – for that has been my experience!), Paul closed his discourse with astonishment, and called it "the riches of God, and the depth," confessing how unsearchable were the judgments of God. He did this almost in the very words of David, who at one time called God's judgments "an immense depth" whose foundations could not be reached by measure or sense; and at another time said that God's knowledge of him and of his own constitution was "a cause of marvel," and of a greater force that he was possibly able to grasp.

28.22. In his words (Psalm 8) it would be a cause of wonderment even if he was to leave all else aside and consider only the nature and constitution of a human being, how we are composed, how we move, and how the mortal is compounded with the immortal; and we can add – how it is that I flow downwards, and yet am borne upwards; and how the soul is circumscribed; and how it gives life and shares in feelings; and how the mind is at once circumscribed and yet unlimited, dwelling within us and yet traveling over the Universe in swift motion and flow; how it is both received and imparted by word, and passes through air, and enters within all things; how it shares in sense, and yet closes itself off from sense? In fact even before we get to those questions we have to consider others such as: what was our first making and composition in the workshop of Nature? And what will be our last formation and completion? What is the meaning of our desire for nourishment and its imparting? And who brought us spontaneously to those first springs and sources of life? How is it that the body is nourished by food, and the soul by reason? What is the pull of nature, and the mutual relations between parents and children, that they should be held together by a spell of love? How is it that species are permanent, and are also different in their characteristics, although there are so many that their individual marks can hardly be described? How is it that the same animal can be both mortal and immortal; the first by the capacity of death, the second by the capacity of regeneration? For one departs, and another takes its place, just like the flow of a river, which is never still, yet ever constant. And we could discuss many more points concerning the different members and aspects of a human being, and their mutual adaptation both for utility and beauty; how some are connected and others disjoined; how some are more excellent and others less comely; how some are united and others divided, how some contain and others are contained, according to the law and reason of Nature. Many things could also be said about voices and ears. How is it that the voice is carried by the vocal organs, and received by the ears, and both are joined by the striking and resounding of the medium of air? Much too could be said about the eyes, which have an indescribable communion with visible objects, and which are moved in harmony solely by the will alone, and are affected in the same way as the mind. For the mind too, with comparable alacrity, is joined to the objects of its thought, as the eye is to the objects of sight. Many things could be said concerning the other senses, which are not so evidently foci of our rational powers. Much could be said about our rest in sleep, and the figments of dreams, or about memory and reminiscence; about calculation, and anger, and desire. In a word, so much could be said about all that sways this Microcosmos we call Man.

28.23. Shall I reckon up for you the differences of the other animals, both from us and from each other; their differences in terms of nature, reproduction, feeding patterns, region, temperament, and social habits? How is it, for example, that some are gregarious and others are solitary; some herbivorous and others carnivorous; some fierce and others tame; some fond of man and domesticated, others untamable and free? And some we might regard as bordering on reason and the power of learning, while others are altogether destitute of reason, and incapable of being taught. Some have fuller senses, others have less; some are immovable, and some have the power of walking; while some are very swift, and others very slow; some surpass in size or beauty, or in one or other of these respects; while others are very small or very ugly, or both; some are strong, and others are weak; some are good at self-defense, while others are timid and cunning, and yet others are devoid of all defense. Some are hardworking and thrifty, others altogether indolent and improvident. And before we address such points as these, how is it that some animals turned out as crawling things, and others were upright; some were attached to one spot, some amphibious; some delight in beauty and others are unadorned; some are married and some single; some temperate and others intemperate; some have numerous offspring and others not; some are long-lived and others have but short lives? It would be a weary discourse to go through all the rest of such details.

28.24. But consider this as well – look at the fishy tribe gliding through the waters, as if they were flying through the liquid element, and breathing its own air, but in trouble when they come in contact with our element, just as we are in the waters. Mark the habits and dispositions of the fish, their intercourse and their births, their size and their beauty, their affection for places, and their wanderings, their assemblings and departings, and their properties which so nearly resemble those of the animals that dwell on land. In some cases they dwell in community, but often there is a great contrast of properties, both in name and shape. And then consider the tribes of birds, and their varieties of form and color, both those which are voiceless and the songbirds too. What is the reason for their melody, and who gave them it? Who gave to the grasshopper the lute in his breast, and their songs and chirruping on the branches when they are moved by the sun to make their midday music, and sing among the groves, and escort the wayfarer with their melodies? Who wove the song for the swan when he spreads his wings to the breezes, and makes melody of their rustling? For I am not going to speak at all of contrived voices, and all the rest that art fakes up against the truth. From where does the peacock, that boastful Persian bird, get his love of beauty and of praise (for he is fully conscious of his own beauty), so that when he sees any one approaching, or when, as the saying goes, he wants to make a show before his hens, raising his neck and spreading his tail in circle around him, glittering like gold and studded with stars, he makes a spectacle of his beauty to his lovers with such pompous steps? Holy Scripture, indeed, admires the cleverness involved in women's weaving when it says: "Who gave to woman skill in weaving and cleverness in the art of embroidery?" And this is a skill that belongs to a living creature endowed with reason, and abundant in wisdom, which reaches up even to the things of heaven.

28.25. You see, my point is to make you stand in wonderment even at the natural knowledge of irrational creatures, and if you can, explain for me its cause. How is it that birds have for nests rocks and trees and roofs, and adapt them both for safety and beauty, suitable for the comfort of their chicks? Where do bees and spiders get their love of work and art from, by which the former plan their honeycombs, and join them together by hexagonal and co-ordinate tubes, and construct the foundation by means of a partition and an alternation of the angles with straight lines; doing all this, as is the truth of the matter, in such dark hives and obscure honeycombs; and the latter weave their intricate webs by such light and almost airy threads stretched in so many different ways, growing from almost invisible beginnings, to be at once a precious dwelling, and a trap for weaker creatures with a view to their enjoyment of food? What Euclid ever imitated these, while pursuing philosophical enquiries with lines that have no real existence, and wearying himself with demonstrations? From what Palamedes came the tactics, and (as the saying goes) the movements and configurations of cranes, and the systems of their movement in ranks and their complicated flight? Who were their Phidiæ and Zeuxides, and who were the Parrhasii and Aglaophons who knew how to draw and fashion such excessively beautiful things? What harmonious Gnossian chorus of Dædalus, ever wrought for a girl the highest pitch of beauty? What Cretan Labyrinth, hard to get through, hard to unravel, as the poets say, and continually crossing over itself through the tricks of its construction ever equalled this? For I will not speak of the ants' storehouses and their storekeepers, of their treasurings of wood in quantities, because of our time constraints, or all the other details which we know are told of their marches and leaders and the good order in all their works.

28.26. Now, if all this knowledge has come within your reach and you are familiar with these branches of science, then turn now and look at the differences of plants; up to the artistic fashion of the leaves, which is adapted both to give the utmost pleasure to the eye, and to be of the greatest advantage to the fruit. Look too at the variety and lavish abundance of fruits, and most of all at the wondrous beauty of such as are most necessary. And consider the power of roots, and juices, and flowers, and odors, for not only are they very sweet, but also serviceable as medicines; and consider the graces and qualities of their colors; or again the costly value, and the brilliant transparency of precious stones. For nature has set before you all things as in an abundant banquet free to all, both the necessities and the luxuries of life, in order that, if nothing else, you may at any rate know God by his benefits, and may be made wiser by your own sense of want than you were at first. Next, I pray you, traverse the length and breadth of earth, the common mother of all, and the gulfs of the sea bound together with one another and with the land, and the beautiful forests, and the rivers and springs abundant and perennial, not only of waters that are cold and fit for drinking, and on the surface of the earth; but also such as running beneath the earth, and flowing under caverns, are then forced out by a violent blast, and repelled, and then filled with heat by this violence of strife and repulsion, bursting out by little and little wherever they get a chance, and hence supplying our need of hot baths in many parts of the earth, and (in conjunction with the cold bath) offering us a cost-free and spontaneous healing. Tell me the origins and meanings of these things? What is this great web unfashioned by any artifice? These things are no less worthy of admiration, in respect of their mutual relations than when they are considered separately. How is it, for example, that the earth stands solid and unswerving? What is it supported on? What is it that props it up, or what does that rest upon in turn? For even reason has nothing that it can lean upon here, only on the Will of God. And how is it that part of the world is drawn up into mountain summits, and part laid down in plains, and all of this in so many different ways? And because the variations are individually small, the earth supplies our needs more liberally, and is made more beautiful by its variety; part being distributed into habitations, and part left uninhabited, namely all the great height of mountains, and the various clefts of its coast line cut off from it. Is not all this a clearest proof of the majestic working of God?

28.27. And with respect to the sea even if I did not marvel at its greatness, yet I should have marveled at its gentleness, in that although so loose an element it stands within its boundaries; and if not at its gentleness, yet surely at its greatness; but since I marvel at both things, I will praise the power that lies in both. What collected it? What bounded it? How is it raised and lulled to rest, as though respecting its neighbor earth? How does it receive all the rivers, and yet remain the same, through the very superabundance of its immensity, if that term be permissible? How does the boundary of the sea stand, even though it is only sand that holds in an element of such magnitude? Have your natural philosophers with all their knowledge of useless details anything to tell us? Those men I mean who really are endeavoring to measure the sea with a wineglass, and judge such mighty works by their own conceptions? Or shall I give the really scientific explanation of it from Scripture concisely, and yet more satisfactorily and truly than by the longest arguments? For there it says: "He has fenced around the face of the water with his command." This is the chain of fluid nature. And how does God bring upon it that Nautilus that inhabits the dry land [namely man] in such a little vessel, and with so small a breath of wind? Do you not stand in wonder at this? Is your mind not simply astonished? That Earth and Sea can be bound together by needs and commerce, and that things so widely separated by nature should be thus brought together into one for the sake of man? What are the first causes of springs? Seek out, my philosopher friend, if you can trace or discover any of these mysteries. And who was it who carved the plains and the mountains for the rivers, and gave them an unhindered course? And how to explain the corresponding marvel, the way the sea never overflows, nor the rivers cease to flow? Or explain what is the nourishing power of water, and what the difference is when some things are irrigated from above, while others drink from their roots, if I may luxuriate a little in my language when speaking of the luxuriant gifts of God.

28.28. And now, leaving aside the earth and the things of earth, let us soar into the air on the wings of thought, so that our argument may advance in due order; and from there I will take you up to heavenly things, and to heaven itself, and even things which are above heaven. Now my discourse hesitates to ascend to that which is beyond; but still it shall ascend, as far as may be possible. Who was it that poured out the air, that great and abundant wealth, not measured to men by their rank or fortunes; not restrained by boundaries; not divided out according to people's ages; but like the distribution of the Manna, received by all in sufficiency, and valued for its equality of distribution; the chariot of the winged creation; the seat of the winds; the moderator of the seasons; the quickener of living things, or rather the preserver of natural life in the body; in which bodies have their being, and by which we speak; in which is the light and all that it shines upon, and the sight which flows through it? And mark, if you please, what follows. I cannot give to the air the whole empire of all that is thought to belong to the air. What are the storehouses of the winds? What are the treasuries of the snow? And who, as Scripture has said, has "given birth to the dewdrops?" Out of whose womb came the ice? Who binds the waters in the clouds, and, most marvelously fixes part of it to stay within the clouds, held there by his commanding Word even though its own nature is to flow out; while he pours out the rest of the water upon the face of the earth, and scatters it abroad in due season, and in just proportions? For he does not allow the whole substance of moisture to go out free and uncontrolled (such a cleansing was enough that occurred in the days of Noah; and he who cannot lie does not forget his own covenant); nor does he restrain it completely so that we should not again stand in need of an Elijah to bring the drought to an end. For "if he should close up the heavens," as scripture says, "who could ever open them?" If he opens the floodgates, who shall ever close them? Who is it that can bring excess or withhold sufficiency of rain, unless it is the one who governs the Universe by his own measures and balances? Indeed what scientific laws can you lay down concerning thunder and lightning, you orators who thunder from the earth, but cannot flash even with little sparks of truth? To what vapors from the earth will you attribute the creation of the cloud, or is it due to some thickening of the air, or pressure or crash of very rare types of clouds, so as to make you think the pressure might be the cause of the lightning crash which makes the thunder? Or what vast compression of air will explain for you the lightning and thunder crash when it breaks loose?

Now if in thought you have thus passed through the air and all the things of air, reach with me even to the heavens and the things of heaven. And let faith lead us now rather than reason; if at least you have learnt from me the feebleness of reason in all those former questions that stood nearer to your condition, and if you have now learned some reason by knowing what things are beyond reason, so as not to be altogether on the earth or of the earth, simply because you are ignorant even of the very fact of your ignorance.

28.29. Who was it then, who spread the sky around us, and set the stars in order? Or rather, first, can you tell me, out of your own knowledge of the things in heaven, what are the sky and the stars; Tell me that, you who do not even know what lies at your very feet, and cannot even take the measure of yourself, but even so feel you need to be busying yourself about what is above your nature, and need to gape at the illimitable? Allowing that you may understand orbits and periods, and waxings and wanings, and settings and risings, and some degrees and minutes, and all the other things which make you so proud of your wonderful knowledge; you have not arrived at comprehension of the realities themselves, but only at an observation of some measure of movement. This has been confirmed by longer practice and the drawing of the observations of many individuals into one generalization leading to the deduction of a law, and finally acquires the name of Science (just as the lunar phenomena have become generally known to our sight); but this is all the basis of this knowledge. But if you are very scientific on this subject, and have a just claim to admiration, tell me what is the cause of this astronomical order and movement? How did the sun come to be a beacon-fire to the whole world, and to all eyes like the leader of some chorus, concealing all the rest of the stars by his brightness, more completely than some of them conceal others? The proof of this is that they shine against him, but he outshines them and does not even allow the fact to be perceived that they rose simultaneously with him, "fair as a bridegroom, swift and great as a giant" (for I will not let his praises be sung from any other source than my own Scriptures) so mighty in strength that from one end of the world to the other he embraces all things in his heat, and there is nothing hidden from his touch, since he fills every eye with light, and every embodied creature with heat; warming, yet not burning, by the gentleness of his temper, and the order of his movement, present to all, and equally embracing all.

28.30. Have you considered the importance of the fact that a pagan writer [Plato] speaks of the sun as holding the same position among material objects as God does among the objects of thought? For the one gives light to the eyes, just as the other gives light to the mind; and the one is the most beautiful of the objects of sight, just as God is the most beautiful of the objects of thought. But who gave original motion to the sun? And what is that power which ever moves the sun in his circuit, though in its nature it is stable and immovable, truly unwearied, and the giver and sustainer of life, and deserving of all the rest of the titles which the poets justly attribute to it in song, since it never rests in its course or its benefits? How does the sun come to be the creator of day when it is above the earth, and of night when it is below it? Or whatever may be the right expressions when one is contemplating the sun? What are the mutual advances and withdrawals of day and of night, and their regular irregularities (if I may use a rather strange expression)? How does the sun come to be the maker and divider of the seasons, which come and go in such regular order, as if interweaving with each other in a dance, standing apart by a law of love on the one hand, and a law of order on the other, and mingle little by little, and each one stealing in upon their neighbor, just as nights and days do, so as not to give us pain by their suddenness. But let this be enough about the sun.

Well then, do you know the nature and phenomena of the moon, and the measures and courses of its light, and how it is that the sun bears rule over the day, and the moon presides over the night; and while She gives confidence to the wild beasts, He stirs up man to go to his work, ascending or descending in the heavens as may be most serviceable? Do you know what is the bond that keeps the Pleiades together, or the fence of Orion as he does who counts the number of the stars and calls each one by their names? Do you know the differences of the glory of each one, and the order of their movement, enough that I should trust you, when by reference to them you weave a web of human arguments, and arm the creature against the Creator?

28.31. What do you think then? Shall we pause here, after discussing nothing further than material and visible things, or, since the Word knows that the "Tabernacle of Moses" is merely a figure of the whole creation (I mean the entire system of things visible and invisible) shall we not pass now through the first veil, and step beyond the realm of sense, in order to gaze into the Holy Place, that is the Intellectual and Celestial creation? But we cannot even see this in an incorporeal way, though in itself it is incorporeal, since it is called (and is) Fire and Spirit. For he is said to "make his angels spirits, and his ministers a flame of fire," though perhaps this term "make" here means preserving them by means of that Word by which they first came into existence. An angel, therefore, is called spirit and fire; spirit, as being a creature of the intellectual sphere; fire, as being of a purifying nature; for I know that the same names belong to the divine Primary Nature. But, relatively to us at least, we must reckon the angelic nature as being incorporeal, or at any rate as nearly so as possible. Do you see how we get dizzy over this subject, and cannot advance to any point, unless it be as far as this: that we know at least that there are Angels and Archangels, Thrones, Dominions, Principalities, Powers, Splendors, Ascents, Intelligent Powers or Intelligencies, all being pure natures, unalloyed, immovable to evil, or scarcely movable; ever circling in chorus round the First Cause (or how else should we sing their praises?), illuminated from out of it with the purest Illumination, or one in one degree and one in another, proportional to their nature and rank, and so conformed to beauty and molded into it that they become Secondary Lights, and can enlighten others by the overflowing largesse of the First Light?

The angels are Ministers of God's Will, strong with both an inborn and an imparted strength; traversing all space, readily present everywhere to all through their zeal for service and the agility of their nature. Different angels among them embrace different parts of the world, or are appointed over different districts of the Universe, as God knows who ordered and distributed everything. They combine all things in one, solely with a view to the good will of the Creator of all; they act as the hymnographers of the divine majesty, eternally contemplating the Eternal Glory, not that God thereby gains an increase of glory, for nothing can be added to that which is already in fullness, or to God who supplies good to all outside himself, but rather glorifying God so that there may never be a cessation of blessings to these first natures who come after God himself. If we have narrated these things as they deserve to be told, it is only by the grace of the Trinity, and of the one Godhead in Three Persons; but if less perfectly than we have desired, yet even so our discourse has gained its purpose. For this is what we were laboring to show: that even to describe the Secondary Natures far surpasses the power of our intellect. Accordingly, much more does it escape the power of our intellect to describe the First Nature and (since I draw back from saying merely the "nature which is above all others") that Only Nature.

St. Gregory of Nazianzus, Oration 29: The Third Theological Oration

On the Son

29.1. These are my arguments therefore, designed to cut short my opponents' readiness to argue, and their recklessness, with its consequent insecurity in all matters, but above all in those discussions which relate to God. But since to rebuke others is no hard thing at all, but on the contrary a very easy thing, which any one who likes can do; whereas to substitute one's own belief for theirs is the part of a reverent and intelligent man; then let us proceed in reliance on the Holy Spirit, that Spirit who among them is held in dishonor, but who among us is adored; and let us now bring to the light our own conceptions about the Godhead, whatever these may be, like some noble and timely birth. Not that I have at other times been silent; for on this subject alone I am full of youthful strength and daring; but the fact is that under present circumstances I am even more bold to declare the truth, that I may not (to use the words of Scripture) by drawing back fall into the condemnation of being displeasing to God. And since every discourse is of a twofold nature, the one part establishing one's own position, and the other part spent in overthrowing one's opponents'; let us first of all state our own position, and then try to controvert that of our opposition. I shall do both things as briefly as possible, so that our arguments may be taken in at a glance (like those of the elementary text books which they have devised to deceive simple or foolish persons), and also so that our thoughts may not be scattered by reason of the length of the discourse, like water which is not contained in a channel, but flows to waste over the open land.

29.2. The three most ancient opinions concerning God are Anarchia, Polyarchia, and Monarchia. The first two are the playthings of the children of Hellas, and may they continue to be so. For Anarchy is a thing without order; and the Rule of Many is factious, and thus anarchical, and thus disorderly. For both these theological positions tend to the same thing, namely disorder; and thus to dissolution, for disorder is the first step to dissolution. But Monarchy is that axiom which we hold in honor. It is, however, a Monarchy that is not limited to one person, for it is possible for unity, if at variance with itself, to come into a condition of plurality; but we hold it to be made out of an equality of nature and a union of mind, and an identity of motion, and a consilience of its elements to unity (a thing which is impossible for created natures) so that though it is numerically distinct there is no severance of essence involved. Therefore Unity having from all eternity arrived by motion at Duality, found its rest in Trinity. This is what we mean by Father and Son and Holy Spirit. The Father is the Begetter and the Emitter; though without passion, of course, and without reference to time, and not in a corporeal manner. The Son is the Begotten, and the Holy Spirit the Emission; (I say this since I do not know how else this can be expressed in terms that wholly exclude material conceptions). But we shall not venture to speak of "An overspill of goodness," as one of the Greek Philosophers dared to say, as if God were like a wine-bowl filled to overflowing, saying this in plain words in his oration on the First and Second Causes. Let us never look on this matter of divine generation as being involuntary, like some natural overflow, hard to be retained, for it is by no means fitting to our conception of the Godhead. Therefore let us confine ourselves within our proper limits, and speak of the "Unbegotten" and the "Begotten" and that which "Proceeds from the Father," as in one place God the Word himself expressed it.

29.3. So, when did these come into being? They are above all "when." But, if I am to speak a little more boldly, I will say "when the Father did." And when did the Father come into being? There never was a time when he was not. And the same thing is true of the Son and the Holy Spirit. Ask me again, and again I may ask in turn: "When was the Son begotten?" And answer you: "When the Father was not begotten." And when did the Holy Spirit proceed? When the Son was not proceeding but begotten, namely beyond the sphere of time, and above the grasp of reason (although we cannot set forth something that is above time unless we avoid (as we would wish to) any expression which conveys the idea of time. But such expressions as "when" and "before" and "after" and "from the beginning" are certainly not timeless, however, much as we may force them; unless indeed we were to take the Æon, that interval which is coextensive with the eternal things, and is not divided or measured by any motion, or by the revolutions of the sun, as time is measured.

How then, if they are coeternal, are they not all alike unoriginate? It is because they are from him, though not after him. For that which is unoriginate is eternal, but that which is eternal is not necessarily unoriginate, so long as it may be referred to the Father as its origin. Therefore in respect of Cause they are not unoriginate; but it is evident here that the cause is not necessarily prior to its effects; for the sun, for example, is not prior to its light. And yet, even so, they are in some sense unoriginate; that is in respect of time, even though you would scare simple minds with your quibbles; for the sources of Time are not subject to time.

29.4. Well how can this generation be passionless? In that it is incorporeal. For if corporeal generation involves passion, incorporeal generation excludes it. And I will ask of you in turn, "How is the Word God if he is created?" For that which is created is not God. I refrain from reminding you that here too is passion if we take the creation in such a bodily sense, as time, desire, imagination, thought, hope, pain, risk, failure, success, all of which and more than all find a place in the creature, as is evident to every one. Indeed I am amazed that you have not ventured so far as to conceive of marriages and times of pregnancy, and dangers of miscarriage, as if the Father could not have begotten at all if he had not begotten in such a material sense; or again, that you did not count up the modes of generation of birds and beasts and fishes, and bring under the category of some one of them this divine and ineffable generation; or even eliminate the Son out of your new hypothesis. But can you not even grasp this, that as far as his generation according to the flesh differs from all others (for where else among us do you know of a Virgin Mother?), so also does he differ in his spiritual generation. In short: he, whose existence is not the same as ours, differs from us also in his generation.

29.5. Who then is that Father who had no beginning? One whose very Existence had no beginning; for one whose existence had a beginning must also have begun to be a Father. He did not then become a Father after he began to be, for his being had no beginning. And he is Father in the absolute sense, for he is not also Son; just as the Son is Son in the absolute sense, because he is not also Father. These names do not belong to us humans in the absolute sense, because we are both fathers and sons, and not one more than the other; and we are of both, not of one only; and so we are divided, and by degrees become men, and perhaps not even men, and then we turn into such as we did not desire [by death], leaving behind and being left behind, so that only the memory of relations remains, without the underlying facts. But, an objector may say, the very form of the expression "He begot" and "He was begotten," inevitably introduces the idea of a beginning of generation. Not necessarily – for what if we do not use this expression, but say rather, "He has been begotten from the beginning" so as readily to evade your far-fetched and time-loving objections? Will you bring Scripture against us, as if we were forging something contrary to Scripture and to the Truth? Why, every one knows that in practice we very often find tenses interchanged when time is spoken of; and this is especially the custom of the Holy Scripture, not only in respect of the past and present tenses, but even of the future; as for instance "Why did the heathen rage?" when they had not as yet raged and: "They shall cross over the river on foot," where the meaning is that they had already crossed over. It would be a long task to reckon up all the expressions of this kind which students have already noticed.

29.6. So much for this point. What is their next objection, full of contentiousness and impudence? The Father, so they argue, either voluntarily begot the Son, or else involuntarily. Thus, as they think, they bind us hand and foot with cords; these however are not strong, but very weak indeed. For, they say, if it was involuntarily he must have been under the sway of some one, and then who exercised this sway? And how could he be God if he was so subject? But if voluntarily, then the Son is a Son out of the divine will; and if so, how can he then be of the Father? In this way they invent a new sort of mother for him, namely the Will, in place of the Father. There is one good point which they may allege about this argument of theirs; namely, that they have finally left aside the concept of passion, and taken refuge in will. For will is not a passion.

Now let us look at the strength of their argument. And from the start I think it is best to wrestle with them at close quarters. I will ask you in return, you who so recklessly assert whatever takes your fancy; Were you begotten voluntarily or involuntarily by your father? If involuntarily, then he was under some tyrant's sway (and what a terrible violence!) And who was the tyrant? You can hardly say it was nature, for nature is tolerant of chastity. If it was voluntarily, then by a few syllables your father is done away with, for you are shown to be the son of will, and not a son of your own father. I pass now to the relation between God and the creature, and I pose your own question back to your own wisdom. Did God create all things voluntarily or under compulsion? If under compulsion, here also is the same tyranny, and one who played the tyrant; but if voluntarily, the creatures also are deprived of their God, and you before all the rest, who invent such arguments and tricks of logic. For a partition is thus set up between the Creator and the creatures in the form of volition. And yet I think that surely the person who wills is distinct from the act of willing; just as he who begets is distinct from the act of begetting; as is the speaker from the speech; or else we all must be very stupid. On the one side we have the Mover, and on the other side that which is, so to speak, the motion. Thus the thing willed is not the child of will, for it does not always result from this; nor is that which is begotten the child of generation, nor that which is heard the child of speech, but rather the child of the person who willed, or begot, or spoke. But the things of God are beyond all this, for with him perhaps the will to beget is indeed generation, and there is no intermediate action (if we may accept this altogether, and not rather consider generation superior to will).

29.7. Will you permit me, then, to play a little upon this word "Father," for your own reckless example encourages me to be so bold? The Father is God either willingly or unwillingly; and how will you escape from your own excessive acuteness? If willingly, when did he begin to will? It could not have been before he began to be, for there was nothing prior to God. Or is one part of him will and another the object of will? If so, he is divisible. So the question arises, as the result of your argument, whether God himself is not the child of will? And if unwillingly, what compelled him to exist, and how is he God if he was compelled – indeed compelled to nothing less than to be God? How then was the Son begotten at all, says my opponent; and how was he created? If, as you say, he was created? For this is a part of the same difficulty. Perhaps you would say, "Created by will and Word." But in this, you have not yet solved the whole difficulty; for it still remains for you to show how will and word gained the power of action. For humanity was not created in this way.

29.8. So how was the Son begotten? This generation would hardly have been any great thing if the likes of you could have been able to comprehend it; you who have no real knowledge even of your own generation, or at least who comprehend very little of it, and of that little are ashamed to speak! But even so, do you think you can know the whole? You will have to undergo much labor before you discover the laws of composition, formation, manifestation, and the bond whereby soul is united to body, or mind to soul, or reason to mind; not to mention movement, increase, assimilation of food, sense, memory, recollection, and all the rest of the parts out of which you yourself are compounded. Can you know which of them belongs to the soul and body together, and which to each independently of the other, and which is received from each other? For those parts whose maturity comes later, even so received their laws at the time of conception. Tell me what these laws are? But even if you can, still you should not venture to speculate on the generation of God; for that would be a matter wholly unsafe. For even if you did know all about your own generation, you cannot possibly know about God's. And if you do not even understand your own, how can you possibly know about God's? For in proportion as God is harder to work out than man, so is the heavenly generation harder to comprehend than your own. But if you assert that just because you cannot comprehend it, even so he cannot have been begotten, it will be time for you to strike out many existing things which you cannot comprehend; and first in the list, surely is God himself. For you cannot say what God is, even if you are very reckless, and excessively proud of your intelligence. First, cast away your notions of flow and divisions and sections, and your conceptions of immaterial as if it were material birth, and then you may perhaps worthily conceive of the divine generation. How was God begotten? I repeat the question in indignation. The Begetting of God must be honored by silence. It is a great thing for you to learn even that he was begotten. But the manner of his generation we will not admit that even angels can conceive, much less you. Shall I tell you how it was? It was in a manner known only to the Father who begot, and to the Son who was begotten. Anything more than this is hidden by a cloud, and escapes your dim sight.

29.9. Well, you say, but the fact is that the Father begot a Son who either was or was not in existence. What utter nonsense! This is a question which applies to you or me, who on the one hand were in existence, as for instance Levi was in the loins of Abraham; and on the other hand came into existence; and so in some sense we are partly derived out of what existed, and partly out of what was non-existent; whereas the contrary is the case with Original Matter, which was certainly created out of what was Non-Existent, notwithstanding that some [Hellenes] pretend that it too is unbegotten. But in this case "to be begotten," even from the beginning, is synonymous with "to be." So on what ground can you base your capricious question? For what is older than that which is from the beginning, if we may place there the previous existence or non-existence of the Son? In either case we destroy its claim to be the Beginning. Or perhaps you will say, if we were to ask you whether the Father was of existent or non-existent substance, that he is twofold, partly pre-existing, partly existing; or that his case is the same as that of the Son; namely, that he was created out of non-existing matter. All this arises out of your ridiculous questions and your sandcastles, which cannot withstand the merest ripple.

Both positions are false, of course, and your question contains an absurdity: it is not that it is too difficult for us to answer. But if your dialectical assumptions lead you to think that one or other of these alternatives must necessarily be true in every case, let me ask you one little question: Is time in time, or is it not in time? If it is contained in time, then in what time, and what is it other than that time, and how does time contain itself? But if it is not contained in time, what is that surpassing wisdom which can conceive of a time which is timeless? Now, in regard to this expression, "I am now telling a lie," admit one of these alternatives, either that it is true, or that it is a falsehood, without qualification (since we cannot admit that it is both). But this cannot be. For of necessity the speaker is either lying, and so is telling the truth, or else he is telling the truth, and so is lying. What wonder is it, then, that as in this case both contraries are true, so in the other case they should both be untrue, and thus your clever little puzzle proves to be merely foolishness? Solve me one more riddle. Were you present at your own generation, and are you now present to yourself, or is neither the case? If you were, and are, present, who were you, and with whom are you present? And how did your single self become thus both subject and object? But if neither of the above is the case, how did you get separated from yourself, and what is the cause of this disjoining? But, perhaps you will protest that it is stupid to make a fuss about the question whether or not a single individual is present to himself; for the expression is not customarily used of oneself but of others. Well, you can be sure of this: that it is even more stupid to discuss the question whether that which was begotten from the beginning ever existed before its generation or not. For such a question arises only as referring to material objects divisible by time.

29.10. Even so my opponents argue that the Unbegotten and the Begotten are not the same; and if this is so, the Son cannot be the same [nature] as the Father. It is clear, without having to say so, that this line of argument manifestly excludes either the Son or the Father from the Godhead. For if to be unbegotten is the essence of God, to be begotten is not that essence; and if the opposite is the case, the Unbegotten is excluded. What argument can contradict this? Choose then whichever blasphemy you prefer, for you are now the inventor of a new theology, if indeed you are anxious to embrace a blasphemy at all costs. In the next place, in what sense do you assert that the Unbegotten and the Begotten are not the same? If you mean that the Uncreated and the Created are not the same, I agree with you; for certainly the Unoriginate and the created are not of the same nature. But if you say that the One who Begot and that which is Begotten are not the same, the statement is inaccurate. For it is in fact a necessary truth that they are the same. For the nature of the relation of Father to Child is this, that the offspring is of the same nature with the parent. Or we may argue again in this form: What do you mean by Unbegotten and Begotten, for if you mean the simple fact of being unbegotten or begotten, these are not the same; but if you mean to refer to the persons to whom these terms apply, how are they not the same? For example, Wisdom and Unwisdom are not the same in themselves, but yet both are attributes of a person, who is the same; and they do not mark a difference of essence, but rather something that is external to the essence. Are immortality and innocence and immutability also the essence of God? If so God would have many essences and not one; or else deity would be a compound of these. For he cannot be all these things and yet without composition, if they are to be held as essences.

29.11. I suppose my opponents do not assert this, for these qualities are common also to other beings. But God's essence is that which belongs to God alone, and is proper to him. Whoever thinks that matter and form are unbegotten elements, of course, would not allow that unbegottenness is the property of God alone (yet we must cast far away from us the darkness of the Manicheans). But suppose that it is the property of God alone. Then what of Adam? Was he not alone the direct creature of God? Yes, you will say. But was he then the only human being? By no means. And why? Well the answer is: because humanity does not consist in the aspect of a direct creation, since that which derives from being begotten is also human. Well, in the same way neither is he who is Unbegotten solely God, though he alone is the Father. But grant that he who is begotten is God too; for he is of God, as you must allow, even though you cling so much to your term "Unbegotten." Then how would you describe the Essence of God? Not by declaring what it is, but by rejecting what it is not. For your word signifies that God is not begotten; it does not present to you what is the real nature or condition of that which has no generation. So, tell me what is the Essence of God? It is for your infatuation to define this, since you are so anxious about his generation too; but to us it will be a very great thing, if ever, even in the future, we should learn this, when this darkness and dullness is done away for us, as he has promised who cannot lie. This, then, may be the thought and hope of those who are purifying themselves with a view to this end. For our part, we will be bold enough only to say that if it is a great thing for the Father to be Unoriginate, it is no less a thing for the Son to have been Begotten of such a Father. For not only would he then share the glory of the Unoriginate, since he is of the Unoriginate, but he also has the added glory of his generation, a thing marvelously great and august in the eyes of all those who are not groveling or completely materialistic in mind.

29.12. But, as they insist on saying, if the Son is the same as the Father in respect of essence, then it will follow that if the Father is unbegotten, the Son must be so likewise. Quite so: that would follow if the essence of God consisted in being unbegotten; and so he would be a strange mixture, "begottenly unbegotten." If, however, the difference is outside the scope of essence, how can you be so certain in projecting this conclusion? Are you also your father's father, so as in no respect to fall short of your father, since you are the same with him in essence? Is it not evident that our enquiry into the nature of the essence of God, if we make it, will leave the issue of personhood absolutely unaffected? But that the term "Unbegotten" is not a synonym of God can be proven in this way. If it were so, it would be necessary that, since God is a relative term, Unbegotten should be relative too; or that since Unbegotten is an absolute term, so must God be, namely "God of no one." For words which are absolutely identical are similarly applied. But the word Unbegotten is not used relatively. For to what could it be relative? And of what things is God the God? Would we not say: "Of all things?" How then can God and Unbegotten be identical terms? Or again, since Begotten and Unbegotten are contradictories, like possession and deprivation, it would follow that contradictory essences would co-exist; a thing which is impossible. Or again, since possessions are prior to deprivations, and the latter are destructive of the former, not only must the essence of the Son be prior to that of the Father, but it must be destroyed by the Father, at least on your hypothesis.

29.13. What now remains of their invincible arguments? Perhaps the last one they will take refuge in is this. "If God has never ceased to beget, the generation is imperfect; and when will he cease?" But if he has ceased, then he must have begun. And so once more these carnal minds bring forward carnal arguments. Whether he is eternally begotten or not, I do not conclude as yet, until I have looked into the biblical statement more accurately: "Before all the hills he begets me." But I cannot see the necessity of their conclusion. For if, as they say, everything that is to come to an end also had a beginning, then surely that which has no end had no beginning. What then will they conclude about the soul, or the angelic nature? If it had a beginning, it will also have an end; and if it has no end, it is evident that according to them it had no beginning. But the truth is that they did have beginning, and will never have an end. Their assertion, then, that whatever has an end had also a beginning, is simply untrue. Our position, however, is, that as in the case of a horse, or an ox, or a human being, the same definition applies to all the individuals of the same species; and whatever shares the definition also has a right to the name; so, in the very same way there is One Essence of God, and One Nature, and One Name; although in accordance with a distinction in our thoughts we use distinct names and that whatever is properly called by this name really is God; but what he is in nature, that he is truly called, if at least we are to hold to the position that this Truth is a matter not of names but of realities. But our opponents, as if they were afraid of leaving any stone unturned to subvert the Truth, indeed acknowledge that the Son is God when they are compelled to do so by arguments and evidences; but they only mean that he is God in an ambiguous sense, and that he only has a partial share in the title.

29.14. And when we make our objections and ask them: "So what do you really mean to say? That the Son is not properly God? Just as a picture of an animal is not properly an animal? And if not properly God, in what sense is he God at all?" And to this they reply, "Why should these terms not be ambiguous, and in both cases be used in a proper sense?" And they offer us then such instances as the house dog and the dogfish; where the word Dog is ambiguous, and yet in both cases is properly used, for there is such a species corresponding to both these named; or they raise up other cases in which the same appellative is used for two things of different natures. But, my dear, in this case, when you include two natures under the same title, you are not asserting by that argument that either is better than the other, or that the one is prior and the other posterior, or that one is to a greater degree and the other to a lesser degree that thing which is predicated of them both; for there is no connecting link which forces this necessity upon them. One is not a dog more than the other, and one less so; either the dogfish more than the house dog, or the house dog than the dogfish. Why should they be, or on what principle? But the community of name is here between things of equal value, though of different natures. But in the case of which we are speaking presently, you actually couple the name of God with adorable majesty, and make it surpass every essence and nature (an attribute of God alone), and then you ascribe this name to the Father, while you deprive the Son of it, and make him subject to the Father, and give him only a secondary honor and worship. Even if you bestow on him an equal title in words, yet in practice you cut off his divinity, and pass malignantly from a use of the same name (implying an exact equality) to one which connects things which are clearly not equal. And so the case of the depicted as distinct from the living person are, in your mouth, an apter illustration of the relations of deity than the instance of "dogs" which I gave before. Or else you must concede to both an equal dignity of nature as well as the common name, even though you introduced these natures into your argument as being different. But in this way you destroy the analogy of your dogs, which you invented as an instance of inequality. For what is the force of your instance of ambiguity, if those whom you distinguish are not equal in honor? For it was not to prove an equality but an inequality that you took refuge in your syllogistic dogs. How could anybody be more clearly convicted of fighting both against his own arguments, and against the Godhead itself?

29.15. If, when we admit that in respect of being the Cause, the Father is greater than the Son, they should hear us as arguing the premiss that he is the cause by nature, and then deduce the conclusion that he is greater by nature also, it would be difficult to say whether they mislead most themselves or those with whom they are arguing. For it does not absolutely follow that all that is predicated of a class can also be predicated of all the individuals composing it; for the different particulars may belong to different individuals. What if I assume the same premiss, namely, that: "the Father is greater by Nature," and then add this other one, "Yet not greater in every respect in terms of nature, nor yet Father by terms of nature." Then what is to prevent me from concluding, "Therefore the Greater is not in every respect greater, nor is the Father in every respect Father?" Or, if you prefer it, let us put it in this way: "God is an Essence: But an Essence is not in every case God"; and what if you should then draw the conclusion for yourself: "Therefore God is not in every case God." I think the fallacy here is evidently the arguing from a conditioned to an unconditioned use of a term, to use the technical expressions of the logicians. For while we assign this word "Greater" to the Father's nature viewed as a cause, the opponents infer it of his nature viewed in itself. It is just as if when we said that such a one was a "dead man" they were to infer simply that it meant he was "a man."

29.16. I cannot refrain from mentioning another point of theirs which amazes me more than the rest. The term "Father," they say, is a name either of an essence or of an action – thinking to tie us hand and foot again. If we say that it is a name of an essence, they will say that we agree with them that the Son must be of a different essence, since there is only one essence of God, and this, so they say, is exhausted by the term Father. On the other hand, if we say that Father is the name of an action, we shall be supposed to be acknowledging plainly that the Son is created and not begotten. For where there is an agent there must also be an effect. And they will then say that they wonder how that which is made can be identical with that which made it. I should myself have been frightened by their clever distinction, if it had been necessary to accept one or other of these alternatives, but really we need to set both of them aside, and state instead a third and truer one, namely: that Father is not a name either of an essence or of an action, but is the name of the relation in which the Father stands to the Son, and the Son to the Father. For, as with us, these names make known a genuine and intimate relation, so too in the case before us they denote an identity of nature between the one that is begotten and the one that begets. But even if we concede to them that Father is a name of essence, it will still bring in the idea of Son, and will not necessarily imply that it is of a different nature, according to common ideas and the force of such names. Or let it be, if you wish, the name of an action. Even then you will not defeat us in this way. The consubstantiality of Father and Son would indeed be the result of this action, or otherwise the conception of an action in this matter would be absurd. You see then how, even though you try to fight unfairly, we easily avoid your sophistries. But now, since we have ascertained the real degree of your invincibility in terms of arguments and sophistries, let us look at your strength in relation to the Oracles of God, to see if you can succeed in convincing us from exegesis.

29.17. Now we have learnt to believe in and to teach the divinity of the Son from the great and lofty utterances of Scripture. And which instances? These: God (The Word) "Who was In the Beginning," and "With the Beginning," and "The Beginning" itself. "In the Beginning was the Word, and the Word was with God, and the Word was God," and "With you is the beginning," and "He who calls her the beginning from generations." Then we learn that the Son is Only-Begotten; for scripture says: "The only begotten Son who is in the bosom of the Father, he it is who has made him known." As regards the Way, the Truth, the Life, and the Light, we have: "I am the Way, the Truth, and the Life"; and "I am the Light of the World." Concerning Wisdom and Power we have: "Christ, the Wisdom of God, and the Power of God." Or with regard to the Effulgence, the Impress, the Image, the Seal we have this: "Who being the effulgence of his glory and the impress of his essence," and again: "The Image of His Goodness," and "It is he whom God the Father has sealed." Also for titles such as Lord, King, He That Is, The Almighty, consider: "The Lord rained down fire from the Lord"; and "A scepter of righteousness is the scepter of your Kingdom"; and "Which is and was and is to come, the Almighty" – all of which passages are clearly spoken of in relation to the Son, with all the other passages of the same force, none of which is an afterthought, or added later to the Son or the Spirit, any more than to the Father himself. For their perfection is not affected by additions. There never was a time when God was without the Word, or when he was not the Father, or when he was not true, or not wise, or not powerful, or devoid of life, or of splendor, or of goodness.

29.18. But so as to stand against all these texts you reckon up for me the expressions which only demonstrate your ignorant arrogance, such as: "My God and your God," or terms such as greater, or created, or made, or sanctified. Add, if you like, the titles Servant and Obedient, or attributions such as gave and learnt, and was commanded, was sent, can do nothing of himself, was told, judged, or willed. And furthermore we have these issues – his ignorance and subjection, his prayer, his asking, his increase, and his being made perfect. And if you like there are even more humble things than these; such as when scripture speaks of his sleeping, his hunger, his being in an agony, and his fear; and perhaps you would make even his Cross and Death a matter of reproach to him? His Resurrection and Ascension I fancy you will leave to me, for in these is found something to support our position. A good many other things you might pick up also, if you desire to cobble together that equivocal and intruded god of yours, who to us is True God, and Equal to the Father. For every one of these points, taken separately, may very easily, if we go through them one by one, be explained to you in the most reverent sense, and the stumbling-block of the letter can easily be cleaned away; that is, if your stumbling is an honest thing and not willfully malicious. But, to give you the explanation in one sentence, it is this: Whatever is lofty you should apply to the Godhead, and to that nature in him which is superior to sufferings and incorporeal; but everything that is lowly, you should apply to the composite condition of him who for your sakes made himself of no repute and was incarnate. Yes, for it is no worse thing to say, "Was made Man," and afterwards was also exalted. If you do this I hope that you will learn to abandon these carnal and groveling doctrines of yours, and study to be more sublime, and to ascend along with his Godhead, so that you will not remain permanently among visible realities, but will rise up with him into the world of thought, and come to know which scriptural passages refer to his own nature, and which to his assumption of human nature.

29.19. For he whom you now treat with contempt was once above you. He who is now Man was once the Uncompounded. What he was, he continued to be; what he was not he took to himself. In the beginning he was, uncaused; for what is the Cause of God? But afterwards, for a cause, he was born. And that cause was that you might be saved, you who insult him and despise his Godhead, only because he took upon himself your denser nature, having converse with flesh by means of Mind. And his inferior nature, the humanity, became divine, because it was united to God, and became one person because the higher nature prevailed, in order that I too might be made God insofar as he was made Man. He was born, but he had already been begotten: he was born of a woman, but she was a Virgin. The first is a human thing, the second divine. In his human nature he had no Father, just so in his divine nature no mother. Both these realities belong to Godhead. He dwelt in the womb, but he was recognized by the prophet, himself still in the womb, leaping before the Word, for whose sake he came into being. He was wrapped in swaddling clothes, but he took off the swathing bands of the grave by his rising again. He was laid in a manger, but he was glorified by angels, and proclaimed by a star, and worshipped by the Magi. Why are you offended by that which is presented to your sight, because you will not look at that which is presented to your mind? He was driven into exile into Egypt, but he drove away the Egyptian idols. He had no form or comeliness in the eyes of the Jews, but to David he was "fairer than the children of men." And on the mountain he was bright as the lightning, and became more luminous than the sun, initiating us into the mystery of the future.

29.20. He was baptized as man, but he remitted sins as God, not because he needed purificatory rites himself, but that he might sanctify the element of water. He was tempted as man, but he conquered as God; indeed he bids us be of good heart because he has overcome the world. He hungered, but he fed thousands; for he is the heavenly bread that gives life. He thirsted, but he also cried out: "If any one should thirst, let them come to me and drink." He promised that fountains should flow from those that believed. He was wearied, but he is the Rest of those who are weary and heavy laden. He was heavy with sleep, but he walked lightly over the sea. He rebuked the winds, and made Peter light as he began to sink. He pays tribute, but it is from out of a fish; indeed, he is the King of those who demanded it. He is called a Samaritan and a demoniac; but he saves the one who came down from Jerusalem and fell among thieves; while the demons acknowledge him, and he drives out devils and sinks into the sea legions of foul spirits, watching the Prince of the demons falling like lightning. He is stoned, but is not captured. He prays, but he hears prayer. He weeps, but he causes tears to cease. He asks where Lazarus was laid, for he was man; but he raises Lazarus from the dead, for he was God. He is sold, and very cheap, for it was only for thirty pieces of silver; but he redeems the world, and that at a great price, for the price was his own blood. As a sheep he is led to the slaughter, but he is the Shepherd of Israel, and now of the whole world also. As a Lamb he is silent, yet he is the Word, and is proclaimed by the voice of one crying in the wilderness. He is bruised and wounded, but he heals every disease and every infirmity. He is lifted up and nailed to the tree, but by the Tree of Life he restores us; indeed he saves even the Robber who was crucified with him. He wrapped the visible world in darkness. He is given vinegar to drink mingled with gall. And who indeed was this? The very one who turned the water into wine, who is the destroyer of the bitter taste, he who is sweetness himself and all our desire. He lays down his life, but he has power to take it again; and the veil is torn in two, for the mysterious gates of heaven are opened; the rocks are split, the dead arise. He dies, but he gives life, and by his death destroys death. He is buried, but he rises again; he goes down into Hell, but he brings up the souls; he ascends to Heaven, and shall come again to judge the living and the dead, and to put to the test such words as yours. If the one aspect should give you a starting point for your error, let the other put an end to it.

29.21. All this, therefore, is the reply we make to those who would set us puzzles. I do not make it willingly as a matter of fact (for light talk and contradictions of words are not agreeable to the faithful, and one Adversary is enough for us), but I do so from necessity, for the sake of our assailants (just as medicines exist only because of diseases), so that they may be led to see that they are not all-wise and not invincible in those superfluous arguments which make the Gospel into something empty. For when we leave off believing, and protect ourselves by mere strength of argument, and by questionings destroy the claim which the Spirit has upon our faith, then our argument is not strong enough for the importance of the subject (and this must necessarily be the case, since it is put in motion by an organ of so little power as the mind). And then what shall be the result? The weakness of the argument, you see, appears to belong to the mystery, and it follows therefore that elegance of language makes the Cross void, as Paul also thought. For it is faith which brings our argument fullness. But may he who proclaims unions and unfastens those that are bound, and who puts into our minds how to solve the knots of their unnatural dogmas, change these men if it is possible and make them faithful believers instead of rhetoricians; Christians instead of that which they now are called. Truly we pray for this and beseech it for Christ's sake. So, be reconciled to God, and do not quench the Spirit; or rather, may Christ be reconciled to you, and may the Spirit enlighten you, even though it is late in the day. But even if you are too fond of your quarrels, we at any rate will hold fast to the Trinity; and by the Trinity may we be saved, remaining pure and without offense, until the more perfect manifestation of that which we desire, in him, Christ our Lord, to whom be the glory for ever. Amen.

St. Gregory of Nazianzus, Oration 30: The Fourth Theological Oration, Which is the Second Concerning the Son

30.1. I have, by the power of the Spirit, sufficiently overthrown the subtleties and intricacies of their arguments, and already generically solved the objections and oppositions drawn from Holy Scripture, by which these sacrilegious robbers of the Bible, these thieves of its internal sense, draw over the multitude to their side, and confuse the way of truth. They do this quite evidently, as I believe all candid persons will acknowledge, attributing to the Deity the higher and diviner expressions, and the lower and more human to him who for us men was the Second Adam, and was God made capable of suffering so as to strive against sin. But we have not yet gone through the passages in detail, because of the haste of our argument. And since you have demanded of us a brief explanation of each of these texts, so that you may not be carried away by the plausibilities of their arguments, we will therefore state the explanations summarily, dividing them into numbers for the sake of carrying them more easily in mind.

30.2. For them the text is always before their eyes: "The Lord created me at the beginning of his ways with a view to his works." How do we respond to this? Shall we bring an accusation against Solomon, or reject his teachings because of his own lapse in his later life? or shall we say that the words are those of Wisdom herself, as it were of Knowledge and the Creator-Word, in accordance with which all things were made? For Scripture often personifies many even lifeless objects; as for instance, "The Sea said" so and so; and, "The Depth said: It is not in me"; and "The Heavens declare the glory of God"; and again a command is given to the Sword; and the Mountains and Hills are asked the reason of their skipping. We do not allege any of these parallels, though some of our predecessors used them as powerful arguments. But let us grant that the expression is used of our Savior himself, the true Wisdom. Let us consider one small point together. What among all things that exist is unoriginate? The Godhead. For no one can tell the origin of God, for such an origin would be older than God. But what is the cause of the Manhood, which God assumed for our sake? It was surely for our salvation. What else could be the cause? Since we find in the Incarnate One clearly both what is created and what gives origin to me, the argument is simple: whatever we find derives from a cause we must refer to the humanity, but all that is absolute and unoriginate we should refer to his Godhead. But is not this text's phrase "created" spoken in connection with a cause? "He created me," so the text says, "As the beginning of his ways, with a view to his works." Now, the works of his hands are truth and judgment; for whose sake "He was anointed with Godhead'; and this anointing refers to the humanity; but the phrase: "He begets me" is not connected with any cause; or else point one out. What argument, therefore, will disprove that Wisdom is referred to as "Creature," in connection with that lower generation of his, but is called "Begotten" in respect of his first and more incomprehensible generation?

30.3. Now let us turn to the issue of his being called Servant, and how he serves many so well, and how it is a great thing for him to be called the Child of God. For in truth he was in servitude to the flesh and to his birth and to the conditions of our life, all with a view to our liberation, and the freedom of all those whom he has saved, who were held in bondage under sin. What greater destiny can befall man's humility than that he should be commingled with God, and by this commingling should be deified, and that we should be thus visited by the Dayspring from on high, that even that Holy Thing that should be born should be called the Son of the Most High, and that there should be bestowed upon him the Name which is above every name? And what else can this name be other than God? And that every knee should bow to the one who for our sake was held in low esteem, and who mingled the form of God with the form of a servant, so that all the House of Israel would know that God has made him both Lord and Christ? For all this was done by the working of the Begotten, and by the good pleasure of the One who begot him.

30.4. Well, let us look at the other of their great irresistible texts. "He must reign," till such and such a time … and "be received by heaven until the time of restitution," and "have the seat at the Right Hand until the overthrow of his enemies." But after this? Must he then cease to be King, or be removed from Heaven? Why, who shall make him cease, or for what cause? What a bold and very anarchical interpreter you must be; since you must have heard also that "Of his Kingdom there shall be no end." Your mistake arises from not understanding that the word "Until" is not always exclusive of that which comes after, but asserts a notion of "up to" that time, without denying what comes after it. To take a single instance: how else would you understand the text: "Behold, I am with you always, even to the end of the world?" Does it mean that he will no longer be with us afterwards? Why would that follow? But this is not the only cause of your error; for you also fail to distinguish between the things that are being signified. He is said to reign in one sense as the Almighty King, both of the willing and the unwilling; but in another sense insofar as his reign produces submission in us, and places us under his Kingship, since we willingly acknowledge his Sovereignty. Of his Kingdom, considered in the former sense, there shall be no end. But in the second sense, what end will there be other than his taking us as his servants, as we enter into a state of salvation. For what need is there to effect submission in us when we have already submitted? After this he shall arise to judge the earth, and to separate the saved from the lost. And then he shall stand as "God in the midst of the gods," that is of the saved; distinguishing and deciding which honor and mansion each one is worthy to receive.

30.5. Let us next consider that subordination by which you subject the Son to the Father. You maintain that he is surely subject to God, yet how can this be if he is God? You propose your argument as if it was about some robber, or some hostile deity. But look at it in this fashion: It was for my sake that "he was called a curse," the one who destroyed my curse; and for me that he was called sin, who takes away the sin of the world; and for me that he became a new Adam, so as to take the place of the old; then just so he makes my disobedience his own as Head of the whole Body. Accordingly, for as long as I am disobedient and rebellious, in terms of my denial of God and my passions, then so long will Christ also be called "disobedient" on my account. But when all things shall be subjected to him on the one hand by the universal acknowledgment of him, and on the other hand by a remaking of the Cosmos, then he himself will also have fulfilled his submission, even bringing me (whom he has saved) to God. For this, according to my understanding, is the meaning of the "subjection" of Christ; namely, that he so completely fulfils the Father's will. But since the Son subjects all things to the Father, so does the Father subject all things to the Son; the one by his work, the other by his good will, as we have already said. And so, he who subjects all, presents to God all that he has subjected, making our own condition his very own. In the same way, so it seems to me, we should interpret the text: "My God, my God, why have you forsaken me?" It was not that he was forsaken either by the Father, or by his own deity, as some have thought, as if the divinity were afraid of the Passion, and therefore withdrew itself from him in his sufferings (for who compelled him either to be born on earth, or to be lifted up on the Cross in the first place?) But, as I said, he was in his own person representing all of us. For we were the forsaken ones, and were formerly despised, but now by the sufferings of him who could not suffer, we were lifted up and saved. Similarly, he makes our folly his own, and our transgressions, his own; and so he speaks that verse of the Psalm, for it is very evident that the 21st Psalm refers to Christ.

30.6. The same considerations apply to yet another passage, "He learned obedience by the things he suffered," which also has reference to his "strong crying and tears," and his "entreaties," and his "being heard," and his "godly reverence." For all of these things he brought to effect in a wondrous way, like a drama whose plot was devised on our behalf. For in his character as the Word he was neither obedient nor disobedient, for such expressions belong to servants, and inferiors, and the one applies to the better sort, while the other belongs to those who deserve discipline. But, in his character as the "Form of a Servant," he condescends to his fellow-servants (more truly to his servants) and takes up a strange form, bearing all of me and all of mine in himself, so that he might consume the bad in himself, just as fire consumes wax, or the sun consumes the mists of earth. And this was so that I may partake of his nature by this blending. In this way he honors obedience by his action, and proves it experimentally by his Passion. For to possess the disposition is not enough, just as it would not be enough in our case either, unless we also proved it by our acts; for action is the proof of disposition.

And we would not be misguided to assume this also, that by the art of his love for man he assesses our obedience, and measures all by comparison with his own sufferings, so that he may know our condition by reference to his own, and know how much can be demanded of us, and how much we tend to give way, taking into the account, along with our environment, our weakness also. For if the Light shining through the veil upon the darkness that is upon this life, was persecuted by the other darkness (I mean, the Evil One and the Tempter), then how much more will the darkness be persecuted, as being weaker than the Light? And why should we be surprised if although he entirely escaped from evil we have been, at any rate in part, overtaken by it? For it is a more wonderful thing that he should have been chased than that we should have been captured – at least to the minds of all who reason rightly on the subject. I will add yet another passage to those I have mentioned, because I think that it clearly tends to the same meaning. I refer to that text: "Insofar as he has suffered, being tempted, he is able to assist those that are tempted." But God will be all in all in the time of restitution; not in the sense that the Father alone will then exist; and the Son be wholly resolved into him, like a torch sent back into a great pyre, from which it was pulled away for a short time, and then put back (for I would not have even the Sabellians injured by such an expression); but the entire Godhead will be all in all when we shall be no longer divided (as we now are by movements and passions), and containing nothing at all of God, or very little, but when we shall be entirely like him.

30.7. As your third point you lay emphasis on the term "greater," and as your fourth you hold to the text: "My God and your God." Well, if he had been called greater, and the word equal had not occurred, this might perhaps have been a point in their favor. But if we find both words clearly used what will these gentlemen have to say? How will it strengthen their argument? How will they reconcile the irreconcilable? For that the same thing should be at once greater than and equal to the same thing is an impossibility; and the evident solution is that the concept of being greater refers to origination; while the concept of being equal belongs to the Nature; and this we acknowledge readily. But perhaps some one else will back up our attack on your argument, and assert, that whatever derives from such a Cause is not inferior to that which has no Cause; since it shares the glory of the Unoriginate, because it is from the Unoriginate. And there is, besides, the issue of the generation, which is for all humanity a matter so marvelous and of such majesty. For to say that the Father is greater than the Son when the latter is considered as man, is true indeed, but is no great thing. For what marvel is it if God is greater than man? Surely this is enough to say in reply to their talk about the issue of being "greater."

30.8. As to the other passages, the reference to "My God" would be used in respect, not of the Word, but of the Word made visible. For how could there be a God of the One who is truly God? In the same way God is Father, not of the One who can be seen, but rather of the Word; for our Lord was of two Natures; so that one expression is used properly, the other improperly, in each of the two cases; but exactly the opposite way to how they are used in respect of us. For with respect to us God is properly our God, but not properly our Father. And this is the cause of the heretics' mistake, namely that they join these two names, which are interchanged because of the Union of Christ's Natures. And an indication of this is found in the fact that wherever the Natures are distinguished in our thoughts from one another, the Names are also distinguished; as you hear in Paul's words, "The God of our Lord Jesus Christ, the Father of Glory." The God of Christ, note, but the Father of Glory. For although these two terms express only one single Person, yet this is not by a Unity of Nature, but by a Union of the two. What could be clearer?

30.9. Fifthly, let it be alleged that it is said of Christ in scripture that he "receives life," "judgment," "inheritance of the Gentiles," or "power over all flesh," or "glory," or "disciples," or whatever else is mentioned. This also belongs to the humanity; and yet if you were to ascribe these things to the Godhead, it would be no absurdity. For you would not so ascribe it as if it were a newly acquired property, but rather as if it were something that pertained to him from the beginning by reason of nature, and not as an act of grace.

30.10. Sixthly, let it be asserted that it is written, "The Son can do nothing of Himself, but what he sees the Father do." The solution of this is as follows: Can and Cannot are not words with only one meaning, for they have many meanings. On the one hand they are used sometimes in respect of deficiency of strength, sometimes in respect of time, and sometimes relative to a certain object; as for instance, "A Child cannot be an Athlete," or, "A Puppy cannot see, or fight with, so and so." Perhaps some day the child will be an athlete, and the puppy will see, or will fight with that other character; though even then perhaps it may still be unable to fight with any other. Or again, the words may be used of something which is generally true. For instance, "A city that is set on a hill cannot be hidden"; while yet it might possibly be hidden by another higher hill being in its line of sight or suchlike. Or in another sense the words can be used of a thing which is not reasonable; such as, "Can the Children of the Bridechamber fast while the Bridegroom is with them?" whether he is envisaged as Bridegroom visible in the bodily form (for the time of his dwelling among us was not one of mourning, but one of gladness), or, considered as the Word. For why should they keep a bodily fast who are cleansed by the Word? Or, again, they are used of that which is contrary to the will; as in, "He could do no mighty works there because of their unbelief," – that is of those who should receive them. Since there is need of both faith in the patient and power in the healer, for a healing to occur, when one of the two fails the other proves impossible. But probably this sense also should be classified as unreasonable. For healing is not reasonable in the case of those who would afterwards be injured by unbelief. The sentence "The world cannot hate you," comes under the same heading, as does also the text: "How can you, being evil, speak good things?" For in what sense is either one impossible, except that it is contrary to the will? There is a somewhat similar meaning involved in the expressions which imply that a thing impossible by nature is possible to God if he so wills; such as that a man cannot be born a second time, or that a needle will not let a camel pass through it. For what could prevent either of these things happening, if God so willed?

30.11. And besides all this, there is the thing that is absolutely impossible and inadmissible, such as that issue which we are now examining. For as we assert that it is impossible for God to be evil, or for him not to exist – for this would be indicative of weakness in God rather than of strength – or for the non-existent to exist, or for two and two to make both four and ten; just so it is impossible and inconceivable that the Son should do anything that the Father does not do. For all that the Father has belongs to the Son; and on the other hand, all that belongs to the Son is the Father's. Nothing then is peculiar, because all things are in common. For their being itself is common and equal, even though the Son should receive it from the Father. It is in respect of this that the text says: "I live by the Father," not as though his Life and Being were kept together by the Father, but rather because he has his Being from the One who is beyond all time, and beyond all cause. But how does the Word see the Father doing, and himself does likewise? Is it like those who copy pictures and letters, because they cannot attain the truth unless by looking at the original, and being led by the hand by it? But how could Wisdom ever stand in need of a teacher, or be incapable of acting unless taught? And in what sense does the Father "Do" in the present or in the past? Did he make another world before this one? Or is he going to make a world to come? And did the Son look at that one and make this? Or will he look at the other, and make one like it? According to this argument there must be four worlds, two made by the Father, and two by the Son. But this is an absurdity! He cleanses lepers, and delivers men from evil spirits and diseases, and quickens the dead, and walks upon the sea, and does all his other works; but in what case, or when did the Father do these acts before him? Is it not clear that the Father impressed the ideas of these same actions, and the Word brings them to pass, yet not in slavish or unskillful fashion, but rather with full knowledge and in a masterly way; or, to speak more properly, like the Father? For in this sense I understand the words that whatever is done by the Father, these things the Son does likewise; not, that is, because of the likeness of the things done, but in respect of the Authority. This might well also be the meaning of the passage which says that: "The Father works even to now, and the Son also"; and what is more this also refers to the government and preservation of the things which he has made; as is shown by the passage which says that: "He makes his Angels Spirits," and that "The earth is founded upon its steadfastness" (though once for all these things were fixed and made) and that "The thunder is made firm and the wind created." For all these things the word was given once, but the action continues on even now.

30.12. Let them quote in the seventh place that: The Son "came down from Heaven, not to do his own will, but the will of him who sent him." Well, if this had not been said by the very one who so came down, we should say that the phrase can be characterized as issuing from the human nature, not from the one who is conceived of in his character as the Savior, for his human will cannot be opposed to God, seeing it is altogether taken into God; but conceived of simply as in our nature, inasmuch as the human will does not completely follow the Divine, but for the most part struggles against and resists it. For we understand in the same way the words, "Father, if it is possible, let this cup pass from me; Nevertheless let not my will but yours be done." For it is not likely that he did not know whether it was possible or not, or that he would oppose will to will. But since, as this is the language of the One who assumed our Nature (for he it was who came down), and not of the Nature which he assumed, we must meet the objection in this way: that the passage does not mean that the Son has a special will of his own, besides that of the Father, but rather that does not have such; so that the meaning would be, "not to do my own will, for there is none of mine separate, but only that which is common to me and you; for as we have one Godhead, so too do we have one will." For many such expressions are used in relation to this Communality, and are expressed not positively but negatively; as, for example: "God does not give the Spirit by measure," for as a matter of fact he does not give the Spirit to the Son, nor does he measure it, since God is not measured by God. Or again, "Not my transgression nor my sin." The words here are not used because he has these things, but because he does not have them. And again, "Not for any righteousness which we have done," for we have not done any. And this meaning is evident also in the clauses which follow. For what, does he say, is the will of my Father – except that everyone who believes in the Son should be saved, and obtain the final Resurrection. Now is this the will of the Father, but not the will of the Son too? Or does he preach the Gospel, and receive men's faith against his will? Who could believe that? Moreover, that passage which says that the Word which is heard is not the Son's but the Father's has the same force. For I cannot see how that which is common to two can be said to belong to one alone, however much I reflect on it; and I do not think any one else can. If then you hold this opinion concerning the Will, you will be right and reverent in your opinion, as I think, and as every right-minded person thinks.

30.13. The eighth passage in hand is, "That they may know you, the only true God, and Jesus Christ whom you have sent"; and "There is none good save one, that is, God." The solution of this appears to me very easy. For if you attribute this only to the Father, where will you place the Very Truth? For if you conceive in this way about the meaning of the phrase "To the only wise God" or "Who only has Immortality, dwelling in the light which no man can approach," or of "To the King of the Ages, immortal, invisible, and only wise God," then the Son seems to have vanished under a sentence of death, or of darkness, or at any rate seems to have been condemned to be neither wise, nor a king, nor invisible, nor God at all, which sums up all these points. And how will you prevent his Goodness, which especially belongs to God alone, from perishing along with all the rest? For my part, I think that the passage "That they may know you the only true God," was spoken concerning the overthrowing of those gods which are falsely so called, for otherwise he would not have added "And Jesus Christ whom you have sent," if the

"Only True God" stood in contrast with him, and the sense of the sentence did not proceed upon the basis of a common Godhead. The phrase "None is Good" meets the tempting Lawyer, who was testifying to his Goodness viewed as Man. For perfect goodness, he says, belongs to God alone, even if a man is called perfectly good. As for instance, "A good man out of the good treasure of his heart brings forth good things." And, "I will give the kingdom to one who is good above you." These are words of God, speaking to Saul about David. Or again, "Do good, O Lord, to the good," and all other similar expressions concerning those of us who are praised, upon whom it is a kind of effluence from the Supreme Good, and has come to them in a secondary degree. It will be best of all if we can persuade you of this. But if not, what will you say to the suggestion on the other side, that according to your hypothesis the Son has been called the only God. In what passage you ask? Why, in this: "This is your God; no other shall be accounted of in comparison with him," and a little further on, "After this he showed himself upon earth, and conversed with men." The final addition proves clearly here that the words are not used of the Father, but of the Son; for it was he who in bodily form dwelt with us, and was in this lower world. Now, if on the other hand, we should insist on taking these words as referring to the Father, and not the imaginary gods, we lose the Father by the very terms which we were pressing against the Son. And what could be more disastrous than such a victory?

30.14. Ninthly, they argue, there is that text "Seeing he always lives to make intercession for us." O, how beautiful and mystical and kind that is. For to intercede does not imply to seek for vengeance, as is most men's way (for in that there would be something of humiliation), but it means that he pleads for us by reason of his Mediatorship, just as the Spirit also is said to make intercession for us. For there is "One God, and One Mediator between God and Man, the Man Christ Jesus." For he still pleads even now as Man for my salvation; for he continues to wear the Body which he assumed, until should make me God by the power of his Incarnation; although "He is no longer known after the flesh" – I mean, the passions of the flesh, the same as ours, sin excepted. For this reason we have an Advocate, Jesus Christ, not indeed as if prostrating himself for our sake before the Father, and falling down before him in a slavish fashion: away with a suspicion so truly slavish and unworthy of the Spirit! For neither is it seemly for the Father to have required this, nor for the Son to submit to it; nor is it just to think such things of God. But by virtue of what he suffered as Man, he persuades the Father to be patient, as his Word and Counselor. I think this is the meaning of the concept of his Advocacy.

30.15. Their tenth objection is the issue of ignorance, and the statement that "Of the last day and hour no man knows, not even the Son Himself, but only the Father." And yet how can Wisdom be ignorant of anything? – that is, Wisdom who made the worlds, who perfects them, who remodels them, who is the boundary of all things that were made, who knows the things of God just as the spirit of a man knows the things that are in him? For what can be more perfect than this knowledge? How can you say then that all things before that hour he knows accurately, and even all things that are to happen about the time of the end, but as to the hour itself he is ignorant? For such a thing would be like a riddle; as if one were to say that he knew accurately all that was in front of the wall, but did not know the wall itself; or that, knowing the end of the day, he did not know the beginning of the night – where knowledge of the one necessarily brings in the other. Accordingly everyone must see that he does know as God, and does not know as Man; if one may separate the visible from that which is discerned by thought alone. For the absolute and unconditioned use of the Name "The Son" in this passage, without the addition of whose Son, gives us this thought, that we are to understand the ignorance in the most reverent sense, by attributing it to the Manhood, rather than to the Godhead.

30.16. If these arguments are sufficient, therefore, let us stop here, and not enquire further. But if not, our second argument stands as follows: Just as we do in all other instances, so let us refer the issue of his knowledge of the greatest events, in honor of the Father, to The Cause. And I think that anyone, even if he did not read it in the way that one of our own students did, would soon perceive that not even the Son knows the day or hour otherwise than as the Father does. For what do we conclude from this? That since the Father knows, therefore also the Son knows, as it is evident that this cannot be known or comprehended by any but the First Nature. There remains for us to interpret the passage about his receiving the commandments of God, and about having kept his commandments, and having done always those things that please him; and in addition the texts concerning his being made perfect, or having an exaltation, and learning obedience by the things which he suffered; and also as regards his High Priesthood, and his Oblation, and his Betrayal, and his prayer to the One who was able to save him from death, and his Agony and Bloody Sweat and Prayer, and suchlike things. Though it must be evident to everyone that such words are concerned, not with that Nature which is Unchangeable and above all capacity of suffering, but rather relate to the passible Humanity. So this is my argument concerning such objections, so far as to be a sort of foundation and memorandum for the use of those who are better able to lead on the enquiry to a more complete elaboration. It may, however, be worthwhile, and will certainly be consistent with what has been already said, instead of passing over without remark the actual titles of the Son (there are many of them, and they are concerned with many of his attributes), to set before you the meaning of each of them, and to point out the mystical meaning of the names.

30.17. We will make a beginning along these lines. The Deity cannot be expressed in words. And this is proved to us, not only by reason, but by the wisest and most ancient of the Hebrews, so far as they have given us grounds for conjecture. For they appropriated certain characters to the honor of the Deity, and would not even allow the name of anything inferior to God to be written with the same letters as the name of God, because to their minds it was improper that the Deity should even to that extent admit any of his creatures to a share with himself. How then could they have admitted that the invisible and separate Nature can be explained by divisible words? No one has ever breathed all of that air, and nor has any mind entirely comprehended, and nor has any speech ever summed up the Being of God. But we merely sketch him out by means of his attributes, and in this way we obtain a certain faint, feeble, and partial idea concerning him, and the best theologian among us is the one who has never claimed to discover the whole truth (for our present limitations do not allow us to see the whole) but has conceived of him to a greater extent than another, by gathering in himself more of the divine Likeness or the Shadow of the Truth, or whatever else we may call it.

30.18. As far as we can reach, therefore the phrases: "He Who Is," and "God," are the special names of his essence; and of these especially "He Who Is," not only because when he spoke to Moses on the mountain, and Moses asked what his name was, this was what he called himself, commanding him to say to the people "I Am has sent me," but also because we find that this name is the one most strictly appropriate. For the name God is still one of the relative titles, not an absolute one, even if (as they who are skilled in such etymologies tell us) it is derived from the idea of "running," or from the term "to blaze forth"; that is from his continual motion, and because he consumes the evil conditions of things (from which fact God is also called "A Consuming Fire"). And the same is the case with the title "Lord," which also is designated as a name of God. "I am the Lord your God," he says, "That is My name"; and, "the Lord is his name." But we are enquiring into a Nature whose Being is absolute, and not into Being as bound up with something else. But Being is, in its proper sense, peculiar to God, and belongs to him entirely, and it is not limited or cut short by any "Before" or "After," for truly in God there is no past or future.

30.19. In relation to the other titles, some are evidently names of God's authority, others of his government of the world; and this viewed under a twofold aspect, the one before, and the other within the Incarnation. For instance the terms Almighty, King of Glory, King of the Ages, Lord of the Powers, or The Beloved, or King of Kings; or again the Lord of Sabaoth, that is Lord of Hosts, or Lord of Powers, or Lord of Lords: these are all clearly titles belonging to his Authority. But the titles: God of Salvation, or of Vengeance, or of Peace, or of Righteousness; or God of Abraham, Isaac, and Jacob, and of all the spiritual Israel which sees God, all these titles belong to his Government. For we are governed by three things, the fear of punishment, the hope of salvation and glory, and the practice of the virtues by which these are attained; and so it is that the Name of the God of Vengeance governs fear, and that of the God of Salvation our hope, and that of the God of Virtues our practice; so that whoever attains to any of these may, as if carrying God within himself, press on to even greater perfection, and even to that divine affinity which rises out of the virtues. Now these are Names common to the Godhead, but the proper name of the Unoriginate One is Father, and the proper name of the Unoriginately Begotten is Son, and that of the Unbegottenly Proceeding (or going) forth is The Holy Spirit. Let us move on then to the Names of the Son, which were our starting point in this part of our argument.

30.20. In my opinion he is called Son because he is identical with the Father in terms of Essence; but not only for this reason, but also because he is of the Father. And he is called Only-Begotten, not because he is the only Son and of the Father alone, and only a Son; but also because the manner of his Sonship is peculiar to himself and not shared by bodies. And he is called the Word, because he is related to the Father as Word is to Mind; not only on account of his passionless generation, but also because of the Union, and of his function of declaring the Father. Perhaps we can compare this relation to that between a Definition and the Thing defined, since this also is called Logos. For, as scripture says, whoever has noetically perceived the Son (for this is the meaning of the phrase "has seen") has also perceived the Father; and the Son is a "concise demonstration" and easy exegesis of the Father's Nature. For everything that is begotten is a silent word of the one who begot it. And if any one should say that this Name was given him because he exists in all things that subsist, he would not be far wrong. For what is there that has existence except by the Word? He is also called Wisdom, as the Knowledge of things divine and human. And how is it possible that he who made all things should be ignorant of the principles of what he has made? And he is called Power, as the Sustainer of all created things, and because he gives to them the power to keep themselves together. And he is called Truth, as being in nature One and not many (for truth is one while falsehood is manifold), and he is named as the pure Seal of the Father and his most unerring Impress. And he is called the Image as being of One Substance with him, and because he is of the Father, not the Father of Him. For this is of the Nature of an Image, to be the reproduction of its Archetype, and of that whose name it bears; except there is more to it here. For in ordinary language an image is a motionless representation of that which has motion; but in this case it is the living reproduction of the Living One, and is more exactly alike than Seth was to Adam, or as any son is to his father. For such is the nature of simple existences, such that it is not correct to say of them that they are Like in one particular and Unlike in another; but they are a complete resemblance, and should rather be called Identical than they should be called Like. Moreover he is called Light as being the Brightness of souls cleansed by word and life. For if ignorance and sin are darkness, then knowledge and a godly life will be Light. And he is called Life, because he is Light, and is the constituting and creating Power of every reasonable soul. For in him we live and move and have our being, according to the double power of that breathing into us; for we were all inspired by him with breath, and as many of us as were capable of it, and insofar as we open the mouth of our mind, even with God the Holy Spirit. He is also Righteousness, because he distributes according to that which we deserve, and is a righteous Arbiter both for those who are under the Law and for those who are under Grace, for soul and body, so that the former should rule, and the latter obey, and the higher have supremacy over the lower; that the worse may not rise in rebellion against the better. He is Sanctification, as being Purity, so that the Pure may be contained by Purity. And he is called Redemption, because he sets us free, who once were held captive under sin, giving himself a Ransom for us, as the Sacrifice to make expiation for the world. And he is called Resurrection, because he raises up from here below, and brings life again to us, who had been slain by sin.

30.21. These names however are still common to the One who is above us, and to him who came for our sake. But others are peculiarly our own, and belong to that nature which he assumed. On this account he is called Man, not only that through his Body he may be apprehended by embodied creatures (whereas otherwise this would be impossible because of his incomprehensible nature) but also so that by himself he may sanctify humanity and be, as it were, a leaven to the whole mass; and by uniting to himself that which was condemned, might release it from all condemnation, becoming for all men all that we are, except sin; namely body, soul, mind and all through which death reaches. In this way he became Man, who is the combination of all these; God in visible form, because he retained that which is perceived by mind alone. He is Son of Man, both on account of Adam, and of the Virgin from whom he came; from the one as a forefather, from the other as his Mother, both in accordance with the law of generation, and yet apart from it. He is Christ, because of his Godhead. For this is the Anointing of his

Manhood, and does not, as is the case with all other "Anointed Ones," sanctify by its action, but rather by the presence in his own fullness of the Anointing One. The effect of this is that: That which anoints is called Man, and makes that which is anointed God. He is the Way, because he leads us through himself; he is the Door, insofar as he allows us in; the Shepherd, since he makes us dwell in a place of green pastures, and brings us up by restful waters, and leads us there, and protects us from wild beasts, converting the wanderer, and bringing back that which was lost, binding up that which was broken, guarding the strong, and gathering them together in the Fold beyond, with words of pastoral knowledge. He is called the Sheep, as being the Victim: the Lamb, as being perfect: the High priest, as being the Offerer. He is called Melchizedek, as being without mother in that Nature which is above us, and as being without Father in that nature which is ours; and without genealogy above (for as it says: "Who shall declare his generation?"). He is also called King of Salem, which means Peace, and King of Righteousness, and is said to receive tithes from the Patriarchs, when they prevail over powers of evil. These are all the titles of the Son. Walk through them: those that are lofty in a godlike manner; those that belong to the body in a manner suitable to them; or rather approach them altogether in a godlike manner, so that you yourself may become a god, ascending from below, for his sake who came down from on high for our sake. In all, and above all, keep to this principle, and you shall never err, either in regard to the loftier or the lowlier titles; Jesus Christ is the Same yesterday and today in the Incarnation, and in the Spirit, for ever and ever. Amen.

St. Gregory of Nazianzus, Oration 31: The Fifth Theological Oration

On the Holy Spirit

31.1. Such then is the account of the Son, and in this manner he has escaped those who set out to stone him, "passing through the midst of them." For the Word is not stoned, but casts stones when he pleases; and uses a sling against wild beasts (that is, words) who approaching the holy Mountain in an unholy way. But, the opponents go on, what have you to say about the Holy Spirit? From where do you bring in upon us this strange God, of whom Scripture is silent? And even those who keep within proper limits in respect to discourse about the Son speak in such a way. And just as we find in the case of roads and rivers, that they often split off from one another and then join up again, so it happens also in this case, through an excess of impiety, that people who differ in all other respects find here some points of agreement; so that you never can tell for certain either where they are of one mind, or where they are in conflict.

31.2. Now the subject of the Holy Spirit presents a special difficulty, not only because when these men have become weary in their disputations concerning the Son, they struggle with greater vehemence against the Spirit (for it seems to be absolutely necessary for them to have some object on which to give expression to their impiety, or life would appear to them no longer worth living). But it is also difficult because we too, worn out by the multitude of their questions, feel like men who have lost their appetite; who have taken a dislike to some particular kind of food, and thus shrink from all food. Just so, we ourselves have started to have an aversion to all discussions. Yet may the Spirit grant it to us, and then the discourse will proceed, and God will be glorified. Well then, we will leave to others who have worked upon this subject for us (as well as for themselves) just as we have worked upon it for them, that task of examining carefully and distinguishing in how many senses the word Spirit or the word Holy is used and understood in Holy Scripture, with the evidence suitable to such an enquiry; and we will let them show how the combination of the two words "Holy" and "Spirit" is used in a peculiar sense. And we will now apply ourselves to the remainder of the subject.

31.3. Our opponents who are angry with us on the grounds that we are bringing in a strange or interpolated God, that is the Holy Spirit, and who fight so very hard for the letter, should know that they are afraid where there is no fear; and I would have them clearly understand that their love for the letter is merely a cloak for their impiety, as I shall make manifest later, when we refute their objections to the utmost of our power. But we have so much confidence in the Divinity of the Spirit whom we adore, that we will begin our teaching concerning his Godhead by fitting to him the Names which belong to the Trinity, even though some persons may think us too bold. The Father was the "True Light which enlightens every man coming into the world." The Son was the True Light which enlightens every man coming into the world. That Other Comforter was also the True Light which enlightens every man coming into the world. Note the: Was and Was and Was; but always Was One Thing. Light repeated three times; but One Light and One Godhead. This was what David represented to himself long before when he said, "In your Light shall we see Light." And now we have both seen and proclaim concisely and simply the doctrine of God the Trinity, comprehending Light from Light in Light. Whoever rejects this, let him reject it; and whoever commits iniquity, let him commit iniquity; but we will proclaim what we have understood. We will climb into a high mountain, and will shout, and if we cannot be heard, below; we will exalt the Spirit. We will not be afraid; or if we are afraid, it shall be fear of keeping silence, not fear of proclaiming.

31.4. If ever there was a time when the Father was not, then there was a time when the Son was not. If ever there was a time when the Son was not, then there was a time when the Spirit was not. If the One was from the beginning, then the Three were so too. If you throw down the One, I am bold to assert that you do not set up the other Two. For what profit is there in an imperfect Godhead? Or rather, what Godhead can there be if it is not wholly perfect? And how can that be perfect which lacks something of perfection? And surely there is something lacking if it does not possess the Holy; and how would it have the holy if it were without the Spirit? For either holiness is something different from him, and if so let some one tell me what it might be conceived to be; or if it is the same, how is it not from the beginning, as if it were better for God to be at one time imperfect and apart from the Spirit? If the Spirit is not from the beginning, then he is of the same rank as myself, even though he may be a little before me; since we must both be parted from the Godhead by time. If he is in the same rank as myself, how can he make me God, or join me with Godhead?

31.5. However, let me reason with you about Spirit from a somewhat earlier point, for we have already discussed the Trinity. The Sadducees altogether denied the existence of the Holy Spirit, just as they did that of Angels and the Resurrection; rejecting, I do not know on what grounds, the important testimonies concerning him in the Old Testament. And as for the Greeks, those who are more inclined to speak of God, and who approach nearest to us, have formed some conception of the Spirit, as it appears to me, though they have differed as to his name, and have addressed him as the "Mind of the World," or the "External Mind," and suchlike. But as for our own sages, some have conceived of him as an Activity, some as a Creature, some as God; and some have been uncertain which of these things to call him, out of reverence for Scripture, so they say, as though the scripture did not make the matter clear either way. And therefore they neither worship him nor treat him with dishonor, but take up a neutral position (or in truth a very miserable one) with respect to the Spirit. And of those who consider him to be God, some are orthodox in mind only, while others venture to be so even with the lips. And I have heard of some who are even more clever, and measure out the Deity; and these agree with us that there are "Three Conceptions"; but they have separated these from one another so completely as to make one of them infinite both in essence and power, and the second infinite in power but not in essence, and the third circumscribed in both power and essence; thus imitating (in a different fashion) that party which calls them the Creator, the Co-operator, and the Minister, and they consider that the same order and dignity which pertains to these names is also sequenced in the reality of the matter.

31.6. But we cannot enter into any discussion with those who do not even believe in the Spirit's existence, nor with the pagan Greek babblers (for we would not be enriched in our argument "with the oil of sinners"). With the others, however, we will argue, and will do so as follows. The Holy Spirit must certainly be conceived of either as in the category of the Self-Existent, or as in that of the things which are contemplated subsisting in another; of which classes those who are skilled in such matters call the one "Substance," and name the other "Accident." Now if the Spirit were an Accident, he would be an Activity of God, for what else, or of whom else, could he be; for surely this is what most avoids composition? And if he is an Activity, he will be effected, but will not effect and will cease to exist as soon as he has been effected, for this is the nature of an Activity. How is it then that the Spirit acts and says various things, and defines, and is grieved, and is angered, and has all the qualities which clearly belong to one that moves, and not just to movement? But if he is a Substance and not an attribute of Substance, he will be conceived of either as being either a Creature of God, or as being God. For anything between these two (as if it were to have nothing in common with God or creation, or as being a compound of both) I cannot imagine anyone could posit, not even those fantasists who invented the mythical goat-stag. Now, if the Spirit is a creature, how do we believe in him, and how are we made perfect in him? For it is not the same thing to believe "In" a thing as to believe "About" it. The one belongs to Deity, the other to any thing in particular. But if the Spirit is God, then he is neither a creature, nor a thing made, nor a fellow servant, nor any of these lowly titles.

31.7. There I have said it out loud for you. Let your slings be fired off; let the syllogism be woven. Either the Spirit is altogether Unbegotten, or else he is Begotten. If he is Unbegotten, then there are two Unoriginates. If he is Begotten, you must make a further subdivision. He is so either by the Father or by the Son. And if by the Father, there are two Sons, and they must be Brothers. And you may make them twins if you like, or the one older and the other younger, since you are so very fond of your bodily conceptions. But if he is begotten by the Son, then perhaps you might even say we get a glimpse of a Grandson God; and nothing can be more absurd than that. For my part, however, if I saw the necessity of the distinction, I should have acknowledged the facts without fear of the names. For it does not follow that because the Son is the Son in some higher relation (inasmuch as we could not in any other way point out that he is of God and is Consubstantial), it would also be necessary to think that all the names of this lower world and of our nature should be transferred to the Godhead. Or perhaps you would consider our God to be a male, according to the same arguments, because he is called God and Father, or that Deity is feminine because of the gender of the word, and Spirit is thus neuter, because it has nothing to do with generation; But if you are foolish enough to join with the old myths and fables, so as to say that God begot the Son by a marriage with his own will, we should then be introduced to the Hermaphrodite god of Marcion and Valentinus who imagined the newfangled Æons.

31.8. Nevertheless, since we do not admit your first logical premiss, which declared that there is no mean between Begotten and Unbegotten, then all at once, along with your magnificent distinctions, away go your Brothers and your Grandsons, just as when the first link of an intricate chain is broken so all the others are broken along with it, and disappear from your system of divinity. For, tell me, what position will you assign to "That which Proceeds," which has started up between the two terms of your division, and is introduced by a better Theologian than you, namely our Savior himself? Or perhaps you have taken that saying out of your Gospels for the sake of your Third Testament, I mean "The Holy Spirit, who proceeds from the Father." Insofar as he proceeds from that Source, he is certainly no Creature; and inasmuch as he is not Begotten he is certainly no Son; and inasmuch as he is between the Unbegotten and the Begotten he is God. And thus escaping the labors of your syllogisms, he has manifested himself as God, far stronger than your distinctions. What then is this Procession? Well, you tell me first what is the Unbegottenness of the Father, and then I will explain to you the physiology of the Generation of the Son and the Procession of the Spirit; but then we shall both of us be frenzy-stricken for prying into the mystery of God. And who are we to do such things, we who cannot even see what lies at our feet, or number the sand of the sea, or the drops of rain, or the days of eternity, much less enter into the Depths of God, and supply an account of that Nature which is so ineffable and transcending all words?

31.9. So, they argue, what is there lacking to the Spirit which prevents his being a Son, for if there were not something lacking surely he would be a Son? We assert that there is nothing lacking – for God has no deficiency. But the difference of manifestation, if I may so express myself, or rather of their mutual relations one to another, is what causes the difference of their names. For it is certainly not some deficiency in the Son which prevents his being Father (for Sonship is not a deficiency), and yet he is not Father. According to this line of argument there must be some deficiency in the Father, in respect of his not being Son. For the Father is not Son, and yet this is not due to either deficiency or subjection of Essence. No, the very fact of being Unbegotten or Begotten, or Proceeding has given the name of Father to the First, the name of Son to the Second, and the name of the Holy Spirit to the third of whom we are speaking, so that the distinction of the three Persons may be preserved in the single nature and dignity of the Godhead. For the Son is not the Father, for the Father is One, but he is what the Father is; nor is the Spirit Son because he is of God, for the Only-begotten is One, but the Spirit is what the Son is. The Three are One in Godhead, and the One is three in its properties. This means that the Unity is not a Sabellian one, but neither does the Trinity countenance their present evil distinctions.

31.10. What is our conclusion? Is the Spirit God? Most certainly. Well then, is he Consubstantial? Yes, if he is God. Well, my opponent may say, if both a Son, and one who is not a Son spring from the same Source and these are both of One Substance with the Source, then I must conclude that there is a God beside a God. Not at all I say. This only happens if you admit that there is another God with another divine nature, making such a Trinity. But since God is One and the Supreme Nature is One, how can I offer you any comparable analogy? Or will you look for it once more in lower regions and in your own material surroundings? It is very shameful, and not only shameful, but very foolish, to take from things here below a guess at what things above are like, and from terms of a fluctuating nature imagine the things that are unchanging. It is as Isaiah says, to seek the living among the dead. But even so I will try, for your sake, to give you some assistance for your thinking, even from such a source. I think I will pass over other possibilities, though I could bring forward many from natural History, some generally known, others more specialist knowledge, of what nature has contrived with such wonderful art in connection with the generation of animals. For not only are likes said to beget likes, and diverse things said to beget diverse things, but also likes can be begotten by diverse things, and diverse things by likes. And, if we may believe the legend, there is yet another mode of generation, when an animal may be self-consumed and thus self-begotten. There are also creatures which depart in some sort from their true natures, and undergo change and transformation from one creature into another, again by the magnificence of nature. And indeed sometimes in the same species a part may be generated and a part not; and yet all remain of one substance; something which is more akin to our present subject. I will just mention one fact of our own nature which every one knows, and then I will pass on to another aspect of the argument.

31.11. What was Adam? A creature of God. Then what was Eve? A fragment of the creature. And what was Seth? The begotten of both. Does it seem to you that Creature and Fragment and Begotten are the same thing? Of course not. But were not these different persons consubstantial? Of course they were. Well then, here it is an acknowledged fact that different persons may have the same substance. I say this, not that I would attribute creation or fraction or any property of body to the Godhead (let none of your contenders logistics be down upon me again), but rather that I may contemplate in these, as on a stage, things which are solely objects of thought. For it is not possible to trace out any image exactly to the whole extent of the truth. But, they say, what is the meaning of all this? For is not the one an offspring, and the other a something else of the One? Did not both Eve and Seth come from the one Adam? And were they both begotten by him? No; but the one was a fragment of him, and the other was begotten by him. And yet the two were one and the same thing; both were human beings; no one will deny that.

Will you therefore give up your strife against the Spirit, arguing that he must be either altogether begotten, or else cannot be consubstantial, or be God; and admit now even from human examples the possibility of our position? I think this would be the best course for you, unless you are determined to be very quarrelsome, and to fight against what is proven to be demonstrable.

31.12. But, my opponent says, who in ancient or modern times ever worshipped the Spirit? Who ever prayed to him? Where is it written that we ought to worship him, or to pray to him, and where have you derived this tenet from? We will give the more perfect reason later, when we discuss the question of the unwritten tradition; for the present it is enough to say that it is the Spirit in whom we worship, and in whom we pray. For Scripture says, "God is a Spirit, and those that worship him must worship in Spirit and in truth." And again, "We do not know, as we should, what we should pray for; but the Spirit itself makes intercession for us with ineffable sighs," and "I will pray with the Spirit and I will pray with the understanding also"; that is, in the mind and in the Spirit. Therefore to adore or to pray to the Spirit seems to me to be simply himself offering prayer or adoration to himself. And what godly or learned man would disapprove of this, because in fact the adoration of One is the adoration of the Three, because of the equality of honor and deity between the Three? So I will not be frightened off by the argument that all things are said to have been made by the Son; as if the Holy Spirit were also one of these things. For it says "all things that were made," and not simply "all things." For the Father was not, nor were any of the things that were not made. Prove that he was made, and then give him to the Son, and number him among the creatures; but until you can prove this you will gain nothing for your impiety from holding to this comprehensive phrase. For if he was made, it was certainly through Christ; I myself would not deny that. But if he was not made, how can he be either "one of the many," or "through Christ?" Therefore, cease this dishonor of the Father by opposing the Only-begotten (for you do no real honor, by presenting him with a creature but robbing him of what is more valuable, a Son), for you also dishonor the Son in your opposition to the Spirit. For he is not the maker of a Fellow servant, but rather he is glorified with One of co-equal honor. Set no part of the Trinity in the same rank as yourself, or else you will fall away from the Trinity. Do not divine the single and co-equally August Nature from either one of them; because if you overthrow any of the Three you will have overthrown the whole. Better take a meager view of the Unity than to venture on a complete impiety.

31.13. Our argument has now come to its principal point; and I am grieved that a problem that was long dead, and which had given way to faith, is now stirred up afresh; yet it is necessary to stand against these babblers, and not to let judgment go by default, when we have the Word on our side, and are pleading the cause of the Spirit. If, so their argument goes, there is God and God and God, how is it that there are not Three Gods? Or how is it that what is glorified is not a plurality of Principles? Who is it who say this? Those who have reached a more complete ungodliness, and even those who are ranked second alongside them; I mean those who have a certain moderation in regard to their views of the Son. For my argument is partly against both of them taken in common, and partly against the latter group in particular. What I have to say in answer to these is as follows: What right have you who worship the Son, even though you have revolted from the Spirit, to call us Tritheists? Are not you therefore Ditheists? For if you deny also the worship of the Only Begotten, you have clearly ranged yourself among our adversaries. And why should we deal kindly with you as towards those not quite dead? But if you do worship the Son, and are thus far along the way of salvation, we will ask you what reasons you have to give for your ditheism, if you also might be accused of it? If you have any word of wisdom among you make me an answer, and open to us also a way towards an answer. For the very same reason with which you will repel a charge of Ditheism will prove sufficient for us against one of Tritheism. And so we shall win the day by making use of our accusers as our advocates, and nothing can be more generous than that.

31.14. So, what is our quarrel and dispute with both parties? For us there is One God, since the Godhead is One, and all that proceeds from him is referred to One, though we believe in Three Persons. For one is not more, and another less, God; nor is one before, and another after; nor are they divided in will or separated in power; nor can you find here any of the qualities of divisible things; because the Godhead is, to speak concisely, undivided in separate Persons; and there is one mingling of Light, as if it were three suns joined one to each other. And so, when we look at the Godhead, or the First Cause, or the *Monarchia*, that which we conceive is One; but when we look at the Persons in whom the Godhead dwells, and at those who timelessly and with equal glory have their Being from the First Cause, then there are three whom we worship.

31.15. What then do we say about their possible objection: "Well, do not the pagan Greeks also believe in one Godhead, as their more advanced philosophers declare? And even among us Humanity is one, namely the entire race; but yet they have many gods, not One, just as there are many men." But in this case the common nature has a unity which is only possible to conceive in thought; and the individuals are parted from one another very far indeed, both by time and by dispositions and by power. For we are not only compound beings, but also contrasted beings, both with regard to one another and with ourselves; nor do we remain entirely the same even for a single day, to say nothing of a whole lifetime, but both in body and in soul we are in a perpetual state of flow and change. And perhaps the same may be said of the Angels, and the whole of that superior nature which is second to the Trinity alone; although they are simple in some measure and more fixed in good, owing to their nearness to the highest Good.

31.16. Nor do those whom the Greeks worship as gods, and (to use their own expression) *dæmons*, need us in any respect to stand as their accusers, for such deities are convicted upon the testimony of their own theologians: some as subject to passion, some as given to faction, and full of innumerable evils and changes, and in a state of opposition, not only to one another, but even to their first causes, whom they call *Oceani* and *Tethyes* and *Phanetes*, and by several other names; and last of all a certain god who hated his children through his lust of rule, and swallowed up all the rest through his greediness that he might become the father of all men and gods whom he miserably devoured, and then vomited forth again. And if these are nothing more than myths and fables, as they say in order to escape the shamefulness of the story, what will they say in reference to the dictum that "all things are divided into three parts," and that each god presides over a different part of the Universe, having a distinct province as well as a distinct rank? But our faith is not like this, "Nor is this the portion of Jacob," says my Theologian. But each of the Persons of the Trinity possesses Unity, not less with that which is United to it than with itself, by reason of the identity of Essence and Power. And this is the account of the Unity, so far as we have apprehended it. And if this account is the true one, let us thank God for the glimpse of it that he has granted us. If it is not, let us seek for a better one.

31.17. As for the arguments with which you would overthrow the Union which we support, I am at a loss to know whether you are making jokes or are actually in earnest. For what is the argument? "Things of one essence," you say, "are counted together," and by this "counted together," you mean that they are collected into one number. "But things which are not of one essence are not so reckoned. And according to this principle you cannot avoid speaking of three gods, while we do not run any risk at all of it, insofar as we assert that the persons are not consubstantial." And so by a single word you have freed yourselves from trouble, and have gained a pernicious victory, for in fact you have done something comparable to men who hang themselves out of fear of death. For to save yourselves trouble in your championship of the *Monarchia* you have denied the Godhead, and abandoned the question to your opponents. For my part, however, even if much labor might be involved, I will not abandon the Object of my adoration. And yet on this point I cannot see where the difficulty is.

31.18. You say, "Things of one essence are counted together," but those which are not consubstantial are reckoned one by one. Where did you get this from? From what teachers of dogma or mythology? Do you not know that every number expresses the quantity of what is included under it, but not the nature of the things? But I am so old fashioned, or perhaps I should say so "unlearned," as to use the word three to refer to number of things, even if they are of a different nature, and to use One and One and One in a different way than connoting just so many units, even if they are united in essence, looking not so much at the things themselves as at the quantity of the things in respect of which the enumeration is made. But since you hold so very close to the letter (although you are contending against the letter), I will ask you take your demonstrations from this source. There are in the Book of Proverbs three things said to go well together, a lion, a goat, and a cock; and to these is added a fourth: namely a King making a speech before the people (I will pass over the other sets of four which are counted up in that book, things of various natures). And I find in the books of Moses two Cherubim counted singly. But now, in your technology, could either the former things be called three, when they differ so greatly in their nature, or the latter be treated as units when they are so closely connected and are of one nature? For if I were to speak of God and Mammon, as two masters, reckoned under one heading, when they are so very different from each other, I should probably be still more laughed at for such a connumeration.

31.19. But to my mind, my opponent answers, those things are said to be connumerated and consubstantial when their names also correspond, such as three Men, or three gods, but not three "this that and the other." What does this concession amount to? It is fitting only for one laying down a law of naming, not for one who is asserting the truth. For must I also assert that Peter and James and John are not three or consubstantial, so long as I cannot say three Peters, or three Jameses, or three Johns?

For what you have reserved for common names we demand also for proper names, in accordance with your arrangement; or else you will be unfair in not conceding to others what you assume for yourself. What about John then, when in his Catholic Epistle he says that there are three that bear witness, the Spirit and the Water and the Blood? Do you think he is talking nonsense? First, because he has ventured to reckon under one numeral things which are not consubstantial, though you say this ought to be done only in the case of things which are consubstantial. But who would ever assert that these are consubstantial? Secondly, because he has not been consistent in the way he has happened upon his terms; for after using three in the masculine gender he adds three words which are neuter, contrary to the definitions and laws which you and your grammarians have laid down. For what is the difference between putting a masculine three first, and then adding One and One and One in the neuter, or after a masculine One and One and One, to use the three not in the masculine but in the neuter, which you yourself disclaim in the case of Deity? What have you to say about the case of the Crab: which may mean either an animal, or an instrument, or a constellation? And what about the Dog, now terrestrial, now aquatic, now celestial? Do you not see that three crabs or dogs are being spoken of? Why of course, you might answer. Well then, are they of necessity all of one substance? None but a fool would say that. So you see how completely your argument from connumeration has broken down, and is refuted by all these instances. For if things that are of one substance are not always counted under one numeral, and things which are not consubstantial can be so counted, and the pronunciation of the name once for all is used in both cases, what is the use of your doctrine?

31.20. I will look also at this further point, which is not without its bearing on the subject. One and one added together make two; and two resolved again becomes one and one, as is perfectly evident. If, however, elements which are added together must, as your theory requires, be consubstantial, and those which are separate be heterogeneous, then it will follow that the same things must be both consubstantial and heterogeneous. No: I laugh at your concept of "Counting Before" and your "Counting After," of which you are so proud, as if the facts themselves depended upon the order of their names. If this were so, according to the same law, since the same things are in consequence of the equality of their nature counted in Holy Scripture, sometimes in an earlier, sometimes in a later place, what prevents them from being at once more honorable and less honorable than themselves? I say the same of the names "God" and "Lord," and of the prepositions "Of Whom," and "By Whom," and "In Whom," by which you describe the Deity according to the rules of art for us, attributing the first to the Father, the second to the Son, and the third to the Holy Spirit. For what would you have done, if each of these expressions were constantly allotted to each Person (when the fact is that they are used of all the Persons, as is evident to those who have studied the question), since you even make them the ground of inequality in terms of both nature and dignity. This is sufficient argument for all who are not totally lacking sense. But since it is a matter of great difficulty for you after you have once started to make your assault upon the Spirit, to check your charge, instead of pushing your quarrel to the bitter end like a furious boar, casting itself upon the lance until you have received the whole wound in your own breast. But let us press on to see what further argument remains to you.

31.21. Over and over again you turn upon us the issue of the silence of scripture [in regard to the Spirit's deity]. But the fact that it is not a strange doctrine, or an afterthought, but rather is acknowledged and plainly set forth by the ancients as well as many in our own day, is already demonstrated by many persons who have treated this subject, and who have handled the Holy Scriptures; and that not with indifference or as a mere pastime, but rather who have gone beneath the letter and looked into the inner meaning, and have been accounted worthy to see the hidden beauty there, and who have been irradiated by the light of knowledge. We, in our turn, will briefly prove the point insofar as it is possible, building on another's foundation in order not to seem to be over-curious or improperly ambitious. But since the fact, that Scripture does not very clearly or very often designate the Spirit God in express words (as it does first the Father and afterwards the Son), is elevated by you into an occasion of blasphemy and of this excessive wordiness and impiety, we will release you from this inconvenience by a short discussion of things and names, and especially of their use in Holy Scripture.

31.22. Some things have no existence, but are spoken of; others which do exist are not spoken of; some neither exist nor are spoken of, and some both exist and are spoken of. Do you ask me for a demonstration of this? I am ready to give it. According to Scripture God sleeps and is awake, is angry, walks, and has the Cherubim for his Throne. And yet when did he become liable to passion, and have you ever heard that God has a body? This issue, therefore, is not really fact, but a figure of speech. For we have given names according to our own comprehension, from our own attributes to those of God. His remaining silent apart from us, and as it were not caring for us, for reasons known to himself, is what we call his sleeping; for our own sleep is such a state of inactivity. And again, his sudden turning to do us good is a waking up; for waking is the dissolution of sleep, just as visitation is the ending of turning away. And when he punishes, we say he is angry; for so it is with us, punishment is the result of anger. And his working, now here now there, we call walking; for walking is change from one place to another. His resting among the Holy Hosts, and as it were loving to dwell among them, is his sitting and being enthroned; this, too, from ourselves, for God rests nowhere more aptly than he does upon the saints. His swiftness of moving is called flying, and his watchful care is called his Face, and his giving and bestowing is his hand; and, in a word, all the other the powers or activities of God is depicted for us in terms of some other corporeal one.

31.23. Again, where do you get your terms "Unbegotten" and "Unoriginate," those two citadels of your position, or we our "Immortal?" Show me these in so many words, or we shall either set them aside, or erase them as not contained in Scripture; and so you are slain by your own principle, the names you rely on being overthrown, and therein the fortress wall in which you trusted. Is it not evident that these titles are derived from passages which imply them, though the words do not actually occur? What are these passages? "I am the first, and I am the last," and "Before Me there was no God, neither shall there be after Me." For all that depends on that word "Am" supports my argument, for it has neither beginning nor ending. When you accept this, namely that nothing is before him, and that he has no older Cause, then you have implicitly given him the titles Unbegotten and Unoriginate. And to say that he has no end of Being is to call him Immortal and Indestructible. The first pairs, then, that I referred to are accounted for in this way. But what are those things which neither exist in fact nor are said? That God is evil; that a sphere is square; that the past is present; that man is not a compound being. Have you ever known a man of such stupidity as to venture either to think or to assert any such thing? It remains to show what are those things which exist, both in fact and in language, namely: God, Man, Angel, Judgment, Vanity (that is, such arguments as yours), and the subversion of faith and the emptying-out of the mystery.

31.24. Since there is so much difference in terms and things, why are you such a slave to the letter, and a partisan of the Jewish wisdom, and a plodding follower of syllables at the expense of facts? If you said twice five or twice seven, and then I concluded from your words that you meant Ten or Fourteen; or if you spoke of a rational and mortal animal, and I concluded that you meant Man, would you think that I was talking nonsense? Surely not, because I should be merely repeating your own meaning; for words do not belong more to their speaker than to him who called them forth. In this case, therefore, I was looking, more to the thoughts they were meant to convey than to the words themselves. And just so, if I found something else included in the meaning of Scripture, but not explicitly or clearly expressed in its words, should I refrain from expressing it out of fear of your sophistical trick about terminologies? This is how we shall hold our own against the semi-orthodox, among whom I may not count you. For since you deny the titles of the Son, which are so many and so clear, it is quite evident that even if you learned a great many more, and clearer ones, you would not be moved to reverence. But now I will take up the argument again a little way further back, and show you, even though you are so clever, the reason for this entire system of [scriptural] secrecy.

31.25. There have been in the whole period of the duration of the world two conspicuous changes of men's lives, which are also called two Testaments, or rather on account of the wide fame of the matter, two "Earthquakes"; the one being the change from idols to the Law, the other from the Law to the Gospel. And we are taught in the Gospel of a third earthquake, namely, from this Earth to that which cannot be shaken or moved. Now the two Testaments are alike in this respect, that the change was not made suddenly, nor at the first movement of the endeavor. And why not – for this is a point on which we must have information? It was so that no violence might be done to us, but that we might be moved by persuasion. For nothing that is involuntary is durable; like streams or trees which are kept back by force. But that which is voluntary is more durable and safe. The former is appropriate to one who uses force, the latter is ours; the one is appropriate to the gentleness of God, the other to a tyrannical authority. And so, God did not think it was fitting to benefit the unwilling, but rather to do good to the willing. And therefore like a Tutor or Physician he partly removes and partly condones ancestral habits, conceding a little of what tended to pleasure, just as medical men do with their patients, so that their medicine may be taken, by being artfully blended with what is pleasant. For it is a difficult thing to change from habits which custom and usage have made honorable. For instance, the first earthquake cut off the idols, but left the sacrifices; the second, while it destroyed the sacrifices did not forbid circumcision. Then, when once men had submitted to the curtailment, they also yielded that which had been conceded to them; in the first instance the sacrifices, in the second circumcision; and became Jews, instead of Gentiles, and then Christians, instead of Jews. They were thus beguiled into the Gospel by gradual changes. Paul is a proof of this; for having at one time administered circumcision, and submitted to legal purification, he advanced until the time he could say, "And I, brethren, if I still preach circumcision, why do I still suffer persecution?" His former conduct belonged to the temporary dispensation, his later conduct to maturity.

31.26. To this I may compare the case of Theology except that it proceeds the reverse way. For in the case by which I have illustrated it the change is made by successive subtractions; whereas here perfection is reached by additions. For the matter stands like this. The Old Testament proclaimed the Father openly, and the Son more obscurely. The New Testament manifested the Son, and suggested the Deity of the Spirit. Now the Spirit himself dwells among us, and supplies us with a clearer demonstration of himself. For it was not safe, when the Godhead of the Father was not yet acknowledged, plainly to proclaim the Son; nor when that of the Son was not yet received to burden us further (if I may use so bold an expression) with the Holy Spirit; in case people might risk the loss even of that which was within the reach of their powers, like men loaded with food beyond their strength, or those who lift up eyes to the sun's light which are still too weak to bear it. But it was done by gradual additions, and, as David says, "Ascents," and by advances and progress from glory to glory, so that the Light of the Trinity might shine upon the more illuminated. This was the reason, I think, that the Spirit gradually came to dwell in the Disciples, measuring himself out to them according to their capacity to receive him; at the beginning of the Gospel, and after the Passion, and after the Ascension, perfecting their powers, being breathed upon them, and appearing in fiery tongues. And indeed it is by "little and little" that he is declared by Jesus, as you will learn for yourself if you will read more carefully. "I will ask the Father," Jesus says, "and he will send you another Comforter, even the spirit of Truth." He said this that he might not seem to be a rival God, or to make his discourses to them by another authority. Again, he says "He shall send him, but it is in My Name." He leaves out the "I will ask," but he keeps the "Shall send"; then again, "I will send," referring to his own dignity, and "Then shall come," evoking the authority of the Spirit.

31.27. You see lights breaking upon us, gradually; and the order of Theology, which it is better for us to keep, which neither proclaims things too suddenly, nor keeps them hidden to the end. For the former course would be unscientific, the latter atheistical; and the former would be calculated to startle outsiders, the latter to alienate our own people. I will add another point to what I have said; one which may readily have come into the mind of others, but which I think is actually a fruit of my own meditations. Our Savior had some things which, he said, could not be borne at that time by his disciples (though they were filled with many teachings), perhaps for the reasons I have mentioned; and therefore these things were hidden. And again he said that all things should be taught us by the Spirit when he would come to dwell among us. One of these things, I take it, was the Deity of the Spirit himself, made clear in later days when such knowledge would be appropriate and capable of being received after our Savior's restoration, when it would no longer be received with incredulity because of its marvelous character. And what greater thing than this did he ever promise, or did the Spirit teach, of all the wondrous things taught and promised concerning the Majesty of God?

31.28. So this is my position with regard to these matters, and I hope it may be always my position, and that of all those who are dear to me; to worship God the Father, God the Son, and God the Holy Spirit, three Persons, One Godhead, undivided in honor and glory and substance and kingdom, as one of our own inspired philosophers not long departed has shown. Whoever is otherwise minded, or who follows the temper of the times, constantly changing their opinion, and thinking of these highest matters most unsoundly, then let such a person "Never see the rising of the Morning Star," as Scripture puts it, nor the glory of its brightness. For if the Spirit is not to be worshipped, how can he deify me by Baptism? But if he is to be worshipped, surely he is an object of adoration, and if he is an object of adoration he must be God; the one notion is linked to the other, a truly golden and saving chain. And indeed from the Spirit comes our New Birth, and from the New Birth comes our new creation, and from the new creation comes our deeper knowledge of the dignity of him from whom it is derived.

31.29. This, therefore, is what may be said as a reply by one who admits the silence of Scripture. But now the swarm of testimonies shall burst upon you from which the Divinity of the Holy Spirit shall be shown to all who are not completely stupid, or total enemies to the Spirit, to be most clearly recognized in Scripture. Look at these facts: Christ is born; the Spirit is his Forerunner. Christ is baptized; the Spirit bears witness. He is tempted; the Spirit leads him up. He works miracles; the Spirit accompanies them. He ascends; the Spirit takes his place. What great things are contained in the notion of God which are not in his power? What titles which belong to God are not applied to him, except only Unbegotten and Begotten? For it was necessary that the distinctive properties of the Father and the Son should remain peculiar to them, in case there should be confusion in the Godhead, which brings all things, even disorder itself, into due arrangement and good order. Indeed I tremble when I think of the abundance of the titles, and how many Names they blaspheme who fall foul of the Spirit. He is called the Spirit of God, the Spirit of Christ, the Mind of Christ, the Spirit of the Lord, and himself is The Lord, the Spirit of Adoption, of Truth, of Liberty; the Spirit of Wisdom, of Understanding, of Counsel, of Might, of Knowledge, of Godliness, of the Fear of God. For he is the Maker of all these, filling all with his Essence, containing all things, filling the world in his Essence, yet incapable of being comprehended in his power by the world; good, upright, princely, by nature not by adoption; sanctifying, not sanctified; measuring, not measured; shared, not sharing; filling, not filled; containing, not contained; inherited, glorified, reckoned with the Father and the Son; held out as a threat; the Finger of God; Fire like God (to manifest, as I take it, his consubstantiality); the Creator-Spirit, who by Baptism and by Resurrection creates anew; the Spirit that knows all things, The Spirit that teaches, that blows where and to how we wills; The Spirit that guides, talks, sends forth, separates, is angry or tempted; The Spirit that reveals, illumines, vivifies, or rather is the very Light and the very Life; The Spirit that makes Temples; The Spirit that deifies; The Spirit that perfects so as even to anticipate Baptism, yet after Baptism which is to be sought as a separate gift; The Spirit that does all things that God does; that divides into fiery tongues; divides gifts; making Apostles, Prophets, Evangelists, Pastors, and Teachers; Spirit that is understanding, manifold, clear, piercing, undefiled, unhindered, which is the same thing as Most Wise and varied in his actions;

who makes all things clear and plain; Spirit of independent power, unchangeable, Almighty, all-seeing, penetrating all spirits that are intelligent, pure, and most subtle (the Angel Hosts I think); and also inspiring all prophetic and apostolic spirits in the same manner although not in the same places; since they lived in different places; thereby showing that he is uncircumscribed.

31.30. Those who say and teach these things, and moreover call him another Paraclete in the sense of another God, those who know that blasphemy against him alone cannot be forgiven, and who branded with such fearful infamy Ananias and Sapphira for having lied to the Holy Spirit: what do you think of these men? Do they proclaim the Spirit God, or something else? Now really, you must be extraordinarily dull and far from the Spirit if you have any doubt about this and need some one to teach you. So important, therefore, and so vivid are his Names. Why is it necessary to lay before you the testimony contained in the very words? And whatever in this case also is said in more lowly fashion, as that "He is Given," "Sent," "Divided"; or that "He is the Gift," the "Bounty," the "Inspiration," the "Promise," the "Intercession for us," and (not to go into any further detail) any other expressions of the sort, is to be explained by reference to the First Cause, that it may be shown from whom the Spirit is, and also so that men may not admit Three Principles as the pagans do. For it is equally impious to confuse the Persons, in the company of the Sabellians, as it is to divide the Natures in the company of the Arians.

31.31. I have very carefully turned over this matter in my own mind, and have looked at it from every point of view, in order to find some illustration of this most important subject, but I have been unable to discover any thing on earth with which to compare the nature of the Godhead. For even if I did happen upon some minute likeness it escaped me for the most part, and left me down below with my example. I picture to myself an eye, a fountain, a river, as others have done before, to see if the first might be analogous to the Father, the second to the Son, and the third to the Holy Spirit. For in these there is no distinction in time, nor are they torn away from their connection with each other, though they seem to be parted by three personalities. But I was afraid in the first place that I should present a flow in the Godhead, incapable of standing still; and secondly that by this figure a numerical unity would be introduced. For the eye and the spring and the river are numerically one, though in different forms.

31.32. Again I thought of the sun and a ray and its light. But here again there is the anxiety that people might get an idea of composition in the Uncompounded Nature, such as there is in the Sun and the things that are in the Sun. And in the second place in case we should seem to give Essence to the Father but deny Personality to the others, and make them out to be only Powers of God, existing in him and not Personally. For neither the ray nor the light is another sun, but they are only effulgences from the Sun, and qualities of its essence. And I was also fearful in case, by this illustration, I should attribute both Being and Not-being to God, which is an even more monstrous position. I have also heard that some one has suggested an illustration of the following kind. A ray of the Sun flashing upon a wall and trembling with the movement of the moisture which the beam has taken up in mid air, and then, being checked by the hard body, has set up a strange sort of quivering. For it quivers with many rapid movements, and is not one rather than it is many, nor yet many rather than one; because by the swiftness of its union and separating it escapes before the eye can see it.

31.33. But it is not possible for me to make use of even this illustration; because it is very evident what gives the ray its motion; but there is nothing prior to God which could set him in motion; for he is himself the Cause of all things, and he has no prior Cause. And secondly because in this case also there is a suggestion of such things as composition, diffusion, and an unsettled and unstable nature: none of which we can suppose in the Godhead. In a word, there is nothing which presents a standing point to my mind in these illustrations from which to consider the object which I am trying to represent to myself, unless one may indulgently accept one point of the image while rejecting the rest of it. Finally, then, it seems best to me to let the images and the shadows slip away, as being deceitful and very far short of the truth. For my part I want to cling to the more reverent conception, resting upon few words, using the guidance of the Holy Spirit, keeping to the end as my genuine comrade and companion that enlightenment which I have received from him, and passing through this world so as to persuade all others also, to the best of my power, to worship Father, Son, and Holy Ghost, the One Godhead and Power. To him belongs all glory and honor and might for ever and ever. Amen.

9 Excerpts from the Treatise "An Exact Exposition of the Orthodox Faith" by St. John of Damascus

Book 1. Chapter 1. That the Deity is incomprehensible, and that we ought not to pry into and meddle with the things which have not been delivered to us by the holy Prophets, and Apostles, and Evangelists. No one has seen God at any time; the Only-begotten Son, who is in the bosom of the Father, he has declared him
The Deity, therefore, is ineffable and incomprehensible. *For no one knows the Father, save the Son, nor the Son, save the Father.* And the Holy Spirit, also, knows the things of God just as the spirit of a man knows the things that are in him. Moreover, after the first and blessed nature no one has ever known God, except the one to whom he revealed himself: something that applies not only to humans, but even to the supramundane powers, even to the Cherubim and Seraphim themselves.

God, however, did not leave us in absolute ignorance. For the knowledge of God's existence has been implanted by him in all by nature. This creation, too, and its maintenance, and its government, proclaim the majesty of the Divine nature. Moreover, by the Law and the Prophets, in former times, and afterwards by his Only-begotten Son, our Lord and God and Savior Jesus Christ, God disclosed the knowledge of himself to us, insofar as that was possible for us. And so, we receive all the things that have been delivered to us by the Law and the Prophets, and the Apostles and Evangelists; and we know and honor these things seeking nothing beyond them. For God, who is good, is the cause of all good, and is subject neither to envy nor to any passion. For envy is far removed from the Divine Nature, which is both passionless and entirely good. Since he knows all things, therefore, and provides what is profitable for each one, he revealed all that was profitable for us to know; but kept secret all that we were unable to bear. So, let us be satisfied with these things, and let us stand by them, not removing everlasting boundaries, nor overpassing the divine tradition.

Book 1. Chapter 2. Concerning things utterable and things unutterable, and things knowable and things unknowable

It is necessary, therefore, that whoever who wishes to speak or to hear of God should understand clearly that both in the doctrine of God and in the doctrine of the Incarnation, not everything is unutterable, and not everything is utterable; neither is everything unknowable, or everything knowable. But the knowable things belong to one order, and the utterable to another; just as it is one thing to speak and another thing to know. Many of the things relating to God, therefore, that are dimly understood cannot be put into fitting terms, but with regard to things above us we cannot do other than express ourselves according to our limited capacity; as, for instance, when we speak of God we use the terms *sleep*, and *wrath*, and *inattentiveness*, as well as *hands*, and *feet*, and similar expressions.

We, therefore, both know and confess that God is without beginning, without end, eternal and everlasting, uncreated, unchangeable, invariable, simple, uncompounded, incorporeal, invisible, impalpable, uncircumscribed, infinite, incognisable, indefinable, incomprehensible, good, just, the maker of all things created, almighty, all-ruling, all-surveying, overseer of all, sovereign, judge; and that God is One, that is to say, One essence; and that he is known, and has his being in three subsistences, in Father, and Son and Holy Spirit; and that the Father and the Son and the Holy Spirit are one in all respects, except in the respect of "not being begotten," that of "being begotten," and that of "procession'; and that the Only-begotten Son and Word of God (who is God) in his compassionate mercy, for our salvation, by the good will of God and the co-operation of the Holy Spirit, being conceived seedlessly, was born uncorruptedly of the Holy Virgin and Mother of God, Mary, by the Holy Spirit, and became of her perfect Man; and that the Same is at once perfect God and perfect Man, of two natures, namely Godhead and Manhood, and in two natures possessing intelligence, will and energy, and freedom, and (in a word) perfect according to the measure and proportion proper to each nature (that is simultaneously to the divinity, and to the humanity, yet to one composite person); and that he suffered hunger and thirst and weariness, and was crucified, and for three days submitted to the experience of death and burial, and ascended to heaven, from which also he came to us, and shall come again. And the Holy Scripture is witness to this and the whole choir of the Saints.

But even so we do not know, nor can we tell, what the essence of God is, or how it is in all, or how the Only-begotten Son and God, having emptied himself, became Man of virginal blood, made by another law contrary to our nature, or how it was he walked with dry feet upon the waters. It is not within our capacity, therefore, to say anything about God or even to think of him, beyond the things which have been divinely revealed to us, whether by word or by manifestation, by the divine oracles, both those of the Old Testament and of the New.

Book 1. Chapter 4. Concerning the nature of Deity: that it is incomprehensible

It is plain, then, that there is a God. But what he is in his essence and nature is absolutely incomprehensible and unknowable. For it is evident that he is incorporeal. For how could what is infinite and boundless, which is formless, and intangible and invisible (in short, what is simple and not compounded) possess a body? How could whatever is circumscribed and subject to passion be immutable? And how could whatever is composed of elements and is resolved again into elements, be passionless? For combination is the beginning of conflict, and conflict the beginning of separation, and separation of dissolution, and dissolution is altogether foreign to God.

Again, how can it be maintained that God permeates and fills the universe? As the Scriptures say, "Do not I fill heaven and earth, the Lord says?" For it is an impossibility that one body should permeate other bodies without dividing and being divided, and without being enveloped and contrasted, in the same way as fluids mix and commingle. But if some should argue that the body is immaterial, in the same way as that fifth body which the Greek philosophers speak about (which body is an impossibility), it will be wholly subject to motion like the heavens. For this is what they mean by the fifth body. Who then is it that moves this? For everything that is moved is moved by another thing. And who again is it that moves that? And so on to infinity, till we finally arrive at something motionless. For the First Mover is motionless, and that is the Deity. And is it not the case that whatever is moved is circumscribed in space? The Deity alone, therefore, is motionless, moving the universe by immobility. This is why it must be assumed that the Deity is incorporeal.

But even to say that God is unbegotten, and without beginning, changeless and imperishable, and possessed of such other qualities as we are accustomed to ascribe to God and his environment, gives no true idea of his essence. For such things do not indicate what he is, but only what he is not. But when we want to explain what the essence of a thing is, we must speak beyond the mere negative. In the case of God, however, it is impossible to explain what he is in his essence, and it is more fitting for us to speak about his absolute separation from all things. For God does not belong to the class of existing things: not that he has no existence, but insofar as he is above all existing things, indeed even above existence itself. For if all our forms of knowledge have to do with what exists, assuredly that which is above knowledge must certainly also be above essence: and, conversely, that which is above essence will also be above knowledge.

God then is infinite and incomprehensible and all that is comprehensible about him is his infinity and incomprehensibility. But all that we can affirm concerning God does not show forth God's nature, but only the qualities of his nature. For when you speak of him as good, and just, and wise, and so on, you do not define God's nature but only the qualities of his nature. Furthermore, there are some affirmations which we make concerning God which have the force of absolute negation. For example, when we use the term darkness, in reference to God, we do not mean darkness itself, but rather that he is not light, but above light: and when we speak of him as light, we mean that he is not darkness.

Book 1. Chapter 8. Concerning the Holy Trinity
We believe, therefore, in One God, one beginning, having no beginning, uncreated, unbegotten, imperishable and immortal, everlasting, infinite, uncircumscribed, boundless, of infinite power, simple, uncompounded, incorporeal, without flux, passionless, unchangeable, unalterable, unseen, the fountain of goodness and justice, the light of the mind, inaccessible; a power known by no measure, measurable only by his own will alone

(for all things that he wills he can achieve), creator of all created things, seen or unseen, the maintainer and preserver of all things, the provider, master, lord and king over all, with an endless and immortal kingdom: having no contrary, filling all, encompassed by nothing but rather himself the encompasser and maintainer and original possessor of the universe, occupying all essences intact and extending beyond all things, and being separate from all essence as being himself hyper-essential and above all things and absolute God, absolute goodness, and absolute fullness: determining all sovereignties and ranks, being placed above all sovereignty and rank, above essence and life and word and thought: being himself the very light and goodness, the life and essence, inasmuch as he does not derive his being from any other, that is to say, of any existent thing: but being himself the fountain of being to all that is; source of life to the living, of reason to those who possess reason; to all the cause of all good: perceiving all things even before they have come to pass: one essence, one divinity, one power, one will, one energy, one beginning, one authority, one dominion, one sovereignty, made known in three perfect *hypostases* and adored with one adoration, believed in and served by all rational creation, united without confusion and divided without separation (a thing which truly transcends thought). For: "We believe in Father, Son and Holy Spirit" into whom we have also been baptized. For this was how our Lord commanded the Apostles to baptize, saying: "Baptizing them in the name of the Father, Son, and Holy Spirit."

We believe in one Father, the beginning and cause of all: begotten of no one: without cause or generation, alone subsisting: creator of all: but Father of one only by nature (namely his Only-begotten Son and our Lord and God and Savior Jesus Christ) and Producer of the most Holy Spirit. And we believe in one Son of God, the Only-begotten, our Lord, Jesus Christ: Begotten of the Father, before all the ages: Light of Light, true God of true God: Begotten, not made, Consubstantial with the Father, through whom all things are made: and when we say "He was before all the ages" we show that his birth is without time or beginning: for the Son of God was not brought into being out of nothing, "He who is the effulgence of the glory, the impress of the Father's subsistence," the living wisdom and power, the Word possessing interior subsistence, the essential and perfect and living image of the unseen God. For he was always with the Father and in him, begotten of him everlastingly and without beginning. For there never was a time when the Father was and the Son was not; but always the Father and always the Son who was begotten of him co-existed. For he could not have received the name Father apart from the Son: for if he were without the Son, he could not be the Father: and if he afterwards had the Son, then he would have become Father later, as if not having been Father prior to this, and he would then have been changed from that which was not Father so as to become the Father. This is the worst form of blasphemy. For we may not speak of God as destitute of natural generative power: and generative power means the power of producing from one's self, that is to say, from one's own proper essence, that which is like in nature to one's self.

And so, in treating of the generation of the Son, it is an act of impiety to say that time comes into play and that the existence of the Son is of later origin than the Father. For we hold that it is from him, that is, from the Father's very nature, that the Son is generated. And unless we insist that the Son co-existed from the beginning with the Father by whom he was begotten, then we introduce change into the Father's subsistence; because, from not being the Father, he would have subsequently become the Father. For the creation, even though it originated later, is nevertheless not derived from the essence of God, but is brought into existence out of nothing by God's will and power, and thus change does not touch God's nature. But generation means that the begetter produces out of his own essence an offspring similar in essence. But the terms "creation" and "making" mean that the creator and maker produces from that which is external, and not out of his own essence, a creation of an absolutely dissimilar nature.

And so, in the case of in God, who alone is passionless and unalterable, and continues always immutable, both begetting and creating are passionless acts. For being by nature passionless and not liable to flux, since he is simple and uncompounded, God is not subject to passion or flux either in begetting or in creating, nor has he need of any co-operation. But in his case generation is without beginning and everlasting, since it is the work of nature and a producing which is from his own essence, that the Begetter may not undergo change, and that he may not be God first and God last, nor receive any accession: while creation in the case of God, since it is the work of will, is not co-eternal with God. For it is not natural that whatever is brought into existence out of nothing should be co-eternal with what is without beginning and everlasting. There is this difference in fact between man's making and God's. Man can bring nothing into existence out of nothing, but all that he makes requires pre-existing matter for its basis, and he certainly does not create it by will only, but first thinks out what it is going to be and pictures it in his mind, and only then does he fashion it with his hands, undergoing labor and trouble, and often missing the mark and failing to produce to his satisfaction the thing he was striving after. But God, through the exercise of will alone, has brought all things into existence out of nothing. Now there is the same difference between God and man in begetting and generating. For with God, who is without time and beginning, passionless, not liable to flux, incorporeal, single and without end, generation is also without time and beginning, passionless and not liable to flux, nor dependent on the union of two agents: nor has his own incomprehensible generation a beginning or end. And it is without beginning because he himself is immutable: without flux because he himself is passionless and incorporeal: independent of the union of two again because he himself is incorporeal (and also because he is the one and only God, who stands in need of no co-operation): and it is without end or cessation because he himself is without beginning, or time, or end, and ever continues the same. For that which has no beginning has no end: but whatever by grace is endless is not necessarily also without beginning, as, we may take as an example, the angels.

And so, the everlasting God generates his own Word which is perfect, without beginning and without end, because God whose nature and existence are above time may not engender within time. But with man clearly it is otherwise, for generation is with us a matter of sexuality, and destruction, and flux, and increase and the body wraps us round, and we possess a nature which is male or female, and the male requires the assistance of the female. But may he who surpasses all things, and who transcends all thought and comprehension, be ever gracious to us.

The holy catholic and apostolic Church, therefore, teaches the existence at once of a Father, and of his Only-begotten Son, who was born of him without time and flux and passion, in a manner incomprehensible and perceived by the God of the universe alone: just as we recognize the existence at once of fire and the light which proceeds from it: for there is not first of all fire and afterwards light, but they exist together. And just as light is always the product of fire, and is always in it and never any time separate from it, just so is the Son begotten of the Father and is never in any way separate from him, but is ever in him. But whereas the light which is inseparably produced from fire, and always dwells within it, has no proper subsistence of its own, as distinct from that of fire (since light is a natural quality of fire), the Only-Begotten Son of God, who is begotten of the Father without separation and difference and always abides in him, does have a proper subsistence (*hypostasis*) of his own distinct from that of the Father.

The terms "Word" and "effulgence," then, are used because the Son is begotten of the Father without the union of two, or passion, or time, or flux, or separation: and the terms "Son" and "impress of the Father's *hypostasis*," are used because he is perfect and has subsistence and is in all respects similar to the Father, except that the Father is not begotten: and the term "Only-begotten" is used because he alone was begotten; alone of the Father alone. For no other generation is like that of the generation of the Son of God, since none other is Son of God. For though the Holy Spirit proceeds from the Father, yet this is not generative in character but processive. This is a different mode of existence, equally incomprehensible and unknown, just as is the generation of the Son. And so, all the qualities the Father has also belong to the Son, except that the Father is unbegotten, and this exception involves no difference in essence or dignity, but only a different mode of coming into existence. We have an analogy in Adam, who was not begotten (for God himself molded him), and Seth, who was begotten (since he is Adam's son), and Eve, who proceeded out of Adam's rib (and thus she was not begotten). These do not differ from each other in nature, for they are all human beings: but they do differ in the mode of their coming into existence.

For one must recognize that the word Unoriginate (*agenetos*) signifies uncreated or not having been made, while the word Unborn (*agennetos*) means unbegotten. According to the first significance, essence differs from essence: for one essence is uncreated (*agenetos*) and another is created (*genete*). But in the second significance there is no difference between essence and essence. For the first subsistence of all kinds of living creatures is *agennetos* but not *agenetos*. While they were created by the Creator, being brought into being by his Word, but they were not begotten, for there was no pre-existing form like themselves from which they might have been born.

So then in the first sense of the word the three absolutely divine subsistences of the Holy Godhead agree; for they exist as one in essence and as uncreated. But with the second signification it is quite otherwise. For the Father alone is ingenerate (*agenetos*), no other subsistence having given him being. And the Son alone is generate (*gennetos*), for he was begotten of the Father's essence without beginning and without time. And only the Holy Spirit proceeds (*ekporeuei*) from the Father's essence, not having been generated but simply as proceeding. For this is the doctrine of Holy Scripture. But the nature of that generation and that procession is quite beyond comprehension.

And this also it is appropriate for us to know: that the names Fatherhood, Sonship and Procession, were not applied to the holy Divinity by us: on the contrary, they were communicated to us by the Godhead, as the divine apostle says, "And thus I bow the knee to the Father, from whom is every family in heaven and on earth. But if we say that the Father is the origin of the Son and greater than the Son, we are not thereby suggesting any precedence in time or superiority in nature of the Father over the Son (for it was through his agency that God made the ages), or superiority in any other respect except causation. And we mean by this, that the Son is begotten of the Father and not the Father of the Son; and that the Father is naturally the cause of the Son: just as we say likewise that fire does not proceed from light, but rather light proceeds from fire. So then, whenever we hear it said that the Father is the origin of the Son and greater than the Son, let us understand it to mean in respect of the causation. And just as we do not say that fire is of one essence and light is of another, so we cannot say that the Father is of one essence and the Son is of another: but both are of one and the same essence. And just as we say that fire has brightness, because of the light proceeding from it, and we do not consider the light of the fire as an instrument ministering to the fire, but rather as the fire's own natural force: just so we say that the Father creates all that he creates through his Only-begotten Son, not as though the Son were a mere instrument serving the Father's ends, but rather as being his natural and hypostatic force. And just as we say that the fire shines and again that the light of the fire shines, just so "All things that the Father does, these also the Son does likewise." But whereas light possesses no proper subsistence of its own, distinct from that of the fire, the Son is a perfect subsistence, inseparable from the Father's subsistence, as we have shown above. For it is quite impossible to find in creation an image that will illustrate in itself exactly in all details the nature of the Holy Trinity. For how could that which is created and compounded, subject to flux and change, circumscribed, formed and corruptible, clearly show forth the super-essential divine essence, unaffected as it is in any of these ways? For it is evident that all creation is liable to most of these affections, and all from its very nature is subject to corruption.

In the same way: "We believe also in one Holy Spirit, the Lord and Giver of Life: Who proceeds from the Father" and abides in the Son: who is the object of equal adoration and glorification with the Father and Son, since he is consubstantial and co-eternal: the Spirit of God, direct, authoritative, the fountain of wisdom, and life, and holiness: God existing and addressed along with Father and Son: uncreated, full, creative, all-ruling, all-effecting, all-powerful, of infinite power, Lord of all creation and not under any lord: deifying, not deified: filling, not filled: shared in, not sharing in: sanctifying, not sanctified: the intercessor, receiving the supplications of all: in all things like to the Father and Son: proceeding from the Father and communicated through the Son, and participated in by all creation, creating, through himself and investing with essence and sanctifying, and maintaining the universe: having subsistence, existing in its own proper and peculiar hypostasis, inseparable and indivisible from Father and Son, and possessing all the qualities that the Father and Son possess, except those of not being begotten or born. For the Father is without cause and unborn: for he is derived from nothing, but derives his being from himself, nor does he derive a single quality from any other. Rather he is himself the beginning and cause of the existence of all things in a definite and natural manner. But the Son is derived from the Father in the manner of generation, and the Holy Spirit likewise is derived from the Father, but not in the manner of generation, but in the manner of procession. And we have learned that there is a difference between generation and procession, but as to the nature of that difference we do not understand it. Furthermore, the generation of the Son from the Father and the procession of the Holy Spirit are simultaneous.

And so, all that the Son and the Spirit have is from the Father, even their very being: and unless the Father is, neither is the Son or the Spirit. And unless the Father possesses a certain attribute, the Son and the Spirit will not possess it: and through the Father, that is, because of the Father's existence, the Son and the Spirit exist, and through the Father, that is, because of the Father having the qualities, the Son and the Spirit have all their qualities; those of being unbegotten, and the quality of birth and the quality of procession being excepted, for in these hypostatic, or personal, properties alone do the three holy subsistences differ from each other, since they are indivisibly divided not by essence but by the distinguishing mark of their proper and peculiar hypostasis.

Further we say that each of the three has a perfect subsistence, that we may understand God not as one compound perfect nature made up of three imperfect elements, but rather as one simple essence, surpassing and preceding perfection, existing in three perfect subsistences. For all that is composed of imperfect elements must necessarily be compound. But from perfect subsistences no compound can arise. And this is why we do not speak of the form as being "from subsistences," but as being "in subsistences." But we speak of those things as imperfect which do not preserve the form of that which is completed out of them. For stone and wood and iron are each perfect in its own nature, but with reference to the building that is completed out of them each is imperfect: for none of them is in itself a house.

And so we say that the subsistences are perfect, so that we may not conceive of the divine nature as being compounded. For compoundedness is the beginning of separation. And again we speak of the three subsistences as co-inhering in being, so that we may not introduce a crowd and multitude of Gods. Owing to the three subsistences, there is no compoundedness or confusion: while, owing to their having the same essence and co-inhering one in another, and being the same in will, energy, power, authority, and movement (so to speak), we recognize the indivisibility and the unity of God. For in truth there is only one God, and his Word and his Spirit.

One ought, moreover, to recognize that it is one thing to look at a reality as it is, and another thing to look at it in the light of reason and thought. In the case of all created things, the distinction of the hypostases is observed in actual fact. For in actual fact Peter is seen to be separate from Paul. But the community and connection and unity are apprehended by reason and thought. For it is by the mind that we perceive that Peter and Paul are of the same nature and have one common nature. For both are living creatures, rational and mortal: and both are flesh, endowed with the spirit of reason and understanding. It is, then, by reason that this community of nature is observed. But in this case the hypostases do not exist one within the other. But each stands privately and individually, that is to say, stands quite separate in itself, having innumerable points that divide it from the other. For they are both separated in space and they differ in time, and they are divided in thought, and power, and shape, or form, and habit, and temperament and dignity, and pursuits, and many other differentiating properties, but above all, they are separated in the fact that they do not dwell in one another but are distinct. This of course is the reason that we can speak of two, three, or many men.

And this may be perceived throughout the whole of creation, but in the case of the holy and hyper-essential and incomprehensible Trinity, far removed from all other things, it is quite the reverse. For there the community and unity are observed in fact, through the co-eternity of the subsistences, and through their having the same essence and energy and will and concord of mind, and then their being identical in authority and power and goodness – note that I do not say similar but identical – and then their movement as by one impulse. For there is one essence, one goodness, one power, one will, one energy, one authority, one and the same, I repeat, not three resembling each other. But the three subsistences have one and the same movement. For each one of them is related as closely to the other as to itself: that is to say that the Father, the Son, and the Holy Spirit are one in all respects, save those of not being begotten, of birth and of procession. But it is by thought that the difference is perceived. For we recognize only one God: and only in the attributes of Fatherhood, Sonship, and Procession (both in respect of cause and effect and perfection of subsistence, that is, mode of existence) do we perceive difference. For with reference to the uncircumscribed Deity we cannot speak of a separation in space, as we can in our own case. For the hypostases dwell in one another, in no way confused but rather cleaving together, according to the word of the Lord, "I am in the Father, and the Father is in Me": nor can one admit any difference in will or judgment or energy or power or anything else at all which may produce actual and absolute separation in our case. This is why we do not speak of three Gods, the Father, the Son, and the Holy Spirit, but rather of one God, the Holy Trinity; the Son and Spirit being referred to one cause, and not compounded or coalesced according to the *synæresis* that Sabellius proposed. For, as we have said, they are made one not so as to commingle, but so as to cleave to each other, and they have their being in each other without any coalescence or commingling. Nor do the Son and the Spirit stand apart, but neither are they separated in essence according to the *diæresis* of Arius. For the Deity is undivided in the midst of things divided, to put it concisely: and it is just like three Suns cleaving to each other without separation and giving out a light mingled and conjoined into one. When, therefore, we turn our eyes to the Divinity, and the First Cause and the Sovereignty and the Oneness and Sameness, so to speak, of the movement and will of the Divinity, and the Identity in essence and Power and Energy and Lordship, all that we can see is unity. But when we look to those things in which the Divinity subsists, or (to put it more accurately), which are the Divinity, and those things which are in it through the First Cause without time or distinction in glory or separation, that is to say, the *hypostases* of the Son and the Spirit, the Godhead appears to us a Trinity that we adore. The Father is one Father, and without beginning, that is, without cause: for he is not derived from anything. The Son is one Son, but not without beginning, that is, not without Cause: for he is derived from the Father. But if you eliminate the idea of a beginning from time, he too is also without beginning: for the Creator of times cannot be subject to time. The Holy Spirit is one Spirit, going forth from the Father, not in the manner of Sonship but in terms of Procession; in such a way that the Father does not lose his property of being Unbegotten because he has begotten, nor has the Son lost his property of being begotten because he was begotten of that which was Unbegotten (for how could that be so?), nor does the Spirit change either into the Father or into the Son because he has proceeded and is God. For a property is quite constant. For how could a property persist if it were variable, moveable, and could change into something else? For if the Father is the Son, he is not strictly the Father: for there is strictly one Father. And if the Son is the Father, he is not strictly the Son: for there is strictly one Son and one Holy Spirit.

Further, it should be understood that we do not speak of the Father as derived from any one, but we speak of him as the Father of the Son. And we do not speak of the Son as either Cause or Father, but we speak of him both as from the Father, and as the Son of the Father. And likewise we speak of the Holy Spirit as from the Father, and call him the Spirit of the Father. And we do not speak of the Spirit as from the Son: but even so we call him the Spirit of the Son. "For if any one has not the Spirit of Christ, he is none of his" as the divine apostle says. And we confess that he is manifested and imparted to us through the Son. For he breathed upon his Disciples, it says, and he said, "Receive the Holy Spirit." It is just the same as in the case of the sun from which come both the ray and the radiance (for the sun itself is the source of both the ray and the radiance), and it is through the ray that the radiance is imparted to us, and it is the radiance itself by which we are illumined and in which we participate. Furthermore, we do not speak of the Son of the Spirit, or of the Son as derived from the Spirit.

Book 1. Chapter 14. The properties of the divine nature

These are the attributes which the Deity possesses by nature: Uncreated, without beginning, immortal, infinite, eternal, immaterial, good, creative, just, enlightening, immutable, passionless, uncircumscribed, immeasurable, unlimited, undefined, unseen, unthinkable, wanting in nothing, being his own rule and authority, all-ruling, life-giving, omnipotent, of infinite power, containing and maintaining the universe and making provision for all: and many similar. He has not received them from elsewhere, but he himself imparts all that is good to his own creations according to the capacity of each.

The hypostases dwell in and are firmly established in one another. For they are inseparable and cannot part from one another, but keep to their separate courses within one another, without coalescing or mingling, but cleaving to each other. For the Son is in the Father and the Spirit: and the Spirit in the Father and the Son: and the Father in the Son and the Spirit, but there is no coalescence or commingling or confusion. And there is one and the same motion: for there is one impulse and one motion of the three hypostases, which is not to be observed in any created nature.

Furthermore the divine effulgence and energy, since it is one and simple and indivisible, assuming many varied forms in its goodness among what is divisible and allotting to each the component parts of its own nature, still remains simple and is multiplied without division among divided realities, and gathers and converts the divided into its own simplicity. For all things desire it and have their existence within it. It also gives to all things their being according to their several natures, and it is itself the being of existing things, the life of living things, the reason of rational beings, the thought of thinking beings. But it is itself above mind and reason and life and essence.

In addition the divine nature has the property of penetrating all things without mixing with them and of being itself impenetrable by anything else. Moreover, it has the property of knowing all things with a simple knowledge and of seeing all things, simply with his divine, all-surveying, immaterial eye; both the things of the present, and the things of the past, and the things of the future, before they come into being. It is also sinless, and can cast sin out, and bring salvation: and all that it wills, it can accomplish, but does not will all it could accomplish. For it could destroy the universe but it does not wish so to do.

Book 2. Chapter 3. Concerning Angels

God is himself the Maker and Creator of the angels: for he brought them out of nothing-ness into being and created them after his own image, an incorporeal race, a sort of spirit or immaterial fire: in the words of the divine David, "He makes his angels spirits, and his ministers a flame of fire": and he has described their lightness and the ardor, and heat, and keenness and sharpness with which they hunger for God and serve him, and how they are borne to the regions above and are quite delivered from all material thought.

An angel, then, is an intelligent essence, in perpetual motion, with free will, incorpo-real, ministering to God, having obtained by grace an immortal nature: and the Creator alone knows the form and limitation of its essence. But all that we can understand is, that it is incorporeal and immaterial. For all that is compared with God who alone is incomparable, we find to be dense and material. For in reality only the Deity is truly immaterial and incorporeal. The angelic nature then is rational, and intelligent, and endowed with free will, changeable in will, or variable. For all that is created is changeable, and only that which is uncreated is unchangeable. Also all that is rational is endowed with free will. Since the angel is rational and intelligent, therefore, it is endowed with free will: and as it is created, it is changeable, having power either to abide or progress in goodness, or to turn towards evil.

An angel is not susceptible of repentance because it is incorporeal. For it is owing to the weakness of his body that man comes to have repentance. It is immortal, not by nature but by grace. For all that has had beginning comes also to its natural end. But God alone is eternal, or rather, he is above the Eternal: for he, the Creator of times, is not under the dominion of time, but above time. The angels are secondary intelligent lights derived from that first light which is without beginning, for they have the power of illumination; they have no need of speech or hearing, but without uttering words they communicate to each other their own thoughts and counsels.

All the angels were created through the Word, and through their sanctification by the Holy Spirit they were brought to perfection, each one sharing in proportion to his worth and rank in brightness and grace. They are circumscribed: for when they are in the Heaven they are not on the earth: and when they are sent by God down to the earth they do not remain in the Heaven. They are not hemmed in by walls and doors, and bars and seals, for they are quite unlimited. Unlimited, I repeat, for it is not as they really are that they reveal themselves to the worthy humans to whom God wishes them to appear, but rather in a changed form which the beholders are capable of seeing. Yet that alone is naturally and strictly unlimited which is un-created. For every created thing is limited by God who created it.

In addition, apart from their essence they receive sanctification from the Spirit: through the divine grace they prophesy: they have no need of marriage for they are immortal. Seeing that they are minds they are in mental places, and are not circumscribed after the fashion of a body, for they do not have a bodily form by nature, nor are they extended in three dimensions. But to whatever post they may be assigned, there they are present after the manner of a mind and energies, and they cannot be present and energize in different places at the same time.

Whether they are equals in essence or differ from one another we do not know. God, their Creator, who knows all things, is the only one who knows. But they differ from each other in brightness and rank, whether their rank is dependent on their brightness, or their brightness on their rank: and they impart brightness to one another, because they excel one another in honor and nature. And clearly the higher angels share their brightness and knowledge with the lower.

They are mighty and prompt to fulfill the will of the Deity, and their nature is endowed with such celerity that wherever the Divine glance bids them, there they are found immediately. They are the guardians of the divisions of the earth: they are set over nations and regions, allotted to them by their Creator: they govern all our affairs and bring us help, and this because they are set over us by the divine will and command and are ever in the vicinity of God. Only with difficulty are they moved to evil, yet they were not absolutely immoveable: but now they are altogether immoveable, not by nature but by grace and because of their nearness to the Only Good.

They look upon God according to their capacity, and this is their food. They are above us for they are incorporeal, and are free of all bodily passion, yet they are not passionless: for the Deity alone is passionless. They take different forms at the bidding of God, their Master, and so it is that they reveal themselves to men and unveil the divine mysteries to us. They have Heaven for their dwelling-place, and have only one duty, to sing God's praise and carry out his divine will. Moreover, as that most holy, sacred, and gifted theologian, Dionysios the Areopagite, tells us: All theology, that is to say, the holy Scripture, has nine different names for the heavenly essences. That divine master in sacred things divides these essences into three groups, each containing three. And the first group, he says, consists of those angels who are in God's presence and are said to be directly and immediately one with him, namely the Seraphim with their six wings, the many-eyed Cherubim and those that sit in the holiest thrones. The second group is that of the Dominions, and the Powers, and the Authorities; and the third, and last, is that of the Rulers, Archangels and Angels.

Some, indeed, like Gregory the Theologian, say that these angels existed before the creation of other things. He thinks that the angelic and heavenly powers were first and that thought was their function. Others, again, hold that they were created after the first heaven was made. But all are agreed that it was before the foundation of man. For myself, I am in harmony with the Theologian. For it was fitting that the mental essence should be the first created, and then that which can be perceived, and finally man himself, in whose being both parts are united.

But those who say that the angels are creators of any kind of essence whatever are but the mouthpiece of their father, the devil. For since they are created things the angels are not creators. But he who creates and provides for and maintains all things is God, and he alone is uncreated and is praised and glorified in the Father, the Son, and the Holy Spirit.

Book 2. Chapter 12. Concerning Man

In this way, then, God brought into existence noetic essence, by which I mean, angels and all the heavenly orders. For these clearly have a noetic and incorporeal nature: and by incorporeal I mean in comparison with the denseness of matter. For the Deity alone is truly immaterial and incorporeal. But he also created in the same way sensible essence, that is heaven and earth and the intermediate region; and so he created both the kind of being that is of his own nature (for the nature that has to do with reason is related to God, and apprehensible by mind alone), and the kind which, insofar as it clearly falls under the province of the senses, is separated from him by the greatest interval. And it was also fitting that there should be a mixture of both kinds of being, as a token of still greater wisdom and of the opulence of the Divine economy with regard to natures, as Gregory the Theologian, expounder of God's being and ways, puts it, and to be a sort of connecting link between visible and invisible natures. And by the word fitting I mean simply that it was an evidence of the Creator's will, for that will is the law and ordinance that is most appropriate, and no one will ever say to his Maker, "Why did you fashion me so?" For the potter is able at his will to make vessels of various patterns out of his clay, as a proof of his own wisdom.

Now this being the case, God creates with his own hands man of a visible nature and an invisible nature, after his own image and likeness: on the one hand he formed man's body from earth, and on the other hand he granted to Man his reasoning and thinking soul by virtue of his own inbreathing; and this is what we mean by "After his image." For the phrase "after his image" clearly refers to the side of human nature which consists of mind and free will, whereas "After his likeness" refers to likeness in virtue, insofar as that is possible.

Furthermore, body and soul were formed at one and the same time, not first the one and then the other, as Origen so foolishly supposed. God made man, therefore, without evil, upright, virtuous, free from pain and care, glorified with every virtue, adorned with all that is good, like a sort of second microcosm within the great macrocosm of the world; another angel capable of worship, compounded, surveying the visible creation and initiated into the mysteries of the realm of thought, prince over the things of earth, but subject to a higher King, of the earth and of the heaven, temporal and eternal, belonging to the realm of sight and to the realm of thought, midway between greatness and lowliness, spirit and flesh: for he is spirit by grace, but flesh by overweening pride: spirit that he may abide and glorify his Benefactor, and flesh that he may suffer, and through that suffering may be admonished and disciplined whenever he prides himself in his greatness. Here, that is in the present life, his life is ordered as an animal's, but elsewhere, that is, in the age to come, he is changed and (to complete the mystery) becomes deified by merely inclining himself towards God; becoming deified, in the way of participating in the divine glory and not by any change into the divine being.

Even so, God made him sinless by nature, and endowed him with free will. By sinless, I mean not that sin could find no place in him (for that is the case with the Deity alone), but rather that sin is the result of the free volition he enjoys rather than an integral part of his nature; which means that he has the power to continue and go forward in the path of goodness, by co-operating with the divine grace, or likewise to turn from the good and take to wickedness; for God has conceded this by conferring freedom of will upon him. For there is no virtue in what is the result of mere compulsion.

The soul, accordingly, is a living essence, simple, incorporeal, in its proper nature invisible to bodily eyes, immortal, reasoning and intelligent, formless, making use of an organized body, and being the source of its powers of life, and growth, and sensation, and generation; mind being but its purest part and not in any way alien to it (for as the eye is to the body, so is the mind to the soul); moreover it enjoys freedom and volition and energy, and is mutable, that is, it is given to change, because it is created. It has received all these natural qualities by the grace of the Creator; from which grace it has received both its being and this particular kind of nature.

We understand two kinds of what is incorporeal and invisible and formless: the one is such in essence, the other by free gift: and likewise the one is such in nature, and the other only relatively so by comparison with the denseness of matter. God, therefore, is incorporeal by nature, but the angels and demons and souls are said to be so by free gift, and relatively so in comparison with the denseness of matter....

Book 2. Chapter 30. Concerning Prescience and Predestination

We ought to understand that while God knows all things beforehand, even so he does not predetermine all things. For he knows beforehand those things that are in our power, but he does not predetermine them, for it is not his will that there should be wickedness nor does he choose to compel virtue. So that predetermination is the work of the divine command based on fore-knowledge. But on the other hand God predetermines those things which are not within our power in accordance with his prescience. For already God in his prescience has prejudged all things in accordance with his goodness and justice.

Bear in mind, too, that virtue is a gift from God implanted in our nature, and that he himself is the source and cause of all good, and without his co-operation and help we cannot will or do any good thing. But we have it in our power either to abide in virtue and follow God, who calls us into ways of virtue, or to stray from the paths of virtue, which is to dwell in wickedness, and to follow the devil who summons but cannot compel us. For wickedness is nothing else than the withdrawal of goodness, just as darkness is nothing else than the withdrawal of light. While we abide in our natural state, therefore we abide in virtue, but when we deviate from the natural state, that is from virtue, we come into an unnatural state and dwell in wickedness.

Repentance is the returning from the unnatural into the natural state, from the devil to God, through discipline and effort. The Creator first made Man male, giving him to share in his own divine grace, and thereby bringing him into communion with himself: and so it was that, like a prophet, he gave the names to living things, with authority, as though they were given to be his servants. For having been endowed with reason and mind, and free will after the image of God, Man was fitly entrusted with dominion over earthly things by the common Creator and Master of all.

But since God in his prescience knew that man would transgress and become liable to destruction, he made from him a female, like himself, to be a help to him; a help, indeed, for the conservation of the race by generation from age to age, after the transgression. For the earliest formation is called "making" and not "generation." For "making" is the original formation at God's hands, while "generation" is the succession from each other made necessary by the sentence of death imposed on us on account of the transgression. This man God placed in Paradise, a home that was both spiritual and sensible. For Man lived in the body on the earth in the realm of sense, while he still dwelt in the spirit among the angels, cultivating divine thoughts, and being supported by them: living in naked simplicity a life free from artificiality, and being led up through God's creations to the One and only Creator, in whose contemplation he found joy and gladness. When God had furnished his nature with free will, then, he imposed a law on him, not to taste of the tree of knowledge. Concerning this tree, we have said as much as is necessary in the chapter about Paradise, at least as much as it was in our power to say. And with this command God gave the promise that, if he should preserve the dignity of the soul by giving the victory to reason, and acknowledging his Creator and observing his command, then he should share eternal blessedness and live to all eternity, proving mightier than death: but if indeed he should subject the soul to the body, and prefer the delights of the body, in ignorance of his true dignity making himself like the senseless beasts, and shaking off his Creator's yoke, and neglecting his divine ordinance, he would be liable to death and corruption, and would be compelled to labor throughout a miserable life. For it was no use for man to obtain incorruption while he was still untried and unproved, in case he should fall into pride and fall under the judgment of the devil. For because of his incorruption the devil, once he had fallen as the result of his own free choice, was firmly established in wickedness, so that there was no room for repentance for him and no hope of change: just as, moreover, the angels also, when they had made a free choice for virtue became, through grace, immoveably rooted in goodness.

It was necessary, therefore, that man should first be put to the test (for man untried and unproved would be worth nothing at all), and being made perfect by the trial through the observance of the command should then receive incorruption as the prize of his virtue. For being intermediate between God and matter he was destined, if he kept the command, to be delivered from his natural relation to existing things and to be made one with God's estate, and to be immoveably established in goodness; but, if he transgressed and inclined rather to what was material, and tore his mind from the Author of his being, I mean God, then his fate would be corruption, and he would become subject to passion instead of being passionless, and would be mortal instead of immortal, and thus dependent on connection and unsettled generation. And in his desire for life he would cling to pleasures as though they were necessary to maintain it, and would fearlessly abhor those who sought to deprive him of these, and would transfer his desire from God to matter, and his anger from the real enemy of his salvation to his own brethren. The envy of the devil, then, was the reason for man's fall. For that same demon, so full of envy and with such a hatred of the good, could not bear to allow us to enjoy the pleasures of heaven, when he himself was kept below on account of his arrogance, and so it was that the false one tempted miserable man with the hope of Godhead, and leading him up to as great a height of arrogance as himself, he then hurled him down into a pit of destruction just as deep.

Book 3. Chapter 1. Concerning the Divine Economy and God's care over us, and concerning our salvation

And so it happened that Mankind was snared by the assault of the Devil, and broke his Creator's command, was stripped of grace and lost his confidence with God, clothed himself with the harshness of a laborious (for this is the meaning of the fig-leaves); and was clothed about with death, that is, mortality and the heaviness of flesh (for this is what the garment of skins signifies); was banished from Paradise by God's just judgment, and condemned to death, and made subject to corruption. Yet, even so, in his compassion, God who had first given Man his being, and who in his graciousness had bestowed on him a life of happiness, did not turn his back. But he first trained him in many ways and called him back, by groans and trembling, by the Great Flood and its destruction of almost the entire race, by confusion and diversity of tongues, by the rule of angels, by the burning of cities, by figurative manifestations of God, by wars and victories and defeats, by signs and wonders, by various faculties, by the law and the prophets: for by all of these means God earnestly strove to emancipate man from the widespread enslaving bonds of sin, which had made life such a mass of iniquity, in order to accomplish man's return to a life of happiness.

For it was sin that brought death like a wild and savage beast into the world to the ruin of the human life. But it was fitting that the Redeemer should be without sin, and not made liable to death because of sin, and further, that his nature should be strengthened and renewed, and trained by labor and taught the way of virtue which leads away from corruption to the life eternal. Finally there was revealed that mighty ocean of love for mankind that characterizes the Redeemer. For the very Creator and Lord himself undertakes a struggle in behalf of the work of his own hands, and learns by toil to become Master. And since the enemy snares man by the hope of Godhead, he himself is snared in turn by the veil of flesh, and so we saw revealed the goodness and wisdom, the justice and might, of God. God's goodness is revealed in that he did not turn his back on the frailty of his own handiwork, but was moved with compassion for him in his fall, and stretched out his hand to him: and his justice is shown in that when man was overcome he did not make any other victorious over the tyrant, and did not snatch man from death by power alone, but in his goodness and justice he made him, who had become the slave of death through his sins, the very one who was once more lifted up as conqueror and rescued, like by like, most difficult though this seemed. God's wisdom is seen in his devising the most fitting solution of the difficulty. For by the good pleasure of our God and Father, the Only-begotten Son and Word of God and God, "he who is in the bosom of the God and Father," of like essence with the Father and the Holy Spirit, who was before the ages, who is without beginning and "was in the beginning," who is in the presence of the God and Father, and is God and "made in the form of God," bent the heavens and descended to earth: that is to say, without humiliation he humbled his exalted station (which even so could not be humbled), and stoops down to his servants, with a condescension that was ineffable and incomprehensible (for that is what the descent signifies).

And God, who is perfect, becomes perfect man, and brings to perfection the newest of all new things, the only new thing under the sun, through which the boundless might of God is manifested. For what greater thing is there, than that God should become Man?

"And the Word became flesh" without being changed, of the Holy Spirit, and Mary the holy ever-virgin, the Mother of God. And he acts as mediator between God and man. He who is the only lover of man was conceived in the Virgin's chaste womb without will or desire, or any connection with man or pleasurable generation, but rather through the Holy Spirit and thus became the first offspring of Adam. And he who is like us becomes obedient to the Father, and finds a remedy for our disobedience in exactly what he had assumed from us, and so he became a pattern of obedience to us, without which it is not possible to obtain salvation.

Book 3. Chapter 2. Concerning the manner in which the Word was conceived, and concerning his divine incarnation

The angel of the Lord was sent to the holy Virgin, who was descended from David's line. For it is evident that our Lord sprang out of Judah, from which tribe no one had turned his attention to the altar, as the divine apostle said: but about this we will speak more directly later on. And bearing glad tidings to her, he said, "Hail highly favored one, the Lord is with you. And she was troubled at his word, and the angel said to her, Fear not, Mary, for you have found favor with God, and shall bring forth a Son and shall call his name Jesus; for he shall save his people from their sins." This is why the name Jesus has the interpretation "Savior." And when she asked in her perplexity, "How can this be, seeing I do not know a man?" the angel again answered her, "The Holy Spirit shall come upon you, and the power of the Most High shall overshadow you. And this is why that holy thing which shall be born from you shall be called the Son of God." And she said to him, "Behold the handmaid of the Lord: be it done to me in accordance with your word."

And so, after the assent of the holy Virgin, the Holy Spirit descended upon her, according to the word of the Lord which the angel spoke, purifying her, and granting her power to receive the divinity of the Word, and likewise power to bring forth. And then was she overshadowed by the enhypostatic Wisdom and Power of the Most High God, the Son of God, who is of like essence with the Father as of Divine seed, and from her holy and most pure blood he formed flesh animated with the spirit of reason and thought, the first-fruits of our compound nature: not by procreation but by creation through the Holy Spirit: not developing the fashion of the body by gradual additions but by perfecting it at once, he himself, the very Word of God, standing to the flesh in the relation of its hypostasis. For the divine Word was not made one with flesh that had an independent pre-existence, but taking up his abode in the womb of the holy Virgin, he unreservedly took upon himself through the pure blood of the eternal Virgin, and in his own hypostasis, a body of flesh animated with the spirit of reason and thought. So it was that he assumed to himself the first-fruits of man's compound nature, himself, the Word, having become a hypostasis in the flesh. So that he is at once flesh, and at the same time the very flesh of God the Word, and likewise flesh animated, that is possessing both reason and thought. This is why we do not speak about a man as having become God, but rather of God having become Man. For being by nature perfect God, he naturally became likewise perfect Man: and did not change his nature nor make the dispensation an empty show, but became, without confusion or change or division, hypostatically one with that flesh which was conceived of the holy Virgin, and animated with reason and thought, and which had found existence in him, while he himself did not change the nature of his divinity into the essence of flesh, nor the essence of flesh into the nature of his divinity, and did not make one compound nature out of his divine nature and the human nature which he had assumed.

Book 3. Chapter 3. Concerning Christ's two natures, in opposition to those who hold that he has only one

Now the two natures were united with each other without change or alteration. The divine nature did not depart from its native simplicity, nor did the humanity change into the nature of God, nor was it reduced to non-existence, nor was one compound nature produced out of the two. For a compounded nature cannot be of the same essence as either of the natures out of which it is compounded, since it is made into one thing out of different things: for example, the body is composed of the four elements, but is not of the same essence as fire or air, or water or earth, nor does it keep these names. If, therefore, after the union, Christ's nature was, as the heretics maintain, a compound unity, he must have changed from a simple into a compound nature, and is no longer of the same essence as the Father whose nature is simple, nor as his mother, who is not a compound of divinity and humanity either. If that was the case he would not be either in divinity or humanity: nor will he be called either God or Man, but simply Christ: and the word Christ will be the name not of the hypostasis, but rather of (what in their view is) the one nature.

We, however, do not hold that Christ's nature is compound, nor yet that he is one thing made out of other things and differing from them in the way that a man is made out of soul and body, or as the body itself is made up of the four elements, but for our part we hold that, even though he is constituted of these different parts he is yet the same one. For we confess that he alike in his divinity and in his humanity, the same one both is, and is confessed to be, perfect God; and that he consists of two natures, and exists in two natures. Further, by the word "Christ" we understand the name of the hypostasis, not in the sense of one kind, but as signifying the existence of two natures. For in his own person he anointed himself; as God anointing his body with his own divinity, and as Man being anointed. For he is himself both God and Man. And the anointing is the divinity of his humanity. For if Christ, being of one compound nature, is of like essence to the Father, then the Father also must be compound and of like essence with the flesh, which is absurd and extremely blasphemous.

How, indeed, could one and the same nature come to embrace opposing and essential differences? For how is it possible that the same nature should be at once created and uncreated, mortal and immortal, circumscribed and uncircumscribed?

But if those who declare that Christ has only one nature should say also that this nature is a simple one, they must admit either that he is God pure and simple, and thus reduce the incarnation to a mere pretence, or that he is only man, as did Nestorius. And how then do we account for his being "perfect in divinity and perfect in humanity?" And when can Christ be said to be of two natures, if they hold that he is of one composite nature after the union? For it is surely clear to every one that before the union Christ's nature was one. But this is what leads the heretics astray, namely that they look upon nature (*physis*) and subsistence (*hypostasis*) as the same thing. For when we speak of the nature of men as one, observe that in saying this we are not looking to the question of soul and body. For when we compare together the soul and the body it cannot be said that they are of one nature. But since there are very many subsistences of men, and yet all have the same kind of nature: for all are composed of soul and body, and all take part in the nature of the soul, and possess the essence of the body, and the common form: so we speak of the one nature of these very many and different sub-sistences; while of course each subsistence has two natures, and fulfills itself in two natures, namely, soul and body.

But a common form cannot be admitted in the case of our Lord Jesus Christ. For neither was there ever, nor is there, nor will there ever be another Christ constituted of deity and humanity, who exists in deity and humanity, at once perfect God and perfect man. And so in the case of our Lord Jesus Christ we cannot speak of one nature made up of divinity and humanity, as we do in the case of the individual made up of soul and body. For in the latter case we are dealing with an individual man, but Christ is not an individual. For there is no predicable form of Christ-hood, so to speak, which he possesses. And therefore we hold that there has been a union of two perfect natures, one divine and one human; not with disorder or confusion, or intermixture, or commingling, as is said by the divinely-condemned Dioscorus, Eutyches, and Severus, and all that impious company: and not in a personal or relative manner, or as a matter of dignity or agreement in will, or equality in honor, or identity in name, or good favor, as the divinely-abhorred Nestorius said, along with Diodoros and Theodoros of Mopsuestia and their diabolical tribe: but rather by synthesis; that is, hypostatically, without change or confusion or alteration or difference or separation; and we confess that in two perfect natures there is only one hypostasis of the Son of God incarnate. We profess that there is one and the same subsistence belonging to his divinity and his humanity, and we admit that the two natures are preserved in him after the union, but we do not hold that each one is separate and by itself, but rather that they are united to each other in one compound subsistence. For we look upon the union as essential, that is, as a true and not imaginary one. We say that it is essential, moreover, not in the sense of two natures resulting in one compound nature, but in the sense of a true union of them in one compound subsistence of the Son of God, and we hold that their essential difference is preserved. For the created remains created, and the uncreated, remains uncreated: the mortal remains mortal; the immortal, remains immortal: the circumscribed, remains circumscribed: the uncircumscribed, remains uncircumscribed: the visible, remains visible: the invisible, remains invisible. "The one part is all glorious with wonders: while the other is the victim of insults."

Moreover, the Word appropriates to himself the attributes of humanity: for all that pertains to his holy flesh is his: and he imparts to the flesh his own attributes by way of communication (*antidosis*) in virtue of the parts interpenetrating one another, and in virtue of the oneness of hypostasis, and insofar as he who lived and acted both as God and as man, taking to himself either form and holding intercourse with the other form, was himself one and the same. So it is that the Lord of Glory is said to have been crucified, although his divine nature never endured the Cross, and also that the Son of Man is allowed to have been in heaven before the Passion, as the Lord himself said. For the Lord of Glory is one and the same with him who is in nature and in truth the Son of Man, that is, the one who became man, and both his wonders and his sufferings are known to us, although his wonders were worked in his divine capacity, and his sufferings were endured as man. For we know that, just as is his one hypostasis, so is the essential difference of the natures preserved. For how could difference be preserved if the very things that differ from one another are themselves not preserved? For difference means the difference between things that differ. Insofar as Christ's natures differ from one another, that is, in the matter of essence, we hold that Christ unites in himself two extremes: in respect of his divinity he is connected with the Father and the Spirit, while in respect of his humanity he is connected with his mother and all mankind. And insofar as his natures are united, we hold that he differs from the Father and the Spirit on the one hand, and from the mother and the rest of mankind on the other. For the natures are united in his subsistence, since he has one compound subsistence, in which he differs from the Father and the Spirit, and also from his mother and from us.

Book 3. Chapter 4. Concerning the manner of the Mutual Communication

Now we have often said already that essence is one thing and hypostasis another, and that essence signifies the common and general form of hypostases of the same kind, such as God, man, while hypostasis (subsistence) marks the individual, that is to say, Father, Son, Holy Spirit, or Peter, Paul. Observe, then, that the names, divinity and humanity, denote essences or natures: while the names, God and man, are applied both in connection with natures (as when we say that God is incomprehensible essence, and that God is one), and with reference to subsistences, that which is more specific having the name of the more general applied to it (as when the Scripture says, "Therefore God, your God, has anointed you," or again, "There was a certain man in the land of Uz," for it was only to Job that this reference was made).

And so, in the case of our Lord Jesus Christ, seeing that we recognize that he has two natures but only one subsistence compounded of both, when we contemplate his natures we speak of his divinity and his humanity, but when we contemplate the subsistence compounded of the natures we sometimes use terms that have reference to his double nature, as "Christ," and "at once God and man," and "God Incarnate"; and sometimes those that imply only one of his natures, such as "God" alone, or "Son of God," and "man" alone, or "Son of Man"; sometimes using names that imply his exaltedness and sometimes those that imply his lowliness. For he who is at once God and man is one reality, being the former from the Father ever without cause, but having become the latter afterwards out of his love for man.

When we speak of his divinity we do not ascribe to it the properties of humanity. For we do not say that his divinity is subject to passion or created. Nor, again, do we predicate of his flesh or of his humanity the properties of divinity: for we do not say that his flesh or his humanity is uncreated. But when we speak of his subsistence (*hypostasis*), whether we give it a name implying both natures, or one that refers to only one of them, we still attribute to it the properties of both natures. For Christ (a name which implies both natures) is spoken of as at once God and man, created and uncreated, subject to suffering and incapable of suffering: and when he is named Son of

God and God, in reference to only one of his natures, he still keeps the properties of the co-existing nature, that is, the flesh, being spoken of as God who suffers, and as the Lord of Glory crucified, not in respect of his being God but in respect of his being at the same time man. Likewise, too, when he is called Man and Son of Man, he still keeps the properties and glories of the divine nature, a child before the ages, and man who knew no beginning; it is not, however, as child or man but as God that he is before the ages, and became a child in the end. And this is the manner of the mutual communication of properties: either nature giving in exchange to the other its own properties because of the identity of the hypostasis and the interpenetration of the parts with one another. Accordingly we can say of Christ: "This our God was seen upon the earth and lived amongst men," and "This man is uncreated and impassible and uncircumscribed."

Book 3. Chapter 7. Concerning the one compound subsistence of God the Word

We hold, therefore, that the divine subsistence of God the Word existed before all else and is without time and eternal, simple and uncompounded, uncreated, incorporeal, invisible, intangible, uncircumscribed, possessing all that the Father possesses, since he is of the same essence with him, differing from the Father's subsistence in the manner of his own generation and the relation with the Father's subsistence, being perfect also and at no time separated from the Father's subsistence: and in these last days, without leaving the Father's bosom, he took up his abode in an uncircumscribed manner in the womb of the holy Virgin, without the instrumentality of seed, and in an incomprehensible manner known only to himself, so causing the flesh which was derived from the holy Virgin to subsist in the very hypostasis that was before all the ages.

And so he was both in all things and above all things, and also dwelt in the womb of the holy Mother of God, but was in it by the energy of the incarnation. He became flesh, therefore, and thereby took upon himself the first-fruits of our compound nature, namely the flesh animated with intelligent and national soul, so that the very subsistence of God the Word was changed into the fleshly subsistence, and so the subsistence of the Word, which had formerly been simple, now became compound, compounded indeed out of two perfect natures, divinity and humanity. It bears the characteristic and distinctive property of the divine Sonship of God the Word in virtue of which it is distinguished both from the Father and the Spirit, and also bears the characteristic and distinctive properties of the flesh, in virtue of which it differs from his Mother and the rest of mankind. Moreover it also bears the properties of the divine nature in virtue of which it is united to the Father and the Spirit, as well as the marks of the human nature in virtue of which it is united to the Mother and to us. And furthermore it differs from the Father and the Spirit and the Mother and from all of us, in that it exists as at once God and man. For this we know to be the most special property of the hypostasis of Christ.

This is why we confess him, even after the incarnation, to be the one Son of God, and likewise Son of Man, one Christ, one Lord, the only-begotten Son and Word of God, one Lord Jesus. We reverence his two generations, one from the Father before time and beyond cause and reason and time and nature, and one in the end-times for our sake, which is like to us and yet above us; for our sake because it was for our salvation; like to us in that he was man born of woman at the fullness of time; and yet above us because it was seedless, and by the Holy Spirit and the Holy Virgin Mary, transcending the laws of parturition. We proclaim him not as God only, devoid of our humanity, nor yet as man only, stripping him of his divinity, nor yet as two distinct persons, but as one and the same, at once God and man, perfect God and perfect man, wholly God and wholly man, the same who is wholly God, even though he was also flesh, and wholly man, even though he was also most high God. And by "perfect God" and "perfect man" we mean to emphasize the fullness and unfailingness of the natures: while by "wholly God" and "wholly man" we mean to lay stress on the singularity and individuality of the subsistence.

And we confess also that there is "One incarnate nature of God the Word," expressing by the word "incarnate" the essence of the flesh, according to the teachings of blessed Cyril. And so the Word was made flesh and yet did not abandon his own proper immateriality: he became wholly flesh and yet remained wholly uncircumscribed. So far as he is body he is diminished and contracted into narrow limits, but inasmuch as he is God he is uncircumscribed, his flesh not being coextensive with his uncircumscribed divinity.

He is then wholly perfect God, but is not simply God: for he is not only God but also man. And he is also wholly perfect man but not simply man, for he is not only man but also God. For "simply" here has reference to his nature, and "wholly" to his subsistence, just as the term "another thing" would refer to nature, while "another" would clearly denote subsistence.

But take note that although we hold that the natures of the Lord permeate one another, yet we know that the permeation springs from the divine nature. For it is this which penetrates and permeates all things, as it wills, while nothing penetrates it: and it is this too, which imparts to the flesh its own peculiar glories, while abiding itself impassible and without participation in the affections of the flesh. For if the sun imparts to us its energies and yet does not participate in ours, how much more will this be true of the Creator and Lord of the Sun.

Book 3. Chapter 12. That the holy Virgin is the Mother of God: an argument directed against the Nestorians

We also proclaim the holy Virgin to be in strict truth (*akribos*) the Mother of God. For inasmuch as he who was born of her was true God, then she who bore the true God incarnate is the true Mother of God. For we hold that God was born of her, not implying that the divinity of the Word received from her the beginning of its being, but meaning rather that God the Word himself, who was begotten of the Father timelessly before the ages, and was with the Father and the Spirit without beginning and through eternity, took up his abode in these last days for the sake of our salvation in the Virgin's womb, and was without change made flesh and born of her. For the holy Virgin did not bear a mere man but true God: and not mere God but God incarnate. And he did not bring down his body from Heaven, or simply pass through the Virgin like a channel, but received from her flesh of like essence to our own and subsisting in his own self. For if the body had come down from heaven and had not partaken of our nature, what would have been the use of his becoming man? For the purpose of God the Word becoming man was that the very same nature which had sinned and fallen and become corrupted, should triumph over the deceiving tyrant and so be freed from corruption, just as the divine apostle puts it, "For since by man came death, by man came also the resurrection of the dead." If the first is true, the second must also be true.

Although he says, "The first Adam is of the earth and earthy; the second Adam is Lord from Heaven," not that he does not say that his body is from heaven, but emphasizes the fact that he is not a mere man. For, take note, he called him both Adam and Lord, thus indicating his double nature. For Adam, being interpreted, means earth-born: and it is clear that man's nature is earth-born since he is formed from earth, but the title Lord signifies his divine essence. And again the Apostle says: "God sent forth his only-begotten Son, made of a woman." He did not say "made by a woman." Therefore the divine apostle meant that the only-begotten Son of God and God is the same as he who was made man of the Virgin, and that he who was born of the Virgin is the same as the Son of God and God.

But he was certainly born after the bodily fashion inasmuch as he became man, and did not take up his abode in a man formed beforehand, as if dwelling in a prophet. No, he himself became man in essence and truth; that is he caused flesh animated with the intelligent and reasonable to subsist in his own subsistence, and himself became the subsistence for it. For this is the meaning of "made of a woman." For how could the very Word of God itself have been made under the law, if he did not become man of like essence with ourselves?

Hence it is with justice and truth that we call the holy Mary the Mother of God. For this name embraces the whole mystery of the dispensation. For if she who bore him is the Mother of God, then indeed he who was born of her is truly God and likewise also man. For how could God, who was before the ages, have been born of a woman unless he had become man? For the Son of Man must clearly be man himself. But if he who was born of a woman is himself God, manifestly he who was born of God the Father in accordance with the laws of an essence that is divine and knows no beginning, and he who was in the last days born of the Virgin in accordance with the laws of an essence that does have a beginning and is subject to time (that is, an essence which is human), must be one and the same. This title (*Theotokos*) truly signifies the one subsistence as well as the two natures and the two generations of our Lord Jesus Christ.

But we never say that the holy Virgin is the Mother of Christ because this title was insultingly proposed by that vessel of dishonor, the defiled and abominable Judaizer Nestorius, in order to do away with the title Mother of God, and to bring dishonor on the Theotokos, who alone is in truth worthy of honor above all creation. For David the king, and Aaron, the high priest, are also called Christ, for it is customary to make kings and priests by anointment: and besides every God-inspired man may be called Christ, but then they are not by nature God. Indeed the accursed Nestorius insulted him who was born of the Virgin even by calling him "God-bearer." Let it ever be far from us to speak of or think of him as God-bearer only, who is in truth God incarnate. For the Word himself became flesh, having been truly conceived of the Virgin, but he came forth as God with the assumed nature which, as soon as it was brought forth into being, was deified by him, so that these three things took place simultaneously: the assumption of our nature, the coming into being, and the deification of the assumed nature by the

Word. And so it is that the holy Virgin is thought of, and spoken of, as the Mother of God, not only because of the nature of the Word, but also because of the deification of human nature, the miracles of conception and of existence being accomplished together, namely, the conception of the Word, and the existence of the flesh in the Word himself. For the very Mother of God in some marvelous manner was the means of fashioning the Framer of all things and of bestowing manhood on the God and Creator of all, who deified the nature that he assumed, while the union preserved those things that were united just as they were united; that is to say, not only the divine nature of Christ but also his human nature; that is to say not only that which is above us but that which is of us. For he was not first made like us and only later became higher than us, but always, from his very first coming into being he existed with the double nature, because he existed in the Word himself from the beginning of the conception. And so he is human in his own nature, but also, in some marvelous manner, he is of God and divine. Moreover he has the properties of the living flesh: for by reason of the economy of salvation the Word received these things which are, according to the order of natural motion, truly natural.

Book 3. Chapter 15. Concerning the energies in our Lord Jesus Christ
We hold, further, that there are two energies in our Lord Jesus Christ. For on the one hand he possesses, as God, and being of like essence with the Father, the divine energy; and likewise, since he became man and of like essence to us, also possesses the energy proper to human nature. But take note that energy and capacity for energy, and the product of energy, and the agent of energy, are all different things. Energy is the efficient (*drastike*) and essential activity of nature: the capacity for energy is the nature from which energy proceeds: the product of energy is that which is effected by energy: and the agent of energy is the person or hypostasis which uses the energy. Further, sometimes the word energy is used in the sense of the product of energy, and the product of energy used in the sense of energy; just as the terms creation and creature are sometimes transposed. For we say "all creation," often meaning creatures.

Note too that energy is an activity and is energized rather than energizes; as Gregory the Theologian says in his treatise concerning the Holy Spirit: "If energy exists, it must manifestly be energized and will not energize: and as soon as it has been energized, it will cease." Life itself, it should be observed, is energy, indeed the primal energy of the living creature, and so is the whole economy of the living creature, its functions of nutrition and growth (that is, the vegetative side of its nature), and the movement stirred by impulse (that is, the sentient side), and its activity of intellect and free will. Energy, moreover, is the perfect realization of power. So, if we contemplate all these things in Christ, surely we must also hold that he possesses human energy.

The first thought that arises in us is called energy: and it is simple energy not involving any relationship: the mind sending forth the thoughts peculiar to it in an independent and invisible way, for if it did not do so it could not justly be called mind. What is more, the revelation and unfolding of thought by means of articulate speech is said to be energy. But this is no longer simple energy that involves no relationship, but it is considered in relation to it being composed of thought and speech. Further, the very relation which he who does anything bears to that which is brought about is energy; and the very thing that is effected is called energy. The first belongs to the soul alone, the second to the soul making use of the body, the third to the body animated by mind, and the last is the effect. For the mind sees beforehand what is to be and then performs it by means of the body. And so the hegemony belongs to the soul, for it uses the body as an instrument, leading and restraining it. But the energy of the body is quite different, for the body is led and moved by the soul. And with regard to the effect, the touching and handling (and so to speak, the embrace of what is effected), belong to the body, while the figuration and formation belong to the soul. And so in connection with our Lord Jesus Christ, the power of miracles is the energy of his divinity, while the work of his hands and the willing and the saying, "I will, be made clean," are the energy of his humanity. And as to the effect, the breaking of the loaves and the fact that the leper heard the "I will," belong to his humanity, while the multiplication of the loaves and the purification of the leper belong to his divinity. For through both, that is through the energy of the body and the energy of the soul, he displayed one and the same cognate and equal divine energy. For just as we saw that his natures were united and permeate one another, and even so we do not deny that they are different but even enumerate them, although we know they are inseparable, so also in connection with the wills and the energies we know their single union, and yet we recognize their difference and can thus enumerate them without introducing separation. For just as the flesh was deified without undergoing change in its own nature, in the same way also his will and energy are deified without transgressing their own proper limits. For whether he is the one or the other, he remains one and the same, and whether he wills and energizes in one way or the other, that is as God or as man, he is one and the same.

We must, then, maintain that Christ has two energies in virtue of his double nature. For things that have diverse natures, also have different energies, and things that have diverse energies, also have different natures. And so, conversely, things that have the same nature also have the same energy, and things that have one and the same energy also have one and the same essence, which is the view of the Fathers, who set forth the godly interpretation. One of these alternatives, then, must be true: either, if we hold that Christ has one energy, we must also hold that he has only one essence, or, if we are solicitous about truth, and confess that he has (according to the doctrine of the Gospels and the Father) two essences, we must also confess that he has two corresponding energies accompanying them. For as he is of like essence with God the Father in divinity, so he must be his equal also in energy. And just as he is of like essence with us in humanity so he must be our equal also in energy. For the blessed Gregory, bishop of Nyssa, says: "Things that have one and the same energy, also have absolutely the same power." For all energy is the effect of power. But it cannot be that uncreated and created nature have one and the same nature or power or energy. But if we were to hold that Christ has only one energy, we would be attributing to the divinity of the Word the passions of the intelligent spirit, namely tears and grief and anguish.

If our opponents should argue that the holy Fathers said in their disputation concerning the Holy Trinity, "Things that have one and the same essence have also one and the same energy, and things which have different essences have also different energies," and that it is not right to transfer to the Economy what has reference to matters of Theology, we shall answer that if this has been said by the Fathers solely with reference to Theology, and if the Son does not retain the same energy as the Father after the incarnation, then assuredly he cannot have the same essence. But to whom of the Fathers shall we attribute this position? Scripture says: "My Father works even now, and I too work": and this, "Whatever he sees the Father doing, these works the Son does also": and this, "If you do not believe Me, believe my works": and this, "The work which I do bears witness concerning Me": and this, "As the Father raised up the dead and gives them life, even so the Son gives life to whoever he wills." For all these texts show not only that he is of like essence to the Father even after the incarnation, but that he has also the same energy.

Again: if the providence that embraces all creation is not only that of the Father and the Holy Spirit, but also that of the Son, even after the incarnation, assuredly since that is energy, then he must have even after the incarnation the same energy as the Father has. But if we have learned from the miracles that Christ has the same essence as the Father, and since the miracles happen to be the energy of God, then it follows that he must have the same energy as the Father even after the incarnation. But, if there is one energy belonging to both his divinity and his humanity, it will have to be compounded, and will be either a different energy from that of the Father, or the Father too will have a compounded energy. But if the Father has a compounded energy, manifestly he must also have a compound nature. But if they should say that together with the concept of energy is also introduced personality, we reply that if personality is introduced along with energy, then the converse must hold good that energy is also introduced along with personality; and on that argument there will now also be three energies of the Holy Trinity just as there are three persons or subsistences, or else there will be one person and one subsistence just as there is only one energy. But the truth of the matter is that the holy Fathers have unanimously maintained that things which have the same essence have also the same energy. And if personality is introduced along with energy, those who maintain that neither one nor two energies of Christ should be spoken of, surely do not maintain that either one or two persons of Christ are to be spoken of?

Take the case of the angel's flaming sword; just as here the natures of fire and steel are preserved distinct, so also are their two energies and their effects. For the energy of the steel is its cutting power, and that of the fire is its burning power, and the cut is the effect of the energy of the steel, and the burn is the effect of the energy of the fire: and these are kept quite distinct in the burnt-cut, and in the cut-burn, although here the burning does not happen except in the cut (after the union of the two), nor can the cut happen except in the burning. But we do not maintain on account of the twofold natural energy that there are two flaming swords, nor do we confuse the essential difference of the energies on account of the unity of the flaming sword. It is the same in the case of Christ. his divinity possesses an energy that is divine and omnipotent while his humanity has an energy like our own. And the effect of his human energy was his taking the child by the hand and drawing her to himself, while that of his divine energy was the restoring of her to life. For the one is quite distinct from the other, although they are inseparable from one another in theandric energy. But since, because Christ has one subsistence, he must also have one energy, then, because he has one subsistence, he must also have one essence.

Again: if we should hold that Christ has only one energy, this must be either divine or human, or neither. But if we hold that it is divine we must maintain that he is God alone, stripped of our humanity. And if we hold that it is human, we shall be guilty of the impiety of saying that he is a mere man. And if we hold that it is neither divine nor human, we must also hold that he is neither God nor man, and of like essence neither to the Father nor to us. For it is as a result of the union that the identity in hypostasis arises, but even so the difference between the natures is not abolished. But since the difference between the natures is preserved, then clearly the energies of the natures will also be preserved. For no nature exists that is lacking in energy.

If Christ our Master has one energy, it must be either created or uncreated; for between these positions there is no energy, just as there is no nature. If the energy is created, it will point to created nature alone, but if it is uncreated, it will signify uncreated essence alone. For whatever is natural must completely correspond with its proper nature: for there cannot exist any nature that is defective. But the energy that harmonizes with a nature does not belong to anything external: and this is manifest because, apart from that energy which harmonizes with its nature, a nature cannot either exist or be known. Through the means by which each thing manifests its energy, the stability serves to confirm its own proper nature.

If Christ has one energy, it must be one and the same energy that performs both divine and human actions. But there is no existing thing which while abiding in its natural state can act in opposite ways: for fire does not freeze and boil, nor does water dry up and make wet. How then could he who is God by nature, and who became man by nature, both have performed miracles, and endured passions with one and the same energy? If Christ assumed the human mind, that is to say, the intelligent and reasonable soul, then unquestionably he has thought, and will go on thinking for ever. But thought is the energy of the mind: and so Christ, as man, is endowed with energy, and will be so for ever. Indeed, the most wise and great and holy John Chrysostom says in his second homily on the exegesis of the Acts: "We would not be wrong if we were to call even his passion an action: for insofar as he suffered all things, he accomplished that great and marvelous work, the overthrow of death, and all his other works."

If all energy is defined as essential movement of some nature, as those who are versed in these matters say, where can one see any nature that has no movement, and is completely devoid of energy, or where does one find energy that is not movement of natural power? But, as the blessed Cyril says, no one in his right senses could admit that there was only one natural energy of God and his creation. It is not his human nature that raises up Lazarus from the dead, nor is it his divine power that sheds tears: for the shedding of tears is peculiar to human nature while the giving of life is peculiar to the enhypostatic life. But yet they are common, the one to the other, because of the identity in subsistence. For Christ is one, and one also is his person or hypostasis; but even so he has two natures, one belonging to his humanity, and another belonging to his divinity. And the glory, indeed, which proceeded naturally from his divinity became common to both through the hypostatic identity; and again on account of his flesh that which was lowly became common to both. For he who is the one or the other, that is God or man, is one and the same, and both what is divine and what is human belong to himself.

For while his divinity performed the miracles, they were not done apart from the flesh, and while his flesh performed its lowly offices, they were not done apart from the divinity. For his divinity was joined to the suffering flesh, yet remaining without passion, and it endured the saving passions, while the holy mind was joined to the energizing divinity of the Word, perceiving and knowing what was being accomplished.

And so his divinity communicates its own glories to the body while it remains itself without part in the sufferings of the flesh. For his flesh did not suffer through his divinity in the same way that his divinity energized through the flesh. For the flesh acted as the instrument of his divinity. Although from the first conception there was no division at all between the two forms (since the actions of either form always became those of one person), nevertheless we do not in any way confuse those things that took place without separation, but we recognize from the quality of its works what sort of form anything has.

Christ, then, energizes according to both his natures and either nature energizes in him in communion with the other: the Word performing through the authority and power of its divinity all the actions proper to the Word, that is all acts of supremacy and sovereignty, and the body performing all the actions proper to the body, in obedience to the will of the Word who is united to it, and of whom it has become a distinct part. For he was not moved of himself to the natural passions, nor again did he of himself recoil from painful things or pray for release from them, or suffer external events, but rather he was moved in conformity with his nature, the Word willing and allowing him economically to suffer this, and to do the things that were proper to him, so that the truth might be confirmed by the works of nature.

Moreover, just as he received in his birth from a virgin super-essential essence, so also he revealed his human energy in a superhuman way, walking with earthly feet on unstable water, not by turning the water into earth, but by causing it in the superabundant power of his divinity not to flow away or yield beneath the weight of material feet. For not in a merely human way did he do human things: for he was not only man, but also God, and so even in his sufferings he brought life and salvation: nor did he energize as God, strictly in the divine manner, for he was not only God, but also man, and so it was by touch and word and such means that he worked miracles.

But if any one should say, "We do not confess that Christ has only one energy in order to do away with the concept of human energy, but we do so because human energy, in opposition to divine energy, is called passive (*pathos*)." And to this we give an answer that, according to this reasoning, even those who maintain that he only has a single nature do not assert this with a view to doing away with his human nature, but because human nature in opposition to divine nature is spoken of as passible (*pathetike*). But really, God forbid that we should ever call the human activity passion, when we are distinguishing it from divine energy. For, to speak generally, we never recognize or classify existence in terms of comparison or collation, because otherwise existing things would turn out to be mutually the cause of one another. For if the human activity is seen as passion because the divine activity is seen as energy, then undoubtedly it would follow that the human nature also must be wicked because the divine nature is good, and so, conversely and by terms of opposite, if the divine activity is called energy because the human activity is called passion, then perhaps the divine nature must be good because the human nature is bad? But then all created things must be bad, and then he must have spoken falsely who said, "And God saw everything that he had made, and, behold, it was very good."

So it is that we maintain that the holy Fathers gave various names to the human activity according to the generic sense. For they called it power, and energy, and difference, and activity, and property, and quality, and passion, not in distinction from the divine activity, but the divine power, because it is a conservative and invariable force. They called it energy, because it is a distinguishing mark, and reveals the absolute similarity between all things of the same class; difference, because it distinguishes; activity, because it makes manifest; property, because it is constituent and belongs to that alone, and not to any other; quality, because it gives form; and passion, because it is moved. For all things that are of God and after God suffer in respect of being moved, insofar as they do not have motion or power in themselves. Therefore, as has been said, it is not in order to distinguish the one from the other that it has been named, but it is in accordance with the plan creatively implanted within it by the Cause that framed the universe. This is why when they spoke of it along with the divine nature they called it energy. For he who said, "For either form energizes a close communion with the other," did something quite different from him who said, "And when he had fasted forty days, he was afterwards very hungry" (for he allowed his nature to energize when it so willed, in the way proper to itself), or from those who hold there is a different energy in him or that he has a twofold energy, or now one energy and now another. For these statements with the change in terms signify the two energies. Indeed, often the number is indicated both by change of terms and by speaking of them as divine and human. For the difference is difference in terms of differing things, but how do things that do not exist differ?

Book 3. Chapter 17. Concerning the deification of the nature of our Lord's flesh and of his will

It is also noteworthy that the flesh of the Lord is not said to have been deified and made equal to God, or made God in respect of any change or alteration, or transformation, or confusion of nature: as Gregory the Theologian says, "From which the one deified, and the other was deified, and, if I may speak boldly, was made equal to God: and that which anointed became man, and that which was anointed became God." For these words do not signify any change in nature, but rather the economical union (I mean the hypostatic union by virtue of which it was united inseparably with God the Word), and the permeation of the natures through one another, just as we saw earlier that burning permeated the steel. For, just as we confess that God became man without change or alteration, so we consider that the flesh became God without change. For because the Word became flesh, he did not overstep the limits of his own divinity nor abandon the divine glories that belong to him: nor, on the other hand, was the flesh, when it was deified, changed in its own nature or in its natural properties. For even after the union, both the natures remained unconfused and their properties unimpaired. But the flesh of the Lord received the riches of the divine energies through the purest union with the Word, that is to say, the hypostatic union, without entailing the loss of any of its natural attributes. For it is not in virtue of any energy of its own but because of the Word united to it, that it manifests divine energy: for the flaming steel burns, not because it has been endowed in a physical way with burning energy, but because it has obtained this energy by its union with fire.

And so the same flesh was mortal by reason of its own nature, and it was life-giving because of its hypostatic union with the Word. And we hold that it is just the same with the deification of the will; for its natural activity was not changed but united with his divine and omnipotent will, and became the will of God, made man. And so it was that, though he wished, he could not of himself escape [the chalice], because it pleased God the Word that the weakness of the human will, which was truly in him, should be made manifest. But he was able to cause at his will the cleansing of the leper, because of the union with the divine will.

Observe also, that the deification of the nature and the will points most expressly and most directly to the existence of two natures and two wills. For just as the burning does not change into fire the nature of the thing that is burnt, but makes distinct both what is burnt, and what burned it, and is indicative not of one but of two natures, so also the deification does not bring about one compound nature but two, and their union in subsistence. Indeed, Gregory the Theologian says, "From which the one deified, the other was deified," and by the words "from which," "the one," and "the other," he most clearly indicates two natures.

Book 3. Chapter 19. Concerning the theandric energy

When the blessed Dionysios says that Christ exhibited to us some sort of novel theandric energy, he is not abolishing the natural energies by saying that one energy resulted from the union of the divine with the human energy: for in just the same way we could speak of one new nature resulting from the union of the divine with the human nature. For, according to the holy Fathers, things that have one energy also have one essence. But rather he wished to indicate the novel and ineffable manner in which the natural energies of Christ manifest themselves, a manner befitting the ineffable way in which the natures of Christ mutually permeate one another, and further how strange and wonderful and entirely new to us was his life as man, and lastly the manner of the mutual interchange arising from the ineffable union. For we hold that the energies are not divided and that the natures do not energize separately, but that each conjointly in complete communion with the other energizes with its own proper energy. For the human part did not energize merely in a human manner, for he was not mere man; nor did the divine part energize only after the manner of God, for he was not simply God, but he was at once God and man. For just as in the case of natures we recognize both their union and their natural difference, so is it also with the natural wills and energies.

Note, therefore, that in the case of our Lord Jesus Christ, we speak sometimes of his two natures and sometimes of his one person: and either one or the other can be referred to one conception. For the two natures are one Christ, and the one Christ is two natures. And so it is all the same whether we say "Christ energizes according to either of his natures," or "Either nature energizes in Christ in communion with the other." The divine nature has communion with the flesh in its energizing, because it is by the good favor of the divine will that the flesh is permitted to suffer and do the things proper to itself, and because the energy of that flesh is altogether salvific, and this is an attribute not of human but of divine energy. On the other hand, the flesh has communion with the divinity of the Word in its energizing, because the divine energies are performed, so to speak, through the medium of the body, and because he who energizes is one and the same, at once God and man.

Note this also, that his holy mind also performs its natural energies, thinking and knowing that it is the mind of God and that it is worshipped by all creation, and still remembering the times he spent on earth and all that he suffered, but it has communion with the divinity of the Word in its energizing and orders and governs the universe, thinking and knowing and ordering not as the mere mind of man, but as hypostatically united with God and acting as the mind of God.

It is this theandric energy, therefore, which makes it plain for us that when God became man, that is when he became incarnate, both his human energy was divine (that is deified), and communing with his divine energy, and his divine energy was communing in his human energy, and each one was observed in conjunction with the other. Now this manner of speaking is called a periphrasis, that is when one embraces two things in a single statement. For just as in the case of the flaming sword we speak of the cut-burn as one, and the burnt-cut as one, but still hold that the cut and the burn have different energies and different natures, the burn having the nature of fire and the cut having the nature of steel; well, in the same way also when we speak of one theandric energy of Christ, we understand the two distinct energies of his two natures, a divine energy belonging to his divinity, and a human energy belonging to his humanity.

Book 4. Chapter 13. Concerning the holy and immaculate Mysteries of the Lord God

The one who is good and altogether good, indeed far more than good; he who is goodness throughout, by reason of the exceeding riches of his goodness, did not wish for himself (that is his nature) only to be good, with no other able to participate in that goodness, so it was for this very reason that he first made the spiritual and heavenly powers: next the visible and sensible universe: next man with his spiritual and sentient nature. All things, therefore, which God made, share in his goodness in respect of their existence. For he himself is existence to all, since all things that exist, are in him; not only because it was he who brought them out of nothingness into being, but because his energy preserves and maintains all that he made: and especially the living creatures, both in that they exist and in that they enjoy life and share in his goodness. But to tell the truth those living creatures that are endowed with reason have an even greater share in his goodness, both because of what has been already said and also because of that rational capacity which they possess. For they are somehow more dearly akin to God, even though he is incomparably higher than them.

Man, however, being endowed with reason and free will, received the power of continuous union with God through his own choice, if indeed he chose to remain in goodness, that is in obedience to his Maker. But since he transgressed the command of his Creator and became liable to death and corruption, the Creator and Maker of our race, because of deep compassion, took on our likeness, becoming man in all things except sin, and was united to our nature. For since he bestowed on us his own image and his own spirit and we did not keep them safe, he participated in our poor and weak nature, so that he might cleanse us and make us incorruptible, and establish us once more as partakers in his divinity.

For it was fitting that not only the first-fruits of our nature should partake in the higher good, but indeed every man who wished it, and that a second birth should take place and that the nourishment should be new and suitable to the birth and thus the measure of perfection be attained. Through his birth, that is, his incarnation, and baptism and passion and resurrection, he delivered our nature from the sin of our first parent and from death and corruption, and he himself became the first-fruits of the resurrection, and made himself the way and the image and the pattern, so that we also by following in his footsteps could become by adoption what he himself is by nature: sons and heirs of God and co-heirs with him. And so, as I said, he gave us a second birth so that, just as we the children of Adam are in his image and are the heirs of curse and corruption, so also being born of Christ we may be in his likeness and heirs of his incorruption, blessing and glory.

Now seeing that this Adam is spiritual, it was fitting that both his birth and food should be spiritual too; but since we are of a double and compounded nature, it is fitting that this birth should be double and the food compounded. So it was that we were given a birth by water and Spirit (I mean, by holy baptism): and the food is the very bread of life, our Lord Jesus Christ, who came down from heaven. For when he was about to take on himself a voluntary death for our sakes, on the night on which he gave himself up, he laid a new covenant on his holy disciples and apostles, and through them on all who believe in him. In the upper chamber of holy and illustrious Sion, after he had eaten the ancient Passover with his disciples and had fulfilled the ancient covenant, he washed his disciples' feet in token of the holy baptism. "Then having broken bread he gave it to them saying: 'Take, eat, this is my body broken for you for the remission of sins.' Likewise he also took the cup of wine and water and gave it to them saying, 'Drink all of you from this for this is my blood, blood of the New Testament, which is shed for you for the remission of sins. Do this in remembrance of me. For as often as you eat this bread and drink this cup, you proclaim the death of the Son of Man and confess his resurrection until he come.'"

If the Word of God is alive and energizing, therefore, and the Lord did all that he willed; if he said, "Let there be light and there was light, let there be a firmament and there was a firmament"; "If the heavens were established by the Word of the Lord and all the host of them by the breath of his mouth"; if the heaven and the earth, water and fire and air and the whole glory of these, and, indeed this most noble creature, man, were perfected by the Word of the Lord; if God the Word of his own will became man and the pure and undefiled blood of the holy and ever-Virgin Mary made his flesh seedlessly, can he not also make the bread his body and the wine and water his blood? He said in the beginning, "Let the earth bring forth grass," and even until this present day, when the rain comes it brings forth its proper fruits, urged on and strengthened by the divine command. God said, "This is my body, and this is my blood," and "Do this in remembrance of me." And so it still stands at his omnipotent command until he come again: for it was in this sense that he said "Until he come": and through the Epiclesis the overshadowing power of the Holy Spirit becomes the rain to this new tillage. For just as God made all that he made by the energy of the Holy Spirit, so also now the energy of the Spirit performs those things that are supernatural and which it is not possible to comprehend except by faith alone. "How shall this be," said the holy Virgin, "Seeing I do not know a man?" And the archangel Gabriel answered her: "The Holy Spirit shall come upon you, and the power of the Most High shall overshadow you." So why do you ask now how the bread becomes Christ's body and the wine and water Christ's blood? My answer to you is: The Holy Spirit is present and does those things which surpass reason and thought.

Furthermore, bread and wine are employed: for God knows man's infirmity: for in general man turns away discontentedly from what is not well-worn by custom: and so with his usual indulgence God performs his supernatural works through familiar objects: and just as in the case of baptism, since it is man's custom to wash himself with water and anoint himself with oil, he connected the grace of the Spirit with the oil and the water, and made it into the water of regeneration, just so since it is our custom to eat and to drink water and wine, he connected his divinity with these elements and made them into his body and blood in order that we may rise to what is supernatural through what is familiar and natural.

The body which is born of the holy Virgin is truly body united with divinity. It is not that the body which was received up into the heavens descends, but that the bread itself and the wine are changed into God's body and blood. But if you enquire how this happens, it is enough for you to learn that it was through the Holy Spirit, just as the Lord took on himself flesh that subsisted in him and was born of the holy Mother of God through the Spirit. And we know nothing further save that the Word of God is omnipotent, true and energizes; but the manner of this cannot be discovered. But we can express it well enough by saying that just as in nature the bread (by the eating) and the wine and water (by the drinking) are changed into the body and blood of the eater and drinker, and do not become a different body from the former one, just so the bread of the table and the wine and water are supernaturally changed by the invocation and presence of the Holy Spirit into the body and blood of Christ, and they are not two bodies but one and the same.

This is why to those who partake worthily and with faith, this is for the remission of sins and for life everlasting and for the safeguarding of soul and body; but for those who partake unworthily and without faith, it is for chastisement and punishment; just as the death of the Lord became for those who believe life and incorruption for the enjoyment of eternal blessedness, while for those who do not believe, and for the murderers of the Lord, it was for everlasting chastisement and punishment.

The bread and the wine are not merely figures of the body and blood of Christ (God forbid!) but are actually the deified body of the Lord itself: for the Lord has said, "This is My body," not, this is a figure of my body: and he said "My blood," not, a figure of my blood. And on a previous occasion he had said to the Judeans: "Unless you eat the flesh of the Son of Man and drink his blood, you will have no life in you. For my flesh is true food and my blood is true drink." And again, "Whoever eats me, shall live." And so in awe and with a pure conscience and certain faith let us draw near and it will assuredly be for us what we believe, doubting nothing. Let us pay homage to it in all purity both of soul and body: for it is twofold. Let us draw near to it with an ardent desire, and with our hands crossed over our breast let us receive the body of the Crucified One: and let us apply it to our eyes and lips and brows and partake of this divine ember, so that the fire of our desire with the additional heat derived from the ember may utterly consume our sins and illumine our hearts, and so that we may be inflamed and deified by our participation in the divine fire. Isaiah had a vision of this coal. But coal is not plain wood but wood united with fire: in like manner so too is the bread of the communion not just plain bread but bread united with divinity. But a body which is united with divinity is not one nature, but has one nature belonging to the body and another belonging to the divinity that is united to it; so that the compound is not one nature but two.

Melchisidek, the priest of the most high God, received Abraham on his return from the victory over the pagans with bread and wine. That table pre-imaged this mystical table, just as that priest was a type and image of Christ, the true high-priest: "For you are a priest for ever after the order of Melchisidek." The temple show-bread was also an image of this bread. And this too is surely that pure and bloodless sacrifice which the Lord through the prophet said is offered to him "From the rising to the setting of the sun."

The body and blood of Christ are meant for the support of our soul and body, and are never consumed and never suffer corruption or waste (God forbid!) but are for our being and preservation, as a protection against all kinds of injury, as a purging from all uncleanness. If men take up base gold, they purify it by a critical burning: symbol of how we shall not be condemned along with the dross of this world in the future. The refining purifies it from defilement and all kinds of calamities; according to the words of the divine Apostle, "For if we would judge ourselves, we shall not be judged. But when we are judged, we shall be chastened by the Lord, so that we shall not be condemned along with the world." This too is what he says, "So that whoever partakes of the body and blood of Christ unworthily, eats and drinks condemnation to himself." So, being purified accordingly, we are united to the body of Christ and to his Spirit and in this way we become the body of Christ.

This bread is the first-fruits of the future bread which is [called in the Lord's prayer] *Epiousion*, or in other words necessary for existence. For the word *epiousion* signifies either the future, that is the One who is for a future age, or else him of whom we partake for the preservation of our essence. Whatever sense the word denotes, it is fitting to speak like this of the Lord's body. For the Lord's flesh is life-giving spirit because it was conceived of the life-giving Spirit. For what is born of the Spirit is spirit. But I do not say this to take away the nature of the body, but rather I wish to make clear its life-giving and divine power.

But if some persons have called the bread and the wine the "Antitypes" of the body and blood of the Lord (as for example as the divinely inspired Basil did), they did not call them this after the consecration, only before the consecration, in other words using this term for the offering. We refer to it also as participation; for through this we partake of the divinity of Jesus. We also call it Communion, and it is an actual communion, because through it we have communion with Christ and share in his flesh and his divinity:

Indeed, we also have communion and are united with one another through it. For since we partake of one bread, we all become the one body of Christ and one blood, and become members of one another, since we are one body with Christ.

With all our strength, therefore, let us be on our guard not to receive communion from the heretics or to offer communion to them; for the Lord said: "Do not give what is holy to the dogs," and "Do not cast your pearls before swine." For if we do this we shall become partakers in their dishonor and condemnation. For if the union given is truly with Christ and with one another, we are certainly freely united also with all those who partake along with us. For this union is effected voluntarily and not against our inclination. And we are all one body because we partake of the one bread, as the divine Apostle says. Moreover in this respect we also find mention made of the antitypes of future things. This does not imply that the elements are not truly Christ's body and blood, but it means that even now we partake of Christ's divinity through them, but in the future we shall partake noetically through simple vision.

Book 4. Chapter 15. Concerning the honor due to the Saints and their remains

Honor should be paid to the saints as to the friends of Christ, and as sons and heirs of God. In the words of John the theologian and evangelist, "As many as received him, he gave them power to became sons of God." So that they are no longer servants, but sons: and if sons, they are also heirs; heirs of God and co-heirs with Christ: and the Lord in the holy Gospels says to his apostles, "You are my friends. From now on I do not call you servants, for a servant does not know what his Lord is doing." And furthermore, if the Creator and Lord of all things is called King of Kings and Lord of Lords and God of Gods, then surely even the saints are like gods and lords and kings. For God truly is, and is called, the God and Lord and King of all these. For "I am the God of Abraham," he said to Moses, "The God of Isaac and the God of Jacob." And "God made Moses a god to Pharaoh." Now of course I am referring to gods and kings and lords not as a matter of nature, but insofar as they have become rulers and masters of their passions, and because they have preserved a true likeness to the divine image according to which they were made (for the image of a king is also called king), and insofar as they are united to God of their own free will and receive his indwelling and are in process of becoming by grace through participation with him what he is himself by nature. Surely, then, the worshippers and friends and sons of God must be held in honor? For the honor shown to the most thoughtful of fellow-servants is a proof of good feeling towards the common Master.

The saints are made the treasuries and pure habitations of God: "For I will dwell in them," God said, "And walk in them, and I will be their God." The divine Scripture also says that "The souls of the just are in the hands of God and death cannot lay hold of them." For death is more the sleep of the saints than their death. For they worked in this life and shall continue to work to the end, and "Precious in the sight of the Lord is the death of his saints." What is more precious than to be in the hand of God? For God is Life and Light, and those who are in God's hand are within life and light.

In addition the Apostle tells us that God even dwelt in the bodies of the saints in a spiritual manner: "Do you not know that your bodies are the temples of the Holy Spirit who dwells within you?" And "The Lord is that Spirit," and "If any one should destroy the temple of God, God will destroy him." Surely, then, we must ascribe honor to the living temples of God, those living tabernacles of God? While they lived the saints stood with confidence before God. Christ our Master made their relics into fountains of salvation for us, pouring forth manifold blessings and making them abound in the oil of sweet fragrance. And no one should doubt this. For if water poured forth in the desert from the steep and solid rock at God's will and from the jaw-bone of an ass so that it might quench Samson's thirst, is it so incredible that fragrant oil should pour forth from the relics of the martyrs? By no means, at least to those who know the power of God and the honor which he accords his saints.

In the terms of the Old Law every one who touched a dead body was considered impure, but these are not dead. For from the time when he that is himself life and the Author of life was reckoned among the dead, we do not consider those who have fallen asleep in the hope of the resurrection and in faith in Christ to be dead. For how could a dead body work miracles? And how could the demons be driven off by them, or diseases dispelled, or sick persons made well, or the blind restored to sight, or lepers purified, or temptations and troubles overcome; and how does every good gift from the Father of lights come down through them to those who pray with sure faith? What hard work would you not undertake in order to find a patron who could introduce you to an earthly king and who would speak to him on your behalf? Are not the saints, then, worthy of honor since they are the patrons of the whole race, and make intercession to God for us?

Of course we should give them honor by building temples to God in their name, bringing them fruit-offerings, honoring their memories and taking spiritual delight in them, in order that the joy of those we invoke may be ours, and so that in our attempts at worship we may never cause them offense. For those who worship God will take pleasure in the things by means of which God is truly worshipped, while his attendants will be angry at all those things than anger God. Let us believers venerate the saints, in psalms and hymns and spiritual songs, by contrition and by pity for the needy, because God also is most truly worshipped in this manner. Let us raise monuments to the saints and visible icons, and let us try to become, by imitation of their virtues, living monuments and icons of them. Let us give honor especially to her who bore God, who is strictly and truly the Mother of God. Let us honor also the prophet John as Forerunner and Baptist, and as Apostle and Martyr, "For among those born of women there has not risen a greater than John the Baptist," as the Lord said, for he became the first to proclaim the Kingdom. Let us honor the apostles as the Lord's own brothers, who saw him face to face and ministered to his passion. "For those whom God the Father foreknew he also predestined to be conformed to the icon of his Son: first apostles, second prophets, third pastors and teachers." Let us also honor the martyrs of the Lord, chosen out of every class, as soldiers of Christ who have drunk his cup and were then baptized with the baptism of his life-bringing death, so as to be partakers of his passion and glory. The leader of them all is Stephen, the first deacon of Christ and apostle and Protomartyr. Also let us honor our holy fathers, the God-bearing ascetics, whose struggle was the longer and more laborious one of the conscience: who wandered about in sheepskins and goatskins, being destitute, afflicted, tormented; "they wandered in deserts and in mountains and in dens and caves of the earth, of whom the world was not worthy." Let us honor those who were prophets before the time of grace, the patriarchs and just ones who foretold the Lord's coming. Let us carefully review their lives, and let us emulate their faith and love and hope and zeal and way of life, and their endurance of sufferings and their patience even to the point of blood; so that we too may be sharers with them in their crowns of glory.

Book 4. Chapter 16. Concerning Icons

But since some find fault with us for venerating and honoring the icon of our Savior and that of the Virgin Lady, and those, too, of the rest of the saints and servants of Christ, let them remember that in the beginning God created man after his own image. On what grounds, then, do we show reverence to one another except because we are made after God's image? For as Basil says, that skilful expounder of divine things, "the honor given to the image passes over to the prototype." Now a prototype is that which is imaged, from which the derivative is obtained. Why was it that the people in the time of Moses all honored the tabernacle which bore an image and type of heavenly things (or rather a type of the whole creation)? For God said to Moses, "See that you make these things after the pattern which was shown to you on the mountain." As for the Cherubim, too, which overshadow the Mercy Seat, are they not also the work of men's hands? And what was the celebrated temple at Jerusalem? Was it not made by hand and fashioned by the skill of men?

What is more the divine Scripture blames those who worship graven images, but offers the same blame to those who sacrifice to demons. The Greeks sacrificed and the Jews also sacrificed: but the Greeks did it to demons and the Jews did it to God. So the sacrifice of the Greeks was rejected and condemned, but the sacrifice of the just was very acceptable to God. For Noah sacrificed, and "God smelled a sweet savor," receiving the fragrance of his right choice and reverence. This was why the graven images of the Greeks (since they were images of false deities), were rejected and forbidden.

But apart from this who can make an imitation of the invisible, incorporeal, uncircumscribed, and formless God? This is why to give form to the Deity is the height of folly and impiety. And so, in the Old Testament, the use of images was not common. But afterwards God in his deep compassion truly became man for our salvation (not as he was seen by Abraham in the semblance of a man, nor as he was seen by the prophets, but truly man in being), and he lived upon the earth and dwelt among men, worked miracles, suffered, was crucified, rose again and was taken back to Heaven. Since all these things actually took place and were seen by men, they were written down for our instruction and remembrance since we were not alive at that time, so that though we did not actually see, we could still hear and believe, and so obtain the blessing of the Lord. But since not every one is literate, or has time for reading, the Fathers gave their sanction to depicting these events in icons, as being acts of great heroism, in order that a concise memorial of them could be formed. Often, doubtless, when we do not have the Lord's passion in mind and we see the icon of Christ's crucifixion, his saving passion is immediately brought to mind, and we fall down and worship (not the material but rather) that which is imaged: just as we do not worship the material of which the Gospels are made, nor the material of the Cross, but that which these things typify. For in what respect does a cross that typifies the Lord, differ from a cross that does not do so? It is just the same also in the case of the Mother of the Lord. For the honor which we give to her is referred to him who was made incarnate of her. And similarly the brave acts of holy men also stir us up to be brave and to emulate their valor and glorify God. For as we said, the honor that is given to these best of fellow-servants is a proof of good-will towards our common Lady, and the honor rendered to the icon passes over to the prototype. But this is an unwritten tradition, just as is the case with the custom of praying towards the East and the veneration of the Cross, and many other similar things.

A certain tale, is told, how when Abgar was king over the city of the Edessa, he sent a portrait artist to paint a likeness of the Lord, and when the artist could not paint because of the brightness that shone from his countenance, the Lord himself put a cloth over his own divine and life-giving face and impressed upon it an image of himself and sent this to Abgar, so as to satisfy his request. The Apostles handed down to us much else that was unwritten. Paul, the Apostle of the Gentiles, tells us in these words: "Therefore, brethren, stand fast and hold the traditions which ye have been taught by us, whether by word or by epistle." And to the Corinthians he writes, "Now I praise you, brethren, because you remember me in all things, and you keep the traditions as I have handed them on to you."

Index

Printed in the USA/Agawam, MA
November 14, 2022

801262.005